Success as a Psychology Major

Dedication

For Annie and Abigail—thank you for supporting me through the ups and downs of writing!

–D.C.

To all of my students, colleagues, and friends who inspired this.

–J.A.H.

Success as a Psychology Major

David E. Copeland
University of Nevada, Las Vegas

Jeremy Ashton Houska
University of La Verne

SAGE

Los Angeles | London | New Delhi
Singapore | Washington DC | Melbourne

SAGE

FOR INFORMATION:

SAGE Publications, Inc.
2455 Teller Road
Thousand Oaks, California 91320
E-mail: order@sagepub.com

SAGE Publications Ltd.
1 Oliver's Yard
55 City Road
London, EC1Y 1SP
United Kingdom

SAGE Publications India Pvt. Ltd.
B 1/I 1 Mohan Cooperative Industrial Area
Mathura Road, New Delhi 110 044
India

SAGE Publications Asia-Pacific Pte. Ltd.
3 Church Street
#10-04 Samsung Hub
Singapore 049483

Acquisitions Editor: Abbie Rickard
Editorial Assistant: Elizabeth Cruz
Production Editor: Karen Wiley
Copy Editor: Celia McCoy
Typesetter: Hurix Digital
Proofreader: Christine Dahlin
Indexer: Maria Sosnowski
Cover Designer: Scott Van Atta
Marketing Manager: Katherine Hepburn

Printed in the United States of America

Library of Congress Control Number: 2019952084

ISBN: 978-1-5443-3471-4

This book is printed on acid-free paper.

20 21 22 23 24 10 9 8 7 6 5 4 3 2 1

Brief Contents

Detailed Contents

Preface

We welcome you to the world of psychology! No matter whether you are a current psych major (or psych minor) taking Introduction to the Psychology Major, the First-Year Experience in Psychology, Careers in Psychology, or General Psychology or are someone interested in learning more about the psychology major—welcome! Even if you are further along in your undergraduate education, it is never too late to learn some important steps that you can take to prepare for your future. Because this book is comprehensive, but not overly technical, it can be used by high school psychology courses as many of the issues we discuss can give students a head start as they prepare to start majoring in psychology in college.

Our main motivation for writing this book came from conversations with graduating psychology students who told us that they wished they had known so many things about the major earlier in their college experience. At the end of our Introduction to the Psychology Major courses each semester, we asked our students for specific feedback about the topics: we asked them to list the three most important things they learned, whether any topics needed additional coverage, if they thought certain topics are not needed, and whether there are any topics missing. We also ask graduating psychology majors for feedback as to how we could have better prepared them for their futures.

Students noted a variety of topics that are related to succeeding as a psychology major, and we have used this important feedback to refine the topics covered in this book. We cover a wide range of topics, including (a) goal setting and avoiding procrastination, (b) practical study skills, (c) adopting the right mindsets (e.g., thinking critically and acting ethically), (d) networking and getting to know your professors, (e) benefits of professional organizations and student clubs, (f) the psychology curriculum and skill development, (g) research involvement, (h) reading psychological research, (i) writing in APA style, (j) career possibilities and preparation, (k) graduate school paths, (l) money issues, and (m) documenting your accomplishments. Our students tell us that all psychology majors will want to keep this book as a reference or guide throughout their undergraduate training!

We look forward to your feedback as you progress in your psychology major. Follow us on Twitter (@Psych_Success), mention us in your tweets, and use the hashtag #SuccessAsAPsychMajor.

PEDAGOGICAL APPROACH AND KEY FEATURES

We hope you find this book one that you can learn from when you start your psychology major and also one that you can consult repeatedly as you progress through your program. Because the first author works at a large public research university and the second author has worked at smaller universities, we have a well-rounded understanding of the priorities at different types of schools. Having both of these perspectives allowed us to write chapters that are relevant to all psychology undergraduates. Our primary role as authors is to serve as your (virtual) guide—supplementing the guidance of your professors at your institution and stimulating meaningful conversations with your classmates.

Writing Style. In order to accomplish this, we present you a comprehensive—but not overly technical—view on how you, too, can become a superstar psychology student. Although our writing style is direct and informative, we convey our points by writing in a manner that is accessible and somewhat conversational. We include a small amount of (often corny) humor and interactive exercises to better engage you in the material because, after all, good educational material needs to capture and keep your attention.

Modular Approach. We organized our book into chapters that each consist of a number of short modules. We hope this helps you focus on brief topics instead of procrastinating when confronted with long, daunting chapters. Modules include practical tips (e.g., avoiding plagiarism, utilizing campus career services) and concrete examples (e.g., CV, APA template). Each module includes the clear and concise coverage of a specific topic, and this information is presented in the following organizational structure:

- Vignettes
- Why Did We Tell You This Story?
- Take-Home Message
- Action Steps

Let us share a bit about these important text features and our reasons for choosing them.

Vignettes. To help you relate to the material, chapters begin with a short description of a student in the context of that topic. These vignettes are based on encounters with past students, though only the names have been changed to protect the innocent.

Why Did We Tell You This Story? This is a quick recap of what you should have gotten out of the vignette, and often a hint (or foreshadowing) about how that story will connect with the themes of the chapter.

Take-Home Message. Take-home messages quickly reiterate the main points from a module.

Action Steps. We include a list of action steps to motivate you to apply what you are learning. Do not worry—these are not busywork! Action steps are designed to have a practical use for students (e.g., conduct an informational interview, locate a scholarship and apply for it). In addition, these action steps balance the need for students to be independent and to take control of their own educational experiences with knowing when and where to seek help. We included these action steps at the end of each module—instead of at the end of the chapter—so that you will be motivated to take action immediately after reading about a specific topic.

References. We have organized these by module and subsection at the end of the book. We want to increase the likelihood that students use them for further reading!

In closing, this book provides many suggestions for how psychology students can succeed. However, we know that not all of you reading this Preface right now are going to remain psychology majors, and some of you psychology majors may move into careers that are not directly related to your field of study. This is perfectly fine—we even cover some of these possibilities in this book. We want you to take the path that is right for you, so that you succeed!

Wishing you much success.

D.C.

J.A.H.

Acknowledgments

We would like to thank Kris Gunawan, Nicole Bies-Hernandez, and Paul Schroeder for sharing ideas and feedback that contributed to the development of this book. We also want to thank Wayne Weiten and Mark Ashcraft for their invaluable advice about authoring a book. We also benefited greatly from the guidance of the team at SAGE—especially Abbie Rickard, who worked with us through every step of this book. We are also grateful for the following reviewers: Brittany Draper, Angelo State University; Rachelle Cohen, Georgia State University; Betty Dorr, Fort Lewis College; Jamie L. Franco-Zamudio, Spring Hill College; Alexandra K. Frazer, Muhlenberg College; Brian A. Johnson, The University of Tennessee-Martin; Kareem J Johnson, Temple University; Courtney Mozo, Old Dominion University; Rachel A. Ritchie, Florida International University; Douglas Smith, Southern Oregon University; Yvonne V. Wells, Suffolk University, Boston; and Jason Whetten, Northern Arizona University.

We are also appreciative of the help from various students who provided input and discussed ideas with us. This includes Katie Larson, Amber Williams, William Ridgway, Jackson Pelzner, Mike Palena, Manthan Satyawadi, Ben Bain, Damien Olivares, Mary Collins, Mary Riley, Abby Voelkner, Alexis Andino, Deana Fritz, Alissa Nowak, Kristine Liang, Alexis Shuey, and Rhiannon Renn. In addition, we greatly appreciate the feedback from the thousands of students who have taken our Introduction to the Psychology Major courses over the years!

About the Authors

David E. Copeland is an Associate Professor of Psychology at the University of Nevada, Las Vegas (UNLV). He earned his PhD in cognitive psychology from the University of Notre Dame in 2003. He has published psychology research articles in journals such as *Memory & Cognition*, *Psychology and Aging*, and *Journal of Experimental Psychology: Learning, Memory, and Cognition* and has co-authored several book chapters. He has been recognized with three teaching awards, an outstanding mentorship award, and an outstanding faculty advisor award (for the UNLV Psi Chi chapter). He has been the Undergraduate Director for the Department of Psychology and a faculty advisor for Psi Chi and has taught a variety of psychology courses at both the undergraduate and graduate levels. In particular, he designed and has been teaching an Introduction to the Psychology Major course for psychology majors and minors at UNLV. In addition, he has supervised and mentored doctoral students who have gone on to careers in both academia and the private sector, has helped numerous undergraduates prepare for and gain admission into graduate school, and has also worked with students to help them find jobs or volunteer opportunities after completing their bachelor's degree.

Jeremy Ashton Houska is Director of Educational Effectiveness at the University of La Verne. Prior to that, he enjoyed serving in a variety of roles including Vice President for Institutional Research, Effectiveness and Design, Director of Institutional Research and Assessment, as well as an Associate Professor of Psychology. His teaching has been recognized with a number of awards, including the Society for the Teaching of Psychology's (Division 2 of the American Psychological Association) Wilbert J. McKeachie Teaching Excellence Award in 2009. He has taught a variety of courses in the psychology curriculum, including the Introduction to the Psychology Major course for first-year students and a section of Introductory Psychology specially designed for psychology majors. As an advisor to organizations such as Psi Chi, he partners with students to design opportunities that foster their professional growth and leadership development. He earned his PhD in experimental psychology from the University of Nevada, Las Vegas; MA in general-experimental psychology from California State University, San Bernardino; and BS in psychology from the University of La Verne.

Welcome to Psychology . . . Now Let's Get Stuff Done

1

1.0 MEET KRIS

© Can Stock Photo/cloudrain

CHAPTER OUTLINE

Kris is a senior, about to graduate with a bachelor's degree in psychology. Throughout college he has been a pretty good student, earning mostly B's in his courses (with some A's and some C's). Recently, Kris met with a professor to see if she could provide some insight into what he could do after graduation. The professor asked him if he were considering graduate school or if he were going to start a career right away, but Kris said that he had not given it much thought until now; he said that he thought he would figure out the next step after graduation.

To get a better idea of how she could help, the professor asked Kris if he had worked as a research assistant. Kris said that he remembered one of his professors asking for volunteers, but he had not bothered to follow up on it. She asked if Kris had completed any internships; Kris shook his head no and said that he did not have time. The professor questioned whether Kris was involved with any student organizations like Psychology Club, and Kris told her that he thought those clubs were only for honors students with straight A's. She pressed on and asked if he had been to the career center on campus, but Kris responded with his own question: "There's a career center on our campus?"

At this point, the professor was still not ready to give up—she checked to see what skills Kris developed in college by asking him if he wrote any papers or did presentations in front of a class. Kris said that he purposely chose professors who had reputations for being "easy." He found the ones who were known for using multiple-choice exams, letting students out of class early, and requiring little outside reading and who did not assign papers or projects.

Why Did We Tell You This Story?

Over the years, we have seen too many students like Kris who did not take advantage of their college experience and who did not take time to prepare for their future. Kris should have been (1) exploring possible career paths, (2) taking challenging courses that made him think, (3) developing skills for a professional career, (4) networking with peers in student organizations, (5) getting valuable experience by working on research or completing an internship, (6) taking advantage of free resources offered by his school, and (7) planning his next step well before finishing college. Although it is not too late for Kris to figure things out, he would have been much better off if he had known the keys to succeeding as a psychology student when he was first starting the major.

As professors, we want to see students like you succeed, so we wrote this book to open up the secrets to becoming a successful psychology major! If you take this book seriously, we will help you find possible career paths, determine whether graduate school is a good choice for you, and describe how you can have experiences throughout college that can help to get you there!

1.1 THE GOOD (AND BAD) ABOUT THE PSYCHOLOGY MAJOR

We would like to welcome you into a world that we both love—psychology! Psychology is one of the most popular majors in college today—according to the U.S. Department of Education (2018), it is the fourth most popular college major (see Figure 1.1). One reason is that students seem to be naturally curious about themselves and other people. Another reason is that psychology seems to funnel its way into almost every aspect of our lives (people are constantly perceiving, thinking, remembering, feeling emotions, and reacting to others). Some students choose psychology because they like the idea of helping people who have problems, whereas others may want to apply psychological knowledge to other fields. It's also possible that you have your own reasons for exploring psychology.

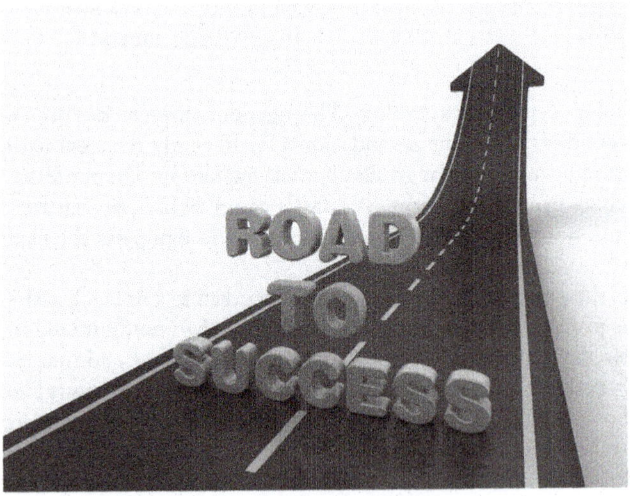

iStock.com/porcorex

FIGURE 1.1

Most Popular Areas of Concentration for Bachelor's Degrees Awarded in 2014–15

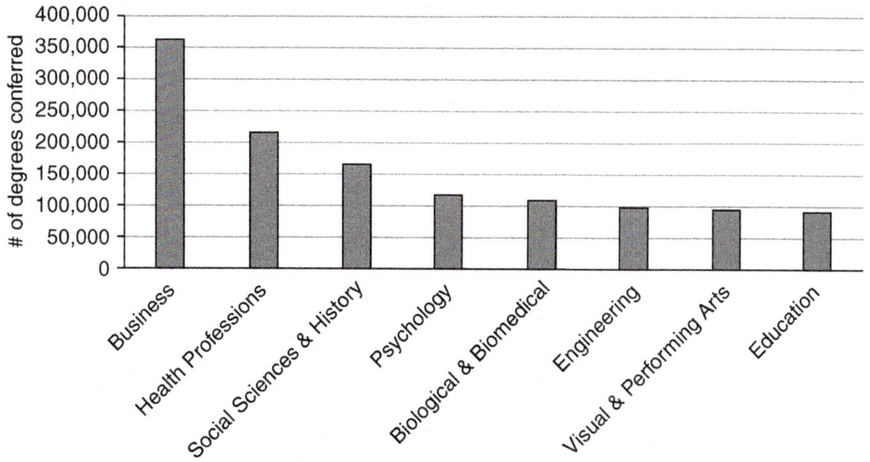

Note: Based on data from U.S. Department of Education, National Center for Education Statistics. (2018). *Digest of education statistics,* 2016 (NCES 2017-094). Retrieved from https://nces.ed.gov/fast-facts/display.asp? id=37.

Regardless of which reason brought you here, you may not have a complete understanding of the pros and cons of psychology as a major. If you told a family member, friend, or academic advisor that you were considering psychology as a major, perhaps that person provided advice about what to expect. We hope that they made you feel excited about your choice of major, but it is also possible that you have heard cautionary tales that scared you. Our goal here is to provide you with a clear picture so that you can dive further into the psychology major as an informed student!

It is likely that there are kernels of truth in both optimistic and pessimistic accounts of psychology as a major. For every driven entrepreneur who attributes her success to what she learned in her psychology courses, there is also likely to be a disillusioned coffee shop barista who laments his experience. Be aware that compelling tales of success or failure tend to stand out in your mind more than the tales of people who simply apply themselves and do well in life. This is due to a cognitive phenomenon worth mentioning here—the availability heuristic (check out Tversky & Kahneman, 1973). Another related idea is the law of small numbers, which is when people mistakenly give more importance to a small number of occurrences that they hear about rather than what happens to most people (e.g., Tversky & Kahneman, 1971).

Our point here is that one person's story—as vivid and compelling as it may seem—should never be the end-all and be-all to your future. Do not stop seeking information once you have heard one story or even a handful of them. Stories can be effective in persuading people (see Green & Brock, 2000), and often they are more powerful than hearing about statistical information (e.g., Betsch, Ulshofer, Renkewitz, & Betsch, 2011). By no means are we saying to discount the information that people share with you. Rather, we suggest you become a relentless and voracious seeker of information. Take in the good and the bad about YOUR major. We will help you get started by sharing some of the things we have seen and heard about psychology.

Negatives About the Psychology Major

There are a number of misconceptions about psychology and its majors (e.g., Brinthaupt, Hurst, & Johnson, 2016)—we listed some of our favorites in Table 1.1. In addition to those, if you have been on the interwebs you may have seen dramatic headlines that disparage certain majors. We noticed a few that described psychology as a "bad major." One described psychology as one of "the worst college majors" (Goudreau, 2012), another as one of "the most worthless college majors" (Trattner, 2018), and two Florida governors questioned the career prospects of psychology majors (Logue, 2016)—one even suggested that psychology students should expect to end up working at places such as Chick-fil-A (Jaschik, 2015).

What should you make of this negativity? Part of this dissatisfaction could stem from ignorance about the field and what the bachelor's degree in psychology will allow you to do. Unlike degrees in applied fields like engineering or nursing that train students for a specific job, the psychology major focuses on teaching you how to think and create. Also, you may be disappointed to learn that an undergraduate bachelor's degree in psychology (a BA or BS) will NOT certify you to start practicing as a counselor, psychotherapist, clinician, or professor—those jobs require additional graduate study (i.e., a master's or doctorate degree).

So, is it time to consider a different major? Of course not—give us a chance to make a case in favor of psychology!

Positives About the Psychology Major

As a psychology major, your curriculum will likely start with an introductory psychology course and then progress to your senior year, when you take in-depth seminar courses and, hopefully, complete a capstone course or culminating project. In between, you will take a journey through Statistics, Research Methods, and a large number of elective courses (we will walk you through some of the many subfields of psychology in Chapter 4). You will gain scientific literacy, quantitative reasoning, and the ability to

TABLE 1.1

Our Favorite (False) Stereotypes and Misconceptions About Psychology (Some Were Inspired by Brinthaupt, Hurst, & Johnson, 2016)

Psychology majors are analyzing everyone that they meet.
Psychologists can read other people's minds.
All psychology majors are trying to figure out their own problems or disorders.
Psychologists have secret labs where they administer electroshock treatments.
All psychology majors become therapists or "shrinks."
Psychology is an easy major because it is based on common sense.

understand, evaluate, and develop empirical research in the social sciences. You will have opportunities to immerse yourself into research, you can dip your toes into the culture of professional conferences, and you will surely get your hands dirty administering studies and playing with data using the statistical software packages of our field (e.g., SPSS, SAS, R, and Excel).

A degree in psychology prepares you with skills that can be applied to a wide variety of careers. These competencies include thinking critically, writing and presenting for various audiences, conducting empirical research, and working with others. In the process, you will gain domain knowledge in statistics, mental disorders, how the mind works, and how people behave. It just so happens that the skills that we just described nicely correspond to a recent article that listed the top skills that employers desire in their new hires (Hart Research Associates, 2018)!

In addition to all of that, psychology can be a gateway to a wide variety of careers. Some are related to mental health or helping others. Psychology can help prepare you to pursue careers in areas such as counseling, therapy, social work, addictions, medicine, or clinical disorders—you may need additional graduate training, but your undergraduate psychology degree is a great start. We also want to emphasize that majoring in psychology does not limit you to those helping fields, as there are many other paths you can pursue, including career opportunities in business, nonprofit organizations, human services, and other areas! We cover this a lot more later in the book when we discuss careers.

Balancing the Good and Bad

As you can see, the positives about the psychology major can outweigh the negatives—it is a matter of informed perspective. Bachelor's-level psychology graduates come away with a toolkit that includes basic scientific skills and, often, an understanding of the "behind the scenes" aspects of empirical research. Additionally, psychology majors glean familiarity, if not a deeper understanding, of subject matter that can be of great use to many industries and work settings.

We wrote this book to educate students like you about this reality. We understand that many students have no clue about what career they would like to pursue, but we want to get you to start thinking about possible careers as early as possible. Even if you have no idea right now, you can still work hard to develop the skills that will be applicable to a variety of careers. Throughout this book, we want to let you know of all of the resources that are available to you to help you be the best that you can be!

We want to end this module on one very important point. No matter what a college diploma can offer students, if you do not take advantage of the opportunities available to you, you may not develop the skills that we described. We expand on this point in much more detail in the next section by distinguishing between a college degree and a college education!

© Can Stock Photo/creatista

Take-Home Message

As you read this book and as you progress in the years to come, we recommend that you devour all of the information you can about the psychology major, career opportunities, and graduate study. Do not be daunted by what may seem challenging or discouraging! We tell our students that it is always best to be an informed optimist rather than a naïve dreamer. Also, keep in mind that no one has ever learned by placing a book beneath their pillow and hoping to learn through diffusion or osmosis—learning takes effort. Take advantage of the opportunities in psychology to learn knowledge and develop your skills!

Action Steps

1. Use this module as an inspiration to connect with current and former psychology majors. Ask them about what they see as negatives and positives to our major. If you want, you can take a moment to fast-forward to the end of this book and check out the advice from people who graduated with degrees in psychology. Use this information to make an informed decision as to whether psychology is the right major for you. And, if you are on the fence and cannot decide if it is a fit or not, finish reading this book before making a decision, as we will provide more information than you could ever imagine about the psychology major.

2. Visit at least one of your professors during their scheduled office hours, or hang around to chat with them after class. In whatever situation works for you, find time to strike up conversations about what you are learning about YOUR major and what suggestions or advice they would give someone new to psychology. You should ask them what they recommend you to do to be successful in the major, how to be in the best position to take the next steps after graduation, and other questions you might have about the major and career opportunities.

iStock.com/alexsl

If you dedicate some time to these actions, you will be well on your way to joining the ranks of the "savvy psych majors" who seek out information on their own. This is a tendency that will suit you well in the years to come. Also, you will hone your skills on how to engage in productive conversations with your peers and mentors. As you will read in the modules to come, you will be most successful if you connect with others in your classes and department.

1.2 DOES A COLLEGE DEGREE GUARANTEE SUCCESS?

It might be tempting to think that a college education is the same thing as a college degree, but the two are a little bit different. A college degree, in and of itself, is a piece of paper (or sheepskin for those of you attending fancy schools) that you can hang on the wall. You might say, "Well, they don't just hand those out to anyone," and that is true to some degree (pun intended), but there is a large amount of variability among those who receive diplomas at graduation. Some graduates have earned honors such as valedictorian or salutatorian because of their incredible grades. In contrast, there are also graduates who may have passed with the minimum grade point average (because they did not bother to read the assigned textbooks)—some of these students may have searched a website like RateMyProfessors.com to find the easiest instructors, particularly ones who did not require papers.

Even though these students may have had completely different experiences in college, all of them end up earning the same degree. The degree is worth the same when it is listed on a résumé or curriculum vitae (CV). So, if a particular job requires a college diploma, all of these individuals can apply (see Caplan, 2018, for a unique discussion on this topic).

A College Education

In contrast to the degree itself, a college education consists of the knowledge, skills, relationships, and the experiences you build along the way (e.g., Bruni, 2018). In psychology, you can read about fascinating (and sometimes controversial) research studies—you can also take part in class discussions about these issues. You can become a research assistant and contribute to scientific studies that might one day be taught in textbooks. You can join organizations and travel to psychology conferences that are nearby or far away. You can ask your instructors or the campus career office for assistance finding an internship that can help you gain work experience. You can develop writing skills that are applicable to a variety of careers. If you find instructors who challenge you, then you can also develop your ability to critically think (we guarantee that this is a skill that can help for the rest of your life).

iStock.com/JohnnyGreig

As you can see, a college education can be very good or it could be just okay (or "meh"). Ultimately, the choice of what you want to get out of college is completely up to you, but you are probably not surprised to learn that we are big proponents of getting a good education. To help you out, we included some suggestions for psychology

TABLE 1.2
An Example of a Good College Education in Psychology

1.	Extensive knowledge about topics (e.g., in psychology)
2.	The use of classroom and study tips that lead to long-term knowledge and knowing how to continue learning throughout life
3.	The ability to write and communicate effectively
4.	Experience in research and/or an internship
5.	Relationships with professors, fellow students, and/or professionals in your preferred career area (i.e., networking)
6.	Knowledge and skills in other areas (e.g., a minor or second major)
7.	The ability to think critically about arguments and to make rational decisions
8.	Knowing how to find reliable information
9.	Learning from setbacks and failures rather than avoiding them or quitting at the first sign of trouble
10.	Enhancing your computer skills
11.	A clear and well-developed plan for achieving your career goals
12.	Awareness of how graduate school can benefit certain career paths (and, if you choose that route, knowledge of how to get into graduate school)
13.	Taking advantage of opportunities that come with your tuition (e.g., advising, career services, job fairs, guest speakers from other schools)
14.	A good monetary situation for yourself (e.g., scholarships that minimize or eliminate the need for loans)
15.	Unique experiences that you will remember your entire life (e.g., travel abroad, completing an honors thesis, attending a professional conference, building friendships, challenging yourself and succeeding)

students in Table 1.2. We think that those of you who take our advice and use college as an opportunity to develop skills, gain long-term knowledge, and try new things will be at an advantage—and you will have those skills and experiences for the rest of your life.

Take-Home Message

As the saying goes, *C's might get degrees, but A's and B's succeed!* We want to expand this and say that average grades can get you the diploma, but skills and experiences can land you the job. So, do more than the minimum—work hard in the classroom and get involved in activities outside of class! Keep in mind that being serious about one's college education does not mean never having any fun. To the contrary, getting involved in your education can be invigorating! Taking part in psychological research can lead to new discoveries. Joining a club like Psi Chi gives you the chance to meet new people and socialize. Taking advantage of study abroad can open up a new way of life to you. In college, there are tons of opportunities that are available, so why not jump right in and reap the benefits? In this book, we make a lot of recommendations as to how you can get all of the advantages of being a psychology major!

Action Steps

1. Take a few minutes to think about whether you are in college for the degree, the education, or both (we recommend this last option!). Decide today whether you want the basic, no-frills, minimal-effort college degree or whether you want to participate in the add-ons that can come with it. The good news is that most of the add-ons do not cost money, just a little bit of your time and effort, but the payoff can be big in the long term!

© Can Stock Photo/soupstock

2. Imagine yourself at graduation—visualize not only what you look like but also the knowledge, skills, and experiences that you have gained as a college student. Imagine yourself so that you are similar to the description in Table 1.1—do you like what you see? If so, then commit to taking action and making that goal your reality. Even if you have already started college on the wrong foot, there is still time to change—start today!

1.3 SUPERSTAR PSYCHOLOGY STUDENTS

Now that you know the importance of a college education, we want to encourage you to aspire to become a superstar psychology student! That is, we want you to strive to get the most out of the psychology major and to be ready to transition to the work world or graduate school. We started with existing research on the topic (Bain, 2012; Martin, 2015; Newport, 2005) and then we also conducted informal interviews with colleagues about this topic. Putting that all together, we developed a list of 12 traits and accomplishments of superstar psychology students.[1] And, for those of you who are interested, there are also descriptions of superstar psychology graduate students, too (see Grover, Leftwich, Backhaus, Fairchild, & Weaver, 2006).

Start by reading through these descriptions. Then, answer the questions in the Self-Assessment to see where you are right now. Finally, use these items as you think about where you want to be in the future!

iStock.com/SIphotography

[1]We understand that the term "superstar psychology student" might sound a little corny, but we like it because it is memorable, it clearly conveys an image of achieving success, and others have already been using it (see Grover, Leftwich, Backhaus, Fairchild, & Weaver, 2006; Martin, 2015). Remember that *any of you* can reach this status if you follow the advice in this book!

Traits and Accomplishments of Superstar Psychology Students

1. Superstar students *actually* use effective study techniques.

   They do not just claim to "know how to study"; they ACTUALLY use good study techniques. Effective study techniques lead to long-term knowledge and good grades.

2. Superstar students take the time to learn APA-style formatting (and word-processing software).

   They pay attention to details in their work and proofread carefully. Everyone makes mistakes—however, those who look over their work so that they can fix mistakes tend to do better. Employers and graduate programs expect people to know how to use popular software like Word, so take the time in college to learn!

3. Superstar students get involved in research.

   This is especially true for those who plan to enter doctoral graduate programs (many of those involve research), but it can also help those who are looking into jobs or master's programs as well. Working on research can help you with data analysis, communication, and critical thinking skills. It can also be a way to earn a good letter of recommendation.

4. Superstar students find an internship to get relevant work experience (and connections).

   Internships can help in a number of ways: they can (a) build your résumé, (b) help you to develop skills, (c) teach you about a career path, and (d) possibly get your foot in the door for a future job. Good Grades + Internship = Better Résumé.

5. Superstar students join a few college clubs and professional organizations.

   The key is not to join every club or professional organization, but to selectively join ones that can help YOU. Clubs allow you to meet others who have similar goals, and they are an opportunity to build skills (and résumé lines) in leadership positions. Professional organizations can provide you with resources (e.g., books, scholarship and grant opportunities, tips on careers or graduate school, etc.).

6. Superstar students apply for scholarships, grants, and awards.

   Scholarships, grants, and awards are easy ways to say the following to employers and graduate programs, "You should hire/admit me because this organization thought highly enough of me to give me money and/or recognition!" Plus, who does not want free money or a pat on the back?

7. Superstar students add a minor (or possibly a second major).

   Having a minor (or second major) can be a nice complement to your psychology training. With the right planning (use campus advising for help!)

Self-Assessment

iStock.com/akinbostanci

The next step is for you to assess yourself on the qualities of a superstar psychology student. For each of the items below, answer "Yes" or "No" based on the current you:

1. Are you actively using effective study skills?
2. Do you know how to properly write in APA-style formatting?
3. Have you worked on research?
4. Have you gained work experience in an internship?
5. Do you have memberships in any professional or college organizations?
6. Have you earned any scholarships, research grants, or awards?
7. Do you have a minor or second major?
8. Do you have strong critical thinking skills related to data and statistics?
9. Do you have a plan for your career and the path to get there?
10. Do you have a clear idea of what specific degree(s) is/are needed for your career goals?
11. Do you know how to properly prepare for graduate school?
12. Do you know how to properly document your accomplishments on a CV and résumé?

this can be built into your course schedule. It can also help you stand out from all of the other college students who did not do it.

8. Superstar students focus on learning statistics and developing critical thinking skills.

   Instead of succumbing to math anxiety, superstar psychology students realize that analytical thinking and the ability to work with data/numbers/statistics is an important skill in today's world (think of all of the data that companies and governments gather—valued employees will be able to work with data).

9. Superstar students figure out what they want to do after college.

   It is okay to not know what you want to do after college, but the sooner you can figure it out, the sooner you can have a concrete goal that you want to reach. Progress tends to happen faster when you have an end goal in mind.

10. Superstar students figure out what degree they need for their career goals.

    Superstar students do not earn a degree and then ask, "Now what can I do with this degree?" Instead, they say "I want to do __, and it requires a __ degree"—then they go after the degree(s) that they need.

11. Superstar students learn how to prepare for graduate school.

    Many psychology-related careers require some graduate training, and graduate school is much more competitive than college. So, if this is a possibility (or even a remote possibility), start preparing early.

12. Superstar students know how to document their accomplishments.

    Most jobs require that you submit a résumé, and graduate school applications require you to submit a CV. So, learn how to build these and what accomplishments will make them impressive!

Take-Home Message

While we use the term "superstar psychology student" because it is catchy and we want you to dream big, we think that each and every one of you can reach superstar status. There is nothing magical to the steps that we described in this module—the key idea is that you have to take action in order to build up these accomplishments. Keep reading this book so that you can learn how to make these happen!

Action Steps

1. How many "Yes" answers (out of 12) do you have from the Self-Assessment? If you did not already do it, please go back and answer the superstar questions for yourself!
2. How many "Yes" answers do you want to have in a year or two? Which ones? How many do you want to have by graduation? Set these aside where you can find them later, and return to your answers here after you finish this chapter and learn more about setting goals. As a preview, we want you to make your goals very specific!

1.4 MOTIVATION FOR COLLEGE SUCCESS—WHAT IS YOUR "WHY"?

Imagine that we asked you to hop on a bicycle today and ride 100 miles without stopping. Some of you (who are cycling enthusiasts) might not mind, but most of you would probably find a way to politely decline that request. Now, instead of us making that request, imagine that a close loved one was 100 miles away, in serious trouble, and the only way for you to get there was by riding a bike—would you do it now? The difference between those two scenarios is that, in the latter scenario, you had a strong motivation (or "why") to complete that daunting task. In the words of Nietzsche (1889), "He who has a *why* can bear almost any *how*."

If you have just started college, then you can see a large number of courses and requirements ahead of you over the next few years. If you have been in college for a few years, then you know that college can be humbling at times. To help you get through this, we want to describe a technique described by Miller (2014). Take a moment and ask yourself, "What is your reason for being in college (and completing your degree)? In other words, why do you stay in college?"

iStock.com/IvelinRadkov

The answer to this can differ among college students. For example, maybe you are a nontraditional student who needs college training to restart a brand-new career path. Perhaps you are a first-generation college student and your family has pushed you to go beyond their educational achievements. In a similar manner, maybe your parents and grandparents sacrificed a lot so that you could have this opportunity and you do not want to let them down. Or is it possible that you have a dream of becoming a neurosurgeon so that you can use your knowledge and skills to save and improve lives? Others might be completing college to set a good example for their kids. For some of you, the answer might be obvious; however, for others, you may have to think a little bit more. Keep in mind that the answer can be different for different people. Regardless of your reason, though, be specific about your motivation. Whatever your reason, write it down!

Take-Home Message

We put you through this exercise because college is a lengthy process that can wear you down at times. When you experience those moments—whether it is the miserable feeling of getting a D on a difficult exam, not seeing an end in sight, questioning your choice of major, or having difficulty finding time to get everything done—refer back to your reason for being in college and wanting to finish. Digging deep down to find that motivation can potentially mean the difference between sticking to it and giving up. We want you to succeed, so find that motivation and remind yourself why you are here!

Action Steps

1. Maybe your "why" is similar to one of the previous responses, but maybe it is different—regardless, we want you to think about and to search for your "why." Make sure that it is personal and specific—try to avoid broad or generic ideas that have little to no impact on you.

iStock.com/Ben-Schonewille

2. Once you have it, write it down and put it where you will see it—use it to remind yourself why it is important for you to put in the effort to succeed!

1.5 SETTING GOALS AND CREATING SYSTEMS TO ACHIEVE THEM

Thus far, we have emphasized the importance of a college education, described the traits of superstar students, and asked you to identify your "why." Although this is a great start, it is just step one. The next step for achieving more is to set goals for what you want to accomplish. Importantly for you, there is research that has demonstrated that setting the right kinds of goals can lead to improved academic performance in college over simply trying to do your best (e.g., Latham & Brown, 2006). However, it is important to keep in mind that goals are most helpful when they are used properly (e.g., Locke & Latham, 2006). In this module, our objective is to help you to understand how to best use goals toward success in college.

Start by Creating Large Goals—Dream Big!

A major purpose of using goals is to give yourself some direction. Without goals, you might drift aimlessly as you may not have anything specific that you are trying to accomplish. Let's fix this by taking a moment and writing down five long-term goals that you would like to accomplish. This can relate to college or a future career or it can be one of the traits of superstar psychology students—these are good choices because goals that require effort lead to higher levels of satisfaction than easy ones (Locke & Latham, 2006).

Keep the Goals Positive!

The way that something is framed or presented can affect your decisions and performance (e.g., Kahneman, 2013). We recommend that you phrase your goal as a positive challenge rather than trying to avoid a negative consequence—the former tends to lead to higher achievement than the latter (e.g., Drach-Zahavy & Erez, 2002). For example, a goal to earn a grade point average of 3.5 or higher is better than a goal to avoid earning any C's or D's—in other words, aim to win instead of trying not to lose.

iStock.com/hadynyah

Break Goals Into Specific Subgoals (and Subgoals Into Even More Specific Daily Goals)

One thing that you will notice about most big goals (e.g., land an internship) is that they are not likely to be accomplished today. Unfortunately, because they seem far out into the future and in the land of "someday," you may not feel very motivated to work toward them today. And, if

FIGURE 1.2

Example of Breaking a Big Goal Down Into Subgoal and Daily Goals.

GOAL: Earn an A on the exam	
SUBGOAL 1: Study	SUBGOAL 2: Get help or clarification
DAILY GOAL 1a: Read Chapter 1	DAILY GOAL 2a: Ask questions in class
DAILY GOAL 1b: Summarize Chapter 1	DAILY GOAL 2b: Visit office hours
DAILY GOAL 1c: Read Chapter 2	
DAILY GOAL 1d: Summarize Chapter 2	
DAILY GOAL 1e: Review chapter summaries	
DAILY GOAL 1f: Create flashcards for key definitions	

you feel that way today, then you are also likely to feel that way tomorrow, next week, next month, next year, and, well, you get the idea.

One secret to avoiding this problem is to break vague and distant goals down into more detailed subgoals (Latham & Brown, 2006). Unfortunately, one mistake that we see students make is that their subgoals are not specific enough! If your goal is to graduate from college, a subgoal might be to complete your Statistics course; however, you might be weeks away from achieving this subgoal. Break this down even further until it is something you can accomplish today (call these daily goals). In this example (see Figure 1.2), your daily goal might be to read Chapter 5 in your Statistics textbook and to complete the assigned problems. The takeaway here is that you need to keep making goals more and more specific until it is something that you can realistically achieve today!

Create a Timeline

Besides specificity, another thing to consider is the timeframe of completing goals. In one regard, this involves setting some type of deadline. Consider these two goals: (a) "I am going to do an internship one day" vs. (b) "I am going to apply for an internship this week." With the former, who knows when "one day" is going to occur? In contrast, the latter pushes you to take action because you have defined a timeframe for it. If possible, we recommend creating timelines by working backward from a deadline. If a class presentation is scheduled for 2 weeks from today, work back from that date to determine what your daily goals can be between now and then.

Build a System for Your Goals

When you have long-term or predictable goals, systems are helpful as a plan of attack for each day or week. Systems are a way to create a routine where you can chip away at a goal, making steady progress until you reach that goal. For example, simply saying "I want to study more" is probably not very effective—but planning that you are going to the library to study from 3:00 p.m. to 5:00 p.m. Sunday through Thursday is a system that is more likely to work. You may already be using systems but you just do not realize it.

If you have ever learned how to play a musical instrument or played a sport, then you probably used a system. In these scenarios, you likely practiced on a regular basis (and improved as a result). If systems can be successful for music or sports, why not try them with college? Set aside specific days and times throughout each week where you can work on courses, papers, or other accomplishments. This can be any time that works for you—right when you wake up, between two courses, or in the evening. Also, these sessions do not have to be very long—they could be as short as 10 minutes or as long as an hour or two—the key is to spread them out.

A final point that we want to make about systems is that you should design them so that you will stick with them—you do not want to set them up to fail. A common mistake that we see is that some people are overly ambitious—they might make plans to study 40 hours per week, but it is not realistic that they will stick with that schedule. So, try to be reasonable when building a system. Another thing to try is to apply the psychological construct of positive reinforcement (e.g., Skinner, 1948). That is, when you stick to your system, reward yourself! Using positive reinforcement will help you to continue following your system in the future.

Take-Home Message

Rather than drifting through college hoping to "do your best," set goals so that you know what you want to accomplish. Remember that most goals tend to be too large to accomplish in one day, so it is important to keep breaking them down into specific subgoals and even more specific daily goals that can be realistically accomplished. A final note about goals is that, if left alone, they are no better than wishes—we could wish for world peace, but that does not mean that it is going to happen. Goals and wishes do no good unless you act on them. So take the first step today!

Action Steps

1. Create a list of at least five long-term goals that you want to achieve (you can refer back to your superstar goals from an earlier module). Keep in mind that this list can be fluid—you can add to it or subtract from it in the future. Once you have your list, break each goal down into more and more specific subgoals; keep going until you can create daily goals.

© can stock photo/nan104

2. Take time to plan a daily/weekly system for when you can work on tasks that you want to accomplish for your courses. Create specific blocks of time that are dedicated to studying and preparing for a certain course. You can also set up certain blocks that are fluid and can be used for whatever course that week has any upcoming big activities such as an exam, paper, or presentation.

3. Get into the habit of starting each day with a list of achievable daily goals and cross them off as you complete them. Some people prefer to write out a list at night (for the next day), and others prefer to create it in the morning—do whatever works best for you.

1.6 OVERCOMING PROCRASTINATION AND GETTING STUFF DONE

Raise your hand if you have ever set a goal but put it off until later because you did not feel like doing it? If it makes you feel better, we (and other professors) raised our hands, too (Ackerman & Gross, 2007). Although you may tell yourself, "I'll feel like doing it tomorrow," the problem is that, when tomorrow comes, you will likely say the exact same thing, putting it off yet another day (Pychyl, 2013). Some of you may even try to convince yourselves that procrastination is actually a productive strategy ("I work better under a lot of pressure!"); unfortunately, though, research suggests that this is not true for most people (Ferrari, 2001). In this module, we will first explore some reasons that we procrastinate. After that, we will provide a number of suggestions for how you can change your ways and procrastinate less.

iStock.com/anyaberkut

What Happens When We Procrastinate (in a Fun Story)

According to Urban (2016), when we are not procrastinating, it is as if our mind is being directed by a *Rational Decision-Maker* who is the captain steering us into reasonable decisions. However, every once in a while, our Rational Decision-Maker receives a visit from the *Instant Gratification Monkey*.

The Instant Gratification Monkey wants to do anything that feels good in the moment—checking websites, downloading apps, eating food—basically anything that you can easily do right now that feels good. The Instant Gratification Monkey has no qualms with steering us off course, leading us to procrastinate.

Urban (2016) continues his tale by introducing one more character—the *Panic Monster*!

© Can Stock Photo / qliebin

iStock.com/VladGans

The Panic Monster wakes up when a deadline gets close because it desperately wants to avoid the negative repercussions of inaction (e.g., a failing grade). As you may have noticed in your own life, the Panic Monster can scare away the Instant Gratification Monkey, which is good in that the task gets done; however, the Panic Monster can bring a lot of stress.

This example illustrates a lot of problems that come with procrastination (Tice & Baumeister, 1997). At first, procrastination may seem good as stress is low—but this is only true while you are putting the task off. When the deadline approaches (and the Panic Monster arrives), the stress ramps up! A side effect (possibly due to this stress) is that procrastinators tend to be sick more often than nonprocrastinators. Another major problem, particularly for students, is that procrastination leads to lower grades.

Why Do We Procrastinate?

One reason that we procrastinate is that we tend to value immediate rewards over future rewards. For example, a number of studies (e.g., Mischel, Shoda, & Rodriguez, 1989) showed that individuals had difficulty resisting an initial offer of a single piece of candy, even when they could wait and receive a larger reward after a delay. This relates to procrastination because, in the moment, you might prefer an activity that is fun right now (e.g., playing on your phone), even though you might earn a high grade later if you worked on that essay today.

We also tend to underestimate the length of tasks and then, because of that, overestimate our ability to get things done. Because of this, we are willing to put things off because we think that we will have plenty of time later. This is dangerous because a research study (Buehler, Griffin, & Ross, 1994) demonstrated that the actual time for students to complete an academic task was nearly twice as long as what those students predicted!

Finally, procrastination can serve as a protection for our self-esteem. If we delay a task and still do well, it is because of our "phenomenal talent and skills." However, if we delay a task but do not end up doing well, we tell ourselves that the poor outcome was due to the time crunch. As you can see, we have a built-in excuse ready to use (Ferrari & Tice, 2000)!

Two Types of Procrastination

So far, we have been mainly focusing on one type of procrastination—this is when we procrastinate but we have the "safety net" of a deadline that can cause us to panic and get the task done. The second type is when we have life plans or bucket-list items that do not have deadlines (e.g., "I want to learn how to speak Italian and travel to Italy"). The problem here is that we can continually put things off with no penalties—this can potentially lead to a lot of regret later in life when we look back at what we did not accomplish.

Regardless of what type of procrastination you are dealing with, imagine how much more productive and successful you could be if you did not procrastinate as much. If you could avoid procrastinating, you could actually make significant progress with your goals!

TABLE 1.3

WHAT-WHEN-WHERE-HOW To-Do List Example

WHAT?	Read Chapter 2 for Research Methods
WHEN?	2:00 to 3:00 p.m. on Monday this week—between my classes
WHERE?	Coffee shop across from campus
HOW?	Online textbook—there is free WiFi for my laptop. Bonus: caffeine will help keep me awake and focused!

TABLE 1.4

IF → THEN Examples

IF I have a break between classes, THEN I will read a chapter for class.
IF I am reading for class, THEN my phone will be turned off and in my backpack.
IF my calendar shows an alert for an exam in 2 weeks, THEN I will create flashcards for studying.

Fortunately for you, a number of psychological researchers have studied procrastination and have come up with ways to reduce it (e.g., Ferrari, 2010; Pychyl, 2013).

One Strategy to Reduce Procrastination

The first strategy you can implement is to go beyond a standard to-do list; this is because a standard list only includes *what* needs to get accomplished (Pychyl, 2013). To go beyond the standard list, you want to add to the "what" by also describing the "when," "where," and "how" as well. For example, if you know that you have to write an essay for class (what), you should also specify that you are going to work on it tomorrow afternoon at 2:00 p.m. (when) in the library (where) by looking up articles in the library database and writing the essay on your laptop (how) (see Table 1.3).

Gollwitzer and Sheeran (2006) recommend that you use "if→ then" rules to increase the odds that you start taking action (see Table 1.4). You can do this by setting up a trigger or cue that will signal that it is time to start working on that essay—for example, you could program a reminder on your phone calendar for 2:00 p.m. tomorrow. To put it in Gollwitzer and Sheeran's terminology, *if* you see the calendar alert, *then* you write the essay. You can also set up cues to create a regular routine or habit. For example, we knew one student who implemented a study routine based on when his young child went to sleep. *If* his child went to bed, *then* he would read or study for an hour (this example is somewhat similar to one described by Pychyl, 2013). You can use anything as a cue, but make it clear!

Ideally, you should take this a step further and prepare for possible distractions (or Instant Gratification Monkeys). For example, you can probably anticipate some likely distractions (e.g., text messages from friends). Once you have identified those possible distractions, plan "if→ then" rules for how you are going to deal with them. With the text message example, you can set up a rule that *if* you are working on a paper, *then* you will turn your phone completely off and stash it in your bag. Avoiding distractions and knowing what you will do can help tremendously!

iStock.com/marekuliasz

A Second Strategy to Reduce Procrastination

The strategy here is easier said than done—if you catch yourself procrastinating, then push yourself to *just get started* (Pychyl, 2013). Sitting there and thinking about the task is probably not going to get you anywhere, so you might as well just get started. The act of getting started is helpful because you can develop momentum for working on the task and you can see that the task itself is not so bad.

In order to get started, you may have to focus on stripping away the emotions that surround a task (e.g., fear of failure, being in awe of the amount of work needed to be done)—these emotions can make the task seem more intimidating. Remember, you do not have to "feel like doing it" to get it done. Another helpful tip here is to think of "what" you have to do in a concrete manner instead of abstractly (e.g., McCrea, Liberman, Trope, & Sherman, 2008). So, instead of dreading that "lengthy paper," think of it as more concrete steps—sitting down to brainstorm, selecting a topic, conducting a simple library search, summarizing articles, etc.

Some Additional Thoughts about Getting Stuff Done

In addition to the strategies we just described, there are a few more suggestions that people can try. First, remember that everyone procrastinates, so do not beat yourself up too much about it. Second, be sure that you value your future self as much as you value your current self—imagine where you want to be in the future (set goals!). If you truly value that future self, then you better start taking steps now to make that happen. You can also better connect to that future by thinking of time in smaller units—think about an upcoming deadline as 14 days instead of 2 weeks (Lewis & Oyserman, 2015). Finally, use a basic psychological principle from operant conditioning—set up plans to reward yourself for getting tasks done.

Take-Home Message

Procrastination is something that happens to everyone, but psychologists have an understanding of why we procrastinate and how we can reduce it. There are a number of strategies described here that you can try in your own life. However, suppose that you follow the steps described previously but after a while you are back to your old habits. What should you do—give up? Of course not! You may not want to repeat the exact same plan that did not work; instead, figure out how you can improve your plan, and then try again. And if that does not work? Reassess your plan again, make some changes, and then try again! But most importantly, try those strategies today (do not procrastinate)!

Action Steps

iStock.com/katleho Seisa

1. Start implementing these strategies in your daily life by picking some tasks where you are currently procrastinating. Start by creating an expanded to-do list and use cues to create "if → then" rules for triggering action (do not forget to account for possible distractions by creating "if → then" rules for those).
2. Pick another task where you are currently procrastinating and **JUST GET STARTED** on it right now. To help with this, (a) strip away any emotions (e.g., fear of failure, not feeling like doing it) and (b) think about the task in a very concrete manner (break the task down into smaller, concrete steps).

1.7 LIVING THE "GETTING STUFF DONE" (GSD) LIFESTYLE

In the world of superheroes, a lucky few are either born with extraordinary powers (e.g., Wonder Woman) or suddenly gain new powers (e.g., Spider-Man); however, in real life, things are not that easy. Real-life musical talents like the Beatles and Beyoncé did not instantly go into the studio to create a masterpiece—they worked extremely hard over time to get to that point. Some of the best athletes might start with physical talent, but they become great by pushing themselves and chipping away at goals (e.g., Grover, 2014).

In college, you are not going to be bitten by a radioactive spider that will give you superstar abilities—you actually have to put in effort by reading books, paying attention in class, and writing papers. If you want to be productive, you have to put in some effort. Most people seem to go through their days on autopilot, wasting time and occasionally reacting to external pressures like deadlines. However, imagine how much you could get done if you adopted the GSD lifestyle!

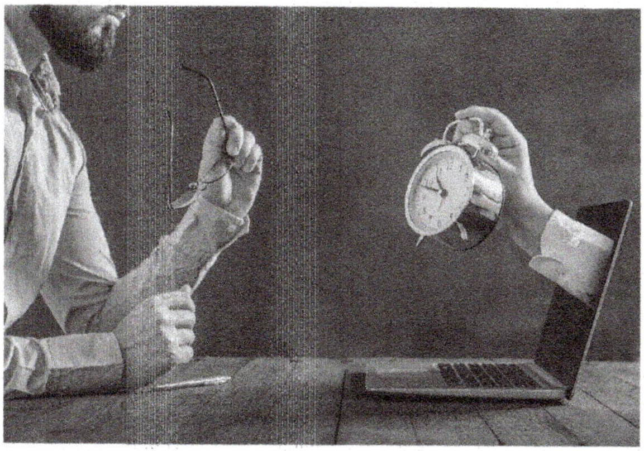

iStock.com/baloon111

Part of the GSD lifestyle is finding time for things that are a priority in life. Seeing that a college education can potentially affect your mental abilities and your future earning potential, we think that it should qualify as a priority. Because it is a priority, you need to find time to do it well. We recognize that you already have constraints on your time (e.g., family responsibilities, a job, etc.), but we bet that everyone can find pockets of time that you may not have noticed—use those moments to get stuff done. As we will explain, you do not have to find large pockets of time; small bits of effort can build up into large accomplishments!

Set Goals—How Many Superstar Psychology Student Accomplishments Do You Want to Achieve?

Instead of drifting through college, use this book to set goals of what you want to achieve. As we noted earlier, people accomplish more when they have a goal (e.g., Latham & Brown, 2006). We did some of the work for you by describing the accomplishments of superstar psychology students. Now you just have to decide which ones are important to you and to then break those down into specific goals so that you can keep making progress toward them. If possible, be very specific by breaking subgoals down so that it is something that you can achieve today. Remember, any step forward, no matter how small, is better than moving backward or standing still.

Plan for Activities to Take Longer Than You Expect

A simple fact of life is that activities take longer to complete than people expect—this is referred to as the planning fallacy (Kahneman & Tversky, 1979). The funny thing about this is that people fall victim to this over and over and over. When we work with students who are writing a thesis (a long research paper), it is not uncommon for them to tell us that they will have it written in 2 months. However, nine out of 10 times, when those 2 months have passed, they only completed about half of the writing.[2]

Our point here is that you should always start early (if possible) so that you can give yourself more time to get things done. If you think you can write a good paper in a weekend, allocate a full week for it. If you think it will take 20 minutes to read a chapter, be realistic and give yourself an hour. When adopting the GSD lifestyle, beware of the planning fallacy!

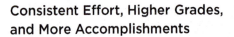

iStock.com/PointImages

Consistent Effort, Higher Grades, and More Accomplishments

Imagine a silly example where college students approached taking courses in a procrastination-like manner—you would put off taking courses for 3½ years and then, when the Panic Monster arrived (Urban, 2016), you would try to cram 100 credits worth of courses into a single semester! Instead, college students follow a more reasonable strategy of taking

[2] We humorously refer to this as the half-life rule—for big projects, when you reach the date you expected to be finished, you will only be halfway to your goal.

approximately three to five courses each semester, making consistent progress on the way to graduation.

Think about it, procrastinating in that college course example sounds ludicrous—so why do we do it with other tasks?

We recommend the approach of making consistent effort—study a little bit here and a little bit there; read a textbook chapter tonight, read another one tomorrow over lunch. Chip away at it! If you could find 1 hour each day to read, there would be no need to cram or panic the night before an exam (see Figure 1.3). If you want to have a lot of experiences in college, then spread them out. Try an internship one semester, work on a research team another semester. However, if you keep putting things off, eventually that exam will arrive or graduation day will be there—without consistent progress, you will not be ready. With the GSD lifestyle, you can choose to be productive now instead of waiting until "someday."

Eat the Frog First!

There is an old saying (sometimes attributed to Mark Twain) that states that, if you start your day by eating a live frog, then, no matter what else happens that day, you can have a sense of accomplishment because you already tackled a difficult task (Tracy, 2017). Now, we are not suggesting that you actually eat a live frog. Instead, this saying suggests that you should dive into your most important and difficult task first.

Suppose that you have two key activities that you want to get done that day—studying for an exam and catching up with friends on social media. "Eating the frog" means that you should study first, followed by catching up on social media. Let's say that you opted to start with the fun activity (with the best of intentions to study later)—it is not difficult to

FIGURE 1.3

Comparison of Consistent Effort vs. Procrastination and Last-Minute Panic

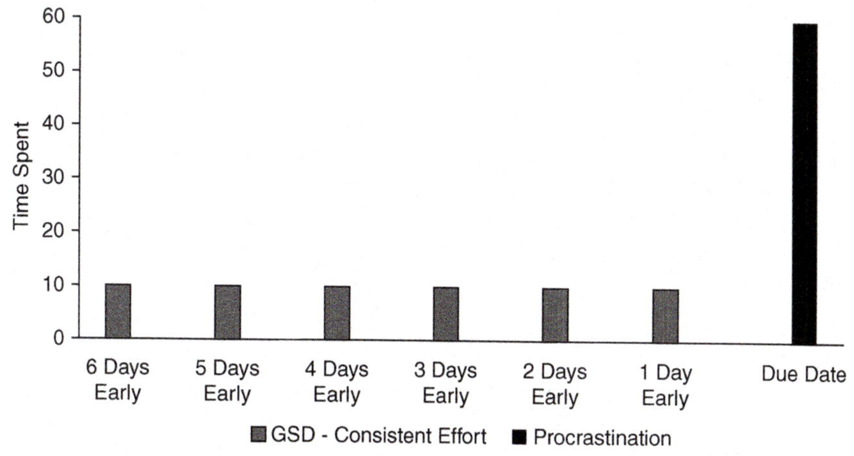

iStock.com/IgorIgorevich

imagine getting sucked into an internet rabbit hole where you start responding to friends and watching videos and then that leads to downloading and playing with some new apps. And, just like that, there is no time (or energy) left for studying. To avoid a situation like this, the GSD lifestyle dictates that you should eat the frog first!

Less Stress

As we discussed in an earlier module, procrastination is an invitation for the Panic Monster (Urban, 2016) to come and visit. In other words, why live your academic life so that it is more stressful than it needs to be? So, get that paper started, build a cushion when planning how long activities will take, read your textbook consistently, and log into your online course more than once a week! A major benefit to the GSD lifestyle is that you should start to feel more confident about your academic performance as you make more progress.

Still Time for Fun and Family

Although productivity may sound like a lot of work, one trick is that you can do it with minimal time and effort. You do not necessarily have to push yourself for hours each day—just be consistent with small amounts of progress. For example, imagine if your current routine consists of attending class, working at a job, spending time with friends or family, and no time spent reading your textbooks—if you increase your daily reading time from 0 minutes to 15 minutes, then your productivity should noticeably improve. In most cases, your friends and family will understand that you need some time to devote to your education, especially if they are supportive of you and your goal to earn a college degree!

Take-Home Message

So, how do you do this? Stop working on autopilot, following your old routine, and floating toward whatever seems easy. Instead, make a true determination to get things done. As we noted in other modules, one key is using a little bit of effort to **JUST GET STARTED** (Pychyl, 2013). Make the conscious choice to live the GSD lifestyle and then take action! If you ever stumble or lose your way, remind yourself "why" you are in college!

Action Steps

1. Make a promise to yourself right now that, as you move through this book, you will take action as you learn about what you can do to improve yourself (eat those frogs!). We cannot say it enough—take action, do not

procrastinate—reap the benefits of the GSD lifestyle!

2. Each and every one of you will run into problems at some point.

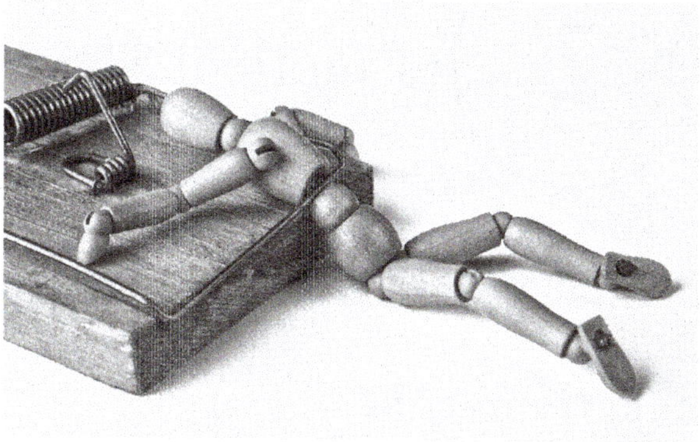

iStock.com/LuisPortugal

There will be a week where a job might demand more hours of your time, there might be nights when the siren call of Netflix or Hulu will be too much to resist—regardless of what happens, studying and schoolwork will likely be a casualty in those scenarios. When that happens, avoid the temptation to give up the entire plan completely. Instead, admit to yourself that you messed up, but then dive right back into the plan. If you have a bad day, a bad week, or even a bad semester, shrug it off and jump back into the GSD lifestyle!

2 Practical Student Tips

CHAPTER OUTLINE

2.0 MEET NICOLE

iStock.com/alvarez

Nicole is a freshman who just declared a major in psychology. She is a first-generation college student, meaning that she is the first person in her immediate family to attend college. Because of that, Nicole did not have any guidance about the simple things in college—this includes things like how to take notes and how to study.

In her General Psychology course she was surprised to see that psychological researchers have learned a lot about how people learn, strategies they can use to better remember information, and what does not matter. This caught her attention because her first year of college was much more challenging than high school. At times she has struggled to retain the material—especially when it was time for an exam. This caused her grades to be a bit lower than she expected.

Nicole may have been struggling, but she was smart enough to realize that she needed to do better. If she did not improve her study strategies, she would probably become frustrated and possibly drop out of college. Even though she always thought of herself as somewhat introverted, she gathered some courage and stopped by her instructor's office to ask how she could improve her approach to studying.

Why Did We Tell You This Story?

We know of a lot of students who have been in similar situations as Nicole. Some are unsure of the most effective study techniques, some hold mistaken beliefs about learning and memory that have been falsified in psychological research studies, and some are familiar with the best study strategies but fail to apply them on an everyday basis. Please read this chapter carefully as we provide a lot of practical advice based on research. And, finally, if you need it, be sure to follow the tips from the previous chapter regarding goals, systems, avoiding procrastination, and the GSD lifestyle!

2.1 DUE DATES? GRADING POLICY? IT'S IN THE SYLLABUS!

Because many students never seem to read the syllabus (e.g., Raymark & Connor-Greene, 2002), one of us created a t-shirt with a simple slogan emblazoned across the front: "It's in the Syllabus!" (the other one has a coffee mug with this slogan). This is frustrating for instructors because the most basic questions about the structure and format of any college course can be answered if students took a moment to read it (Doolittle & Siudzinski, 2010). So, we want to begin this chapter by providing some professorly advice. For almost any question you have about the structure and policies of a course, the answer is probably in the syllabus!

It Is Not Just a Boring Legal Document

Please read your syllabi at the beginning of a semester! We admit that syllabi contain jargon that can be boring—the reason is that college administrators require instructors to include a bunch of university policies. However, there are a lot of important course details spelled out in your syllabi (Harrington & Gabert-Quillen, 2015)—here are some highlights that you should always read:

1. **Professor Contact Information.** Does your professor prefer email, text messages, or phone calls? Pay attention because that is what they will monitor. Also, we check our messages and try to respond within 2 business days—so please do the same!

2. **Office Hours and Appointment Policy.** We highly recommend that you take advantage of office hours! You can use them to (a) get help with difficult topics, (b) prepare in advance for a big project (ask for additional tips), or (c) ask questions about your major, a career, graduate school, research, student clubs, or anything else you want to learn about.

3. **Course Objectives and Learning Outcomes.** Knowing these can help you get more out of the class. Also, these can be a hint as to what is most likely to appear on an exam. Also, pay close attention to skills that you will develop in the course (we expand on this idea in later chapters).

4. **Attendance Policy.** Regardless of the course attendance policy, follow this rule—always attend class! However, knowing the policy will be helpful if an emergency or illness occurs.
5. **Assignment Due Dates and Exam Dates.** Put these in your planner or your phone calendar immediately! Set alarms in your phone to remind yourself at least 1 week in advance.
6. **Assigned Reading and Weekly Topics.** Class sessions are infinitely more productive and interesting when you have prepared by completing the readings. So, please read!
7. **Grading Policies.** One thing that always surprises us is the number of students who ask, "What is my grade?" This is so important that we will present an entire section on this.

Grading Systems

Grades are an evaluation of student performance and academic skills (e.g., Pattison, Grodsky, & Muller, 2013). Most courses use letter grades (some include pluses and minuses), but some might simply indicate whether you passed or failed. Courses may differ as to whether you gain points for correct answers or lose points for errors; mathematically, these are the same, but they can potentially affect student performance (e.g., Bies-Hernandez, 2012). Regardless of which system is being used, the syllabus should always describe the system being used—so read your syllabus! In the following, we review some of the common grading systems.

Add-Up-Points System. This is a common system where each activity (e.g., quiz, exam, paper) is worth a certain number of points. You simply add up the points that you earned (total points) and then divide that by the total number of points that those tasks were worth (possible points)—this gives you your overall grade percentage. You can then look up the grading scale in the syllabus to determine the letter grade. An advantage of this system is that you can calculate hypothetical grades by estimating how well you think you will do on remaining activities. We have an example calculation in Table 2.1 (the grade in the example is based on a typical grading scale where an A is 90–100%).

Weighted-Tasks System. This is similar to the previous system, but here each task category is worth a percentage (weight) of your grade. The calculations are slightly more complex than adding up the points—you have to calculate the percentage for each category, multiply that by the percentage that the category is worth, and then add those values up. We have an example calculation in Table 2.2 to illustrate this idea. You would then look up to see where your calculated overall grade percentage falls on the syllabus grading scale (the example is based on a typical grading scale where an A is 90–100% and a B is 80–89%).

Curved-Grade System. A real *curve* involves ranking students against each other based on their scores. The top students earn an A, students with the lowest scores earn an F, and

TABLE 2.1

Add-Up-Points Example

Course Activity	Points Earned	Points Possible
Quizzes	15	20
Exams	99	100
Totals	114	120

Overall Grade 95% (Points Earned / Points Possible)
Grade: A

TABLE 2.2

Weighted-Tasks Example

Activity	Weight	Points Earned	Points Possible	Weighted Score
Quizzes	20% of grade	50	50	20%
Exams	80% of grade	85	100	68%

Weighted Scores = [(Points Earned / Points Possible) × Weight]
Overall Grade 88% (Sum of Weighted Scores)
Grade: B

the rest are in the middle. One advantage of this system is that you can earn a high grade if you outperform your classmates—however, a very big disadvantage is the possibility that you might have good scores, but if your classmates did better, you might earn a lower grade. In the example in Table 2.3, even though Roberto earned a high score (which might normally be an A), others were ranked above him causing his grade to be lower). Finally, another disadvantage is that you cannot calculate a hypothetical final grade if you do not know your classmates' scores.

Outcome-Based System. This system is designed so that you have to complete a certain number of activities to a satisfactory level to earn a particular grade. For example, you may have to complete eight activities to earn an A, but smaller numbers of completed activities might correspond to lower grades. An advantage of this system is that you simply have to complete the tasks (at a satisfactory level); however, a possible disadvantage is that instructors might not allow re-submissions.

Take-Home Message

Although we admit that there is boring policy information in your course syllabi, do not let that overshadow the many pieces of useful information. Your syllabi are important for planning out your semester. If you ever have a question about the course, check the syllabus first before you reach out to your professor. What is the professor's email address? When are the exams? Is there a paper? How much is the paper worth? What do you need to score to earn an A? The answer to all of those questions is simple—IT'S IN THE SYLLABUS!!!

TABLE 2.3
Curved-Grade Example

Rank	Student	Points Earned	Possible Points	Grade
1	Tyra	99	100	A
2	Emily	98	100	B
3	Sandra	95	100	B
4	Roberto	94	100	C
5	Carmen	83	100	C
6	Jacob	78	100	C
7	Nathan	77	100	D
8	Michelle	76	100	D
9	Alexis	75	100	F

iStock.com/DjelicS

Action Steps

1. Do not just stash your syllabi away or put them in the trash—actually read through your syllabi and keep them somewhere so that you can find them later. Most importantly, use a calendar to note your reading, assignment due dates, and exams. Use the information from all of your syllabi to create a well thought-out plan for the semester.
2. All students should monitor their grades as they move through a course—if you need help with the math, use spreadsheet software like Microsoft Excel. Set up columns and rows for every graded activity listed in the syllabus. Enter all of your scores (do not forget to add zeroes for any missed or skipped activities) and you can see your current grade status. If you have an Add-Up or Weighted-Total system, you can calculate hypothetical final grade outcomes toward the end of the semester by considering the best- and worst-case scenarios.

2.2 CLASSROOM AND NOTE-TAKING TIPS

Many students think that taking notes is really easy. All you do is copy words from a PowerPoint slide into a notebook. And, if you can do it faster by using a laptop, borrowing someone else's notes, or downloading the professor's slides, then even better—right? *Wrong*. In this module, we are going to debunk some of the myths about note-taking and productive classroom behaviors, and offer practical advice.

Attend Class or Skip?

iStock.com/FatCamera

Skipping class, playing hooky, cutting, or ditching—regardless of what you call it, our advice is simple: DO NOT DO IT! If you spent thousands of dollars for a car, would you leave it parked in the garage and never drive it? Well, if you (or your parents) are paying thousands of dollars for college, why skip classes? If you do not care about money, here is something that should get your attention—studies have shown that better class attendance is clearly related to higher grades. In fact, attendance is a better predictor of college achievement than SAT scores, high school GPA, or study habits (Crede, Roch, & Kieszczynka, 2010). So, unless you are going to have a life-changing day away from campus, just go to class.

Do Not Plan to Rely on a Classmate's Notes

Some students may rationalize that they can learn just as much by copying a classmate's notes, and they mistakenly think that getting the notes is just as good as attending class that day. However, there are a number of problems with this approach. First, students assume that a classmate's notes will make sense to them—however, in reality another student's phrasing and abbreviations may seem like gibberish to you (see photo of the handwritten notes—can you make sense of any of that?!?). Even worse, the notes might be sparse and might be missing key pieces of information. Lastly, keep in mind that the student who took the notes may simply not be a very good note-taker.

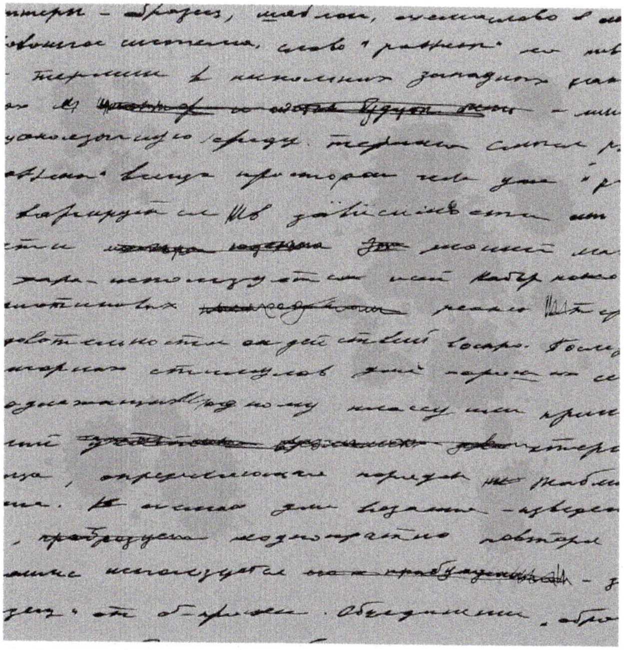

© Can Stock Photo/katyau

Come to Class Prepared—Then Ask Questions

Come to class prepared—read the assigned pages before you come to class. In our experiences, students enjoy lectures and discussions a whole lot more when they already have some familiarity with the topic. When you have some prior knowledge about a topic, you will be more confident about speaking in class; when this happens, you get much more out of your

© Can Stock Photo / Leaf

class sessions. In contrast, when concepts are brand new and unfamiliar, we tend to not be as interested.

In addition, class can be more interesting and pass more quickly when you actively participate! And remember, participating is more than just attending class—add or ask something meaningful (e.g., Dunn, 2019). Do not stress over this, though, as you can start with something easy—answer a question that the professor poses to the class. You could also ask the professor to clarify or give another example when a difficult concept is presented. And do not worry about looking dumb—people around you may be daydreaming or paying attention to their phones instead of you anyway!

Participating in class is also a way for you to get your professors to notice you in a positive manner. As you read through the rest of this book, you will learn that building relationships with professors is reported as one of the best parts of college by past graduates. When you are close to graduation, you will need to secure strong recommendation letters from professors who know you well. So, get started earning those rec letters every class session!

Where Should You Sit?

Professors sometimes refer to the first few rows and the middle of a classroom as the "high achiever" seats—there are some studies that support this idea (e.g., Marshall & Losonczy-Marshall, 2010), but there are also studies that show no connection between seat location and grades (e.g., Kalinowski & Taper, 2007). When students are asked about their seat selection, they provide various reasons—(a) some sit near the front to get a better view or to participate more in discussions, (b) some sit near the back (or sides) to avoid interactions, and (c) many sit wherever their friends are located (Smith, Hoare, & Lacey, 2018).

Ultimately, where you sit is up to you, but we have some ideas that you might consider (see Table 2.4). First, there may be more opportunities to participate in (and learn from)

TABLE 2.4

Our Top Five Reasons Not to Sit Toward the Back in Class

1. Other students, in front of you, might be using phones or laptops (and this can draw your attention).
2. You may be more tempted to look at distractions on your own phone or laptop if you are "hidden" in the back of the room.
3. It can be difficult to hear soft-spoken instructors when seated in the back.
4. It might be more difficult to read slides or the board when seated farther back.
5. Most of the class discussion activity happens toward the front of the room (and, if you want to learn, you want to participate in these discussions).

discussions when you sit toward the front (e.g., Smith et al., 2018). Second, consider distractions—there may be more of them in your line of sight if you sit in the back. For example, some students are not using laptops to take notes—they are updating social media, shopping, and looking at videos. If you are behind one of these students, what do you think will catch your eye? Finally, although it can be enjoyable to sit with your friends, this can be problematic if they are not taking the class seriously. There is evidence that groups of friends who sit together earn similar scores (e.g., Smith et al., 2018)—so, you might reconsider your seat if you have a group of friends who may bring your performance down. Our point is that you are in class to learn, and any distractions may prevent that.

© Can Stock Photo/lisafx

Taking Notes

First and foremost, taking notes is a good thing—it can help retention (Bui, Myerson, & Hale, 2013), particularly for deeper levels of learning (Bohay, Blakely, Tamplin, & Radvansky, 2011). Although there are different ways to take notes, we include some general recommendations here. One thing to keep in mind is that you should do your best to be an active note-taker—try not to be a mindless zombie who writes without thinking about the ideas. Underline ideas that seem most important, draw lines to connect related ideas, and add your own thoughts. If you catch your mind wandering and know that you missed something, take note of that so that you can ask a classmate or check the book later. And if an idea does not make sense to you, stop and ask a question.

Does the instructor provide anything? Some instructors will provide handouts of their class slides, some will provide an outline, and others might not provide anything. If your instructor provides slides or an outline, do not be tempted to think that you do not need to take notes! Use the handouts as a starting point, and then add to them. Jot down examples that illustrate concepts. Draw a diagram that is presented in class. Circle or highlight ideas that seem to be most important. Mark ideas that you find especially difficult so that you can focus on them more later.

Pay attention to what is said. When instructors use PowerPoint, some students think they only need to copy everything that is on the slides. These students take this further by taking a "mental break" after they finish copying the current slide and do nothing until the next slide appears. If this is you, you are likely missing out on interesting examples or connections that your instructors are describing aloud.

Pens vs. laptops. Computers can be beneficial for students, but there are two major reasons that you should think twice before using your laptop in class. First, there can be a small learning benefit when students take notes *by hand* than when they take notes on a computer (Morehead, Dunlosky, & Rawson, 2019; Mueller & Oppenheimer, 2014). A second reason that you might reconsider using a laptop is that there are far too many potential distractions—discussion boards, social media, shopping. These activities are negatively related to class performance (Ravizza, Uitvlugt, & Fenn, 2017). The research from cognitive psychology about multitasking tells us that, when we try to do two things, there is a cost in performance (e.g., Finley, Benjamin, & McCarley, 2014).

We recommend that, when deciding between a pen and a laptop for taking notes, you take a few things into account. First, which fits the situation best? If the professor lectures very quickly and does not provide handouts, you may want to type notes so that you can keep up. However, if there are a lot of diagrams or formulas (which are difficult to type), or the lecture pace is slow, then pen and paper might make the most sense. Second, know yourself—if you have been tempted by electronic distractions in the past, then you will likely find yourself distracted again if you use a laptop in the future! Speaking of electronic temptations . . .

Turn your phone off and put it away. We know that this is downright offensive to some people, but we recommend you turn your phone off AND put it away. Unless a family member is in the hospital or your partner is 9 months pregnant, you can survive a little while without your phone. Having a cell phone present—not even using it, just the fact that it is there—can lead to lower levels of attention and worse performance on a task (Thornton, Faires, Robbins, & Rollins, 2014). And, if you cannot fathom the idea of turning off your phone, then you may want to explore the possibility that you have an addiction—see Yildirim and Correia's (2015) questionnaire that assesses nomophobia (fear of being without one's phone).

© Can Stock Photo/Antonio_Diaz

Are you a visual learner or verbal learner? If we had a nickel for every time students told us that they are either visual or verbal learners, then we would be rich (well, actually, we might not be rich, but we could probably buy a new smartphone at least). Anyway, our point is that some students have learned a "scientific fact," that people are either visual or verbal learners; however, as noted by Brown, Roediger, and McDaniel (2014), there is no scientific evidence that supports the claim that "visual learners" learn better from visual materials or that "verbal learners" learn better from verbal presentations. So, drop that myth and embrace *this* instead—it is more important that you process the information deeply (Craik & Lockhart, 1972) no matter how it is presented.

Using your notes later. Every week (or every other week), take the notes from that time period and condense them to one page. This next warning is very important, though—do not simply recopy your notes! This is typically a waste of time as the mental effort required to do so is very superficial. Instead, you should take the ideas and think about them. Which concepts are most important? Which concepts are most related to each other? Which topics apply most to your life? Which ones do you understand the best? The least? What is most likely to be on an exam?

Once you have thought through those questions, then write out a one-page summary—a nicely organized explanation of what you learned. One way that you think about this is to pretend that you were writing a summary to help out a fellow student who missed class for the past week or two. When you think about the information in this manner, you are thinking about it much more deeply (Craik & Lockhart, 1972) and this builds associations in memory.

Reflect on your note-taking approach. A final point that we want to make is that you should occasionally reflect on your note-taking strategy (e.g., Boch & Piolat, 2005). For example, you might ask yourself if you are happy with your notes and if they have been helpful. Consider comparing your notes to a classmate's notes—does that person do things that seem more helpful? And if you find yourself at a loss because your note-taking approach does not seem to help you prepare for exams, then seek out help right away! Most institutions have student centers to help with this type of skill (if you cannot figure out where to get help, ask your professors—they will know about campus resources).

Take-Home Message

Always go to class—do not pass "Go," do not collect $200—go directly to class (that was a reference to the Parker Brothers' board game *Monopoly*). When in class, sit toward the front and pay attention. If you catch your mind starting to wander, try to change things up by moving around or asking a question. Speaking of asking questions, try to participate in every class as it will help you feel more connected to the discussion. Finally, no one wants to hear this, but it is in your best interest to turn your smartphone completely off and to stash it out of sight (some of you might want to do this with laptops, too).

Action Steps

iStock.com/Django

1. If you are not already doing this, sit closer to the front in all of your courses. If any of your friends tease you about sitting in the front, just tell them that you need to pay attention and do well. Be careful that you do not slip farther toward the back of the room in the courses you do not care as much about—those are the ones where you probably need to sit toward the front the most.
2. Get in the habit of taking good notes. One important aspect is to make sure that you are an active note-taker, not a passive transcriber. Jot down questions, insights, or points of confusion as you take notes. And, if you want help to improve your note-taking skills, drop in and visit a student center on your campus that is there to help (if you do not know where to go, ask your professors).

2.3 STUDY SKILLS—STUDY LIKE A CHAMPION!

Based on our interactions with students, we expect that some might be tempted to skip this topic because they think that they already know the best ways to study. However, have you ever thought or said anything like the following phrases?

"I don't have enough time to study."

"Cramming the night before a test has been good enough in the past."

iStock.com/fizkes

"I would rather <insert time-wasting activity here> than study."

We ask that you give us a chance here—read this module and try some of these techniques (see Table 2.5). These approaches are all backed up by research, so we promise that, if you give these a real chance, you will notice significant improvement in your learning (and grades). We also encourage you to be proactive and adopt these strategies on your own—do not rely on your instructors to always remind you of how you should be studying (e.g., Hunter & Lloyd, 2018).

Distributed Practice

If you only choose one tip from this module, please avoid cramming and spread out your studying. Years of research has consistently shown that spreading out your studying is a very effective way to learn (e.g., Kornell, Castel, Eich, & Bjork, 2010)—this is especially important if you want to retain the knowledge for the long term (which should be your goal). Some students misinterpret this tip to mean that they have to study more. Although it would be good to spend more time studying, this does not have to be the case for distributed practice to be effective. For example, if you were going to spend a total of 4 hours, instead of trying to cram for 4 continuous hours the night before the exam, you could distribute your studying across eight different nights (30 minutes per night). In either scenario, you are spending a total of 4 hours studying—but, the second approach is a much more effective way to learn. One big reason for this leads us to our next tip. . .

TABLE 2.5

Our Top Five Study Tips

1. Distributed practice—spread out your studying of a topic across days or weeks
2. Study in chunks—avoid lengthy cramming sessions on the same topic
3. Set a goal—if you know what you want to accomplish, you will know when to stop
4. Read—time in college classes is limited, so you have to spend time learning on your own
5. Test yourself—embrace quizzes as a chance to practice for upcoming exams

Study Each Topic in 15- to 60-Minute Chunks

Imagine that we asked you to work at the airport—your job is to scan carry-on luggage and watch for banned items (e.g., guns, knives, 5-ounce bottles of water, etc.). At first, you might find it interesting and you might get excited as you identify some objects. However, after a while, your performance will drop off—this is normal and to be expected. The reason is that it is difficult to maintain attention on the same thing for a long period of time (Howe, Warm, & Dember, 1995).

Because of that, we recommend that you only study for up to 60 minutes on the same topic. At that point, take a short break or switch to a different topic or course. Once you go beyond an hour on the same topic, the effectiveness of your studying will diminish. However, we also understand that you cannot always find 60-minute chunks to study. If that is the case, start small—try to find 15–20 minutes here and there when you can do a little bit of studying. If that is successful, you can always make those sessions longer.

Make a Goal for Each Study Session

Rather than cracking open your books and notes and broadly declaring that right now it is "time to study for 45 minutes," set a specific goal of what you want to accomplish. For example, you may want to read Chapter 5 and to take notes on the key terms. If you finish that in 30 minutes, then reward yourself by taking a break. In other words, stop thinking of yourself like an employee who gets paid by the hour; instead, work until you finish the task. A second reason for making a goal is that it gives you a purpose—when you find yourself bored and wanting to go outside, remind yourself that you just need to complete the goal before going off and doing something else.

Complete the Readings

Read the book! Read assigned articles! It might be tempting to adopt the mindset of "read as little as possible," but please try to resist that approach. Instead of thinking of reading as a chore, think about it as a way to explore new topics (that's a big reason why you chose to study psychology, right?). Some students think that all of the material worth knowing is covered during lecture or in demonstrations, but a great deal of knowledge can be gained by focusing on completing the assigned reading outside of class (e.g., Copeland, Scott, & Houska, 2010). Also, remember that having a foundation of knowledge (from reading) can help you learn more during class lectures and discussions (e.g., Cerbin, 2018).

© Can Stock Photo/michaeljung

Finding time. It is not that difficult to find time to read, but you must make it a priority. For example, do you need to watch 4 hours of television in one night, or can you survive on 2? We understand that your friends are all going out at night and that you will become a social pariah if you stay home, but try this—read for a little bit and then reward yourself by going out afterward. And you might have a lot more fun because you will be more relaxed knowing that you did the reading.

Should you read before or after class? There are pros and cons to both approaches, but our recommendation is to read before class. If you do not fully understand all of the topics from the reading, you can jot down questions and then ask them in class.

Avoid sleep-reading! Most people have experienced this at some point—as you are reading a page, you realize that you have no memory for what you just read. One way to get around this is to limit your studying to 60-minute chunks of time. A second approach is to give yourself a goal while reading—you will focus more if you are trying to figure out what ideas mean and how they connect. Finally, another tactic is to take time to summarize what you just read. This is especially helpful if you put the ideas into your own words; the *generation effect* (Slamecka & Graf, 1978) is a phenomenon where you remember information better if you generate it yourself rather than when you passively receive it (or blindly repeat it from someone else). An added bonus is that now you will have a summary to use when you study later!

Pick a Good Spot

Some people study more effectively in complete silence, whereas others prefer a little bit of background noise. Find what works best for you—you might find that your preferences change based on the topic you are studying or possibly based on your mood. However, we want to warn you not to kid yourself and think that you can study effectively in a distracting environment. Turn off the television, put away your phone, and consider staying away from friends.

Shutterstock / patpitchaya

Use Mnemonics

If courses require you to memorize information, we recommend that you try using mnemonics—it is possible for anyone to have a great memory by applying mnemonics properly. These can be simple, such as (a) creating a vivid image of the information, (b) altering the information into something funny or interesting (e.g., to remember one of the primary functions of the amygdala, think of it as an emotional person named Amy G. Dala), or (c) using acronyms (e.g., PET for positron emission tomography) or acrostics (e.g., Please excuse my dear Aunt Sally for the mathematical order of operations). All of these techniques are simple and you can personalize them for yourself (see Carney, Levin, & Levin, 1994, for examples of various mnemonics).

If you want to remember something really well, then you could try a formal mnemonic. These techniques have been around since Ancient Greece (when a strong memory was useful because it was difficult to find a place to charge your smartphone) and, with a little effort, they can work really well. With the *Peg-Word* mnemonic you can pre-memorize number rhymes such as, "One is a bun, two is a shoe..." Then, you associate the list of new information with each rhyme (e.g., think of the first item in a hotdog bun, the second item in an old pair of shoes, etc.). This structure also allows you to keep the information in sequential order. Other formal mnemonics include the *Memory Palace* or *Method of Loci*—look these up or ask your instructors about them. Regardless of which you use, the payoff can be huge because these mnemonics can help you retain a lot of information!

Test Yourself

© Can Stock Photo / Leaf

Most people think that exams or quizzes are only used to test what someone has learned. However, a lot of research has shown that tests improve memory better than re-reading (Agarwal & Bain, 2019; Chan, McDermott, & Roediger, 2006)! Of course, you must first read or hear the information initially, but, after that, follow it up with a practice test or quiz rather than re-reading your notes or the book. Importantly, though, do not have your notes or book open in front of you—try to recall the answer from memory. You can do this with flashcards—again, try your best to answer the question from memory before you look at the answer!

Testing is beneficial because it can help you evaluate what information you can and cannot recall (Son & Kornell, 2008). Second, testing yourself is a way to practice what you will be doing on the actual test (Roediger & Karpicke, 2006). During the real test, you likely will not have your notes or book in front of you—you will have to recall information from memory. Why not practice what you will actually be doing on the test? Finally, a third benefit is that testing yourself on some pieces of information can even improve your memory for related information that was not tested (Chan et al., 2006). In other words, you do not necessarily have to test yourself on every single fact to see a memory benefit.

Build a Foundation, Then Add Ideas

Have you ever tried to learn a new language? It tends to be difficult at first because you have no prior knowledge to serve as anchors, and you do not have a clear idea of how to organize the information. The same is true when you try to learn a new subject area in college. Despite this problem, we sometimes see students who keep plowing forward and reading new chapters even though they do not understand the initial ones. When you do this, you have not established a foundation to help you connect and organize the new ideas. Our recommendation is to start slowly and to make sure that you can establish a small foundation of knowledge in the new topic area. Once you do this, then you can start linking new ideas to the foundation. And, if you are having problems in a class, utilize your professor's office hours early in the semester!

Take-Home Message

A lot of students think that they know the best ways to study and learn, but unfortunately these "common sense" approaches are not always backed up by research. As we said earlier, if you only apply one of our recommendations, you should spread out your studying across days and weeks instead of cramming it all in one night. It is okay to keep the study sessions short—just be sure to set goals for what you want to accomplish each time and to complete the assigned readings! You do not have to apply all of the advice that we provide here, but try out some of these ideas—put the information you learn into your own words by summarizing ideas, create mnemonics to make material more memorable, and test yourself as a way to practice for your upcoming exams.

iStock.com/AndreyPopov

Action Steps

1. Find small chunks of time in your days when you can do a little bit of reading or studying. Make sure that these occur across several days (or every day) of the week so that you can spread out your studying.
2. In addition to using distributed learning, apply at least two of the tips to your studying approach this semester. For example, if you previously avoided reading, start incorporating that into your routine (starting this week). If you never tried testing yourself, start out with flashcards (some apps have made it easy to create these). The important thing is that you use methods that are supported by research and, most importantly, that you actually use them!

2.4 QUIZ AND EXAM TIPS

Do you despise tests? Sure, we all do (professors, too—we have to spend time making them and grading them). In this module, we hope that we can lessen your hatred or anxiety associated with tests by providing you with some important information. We first focus on test anxiety and some steps you can take to deal with it. After that, we describe a number of tips to help you improve your performance on different types of tests.

Dealing With Test Anxiety

It is not uncommon to feel anxiety before and possibly during a test. So, rest assured that you are not alone if you feel this way. Also recognize that a little bit of jitters can actually be a good thing—when your body is at an increased arousal level, performance can be better; however, you do not want to be too anxious as too much arousal might not be helpful.

One of the best ways to lessen test anxiety is to spend time preparing beforehand. We just covered a whole bunch of classroom and study tips in this chapter, so use those to prepare yourself. It can also be helpful to start a test with the right mindset. Knowing that you are prepared should give you confidence that you can do well, but tell yourself that it is not necessary to be perfect—it is okay to make some mistakes. Also, remind yourself that this one test does not define who you are—if you do well, then great; but, if you do not do well, it can be a learning experience (we have more on the topic of failure in the next chapter). Even the best and brightest superstar students have times when they do not do well.

On the day of the test, arrive early enough so that you are not rushed and can find a comfortable seat. If you find that you are feeling very anxious, we have two things that you might try. One approach is to pull out a sheet of paper and spend a few minutes writing about your worries—this act can help "offload" the anxiety and has been shown to improve test performance (e.g., Ramirez & Beilock, 2011).

iStock.com/mapodile

A second approach is to try a simple focused breathing exercise (e.g., Clinton & Meester, 2019). Start by closing your eyes, then slowly inhale for about 7 seconds, followed by a slow exhale for 7 seconds—repeat as needed (you might need a few repetitions before you feel better). Finally, use the following test-taking tips that we provide below—knowing and applying these can increase your confidence and, hopefully, improve your performance!

Embrace Quizzes—They Help You Learn

As we noted in the previous module, one big misperception that many students have about quizzes is that they are simply a tool to measure how much you have learned. However, there is a large body of research that has shown that testing is also an important learning tool (Roediger & Karpicke, 2006)! So, instead of dreading those pop quizzes, embrace them—the goal is to improve your memory so that you can do better on the exam and remember the information better later!

Tips for Multiple-Choice Questions

One common form of testing is the use of multiple-choice questions. Multiple-choice questions can be very specific, asking for detailed knowledge such as definitions or asking you to differentiate between a set of terms. Although many students assume that multiple-choice questions are easier than other types of questions, such as essays or short answers (after all, the answers are right in front of you), that is not always the case (see Table 2.6 for a summary of our tips).

1. Our first tip for multiple choice is to try and answer the question before you look at the choices. If you have been studying by using practice tests to recall information, then you should be prepared to do this. If you can recall the answer, then simply look for it among the choices. But, make sure that you read through all of the choices as sometimes the instructions will be to choose the BEST answer.

2. Our second tip is to scan the choices and cross out the ones that are obviously wrong. When there are four choices, even if you do not know the answer, you have a one in four (25%) chance of answering it correctly. However, if you can eliminate one choice, then that improves your odds to one in three (33%). If you can eliminate two choices, your odds are one in two (50%). And if you can eliminate three choices, then all that you have left is the answer!

3. If you are not sure about a particular question, mark that question so that you know to come back to it later. There are two reasons that this can be helpful. First, by letting the question incubate, sometimes the answer will come to you later (e.g., Vul & Pashler, 2007). Second, you may find a hint to the answer as you read through the other questions on the exam—that is, it is possible that another question might provide a retrieval cue to help you with that earlier question.

4. Proofread your test to make sure that you answered every question. Of course, this assumes that there is no penalty for incorrect guessing (some standardized tests like the SAT penalize for guessing, but most professors do not use this approach). One of the most frustrating things that we see is when a student leaves a question blank—as we noted earlier, with four choices you have a 25% chance of guessing correctly; however, if you leave it blank, you have a 0% chance!

5. These final tips should be used with caution, as they only apply to poorly designed tests. Some instructors will make the correct answer the longest choice. A reason for this is that they carefully write out the correct answer, but may not take as much time to write out comparable incorrect choices. Also, some instructors will only include an option of "All of the above" or "None of the above" when it is the correct choice, so if you happen to be stumped by a particular question, you can try that choice. However, as we noted, do not blindly apply these strategies—only rely on them when you are in trouble and have no idea which answer to select.

TABLE 2.6
Multiple-Choice Question Tips

What are some good tips for answering multiple-choice questions?

a. Answer the question before looking at the choices
b. ~~Never cross out answers that are clearly wrong~~
c. Mark difficult questions so that you remember to return to them later
d. Proofread to make sure that you answered all questions
e. Choices (a.), (b.), and (d.) are all correct

Tips for Short Answer and Essay Questions

Short answer and essay questions are different from multiple choice in that they do not provide choices. Instead, your task is to retrieve the information from memory. Here are some tips for these types of questions.

1. Be sure to insert keywords into your answers whenever you can. The reason for this is that short answer and essay questions are more difficult to grade than multiple-choice questions. So, be crystal clear with your response as instructors will likely notice keywords when they are scoring responses.
2. Our second tip is to use margins, the back of the page, or scratch paper to create a rough outline of your answer. An organized response tends to be graded as better than a jumbled mess of a response. We do not expect you to write out a full outline—all that we are suggesting is that you jot down some ideas to help you organize your thoughts for the answer that you write.
3. Before you move on to the next question, check to see that you *actually answered the question* that is asked. In some cases, students might write a lot of information but they forget to actually answer the question. Yes, being able to include a lot of information is important, but it is even more important to demonstrate that you understood what was asked.
4. As we suggested in the multiple-choice tips, if at first you cannot think of a response, then read through other questions on the exam to look for hints or keywords that you can use. Often times, other questions (or even choices listed in a multiple-choice question) can trigger a memory that can help you.
5. Our final tip is for a situation in which you are completely clueless as to what to write. If you leave it blank, you are guaranteed to earn zero points. One approach that you can try is to pose a hypothetical question that is somewhat related to the question on the exam and to answer that. Here, you are demonstrating that you have knowledge on a relevant topic, and if the grader is lenient he/she may give you partial credit for trying. Keep in mind, though, that it might not work; however, trying this approach is better than a guaranteed zero for leaving it blank.

Additional Exam Tips

But wait, there's more—here are a few more exam tips that you can use! These can be helpful no matter what types of questions are on the exam.

1. Be sure to read the instructions—sometimes there are surprises in the instructions. For example, a generous instructor may inform you that you are allowed to use your notes, a calculator, or possibly work with others. You may also find that, instead of having to answer all of the questions, you are allowed to skip one. Always read the instructions before you begin!
2. Along this same line, be sure that you read questions carefully. For example, some questions may insert a word that can completely change a question—"Which of the following psychologists was NOT a behaviorist?"—if you miss the word "not" then you might look for names like "Watson" or "Skinner."
3. In traditional in-person classes, check with your instructors to see whether you are allowed to ask questions during an exam. If they allow it, ask them for clarification if you encounter a confusing question or one that is extremely difficult to answer. The instructor may rephrase a question for you that might make it clearer!
4. Our final tip is to save your old exams and to learn from them. For example, many instructors will hand back old exams and go over the correct answers. Do not just look for your grade and celebrate (if you did well) or pout (if you did poorly). Also, do not use this as a moment to beg for more points or to complain about scoring. What you should be doing is reinforcing the information you knew and learning from the questions you missed. Use this time to learn!

Take-Home Message

When you think about tests, remember that they are not only useful for evaluating what you know but can also be beneficial for learning. This can be done by participating in quizzes before an exam or by testing yourself. You can also review an old exam to reinforce the answers you knew and to learn from your mistakes. In terms of taking tests, there are a number of tips that we outlined in this module that you can use to improve your performance. Please take the time to learn these strategies as your future self may thank you for the higher grade point average.

© Can Stock Photo/jannoon028

Action Steps

1. Keep a copy of this module and/or your notes from this module and review them before every exam (we recommend printing a copy and putting it on a bulletin board near where you study). After a while, you will hopefully start to implement these strategies automatically.

2. It is possible that you have a preference for certain types of exam questions—in our experience, most students prefer multiple-choice questions because they think they are easier. But, regardless of your preference, accept the fact that exams can have any types of questions—when you embrace that fact, you can be better prepared for anything.

2.5 LEARNING FROM GRADED ACTIVITIES

How many of you have done the following? After receiving a graded copy of your paper back from the instructor, you immediately look for the grade or score. If you earned an A, then you pat yourself on the back and *never look at it again.* If you did not earn an A, then you flip through the paper trying to assess whether the feedback seems to justify the grade. At that point, you stuff the paper away and *never look at it again.* We use this example to illustrate an important point—most students either ignore feedback or they only care about the feedback to the extent to which it justifies the grade. Our goal in this module is to explain how students can use grades and feedback to improve both their learning and their performance in the course.

Papers and Essays

iStock.com/Lamaip

In our ideal classroom, all papers would consist of three parts—(1) a student's initial draft, (2) specific, actionable feedback from the instructor or classmate(s), and (3) an improved version written by the student. In this scenario, you should ALWAYS use the feedback when revising your paper. In addition to using the feedback, re-read the instructions or grading criteria for the paper; this will help you to better assess your work before you re-submit it (see Wiggins, 2012).

Even if you do not have to turn in a revision, we recommend that you use any professor feedback to make actual edits to your paper. With computer software like Word or Google Docs, this should be pretty easy (it's not like you have to re-type the entire paper from scratch using a typewriter!). Editing your work will help you improve your writing. Also, you never know if, in the future, an award, graduate school, or job ad will ask you to submit writing samples—your improved revision will be a much better sample than the original draft!

Exams and Quizzes

Some professors (like us) will review exams when we hand them back to students because it can be an important learning activity. First, you can see which answers you missed—this will help you understand what topics you do not fully understand. If your course has cumulative exams, then this benefit should be readily apparent—that topic might be asked about on a future exam! However, even if you do not have cumulative exams, use this time to learn from your mistakes. A second reason to review an exam is that you might gain a better grasp of what types of information are most important to the instructor—this can be very valuable for future exams in that course.

Do Not Get Offended—Learn to Take Criticism

iStock.com/AntonioGuillem

We have seen too many students who end up moping if their exam or paper grade is not as high as they had hoped—be careful not to make this mistake. Hold your head up! It's just one score, not the end of the world! Things could be worse! Are those enough clichés to make our point clear? Yes, the grade might not be what you wanted, but do not go straight to your professor with a negative attitude. An interesting psychological phenomenon to keep in mind is that people have a tendency to consider themselves and their work as above average (Kruger & Dunning, 1999).[1] In other words, you are not always the best judge of your own performance. You may think that your essay should have earned an A+, but you have to acknowledge that you are biased when judging your own work.

If you are feeling frustrated or upset by an exam score, check your errors with your notes and possibly the textbook—try to figure out what you got wrong or misremembered. With a paper, keep in mind that professors try their best to grade fairly and to provide helpful feedback. So, do not take a poor grade personally—trust us, the professor is not out to get you! Instead, review the feedback to learn why you missed points or what you could have done better.

If you are still unsure as to why your grade was recorded as it was, then wait 48 hours and come back to it. When you first get a grade back, it is easy for expectations or emotions to influence your views; after a couple of days, you can look at the errors and feedback more objectively. At that point, if you still have questions, set up an appointment with your professor (or visit during office hours). Try to view that meeting as an information-seeking session and not an attack or an interrogation—ask about how you can improve. Feedback about how you can improve is the most useful tool for your future performance (see Cheng, Liang, & Tsai, 2015).

Contrast this approach with one characterized by acting out of anger or frustration. If you approach or email your professors with a defensive tone, they will probably be less willing to help. Put yourself in the professor's shoes—would you want to help a student who acts combatively and only seems to care about the grade or one who acts calmly and seems

[1] In what might be the funniest example of this phenomenon, people made judgments about who would go to heaven (Stanglin & Gross, 1997). A large majority thought that Mother Teresa, a woman nominated for sainthood, would go to heaven—but, the interesting part was that respondents rated *themselves* as the most likely to go to heaven!

interested in improving and learning? Remember, college is primarily about the learning process and acquiring skills—grades are a part of it, but not the most important part.

Take-Home Message

Grades are not just an endpoint of an assignment or exam—be sure that you take time to learn from your graded work! Before you see a grade, prepare yourself that the grade might be lower than you were expecting. If it is lower than you hoped, then (a) check exam errors by referencing your notes or textbook—for a paper, try to consider the feedback objectively, (b) if you still have questions about the grading, wait 48 hours until you set up a meeting with your professor, and (c) finally, go into the meeting with a calm demeanor with the goal to learn, not to fight over a grade!

Action Steps

iStock.com/ Coompia77

1. Make a special effort to attend class on days when papers and exams are returned. This is a great opportunity to start learning from your mistakes.
2. Make it a habit that, when a paper is returned to you with feedback, you use the comments to revise the paper right away. By doing that, you can improve your writing skills and you can save that improved paper to possibly use as a writing sample in the future (see our later chapter that covers how to document your accomplishments)!

2.6 ADVANTAGES AND DISADVANTAGES OF BEING AN ONLINE STUDENT

In some ways, the increase in the number of online courses over the past decade has been very helpful for both colleges and students. However, with every benefit, there are bound to be some costs. This module briefly considers the pros and cons of online courses. We do not want to come across as grumpy old men who hate technological progress (back in our day, we chiseled class notes into stone tablets!). To be sure, there are some considerable disadvantages that online students encounter (especially students who try to do all or most of their education online)—*but*, there are some ways that online students can try to overcome them.

Advantages

An obvious advantage is that online students can work from home instead of having to physically be on campus. This can save time as students can work on their own schedule. Besides the constraints of due dates, students can choose to listen to lectures, read materials,

© Can Stock Photo/deandrobot

and take exams when they want. This can be a tremendous advantage for students who have to balance a work schedule on top of a class schedule.

A second advantage is that there are many resources available online. For example, library resources can be accessed via college websites, large psychology organizations have websites that contain a lot of useful information, and search engines like Google make a lot of information very accessible. If you do not know how to do something you can conduct an online search right away while working on a computer or phone.

Disadvantages

Although the advantages listed previously can be quite helpful, we have to warn that too much of a good thing can have potential disadvantages for students. The occasional online course can be a nice change of pace for one's schedule; however, when students try to complete an entire degree program online, there are some disadvantages. We share these, not to derogate online students or programs but to inform and caution those considering virtual instruction.

Several years ago, the *Massive Open Online Course (MOOC)* movement was seen as a panacea for many of higher education's problems—access to all, reducing overhead costs, and so on. However, this grand experiment is now all but dead in the water due to low completion rates for these online courses (see The Hechinger Report, 2015). Still, you will likely have the opportunity to take several, if not more, online psychology courses in the years to come. It is important to note that even the most pedagogically sound online courses lack opportunities to apply and integrate new skills and knowledge (Margaryan, Bianco, & Littlejohn, 2015). Moreover, students and professors often cannot engage in simple—but effective—instructional techniques such as the Socratic Method (see Chesley, 2013) in virtual classrooms.

Besides the instructional challenges associated with online courses, students should not overlook very practical considerations. When you are not physically on campus, getting involved in activities like serving on a research team can be very difficult. As with many jobs, most professors want to meet research assistants in person. Also, because human participants' data need to be protected for ethical reasons, a lot of coding and analyses must be done on secure computers (i.e., on campus, not online).

As we noted with our classroom tips earlier, students should do their best to avoid distractions. Unfortunately, potential distractions are also prevalent for online courses, as students report taking part in a variety of distracting activities (e.g., music, video games, phones) while viewing online lectures (Blaisman, Larabee, & Fabry, 2018). Not surprisingly, students remember significantly less information from the lectures when distracted.

Another problem is that getting to know professors can be more difficult. Sure, you can have conversations over email (or FaceTime or Skype); we all communicate with people electronically. However, in-person (i.e., face-to-face) communication can be more memorable (which is important if you want professors to remember you and possibly write a letter of recommendation for you!). Networking and professional growth can potentially suffer because you may miss out on in-person campus activities and meetings. Organizations like Psi Chi (the international honor society in psychology) may hold meetings on your campus with guest speakers and informative panels. Student organizations may not have the time or resources to record these meetings and post them online; plus, you miss out on the chance to meet other students who attend these meetings.

One thing that students might not always consider is that there is slightly less trust between professors and students online because cheating can be perceived as a major issue (e.g., Trammell, Morgan, Davies, Petrunich-Rutherford, & Herold, 2018). This is because of the online environment—without using excessive methods (e.g., anti-cheating services), professors can never know for sure whether it is the student who is doing the work or taking the test. Also, students might be tempted to use notes, materials, or search engines to help with exam questions. Because of these issues, instructors have a tendency to make online exams more difficult; these more difficult exams may require more critical thinking and connecting of ideas rather than simple rote memorization of terms. Also, to ensure that students are learning and completing ideas, there are likely going to be more writing assignments so that students can demonstrate understanding, whereas, in a classroom, instructors can simply ask a question aloud to check for understanding.

A final problem that online students may encounter is that not all courses needed for a degree will be offered virtually. Although online course offerings have expanded a great deal in recent years, because it is a relatively new process, not all subjects are offered. For example, some courses that require in-person interaction for skill development might not work best in an online environment.

Overcoming Disadvantages

The easiest way, if possible, to overcome these disadvantages is to mix in some time on campus with the online courses—that is, instead of taking your entire psychology curriculum online, take some in-person courses from professors you want to meet, and then be sure to interact with them (e.g., participate during class discussions, speak with the professors during office hours). In addition, you can join student clubs or attend meetings held by campus organizations. This approach will give you the best of both worlds—flexibility with some online courses along with networking opportunities on campus.

If spending time on campus may not be possible, there are some things that students can do. First, try to take more than one course from the same professor and, when doing so, be sure to communicate with the professor so that he or she will get to know you. Keep in mind that the goal is not to pester the professor; it is to build an online professional relationship so that he or she will remember you (in a positive manner). Along this line, it may be helpful to use (professional-looking) photos in your profile or email—this will help the professor to put a face to the name. Also, if you ever do plan a trip to campus, set up a face-to-face meeting with some of your professors.

Another tip is to contact research groups and ask about opportunities to participate from afar. When you contact them, be sure that you are up front with them about your situation and why you cannot be on campus. Be prepared to hear a lot of rejection (e.g.,

"Thanks for your interest, but we need our research assistants to work on campus…"), but you will never know if you do not try.

Another approach, if you live far from campus, is to look for student organizations, research projects, or resources at a school that is nearby; in some cases, they may allow you to participate. However, keep in mind that you may have to be a student at that institution, so you might have to weigh the pros and cons as to whether signing up for credits is worth it (and whether it will affect your graduation timeline at your current school). Both of us have accepted requests made by students from other schools (who were going to be near our campus over the summer) to work on research over the summer, so this is a real possibility.

A final idea is to consider attending a "student-friendly" annual research conference held by a professional psychological organization (for details on this, see our modules on psychology organizations). Before the conference, contact the Psi Chi officers at your school to see if there is a group of students planning to attend the conference. If there is, arrange plans to meet with them. You can also look through the conference schedule and find professors and students from your school who will be presenting—for example, you can attend their poster presentations and introduce yourself.

Prepping for Success in an Online Course

Imagine if your online instructor asked, "How many assignments and quizzes do you plan to miss this semester?" Of course, almost all of you are going to say zero—but our experiences with online courses is that nearly half of you will miss at least one activity, and some of you will miss a large number of activities. Because we want all of you to succeed, we want to help you minimize this possibility. The following tips introduce common situations that we have seen, along with solutions for how to deal with the problem.

1. **Situation:** Good online instructors will send out at least one reminder email each week, but, if you never check your email, you will not see those emails.

   Solution: Check your email daily—one way to do this is to add your email to your smartphone. If you never check your school email, set it up so that it automatically forwards messages to an account that you actually do check.

2. **Situation:** With in-person courses, you have set days/times for class; with online courses, you are free to work whenever you want. However, that freedom brings the possibility that you may forget about the course.

   Solution: Set up a block of time that you can consistently set aside each week to work on your online course. Pick a day before the due date, as some activities will require more time and effort.

3. **Situation:** Different weeks may require different amounts of time and effort.

   Solution: When you finish a module, take a few minutes to look ahead for what is required for the next one. This can give you a "heads up" as to whether there are any activities that will require you to invest more time or to start early.

4. **Situation:** Sometimes we need external cues to remind us to do something.

   Solution: If you use a hardcopy planner, write in your assignments and due dates. If you prefer the electronic calendar on your smartphone, program it to send you weekly reminders about assignments and due dates.

© Can Stock Photo/AntonioGuillem

5. **Situation:** When you attend an in-person class, you might chat with the people sitting around you (sometimes you remind each other about deadlines).

   Solution: Reach out to your classmates and see who else is interested in creating a peer "reminder" or "accountability" group. Use a smartphone app (like *GroupMe*) to text each other reminders each week.

Take-Home Message

Online courses have some advantages over traditional, in-person courses. However, before you dive into them, be sure that you are aware of the disadvantages—especially if you want to complete all or most of your courses online. There are some steps, outlined previously, that you can take to mitigate these issues; however, to get the most out of your college experience, including the resources on campus and the networking opportunities, we highly recommend that students spend significant time on campus (if possible). As you will see in a lot of areas in this book, a lot of our recommendations for preparing yourself for a career or graduate school are easier if you spend at least part of your time on campus instead of exclusively working from home and taking all of your courses online.

Action Steps

1. If you are in an online course right now, apply the tips that we described in this module. Do it right away so that you can benefit (and decrease the odds of procrastination).

2. If you take most of your courses online, mix it up in the future by adding some in-person courses. In addition (or if that is not possible), figure out ways to get involved on campus by meeting professors or attending campus events.

iStock.com/ asiseeit

3 Adopting the Right Mindsets—Deep Learning, Critical Thinking, and Ethics

CHAPTER OUTLINE

3.0 MEET EMERSON

iStock.com/sam thomas

Emerson was a seemingly stellar student—with a 3.8 GPA and the successful completion of courses like Research Methods and Statistics. Now, as a senior, Emerson was taking a Capstone Senior Seminar course that included (a) an assessment exam to determine what they learned throughout the major and (b) an APA-style research proposal. So far, this sounds like another tale about a superstar psychology student, right?

Unfortunately, this is not one of those tales. When it was time to take the senior assessment exam, the concepts seemed very familiar, but Emerson had to guess for a lot of questions. When it came to the research paper, they became really nervous when the instructor covered the instructions that included (a) proposing a psychological experiment, (b) identifying independent and dependent variables, (c) explaining what statistics could be used, and (d) writing out citations and references in perfect APA-style formatting. Emerson thought back to some old choices they made while in college—for example, selecting instructors who had a reputation for not requiring a paper, cramming the night before exams, and opting for an "easy" Statistics instructor because they just wanted to pass with minimal effort (after all, why would a psychology student need to know math?).

With much trepidation and frustration, Emerson pulled through and submitted a mediocre paper. But this course caused Emerson's GPA and confidence to both fall to their lowest levels.

Why Did We Tell You This Story?

Even high-performing students like Emerson can be hampered by maladaptive beliefs and strategies. Emerson, at the end of college, had not retained much knowledge and had not taken time to develop important skills. Fortunately for you, being aware of these common pitfalls can prevent you from falling into the situation that Emerson fell into. If they could have done it all over again, Emerson should have (1) focused on long-term, deep learning, (2) not prioritized grades over learning and skill development, and (3) not been afraid of a challenge.

3.1 APPROACHES TO LEARNING

In our opinion, this module really touches on the foundation of your mindset as a student. In fact, we would argue that this might be one of the most important issues that can affect your overall college experience. To begin our exploration, let's start with a simple question—"What goals do you have for your courses this semester?"

iStock.com/marrio31

Although there are a variety of answers you might give, they probably fall into one of the following categories: (1) earn a good grade, (2) learn a lot of facts, (3) understand how things work, or (4) develop a skill. In this module we will cover these different types of learning goals along with some pros and cons of each approach.

Strategic Learning—"I'm Here for the Grades"

If your childhood was anything like ours, you might have had parents who expected you to earn high grades (or parents who scolded you for poor ones). Or maybe you received some type of reward or bribe for earning high grades. Although parents who do this have the best of intentions, one problem with this is that it can put grades up onto a pedestal so that grades themselves become the goal—this is sometimes referred to as a strategic learning style (e.g., Bain, 2012).

Although we think that it is worthwhile to aim for high grades, one problem with grades is that they are not always clearly related to what you have mastered from the course. Perhaps you did well on your exams. Or, maybe you racked up a lot of participation points and bumped up your score with extra credit that resembled busy-work. Was the instructor strict or lenient when it came to grading? Our point here is that no one can tell from your transcript how much you truly learned in a particular class. So, although aiming for high grades is a good goal, we think that grades should not be the ultimate goal when in school.

Putting grades into perspective. Although we love the aspirations of most students who want to do well in college, we want to make sure that all of you are realistic about grades. In most cases, not everyone will earn an A (or even a B). As McCullough (2014) notes, if you give a trophy to everyone, the trophy becomes meaningless—the same is true for grades. So, please understand that, although we want you to earn high grades, getting an A at all costs is not part of the game (especially if it includes begging, cheating, or pleading!).

We understand that good grades can be helpful for graduate school or scholarship applications, and some employers may ask about grades. However, one sobering reality is that grades do not matter after you are admitted into a graduate program or after you get your first job—after that point, no one else in the future will ask about your grades. In fact, grades are not always important when applying for a first job—one study showed that only 37% of recent college graduates were asked about grades during the hiring process (Arum & Roksa, 2014)! As for graduate school, it is possible to earn an F during college and still get into a PhD program (do not tell anyone else, but one of the authors of this book can attest to that).

When a focus on grades goes awry. Most students do not do this, but, in some extreme cases, there are a few students who think that grades are so important that they are willing to treat them as something that can be negotiated. In these scenarios, otherwise intelligent and rational students may behave in ways that are known by the term *grade grubbing* (e.g., Fendrich, 2009; Roderick, 2011). This includes emphasizing grades more than learning, conveying this attitude to professors, and pestering them for higher grades that were not earned.

Our advice is simple—please avoid these behaviors! Remember that professors are simply evaluating the work that is submitted to them. The truth is that professors do not like assigning low grades any more than students like receiving them. Most professors want their students to do well, but the grade must be earned in a manner that is fair to all students in the course (see Vernon, 2019, for a professor's perspective on grading).

Please do not take any of this the wrong way. By no means are we saying that you should stop striving for high grades—we want you to set your sights on earning a high grade point average on your quest to become a superstar psychology student! However, we want you to go about it the right way (see Table 3.1).

TABLE 3.1

How Much Do You Agree With the Following Items? Then Check the Key to See What Your Answers Indicate.

1. I typically prepare for an exam by memorizing information.
2. I like to compare ideas and evidence, and to then draw my own conclusions.
3. I prefer that exams ask about information that was explicitly covered in class.
4. I try to connect ideas from class to situations in my own life (or the real world).
5. Most of the time, I just want to get through my classes with a good grade.
6. Some ideas from lecture motivate me to look into the topic outside of class.

KEY: If you have more agreement with the odd-numbered items, then you might have tendencies toward surface learning; if you connect more to the even-numbered items, then you might have more of a deep learning approach.

Surface Learning—"I Want to Win Trivia Games!"

© Can Stock Photo/MicroOne

Another approach is to prepare for any "who," "what," or "when" question that might appear on exams. Many students have learned that blindly memorizing and then regurgitating facts on an exam leads to positive outcomes. Unfortunately, the structure of some college courses can contribute to students adopting a *surface learning* mindset like this—too many courses focus way too much on the learning of facts, and it is not uncommon to find courses that rely on multiple-choice exams that ask you questions such as "Who was known for plotting the forgetting curve by testing himself on nonsense syllables?"

One drawback to this approach is that, although this information is useful and important, being able to answer these questions only requires a shallow understanding of the information—it does not convey whether you know how to apply what was learned. A second drawback is that memorizing individual facts tends to lead to lower levels of long-term memory retention than when you integrate the information into a deeper level of understanding (e.g., Radvansky, 1999). For example, you might be surprised to learn that students who passed an introductory psychology course (which relied on multiple-choice tests) only retained approximately 50–70% of the content when they took a follow-up test 2 or 3 years later (Hard, Lovett, & Brady, 2019; Landrum & Gurung, 2013). In other words, memorizing facts does not always lead to long-term retention.

So, should you ignore facts when you are reading or studying? Of course, not—you need a foundation of information in memory. However, do not stop with the facts—instead, learn the information by piecing it together into a knowledge base. This leads us to our next idea…

Deep Learning, Part 1—"*Why* Is One of My Favorite Words"

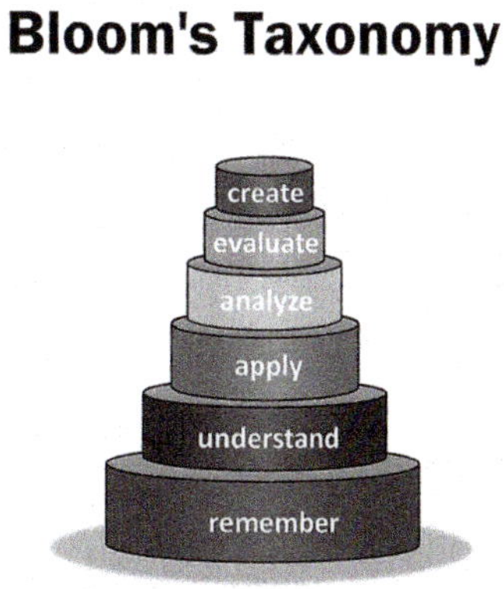

Shutterstock

Many educators and researchers argue that students should look at the material from a deeper perspective (e.g., Bain, 2012) and that students should strive to retain underlying themes that can be found in different psychological topics (e.g., Gerow, 2010). Some of you may have heard of *Bloom's taxonomy of learning*, which describes learning as occurring at different levels (e.g., Anderson & Krathwohl, 2001; Bloom, Engelhart, Furst, Hill, & Krathwohl, 1956). In a nutshell, the lowest level of learning is *remembering*—basically, this is what we discussed in the previous section. Moving beyond that, we get into *understanding, applying*, *analyzing*, *evaluating*, and *creating* information—this is referring to a level of learning that goes beyond the simple memorization of facts. Here, you start to think about, interpret, and connect ideas—this should be the goal of learning! And, as an added bonus, research from cognitive psychology is pretty clear that information that is processed more deeply is typically better recalled than information processed at a shallow, or surface, level (e.g., Craik & Lockhart, 2008).

We hope that you will have to *apply*, *analyze*, *evaluate*, and *create* (the fun one!) in your psychology classes. Look for professors who emphasize those levels, not just those who are known to be easy graders! Please do not approach your college career like a trivia buff collecting facts for a game show—instead, think about how you will apply the information you are learning to your own life and future career. Also, seek out opportunities to create (research experiences are a great place to do this). As part of this process, you will develop skills that will prepare you for wherever you go next in life. Speaking of skills, let's discuss them in more detail.

Shutterstock

Deep Learning, Part 2—"Developing Skills"

You might not know it yet, but the American Psychological Association (APA) is more than an organization that creates formatting rules for how to write a paper. Relevant to you, the APA also outlines a set of skills that undergraduate psychology majors should develop (American Psychological Association, 2013). These are skills that you should be working on every semester as you progress through the major!

1. Interpret, design, and conduct basic psychological research.
2. Demonstrate effective writing for different purposes.
3. Exhibit effective presentation skills for different purposes.
4. Interact effectively with others.
5. Apply psychological content and skills to career goals.

All of these goals are worded in terms of things you should be able to *do* or *demonstrate* to others. So, how should you go about gaining these valuable skills? We have a simple recommendation for you—put a little bit of time and effort into choosing your classes.

For example, every psychology student has to take Research Methods, but in most cases you will have some choice when it comes to the instructor. We know that some students choose sections based on the day and time they are offered, whereas others look for professors who are known for being easy—we do not want you doing those things! Instead, look for professors who will help you develop useful skills. For example, does an instructor include an oral presentation requirement in Research Methods? Is there a Cognitive Psychology class that includes a group project? A Capstone Senior Seminar class that focuses on a research paper? Look for these and choose the course sections that will help you improve yourself by developing these skills (we have much more on skills in the next chapter).

Take-Home Message

What is your approach to learning—are you more of a surface learner or a deep learner? In case you missed it, you can do a rough assessment by seeing how well the items in

Table 3.1 describe you. Keep in mind that a learning approach is not fixed and it can sometimes vary based on the topic or course. Ultimately, the approach you use in your courses is up to you, but our advice is that grades should not be the primary goal—grades should be a by-product of effective deep learning. In other words, if you learn the material and develop skills, good grades should follow.

As we wrap things up, we want to emphasize one last point. Remember the research that we mentioned earlier about students retaining less content from a psychology course as the years went by? Well, when students in one of those studies were asked an open-ended question (as seniors) about what they took away from their course, the most common responses revolved around learning foundational knowledge, developing skills, and their perspectives of others (Hard et al., 2019). In other words, although you can learn content from your psychology courses, your psychology courses can also help you develop skills and apply what you learn to your life.

Action Steps

1. Reflect on your typical approach to learning (described earlier). Are you happy with your approach? If not, take steps starting today to make a change—start setting goals for how you want to approach a class and for what you want to get out of it.

2. Use backward design (Wiggins & McTighe, 2005) to prepare for valuable skills. Here is the approach:

(a) Focus on results by asking, "What do you want to know, be able to do, or demonstrate to other people?"

(b) Monitor your achievements by identifying your measures of success and listing them. Earn bonus points if a professor agrees that your standards are appropriate.

(c) Prepare yourself for success by following our advice from this module—request course syllabi to see which class sections can help you the most. Also, ask your professors for suggestions on how you can reach your measures of success.

iStock.com/asiseeit

3.2 ADOPTING A CRITICAL THINKING MINDSET

One of the ways that you can move from a surface (or strategic) approach to a deep learning approach is to embrace a critical thinking mindset (you might also hear terms such as *reasoning* or *analytical thinking*). Essentially, this involves focusing your efforts at using the higher levels of Bloom's taxonomy, such as analyzing and evaluating information (e.g., Anderson & Krathwohl, 2001). Developing critical thinking skills is easier said than done, but you should feel better knowing that it is emphasized in higher education (e.g., Huber & Kuncel, 2016) and that it is actually possible to enhance your reasoning

Library of Congress

abilities (e.g., Nisbett, 2015). In this module we will scratch the surface of critical thinking by providing a few helpful suggestions for adopting a critical thinking mindset.

Be Skeptical

When it comes to critical thinking, one of the first pieces of advice is to be skeptical. What we mean by this is to not always blindly accept information that you encounter. To help us illustrate what we mean, let's consider a quote that we recently came across:

> *"Don't believe everything that you read on the internet."*
>
> —Attributed to Abraham Lincoln

On the surface, this sounds like good advice (consistent with what we are saying here), but some of you may have noticed something funny about this attributed quote. If you have not noticed the humor here, think about the following—in what century was Abraham Lincoln alive (HINT: not this century)?

So, whether you stumble across a (fake) quote like this online, read a post on social media, or learn something new, do not blindly accept it as true. What or who is the source of the information, and is that source trustworthy? Are people trying to convince you of something? If so, what is their perspective or goal? When it comes to psychological knowledge, does the information come from "somewhere online" or does it come from a more reliable source such as a journal article or textbook? Both news media and social media sources have been known to exaggerate a finding, report a study inaccurately, pass along outdated information, or sensationalize an odd or counterintuitive outcome. So, you may want to consider using an academic textbook or research article as the source of your information. Speaking of research . . .

Is There Any Evidence for That Claim?

When adopting a critical thinking mindset, an important consideration is to understand the difference between claims that are backed by evidence and those that are either vague or unsubstantiated. For example, when it comes to dating relationships, some people rely on the folk wisdom that "opposites attract," but others may contradict that by saying that "birds of a feather flock together" (see Table 3.2). One big problem with "common sense" statements like these is that they are not very specific and are not applied to any particular context. Another problem is that statements like these can sometimes be unfalsifiable. For example, does "opposites attract" mean that they will always attract, sometimes attract, or occasionally attract? Or does it only apply to magnets?

As you have learned (or will learn) in your General Psychology course, one of the key goals of psychology is to empirically test ideas. For example, as we noted in an earlier chapter, it might intuitively make sense that matching your preferred learning style to how an instructor structures class is the best approach. However, a whole bunch of psychological research has shown that this does not matter (Brown, Roediger, & McDaniel, 2014).

TABLE 3.2
Some (Contradictory) Common Sense Sayings

Opposites attract . . . but birds of a feather flock together.
You cannot judge a book by its cover . . . but the clothes make the man.
Better safe than sorry . . . but nothing ventured, nothing gained.
Two heads are better than one . . . but too many cooks spoil the broth.
Look before you leap . . . but he who hesitates is lost.
The grass is always greener on the other side . . . but there's no place like home.
Absence makes the heart grow fonder . . . but out of sight, out of mind.

Another example is that a surprising number of adults believe in supernatural phenomena such as ghosts, telepathy, clairvoyance, or psychokinesis, even though there is no consistent evidence to support the existence of them (e.g., Bouvet & Bonnefon, 2015). Although these beliefs tend to be harmless, they can be related to how you think about other aspects of the world (e.g., Pennycook, Fugelsang, & Koehler, 2015)—that is, the acceptance of these types of beliefs is related to lower levels of analytic thinking about other topics. So save your exploration of supernatural topics for fictional books or movies. Speaking of fictional stories...

The Power of Stories

Clearly we know that people can be influenced by stories—have you noticed that we begin each chapter with a short tale about a student? Stories can be effective because they pull us in—we want to learn about people (especially people to whom we can relate), we like tracking goals, and we want to find out what is going to happen next (e.g., Zwaan, 1999). The great part about stories is that they can be informative, memorable, and entertaining.

Unfortunately, there can be a downside to stories (e.g., Kida, 2006). Unlike research (which is typically based on multiple observations or a large sample), a story might only illustrate a single case or perspective. Imagine that a classmate shares a story about a difficult course project and then tells you to avoid that class at all costs. Should you reconsider that course? Maybe—but we would recommend obtaining more information. Even though your classmate had a bad experience, it is possible that other students enjoyed the course and learned a lot. Perhaps this classmate procrastinated, which led to the need to rush through a big project at the last minute. Our point is this: a story can potentially be useful (and memorable), but, because it typically only illustrates a single case, it could be describing an outlier instead of the typical experience.

Consider Other Views

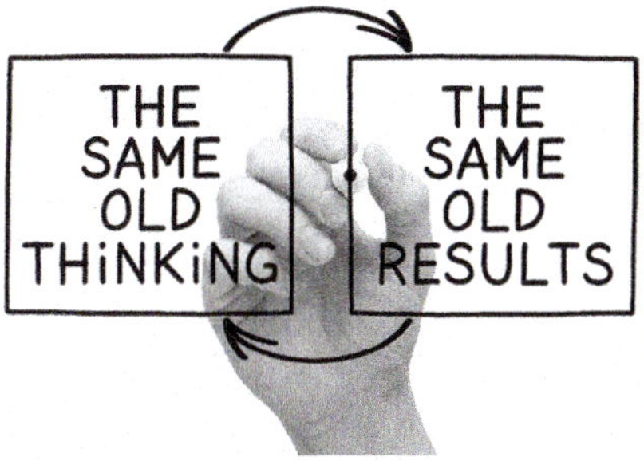

iStock.com/IvelinRadkov

One of the things that you should learn as a psychology major is that the world is diverse—there are people who have different experiences, interests, and viewpoints than yours. Things that might seem very obvious to you might be viewed very differently by others. For example, a college might propose a small tuition hike to have extra money for student support services. However, a student from a poor family might have to work additional hours (or drop out) if tuition is raised just a small amount. One way to adopt a critical thinking approach is to consider arguments that run counter to what you currently believe. So, if you think that a tuition hike is good, consider why it might be bad, or vice versa (e.g., Catapano, Tormala, & Rucker, 2019).[1]

Considering other views can also involve how you mentally represent an idea. As an example, when we talk to college students, most talk about their time in college as if it is open-ended and seemingly endless. This can be problematic because it might lead to procrastination—because graduation is "sometime in the future," there is little urgency to take action and get stuff done. An alternative perspective is to represent your time in college as blocks of time (this idea was inspired by Urban, 2014). For example, if we assume that college will take 4 years to complete, and that there are 12 months in each year, it can be represented like the depiction in Figure 3.1.

If you are like us, this new representation caused the time period to suddenly seem much shorter—graduation is right around the corner! In this graphical representation, we can clearly see that there are a limited number of months to get stuff done (even fewer if you plan to spend your summer at the beach). When we represent your time in college like this, procrastinating (when it comes to applying our superstar tips) no longer seems to be a good idea.

Try New Solutions

Sometimes things are working well in life—if this describes you, then keep it up! However, there are other times when things are not working out as well. As professors, we see some struggling students who tell us that they want to improve their grades. Unfortunately, far too often the solution to this problem is a declaration that they will try to "study more." Although that intention is good, this might not be helpful if poor study strategies are being used. As we noted in our classroom and study skills discussion in a previous chapter, it is important to apply the correct strategies such as taking good notes, paying attention in class, actually reading the assigned book, and spreading out your studying. If the current approach is ineffective, the simple solution of doing more of it is not likely to work out well. If you want things to change, then you may have to change your approach—but be

FIGURE 3.1

A Month-by-Month Depiction of One's Time in College. We Highly Encourage You to Use This to Plan Out How and When You Are Going to Tackle Your Superstar Accomplishments!

	1	2	3	4	5	6	7	8	9	10	11	12
Year 1												
Year 2												
Year 3												
Year 4												

[1]One word of caution—be careful of taking this too far and adopting another person's perspective (i.e., putting yourself in their shoes). If you think that this "other person" has different values than you, this might make you more resistant to the counterargument (e.g., Catapano, Tormala, & Rucker, 2019).

sure to take some time to think about the appropriate strategy to use!

iStock.com/FG Trade

Categorical Thinking

People have a tendency to think about the world in a binary or categorical manner. For example, students are either psychology majors or some other major; people are male or female. We think of the world in a black-or-white manner because it is simpler to do so—however, life has a lot of gray areas and things are not always easily categorized. Students can have more than one major, and some people (like Emerson, the student in the chapter opening) do not identify with either of the traditional genders (e.g., Huston, 2015). Here is another example for those of you who are into psychological issues—whenever you are asked if something is a result of *nature* or *nurture*, it is often the case that the answer is *BOTH*.

Our point here is that we often rely on categories because they can simplify our thinking. But try to resist the temptation to think of everything in a black-or-white manner. And, if it makes you feel any better, psychological researchers are sometimes prone to oversimplified categorical thinking, too—such as labeling people as introverts or extroverts or categorizing people as having either a high or a low working memory span (e.g., Young, 2016).

Take-Home Message

In our view, the ability to think critically is one of the most important skills to develop. It can help with understanding concepts and issues, identifying pros and cons, and becoming more resistant to arguments (or sales pitches) with little substance. In this module, we introduced a number of issues that can help with critical thinking, but we could go on even longer. Although our space here in this chapter has run out, pay attention to various tidbits about critical thinking that we slip into other chapters of this book.

Action Steps

© Can Stock Photo/miceking

1. Be willing to challenge your own beliefs about the world.

   A great starting point is to check out a book such as *50 Great Myths of Popular Psychology* (Lilienfeld, Lynn, Ruscio, & Beyerstein, 2010) or a research article such as *Myths and Misconceptions in Popular Psychology* (Furnham & Hughes, 2014). Unless you have already taken a lot of psychology courses, you probably hold some of those myths—if you do, read more about the topic so that your beliefs are more consistent with what we learn through psychological research.

2. There are a lot of books out there that focus on critical thinking that you should read. These are two of our favorites (the full information is in the references)—we like these because they have interesting examples related to psychology:

   - *How to Think Straight About Psychology* by Stanovich (2018)
   - *Mindware* by Nisbett (2015)

3.3 REGRETS, FAILURE, AND LUCK—CHALLENGE YOURSELF!

If you think that the idea of failure is one of the worst things that can happen in life, and that it should be avoided at all costs, there are two ways we can structure our lives. First, no matter the outcome of a task, everyone gets rewarded (trophies for everyone who participated!). This might sound good at first, but this approach can be problematic because it can teach people that actual performance and outcomes do not matter. The second way to avoid failure is by not even trying at all—if you do not try, you cannot fail (or succeed). We do not like either of those approaches—in fact, we think that failure can potentially be helpful, or at least a sign that you are doing things the right way. Our goal with this module is to explain why failure is something that can be embraced—with the right mindset, you can actually learn more from failure than from success.

iStock.com/deimagine

Failure Happens More Often Than You Think

Did you ever interview for a job and not get one? Have you ever applied for a scholarship only to find out that you were not selected? The point is that most, if not all, people have experienced failure at some time in their lives. Even though you may not have succeeded at something, does that make you a complete failure? Of course not! People fail every single day, the world does not end, and they keep moving forward. The lesson here is that failure happens to successful people, it happens to rich people, and it can happen to you (see Kipman, 2018, for some examples of successful people who have experienced failure).

Which Regret Is Worse—Failing at Something or Not Even Trying?

"'Tis better to have loved and lost than never to have loved at all."

—Attributed to Alfred Lord Tennyson

Have you ever heard about an opportunity—such as an internship, job, or research position—but were too afraid to apply? Have you ever considered taking a course that you thought might be interesting but avoided it because you were scared that it might be too difficult? The worst part of these situations is that, in the future, you may seriously regret that you never even tried.

Psychological researchers have examined two types of regret—regret from not trying and regret from trying and failing. Although the latter has a short-term effect on us, regret from not even trying has a greater effect on us in the long term (Gilovich & Medvec, 1995). This point is important, so we will repeat it—regret is more powerful when you do not try than when you try something but fail. Imagine yourself in the far-off future, when you are on your deathbed reflecting on your life. At that point, is it going to matter that you tried in life and suffered some minor setbacks? Probably not—at least you made an attempt! But, if you never even tried some things, you will likely rue the fact that you have no idea if you could have succeeded.

Learn From Failure

We are not going to sugarcoat things—most of the time, success is better than failure. Earning a scholarship, getting into graduate school—those are fantastic things. However, you can still learn important life lessons if you are not selected for that scholarship or are not admitted into a particular graduate program. When you fail at something, you have an opportunity to analyze the situation and improve yourself so that your odds of success go up when you try again. For example, people do not always get admitted to the first school that interviews them. But, after learning about the process and what questions to expect, the next interview might go much better. The point is that, if you try in life, failure is going to happen; but, you have to learn from the failures so that you can increase the probability of success on your next attempt. Before you continue reading, complete the activity in Table 3.3.

One of the reasons that we discuss the topic of failure is because it can interact with the mindset you adopt regarding your abilities (e.g., Dweck, 2006). You see, there are some who hold a *fixed view*. In a simplified manner, this suggests that some people are born smart and others are not. In contrast, an alternative view is to have a *growth mindset* (our recommendation!)—in this perspective, intellectual abilities are not completely set in stone and can be changed through effort. Importantly, students who adopt this mindset fare much better in school than those who approach it as a fixed trait.

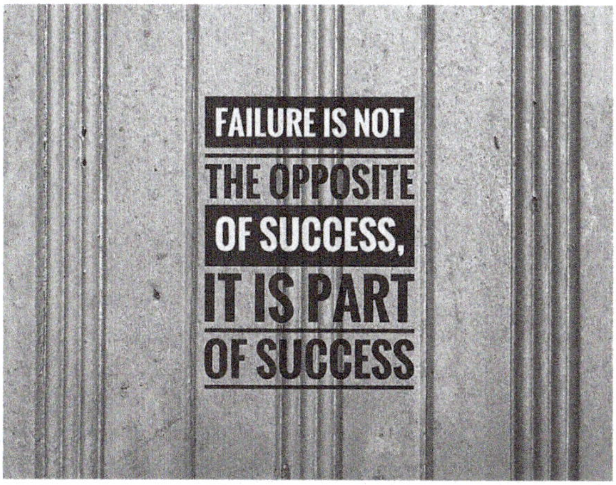
FAILURE IS NOT
THE OPPOSITE
OF SUCCESS,
IT IS PART
OF SUCCESS
Shutterstock

Let's consider a practical example. We bet that you have seen (or will see) students who, upon having difficulty in a Statistics course, will throw up their hands and give up—they

TABLE 3.3

How Much Do You Agree With the Following Items? Then Check the Key to See What Your Answers Indicate.

1. If I am honest with myself, I feel more intelligent when tasks are easy.
2. Life can be broken down like this—some people are good at math, and others are not.
3. I typically avoid things that seem like they are going to be challenging.
4. When a project is hard, I spend more time and effort because I want to succeed on it.
5. I am okay with making the occasional mistake because I can learn from it and improve.
6. Even though I might not succeed, I am willing to try because my efforts might pay off.

KEY: If you have more agreement with the first three items, then you might have tendencies toward a fixed mindset; if you connect more to the last three items, then you might identify more with a growth mindset.

Growth Mindset
- I can learn anything I want to
- When I'm frustrated, I persevere
- I want to challenge myself
- When I fail, I learn
- Tell me I try hard
- If you succeed, I'm inspired
- My effort and attitude determine everything
Fixed Mindset
- I'm either good at it, or I'm not
- When I'm frustrated, I give up
- I don't like to be challenged
- When I fail, I'm no good
- Tell me I'm smart
- If you succeed, I feel threatened
- My abilities determine everything

Shutterstock

may claim that they have math anxiety (e.g., Ashcraft & Moore, 2009) and that they will never be good at math (a fixed view). In contrast, if you have a growth perspective, even though you had a setback in that course, you are more likely to put in the time and effort to keep improving. If you are interested in making real progress academically, growing your academic knowledge, and getting the most out of your psychology experience, seek out the experts at your institution—your professors are there to help you grow.

Create More Luck in College and in Life

Thus far, we have been talking about failure, which is a somewhat negative topic. So let's switch gears and discuss a more positive topic—good luck. Most people want more good luck, but is luck something that happens to you? Or is luck something that people can create by adopting the right mindset? This is connected to the psychological ideas of an *internal* or *external locus of control* (e.g., Ng, Sorensen, & Eby, 2006; Rotter, 1966). The former is when people think that their behaviors determine what happens in their lives, whereas the latter is when people think that their behaviors do not have as much of an effect on life outcomes. People with an internal locus of control are more likely to work hard, take control of situations, and try to make things happen. People with an external locus of control are more likely to believe in concepts like fate and that outcomes are due to chance. The reason that we introduce these terms is that we want to convince you to approach life with an internal locus of control—here are a few ways that you can do this to try and create more good luck in your life (see Table 3.4).

TABLE 3.4

Examples of Steps Students Can Take for Creating More Luck

Try New Things and Get Involved.

- Join student clubs and professional organizations.
- Get involved with research, volunteering, service learning, or an internship.
- Utilize your professors' office hours and learn from them (learn more about class topics or about opportunities outside of the classroom).

Be Prepared and Work Hard.

- Spread out your studying across different days—do it consistently.
- Apply more than once (for scholarships, opportunities, awards, etc.).
- Write multiple drafts of a paper (you are not likely to write the perfect paper the first time—it will improve with edits).

Be open to new experiences. One way to create good luck is to be open to new experiences. Try something different—join a professional organization, participate in a student club, or visit your professors during office hours. When you open yourself up to new experiences and meet new people, you can discover new opportunities. A student you meet in a club might tell you about an internship; a professional organization might advertise a book that provides advice for the field you are considering; a professor might invite you to join a research team. Our point here is that there are opportunities all around us. Step one is to put yourself out there so that you can learn about them—then step two is to take advantage of those opportunities!

Be prepared and work hard. Another way to create good luck is to be prepared. Instead of attributing your exam performance to luck, we recommend that you use our classroom, study, and exam tips to be properly prepared. One thing that usually goes along with preparation is hard work. Imagine two students—the first earns a scholarship, but the second does not. Could the difference between them be a result of luck? Sure, but it could also be due to hard work. In our experience, the students who earn scholarships are the ones who work hard and apply to a bunch of them (instead of just one). Our point here is that some people who appear to be lucky may simply be people who try a little bit harder (and smarter). When you work hard you can create more opportunities for success to occur!

Take-Home Message

Despite the fact that failure happens to everyone, many people try to avoid failure when they can. However, failure is typically not as bad as we anticipate it to be; not trying (or not challenging ourselves) can lead to more regret over the long term. Failure can be useful because it can be a powerful learning tool. For example, professors like us would prefer to mentor a student who tried and failed (but was still willing to keep going) over a student who did not try at all. In the former case, even though that student failed, he or she is likely to have learned a lot from that experience.

Action Steps

1. Make a list of some dreams or goals that you want to achieve but have avoided because of a fear of failure. Think critically about whether failure in that situation would really be so bad or if, at a minimum, it could be a phenomenal learning experience. If so, take action and work toward that goal. If you fail, adopt the mindset that you can improve—assess what could have been done better, make changes, and consider trying again.

2. Create your own luck in areas that are important to you. Right now, make a list of two or three things that are important to you (e.g., finding a job, joining a research team, earning a scholarship, etc.). Next, decide right now how you are going to work hard and increase the odds of good luck occurring for you. For a more thorough description of how to change your luck, see Wiseman's (2004) tips (the complete reference can be found with the other references at the end of the book).

3.4 THINKING ABOUT ETHICS IN COLLEGE AND IN PSYCHOLOGY

When we introduce the topic of ethics to our students, many of them roll their eyes and tell us that it is mostly common sense rules about right and wrong. However, as we pointed out in an earlier module on critical thinking, *common sense* is a pretty flimsy argument. Regarding ethics, although it is true that some ideas are intuitive, people do not always consider the consequences of unethical actions. On top of that, a sizable percentage of people will admit to taking part in (or observing) unethical behaviors—sometimes there are outside pressures that push people in this direction (e.g., Carucci, 2016). In this module, we are going to discuss the benefits of adopting an ethical mindset as well as the drawbacks to not acting in an ethical manner. We are going to focus on two areas that are highly relevant to psychology students—(a) ethics as a student and (b) ethics related to the field of psychology.

Real-World Examples of (a Lack of) Ethics

Unfortunately, it is not too difficult to find examples of people acting in unethical ways in college settings. In one case, over 100 students were caught collaborating on an exam (e.g., Robbins, 2012). In another situation, athletes received extra assistance from tutors (e.g., sharing exam answers, writing papers for others, taking a test for someone else) in order to pass online courses (e.g., Dinich, 2009). Parents even get involved, too—in an attempt to get their children into college, numerous parents lied about their child's accomplishments or abilities and also paid others to take exams for their children (e.g., Wamsley, 2019).

iStock.com/Michail_Petrov-96

Sadly, the unethical behavior does not stop with students and parents. There are examples of a small number of psychological researchers who were discovered to have fabricated data and then published articles based on those dishonest actions (e.g., Bartlett, 2012, 2015). In addition, other researchers have admitted on anonymous surveys (John, Loewenstein, & Prelec, 2012) that they have been involved in questionable research practices such as rounding off statistical values or excluding a research participant for no apparent reason (if you are a research geek like us, you might be interested in a website that tracks retractions of published scientific papers for reasons as simple as a misprint or as extreme as fraud—see www.retractionwatch.com). Finally, a group of psychologists was criticized for unethical behavior regarding their stance on torture (e.g., Handelsman, 2017).

Why did we just rattle off all of these examples? Are we telling you to go ahead and cheat because others are doing it? Of course not! We listed these examples because they exemplify that cheating and other unethical behaviors happen, we need to be aware of them, and we need to learn from them. As we noted in the opening of this module, ethics are not just an application of common sense—these are issues that should be thought about and discussed (e.g., You, Ruiz, & Warchal, 2018).

Ethics as a Student—Cheating

Cheating can roughly be broken down into four categories (e.g., McCabe, Butterfield, & Trevino, 2012; McKibban & Burdsal, 2013; Schmelkin, Gilbert, Spencer, Pincus, & Silva, 2008):

1. Exam cheating
2. Paper cheating
3. Interactive cheating
4. False personal excuses

Exam cheating is an obvious one, and it can take various forms—this could be looking at someone else's answers, sneaking in a cheat sheet, using an electronic device when you are not supposed to use one, or using a textbook for an online exam when it is supposed to be a closed-book exam. You might think you are being sly with your methods (see Table 3.5)—such as putting your hand on your forehead while glancing at classmates' answers, wearing a baseball cap with answers on the brim, or storing answers on a phone or calculator—but professors have seen these attempts at cheating (and many more). If you are caught, there are two probable outcomes—you may receive a warning (and a loss of respect from your professor), but you might also fail the exam (or possibly the course!).

iStock.com/lisafx

Paper cheating can take a few different forms. The first is creative padding. This refers to actions such as adding sources to your reference list that you did not actually read or use. A second form of paper cheating is taking credit for others' work—this includes scenarios such as having someone else write your paper but turning it in as if it is your writing. Finally, another form of paper cheating is

TABLE 3.5

A Few (True) Stories of Unsuccessful Cheating Attempts

- A student copied answers from a classmate during an exam. Unfortunately for the student, he was naive to the fact that the classmate had a different version of the exam (with slightly different questions and answers).
- A professor figured out that a particular student was copying exam answers all semester from a high-achieving classmate. Unfortunately for the student, before the final exam (which was worth a large percentage of the grade), the professor arranged for the high-achieving student to answer every question incorrectly.
- A student, who was not the best writer, plagiarized by copying and pasting text from a research article directly into her paper. Unfortunately for the student, the plagiarized text was obvious to the professor as it clearly stood out from the rest of the paragraphs—it was in a different font!

plagiarism—taking someone else's words or ideas without giving proper credit (we will cover plagiarism in more detail in a later chapter when we cover writing). These types of cheating are serious and can be thought of as a form of academic theft or stealing.

Interactive cheating is when students work together when they are supposed to be working independently. This could be sharing answers during an in-class exam, working together for online assignments or exams, or collaborating on a paper that is supposed to be done on one's own. Do not take this the wrong way though—there are times and places when working together is encouraged (e.g., studying before an exam, helping someone with practice problems, developing a group project)—however, when you are supposed to work independently, then collaboration is a big no-no.

The final type of cheating, false personal excuses, is when students lie to a professor to gain some academic benefit (for a humorous take on this issue, see Adams's [1999] article on "The dead grandmother/exam syndrome"). This could be to get an extension on a paper, delay taking an exam, have an assignment waived, or increase one's grade. Although some students tell us that this form of cheating is "not a big deal," we disagree—this type of behavior can give students an advantage over their peers, which is not fair to the other students in the course (and one thing that we have learned over the years as professors is that students value and appreciate fairness by instructors).

iStock.com/asiseeit

Before we move on, we want to be clear that we are talking about *lying* or *falsehoods* here. If you have a legitimate reason for needing a delay or another attempt, such as a serious illness or emergency family situation, please notify your instructors about those circumstances! Instructors recognize that unplanned or extreme life events happen, and they will work with you to help.

Why students cheat—should you do it? One explanation for why students cheat is that some have their primary focus on grades (e.g., McKibban & Burdsal, 2013).

For example, earlier in this chapter, we discussed the mindset of being a strategic learner where grades are emphasized more than learning (Bain, 2012). It is also possible that students rationalize cheating in special circumstances—for example, they may think that it is okay to cheat in courses that are particularly difficult or in courses where they do not care about the material (e.g., Anderman & Won, 2019). Cheating can also be a move made out of desperation—if students do not believe that they can meet the course expectations (to pass), they may be more inclined to cheat (e.g., Davy, Kincaid, Smith, & Trawick, 2007).

Other proposed reasons for cheating relate to what students see in the world. Sadly, it does not take much effort to see well-publicized examples of cheating in society—tax evasion, politics, sports, and corporations skirting the rules (e.g., Callahan, 2004). There can also be an influence from what they observe from their peers—this can work both ways in that there can be peer pressure to cheat or possibly influence from peers not to cheat (McCabe et al., 2012). Read through Table 3.6 and think about whether any of those statements are good justifications for cheating.

One issue with cheating is that some people mistakenly think of it as a victimless crime (e.g., Miller, Murdock, & Grotewiel, 2017). But, when cheaters obtain higher grades, then their classmates might be harmed if their academic performance is compared to those who cheated. For example, an honest student who earned solid grades might lose out on a job, award, or graduate school admissions if they are competing with someone else who has inflated grades as a result of cheating. Also, cheaters can hurt themselves if they miss out on an opportunity to truly learn information or skills. They can also have feelings of guilt if they obtain recognition or rewards that were unearned.

Our advice about cheating. Our advice is simple—do not cheat! It is not a victimless crime (Miller et al., 2017). As we noted earlier, it puts grades up on a pedestal so that they are emphasized above learning (McKibban & Burdsal, 2013). Cheating can also create feelings of mistrust among students (when students see their classmates doing it) or between students and instructors. If these arguments were not enough, then understand that the potential punishment is not worth it—cheating can lead to a loss of respect, failing grades, and possibly disciplinary action such as expulsion.

Ethics in Research and Applied Professions

Besides the ethical issues that apply to your life as a student, there are also ethical issues related to psychological research and careers. The American Psychological Association has

TABLE 3.6

Think About It—Are Any of the Following a Good Justification for Cheating in College?

- I really want an A in a course.
- The course is required but is unrelated to my goals or interests.
- I am in danger of not passing a course.
- A lot of people cheat in the world—I should do it, too, if I want to get ahead.
- I know that some of my friends or classmates are cheating.
- Why not? After all, it seems to be a victimless crime.

listed a set of five ethical principles for the field of psychology (American Psychological Association, 2017)—these are listed in Table 3.7. As we go through these, you will notice that, although each principle has a slightly different focus, there is some overlap across them. Also, some of the ideas expressed in these principles may emerge elsewhere in this book when we discuss other topics (e.g., student research opportunities involve consent, debriefing, and Institutional Review Boards [IRBs]).

Principle A: Beneficence and Nonmaleficence. The fancy words in this first principle refer to the idea that people in psychology should strive to help others and do no harm. This can be in a professional setting or a research setting. Importantly, this also includes animals used in research as well. If there are scenarios when harm cannot be avoided, steps should be taken to minimize it as much as possible.

Principle B: Fidelity and Responsibility. To put it simply, the second principle states that you should prioritize the needs of those with whom you work. This means building trust by being clear and transparent about roles and situations. For example, therapists should reassure clients that they are there to help the clients. Another aspect to this is to minimize, eliminate, or disclose conflicts of interest that might be present.

Principle C: Integrity. This principle comes down to this—be accurate and honest. Do not lie, deceive, or take advantage of others. It is understood, though, that some research studies might require deception—in these cases, any harm should be minimized and explanations should be provided afterward.

Principle D: Justice. The fourth principle focuses on being fair to everyone and avoiding biases. For example, a practicing psychologist should treat people similarly regardless of their background or ethnicity. People should also be aware of their limitations or biases and how these can affect others.

Principle E: Respect for People's Rights and Dignity. This last principle reflects the goal to be respectful of the fact that people have differences based on factors such as age, gender, culture, race, religion, disability, or socioeconomic status. That is, people in psychology should be mindful of these differences and to avoid any biases based on them. In addition, this principle emphasizes people's rights of privacy and confidentiality.

Ethical Dilemmas to Consider

One thing to keep in mind is that ethical issues can seem straightforward when you read about them but life scenarios can sometimes make them seem more complicated (remember what we talked about back in the critical thinking module—instead of clearly

TABLE 3.7

American Psychological Association's Ethical Principles

Principle A—Beneficence and Nonmaleficence
Principle B—Fidelity and Responsibility
Principle C—Integrity
Principle D—Justice
Principle E—Respect for People's Rights and Dignity

being black or white, some issues can fall into gray areas). So, before we wrap up this module, we are including some hypothetical ethical scenarios for you to consider. For each of these scenarios, think about what you might do if you were in those circumstances and whether anyone might be harmed based on the actions that are taken.

- You are taking an in-class exam and you notice that two classmates are secretly using their phones to look up and share answers. The instructor has not noticed what those two students are doing.
  - What would you do?
  - Would anyone be harmed in this scenario (this could be you or others)?
- You are taking an online course and a friend of yours happens to be in that same course. As the first exam approaches, your friend makes a remark that the two of you should meet up with your laptops to take the exam together. He says that everyone in online courses collaborates or cheats and that the two of you would be silly not to do it.
  - What would you do?
  - Would anyone be harmed in this scenario (this could be you or others)?
- You are writing a paper for class that must follow APA-style formatting rules. The paper is due in a few hours and, due to some ill-advised procrastination, you are just getting started. One problem is that you do fully understand some of the ideas from a research paper that you are going to cite. The author of the paper described the ideas in a way that seems so intelligent, but, if you described it, your words would be a jumbled mess of nonsense. You think about inserting a sentence or two directly from the research paper.
  - What would you do?
  - Would anyone be harmed in this scenario (this could be you or others)?
- While in college, you recognize the importance of creating (or updating) your résumé. As any good student would do, you ask others for feedback. One person gets back to you and tells you that your list of experiences and memberships is a little short. She tells you that she had that same problem but then addressed it by signing up for a bunch of student organizations that she could include on her résumé. When you ask how she had the time to participate in all of those, she laughs and tells you that she does not really participate—she just signed up with the organizations so that she could list them. She said that everybody lies on their résumé and that, in the grand scheme of things, something like this was nothing.
  - What would you do?
  - Would anyone be harmed in this scenario (this could be you or others)?
- You are taking a Research Methods course, and the course has surprisingly been fun because the professor had everyone work in groups to design and conduct their own research experiment. After collecting data from your classmates for your group's project on extrasensory perception—predict the Zener card (circle, star, cross, wavy lines)—you notice that the results almost reached statistical

significance. If you removed one student from your data, who had zero correct answers, the results would be statistically significant.

  - What would you do?
  - Would anyone be harmed in this scenario (this could be you or others)?

- You are volunteering at a suicide hotline center. You have learned some of the basics about how to work with people who are having a very difficult time—listening, staying calm, and keeping everything confidential. One day, you receive a call from someone who shares their problems along with a lot of personal information. In addition, the person talks about causing harm to his family (in addition to himself).
  - What would you do?
  - Would anyone be harmed in this scenario (this could be you or others)?
- You are working on a research project with a professor and some graduate students. The current project is examining whether or not a certain app is effective for students to improve their learning and test scores. You happen to notice that this app looks familiar—when you look more closely, you notice that it was developed by a software team and your mother was a part of that development team. You think that you should tell the professor about this, but it is possible that she might remove you from the research team, leading to your missing out on this research experience.
  - What would you do?
  - Would anyone be harmed in this scenario (this could be you or others)?

Take-Home Message

Our experience as professors has taught us that some people value learning about ethics, whereas others do not think they need to spend time thinking about these "common sense" ideas. However, if this latter argument were true, then we would not see so many instances of unethical behaviors in society (and in college). We agree with others that ethics are an important topic that should be focused on and discussed in college (e.g., You et al., 2018). So, please heed our warning and take the time to think through the issues and scenarios that we present here—part of becoming a superstar psychology student is doing things the right way and earning one's accomplishments. Finally, just like we noted in the critical thinking module, keep an eye out for further discussion of ethical issues elsewhere in this book.

Action Steps

1. Take a moment to think about a time when you acted in an unethical manner (or were tempted to do so). Would you consider that behavior to be a victimless crime—how would others possibly be affected? How were you affected?
2. Go through the ethical scenarios that we provided in this module. What would you do in those scenarios?

Even better, discuss with your classmates what each person would do—is there agreement?

Navigating the Psychology Curriculum and Meeting Your Professors

4

4.0 MEET P.J.

iStock.com/LSOphoto

CHAPTER OUTLINE

P.J. was a high achiever and liked the idea of helping people, so when he started college he had interests in choosing psychology as his major. However, P.J.'s parents pushed him to major in something (they believed) practical on his way to a potentially high-paying career. Because his parents could be persuasive (and because they were paying some of his tuition), P.J. decided to pursue a career in medicine and major in biology (like most pre-med students).

When P.J. met with an academic advisor to declare his major and learn about the courses he would need, they talked about his goals and interests. P.J. was surprised to hear that, with a little bit of planning, it would make sense for him to double-major in biology and psychology. The academic advisor opened P.J.'s eyes as to how and why this made sense for him.

First, P.J. learned that double-majoring was not that unusual—as long as one's course schedule was planned out carefully, it was still possible to finish all of the requirements in 4 years. Second, P.J. learned that psychology was an important part of being a pre-med student—the updated version of the Medical College Admission Test (MCAT) has a significant portion devoted to psychology topics. Third, the academic advisor told P.J. that, whereas mastering the biology content (e.g., anatomy) was important for a career in medicine, the best doctors were the ones who knew how to connect with and clearly communicate with patients.

Why Did We Tell You This Story?

A lot of students tell us that they enjoy psychology but that they also have other interests. In this chapter, we cover the areas that can be explored and the skills that can be developed as a psychology student—we also consider possibilities for how students can combine their interest in psychology with other areas (e.g., adding a minor or second major). Finally, we emphasize the importance of learning from (and communicating professionally with) your professors as well as an academic advisor.

4.1 TYPICAL PSYCHOLOGY COURSES

According to faculty, understanding the psychology curriculum might be one of the most important topics for students (Landrum, Shoemaker, & Davis, 2003). Our students agree, as they have made it clear to us that they want to have a better understanding of what psychology courses they are likely going to take as an undergraduate. In this module, we will talk about psychology courses broadly, so keep in mind that the specific courses at your institution might be a little bit different. Also, because there is not much of a distinction between psychology programs that award a Bachelor of Arts and those which award a Bachelor of Science (Pfund et al., 2016), we will not make any distinctions here.

The Psychology Curriculum

As with most college majors, courses in the psychology curriculum are categorized into levels (e.g., 100, 200, 300, and 400 levels). A general rule of thumb is that courses with a higher numerical value, for example, the 400 level, will be more difficult and demanding than those at the lower levels. Also, as a general rule, students should take the courses at the lower levels before the courses at the upper levels.

General Psychology and Introduction to the Psychology Major

The psychology sequence begins with General Psychology (e.g., "PSY 101")—this course provides a broad overview of psychology content areas, landmark studies, and current streams of thought (e.g., Gurung et al., 2016). It is common for General Psychology courses to introduce students to psychological research through a lab section (e.g., Peterson & Sesma, 2017) or participation in research studies (e.g., Rocchi, Beaudry, Anderson, & Pelletier, 2016). In addition to PSY 101, some programs offer an Introduction to the Psychology Major course that provides advice for what students can do to get the most out of their psychology experience and become viable candidates for jobs or graduate school (Roscoe & McMahan, 2014). If an instructor has you read this book, then you are likely in one of these courses.

Stats and Methods—Important (and Underappreciated)

After PSY 101, there are typically a few required courses for most psychology students: Statistics and Research Methods. In Statistics, you will learn different quantitative approaches that are used to analyze research data. For example, you can learn about detecting patterns in data sets and whether a specific clinical treatment is effective or not. For Statistics, it will probably help if you have adequate training in college algebra beforehand.

iStock.com/Halfpoint

In Research Methods, you will learn the proper methods of conducting a scientific research study in psychology. You will also learn how to write an APA-style research paper. Do not be intimidated by this, though; your instructor will walk you through it. Also, if you are lucky, you may be able to conduct your own mini-experiment in this class.

In our view, it is important to take Statistics and Research Methods early because they help prepare you for many other psychology courses—an understanding of statistics and methods will allow you to better understand the psychological theories and research taught in your other psychology courses. Knowledge of statistics and methods is also useful in your everyday life. How many times have you heard news stories that report a correlation (sometimes described as a relation between two things) or perhaps a claim that one thing causes another (see Vigen, 2015)? With knowledge of statistics and research methods, you can better judge how believable these claims are and make better life choices.

Another point we must make about statistics is that some people avoid it because they may have a little bit of math anxiety (Ashcraft & Moore, 2009). Keep in mind that most (or all) college students can develop quantitative skills with a little bit of effort (see our discussion of mindsets in another chapter). Even if others pick it up more quickly, that does not mean that you *cannot* do math. Indeed, one of the biggest mistakes that students make about math is giving up without trying (Dweck, 2006). We will refrain from inserting an inspirational quote here, but do your best to embrace the challenge of learning!

Psychology Foundation and Elective Courses

Moving on in the curriculum, there is typically a set of foundational or core courses that cover the major research domains in psychology. According to Norcross and colleagues' (2016) summary, 90% of programs offer courses that cover the following areas:

- Abnormal Psychology—psychological disorders
- Cognitive Psychology—how people think and remember
- Developmental Psychology—how children and adults change throughout life
- Personality—how people's traits contribute to behavior

- Physiological Psychology/Neuroscience—explore the brain's structure and functions
- Social Psychology—how people interact and affect others.

At many schools, students have a little bit of freedom to choose elective courses to complete their psychology requirements. Most institutions offer a wide variety of courses, and the specific topics may depend on (a) the expertise and interests of the faculty and (b) how popular the course is with students. Some schools may organize courses into "tracks" that are organized around major areas, such as clinical psychology, neuroscience, or development.

Navigating Through Psychology's Subfields

One thing that you likely noticed about psychology is that it is a very broad field consisting of a large number of subfields. In fact, the American Psychological Association (APA) lists over 50 different divisions that focus on different subfields! We list some of the subfields of psychology in Table 4.1, but keep in mind that this is not exhaustive and that some areas can be broken down even further.

iStock.com/asiseeit

Some students can feel overwhelmed by the variety of areas in psychology—should you take courses involving neuroscience, development, or psychological disorders? If you know which area interests you the most, then take courses in that area. For example, if you are pursuing a career where you will work with children, then look for courses related to developmental psychology (or perhaps child behavior issues).

However, if you are unsure, then our advice is to read about the different areas (as a starting point, go to www.apa.org and search for "divisions") and to sample courses to see if any pique your interest. You might also speak with an academic advisor or professor. Learning more about the subfields is important because your impression of an area might be different than what it actually involves. After you learn more about the subfields, you can either choose one area to focus on or you can take a breadth approach and fill your schedules with courses from different areas of psychology (this is perfectly fine—a lot of students take this approach). One of the best parts of the breadth approach is that, as you progress through your courses, you can take key findings from different areas and apply them to your life and career preparation!

TABLE 4.1

A Sample of the Subfields of Psychology (Listed Alphabetically)

Clinical psychology	Cognitive psychology
Consumer psychology	Counseling psychology
Culture, ethnicity, and race	Developmental psychology
Educational psychology	Engineering psychology
Environmental psychology	Evolutionary psychology
Experimental psychology	Forensic psychology
Gender and sexuality	General psychology
Health psychology	Humanistic psychology
Industrial and organizational psychology	Media psychology and technology
Military psychology	Neuropsychology
Neuroscience and comparative psychology	Pediatric psychology
Perception	Personality
Psycholinguistics	Psychopharmacology and substance abuse
Psychotherapy	Quantitative and qualitative methods
Rehabilitation psychology	Religion and spirituality
School psychology	Social psychology
Sport psychology	

Unique Courses

At some institutions, one thing to watch out for is the special topics seminar that occasionally pops up on the schedule. There also tend to be some variable credit courses available. For example, if students get involved with research, they might be able to sign up for research credits. Also, some students might find an opportunity to take a Directed Readings course or Independent Study course—for these, you typically meet with a professor on a regular basis by yourself (or with a very small group of students) to discuss articles or a topic that is not covered in an existing course.

Finally, most psychology programs have a senior-level capstone—this might be an experience (e.g., involvement in the community, a unique project, working on research) or a class. If it is a course, it may focus on having students integrate what they have learned throughout the major and reinforcing their skills in some way. Sometimes the course will be in a seminar format, in which students will explore a specific and unique topic. Other times, it will be centered around the creation of a research project. Regardless of the format, the capstone is a nice way to wrap up your major and prepare for your next steps!

TABLE 4.2
Example Plan for Undergraduate Psychology Majors

This is a general timeline for students at our institutions. Because your institution's requirements may be different, we strongly encourage you to *write out the plan for you*! If you need help, work with an academic advisor.

FRESHMAN YEAR

- Courses:
  - General Psychology, Introduction to the Psychology Major
  - General university requirements
- Summer Activities (after this year):
  - Meet with an advisor and catch up on courses if you fell behind
  - Decide if psychology is the right major for you
  - Decide whether you want to pursue a minor or second major

SOPHOMORE YEAR

- Courses:
  - Statistics, Research Methods, psychology foundational and elective courses
  - General university requirements
  - Courses for minor or second major (if applicable)
- Summer Activities (after this year):
  - Meet with an advisor and catch up on courses if you fell behind
  - Look into opportunities such as internships, research, or study abroad

JUNIOR YEAR

- Courses:
  - Psychology foundational and elective courses
  - General university requirements
  - Courses for minor or second major (if applicable)
- Summer Activities (after this year):
  - Meet with an advisor and catch up on courses if you fell behind
  - Look into opportunities such as internships, research, or study abroad

SENIOR YEAR

- Courses:
  - Psychology Senior Capstone, psychology electives
  - General university requirements
  - Courses for minor or second major (if applicable)
- Summer (after this year):
  - Take your next steps (e.g., job or graduate school)!

Take-Home Message

The courses you take in psychology, and the order in which you take them, are carefully designed by expert faculty (see Table 4.2 for an example from our institutions).

Thus, do your best to adhere to your institutional policies and program recommendations so you can get the most out of your degree program. Also, be sure to keep an eye out for the "unsung" courses (e.g., Statistics and Research Methods) and opportunities you can take advantage of in the summer. Although we covered the basics of the psychology curriculum, keep in mind that your institution is likely to offer some exciting courses based on the expertise of your faculty!

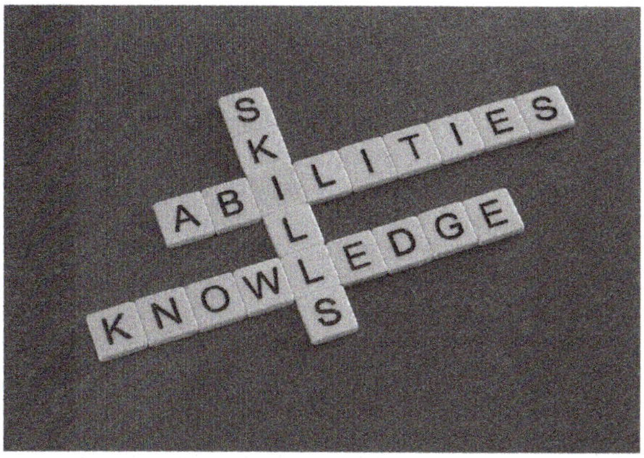

iStock.com/Silense

Action Steps

1. If your psychology program or institution's undergraduate catalog provides a roadmap of what to take each year to keep on track, save it, print it out, and add notes to it. We recommend building your own course plan, similar to what we did in Table 4.2.

2. Find out if your institution offers summer psychology courses. If they *do*, make plans to maintain your academic progress through the warmer months of the year. One word of caution, though—do not overdo it with classes over the summer! One or two courses is probably a good number—we have seen some students burn out after taking too many summer courses.

4.2 SKILLS YOU DEVELOP AS A PSYCHOLOGY MAJOR

As we noted earlier in this book, one of the big misconceptions about college is that the ultimate goal is to get through the required courses with the least amount of effort as possible. But consider this—have you ever stopped to wonder how many people are earning college degrees today? A college degree used to mean that you were part of an elite group of educated people—but, in today's world, a bachelor's degree is much more common, meaning that the degree alone will not make you stand out from the crowd. So, let's change your approach to college. In addition to building a knowledge base, let's focus on developing skills as well.

iStock.com/PeopleImages

Learning Outcomes

When it comes to what learning outcomes you should take away from the psychology major, the go-to resource is the *APA Guidelines for the Undergraduate Psychology Major* (American Psychological Association, 2013). You might be surprised to learn that only

TABLE 4.3
APA Guidelines for the Undergraduate Psychology Major

1. Knowledge Base in Psychology "Students should demonstrate fundamental knowledge and comprehension of the major concepts, theoretical perspectives, historical trends, and empirical findings to discuss how psychological principles apply to behavioral problems" (American Psychological Association, 2013, p. 17).
2. Scientific Inquiry and Critical Thinking "The skills in this domain involve the development of scientific reasoning and problem solving, including effective research methods" (American Psychological Association, 2013, p. 20).
3. Ethical and Social Responsibility in a Diverse World "The skills in this domain involve the development of ethically and socially responsible behaviors for professional and personal settings in a landscape that involves increasing diversity" (American Psychological Association, 2013, p. 26).
4. Communication "Students should demonstrate competence in writing and in oral and interpersonal communication skills" (American Psychological Association, 2013, p. 30).
5. Professional Development "The emphasis in this goal is on application of psychology-specific content and skills, effective self-reflection, project management skills, teamwork skills and career preparation" (American Psychological Association, 2013, p. 33).

one of the five guidelines (#1—"Knowledge Base in Psychology") is related to content knowledge—the rest focus on skill development (see Table 4.3). This means that you will be developing skills as you progress through the psychology major (Hettich, 2014). In the following sections, we go through each of the recommendations and skills highlighted in the guidelines (and most of the skills are also discussed further elsewhere in this book).

Knowledge Base in Psychology

As we noted in the previous module, you are going to take different psychology courses that cover a variety of topics. Not only will you be learning facts, but you will also be learning about theories and underlying themes. We are not going to spend much time on this guideline, though, as earlier chapters in this book addressed study skills and adopting a deep learning mindset that can help in this area. Instead, we are going to spend more time building on the other four learning outcomes set forth by APA by presenting several skills and tendencies you should work toward developing.

Scientific Inquiry and Critical Thinking

Interpreting and Critiquing Information. This skill is extremely important—not just for a career, but also in life. Adopt a critical thinking mindset and do not simply take other people's word for things—interpret the evidence for yourself. Critical thinkers will investigate an issue using logic, thinking probabilistically, looking for evidence, and examining the trustworthiness of a source (e.g., Nisbett, 2015). Using these strategies, a critical thinker can determine whether a claim is likely to be true, false, or untestable. For example, you may have heard claims that childhood vaccines cause autism. Is that true? You could approach this from a number of angles. One approach is to look at the credibility of the source of the claim (celebrities) versus the credibility of a source that denies the claim (scientists). Another approach is to look at evidence in research studies that have examined the issue (e.g., Flaherty's 2011 article entitled *The Vaccine-Autism Connection: A Public Health Crisis Caused by Unethical Medical Practices and Fraudulent Science*).

Analyzing Data. We were disappointed to learn that Statistics is rated as one of the least popular college courses (Newman, 2017). This is unfortunate because data and statistical analyses are a core component of the field of psychology, as they help us gather evidence about human behavior and abilities (Feldman, 2017). From a practical perspective, with so much data about people available to technology companies today (e.g., Singer, 2018), people who can analyze data are in demand. As technology continues to evolve, it will likely be able to gather even more detail about all of us. In this modern world, the ability to code, analyze, and interpret data is a skill that you should develop, not one you should avoid! So, embrace a statistics course, and consider taking more than one (see Friedrich, Childress, & Cheng, 2018 for a discussion of what can be learned in statistics courses).

Ethical and Social Responsibility in a Diverse World

Ethics. When it comes to ethics, sometimes learning what *not* to do can be just as important as learning what you *should* do. For example, in the context of psychological research, most students learn about ethically questionable studies such as Watson and Rayner's (1920) *Little Albert* study or Zimbardo and colleagues' *Stanford Prison* study (see Zimbardo, 2007). As a result of studies like these, psychologists have agreed to adopt a system that includes ethical safeguards, such as informed consent. It is important for students to learn to treat others with respect and recognize what is not acceptable (see our discussion of ethics in another chapter).

Diversity, Equity, and Inclusion. Ideally, institutions of higher education should be intellectually challenging learning spaces. College students should find themselves engaging in new and different experiences and encountering points of view different from their own. If this has not been the case yet, what are you waiting for? Step out of your comfort zone, try something new, or do something differently. For instance, listen to a speaker on a topic you know nothing about, sit with a classmate you have yet to meet, or take that obscure elective course (rather than the easy one). Your college or university is a learning community where you can witness diversity of thought, so be sure to engage in it!

iStock.com/Steve Debenport

iStock.com/SeventyFour

It is also important to remember that higher education is a microcosm of society. You will encounter people of many ethnic and gender identities, varied socioeconomic statuses, and different personalities. Because of these factors and life experiences, the people you meet are likely to hold worldviews different from your own. Thus, it is important to learn as much as you can about diverse groups and how their personal histories shape how they experience life. As a psychology student, you will work alongside students who come from backgrounds different from your own. Take advantage of this rich experience—college life can be a whole lot of fun if you embrace it.

Communication

Writing. Good writing not only conveys a positive first impression, but it is also a skill useful in almost any high-paying job. Writing is a way to communicate your ideas, and good writing can be interpreted as a sign of education and competence. Imagine reading an article that is filled with spelling and grammar mistakes—sure, you can tolerate it, but those errors can possibly influence how you process the content of the message.

Despite what some of you may think, we are not born either with or without writing talent—writing is a skill that is developed through practice. Much like our earlier advice about math—the key idea here is the word *practice*! Unfortunately, we see a lot of students either try to avoid writing classes completely or, if that is not possible, they spend the least amount of time possible on writing assignments. This is the wrong approach—in college, take advantage of the safe space to write more! So, instead of whipping up a paper the night before it is due, start it a week early, ask your professor for feedback, and then use that feedback to make the final product even better. By doing that, you will be one step ahead of your fellow students when it comes to improving your writing.

Speaking/Presenting. Writing is not the only way to communicate your ideas—you also need to be proficient at speaking and presenting (something that you have to do in a lot of jobs). As with writing, college is a great time to practice this skill. If the thought of class presentations makes you anxious, consider this: When you give a presentation in a college class, your audience consists of students who are not paying attention because they are bored and students who are nervous about their own presentation. When we put it like this, is there any reason to be intimidated by that audience? So, do not avoid those classes that include presentations—use them as an opportunity to improve your presentation skills (and use our other presentation tips that we cover in a later chapter).

Professional Development

Hard Work and Perseverance. The simplest skill, but probably one of the most difficult to implement, is to work hard. If you want to get better at something, then practice it! You can get better at almost anything by working at it. We are sure that most of you will agree with that advice, but how many of you regularly follow it? As a starting point, use the anti-procrastination efforts we described back in Chapter 1!

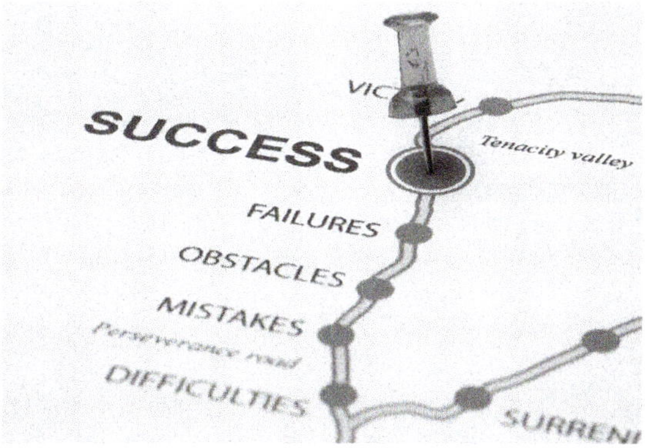

iStock.com/esolla

Acceptance of Failure. If you never fail, it probably means that you are never putting yourself in a position where you might fail. As we note in Chapter 3, failure is okay as long as you learn from it and grow. If you need more evidence that failure is not a recipe to a lifetime of disaster, check out any of the various articles online about successful people who have experienced failure in their lives (e.g., LoCascio, 2016).

How to Work in Groups. A lot of students tell us that they dislike group projects. However, keep in mind that many tasks in the work-world are too difficult to accomplish by oneself, and some tasks require the contributions of different specialists. Also, bosses or managers likely do not want the success of a project to depend solely on one person; instead, they assign projects to a team. All of these factors contribute to the likelihood that you will work as part of a group during your career. So, take time in college to learn how to work productively with others.

Complete Work on Time. We find that there are students who hate deadlines—some may even resort to calling them "arbitrary" or "pointless" when they fall behind in a course. However, there are other students who turn assignments in on time and would think it is unfair if other students are allowed to turn them in late. In other words, professors like us cannot win whether we try to enforce deadlines or we try to be lax when students need more time. Although there are arguments in favor of (e.g., Kreuter, 2012) or against (e.g., Boucher, 2016) the enforcement of deadlines in college, we want you to take a minute to imagine the following scenarios.

Imagine that you (or your company) are competing with others—this can be anything, such as creating a product or providing a service. In this competitive environment, who is more likely to win, the person on time or the person lagging behind? Imagine that it is April 15 and your taxes are due—do you think the Internal Revenue Service (IRS) thinks that it is important to submit your taxes on time (here is a hint—there are financial penalties for filing late)? Imagine that 200 people are applying for a spot in a clinical psychology graduate program—with so many applicants to choose from, do you think the admissions committee cares much about an application that arrives a week late?

Our point here is that, like it or not, deadlines matter in different aspects of life. While in college, it is probably a good idea to get used to completing work on time. But, you can breathe easier knowing that most professors are willing to make exceptions for extreme circumstances or emergencies.

Take-Home Message

As we noted previously, look for courses and other opportunities that can help you develop these skills—these are opportunities for you to improve. Also, keep in

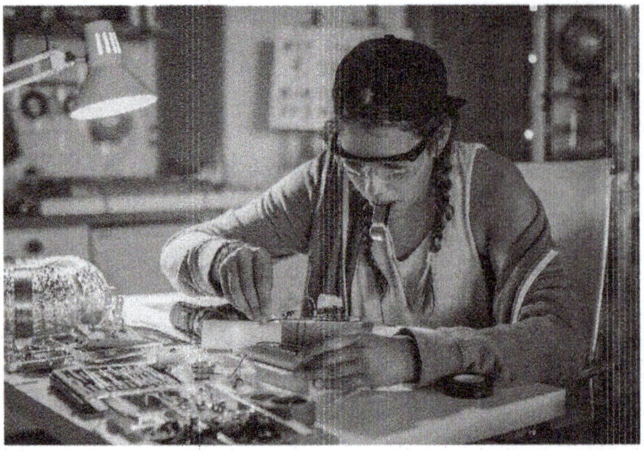

iStock.com/svetikd

mind that the skills covered in this module are not a complete list—there are plenty of other practical skills that might be important for you. For example, you could learn (a) a foreign language, (b) how to program, (c) how to budget and manage your own finances, (d) accounting information to run your own business, (e) how to persuade others, (f) how to improve your memory, (g) how to appreciate art, (h) how to negotiate, or any other skill that is important to you!

Action Steps

1. Review the actual APA Guidelines 2.0 (American Psychological Association, 2013). Pay close attention to the "Attributes Inferred From Successful Demonstration" section of the learning outcomes (e.g., Curious, Open-Minded, Precise). Determine several attributes you would like to possess and be able to demonstrate. Revisit this list periodically to determine whether it still fits your personal goals and whether you are intentionally working toward these attributes.

2. Once you have determined this initial list, jot down some opportunities to develop these attributes. Here is a tip—take a look at your course syllabi (most professors include student learning outcomes)!

4.3 DOUBLE-MAJORING OR PICKING UP A MINOR

Except for some rare circumstances, all college students have a major—in some cases, it might be a broad term like "interdisciplinary studies," but it is a focus nonetheless. In addition to a major, some students will complete a minor, and some high achievers may complete two majors (e.g., Del Rossi & Hersch, 2016; Pitt & Tepper, 2012). Should you consider a minor or double-major? You might think to yourself, "That sounds like a lot of work—I can barely get through one major. Why would I ever need to do that?" Well, a minor or double-major is not for everyone, but in many circumstances it can be a helpful addition. In this module we cover some pros and cons of minors and second majors as well as some tips for picking one that can complement your psychology major.

Reasons for a Minor or Second Major

We list some of the reasons for adding a minor or second major in Table 4.4. One reason is that there can be complementary knowledge and skills that can be developed from two areas (e.g., Pitt & Tepper, 2012). The thinking is that this can potentially help with jobs or graduate school applications (e.g., Slatalla, 2008). An example of this

TABLE 4.4

Top Reasons for Adding a Minor or Second Major

- Two areas can better prepare you for a career or graduate school
- Build practical skills
- You have an interest in more than one area

would be to combine psychology and biology for someone who is planning to attend medical school—biology will provide you with the foundation for understanding anatomy and diseases and then psychology can help you to better understand people.

iStock.com/KatarzynaBialasiewicz

There are also cases where students choose a major because they like it but then realize that it is not necessarily the most practical major for getting a good job (e.g., Zafar, 2011). In these cases, they can pair that major with another field (that is believed to be practical for getting a job). For example, you might have a passion for art history, but you might recognize that there are likely more job opportunities in business. In this case, you could combine both to get a balance between passion and practicality.

Along this line, one recent study showed that a double-major of a liberal arts major (like psychology) combined with either business or a STEM (science, technology, engineering, and math) field led to higher incomes than having just a liberal arts major (Makridis, 2017).

Finally, if you are like most psychology majors, then you have a passion for psychology—but some of you may also enjoy a second, related topic area. For example, perhaps you are fascinated by music or Shakespeare. A minor or second major in that second area can be a way for you to explore both of those interests.

Which to Add—A Minor or Second Major?

The reality is that adding a minor or second major means that you have more required courses to complete. However, with some careful planning, you may be able to use the minor or second major courses to fulfill your institution's elective requirements (e.g., general education). This is indeed possible, as one study showed that students who double-major do not take any longer to graduate than those with a single major (Del Rossi & Hersch, 2016)! The key is to plan it out, and we strongly recommend that you meet regularly with an academic advisor to get help (we have more tips about meeting with academic advisors later in this module).

Adding a second major is going to be more complex than adding a minor, so adding a minor may be more feasible for most students. Also, keep in mind that, if you double-major, you may spread yourself too thin and you may not be able to reach the levels of success that you could reach if you only focused on one area. For example, if you are busy taking additional courses for a second major, you may not have time to get involved with superstar activities that can prepare you for life after graduation (Pitt & Tepper, 2012). With a minor, you can still have time for those activities.

Choosing a Minor or Second Major

Choosing a minor or second major depends on your interests and goals. Students with goals to start their own therapy practice may consider combining psychology with business. Students interested in a cognitive science graduate program might look at a complementary topic such as neuroscience or philosophy. As we noted earlier, some students may simply want to complete a minor in something that they find interesting.

© Can Stock Photo/fizkes

Finally, others might want to develop a skill—theater or public speaking might be good to practice speaking in front of groups, computer science might help with programming, and a foreign language might prepare you to work within new settings.

One way to consider how a minor or second major might complement your psychology major is to have a discussion with an advisor or professor about how the two fields are connected (e.g., Sadigh, 2017). For example, you could ask yourself a question such as, "How will a minor in ___ make me a better worker in my intended career field?" Table 4.5 contains some examples of how you can combine psychology with another area—please note that this is not a complete list as there are a lot of other combinations that you could choose. Search your school's catalog and website for a list of minors or majors to see a complete list of options.

TABLE 4.5

Possible Topics for a Second Major or Minor for Various Career Areas

Career Area → Combine Your Psychology Major with this Second Major/Minor
Cognitive Science → Neuroscience or Philosophy
Computers/Programming → Computer Science
Counseling → Counseling or Human Services
Entrepreneur → Business or Entrepreneurship
Forensics → Criminal Justice
Human Factors → Engineering
Law → Political Science or History or Criminal Justice
Law Enforcement → Criminal Justice
Linguistics → Foreign Language
Management → Business
Marketing → Marketing
Medicine → Biology or Chemistry
Neuroscience → Neuroscience

Public Speaking → Theater or Public Speaking
Sales → Hospitality or Communication
Social Worker → Social Work
Teaching → Education
Therapist → Marriage and Family Therapy
Therapist w/own practice → Business or Accounting
Treatment → Addictions
Writing/Journalism → English or Communication

Take-Home Message

If you do not complete a minor or double-major, is it going to derail your post-graduation plans? Of course not—as we noted earlier, we are not recommending this for everyone. In many cases, immersing yourself completely into your psychology major will help you prepare for your future. However, adding a minor or second major can have advantages. For example, (a) you can explore two different topic areas, (b) you can build additional skills and knowledge that can better prepare you for your future career, and (c) it could possibly be a tie-breaker in your favor if your fellow job or graduate school applicants are evenly matched with you (but did not do it). Also, with so many elective credits required for graduation, why not fill those by exploring a topic area in more depth rather than taking a bunch of unrelated elective courses?

Action Steps

1. Consider whether a minor, or possibly a second major, makes sense for you. Think about your interests and career possibilities. Think about whether two fields would complement each other nicely.
2. Make an appointment with an advisor to discuss the practical scheduling issues about adding a minor or second major. For example, would you have to take summer courses or delay graduation in order to finish all of the requirements?

4.4 MEET YOUR PROFESSORS

In this book, we regularly encourage you to improve yourself by doing well in your courses. But, we also want to encourage you to do more outside of class as well. In this module we are going to walk you through the value of meeting your professors. As a preview, one reason is to get help when you are struggling. It is also recommended that college students find a mentor to listen and possibly share advice—this can be a professor who helps to guide you through college or prepare for your future or to assist in an activity such as research (e.g., Ritzer, 2018). The good news is that most professors truly are enthusiastic about helping students (e.g., Vernon, 2018a). But, first, we want to give you a little background about the different types of faculty (including the variety of job titles you might see) and the different responsibilities included in their jobs (in addition to teaching). The better you understand the lives of professors, the better prepared you will be when you meet with them.

iStock.com/XiXinXing

Different Types of Faculty

Before starting college, you might have had a stereotype of professors being middle-aged or older with an affinity for tweed clothing. But, if you have taken a handful of college courses, then you know that this is just a stereotype and not reality. Like many occupations, professors have diverse backgrounds—they can be young or old, they can come from a variety of cultural and ethnic backgrounds, and some may have even been first-generation college students (e.g., Whitaker, 2018). However, one thing that they tend to have in common is that they are well educated (Clauset, Arbesman, & Larremore, 2015).

Full-Time Faculty. In higher education, there are typically two broad categories of instructors—full-time and part-time faculty (e.g., Hailstorks, Stamm, Norcross, Pfund, & Christidis, 2019). Most full-time professors have an advanced degree (many have a PhD), and you will likely find these professors listed on the department or college website with a little blurb about their area of expertise, degree(s), and job title. Full-time faculty members can have a variety of titles (see Table 4.6). It is important to note that, no matter the title, these individuals are all professors—the different titles refer to subtle differences in their roles or their accomplishments. For example, newly hired faculty are often Assistant Professors, then after years of experience they might be promoted to Associate Professor or Professor.

© Can Stock Photo/racorn

In addition, many full-time faculty members can earn tenure by establishing a solid record of work. Although the expectations for tenure can vary at different institutions, tenure essentially means that a professor cannot be fired for arbitrary reasons. This gives tenured professors the academic freedom to teach or conduct scholarly work on unpopular, sensitive, or controversial topics without fear of political repercussions.

Part-Time Faculty. The second category of professors includes part-time or adjunct instructors. These individuals typically have advanced degrees (but sometimes they are graduate students who are still completing their degree), have a focus on teaching, but are not permanent members of the faculty. However, just because they are not full-time, that does not mean that they are any less knowledgeable or capable in the classroom—everyone

TABLE 4.6

A Variety of Job Titles That You May See for Full- and Part-Time College Faculty

Full-Time Faculty

- Assistant Professor
- Associate Professor
- Professor
- Lecturer
- Faculty in Residence

Part-Time Faculty

- Part-Time Instructor
- Instructor
- Adjunct Professor
- Visiting Professor
- Graduate Student

who is hired to teach a college course has expertise in that subject area (see Table 4.6 for various job titles for part-time faculty).

What Faculty Do

Many people who have never been to college think that professors live an easy life—show up to campus a few times a week to teach (or possibly conduct an online course from home)—but the reality is that professors have a lot of responsibilities. Although most part-time faculty focus on teaching, most full-time faculty divide their efforts among three areas: teaching, conducting scientific research, and service responsibilities (e.g., designing the psychology curriculum, critiquing articles for peer-reviewed journals). However, the emphasis of these areas differs depending on their job expectations and the type of institution where they work.

© Can Stock Photo/stokkete

At a research university, there are more expectations that professors regularly publish research articles and present their research at conferences. At liberal arts or community colleges, most professors focus on being excellent teachers first, but they may also be expected to provide undergraduate students regular opportunities to get involved in research. Of course, there are always going to be exceptions to these descriptions, but this is a general distinction to help you better understand the jobs of professors (see Vernon, 2018a, 2018b, 2018c, 2018d, 2019, for a series of articles that describe the work lives of professors).

Why Meet Your Professors?

We think that it is important for students to build professional relationships and friendships with their professors (e.g., Newport, 2005). Professors often know about opportunities for students in your major—this might be a funding announcement, a research opening, or an award that would be a good fit for you. If you are struggling in class, you can ask your professor for help. Professors can also provide graduate school or career advice. Finally, professors might have connections with people that might be helpful for you—they may know former students who are working in the community or a professor at a graduate program where you are applying. We could keep going on, but hopefully you get our point!

© Can Stock Photo/Nandyphotos

How to Meet Your Professors

Some students tell us that they are shy and are not confident approaching a professor—some even tell us that they think of professors as intimidating (e.g., Olatunji, 2000). But remember that professors are human beings just like you—and a lot of professors are also shy (or, in our case, a little bit nerdy). The good news is that most professors are friendly and are willing to talk if you give them a chance. A lot of psychology professors pride themselves on not only being excellent in the classroom, but also having qualities such as being approachable, accessible, and good listeners (Keeley, Ismail, & Buskist, 2016).

One of the best ways to meet your professors is to stop by during their office hours (e.g., Condis, 2016). If their office hours overlap with your classes, you can email a professor to schedule a time for a meeting. Office meetings are great because the professor can spend time focusing on your questions or providing help. There are many different things that you can talk about—ask for clarification about a tricky concept from class; ask if there are any books that they recommend so that you can learn more about a class topic; you could even discuss a movie that relates to a class topic. If you are not good at initiating conversations, you can ask something like this:

- "I want to learn more about internship opportunities, but I do not know how to start."
- "I read about your research on your website—are you taking new research assistants?"

- "I am interested in graduate school. What did you do to prepare and learn about graduate school when you were a psychology major?"

If you have a specific question you want to talk about, then go ahead and approach that topic. But, if not, go ahead and try any of the topics we listed. However, we do have one request—please be authentic. That is, only ask about a topic that you have genuine interest in—do not feign interest in a topic.

A final point here is that, if you have a quick question, you could also try to catch a professor before or after class. However, be aware that, whereas some professors are okay with this, others may not have much time to chat because they are pressed for time (e.g., they are making last-minute preparations for class, they have to run off to teach another class, they have to attend a meeting, etc.). So please cut them some slack if they seem busy—try to catch them during office hours when they have that time set aside for students.

Take-Home Message

© Can Stock Photo/edharcanstock

So, why did we provide so much detail about professors?

First, there are many misconceptions about what professors actually do—especially outside of the classroom. Second, and more importantly, this little peek behind the curtain will allow you to better understand and connect with your professors. Talking with your professors and building professional relationships with them can be very helpful—this is true if your goal is to work after college or if you are thinking about graduate school. And, as an added bonus, you just might find that some of your professors are very interesting people!

Action Steps

1. Check out your school's department or college website and see the different titles and positions held by the different faculty members. If the job titles at your institution are not clear to you, ask one of your professors to explain them.
2. If you want to understand professors even more, watch interviews from university professor Dr. Bill Buskist (http://youtu.be/8vmboTEFHrk) and community college professor Dr. Saundra Ciccarelli (http://youtu.be/NTdbhLVG6eA). Listen for some of the common themes and differences between professors at these different types of institutions.
3. Select a professor (or more than one) that you would like to talk with and make a plan—are you going to approach him or her after your next class? Are you going to email him or her right now to request an office appointment? Set it up!

4.5 COMMUNICATING WITH PROFESSORS (AND OTHERS)

In this module we want to help you interact with professors by going over the basics of professional communication. Importantly, the advice in this module can be generalized to communication in many other life situations, such as the workplace. We are going to cover how to address professors, how to communicate with professors, and exceptions to these guidelines. We know that some of you may want to skip this module because you think it is beneath you, but we implore you to please read this carefully and apply our tips!

iStock.com/SIphotography

Using Formal Titles

Consider these scenarios: If you had an opportunity to meet one of your state's senators, would you greet her with, "Hey Diane, what's up?" If you were in the military and asked if you understood a set of orders, would you reply with, "I got it, Bob!"? Or would you respond with, "Yes, Sergeant!"? We hope that you see our point here is that you should address people formally, as a sign of respect and acknowledgment of their position or education.

College professors are experts in their fields, and most have earned an advanced degree (Stoloff, Sanders, & McCarthy, 2005)—this could be a master's, PhD (Doctor of Philosophy), PsyD (Doctor of Psychology), JD (Juris Doctor), or MD (Doctor of Medicine). Because most professors have an advanced degree, it is polite to refer to them as Professor Houska or Dr. Houska rather than as Mr. Houska.[1] Because "Doctor" is commonly used for medical doctors, we recommend using "Professor" as your go-to-title (but either is okay). Just be sure to use these respectful titles for all professors, no matter their gender or age (e.g., Gulliver, 2014).

Please be aware that you will find that different professors have different preferences about how to address them (e.g., Kreuter, 2011). Some may not care how you address them, some might make subtle suggestions (e.g., "Welcome to class—I am Professor Copeland"), some might encourage you to use their first name, and some might not tell you anything. To help you navigate through all of this, use the flowchart in Figure 4.1 for good rules-of-thumb as to how to address your professors.

Basic Communication Guidelines

Although you may find the occasional professor who accepts text messages, most of the time you will be communicating with them via email (or possibly a phone call).

[1]As a quick side note, you may think that Mrs. and Mr. are short for Missus and Mister, respectively; but, historically, those two abbreviations corresponded to Mistress (did you ever wonder why there was an "r" in that abbreviation?) and Master. After learning that, do you really want to refer to your professor as either Mistress or Master? Professor or Doctor sounds a lot better now, right? Anyway, it's a sign of respect, so we recommend using these terms.

FIGURE 4.1

How to Address Your College Professors (In Person or via Email). Different Professors May Have Different Preferences, but This Chart Should Help You Avoid Offending Anyone!

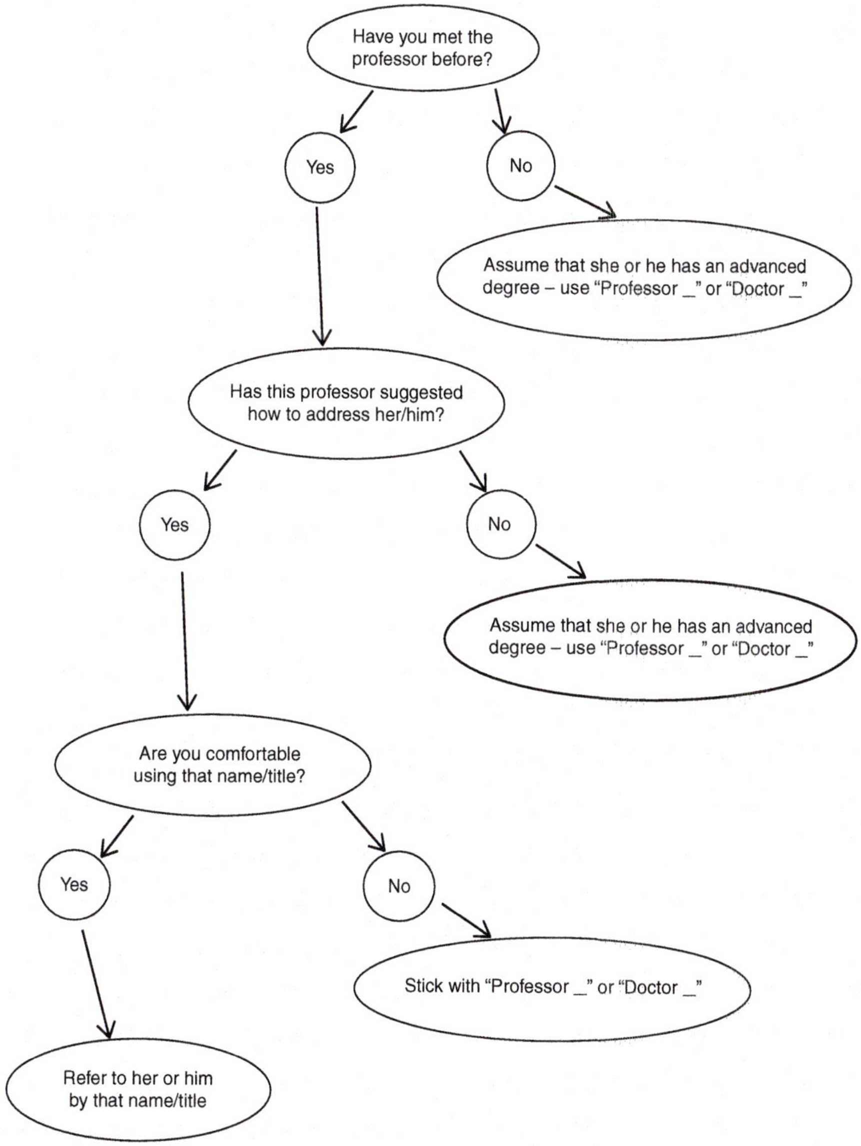

Many students believe that they communicate effectively, but in our experience most have room to improve. So, let's run through some guidelines (also, see the examples of good and bad emails in Figure 4.2).

iStock.com/jacoblund

- Before reaching out, check the course syllabus to see if the professor has a preference for email or phone communication. If you try using a nonpreferred method, you might get a delayed response (or no response at all).
- Address the person with respect and use a proper title if appropriate (explained previously). For example, starting with "Professor Howard" is preferable to "Mrs. Howard," "Howard," or diving right into the message.
- Always include sufficient context so that the other person knows who you are. What is your name? Are you a student in the professor's class? If so, which class?
- Clearly state your question or problem. For example, we have received emails like this, "The form says that it needs a signature from a professional reference. thanks" but then there was nothing else. From that message, it was not clear what the student needed (e.g., "the form" is a very vague description; also it is not clear, but it seems as though the student is asking the professor to be a reference).
- If there is a problem, convey what you have already done to try and solve the problem on your own. Did you check the syllabus? Did you re-read the assignment instructions? Did you already contact the campus computer center for a technology issue?
- Be polite and use proper spelling and grammar—you are not texting a friend about shopping, video games, or going out.
- If possible, use a university or college email account instead of a personal account. The email address "JHernandez@smithcollege.edu" is much more professional than "princessjenna@gmail.com."
- People have lives outside of work (and this includes sleep). So, if you call or email outside of normal working hours, they may not respond until the next workday.
- Please remember that your professors are real-life human beings with feelings, just like you. So, do not berate them as if you are leaving a scathing online review.

Social Media

You may find that some of your professors are incorporating social media into their classes (e.g., Chamberlin, 2013). For example, some classes have shown that Twitter could be used to improve students' memory for class topics (Blessing, Blessing, & Fleck, 2012). That is great for those professors who choose to embrace social media. However, please understand that not all professors want to be social media "friends" with students (e.g., Kolowich, 2010)—so,

FIGURE 4.2

Examples of Bad and Good Emails From a Student to a Professor

BAD EMAIL:

FROM: gamerdude420@gmail.com
SUBJECT: your class

Hey Mr. Copeland, what assignments were due during the first week? Is it oakay if i turm them in late cuz i did not realize things were du that weak?

John

GOOD EMAIL:

FROM: john.nguyen@ungl.edu
SUBJECT: question about late assignment in PSY 101

Professor Copeland, my name is John Nguyen from your online PSY 101 (section 2) course this semester. I missed the deadline for the week 1 assignment — this was my fault as I did not carefully check the deadline. I understand that this might not be accepted for full credit (I saw the syllabus policy about deducted points for late work), but I would appreciate your feedback on this assignment so that I will be prepared for the upcoming chapters. Thank you in advance for any feedback you are willing to provide.

John Nguyen
****

do not engage your professors on social media unless they explicitly invite you (e.g., Crowder, 2016). And please use good judgment when interacting with professors (or anyone) online!

Take-Home Message

One key message to take away from this module is this—no matter how you are interacting with professors, always be polite and professional! If they have not explicitly told you how they prefer to be addressed, always err on the side of formality. When you write an email, be clear about who you are and why you are emailing (and do not forget to proofread). It might seem like we are spending too much time on a trivial issue, but effective professional communication skills will benefit your future. So, do not limit what you learn here to communicating with professors—be professional in all of your educational and career communications.

© Can Stock Photo/YakobchukOlena

Action Steps

1. When you email an instructor, keep in mind that you are writing a professional message to your professor, not a text message to a friend. In addition, remember that professors interact with many students, so please be specific when you send a message.

2. Although we tried to cover the important points on this topic, we could not cover everything in this short module. So, if you want to learn more about communicating with professors, we highly encourage you to check out Bremen's (2012) book titled *Say This, Not That to Your Professor: 36 Talking Tips for College Success*.

4.6 MEETING OTHERS AT YOUR INSTITUTION

© Can Stock Photo/koldunova_anna

At this point, you probably have a good idea of why (and how) you should meet your professors. But, we think you should do more—for example, you can benefit a lot from meeting others in your department (e.g., Newport, 2005). We recommend that you meet (a) the department office staff, (b) other students in your major, and (c) graduate students (if your department has a graduate program). In addition, we think that it is very important for you to regularly meet with an academic advisor. Let's go through these, one by one, so that we can explain why it is important for you to meet each group.

Meet the Department Office Staff

Ask people who actually runs a department, and most will point to the office administrative assistants (e.g., Kim, 2014; Lapowsky, 2014). Most professors are experts in their areas of expertise, but they can be clueless about how the school and the department operate. Thus, the office staff can help you with all sorts of issues. For example, they know (a) what courses are being offered and when, (b) what courses are in the catalog but are never offered, (c) how to contact student organizations, (d) how to find certain professors, (e) when guest lectures are scheduled, and (f) possibly how to get onto a waiting list when a course is full. So, the next time you find yourself walking past the department office, stop by and say hi—you might want to have a good relationship with the office staff if and when you need help!

Meet Other Psychology Students

When we say that you should meet other students, we do not mean that you should try to meet every single psychology major—after all, some schools have over a thousand psychology majors! But, you should start by meeting students sitting nearby in your classes—just introduce yourself as you are waiting for class to start. You never know if you will find someone who might become your new best friend, a study partner, or someone who might know about unique opportunities (e.g., how to get onto a research team or information about an internship). Sometimes your classmates have already taken a class from your professor, so they might provide tips.

You should also seek out students with similar goals and interests as you. For example, if you want to find students who are interested in graduate school, then attend Psi Chi or Psychology Club meetings—these groups tend to have a lot of graduate-school-bound students. Go and chat with other students, especially the club officers (they typically wear club t-shirts or are the ones running the meetings). Do not be intimidated to talk to other students—if you are both attending the meeting, then you already have something in common!

Meet Graduate Students

If your institution has a graduate program, then you should get to know the graduate students (e.g., Hart, 2002; Wlotko, 2002). You can find them in research settings, teaching courses (usually PSY 101), attending talks hosted by the department, or at any events that offer free food (graduate students are known for having low-paying stipends and student loans). You may even find some who participate in student clubs like Psi Chi (sometimes in a mentor role).

Graduate students are a great resource because, in most cases, they were recently just like you—trying to figure out how to succeed as an undergraduate psychology major. Most are willing to answer your questions, and they can provide tips about what they did well and maybe what they wished they had done. Also, graduate students are typically younger than professors, so you might not be as intimidated by them. In addition, getting to know a graduate student might be a way to get involved with a research team.

Meet with an Academic Advisor

College advisors are an invaluable resource to students (see Table 4.7)—they (should) know the curriculum and graduation requirements inside and out, and they can guide you through your major (and, if applicable, your second major or minor as well). One advising blog describes a college advisor as someone who is your "college amusement park fast-pass" (Gibson, 2017). We love this description because advisors can show you the most efficient way through the curriculum requirements so that you do not get stuck making slow progress like those students who skip their advising appointments (or those waiting 4 hours for one ride at Disney World).

How else can advisors help? Advisors can help in other ways, too. Some advisors might even point you toward the professors with the best teaching reputations. Advisors should also know the courses that are the most challenging, so they can make sure that you do not accidentally schedule Statistics, Organic Chemistry, Calculus, Latin, and Thermodynamics all together in the same semester. Advisors are well versed in how to get added to a wait list, how to drop a course (if you find yourself in over your head), and how to submit a petition so that you can skip a class you do not need (e.g., you might skip a history requirement if you scored well on an Advanced Placement History exam). Advisors can also tell you things such as whether you can earn credit for working on research.

College advisors might also have a good idea of what the superstar students are doing outside of class. Seriously, we highly recommend that you ask your advisor for tips about what you can do on campus in addition to your classes! If you are considering a study-abroad program, advisors can help you fit that into your plan. Some advisors can also answer your questions about career possibilities, career planning, and preparing for graduate school. Even if they do not have an answer to your specific question, they can point you toward resources or other places on campus where you can find help.

If you find yourself struggling in college, advisors can talk with you about your difficulties and explore your options. Can you benefit from tutoring? Advisors can point you in the right direction. Should you consider switching majors? Advisors can help you figure out how the courses you have already completed will fit with new potential majors. Are you behind in your graduation timeline because of a failed or dropped course? Advisors can help you find summer courses so that you can get back on track. Do you have family issues and need to step away from college for a semester? Advisors can work with you to figure out the right course of action.

TABLE 4.7

Top Reasons to Meet Regularly With an Academic Advisor

- Stay on track to graduate
- Choose the best instructors
- Plan courses and schedules
- Manage a minor or double-major
- Adding, dropping, or bypassing courses
- Learn about resources at your institution (e.g., tutoring)
- Discover opportunities in your major (e.g., research)
- Discuss career or graduate school plans

How often to visit advisors? You should meet with your advisor(s) regularly, at least once a year, if not once a semester. The reason for this is that there are a lot of requirements and you want to make sure that you are on the right path to graduation. And, if you want to get the most out of your visit with an advisor, please spend a little bit of time to prepare beforehand. What we mean by this is that you should review your course history, explore the course options for the upcoming semester, and jot down any questions that you want to ask. If you take these steps before you arrive, you will be prepared to discuss the topics and options that are most important for you.

Take-Home Message

As we noted in an earlier module, there are a lot of benefits to meeting your professors. However, do not limit yourself to just meeting the faculty—meet your department's office staff, your fellow students who share your interests and goals, and graduate students (if your department has a graduate program). And please do not forget about the importance of meeting with an academic advisor regularly—their job is to help you navigate your way through college, so take advantage of this assistance. Each of these groups can provide you with helpful information and possibly connect you to opportunities and resources.

Action Steps

1. The next day you are on campus—whether it is today, tomorrow, or next week—stop by the department or college office and say hello to the office staff. If you have a question that they might be able to answer, then ask. If you cannot come up with a question, then ask if they can point you to any resources for psychology-related careers, graduate school, or about any student clubs related to psychology.

2. If you do not have an advising appointment for this semester, make one now. Seriously—call, email, or stop by to make an appointment today. To make your advising appointments more productive, take stock of where you have been (e.g., your transcript) and what you want to do (e.g., majors/minors, career goals) and jot down any questions about your college journey; do not worry about asking a dumb question—the only dumb questions are the ones you do not ask.

Research, Teaching, and Service Opportunities

5

5.0 MEET TRINITY

© Can Stock Photo / michaeljung

CHAPTER OUTLINE

Before taking General Psychology (PSY 101), Trinity thought that the field of psychology was all about mental disorders and gender differences. Her perception of psychology was that the field was all about helping people and striving toward a career as a therapist or counselor. She was also confused when she saw courses like Statistics and Research Methods—why would she need those courses if her future career were going to focus on listening to people's problems?

After taking PSY 101, Trinity recognized one important detail—almost everything known about all of those psychology topics was a result of research studies! And psychology research was not boring at all. In fact, more than anything, research was based on curiosity and the drive to put one's ideas to the test. Courses like Statistics and Research Methods were important because they taught students the tools and strategies that can be used to be as objective as possible while conducting research.

During the last week of the semester, Trinity's psychology professor announced that she was conducting a study and that she needed student volunteers to help her administer surveys and conduct follow-up interviews. Trinity jumped at the opportunity and spent a few hours each week on the project. She spent time recruiting participants from campus, administering the surveys and interviews, and coding the responses with other students. At the end of the semester, she was amazed that the professor wanted to hear her thoughts on how to improve the interviews for the future!

Why Did We Tell You This Story?

For a psychology major, there are some amazing learning opportunities that take place out of the classroom. Like Trinity, you can likely get involved with research, but there are other possibilities as well—such as working as a teaching assistant or getting involved in service learning activities. The key idea, though, is that you have to take advantage of these opportunities!

5.1 SUCCEEDING WITH RESEARCH

iStock.com/A-Digit

In a course such as General Psychology you may have had the opportunity to participate in psychological research studies by filling out a survey or taking part in an experiment. This is an important component of research—without participants, there would not be any data! However, many students do not realize that there is another (perhaps more valuable) way to participate in the scientific enterprise—this is to work on preparing, running, and analyzing psychological research projects. This module will introduce why research involvement is something that you should consider!

Who Conducts Research?

If you guessed "professors," then you are on track! But, because research can be a demanding and time-intensive process, professors need help. Most professors collaborate with other professors, and they also work with graduate students who are in the process of earning their advanced degree (like a master's, PhD, or possibly a PsyD). In addition, many professors also need help from undergraduates like you!

Research Opportunities in Your Psychology Program

As we mentioned in the opening, it is fairly common for students in PSY 101 to participate in psychology research studies (Miller, 1981). Most students report that research participation is a positive learning experience (Miles, Cromer, & Narayan, 2015). For example, students have reported that they learned about the research process, they thought the experiment might lead to valuable results, they found the tools (e.g., electroencephalograph [EEG]) interesting, they recognized that psychologists are conducting actual science, or they simply enjoyed participating (Moyer & Franklin, 2011).

Although it is a great first step to participate in a research study, to truly get involved in research you have to first learn more about it! Most psychology programs offer a number of courses that emphasize research (Perlman & McCann, 2005), and in most programs one of these courses is Research Methods (Norcross et al., 2016). Students who take this course will learn about experimental techniques, and some lucky students will have a chance to actually design an experiment of their own (e.g., Perlman & McCann, 2005). Keep in mind that this will not likely be groundbreaking research published in a peer-reviewed journal, but it is an excellent opportunity to develop some skills. And, after that course, you might be ready for another step up—to participate on a research team!

Why Get Involved With Research?

Develop Skills. One benefit to research involvement is that students can develop soft skills that are needed whether they are pursuing a career after graduation or are planning to go to graduate school (e.g., Landrum & Nelsen, 2002). These soft skills include working with others in a group setting, time management, and leadership. A second benefit is that students can also develop technical skills, such as the ability to work with data, use computer software, and develop experiment materials. These skills can be helpful for a career (most employers want to see that you can learn how to use new software) and are definitely helpful if you are going to graduate school (these are all things that you will do in graduate school).

Gain Experience for Graduate School. Many programs, particularly PhD programs, expect graduate students to produce original research. So, it is not at all surprising that getting involved in research early as an undergraduate is a top tip on how to get into graduate school (e.g., Cynkar, 2007). Surveys of professors from clinical and counseling PhD programs also support this—for example, knowledge of scientific methods and the fit (in terms of research topic interests) with a potential graduate school mentor are rated as some of the most important factors contributing to admission to graduate programs (Karazsia & Smith, 2016). So, if you are considering graduate school, it is a very good idea to get involved in research!

Connect with Professors and Earn Letters of Recommendation. Besides being involved in the research process, another benefit to working on research is that you get to work more closely with professors and graduate students. If you need letters of recommendation for graduate school (TIP: if you are going to graduate school, you WILL NEED letters of recommendation), a professor who knows you really well because of your time spent on a research project will be able to write you a much stronger letter than a professor who only knew you from class. Because many graduate programs expect you to participate in research, get a recommendation letter from a professor who can vouch for your research experience!

Earn Research Funding. You might be surprised to hear this, but there are opportunities to earn money for participating in the research enterprise (we provide more information about this in our chapter that covers money issues). For example, groups like Psi Chi (the International Honor Society in Psychology) and the American Psychological Association (APA) offer research and travel grants that defray costs of traveling to a psychology conference to present your work. You might also find opportunities available through your institution—for example, the McNair Scholars program offers research stipends to students from underrepresented groups.

Contribute to Something Potentially Important. As you move through your psychology courses, you will read about thousands of different research studies that have helped us better understand human thinking and behavior. Those studies were conducted by professors and students—just like the experiments currently under way on your campus. Although not every research study is going to end up cited in a textbook, all research studies are valuable. For example, some studies are important because they replicate the findings of an earlier study—replication helps to strengthen people's confidence in an outcome. Other studies might lead to data that support (or falsify) theoretical claims.

iStock.com/Arnon Mungyodklang

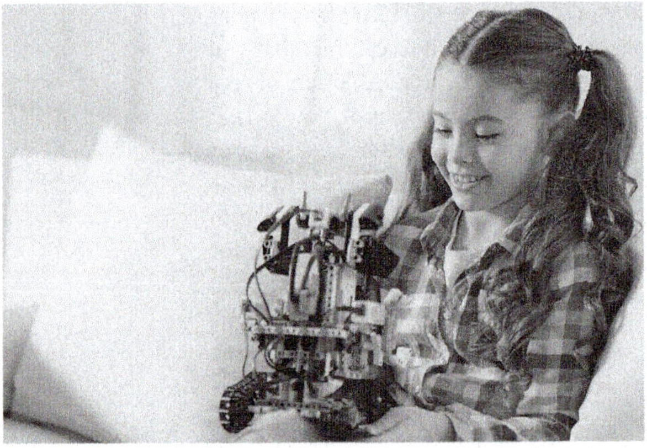

© Can Stock Photo/yacobchuk

Take-Home Message

Most students tell us that they like the topics from the field of psychology, but they are not always sure about whether they like research. If this sounds like you, it is important for you to understand that the knowledge base in psychology results from empirical research. If you notice the design of the psychology curriculum, there are opportunities for you to learn about and to develop research skills—this is why Statistics and Research Methods are such important courses (e.g., Perlman & McCann, 2005). One of our favorite TED talks was one that showed that research should not be intimidating—with some guidance, even kids can do it (Lotto & O'Toole, 2012). So, unleash your inner curiosity about psychology topics and get involved with research![1]

Action Steps

1. List your thoughts about getting involved in psychological research; list both the positives and negatives. Now, take a look at your department's website. What are three or four of the most interesting research projects or topics that you read about? Why? Set aside your thoughts for Action Step 2.

[1] Many students tell us that they imagine college research occurring in a lab setting with everyone wearing white coats. The reality is that most psychology research experiences will not involve white coats, and many may not even take place in a lab (however, you may find that some do). But, even without those things, rest assured that your psychology research experience is still a science-based endeavor.

2. Watch Lotto and O'Toole's (2012) TED Talk titled *Science Is for Everyone, Kids Included* (the full reference is available toward the end of the book). Keep a sheet of paper nearby as you watch their talk. On this sheet, jot down points you find interesting, but also have a critical eye. Are Lotto and O'Toole's points appropriate or relevant to psychology majors considering research?

5.2 THE LIFE OF A RESEARCH ASSISTANT

© Can Stock Photo / 4774344sean

At this point, we may have piqued your interest about the importance of getting involved with research. But, before you make the leap, you are probably wondering, "What exactly would I be doing?" What you do depends on the type of research and what kind of help is needed; however, we will go over the most common types of research activities (e.g., Kardash, 2000) as well as some less-common ones (see Miller et al., 2008, for descriptions of undergraduate research experiences at various institutions). To get a better idea of what you might do at your institution, you can explore your department or college website for research activities, and you can also ask professors, graduate students, or undergraduates who already work on a research team.

Working With Professors and Graduate Students

In most cases, you will work on research with a professor; and at large research schools you may find that you will spend a lot more time working with graduate students. Do not worry; this is not a bad thing! Graduate students work directly with professors and have experience with conducting research studies. Because they need to be productive in order to succeed themselves, they will need your help with different aspects of the research process, and most will take the time to teach you valuable skills. Plus, in most cases, graduate students were recently in your position as an undergraduate, so they know your perspective. Finally, rest assured that graduate students are in communication with professors about your accomplishments and progress in the lab.

iStock.com/valentinrussanov

Library Searches and Reading Articles

In most cases, your professor has been studying a topic for a while (in some cases, they may have been studying the topic for decades). In other words, the professor is already an expert on the topic. Because you will need to learn about the topic, you might be assigned the task of reading some key research articles so that you can become more familiar with the topic. In some cases, a professor or graduate student might be starting a new line of research on a topic. In these scenarios, you might be asked to help find relevant articles, especially recently published ones. So, you may need to conduct library searches using databases like PsycINFO, Web of Science, or possibly Google Scholar. We provide a lot of tips for finding and reading research articles in a later chapter in this book.

Working With Humans or Animals

All of the members of a research group will learn about the ethics involved with research. If the research involves humans, then you will learn about consent, privacy, confidentiality, debriefing, deception, and special populations such as children or prisoners (e.g., Kennison, Jacobs, & Montgomery, 2010). All institutions that conduct research with human participants will have an Institutional Review Board (IRB) that sets research rules and evaluates experiments from an ethical perspective (e.g., what is the likelihood that participants will be at any risk for adverse effects?).

On many research teams, undergraduates will help recruit and schedule human participants. In large research universities, this will typically involve using a participant pool (often PSY 101 students participate to fulfill a course requirement) along with an online platform like Sona Systems that allows you to advertise an experiment with appointment times. Because some smaller colleges might not use a participant pool, you might have to advertise your study in psychology courses (e.g., as an extra credit opportunity) or post flyers on campus. In some cases, you might need special arrangements to recruit participants. For example, if the study needs older adults you might advertise at local community centers. If your study was focused on children, you might recruit students from local schools (and also obtain parental consent). Studies that focus on psychological disorders can be even more difficult because of confidentiality and privacy issues. Because of these types of concerns, remember that all human subject research must be supervised by a professor and must also be approved by an IRB!

Some psychology programs may be conducting animal research. Most animal research involves rats and mice, but there is some research involving birds, monkeys, and other primates. Institutions that conduct animal research will have an Institutional Animal Care and Use Committee (IACUC) that oversees the research and treatment of animals. This is done to make sure that the animals are treated in a fair and ethical manner (e.g., Capitanio, 2017). Because the animals live in the lab or in a nearby facility, you may be asked to assist with animal care—this might involve feeding, cleaning, or handling the animals.

Preparing Research Studies

All research projects need to be planned out with a clear design—an experiment should test the main hypotheses and minimize the effects of confounding variables. Some research teams may ask for your input in this process—this is important because sometimes professors immerse themselves so deeply into an idea as a researcher that they lose sight of the perspective of participants. In addition, you may be asked to help put a study together. Some studies use surveys or scales that have already been used in earlier research—you may be able to get these from published articles. However, other experiments may need brand-new stimuli. In these cases, you might be asked to search the web for resources (e.g., locate photos that fit the experiment criteria) or you might be asked to help create study materials (e.g., create lists of rhyming words).

Although some studies are administered using paper-and-pen methods, most research studies nowadays are conducted with computers. This means that the experiment or survey might need to be programmed. Some professors may recruit research assistants who have specialized computer skills, and others may train you on the basics—especially if they use fairly simple software such as Qualtrics, SurveyMonkey, E-Prime, or Google Forms.

Collecting Data

Research depends on outcomes, so unless you already have access to a data set that you can use to answer your research questions, data will have to be collected. In animal labs, there are a variety of approaches (e.g., Bedwell, 2016). For example, researchers may focus on a rat's behavior when presented with choices or they might examine the effects of stress on an animal. In other cases, the experiment may focus on the effects of a certain drug or on the activity of a specific brain region.

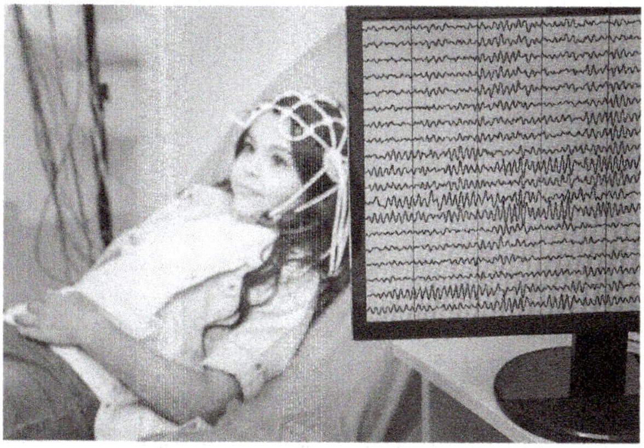

iStock.com/yacobchuk

For human research, you might learn how to conduct basic surveys or how to administer a specific psychological test. Sometimes a survey can be posted online, but, in other cases, data collection might be as simple as sitting participants at a desk and starting a computer program. If a study involves a psychological construct like depression or visual-spatial working memory, then you will likely have to measure that construct with a scale or test. You may also find that some research teams have access to specialized equipment or technology—this might be something like an electroencephalograph (EEG), transcranial magnetic stimulation (TMS), or an eye tracking device. In these cases, you might even be trained how to use it so that you can run participants in an experiment!

Other psychological research will take place in a variety of settings. Researchers who want to learn about child development may go to an elementary school. Studies that are concerned with clinical populations may need to go to mental health centers or hospitals. A research team that explores autism might collaborate with a center that specializes in teaching and reinforcing specific behaviors for autistic children. Researchers who study teaching and learning might go to classrooms. Sports psychologists might work with athletes in training facilities. To put it simply—in many research scenarios, you go to where the people of interest can be found.

Working With Data and Experiment Outcomes

Undergraduate team members also help with coding and analyzing data. In some cases, tasks are relatively simple—such as entering participant responses or scores into a spreadsheet. Sometimes, though, the data can be more complex. For example, open-ended questions can elicit a variety of responses—some of these may be ambiguous or difficult to interpret. Research assistants might be asked to code or categorize the participant responses based on a set of guidelines.

Although some research groups might have the professor and graduate students handle all statistical analyses, others might teach undergraduates how to conduct them. This might involve calculating the mean (average) from a set of scores or possibly creating a graph. In some cases, you might learn how to conduct statistical analyses such as an analysis of variance (ANOVA) or a linear regression. Do not let this scare you—most professors know that undergraduates have only taken one or two statistics courses and are still learning software like Excel, SPSS, and R, so you will likely receive training on how to do these types of analyses.

Other Responsibilities

Most research groups will hold regular meetings—these might be weekly, biweekly, or a few times each semester. These can be small (e.g., you and the professor) or large (e.g., the professor, graduate students, and all of the undergraduate assistants)—it all depends on the group and the professor's preferences. In these research meetings, a professor may want status updates about ongoing projects. In other cases, meetings can be used to lay out plans for future projects, discuss relevant articles, or conduct training on a specialized method or software. These meetings are also a safe environment for undergraduates and graduate students to practice research presentations (e.g., a practice session before going to a conference).

A Thesis or Co-Authorship (on a Presentation or Paper)

Our last point is geared toward those advanced students who are seriously pursuing graduate school. For these students, you might ask a professor about the possibility of doing a senior thesis or an independent project (see Hamm, 2008, and Woody, 2008, for the student and professor perspective of an independent project, respectively). One of the best parts of an undergraduate thesis is that it follows a very similar process to what graduate

TABLE 5.1

Differences Between a Thesis (or Research Paper) and a Class Paper

Thesis (or Research Paper)

- An original research project that includes a review of literature, a description of the project, and the results of the completed project.
- Propose and defend the project to a committee of professors.
- Written across months—typically consists of a large number of drafts.

Class Paper

- This is typically a review of literature or a research proposal.
- Submit the paper to an instructor.
- Written across days or weeks—typically consists of a few drafts.

students do when they are working on their master's thesis. Students will typically work on a research project from start to finish—this includes planning the study, collecting data, writing up an APA-style research paper, and (often) defending the project in a formal defense to a committee of professors (see Table 5.1 for differences between a thesis and a class paper).

If you cannot do a senior thesis, then you may talk to your professor about possibly earning co-authorship on a conference presentation or, in rare circumstances—co-authorship on a manuscript. Conference presentations are an excellent experience to help prepare you for graduate school. Plus, attending a scientific conference and presenting there can be an exciting and very enjoyable learning experience!

Which Is Better—One Research Position or Two (or Three)?

Over the years, students have asked us whether they should work on research with one professor or more than one. Unfortunately, there is no perfect one-size-fits-all answer to this question—so, let us speak generally here. Certainly, there are benefits to continuously working with one professor—he or she will get to know you really well, and you will gain more skills and build up more trust. This could lead to a poster presentation at a conference or possibly co-authorship on a paper. However, you may want to work with a second professor to gain broader experience and new skills from being on different projects—and you might also want to try and earn a second strong letter of recommendation. But, be careful! Our general advice is to not spread yourself too thin, unless you really can handle the extra responsibilities.

Take-Home Message

In this module, we went over some of the possible tasks and responsibilities that you might have as a psychology research assistant. Remember, though, that research projects can vary quite a bit—they (a) focus on different topics, (b) have different types of participants (e.g., young adults, older adults, children, animals, special populations), (c) can take place in different types of settings, (d) may use different computer software, and (e) could utilize different types of equipment. Because of all those factors, the specific experiences of undergraduate research assistants often vary from situation to situation. But, we hope that this module provided a good overview for you—you should now have a pretty good idea of what goes on behind the scenes in research groups!

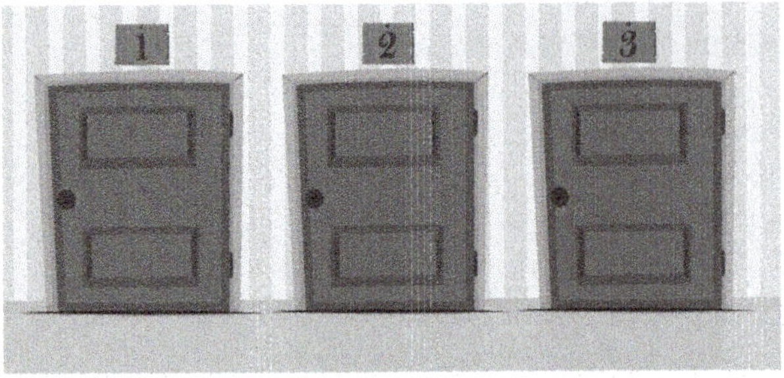

© Can Stock Photo/bluering

Action Steps

1. Think seriously about whether you want to become involved with a research group. (Remember: if you are going to graduate school, then you should definitely participate; however, there are also a lot of benefits for those who are not considering graduate school). If you decide to get involved, write down up to three professors you might like to work with: 1) ___________, 2) ______________, 3) ______________.
2. If you do end up working on research, take Newport's (2005) advice and "pay your dues." This means that, when you start, be humble, be willing to do whatever is asked of you, and learn from those tasks. As you gain more experience, then you can ask for increased responsibilities.

5.3 HOW TO BECOME A PSYCHOLOGY RESEARCH ASSISTANT

© Can Stock Photo/4774344sean

After we sell students on the importance of becoming a research assistant and what they might do, the next question we tend to hear is, "How do I do it?" In this module, we will cover a few different approaches. As you go through the process, be confident that professors really are looking for undergraduate research assistants (e.g., Wayment & Dickson, 2008), so they will be receptive! We will also walk you step-by-step through the construction of an email that you can send to a professor. If you are attending a smaller institution such as a liberal arts college, do not worry; you will likely have opportunities for research (Kierniesky, 2005). Even though research positions might not be advertised as much at smaller institutions, you can talk to professors who might be conducting research—for example, meet with professors after class or speak with your classmates to find out which faculty members are most likely to help you!

Should You Work as a Research Assistant Right Now?

Before you even start looking at research possibilities or talking to professors, you need to do a quick assessment of yourself. First and foremost, do you really have time to devote to research? If you are spread too thin by taking too many credits and working at a job, then it might not be a good fit for you. If you are not a responsible adult, then it might not be a good fit. If you do not yet have a clear understanding of the research process (e.g., from a Research Methods course) and do not understand the difference between independent and dependent variables, then research might not be a good fit . . . yet.

You may also want to assess your future goals. For example, if you are planning to earn a doctorate in psychology, then research experience is a must! If you are considering a master's program in an applied area such as counseling, then research experience will probably be helpful (the letter of recommendation will definitely be helpful!). If you are planning to get a job right after graduation, then research may be a good fit as it can help you develop some skills. See Table 5.2 for a summary of the key reasons why you should get involved in research.

When Is a Good Time to Join?

There is no one right answer for this, as different professors may give you different advice. However, if we had to give one answer for all our readers, we would recommend this: *the earlier the better!* We understand that most students are not going to be ready for research during their freshman year, as you are still getting adjusted to college life; however, if you are a high achiever who does really well in your courses, then we say—GO FOR IT! One thing that is clear, though, is that you should not put it off until your senior year.

Keep in mind that, if you are a freshman or sophomore, you may be competing with juniors and seniors who have taken more courses and who may have more relevant experience than you (e.g., more research-related courses, previous research experience, or member

TABLE 5.2

Reasons That You SHOULD Get Involved in Research as an Undergraduate

- You are curious and want to learn more about psychological research.
- You are planning to attend graduate school and/or you want to develop soft and technical skills for a future career.
- You have the time to commit to it.
- You have completed (or are in) courses such as Statistics and Research Methods.
- You want to build professional relationships with professors and/or graduate students.

of an honors society). If this happens, do not despair! Get over any feelings of rejection or negative vibes, and try to learn something from the situation. You may want to (politely) ask a professor if there is anything you can do to be more competitive for a research position in the future.

You might also be wondering, "When, during the year, is the best time to apply?" Again, there is no right answer for this, as you can probably apply at any time during the year. But, late October or early November for the upcoming spring semester and late March or early April for either the upcoming summer or fall semesters seem to make the most sense. This is because, at those time points, professors will start to plan for the upcoming semesters as they will have a pretty good idea of which of their current research assistants will be continuing to work or moving on (e.g., graduating).

Explore Possibilities and Rank Them

If your psychology department advertises research opportunities on their website, then browse the site so that you can explore what type of research is occurring at your institution (Lai, Margol, & Landoll, 2010). However, if your department does not list research opportunities on its website, then you can try a couple of other approaches. For example, your department will certainly have a list of faculty members on its website—explore faculty websites to get a sense of who is active in research. One clue to this is to look for a professor's bio or curriculum vitae (CV) on the department site. A second approach is to pay attention in class as to whether your instructors describe their own research studies—most professors who conduct research will find ways to slip these golden nuggets into their lectures. Finally, consider attending Psi Chi or Psychology Club meetings on your campus (we cover this in another chapter)—if research is happening in your department, the student officers will know about it!

Once you have explored the research possibilities, create a list to rank them in order of your preference (Lai et al., 2010). For example, if you are interested in a clinical psychology graduate program, you may want to first consider getting involved in clinical research. Keep in mind, though, that the research experience you gain as an undergraduate does not have to be a perfect match with your eventual career or grad school path. After all, the priority here is to develop general research skills.

Follow the Website Application Instructions

As you browse the department websites, look for specific application instructions. If instructions are listed, follow them! Usually this will take the form of something like, "If interested, email Professor ___." Some may even request specific information, such as (a) your name, (b) email, (c) major, (d) GPA, (e) year in school, (f) post-graduation plans, (g) why you want to be a research assistant, and (h) your past research experience.

No Instructions? No Problem! Send an Email

If there are no instructions, then it is up to you to contact the professor and sell yourself. You can meet with a faculty member or graduate student in person, or you can contact them by sending an email. Either approach can work—just use your judgment as to what seems most appropriate in your situation. For example, if you know a professor really well, you might feel comfortable talking in person. You can do this casually (e.g., talking after class or showing up during office hours) or slightly more formally by emailing to schedule a meeting. One thing to keep in mind is that you might want to have a CV prepared, in case the professor wants to see yours (Shah, Savage, Ortiz, & Lai, 2018).

© Can Stock Photo/duiwoy55

If you have never met a particular professor, then email might be the preferred route. Here are some ideas to keep in mind if you send an email (for more email tips, see Shah et al., 2018):

1. Be professional (how do you properly address a professor?).
2. Clearly state your interest in becoming a research assistant and why you want to get involved in that research area—be authentic. Demonstrating that you did your homework by reading about the research online is a good step to take.
3. Indicate when you want to start (summer? fall? right away?) and how long of a commitment you are willing to make (one semester? two semesters?)—keep in mind that some professors prefer a two-semester commitment.
4. Sell yourself—take the perspective of professors and lab managers. What skills, experience, and course achievements do they want the most in a potential research assistant (see Table 5.3)? Do you have a great GPA? Prior research experience? Have you earned any awards or scholarships? Are you an honors student? Are you responsible and professional? Have you taken any courses from this professor? If so, how did you do in that course? Is there someone who would recommend you? If you are early in college and do not have many achievements (yet), focus on your motivation, goals, and willingness to learn.

Other Considerations—Ethics Training? Earn Credit or Volunteer?

As we mentioned earlier in this chapter, all psychological research must be approved by an ethics committee—an IRB for human research or IACUC for animal research. Essentially, this process ensures that research studies conducted at your school follow ethical guidelines. We mention this here because some institutions require that anyone who works on research (e.g., professors, graduate students, and undergraduates) has to complete ethics training (yes, professors have to do this, too). In most cases, this involves completing an online tutorial. Be sure to find out if this is a requirement at your school! If it is, consider

TABLE 5.3
Ten Ways That You Can Sell Yourself as a Good Potential Research Assistant

1. Prior research experience
2. Good grades or GPA
3. Awards, honors, or scholarships
4. A genuine interest in the research area
5. Completion of (or enrollment in) courses such as Statistics and Research Methods
6. Soft skills that you can describe and back up (e.g., examples of being responsible, experience conducting library searches for a paper, prior experience working effectively with a group)
7. Motivation to pursue graduate school or a specific career field
8. A connection to that professor (e.g., "I earned an A in your Statistics course")
9. Willingness to work on any research tasks that are needed
10. Availability or flexibility in your schedule

completing the ethics training before you reach out about becoming a research assistant—if you do that, you can mention that you have already completed the ethics training as part of your email.

Another consideration is whether you will be volunteering or you will be earning course credit. At some institutions, you might have the option (or be required) to earn course credit while you work as a research assistant. For example, there might be an Independent Study, Independent Research, or Supervised Research Experience course listed in your school's catalog. Check with your professors to see what they recommend (or require).

Waiting (and Trying Again)

Because psychology is a popular major and there are a limited number of research assistant positions in your department, this can be a competitive process. Keep in mind that you *may* get turned down—do not worry about it, as this happens to most students. If that happens, try for other positions or improve yourself before contacting the same professor again. However, we want to warn you against simultaneously sending out a mass email to various professors. A mass email will not be personalized to that professor—personalized emails that show you did your homework are always more effective (see our previous advice).

Take-Home Message

A lot of students reach out to us because they know about research positions, they know that they want to get involved ... but they are just not sure how to become a research assistant. You should not have this problem because we just walked you through the steps you can take to get involved. Remember, if you want research experience, do not wait until your senior year—that is too late (if you are applying to graduate school, you will be sending applications in the fall of your senior year)! Also, if you cannot join your preferred research team, remember that any research experience is better than no experience!

Action Steps

iStock.com/s-cphoto

1. If your institution has research opportunities posted on the department website, start browsing them and rank which ones interest you the most. If your institution does not advertise research positions, talk to your professors (or fellow students) to learn about which ones are doing research and might need undergraduate assistants.
2. Apply to your top choice—if you get rejected, improve your presentation of yourself for the next attempt, then apply to your second choice. Wash, rinse, and repeat as necessary.

5.4 BECOME A TEACHING ASSISTANT

© Can Stock Photo/4774344sean

In this book, we spend a lot of time discussing the importance of getting involved in research. However, that is not the only academic opportunity out there for psychology students. At some institutions, you might have the chance to work as a teaching assistant (sometimes this position is referred to by its abbreviation—TA). Not all departments and institutions use teaching assistants, but if this is a possibility for you at your institution, we think that there can be some helpful benefits to this type of role—as noted by Appleby (2019), "being a [teaching assistant] is one of the most valuable and satisfying experiences you can have during your undergraduate career." And, after all, instead of being graded on papers and exams, doesn't it sound nice to help others prepare for those activities? In this module we will describe some of the advantages to being a teaching assistant as well as some responsibilities and things to keep in mind.

Why Work as a Teaching Assistant?

As we mentioned in the opening to this module, some departments will have teaching assistant opportunities, but some may not. If they do, they may have existing procedures for becoming a teaching assistant, so check with your department for this. Usually this will be listed on a department website or in the course catalog or you can check with a professor or academic advisor. If you do not see anything posted on how to become a teaching assistant, check with your professors to see if they might be open to the possibility of you working with them.

TABLE 5.4

Top Benefits to Working as a Teaching Assistant

- Better mastery of the course material
- Development of soft skills (e.g., presenting, motivating others)
- Building of a professional relationship with a professor (and potentially earning a letter of recommendation)
- A new perspective of how courses are designed and operated by professors
- An opportunity to see if you enjoy a teaching-related role and to potentially develop skills related to education-related careers
- A feeling of pride for helping other students

What you get out of being a teaching assistant is going to partially depend on your responsibilities. In most cases, you will be helping other students and a professor. For example, as a teaching assistant you might be asked to

- Hold review sessions before exams
- Tutor students who are struggling
- Review student paper drafts
- Provide feedback on low-stakes homework assignments
- Make suggestions to the professor for new exam questions
- Help build course materials
- Grade student work[2]

Regardless of your specific duties, in most cases you can count on a few benefits (see Table 5.4). First, you will likely reinforce your mastery of course material—as Ebbinghaus (1885) demonstrated, overlearning is a good way to ensure long-term retention of information. A second benefit is that you can improve your soft skills such as speaking in front of groups, explaining concepts in an easy-to-understand manner, motivating others to persist and succeed, or learning how to deal with ethical scenarios. Finally, a third possible benefit is that, if you do a good job, you might earn a letter of recommendation from a professor. When professors see you working hard and responsibly, they are likely to support you when you need help later—for example, if you apply for scholarships, awards, internships, or graduate school.

Things to Consider

Did you succeed in that course? In most cases, professors will want an undergraduate teaching assistant to have already taken the course and done well in it. The good news is that this means that you should already have a pretty good grasp of the course topics.

[2] Not all faculty are comfortable with undergraduates grading the work of other undergraduates. Because of that, undergraduate teaching assistant responsibilities might involve helping in a number of ways but not always helping with grades.

Also, an added bonus is that research from cognitive psychology suggests that teaching others is a great way for you to improve your own mastery of the material (e.g., Koh, Lee, & Lim, 2018).

Time commitment. If you are thinking about becoming a teaching assistant, first, assess whether you have enough time to devote to it. Being a teaching assistant can be as time consuming as taking a course (if not more!), so be realistic about the time requirements. Some professors may want you to attend class, but some might be okay if you are available to help students outside of class. In addition, keep in mind that you might need to complete some training (or take a course) before becoming a teaching assistant (e.g., Hogan, Norcross, Cannon, & Karpiak, 2007).

Course credit. Another consideration is whether you will volunteer or earn course credit as a teaching assistant—again, this might vary across institutions. Most professors will likely prefer that their teaching assistants earn academic credits, and this is completely understandable. This holds them accountable because they are being graded on their performance. Students should also welcome this arrangement as the teaching assistant experience will be formally documented on their transcript.

Ethics. One important ethical issue to be aware of is the right to privacy. In a teaching assistant role, this refers to keeping grade-related information confidential (Family Educational Rights and Privacy Act, 1974). Scores and grades are only to be shared with the course professor and the student involved—no one else! This means that you should never disclose any grade information to other students, other professors, the media, or even parents! If you ever find yourself in an unclear or awkward situation where someone, besides the student, is asking for grade-related information, contact the professor immediately.

Another important ethical issue may arise if you happen to have friends who are in the class. If you are in this situation, disclose this to the professor right away and make sure that you treat those friends just like all the other students in the class—some friends may try to persuade you to give them unfair advantages in a class (e.g., Appleby, 2019). Along this line, in schools with athletic teams, there might be pressure to help student-athletes stay eligible to play in games (e.g., Wolverton, 2015). If you ever feel any pressure—from the student-athlete, fans of the team, or anyone—talk to your professor immediately. In some cases, the professor might switch you to a different course so that there are no awkward situations.

Take-Home Message

There are a lot of academic opportunities available to undergraduates—at some institutions, one of them is being a teaching assistant. When you work as a teaching assistant, you can reinforce your knowledge of the course material, and you can work on key skills such as communicating clearly and explaining difficult concepts to others. Although this can be a great opportunity for high-achieving students, we want to stress the following—even though you did well in a course, it does not mean that being a teaching assistant will be easy. Teaching is an acquired skill, so do work closely with a professor to gain honest feedback and tips to improve!

© Can Stock Photo/imtmphoto

Action Steps

1. Check your college or university course catalog now to see if there is a course on the books for students to earn credit as a teaching assistant.

2. In our experience, lower-level courses like General Psychology (PSY 101), Statistics, or Research Methods are the ones that are most likely to use undergraduate teaching assistants. If you did well in one or all of those courses, reach out to a professor who regularly teaches the class to find out if there are any teaching assistant opportunities.

5.5 ANOTHER TYPE OF EXPERIENTIAL LEARNING—SERVICE LEARNING

Besides research and teaching positions, students may have the opportunity to learn and grow through service activities. One way to do this is to participate in a college course that includes a service learning component. Service learning is more than just simply volunteering or helping in the community—service learning also includes applying concepts learned in class, developing skills that are focused on in a class, and possibly reflecting on the activity in some way (e.g., Bringle & Hatcher, 1995). In other words, it is a combination of community work with academic learning. One important thing to remember is that service learning is not the same thing as an internship—an internship is more about gaining experiences or making networking connections for a career. In this module, we provide some examples of service learning and also provide reasons that it might be a great option for you.

Benefits of Service Learning

There can be quite a few benefits of service learning activities for students (e.g., Celio, Durlak, & Dymnicki, 2011; also see Table 5.5). One thing that might catch your attention is that service learning experiences have been described by professors and students as "transformational" or "eye-opening" (Shor, Cattaneo, & Calton, 2017). These terms are used because students report being emotionally affected by the experience, and some also report a change in their attitude about an issue, person, or group. For example, service learning with community mental health organizations led students to have an increased awareness of how mental disorders can influence people's lives, beyond what you can get from just reading about it in a book (e.g., Michaelson, 2018).

Another reason that service learning is important is because it fits with the APA Guidelines for the Undergraduate Psychology Major—specifically, it relates to developing socially responsible behaviors in applied and diverse settings (American Psychological Association, 2013). An important value of service learning is that it can promote civic learning—this refers to the idea that students can do service as a means of learning as well as learn the importance of service work (Bringle, Reeb, Brown, & Ruiz, 2016). Remember that being a psychology student is not just about learning content in college—you want to develop skills, have experiences, and learn how to work with others in a complex world.

TABLE 5.5
Top Benefits for Students From Service Learning

- Better understanding of the perspective or experiences of others
- Meet new people
- Improved attitudes toward civic engagement
- Better mastery of course material
- Development of a skill (e.g., communication, critical thinking, connecting with others)
- A change in oneself after a new or unique experience

Finally, another benefit to service learning is that it can improve student learning. In other words, students learn more when service learning is included in a course. In some cases, the experience can improve students' knowledge of the course content (e.g., Fleck, Hussey, & Rutledge-Ellison, 2017). In other cases, service learning led to noticeable improvements in students' critical thinking (e.g., Campbell & Oswald, 2018).

Examples of Service Learning Related to Psychology

We found several examples of service learning that have been used with college psychology courses (Campbell & Oswald, 2018; Chan, Ng, & Chan, 2016; Fleck et al., 2017; Michaelson, 2018; Shor et al., 2017). Although these examples came from a variety of psychology courses, including Abnormal Psychology, Community Engagement for Social Change, Community Psychology, Developmental Research Methods, and Lifespan Human Development, they had some common components—namely, most of them involved some type of reflection activity such as writing essays or journals on what was learned or participating in class discussions about their experiences. In some cases, there were specific tasks used to measure knowledge, skills, or attitudes.

In terms of the actual service learning activities, these varied slightly across the examples that we found. Some involved community home visits (e.g., visiting older adults who lived alone), after-school tutoring, community shelters (e.g., the homeless), working with a Boys & Girls Club, or activities in mental health treatment settings (e.g., support groups or psychiatric units). In some cases, students were assigned a particular setting, whereas in others, they had options or could identify their own preference. The service learning activities also varied in terms of the student outcome goals—increasing awareness about mental health issues, experience working with people from diverse backgrounds, greater feelings of civic engagement, mastery of course content, or a skill improvement (e.g., critical thinking).

No Service Learning Opportunities? Consider Volunteering

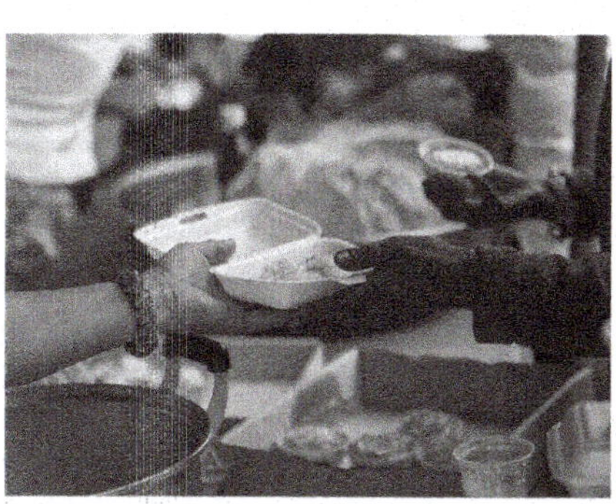

© Can Stock Photo/kuarmungadd

Keep in mind that not all departments or institutions will have opportunities for service learning. In these cases, you can still get involved with service activities by volunteering (not associated with a course). We see some students who go out themselves and find opportunities—this might be volunteering at a mental health clinic, working with children (e.g., tutoring, basic skills training), or helping an existing organization with a worthy cause. If you are not sure where to start, we highly recommend that you look into student clubs at your institution—for example, Psi Chi chapters regularly emphasize and organize volunteer opportunities for students (e.g., Ritzer & Sleigh, 2019).

Things to Keep in Mind

When some people get involved with service activities, they may naively think that any service that they provide to others is a good thing. However, there is an old saying that "*no good deed goes unpunished*"—this can be interpreted to mean that just because your desire is to do something good, it may not always be received or interpreted that way (e.g., Ehrenfeld, 2016). So, please consider the following ideas before blindly diving into service work (e.g., Ritzer & Sleigh, 2019).

First, be sure that the service is actually needed and wanted. Second, listen to those you are going to be helping—they may provide insights as to what could and should be done. Third, be sure that you do not accidentally cause harm in any way while you complete your service activity—be aware that your presence and actions might have unintended consequences. For example, this could be as simple as driving to a senior community and taking up a parking spot near the entrance that an older adult needed. And, lastly, always be respectful of others—be careful not to come across as condescending or possibly as insensitive to those who are different than you.

A final point that we want to make is that there are a lot of different ways to provide service, and you should be aware of how much time and effort that you can commit to any activity. Some people prefer to do one-time activities such as fundraisers or donating and participating in a walk (or 5K) for a particular cause. These activities can be helpful, but remember that you are not likely to get the same learning benefits from them as you would from something that is more involved (such as many of the activities that were described earlier in this module).

Take-Home Message

Service learning is a potentially unique experience in that it combines classroom learning with a service activity that takes place outside of the classroom. Students like these experiences because they can help concepts from class seem real, and professors like them because they improve student attitudes, knowledge, and skills (as we note elsewhere in this book, one of the overlooked aspects of college is the development of skills). So, if you are contemplating service learning or simply volunteering (either on your own or as part of a club), remember that one of the reasons many people choose to study psychology is because they want to help others (e.g., Ritzer & Sleigh, 2019)!

Action Steps

1. See if there are service learning opportunities in courses at your institution—you may have to ask your professors or an academic advisor. If there are options, work with an academic advisor to build it into your schedule.

2. If you identify a service learning opportunity, reach out to the instructor to find out about (a) the experience itself as well as (b) the expected learning outcomes (i.e., what you can expect to take away from the course—this can be knowledge, experiences, or skills).

Finding, Reading, and Thinking About Psychology Research

6

6.0 MEET HAYLEY

CHAPTER OUTLINE

Already, as a sophomore, Hayley was assigned journal articles to read in a few of her psychology courses. She was a complete novice when it came to reading articles, and, when she downloaded her first article, parts of it looked overly complex—there were terms she did not know, graphs, formulas, and statistical symbols. She was not sure where to look for information—should she start at the beginning? One piece of good news was that she figured out right away that the abstract was a big help. The only problem was that it only provided a broad overview. She still had a lot of questions about the research study, and just reading the abstract was not enough to make her feel confident to write an essay about what she learned from this article.

Hayley did not want to fall behind in class, so she showed up at her professor's office the next day during his office hours. She explained that research articles were new to her and that she needed help navigating through it. Hayley was relieved when the professor walked her through the various sections of a research article, explaining what to expect and what to look for in each section. He provided a list of questions that she could use as a guide when she read through a research article. Her professor even taught her some shortcuts to look for in the statistics so that she would not have to interpret every single symbol and equation. Her professor told her that things would make even more sense after she completed her Statistics and Research Methods courses later in the year.

Why Did We Tell You This Story?

A lot of new psychology majors find themselves in a similar situation as Hayley—you are probably familiar with textbooks, but you may have never actually read a research article before. In this module, we try to make this aspect of the psychology major less intimidating by walking you through the process of understanding different types of sources, finding articles, reading them, and then thinking critically about them. One thing that we want to emphasize is that, if you ever feel lost or unsure about finding or interpreting articles, do not be afraid to seek help. You can ask your professors (visit during their office hours or bring up points of confusion during class discussions) or you can utilize an often-overlooked, but tremendously helpful, resource—the librarians at your campus library!

6.1 LIBRARY SKILLS, PART 1—EVALUATING SOURCES

As you progress through college, you are going to be asked to read research articles, textbooks, and possibly news stories. There will also be times when you are asked to write a paper and will need to search for and evaluate information on your own. To help with this, you will need some basic library skills so that you can ask critical questions such as, "*Is Wikipedia a good source?*" (we will repeat this a few times in this chapter, but never forget that, if you ever need assistance with evaluating or finding sources, librarians are there to help). When evaluating sources, we recommend paying attention to three key ideas: (1) Is the source credible (or perhaps biased)? (2) Does the information come from a direct source (i.e., first-hand information straight from the horse's mouth) or a second-hand account (i.e., one that summarizes what another person has done or seen)? And, (3) is there agreement or consensus about an issue? Let's take a deeper look into each of these considerations.

Source Credibility and Conflicts of Interest

Suppose that you heard about a brain game app that was advertised to increase your cognitive abilities (see Simons et al., 2016, for a discussion of research on this topic). When making claims about the app's benefits, who is more credible—a psychology professor who studies memory or your next-door neighbor Bob who is a tennis instructor? Nothing against Bob, who might be a great guy, but we are listening to the psychology professor for this one (we will trust Bob when we need help with our backhand).

Let's take this example a step further, though. What if we also told you that the professor had received financial backing from the app developers? Would you consider that this professor might potentially be biased toward that app? The good news about most credible research journals is that they ask authors to disclose any sources of funding or conflicts of interest. Our point here is that you want to consider the source (credible or not credible?), and you also want to consider the source's motivations.

Primary vs. Secondary vs. Tertiary Sources

As a child, you may have played a *telephone game*, which starts with one person whispering a message to a second person, and then the second person relays the message to a third person, and then that continues until the message reaches the end of the chain. The fun in this game is that the message conveyed to the final person in the chain can end up being drastically different from the original message (see Table 6.1). This happens because people in the chain may embellish it, summarize it incorrectly, or simply misremember part of the message, (e.g., Bridge & Paller, 2012; Lee, Gelfand, & Kashima, 2014). Most of you have seen the same phenomenon in real life—for example, gossip is notorious for becoming slightly altered as it is passed from person to person.

iStock.com/Gisellefissak

The unfortunate aspect is that this can also happen with scientific research. Because of that, psychologists like to rely on primary sources, which are articles that provide a direct account of a study by the people who actually conducted the research. One indicator of a primary source is that it typically contains all of the following sections of an APA-style research report (we cover this more later): introduction, method, results, and discussion; however, books can also be a primary source. A primary source is considered the best type of source because it is an original account of research before it is potentially altered or interpreted by others. This is a major reason that psychological historians rely on this type of source (e.g., Watrin, 2017) and why most psychology instructors assign primary sources for class readings (e.g., Oldenburg, 2005).

One step removed from a primary source is a secondary source—this includes most textbooks and review articles. In this book, we are not conducting all of the research that we describe—we are experts in the field who are summarizing studies that were conducted by others. We did our best to accurately convey the studies we cited in this book, but, like the telephone game, there is a possibility that we changed an idea slightly (but we hope not!). As an example, even one of psychology's preeminent historians, Edwin Boring, may

TABLE 6.1

Example of a "Telephone" Game Message, With Small Changes Made by Each Person in the Chain (See Underlined Portions). Notice That the First and Final Messages Are Very Different, Even With Only Small Changes Occurring at Each Step.

Original:	The mouse tried to escape the doldrums by tending to his crops with his friends.
2nd Person:	The mouse tried to play the drums by tending to his crops with his friends.
3rd Person:	The mouse liked to play the drums while talking to the cops with his friends.
4th Person:	Mickey Mouse played the drums while talking to the cops who were his friends.

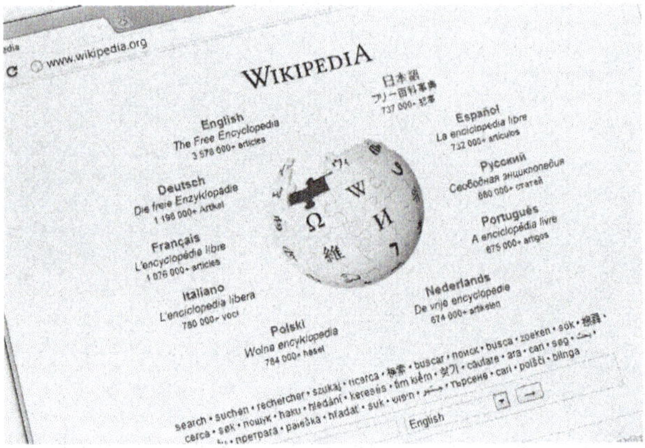

iStock.com/tomch

have translated some classic taste bud research incorrectly that had been written in German (Association for Psychological Science, 2003). Our point here is that, whereas most secondary sources are trustworthy, this example shows that even a secondary source written by one of the field's brightest luminaries can get something wrong (i.e., primary sources tend to be better than secondary sources).

The final level of source is a tertiary one—this includes general sources like dictionaries, encyclopedias, blogs, and online sites like Wikipedia. These are general accounts that can give you an introduction to a topic but should be avoided as a documented reference or source because they are far removed from the primary account (e.g., Turabian, Booth, Colomb, & Williams, 2013). Let us repeat this point—as a general rule—*do not* include a tertiary source as one of your references. This may be easily confused by students who use "research starters" in institutional databases such as EBSCO (see EBSCO Help, n.d., for more details). Even though you are doing the right thing using your library's databases—be careful! Research starters are often encyclopedic entries similar to what one would see in Wikipedia (rest assured—we will revisit Wikipedia again later in this chapter!).

So, to summarize (see Table 6.2)—trust peer-reviewed primary source articles the most, as they are original accounts of research and because other scientific researchers have reviewed and critiqued them in order to deem them acceptable to publish. You can generally trust secondary sources, especially when they are written by experts in the field, but if possible, stick with a primary source. Finally, trust tertiary sources the least, as they are the furthest removed from the original work. Finally, if you are going to use secondary or tertiary sources, do not stop with them—use them to point you toward primary sources (e.g., Lee, 2013).

TABLE 6.2

Notable Pros and Cons of Different Types of Sources

Primary Source
Pro: An original account of the work or event
Con: It can sometimes be difficult to find
Con: It might be written using specialized or field-specific language
Con: It could be a unique outcome or observation that does not reflect the big-picture patterns
Secondary or Tertiary Source
Pro: It can often be a summary of multiple primary sources
Pro: It can point you toward primary source material
Con: It can include misinterpretations, biased interpretations, or errors in the reporting of primary source material
Con: It can be incomplete (e.g., leave out important details)

Is There Agreement?

Even when dealing with primary sources, another consideration is whether there is agreement among multiple credible sources. This is important because it is possible for an occasional study to observe results that might be described as unique, spurious, odd, surprising, or a fluke. For example, most of you know that, on average, males tend to be taller than females. However, what if we ran a study that included an average group of men and compared them to a group of women that included basketball and volleyball players (who tend to be taller than average)? Our study would break from the standard finding by showing that the women were significantly taller than the men!

We mentioned a real-life example earlier in this book. Consider the claim that vaccinations could potentially lead to autism—this was refuted by a large swath of research that did not support that idea (e.g., Flaherty, 2011). The point here is that any single study can produce unusual results, and because of that, you should give more weight to a group of studies (assuming that they were all done reasonably well) that converge on similar outcomes (e.g., Stanovich, 2010). This is a reason for the big push in the field of psychology to replicate findings that are primarily based on a single study (e.g., Baker, 2015).

Take-Home Message

One important skill to develop as a student is to be a critical consumer of information. Along that line, before you even evaluate the information itself, it is important to understand the source of the information. For example—is it credible? Is it biased? If you want to know about a psychology topic or a research study, then we highly encourage you to go straight to the source—utilize primary sources instead of relying on second-hand (or third-hand) explanations. If psychology articles seem intimidating to you, then do not worry—keep reading this chapter and we will guide you through the process of first searching for them and then reading them.

Action Steps

1. When browsing the web or social media, be more cognizant of the source of the information you are consuming. Is it a primary, second-hand, or third-hand account? Can you even figure out the source? Does it seem credible?

2. The next time you learn about an amazing or surprising claim that is based on psychological (or scientific) research, see if it is just a single study or if it is based on a pattern of studies. For example, we have seen plenty

iStock.com/selimaksan

of news stories that talk about the latest research on what is healthy (or not healthy)—are these claims based on a single study or a set of studies that lead to a common outcome?

6.2 LIBRARY SKILLS, PART 2—USING DATABASES TO FIND SOURCES

So far in this chapter we have hammered home the point that, if possible, you should be seeking out primary source articles (especially those which are peer-reviewed). You might be wondering where you can find these valuable sources of information. In this module, we will walk you through two of the most commonly used databases in psychology. The good news is that you can probably do it all from your computer—but, please keep in mind that visiting a library can be extremely helpful; librarians are there to help you. Our students tell us that this chapter and the next are some of the most useful as they can start applying this knowledge in their other courses right away! When you finish this chapter, we hope that you will agree with the following idea: "*Why would anyone use Wikipedia or some random site found from a Google search, when we are so lucky to have access to these specialized library resources?*"

© Can Stock Photo/viperagp

PsycINFO

Your instructors, librarians, esteemed grad students, and other superstar students will likely mention PsycINFO as their go-to library database (PsycARTICLES is another database that is fairly similar). As the name suggests, PsycINFO is a specialized, discipline-specific database for psychology and a great tool for finding published research. The good news is that this database tends to be fairly intuitive for most students to use. That said—our key recommendation is to click "Advanced Search" so that you can include multiple search terms.

Besides the advanced search option, consider utilizing the "Cited References" and "Times Cited in This Database" options that appear in your search results. The former is a list of older articles that are cited in the paper, and the latter is a list of newer articles that cite the paper. These citation tools can be extremely helpful for finding additional articles that are relevant to your topic.

For instance, imagine that you are trying to figure out whether your professor's classroom policy of outlawing laptops, smartphones, and other electronic devices is supported by any scientific research.

Suppose That Your PsycINFO Search Leads You to the Following Articles:

iStock.com/FatCamera

- Lopresti-Goodman, Rivera, and Dressel (2012)—*Practicing Safe Text: The Impact of Texting on Walking Behavior* (this one is not quite right for your topic)
- Bjornsen and Archer (2015)—*Relations Between College Students' Cell Phone Use During Class and Grades* (this one is a great fit!)

If you select that second article, you can now see a summary of the study (this is called an abstract). If, after reading that abstract, you still think that this article is a good fit, then you can click on "Cited References" to find links to older articles related to your topic. If you click the "Times Cited in This Database" option, you see a bunch of even *newer* articles on this topic! This is great because, when starting a term paper, it is always better to have more sources than you think you need (you will likely pare down your list in the outlining and editing stages anyway).

Try not to be one of the students on the other side of the continuum (with very few sources). One big mistake that we see students make is finding the first three articles that match their keyword and then stopping. Please do not do this—just because those articles were the first that appeared does not mean that they are the best or most relevant for your research. In our previous example, the first article we found was about *texting and walking* (not the best fit for our topic)—that is why we kept exploring!

We encourage you to keep looking for a little while so that you can find articles that are the most relevant to the goals of your research. You might find even more relevant articles if you try out different search terms (a thesaurus can help). Another consideration is to explore alternative possibilities—for example, a more exhaustive search *may* reveal peer-reviewed articles that support the *opposite* finding (remember what we said earlier—different peer-reviewed articles can support different conclusions). In the technology example, if you continue searching you will ultimately see that the evidence overwhelmingly converges on the idea that technology (especially social media) in the classroom can disrupt learning. We hope you follow our emphasis here—do not be satisfied with the first articles you find—keep digging. And, as an added bonus, we hope you also take away our other lesson on the detrimental impact that technological distractions can have on classroom performance.

Web of Science

Sometimes, we can learn more about a topic when we can collect knowledge from other disciplines. With our previous example of using technology in the classroom, there may be journals in the areas of communication, media, computer science, and education that also shine a light on this topic. If you want to consider interdisciplinary research, Web of Science (or Web of Knowledge) will help you access peer-reviewed scholarly research from other areas.

Web of Science functions similarly to PsycINFO. You can add additional search terms and you can select options to narrow your search. When you find a key article, you can click "Times Cited" to see newer articles that have cited this particular paper.

iStock.com/payphoto

A Journal's Impact Factor

A key feature of Web of Science is "Journal Citation Reports." You can use this to search for a specific journal and learn its impact factor—this refers to how often articles that are published in that journal are cited in recent years (see Table 6.3). A high number reflects that the journal's articles are cited very often, whereas a smaller number indicates less popularity. High-impact journals (e.g., *Annual Review of Psychology*, *Psychological Bulletin*, and *Psychological Review* are often in this category) publish articles by thought leaders in our field that cover some of the most important and influential issues. But, keep in mind that a lot of these are *review articles*, which are considered secondary sources. One great thing about review articles is that they typically summarize patterns that emerge among primary source articles—in other words, is there converging evidence?

If you are more interested in primary sources, there are a lot of quality journals that publish empirical articles (primary research) that have lower (but respectable) impact factor ratings—this is okay! These journals tend to have lower ratings because they publish

TABLE 6.3

Examples of Journal Impact Scores Based on 2018 Data Observed From Web of Science

Broad Topic Journals	
Annual Review of Psychology	19.755
Psychological Bulletin	16.405
Current Directions in Psychological Science	4.481
Specialized Topic Area Journals	
Journal of Neuropsychology	2.468
Memory & Cognition	1.950
Journal of Social Psychology	1.102

research in a specific topic area in psychology. For example, *Memory & Cognition* is a journal that publishes quality studies, but it is cited less because it only focuses on research that is relevant to researchers in cognitive psychology.

So, remember that impact factor ratings are influenced by how much that journal's articles are cited but that this can be influenced by how broad or specialized the journal is. Quality journals that publish review articles in many different topic areas will have the highest impact ratings. Specialized journals that publish quality research will be a little lower, but still respectable. The journals to be skeptical about are the ones that have very low impact factor ratings even though they publish articles from a variety of psychology topics. If you are ever unsure about the quality of a journal, check with your professor or a librarian—they can help you out!

Google Scholar

iStock.com/brightstars

Google Scholar also indexes peer-reviewed academic journals, but it is not as thorough in psychology as the databases we already discussed. To us, the key benefit of using Google Scholar is that it can fill in the cracks. For example, consider those pesky articles that you find on a PsycINFO search, but they do not have a link to the full article (i.e., it is not available through your library). In these scenarios, Google Scholar can *sometimes* help you out. If you type in the article title (TIP: type the name exactly and put it in quotes), year, journal, and the author(s), you might find copies of articles or preprints of "in press" work that are available for download. Also, rather than filing that interlibrary loan request and waiting, you may gain quicker access to obscure specialized journals or international sources through Google Scholar.

Here is one more warning—Google Scholar has been criticized for focusing more on overall coverage or number of holdings rather than the quality of the journals in its database (see Fagan, 2017, for a review of research on Google Scholar). That is understandable—Google searches everything! Also, sometimes you will find what is referred to as "grey literature," such as conference proceedings, PowerPoint slides, working papers, and unpublished manuscripts; unlike primary source articles, these may not have been peer-reviewed (and, because of that, many instructors will not like you using them as sources). You might also encounter lower-quality work published in predatory or "pay-to-play" journals (instead of subjecting work to an intensive peer-review process, some journals will publish papers with much less scrutiny as long as you pay a fee—see Kolata, 2017, for more on this). So, in closing, Google Scholar—although free and expansive—never should be your first step in research. It can, however, be a supporting resource if used carefully.

Wikipedia and Google—The Wrong Ways to Search

Let's take a minute to consider the easy route of relying on Wikipedia. Wikipedia is a pretty cool initiative—we appreciate the power of crowdsourcing and the ongoing initiatives to increase the quality of Wikipedia entries, such as the Association for Psychological Science's *Wikipedia Initiative* (e.g., Winters, 2011) as well as *Wikipedia's Visiting Scholars* program (e.g., Zahneis, 2018). Because Wikipedia could be described as a secondary (e.g., Lee, 2015) or a tertiary source (e.g., Turabian, Booth, Colomb, & Williams, 2013), it can be a useful way to gain an *initial* understanding of a topic. But, it is not on the same level as most secondary or tertiary sources such as textbooks or review articles. It should NEVER be your go-to source for research papers:

1. First, for a primary source (e.g., journal article) or a secondary source (e.g., textbook), you can clearly check out the credibility of the authors; for Wikipedia, you cannot do this as entries can be edited by anyone.
2. Second, most primary and secondary sources are reviewed by experts in the field; Wikipedia posts may or may not be reviewed by experts in the field.

In a similar manner, conducting a regular Google search can potentially lead to good information (there is some reputable information posted online). Unfortunately, though, there is also a lot of error-filled, biased, or legitimately fake information online as well. The benefit to using the databases we recommended earlier is that you do not have to worry as much about sifting through bad information. So, our advice is that you might use Wikipedia or Google to start your search—perhaps by becoming familiar with the basic idea of a topic area. But please do not stop there—use better tools! To draw upon the opening of this chapter one more time—when you have access to good databases through your institution's library, why stick with the (potentially) less-trustworthy processes such as Wikipedia or a regular Google search?

iStock.com/stevecoleimages

Take-Home Message

To find primary source psychology articles, use your library's search engines—PsycINFO, PsycARTICLES, and Web of Science are great ones. If you must use search strategies such as Wikipedia or a traditional Google search, please only use those to get acquainted with the topic—then move on to primary sources. And, if you are ever "lost" trying to conduct research, talk to librarians—they are very knowledgeable about sources and how to find them. Finally, do not "blow off" or ignore this opportunity to learn about library searches—you will need these skills in your psychology courses!

Action Steps

1. Practice using the library search engines. They are fairly easy to use, but try them out now so that you will be confident using them when you are assigned your next psychology paper!
2. Pick any psychology topic that interests you and compare the results you get when using PsycINFO or PsycARTICLES to the results you get when using Google (or your favorite general web search engine). Our bet is that you might find *some* peer-reviewed scholarly articles using Google, but you will also find a bunch of random sites; in contrast, PsycINFO and PsycARTICLES will lead you to a lot of relevant peer-reviewed primary source articles!

6.3 A (RELATIVELY PAINLESS) INTRODUCTION TO APA-STYLE FORMATTING

Many people (including us!) like to visit the beach for a quick getaway—and often, someone will bring a volleyball. But many times, there is not a full squad (or an odd number of people) to play a proper volleyball match. Because of this, the rules get adjusted to adapt to the (sometimes changing) numbers of players. And, as the day goes on, undoubtedly someone changes the rules in an effort to gain an advantage! Those of us who enjoy order and consistency end up being frustrated—and people watching the game may have no idea what is happening (because there are no set rules). Anyone can make up a new rule at any time—so neither the players nor the friends who are watching understand the game being played.

iStock.com/andresr

So, why did we just introduce you to our rule-less beach game? Imagine if there were no rules for how research articles were written—writers could change the rules (just like the volleyball players) and include as much or as little background about their experiments that they wanted or they could organize their papers in unique (or unusual) ways. This would make it very difficult for all of us to understand articles (just like the spectators had no idea what was happening in the volleyball game). Because of that, the field of psychology has agreed upon a set of rules for psychology papers (American Psychological Association, "2019")—these APA-style formatting rules are used to avoid potential confusion and to add clarity to papers and books (e.g., Bentley et al., 1929; Breitenbach, 2014). So, let's spend some time learning the rules!

Why Learn APA-Style Formatting Rules?

- APA style was developed to standardize scientific writing.
- APA style is used for college papers and research articles.
- Uniform style helps everyone scan articles quickly for key information.
- When everyone follows the same rules, readers do not have to waste time figuring out where to find specific info or the origins of specific ideas/findings.
- Learning the citation and reference rules can help writers avoid plagiarism.

In other words—this standardized set of rules makes the process of finding, reading, and writing up research more efficient (and fair). Imagine how long all of these steps would take (and how frustrating it would be) without a commonly agreed-upon set of rules!

Where to Find Help With APA-Style Formatting

In this chapter, we help you with the basics of APA style so that you can understand psychology articles. We follow that up with the next chapter, where we provide some tips about writing a paper in APA style—this also includes help with building an APA template for yourself that you can use for any future papers! Although our advice is meant to get you started, you might find that you need more help (see Table 6.4).

The book. The book to use is the American Psychological Association's (APA) *Publication Manual* (American Psychological Association, 2020)—in this book, APA describes the current set of APA-style formatting rules. We do not think that anyone ever reads this from start to finish, but it is invaluable because you can look up specific formatting rules (use the index or table of contents) and it also includes a few excerpts of example papers.

iStock.com/Yuri_Arcurs

The website(s). If you do not want to purchase THE BOOK (or other versions of it), you can use the APA Style CENTRAL website (http://www.apastyle.org/). This website is fairly new, and originally it did not seem to be as detailed as the book, but every time we return to the site we have noticed that it has been growing with more information added. It now includes tutorials, frequently asked questions, and sample papers. So, feel free to check it out! And, if you are interested, check out Breitenbach's (2016) brief history of APA style. A final note is that there are other APA-style resources on the web—for example, many of our students like using the Purdue OWL website.

Types of APA-Style Papers

As you browse through psychology research, you will come across two types of APA-style papers: (1) review papers and

TABLE 6.4

Our Top Recommendations for Finding Help with APA-Style Formatting

- *Publication Manual of the American Psychological Association*—you can look up any rule in this book, plus it contains examples of different paper sections
- APA Style CENTRAL website—a lot of tips and explanations for different formatting rules
- Purdue OWL website—a lot of great examples, especially for citations and references
- Librarians—most librarians are experts with the major styles of formatting such as APA style

(2) empirical papers (see Table 6.5). *Review papers* are those which assess the current state of knowledge about a particular topic. You will also hear these papers referred to as "lit reviews" as they require gathering a large number of relevant articles on the topic, making sense of them, summarizing the highlights, and synthesizing them. That latter step is the intellectual challenge—after all, these papers go a step further than simply regurgitating what other researchers have done in the past. They categorize, order, and comment upon the research (by identifying patterns, differences, and unanswered questions). Some psychology journals that focus on review papers are *Psychological Review* and *Current Directions in Psychological Science*.

In contrast to review papers, empirical papers present data collected by the researchers themselves (i.e., a primary source!). When you get to a course such as Research Methods, you will likely write up an empirical paper using the rules of APA style. The key aspect of an empirical paper is that it is a first-hand account of an experiment from a research study. Although these papers review theories and prior work on the topic, the main focus is on its experiments and findings.

Sections of an APA-Style Paper

It is time to start becoming familiar with the APA-style rules, but please note that review and empirical papers are slightly different. APA-style *empirical* papers will

TABLE 6.5

Comparison of Review and Empirical Papers

- Review Papers
  - Critical evaluation of previously published studies and theories
  - Big emphasis on a review of the literature (typically no Method or Results sections)
- Empirical Papers
  - Description of original research
  - Includes all major APA sections (including Method and Results)

contain all of the sections described in this section. However, APA-style *review* papers will only contain some of the sections (they typically do not include the method and results sections).

Title. The title is exactly what it seems—a clear and concise description of the paper. Most psychology papers have straightforward (some might say boring) 10- to 12-word titles ("The Effects of This on That"). However, there has been a trend in recent years for some authors to create witty titles that make a popular culture reference or include a pun (some people think these are funny and harmless, and others do not care for them). The following articles that were published on the same topic nicely illustrate the contrast between these approaches to titles:

- Bjorsen and Archer (2015)—*Relations between college students' cell phone use during class and grades*
- Gingerich and Lineweaver (2014)—*Omg! Texting in class = u fail:(*

Abstract. The abstract is a summary paragraph of the entire article. It can convey the topic explored, what was done, what was found, what was learned, and a take-home point or two—but not much extra detail (so do not rely on only reading the abstract; you will not have a complete understanding of the article). The length of an abstract will vary slightly from journal to journal (or professor to professor), but a quick survey of some journals shows that many fall in the range of 150 to 250 words.

Introduction. This is the first major section in the body of the paper. It will typically start off with an opening paragraph that describes the general topic and will (hopefully!) clearly state the goal of the paper. After that, the introduction will include a *lengthy* review of relevant theories and previous studies that have explored the topic. At some point you will find out the "why" and the "what." Why was the research conducted? What is the problem to be answered by the research study or in this literature review? Finally, at the end of the introduction for empirical papers, you should see a brief overview of the research studies along with some hypotheses (i.e., predictions) for the outcomes of them.

Method. This section contains details about the participants (or, in the case of animal research—the subjects). For human participants, it will include information such as gender, age, the number of participants, and any other relevant attributes. This section will also describe the study materials and procedure *in detail.* Typically, this is at the level of detail so that others can read it and attempt to replicate the study.

Results. In this section, you will find the measurements (i.e., data) collected in the study. Sometimes this information will be included in tables or figures (e.g., graphs). In addition, this section will include statistical analyses that were conducted on the collected data. In our experience, the reports of the statistical outcomes tend to be the most complex and confusing part of the paper for college students. To help with this, later in the chapter we will provide some tips for interpreting results that will simplify things for you.

Discussion. Unlike the previous section, which can sometimes feel like trudging through the murky waters of complex statistics, this section will explain the results to the reader. The second goal of the discussion is to return to themes mentioned in the introduction, address unanswered questions, and otherwise attempt to tie up loose ends from earlier in the paper. For example, future directions or limitations of the study might be included here.

References. In other writing formats, such as MLA and Chicago, this section might be called something like "Bibliography" or "Works Cited." This is where the articles and books that were cited throughout the paper are listed. Note that these are not "Recommended Readings"—every article cited in the paper is included in the references. APA style has VERY SPECIFIC formatting rules for references—to help you out, we cover this in the next chapter. For now, just understand that the sources are arranged in alphabetical order, based on the first author of each source.

Take-Home Message

Formatting rules set the guidelines for producers and consumers of scholarly work. Although these formats may take some time to master—or keep from being confused among one another (see Breitenbach, 2014, for some of the differences between MLA and APA)—learning these rules will make your life easier. Imagine the chaos if researchers could create their own paper sections and citation formats! It would take much longer for you to find what you need, and you might become really frustrated because of that. So, keep in mind that the earlier you learn APA style and apply it—the better.

iStock.com/borevina

Action Steps

1. We understand that a lot of you may have learned MLA formatting and are not thrilled at having to learn a new system (e.g., see Breitenbach, 2014). If this applies to you, that's okay, but do your best to get over the frustration so that you can dive right into learning APA style. The sooner you learn it, the better you will be able to read, understand, and write psychology articles!

2. To better understand the origins of APA-style formatting, consider Bentley and colleagues' (1929) manuscript instructions—we especially want you

to think about the excerpt from the upper portion of page 58, "*Authors presenting scientific articles for publication are expected to be literate and self-critical. They should not be surprised or resentful when careless and illiterate manuscripts are declined and returned. A badly prepared manuscript always suggests uncritical research and slovenly thinking.*" In your opinion, is this okay, or is it a bit harsh?

6.4 PRACTICAL ADVICE FOR READING PSYCHOLOGY RESEARCH PAPERS

Now that we have introduced you to the sections of APA papers, let's go over some practical tips for how to read through a research article (you might be happy to know that we are recommending that you skip some sections—*for now*). There are a number of different reasons that you might be reading psychology journal articles: (1) it might be a class assignment, (2) you are writing a research paper, (3) you want to learn about a specific topic because you are working as a research assistant, or (4) you might have a professor who challenges you to find articles on a particular topic. Regardless of your reason, journal articles can be intimidating because of the statistics and research jargon. Our goal here is to lessen that intimidation by providing tips that can help you navigate your way through an article (for some guided questions to help with reading an article, see Sego & Stuart, 2016).

© Can Stock Photo/dolgachov

Learn From the Title, Year, and Abstract!

Do not just "read" a title... read *into* it. Titles always give you a clue about the topic, and some titles will explicitly describe the experimental outcome (for more on this, see Lee, 2010). For instance, some titles tell you directly what they found, whereas other titles might be a bit more coy in terms of revealing the findings. So be sure to read through titles as they can provide more information than you might have thought!

The publication year is important because it can convey the current relevance of a study. For example, consider Miller's (1956) article on memory, "*The magical number seven, plus or minus two.*" This classic work is clearly important in terms of historical significance, but there are a whole slew of more recent articles that built upon that older paper by updating or refining the theoretical explanations. Also, keep in mind that, in some cases, it is also possible that an older study may have been falsified by later studies! So, although older studies are worthwhile to read, explore more recent articles to see the current state of that research area.

Always read the abstract—it will provide a nice overview of what was studied and what was learned. If you are conducting a library search, use the abstract to decide whether the article is a possible fit for the topic you are researching. If the article is useful, save it, and then keep looking for more that are even better fits (the odds are low that the first article you encounter in a search is going to be the most relevant for your goals). Think of this process like a triage center at an emergency room—you are gaining a basic understanding of the article to determine whether it goes into the category of (a) highly relevant to your topic, (b) possibly relevant, or (c) not relevant.

Before we move on, we want to provide a warning here. If you decide that an article is relevant, do not stop reading at the abstract—we see too many students who only read the abstract and try to act like they fully understand a research article. Do not do this—it will be obvious to your professors as your description of the article will lack deeper meaning and you will not be able to answer any nonsuperficial questions about the research study!

The Introduction (Experiment Overview and Hypotheses)

Once you have decided that an article is relevant for you, the next step is to dive more deeply into some of the details. Read the opening paragraphs of the introduction carefully to learn about the goals of the study. Then skim the following paragraphs that describe prior research and the major theories related to the topic. Finally, carefully read the end of the introduction where you will typically find an overview of the experiment(s) as well as some hypotheses (i.e., predictions) for the outcomes. This is a good spot to learn about the research study without getting lost in the details of the experiment. So, to recap—during your first pass through an article, read the opening paragraphs, note some of the key theories, and then focus on the final paragraphs.

Skip the Method and Results (for Now)

Yes, you read that section header correctly—we are indeed encouraging you to skip over some sections of the journal article (for now). The reason is that these sections tend to be VERY detailed and VERY dense, and at first it is more important for you to understand the main ideas of the paper. However, once you identify an article as being relevant and important for you, then it is time to come back and read these sections—we provide a number of tips in the next module to help you with this (e.g., Christopher & Walter, 2006)!

Discussion and Conclusion

Similar to the introduction, the key areas of interest for you (during your first pass through the article) are the first couple and last couple of paragraphs of the discussion. In most articles, the initial paragraphs will describe the findings in clear language without any statistical jargon. The middle of the discussion will connect how the results of the study fit in with the findings of past research. As you continue through this section, you are likely to encounter ideas for future studies that should be conducted to answer questions or the ambiguous patterns in the data that need rectifying. Sometimes, depending on the journal, authors will speak to how their research can be applied in the real world.

iStock.com/South_agency

As you get to the very end of the discussion, you will likely see some of the main points (or conclusions) reiterated by the authors. This should include the authors' take-home point of their work. If you find the conclusion repetitive, then that is an indication that you have been reading closely!

Take for instance the following conclusion from a published study (Yeager & Dweck, 2012, p. 312):

As students move through our educational system, all of them will face adversity at one time or another . . . ***We have found that what students need the most is not self-esteem boosting or trait labeling; instead, they need mindsets that represent challenges as things that they can take on and overcome over time with effort, new strategies, learning, help from others, and patience. When we emphasize people's potential to change, we prepare our students to face life's challenges resiliently.*** [Our emphasis added.]

Conclusions like this will orient your attention to what really is important—big picture thinking—in the midst of unfamiliar jargon, statistics, and pages of literature review. This recap can assist in sorting and categorizing the research you are collecting. And, in some cases, you will witness a powerful, resounding close to an article much like that seen in the previous paragraph. As an added bonus, we hope that this example also stimulated some reflection about your own resilience!

Take-Home Message

If you find yourself reading every article from start to finish (from word 1 to word 6317)—you are doing it wrong! Be strategic about how you approach psychology articles. As you wade through titles, years, and abstracts, do an emergency room triage to evaluate how relevant the articles are for your purposes. Once these sources have "made the first cut," zoom in toward particular sections—namely, the introduction, discussion, and conclusion. We let you skip the method and results for now, but if this is an article that you want to learn even more about, you will want to dive into those sections, too. And, lucky for you, the following modules provide some tips to help you understand those sections!

Action Steps

1. Earlier in this chapter, we provided quite a few examples about the negative effects of tech (e.g., texting) in the classroom. But, what about texting and driving? And, what kinds of people are most prone to doing so? Check out Sanbonmatsu, Strayer, Medeiros-Ward, and Watson (2013). Your first step is to practice your library search skills (as a reminder, we recommend PsycINFO) to find this article!

2. Once you have downloaded the Sanbonmatsu et al. (2013) article, it is time to apply the strategic reading steps you learned in this module (the following provides some guidance).

© Can Stock Photo/feri

   a. First, analyze the title—anticipate how you might use the angle of this research in your examination of multitasking with technology in the classroom.

   b. What does the year tell you about the current relevance of this research? Is it up-to-date?

   c. Next, skim the abstract. Answer these key questions: What did the researchers do? What did they find? What do these results mean (or might suggest for your research question)?

   d. Hone in on the beginning and end of the introduction. What was the goal of the study? What did the researchers hypothesize? Why did they predict what they did?

   e. Lastly, go to the beginning and end of the discussion. What did the researchers find? How do these findings fit in with similar research? What kinds of limitations or cautions do the researchers acknowledge?

   f. BONUS TASK: How might you apply the work of Sanbonmatsu et al. (2013) to a classroom setting? What might this research suggest about students who perceive themselves to be multitasking experts in the classroom?

6.5 UNDERSTANDING THE METHODS AND RESULTS

In the last module, we walked through the initial steps for interpreting a psychology research article. In this module, we will take things a step further by covering some basic topics related to psychological research—this includes variables, data, and some of the statistics used. The topics here will help you better understand the descriptions of the methods and results that are reported in a research article (e.g., Christopher & Walter, 2006). If you are going to make it through the psychology major (or the whole way through a research article), you need to have a firm grasp of these topics (if you happen to have been using Sego & Stuart's [2016] guided questions from the previous module, a number of them also apply here).

Descriptive and Correlational Research

One of the first things you want to determine about a research study is whether it is descriptive or experimental. Descriptive research usually consists of a large number

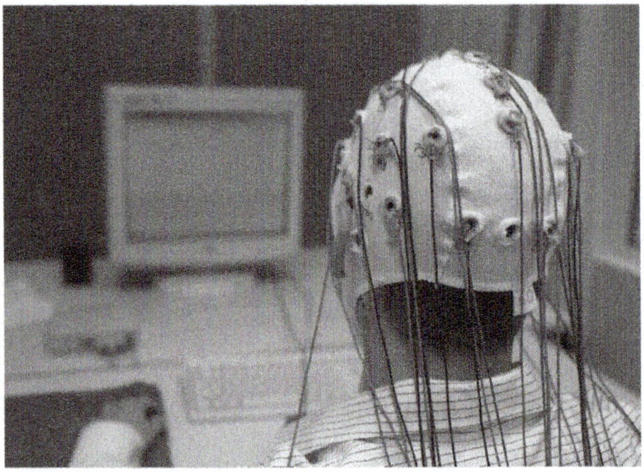

iStock.com/fotografixx

of measurements and then a summary of the patterns of how those measurements relate to one another. These measurements can be based on people's performance on a task, the measurement of a psychological construct using a scale or survey, a measurement of brain activity, or a simple value such as someone's age. One way to identify this type of research is to look for key statistical terms such as correlation or regression.

With this type of research, you want to keep in mind that the researchers are simply observing, measuring, and describing patterns. There might be statistics involved, but the essence of the study is the measurement and description of patterns. The key thing is that, with this type of research, there is no manipulation and, hence, no experiment—which just happens to be what we cover next!

© Can Stock Photo/websubstance

Experimental Design

As you may have already learned, to truly learn whether one thing causes another, we must conduct a well-designed experiment. The first rule is that you must compare at least two different conditions. This could be done by using two different groups, such as a treatment group and a control group. Another possibility is that we could test the same set of people twice—first in one condition, then in a second condition. In this case, the same group of people could serve as their own control group. So, to summarize, we can conduct an experiment by either comparing two separate groups of people (called a *between-subjects design*) or by testing the same people twice, once in each condition (called a *within-subjects design*).

Variables

In an experiment, the key difference between the groups or conditions is called the *independent variable*. For example, suppose we wanted to test whether there was a difference in test scores when people drank coffee before an exam compared to when they did not. The presence or absence of coffee would be the independent variable. In another example, if we were interested in whether males and females differed in how much they liked dark chocolate, then gender would be our independent variable. The take-home point is that the independent variable refers to the key manipulation in the experiment (i.e., what groups or conditions are you comparing to each other?).

iStock.com/HbrH

In both of the previous examples, if we wanted to know whether there was a difference in outcome between the groups or conditions, we must measure something to get scores. What you measure in an experiment is called the *dependent variable.* A way to remember this is that the outcome of interest (the dependent variable) *depends* on the manipulation of (or variation in) the independent variable. So, in the earlier examples, exam performance and rated preference for dark chocolate (respectively) would be the dependent variables. These outcomes *depend* on how much coffee was administered or the participants' gender (the independent variables).

Statistics and *p*-Values

© Can Stock Photo/Muk_Photo

In most psychological experiments, researchers use statistical analyses to determine whether groups or conditions are clearly different in some outcome. For a simple experiment with two groups or conditions (such as studying the effect of coffee on exam performance or how gender plays a role in chocolate preference), researchers typically conduct a statistical test—some common ones are a t-test or analysis of variance (ANOVA). On a basic level, these statistical tests compare your group scores to determine whether we can confidently interpret them as "different."

When researchers use t-tests or an ANOVA, a simple way to interpret whether the groups are significantly different is to look at the reported probability value or "*p-value.*" Many studies in psychology follow the arbitrary standard of 0.05 as the cutoff; so, if a *p*-value is less than 0.05, then it is interpreted as a significant difference in the outcome between the groups or conditions. So, regardless of whether the *p*-value was 0.049, 0.030, or, 0.001, you could say the groups are statistically different (because all of those values are below 0.05). But, if the *p*-value is greater than or equal to 0.05 (even if it is 0.051), then we should interpret the groups as not being statistically different. However, keep in mind that this is not the same as being equal; they are simply not different enough, statistically speaking.

Keep in mind that, because we are assuming that most of you are novices when it comes to research methods and statistics, we are keeping things very simple here. For a more-detailed coverage of the logic of p-values and the do's and don'ts, see Reinhart (2015) or any standard Statistics textbook. However, as we noted previously, we are trying to keep things simple here and we want to describe some of the common practices that you will encounter in psychology articles![1]

Graphs and Error Bars

Another way to look for a difference between groups is to compare the groups' average scores while also taking into account the graph *error bars*. Error bars indicate how much scores are spread out for a group or condition, and they provide an extended range around the average that we have to recognize. As an example, consider the graph displayed in Figure 6.1. Here, Group A has an average score of 11 and Group B has an average score of 15. Even when taking into account the error for both groups, we can see that the entire error bar range for Group A is lower than the entire error bar range for Group B. Because the error bars do not overlap at all, this indicates that Group A and Group B are significantly different from each other.

FIGURE 6.1

Error Bars That Do Not Overlap Indicate That the Group Scores Are Different.

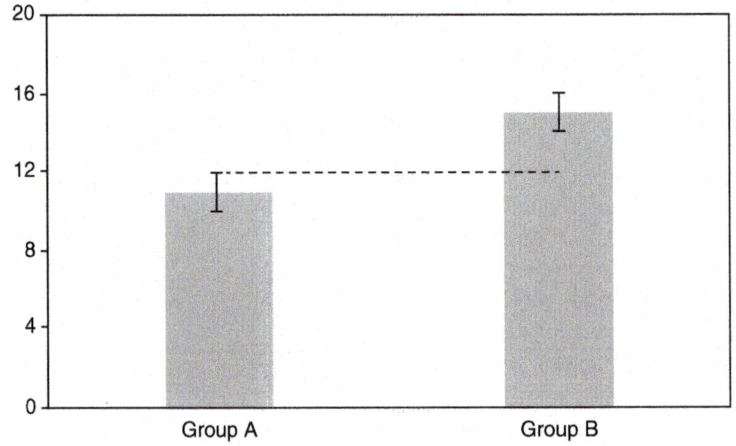

Note: The Dashed Line Was Added to Clearly Show That the Error Bars Do Not Overlap.

[1]It is worth mentioning here that not everyone agrees with the p-value cutoff of 0.05—many statisticians and researchers (see Johnson, 2013) advocate for more stringent criteria for significance testing (i.e., $p < 0.01$, $p < 0.005$, $p < 0.001$). There is also debate as to whether researchers should even be using statistical tests that rely on p-values (e.g., Cumming, 2008, 2013). It is likely that the statistical approaches used to test outcomes will continue to evolve, and some statisticians may lead the move away from null hypothesis statistical testing (NHST) in psychology (see Wasserstein, Schirm, & Lazar, 2019, for more on the world beyond "$p < 0.05$"). However, many past studies have used p-values, so it is worth knowing this!

FIGURE 6.2

Error Bars That Overlap Suggest That the Group Scores Are Not Different.

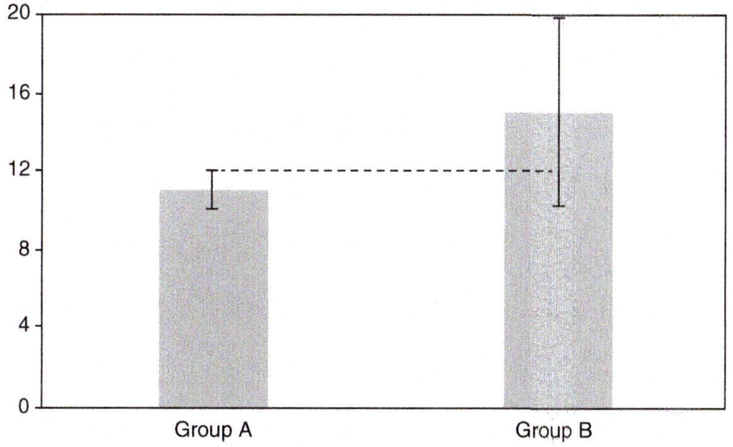

Note: The Dashed Line Was Added to Show That the Top of Group A's Error Bars Overlaps With the Error Bar Range for Group B.

Figure 6.2 displays a slightly different graph, with the same average scores of 11 and 15. However, here, the error bars for Group B are very large. Because the error bars overlap with each other, we cannot say that the groups are different from one another. Even though the average scores are the same as they were in Figure 6.1, the error is large enough here for the error bars to overlap, so we cannot be confident that the groups differ from each other.

To put it simply, a key take-away here is to look for graph error bars—these are very informative. Error bars that do not overlap indicate that the groups are significantly different from each other. Error bars that overlap indicate that the groups cannot be interpreted as different. Finally, graphs that do not include error bars may be ambiguous as you are missing an important piece of information!

Graphs and Misleading Presentations

Another point that we want to make about graphs is to examine them closely to make sure that they are not misleading. One part of a graph to consider is the *y-axis*. Most of the time, the y-axis should have zero as a starting point. However, sometimes the graph has a smaller range (starting above 0) that gives the impression of "zooming in" on the graph. For example, consider the different impressions given by Figure 6.3 (which starts at 0) and Figure 6.4 (which has a smaller range)—Figure 6.3 suggests that there is no difference between the groups, but Figure 6.4 suggests a very large difference between the groups.

A final point to make is that, in Figure 6.4, you might be tempted to conclude that Group A had an extremely low score (because the bar for Group A is so low). However, it only appears low because the y-axis was altered to 10.5 instead of starting at 0. So, watch the scale on the y-axis! If it does not start at (or near) 0, it may mislead you by making

FIGURE 6.3

Y-Axis Scale Starts at 0, Suggesting That the Groups Have Similar Scores.

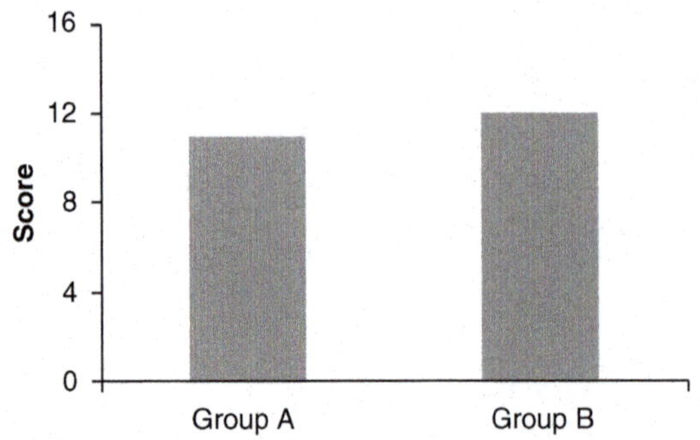

FIGURE 6.4

The Same Data as in Figure 6.3, but Here the Y-Axis Scale Is Zoomed in, Creating a Misleading Difference Between the Groups.

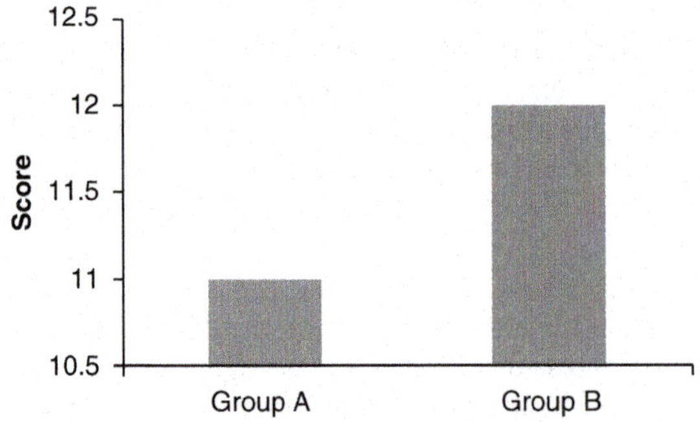

the group scores look more different than they really are, or convey that a score is lower or higher than it would be if 0 were used as the starting point. To bring this point home, check out some additional examples that are discussed by Robbins (2011, 2012).

Take-Home Message

In this module, we covered some basics to help you better understand research designs and statistical (or graphical depictions of) results. To help make this material stick, we strongly recommend that you practice applying this knowledge—we have had many students over the years express to us how much better they had learned once they wrestled and played with the concepts themselves. We provided some practice articles at the end of this chapter that you can use. To make things more interesting, you can also apply these to actual research articles. We encourage you to get into the literature and practice your grasp of these new concepts (see the action steps that follow)!

Action Steps

1. Find several empirical articles on a topic you find interesting. These can be about dogs (Gosling et al., 2003), beards (Dixson & Rantala, 2016), or some other topic that interests you. When you have some articles, see if you can identify some of these key aspects of the study (e.g., Christopher & Walter, 2006):

iStock.com/ChristopherBernard

   a. See if you can determine from the abstract alone whether the research approach was descriptive or experimental in nature (HINT: look for phrases like "experimental conditions" or that "participants were randomly assigned" to them). If you are unsure, or cannot determine this from the abstract, read through the description of the experiment to make certain.
   b. What are the independent and dependent variables for the study? If it is an experiment, is it a between-subjects or a within-subjects design?
   c. For an experiment, were the groups or conditions significantly different from one another? For a correlation, was there a significant relation between variables?
   d. Now here comes the fun part! Think like a psychological scientist—how could you modify or improve this study? Is there a different independent variable that might affect the dependent variable?
2. Besides consuming psychological and social science research, it is helpful to keep up with additional examples in other domains. We like to follow the *New York Times* feature, *What's Going on in This Graph?* We encourage you to check out this column (https://www.nytimes.com/column/whats-going-on-in-this-graph) as it focuses on a valuable skill set—the ability to read and evaluate data visualizations.

6.6 CRITICALLY THINKING ABOUT PSYCHOLOGICAL RESEARCH

Now that you are becoming familiar with finding peer-reviewed research articles and efficiently extracting the key highlights from them, it is also important to use these skills to improve your critical thinking skills (e.g., Lanagan-Leitzel & Diller, 2018). Your instructors will expect this! Simply describing and summarizing "what they did" and "what they found"—and stopping right there—is not the end of the process. Thinking critically about the research you are consuming means that you are identifying potential flaws, applying findings to new situations, and evaluating it in new ways. You can apply some of the critical thinking concepts that we discussed in an earlier chapter, but in this module, we will equip you with some new tools and terms to consider as you carefully read research articles!

Confounding Variables

In a simple psychological experiment, there should only be one difference between the groups or conditions—this is the manipulation of the independent variable. Ideally, we would like for our groups or conditions to be nearly identical except for the independent variable. Unfortunately, in practice, it is impossible to do this—there are almost always going to be a few unwanted differences between the groups and conditions. Any difference between the groups or conditions, aside from the independent variable, that could potentially cause a difference in outcome between the groups or conditions is called a *confounding variable* (sometimes it is simply called a *confound*). As you might have guessed, confounds are bad because, when they are present, you can never know whether it was the confound or the independent variable that caused the difference in outcome between the groups or conditions.

iStock.com/AntonioGuillem

Keep in mind that some confounds are bigger threats than others. For example, if we do not think that gender matters in an experiment, and one experimental group has a larger male-to-female ratio than the other group, then this might not be such a big deal. However, remember the "coffee" example from the last module? We could have people drink (caffeinated) coffee before an exam, and then, later, let them drink decaf coffee before another exam. Suppose that the first exam consists of simple addition and the second exam consists of fraction and exponent problems. In this example, if people scored higher on the first exam than on the second exam, it might be because of the independent variable (coffee/caffeine)—however, it could also be due to the more difficult math on the second exam! With confounds, we cannot be sure if an observed difference between groups was due to our independent variable manipulation or the confounding variable.

Could we improve the coffee study to eliminate that confound? Sure! Our recommendation would be to randomly assign participants (you could use a random number generator—see Random.org for an easy way to do this) to two different conditions:

(1) caffeine for the first exam, then decaf for the second exam or (2) decaf for the first exam, then coffee for the second exam. If the caffeine scores were still higher in this new version of the experiment, then we have more confidence that it was due to the caffeine manipulation (because half of the participants had coffee for exam 1, and the other half had coffee for exam 2). This is now a better experiment because steps were taken to reduce or eliminate that confound.

Bias

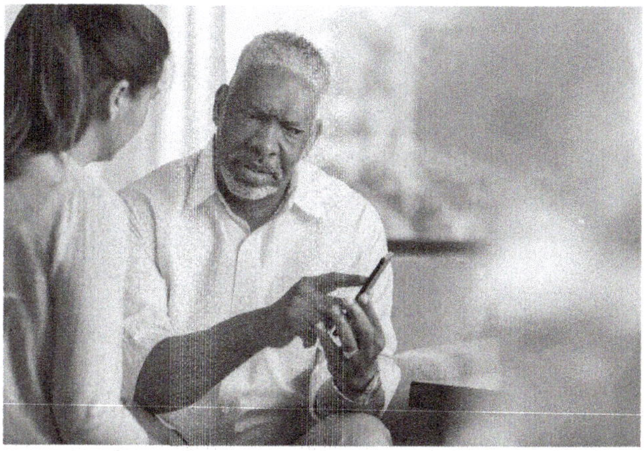

iStock.com/asiseeit

In addition to confounds, experiments can be flawed if the materials or procedures are biased toward a particular group or condition. For example, imagine if you were comparing the performance of young and older adults and we administered the task on a smartphone. Because young adults are much more likely to regularly spend time on smartphones, this method might be biased in favor of those young adults (you might also argue that the small fonts on smartphones can be a bias against the older adults). What might be a better, less-biased way to conduct this study? We could administer the task on a computer with a bigger screen and bigger font—or perhaps administer it using paper and pencil.

It is also possible to have a biased sample. For example, if you were interested in perceptions of prejudice, the racial background (or perhaps the age) of participants can be important (e.g., Carter & Murphy, 2015). If you only collected data from a group of mainly white college students, then your results might not reflect the perceptions of the general population. Many psychology studies rely on college student participants because they are conveniently available—but are these college students truly representative of all humans (see Stanovich, 2010, for a discussion of the "college sophomore problem")? The good news is that, in a lot of research, the college sophomore sample does not matter—however, there are plenty of topics in which participant samples do matter.

Correlation Is Not Causality

Different research approaches affect what types of conclusions you can draw from them. One of the best parts of experiments is that they allow you to draw inferences that one thing causes another. This is because, in a well-controlled and randomly assigned experiment, the two groups are assumed to be the same except for one change—the cause of the difference.

Shutterstock

In contrast, correlations are, for the most part, simply descriptive. For example, if attendance and grades are positively correlated, we can say that, as attendance increases, grades go up—but we cannot say that increased attendance causes higher grades (unless we run a true experiment). For example, what if we told you that ice cream sales was positively correlated with instances of sunburn—you cannot infer that ice cream causes sunburn. We highly encourage you to check out Vigen's (2015) book (*Spurious Correlations*) or the Spurious Correlations website (http://tylervigen.com/discover) for some memorable noncausal relationships involving margarine, celebrities, and falling from trees!

One final thing to consider is that sometimes correlations are dressed up as more-complex statistics such as multiple regression. Techniques like this tend to be better than simple correlations, as there is a better attempt to statistically control other factors. However, as Nisbett (2015) notes, this type of analysis is still not as good as an experiment when it comes to drawing inferences about causality.

iStock.com/kasayizgi

Self-Reports vs. Actual Behavior

Another critical view of psychological research is to examine whether a study is observing actual behavior or people's thoughts about how they might behave. A lot of psychological research studies do the latter because asking people what they think they would do is a lot more convenient than designing an experiment around a behavioral situation. However, there can be significant differences between what people think they would do compared to what they would actually do (e.g., Baumeister, Vohs, & Funder, 2007). For example, people were twice as likely to administer a shock to an animal when placed in a real-life scenario compared to when they were asked about a hypothetical version of it (Bostyn, Sevenhant, & Roets, 2018).[2]

Sample Size and Converging Evidence

We mentioned this earlier (toward the beginning of this chapter), but this is important so we want to emphasize it again. Which is more trustworthy—hearing about the experience of one person or hearing about the experiences of hundreds of people? Which is a stronger case, a single study with a particular result or a set of studies that have agreement on a result? Most of you probably recognize that the latter is likely to be more trustworthy in both examples, but many showed that people still cannot resist giving some weight to the very small sample or even a single case (e.g., Wilson & Brekke, 1994)! So, although those interesting psychological case studies (or isolated articles with a unique finding) can be compelling, resist the urge to overgeneralize from one or a very small number of observations. As we stated earlier, check for converging evidence from more than one research study (e.g., Stanovich, 2010).

Take-Home Message

Although psychological researchers do their best to design well-thought-out studies, it is difficult to control for everything—so there will always be flaws (e.g., Uttal, 2003). With your new knowledge, you can look for potential problems in psychological studies—and hopefully you can get involved with psychological research (see our earlier chapter on joining a research team) so that you can experience research firsthand. Finally, here is one last thing to keep in mind—if you are ever critiquing psychological research (whether it is an article, a conference poster, or a classmate's work), do not be a jerk! Although it is important to understand the flaws of research studies, studies are conducted by people, and people have feelings. So, please use some tact when critiquing other people's research studies (e.g., Sternberg, 2006).

Action Steps

1. To help you practice what you just learned about interpreting and critically thinking about psychological research, please take some time to look up some articles (use your library skills to find articles on any topic that you think is interesting) and take the following steps:
   a. Identify the independent variable(s).
   b. Identify the dependent variable(s).
   c. Determine whether each experiment is a within-subjects or between-subjects design.
   d. Look for *p*-values and graph error bars to see whether they convey significant differences between the experimental conditions/groups.

[2]For those of you who are concerned about the safety of the animals (mice) in this study, rest assured that no actual shocks were administered!

2. The next step is a little bit more difficult—are there any biases or confounds in the articles? This can be in the sampling of participants, the design of the study, or the interpretation of the results. One word of warning is that this might be difficult with research that goes through a stringent peer-review process and is accepted into high-impact journals. See if your instructor can recommend some journals that may publish lower-quality research studies (you can do this on your own by looking for journals that have *very low* impact scores)—you might be more likely to see confounds or biases in these studies.

Writing Papers and Presenting

7

7.0 MEET ALEX

Shutterstock

CHAPTER OUTLINE

Alex was a college sophomore, and she was not too keen about writing papers. She typically started a paper the day before it was due and sometimes had to stay up late to get it finished. Although this paper-writing strategy did not lead to stellar grades, it was good enough to earn passing grades—however, she felt like it was the same struggle each time that she wrote a paper.

In her Research Methods course, Alex had to write a literature review and—true to form—she wrote it the night before it was due. When she received her paper back a week later, she flipped through the pages to look for her grade. She saw a lot of comments from her professor in the margins of each page, but she could not find a grade. She ignored those comments and checked again, but there was no score.

After class, she approached her professor and asked about her "missing grade." She was surprised to hear him say that this paper was not graded! He explained that it was a first draft of the paper and that she should use the feedback he provided as a starting point for improving it. This was new to Alex, as she never really looked at professors' comments on her papers (after all, they seemed pointless—her previous instructors had never had her revise her work); she only ever checked to make sure that she earned a high-enough score.

The professor explained that his perspective on writing was that it was a skill that required practice and that a great way to improve is to learn from feedback and to make changes in order to create a better paper. That was why he required students to write more than one draft of a paper.

Why Did We Tell You This Story?

Unfortunately, as professors, we see too many students who write papers at the last minute, write only one draft, and never bother using the feedback provided. As we note throughout this chapter, writing is a skill that can be improved if you work on it. Students should be focusing on the content of the paper, writing multiple drafts, possibly getting feedback from someone else (either the professor or a classmate), and double-checking it for correct APA-style formatting. In this chapter, we provide some tips for writing psychological papers, suggestions for improving your word-processing skills, and some guidance (and shortcuts) for properly using APA-style formatting.

7.1 WRITING A RESEARCH PAPER

If you have not done so already, you will have to write a research paper for one of your psychology courses. In some cases, this may involve conducting a small experiment or administering a brief survey (e.g., in a Research Methods course) and writing an empirical paper. However, it might not be practical to collect data for a class—because of that, a lot of the papers assigned in psychology courses are either literature review papers or research proposals (see the previous chapter for a comparison of empirical and review papers). In this module, we provide some guidance for writing style and about what types of information you want to include (American Psychological Association, 2020). We also provide some practical tips that will improve the quality of your papers (e.g., Ishak & Salter, 2017).

Reviewing Research Literature

When writing a research paper, you want to make sure that you are focusing on real evidence that has been learned in research studies. When you make claims or express viewpoints, back it up with evidence and citations (see our advice elsewhere in this chapter to paraphrase and cite!). And, when you write a research paper, one source is not going to cut it—you need to cite multiple sources. If you do not have much experience with research papers, ask your professors for how many sources they expect. Building on this, you also want to make sure that you use the most relevant and most up-to-date sources that you can find.

iStock.com/sarah5

Make Sure That Your Paper Tells a Story!

When it comes to student papers, one piece of bad news is that those who do not have much writing experience tend to write papers that do not have much structure. However, the good news is that you can work on this skill. To improve as a writer, try to work on the organization of your papers (see Table 7.1). For example, always make sure that you include an opening paragraph that introduces the paper and your goals and then wrap up the paper with a closing paragraph that reviews the goal and summarizes the key points.

TABLE 7.1

Tips for Writing an Organized Paper

- Start with an opening paragraph
  - State the goal of the paper in the opening.
  - Consider introducing a real-life example to illustrate the main topic.
- The review of literature goes in between the opening and the conclusion.
  - Check to make sure that the literature review paragraphs are in a good sequence. Are similar topics grouped together? Does it build an argument?
  - Add transitions (or subheadings) to the beginning of paragraphs to improve flow.
- Finish with a concluding paragraph
  - Clearly state the key points that the reader should remember.

Between those paragraphs is where you include the information that you research. As a beginner, it is okay to write with one paragraph dedicated to each study that you are describing. However, as you develop your writing skills, your paragraphs will reflect ideas instead of individual studies—this means that your paragraphs will become densely packed with multiple citations in support of an idea (rather than one single study). An important point, regarding structure, is that you should think about the flow of ideas in the body of your paper. If the sequence of ideas does not make sense, then reorganize your paragraphs to help your reader better follow your thinking.

Before we move on, we have to mention something that a lot of students overlook. Once you have your paragraphs in a good sequence, be sure that your paragraphs have transitions! Without transitions, paragraphs seem like they are independent from each other, and they do not flow together very well. What do we mean by transitions? Use language that signifies that you are moving on from the previous paragraph—"In addition to that earlier work...," "In contrast to those results...," "Furthermore...," or "Finally..." The basic idea is that you want to make a small connection to the paragraph that you just finished. If you are drastically changing ideas, and a transition does not seem to fit, then you may want to use a section header to clearly indicate that you are changing topics—psychological writing tends to include more subheaders than other disciplines (e.g., Madigan, Johnson, & Linton, 1995).

Some Tips on Writing Style

When writing, it is good practice to err on the side of formality unless you are told explicitly to do otherwise (e.g., Ishak & Salter, 2017). What do we mean by that? A research paper is neither an opinion piece nor a message sent to your friends. So, be careful that your writing is not too casual or conversational. Research papers are not the place to try out new jokes or to use abbreviations you might find in a text message. Keep the paper serious and professional—if you really want to include a joke, save it for when you do an oral presentation based on your paper (we have presentation tips later in this chapter).

Another aspect of writing style is whether it includes cautious or definitive language. Remember that it is possible for any psychological study or theory to be flawed, inconsistent with other studies, or falsified at some point in the future. Because of this, you should avoid writing with definitive phrasing—instead, be more cautious when describing results,

TABLE 7.2

When Writing About Psychological Research, Avoid Making Definitive Statements and Instead Adopt a More-Cautious Tone

- Cautious (or Tentative) Phrases to Use
  - "The results suggest . . ."
  - "These outcomes are consistent with . . ."
- Definitive Phrases to Avoid
  - "This study proved that . . ."
  - "It is clear that X causes Y . . ."

outcomes, or patterns (e.g., Madigan et al., 1995). We listed some examples of good and bad phrases in Table 7.2.

A final note about writing style is that you should strive to write in a civil tone (e.g., Madigan et al., 1995). This means that you should not be mean-spirited or overly negative with criticism. You should also avoid personalizing any critiques. One way to do this is to focus your critique on the studies or papers themselves, not on the authors of a paper. For example, consider the following two ways of critiquing a study:

- "Houska's (2019) study was clearly flawed, which caused his results to be completely meaningless."
- "The study included a potential confound, which may have led to that unique pattern of results (Houska, 2019)."

The first sentence includes a negative tone and is phrased in a way that the critique is aimed directly at the author. In contrast, the second sentence is more civil and aims the criticism toward the study instead of the author. Remember that the goal of research papers is to evaluate (and hopefully advance) research, not to attack others and put down their hard work.

iStock.com/Malex92

Small Errors Matter

Although professors do not expect students to always be perfect, most of them want to convey that errors matter. A popular book on writing and grammar emphasized this point by drastically changing the meaning of a sentence by adding or subtracting a comma (Truss, 2003):[1]

- "Eats shoots and leaves"
  - <a description of what panda bears eat>
- "Eats, shoots and leaves"
  - <criminal activity by a hungry panda bear>

[1] We recommend this book—it actually makes grammar topics fun (and, yes, the actual title is "*Eats, Shoots & Leaves*")!

Although that example is fun, minor errors like this can have real consequences. For example, one company had to pay out *$5 million* to their employees because a comma was left out of a sentence—the missing comma changed the intended meaning of a rule that led to employees earning a lot more overtime money than intended (Victor, 2018)! Our point here is that small errors matter in writing—one small change in punctuation, spelling, or spacing can change the meaning of what is being conveyed. So, be careful as you write, and take the time to proofread your work for errors.

Do Not Wait Until the Deadline to Start

When writing a paper, is it possible to start the night before it is due, write one draft, and end up with something good? Of course, it is possible—but, just like relying on just one attempt if you were taking a selfie, we bet that you could do better if you worked at it a little more. Writing is difficult and, like most difficult things, it can get better with more time and effort.

So, instead of procrastinating (watch out for that instant gratification monkey—see Urban, 2016), we highly recommend starting a paper a week before it is due (or at least a few days early). When you revisit your paper the next day, you will be astonished by how much of it could be improved (this happens to us, too—sometimes when we look at an earlier draft of our own writing it literally makes us cringe). We have seen students raise their paper grades by one or two letter grades by simply writing additional drafts of their paper.

There is one more thing that you can do—pair up with a classmate and, after each of you has written an early draft, swap papers and give each other feedback. Sometimes, it is much easier to detect errors when reading someone else's paper than your own. You can even check with your professors to see if they are willing to look over an early draft of your paper—if they are willing to do this, be sure to give them a few days to get back to you—yet another reason to start early!

Take-Home Message

You will become very familiar with research papers of two main varieties in psychology: literature reviews and research proposals. These are writing assignments with a purpose: to tell a *research* story. To convey your story in the most convincing manner, be sure to maintain a formal tone throughout your writing and rely upon scholarly sources as evidence for your points. We realize that this next suggestion is easier said than done—always allow yourself more time than you think you need to draft, edit, and polish your writing assignments (focus on organization, add transitions, and proofread). Much like perfect one-shot selfies, perfect one-draft writing projects are elusive!

© Can Stock Photo / deandrobot

Action Steps

1. Whenever you are assigned a paper, immediately set a reminder in your calendar for 1 week before the deadline. And, when that alarm/reminder eventually pops up, take it seriously and get started so that you can write more than one draft of your paper. Also, take it one step further—swap papers with a classmate and give each other feedback!

iStock.com/Wavebreakmedia

2. Use the tips in this module to improve the quality of your psychology papers. To help, we included a brief checklist of questions to ask yourself:
   - Is there good organization (opening, body, and conclusion)?
   - Are there transitions or subheaders when starting new paragraphs?
   - Are there multiple sources cited?
   - Does the paper use formal (not casual) language?
   - Do the descriptions of outcomes use cautious (not definitive) phrasing?
   - Do the critiques avoid overly negative or personalized phrasing?
   - Did you proofread for minor errors?

7.2 PLAGIARISM—DO NOT DO IT!

In our experiences, most students know that plagiarism is bad and that it is something to avoid. However, not all students are clear about what is meant by the term (e.g., Gullifer & Tyson, 2010). As we will point out, there are some misconceptions about what types of behaviors are wrong. On top of that, it is also not always clear to students why some types of plagiarism are such a bad thing. In this module, we try to clearly convey different types of plagiarism, why people do it, the consequences to plagiarism, and, finally, how to avoid doing it yourself.

What Is Plagiarism?

One thing to keep in mind is that people may have misconceptions about what constitutes plagiarism (e.g., Gullifer & Tyson, 2010). For example, some students think that copying and pasting from another source (without citing and/or quoting) is a minor issue (or not cheating at all), whereas faculty tend to think that this is a serious issue (McCabe, Butterfield, & Trevino, 2012). To help you out, we will try to be clear by describing a few rules that you should always follow when writing (see Table 7.3).

TABLE 7.3

Rules to Follow to Avoid Plagiarism (and Advice About What to Do Instead)

- Do not copy text verbatim from another source!
  - Put it into your own words and cite that source.
- Do not copy and paste sentences or paragraphs from the internet!
  - Put it into your own words and cite that source.
- Do not describe other people's ideas without giving them credit!
  - Put it into your own words and cite that source.
- Do not try to pass off someone else's writing as your own!
  - This is simple cheating—*you* need to write *your* own paper.
- Do not copy and paste sentences or paragraphs from old papers that you wrote!
  - This is self-plagiarism (yes, this is a real thing)—start new papers from scratch.

We hope that the items in Table 7.3 clearly convey that copying words and ideas from others (without giving them credit) is plagiarism. However, you might not have been aware that there is such a thing as self-plagiarism (e.g., American Psychological Association, 2020). For example, reusing your own text from an earlier paper that you wrote is a form of plagiarism. So, if you have ever thought about recycling parts of a paper (or an entire paper) that you turned in for a previous course, think again—that is self-plagiarism. If you think that you would never get caught doing this, remember that many professors use software such as TurnItIn—this software is used to compare student papers to writing that is already in its database (and then it adds the new paper to its database!).

What Is Not Plagiarism?

For clarity, we also want to describe what does not fit under the umbrella of plagiarism (Purdue Online Writing Lab, 2019). First, if it is your own ideas or observations, then this is okay. Second, you are okay if you are describing your own original research study. Finally, if the information is thought to be common knowledge, then you may not need to cite. However, if you are writing a paper about any of these things, and then you also include ideas from other sources, be sure to cite those!

Why Is Plagiarism so Bad?

Plagiarism is bad, whether it is done intentionally or not. First of all, it demonstrates poor ethics as you are stealing someone else's ideas and words—this goes against the American Psychological Association's (2017) third ethical principle regarding stealing, cheating, misrepresentation, and fraud. In the academic world, words and ideas are the currency—students and professors work hard to come up with new and interesting ideas about psychological topics. Trying to pass off someone else's work as your own is dishonest and unethical. Another reason that plagiarism is bad is that it can reflect laziness, and

it is inconsistent with the whole purpose of being in school to earn an education. Think about this in the context of writing—part of the writing process is digesting and thinking about ideas, and, if you copy and paste someone else's work, you probably are not thinking deeply about the ideas.

Besides being unethical, there is a wide range of possible consequences for acts of plagiarism—some acts are thought to be more serious than others (e.g., Evering & Moorman, 2012). In a college course, you might receive a failing grade on the assignment or possibly in the course. In addition, you might be referred to a disciplinary committee at the institution—this committee might add another penalty (e.g., suspension) or it might require some type of remedial training regarding best writing practices. In some cases, there can be legal consequences for plagiarizing (e.g., Morrow, 2009). And, finally, plagiarism can have negative consequences on people's reputations. One interesting line of research showed that these negative effects on one's reputation can even be observed among 6-year-old children (e.g., Shaw & Olson, 2014).

Why Do People Plagiarize?

There can be a number of simple reasons that people plagiarize. For example, it might be convenient to copy text, especially if someone is in a hurry to get a paper done at the last minute (e.g., Sheehan, 2014). In some cases, students might not see the value in an assignment and they may plagiarize as a shortcut just to get the task done (e.g., Evering & Moorman, 2012). A third reason for plagiarism might be a misunderstanding of what types of actions count as plagiarism (e.g., Gullifer & Tyson, 2010). Finally, some might plagiarize if they are not confident in their ability to paraphrase and cite correctly (e.g., Ishak & Salter, 2017)—we will expand a bit on this idea.

Avoiding Plagiarism

So, how can you avoid plagiarism? First, do not self-plagiarize—every time that you write a paper, write a *new* paper! Second, when dealing with other people's ideas, use the paraphrase-and-cite approach. It is okay to write about other people's ideas, but remember that *you are writing about them* (and citing them), not copying them. So rephrase ideas and make sure that you include a citation (e.g., Cooper, 2016). Also, remember this—the rule is NOT "paraphrase or cite"; the rule is "paraphrase AND cite" (see Turnitin, 2016, for some great examples of what not to do—the full website information is in the references)!

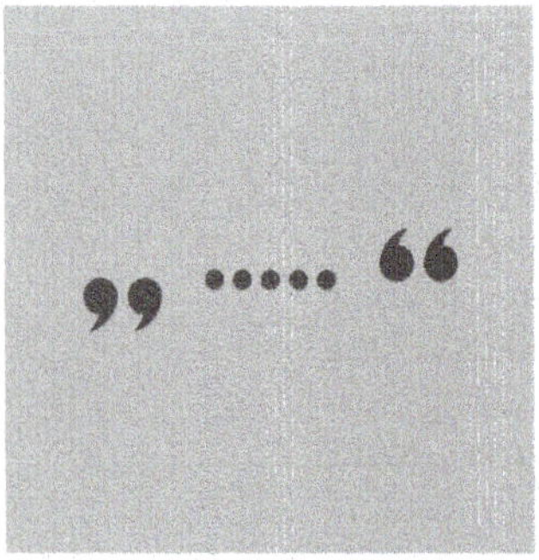

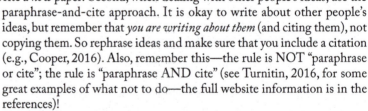

At this point, you might be wondering whether or not you should use quotes. Although you can include quotes in a paper, our recommendation is to avoid them altogether, or to at least minimize your use of them (e.g., Cooper, 2016; Ishak & Salter, 2017). When you quote, you are essentially copying and pasting with quotation marks—using a quote does not signify that you truly understood the ideas, as you are simply repeating someone else, not explaining what was meant. In addition, when you use quotes, you are mixing someone else's writing style with your own writing—this can potentially break up the flow of your writing. Instead of quotes, we recommend the paraphrase-and-cite approach.

Another strategy for avoiding plagiarism is to take advantage of online tools that can be used to detect any similarities in your paper compared to papers in its large database (e.g., Cooper, 2016). It is common for professors to check student papers for plagiarism using an online service such as Turnitin or iThenticate—but you can look for others that are available to anyone such as HelioBLAST or SafeAssign (this last one is available if your institution uses the Blackboard learning management system). These tools might not be as helpful with a short paper that only has a few references, but they can be very helpful if you write a lengthy paper such as a thesis. A final point here is that, now that you know that your professors are using tools like this, you should have extra motivation to avoid plagiarizing.

Take-Home Message

The take-away message here is put ideas into your own words and—most importantly—be sure to cite the original work to give that (or those) author(s) credit. And, speaking of citing work, we just so happen to cover that topic in the next module—so, keep reading! As we noted in this module, plagiarism is considered a serious offense by many professors, so please take the time to learn about it so that you can avoid making any mistakes. If you ever need help with this process, check with your instructor or visit a writing center on your campus.

Action Steps

© Can Stock Photo / robwilson39

1. In the world of writing, plagiarism is stealing—it is the theft of someone else's ideas and/or words. So, always follow this mantra: *paraphrase and cite*! If you are unsure how to cite, read the next module carefully.
2. If you are having difficulty with paraphrasing, we recommend that you check out Turnitin (2016). The website (https://www.turnitin.com/static/plagiarism-spectrum/) has a great list of examples of different types of plagiarism so that you can get ideas of what not to do!

7.3 APA CITATIONS AND REFERENCES

When writing an APA-style paper, students tend to have difficulty with citations and references. Citations are when you mention a source in the body of your paper—it is possible for the same source to be cited more than once in your paper. References are a complete list of all of the sources that were cited in the paper (each source is listed once at the end of your paper). We know that some of you might be tempted to look for a shortcut, such as one of the citation generators that are available online; however, keep in mind that there have been complaints that many of these produce citations or references with formatting errors in them (e.g., Stevens, 2016; Zafonte, 2018)! Because of that, we want to walk you through the process so that you can do it on your own. Now, let's get into some of the nuts and bolts (and overlooked subtleties) of citations and references.

When to Cite

Cite early! Cite a source right away, in the very first sentence that you mention the ideas from the source. Do not wait until the end of a paragraph—cite when you first introduce an idea. Within a paragraph, you do not have to continue citing the same source as long as you are unambiguously referring to the same source. However, if you describe ideas from two or more different sources within the same paragraph, then you have to cite again to be clear which source is being described.

As we just noted, you do not have to continuously cite a source within a paragraph (as long as you are clearly referring to the same source). However, when you start a new paragraph, you should cite again—even if you are still discussing the same source. A new paragraph indicates to the reader that a new idea is being presented, so readers might not be sure whether you are still discussing the same source. Citing again makes it crystal clear to the reader that you are giving credit to that source.

iStock.com/ogichobanov

Order of Authors

One thing to keep in mind with citations is that you must always keep the authors listed in the order they were listed in the source! The author order is important (e.g., Venkatraman, 2010)—in most psychology articles, the first author contributed the most, the second author contributed the next most, and so forth. In some subfields of psychology, such as neuroscience, these rules are tweaked slightly in that the most senior researcher might be listed last; however, you should still keep the authors listed in their original order!

How to Cite

For APA-style citations, you should always include the authors' last names (in their original order!) and the year of publication. There are two ways that you can write it out: (a) *narratively*—including the source author name(s) as part of the sentence or (b) *parenthetically*—putting the citation inside of parentheses (see McAdoo, 2017, for more on this). The choice of which approach to use is yours—it pretty much depends on how you want to structure your sentences. And you do not have to pick one approach and stick with it—you can switch it up in your paper. One thing to note is that parenthetical citations seem to be more common than narrative ones—this reflects the idea that writing should focus on the research itself, not on the researchers (see our discussion from earlier in the chapter that the ideas and research findings should be the main focus of your writing, not *who* conducted the research).

iStock.com/ogichobanov

To insert a citation narratively (i.e., as part of the sentence), include all of the authors' last names in the sentence and then immediately follow that with the publication year in parentheses. When there is more than one author, use the word "and" before the final author. If putting the citation inside of parentheses, list the authors followed by a comma and then the year. Here, if you have more than one author, use an ampersand ("&") before the final author. See Table 7.4 for some examples.

You might also find that you want to cite more than one source at the same time. For example, you might have two sources that support the same point, or you might cite multiple articles that examined the same basic topic. When citing more than one source at the same time, you are most likely going to put them inside of parentheses. In this scenario, separate each citation with a semicolon and list them alphabetically by the last name of the first author from each source. For example, the hypothetical citation "Ash & Paul, 2016" would be listed before "Cox & Allen, 2015" because "Ash" comes before "Cox" alphabetically. This would result in a final reference that looks like this: (Ash & Paul, 2016; Cox & Allen, 2015).

TABLE 7.4

Examples of Different Types of APA-Style Citations

Citation as part of the sentence:
Copeland and Larson (2017) demonstrated that...
Citation inside of parentheses:
One study (Houska & Schroeder, 2017) revealed that...
Multiple citations together:
...showed a clear effect (Bies-Hernandez, 2017; Palena, 2016).
When there are three or more authors:
Gunawan et al. (2018) controlled for...

Another common scenario regarding citations is that you might have a source with three or more authors. If you have three or more authors, instead of listing all of the authors every single time you cite that source, APA style will let you use an abbreviation instead. Take for instance a hypothetical article co-authored by Gunawan, McMullen, and Severe in 2018. In cases like these, just write the first author's last name followed by "et al." and then the year: Gunawan et al. (2018).

Number of Citations and References

There are no rules as to how many citations and references should be included in a paper, but please remember these two rules about citations and references. First, any source that is cited must be in the references. Second, any source listed in the references must be cited. The reason for this is that, if you describe and cite a study, you include the reference so that interested readers can easily find it. Also, there is no point in listing a source in the references if it is never discussed and cited in the paper. So, do not try to reach a professor-imposed number of sources by including more sources in the references unless you actually discuss them in your paper (and cite them)!

APA-Style References

Now that you know the basics of citing sources, let's turn our attention to the formatting of references. This can be tricky because APA-style rules require different types of information and subtle formatting differences for different types of sources. APA style is very specific about the order of information, indents, spaces, capitalization, italics, and punctuation—so please pay attention to details when writing out references. To help you out, let's cover some rules followed by some examples.

Keep authors in the same order they were listed in the source—each reference starts with the first author's last name.

1. Your entire References section should be double-spaced.
2. Start a new reference on a new line.
3. The first line of *each* reference should be left-aligned, but the non-first lines of *each* reference (e.g., second line, third line, etc.) should be indented.
4. Alphabetize the list according to each source's first author (if two sources have identical authors, put those in chronological order).

We recommend always having examples handy so that you can model your references from them. We include some examples (see Figure 7.1), and we will also include some later in this chapter when we walk you through the step-by-step process of building your very own APA template.

Take-Home Message

It is very important to note that APA-style citations and references are different from those used by other formatting styles such as MLA or Chicago. APA citations focus on including the author surnames and publication year in the text—this is in contrast to the

FIGURE 7.1

Example References for a (a) Journal Article, (b) Book, (c) Book Chapter, and (d) Website.

(a) Journal article:

Lastname, F. M., & Lastname, F. M. (Year). Title of article: Pay attention to capitalization. *Title of Journal, volume number*(issue number), page number-page number. doi-or-url-if-available

(b) Book:

Bookauthor, F. M. (Year). *Full title of book.* Publisher. doi-or-url-if-available

(c) Book chapter:

Chapterauthor, F. M., & Chapterauthor, F. M. (Year). Chapter title: Pay attention to capitalization. In F. M. Editor (Ed.), *Full title of book* (pp. page number-page number). Publisher. doi-or-url-if-available

(d) Website:

Webauthor, F. M. (Year, Month Day). *Title of post, blog, or article.* Website. https://www.includethefullwebaddress.com

footnote-bibliography style (Hume-Pratuch, 2014) with which many students are familiar (see Houska, 2015, for an APA-style manuscript reworked for a Chicago-style journal). Because of the detailed specifications for APA citations and references, we strongly recommend keeping good examples handy that you can use as a guide. Even better, in the next module we walk you through the creation of an APA-style template that you can use. We include reference examples in the template so that you will always have them to guide you as you start a new APA-style paper—you can even add some of the examples from this module to your template!

Action Steps

1. You can use our example references or other examples, but keep some example references somewhere you can find them. Even better, follow the advice in the next module for building your own APA template—be sure to include example references because you will want the reminders the next time you write an APA-style paper!
2. If you ever find yourself in a situation where you need examples of citations, check out the numerous examples spread out throughout this book.

7.4 CREATE YOUR OWN APA TEMPLATE

We have said it before, and we will say it again—most of you are going to be writing a lot of APA-style papers as you move through college. As a way to simplify your life, we recommend that you take the time right now to build your very own APA template (e.g., Zafonte, 2018). We are serious about this—if you take some time to do it right now, you may never have to worry about the basic formatting rules ever again! Also, if you do it right, you will not have to fear losing points for basic formatting errors on any future papers. If that sounds like a good trade-off for a little bit of time right now, then continue through this module. As you move through the steps to build your own APA template, be sure to refer to our examples to make sure that your template resembles ours!

Initial Steps for Building Your APA Template

For word processing, some of the most common programs that we see are Microsoft Word, Google Docs, and Pages. One thing to understand is that the main formatting steps should be somewhat similar across these, but the specific commands and procedures might vary slightly (they each have their strengths and weaknesses). As we walk you through the building of your APA template, if you are not sure how to do any of these actions, please refer to our discussion of computer skills and ways to find help in the next module. If you do not know how to do something, take some time now to figure things out!

© Can Stock Photo / dolgachov

Margins. Set your margins to 1 inch on all sides. Some word-processing programs have this as the default, but others might have slightly larger margins. As you set the margins, please do not try the old trick of increasing the margins as a way to try to make a paper longer—that tends to be obvious to most professors (we also know about extra-long titles, increasing line spacing, the period trick, etc.).

Font. Go with a standard font and size such as Times New Roman 12, Arial 11, or Calibri 11. With most programs, the font and font size are typically visible on the main toolbar.

Double-spacing. Most students *think* they know how to double-space, but some word-processing programs use spacing that is not-quite-double-spaced. The first step is to set the line spacing to double—after that, you must also make sure that your program is not adding additional space either before or after your lines. If you do not check on this, you may find that every time you hit <ENTER> or <RETURN> you will get a line space that is slightly larger than double-spaced.

Page 1—Title Page

Although the top page headers and page numbers are the very first things that you see in an APA-style paper, we are going to save our coverage of these until later. The reason is that the steps for doing this can be slightly complicated in certain word-processing software. So, let's start with some easier steps!

FIGURE 7.2

SHORTENED TITLE 1

Title Is Centered

John Q. Smith

University of Nevada, Las Vegas

PSY 200: Introduction to the Psychology Major

Professor Copeland

April 1, 2022

For a professional paper, you are going to include three key pieces of information on the first page—the title (be sure to capitalize it correctly), your professional name, and your institution (see Figure 7.2).[2] Start the title a few double-spaced lines down from the top and make the font bold for the title. We recommend typing "Title is Centered" (without the quotes) for your title—write it with that capitalization to remind you that all of the major words in the title should be capitalized here. Insert a blank double-spaced line beneath the title, and then on the following (double-spaced) line, type your professional name. Because there can be others out there who share your first and last name, use your full name, including any middle initials (American Psychological Association, 2020). After that, type your institution's name. Be careful not to use abbreviations, and also be mindful as to the proper way to write out the name. For example, one of your authors works at UNLV and that is written out as "University of Nevada, Las Vegas" (most people do not know about the comma in the name). For student papers, you may also include additional information on the lines below the affiliation. This includes the (a) course number and name, (b) instructor, and (c) assignment due date. In most cases, this information can be found in your course syllabus—yet another reason to check that syllabus (see our discussion of syllabi in a previous chapter)!

Make sure that all pieces of information are properly centered, and take your time to do this correctly. Do not try to line it up yourself manually (e.g., with spaces or Tabs) as it rarely turns out perfectly centered when you do it this way. Please use the center-align process in your software (usually this is as simple as clicking a button or icon in your top toolbar). A second error is that, in some cases, text ends up off-center (e.g., shifted slightly to the right) because an indent (e.g., Tab) was accidentally included before centering the text.

Inserting a page break. The final step for page 1 is to get to the top of page 2. Some of you might be tempted to repeatedly hit <ENTER> or <RETURN> until you reach page 2—

[2] APA style also includes an "Author Note" on page 1—full contact information for the authors, acknowledgments, any conflicts of interest, and the person to contact for questions. We left this out because the majority of our peers told us that they do not require this on student papers. However, feel free to include it if you wish.

FIGURE 7.3

SHORTENED TITLE	2

Abstract

This is a concise summary paragraph of the entire paper (do not indent).

please do not do this as this can lead to problems. For example, suppose that we did this but then had to go back to page 1 and add something else (e.g., maybe you decided to drop the title farther down a couple of lines). This small change on page 1 will knock everything on page 2 down as many lines as you added. This is problematic because we want a particular section header on page 2 to always be on the top line! So, to avoid accidentally knocking our upcoming page 2 section header from the top line of page 2, please insert a page break—this will jump you to the top of page 2 and it can prevent future problems.

Page 2—Abstract

If you thought that the title page was easy, then you will be pleasantly surprised to learn that page 2 is even easier (see Figure 7.3). On the top line, centered and in bold, type "Abstract" as that is the section header that goes here. The text for the abstract goes on the next double-spaced line down—it is important to note that, unlike traditional paragraphs that are indented slightly, this text should be left-aligned (not entirely to the left; after all, there is a 1-inch margin on the left side). Here, type some text to remind you what goes into the abstract—you should also include a reminder that this abstract paragraph is not indented. We recommend typing this: "This is a concise summary paragraph of the entire paper (do not indent)." At this point, we are going to jump to the top of page 3 by inserting another page break.

Page 3—The Body

Introduction. On the top line of page 3 (see Figure 7.4), centered and in bold, repeat the full title exactly as you typed it on page 1. On the next line, start a normally indented paragraph, and we recommend typing the following: "Introduce the topic and review the research literature (Lastname & Lastname, Year)." This paragraph represents your introduction, or literature review, section—because literature reviews include a lot of citations, we included one in the example text (NOTE: it corresponds with the reference example that we have you add on page 4). Keep in mind that, unlike most other sections of an APA-style paper, you DO NOT write "Introduction" above the section—you write the full title on the top line of page 3.

FIGURE 7.4

SHORTENED TITLE 3

Title Is Centered

Introduce the topic and review the research literature (Lastname & Lastname, Year).

Method

Participants

Describe the participants or subjects.

Materials

Describe the experiment materials in detail.

Procedure

Describe the step-by-step experiment procedure.

Results

Report the statistics and patterns.

Discussion

Explain the findings, describe limitations, and explore future directions.

Method. On the next line, type your next section header: "Method" (centered and in bold). Within this section, you are going to include three subsections that each have their own paragraph. The first subsection is "Participants" (left-aligned and bold)—on the line below that header include text for its indented paragraph by typing, "Describe the participants or subjects." The next subsection is "Materials" (left-aligned and bold); include the following indented text below: "Describe the experiment materials in detail." The third subsection is "Procedure" (left-aligned and bold). Beneath this, indent and type "Describe the step-by-step experiment procedure."

Results. On the next line, you will include the next section header: "Results" (centered and bold). Below this section header, type this reminder text (left-aligned and indented like a normal paragraph): "Report the statistics and patterns."

Discussion. The next section header is "Discussion" (centered and bold). On the following line, insert an indent and type a reminder of what goes in this section: "Explain the findings, describe limitations, and explore future directions." At this point, we are ready to jump to the top of the next page, so insert another page break!

FIGURE 7.5

SHORTENED TITLE 4

References

Lastname, F. M., & Lastname, F. M. (Year). Title of article: Pay attention to capitalization. *Title of Journal, volume number*(issue number), page number-page number. doi-or-url-if-available

Page 4—References

On the top line of page 4 (see Figure 7.5), add the section header "References" so that it is centered and in bold. On the next line, you are going to write out an example reference (as we noted in the previous module, we recommend avoiding the unreliable citation or reference generators online that can contain errors—Stevens, 2016; Zafonte, 2018). One tricky part of references is that, for each and every reference that you list, only the first line is left-aligned—non-first lines of each reference are indented (e.g., second line, third line, etc.). This is typically called a "hanging indent" (if you are not sure how to do this, see our tips for getting help in the next module).

We recommend the following example reference for your APA template, as you will most likely use journal articles as your sources. We tried to include subtle formatting tips in the various parts of this example reference:

Lastname, F. M., & Lastname, F. M. (Year). Title of article: Pay attention to capitalization. *Title of Journal, volume number*(issue number), page number-page number. doi-or-url-if-available

There are a number of other types of references that you might use in a paper, and every type you can think of is listed in the APA Publication Manual (American Psychological Association, 2020)—we also included a number of examples in the previous module. So, you might consider including examples of the more common types in your APA template. Also, do not forget that, when you write out a reference for a source, keep the authors in their original order (e.g., Venkatraman, 2010).

The Grand Finale—Headers and Page Numbers

There are slightly different APA style guidelines for the headers of professional papers and student papers. For professional papers, in the top header on every page you are going to include a running head (basically, a shortened version of your title written in all capital letters) aligned to the left, with page numbers aligned to the right. For student papers, unless your instructor requires a running head, you can just insert page numbers in the top header that are aligned to the right. Some word-processing programs make the headers and page numbers simple, but others make them more complicated.

We recommend including a running head in your APA template, and you can always delete it if your instructor does not require it. For your template, you might click in the top header space and type this: "SHORTENED TITLE" (set it so that it is left-aligned). In addition, insert a right-aligned page number on the same line in the header. This same header and page number setup should appear in the remaining pages of the paper.

Take-Home Message

We cannot emphasize this point enough—take the time now to create your very own APA template. Trust us, building a template now will save you time and effort later. Some of our students have told us that this was invaluable because they used it for papers throughout most of their psychology courses! One final thing to keep in mind is that, if you have to write a paper that is slightly more complicated, such as having more than one experiment or having even more levels of subheaders, you may have to make some adjustments to the formatting of your section headers in the body of your paper. Because that is beyond the scope of what we can cover here, we refer you to the APA Publication Manual for those formatting guidelines (American Psychological Association, 2020). And, finally, if you do not know how to do any of these formatting steps, please keep reading—we provide tips in the next module.

Action Steps

1. Follow the steps described previously to create your very own APA template. Save it where you will find it later because you are going to use this in future courses.
2. When you are assigned an APA-style paper in future courses, open this file and replace your reminder text with the actual text for your paper. However, because the basic formatting is completed, and you have reminders for the various sections, you will save yourself a lot of work, and hopefully some points, too (fewer deductions for formatting errors)!

7.5 COMPUTER SKILLS THAT YOU NEED TO KNOW

Your college courses will require you to use various types of common software—word processing (e.g., Google Docs, Word, Pages), spreadsheets (e.g., Google Sheets, Excel, Numbers), and presentations (e.g., Prezi, PowerPoint, Keynote). It is worth it for you to learn how to use these programs now so that you can focus your energy on the content of your papers,

iStock.com/Roman Didkivskyi

iStock.com/sefa ozel

data sets, and presentations instead. In addition, these programs are used by a large number of companies and organizations around the world. To put things into perspective, career advisors do not recommend listing proficiency in Microsoft Office as a skill on your résumé—this is because it is assumed that you already have those skills (e.g., Bahler, 2018; Hamer, 2019). We will provide some tips in this module, but if you do not know how to use these programs, take the time now to teach yourself!

Improving Your Word-Processing Skills

Very few people know how to do everything in word-processing software like Word, Pages, or Google Docs. Even though we have been using some of this software for years (or decades), we recognize that we can always learn new things. So, please, even if you think you know the basics, take your time to read this section and heed our advice to improve your word-processing skills. One key thing that we want to emphasize is that you can learn without having an instructor hold your hand through the process. So, become an independent learner and take some responsibility to teach yourself some basic skills! But, rest assured that, if you need assistance, most institutions will have computer labs or tech support staff available.

Word-Processing Skills You Need

We see too many students who try to get by in word-processing software by using their own (sometimes clunky) procedures instead of the ones that work best for the software. For example, as we mentioned in the previous module, a big mistake that we often see is that students will repeatedly hit <ENTER> or <RETURN> when they want to move to the next page. Although this can work, it can also lead to some annoying problems (use the advice from earlier and insert page breaks).

In Table 7.5, we included a list of some common formatting procedures that you should know—especially when you are trying to apply APA-style formatting rules to your paper (for a list of even more basic word-processing skills, see Gecawich, 2017). Even if you think that you are doing it properly, double-check to make sure that you are doing it right. For example, we noticed that, in some software, students think they are double-spacing correctly—however, unbeknownst to them, there are other settings that might need to be adjusted to make sure additional line spacing is not being added before or after a line.

In addition to knowing how to format correctly, it can be helpful to learn shortcuts. These can make you a lot more efficient in your word-processing software. For example,

TABLE 7.5

Important Formatting Procedures You Need to Learn for Software Like Word, Pages, and Google Docs

- Insert a page break
- Adjust margins
- Align text
- Bold, italicize, underline
- Line spacing
- Indents (and special types of indents)
- Inserting page numbers
- Adding a header or footer

instead of reaching for your mouse (or trackpad) and searching for the copy or paste icon, learn the keyboard shortcut for those actions. The more that you write, the more thankful you will be for knowing some shortcuts.

Here is another thing to keep in mind—please do not ignore or turn off the grammar/typo/proofreading options. And when you see a notification of a possible error, check it out—if there is indeed an error, fix it. Some word-processing software also includes another great proofreading option. If you turn on the option to show formatting marks (this is sometimes conveyed by the ¶ icon), you can check for proper spacing, tabs, and page breaks—we certainly use this when we are grading student papers for proper formatting!

Ways to Get Help

If you are unsure how to do something in your word-processing software, one piece of good news is that there are multiple ways to find solutions (see Table 7.6). One useful approach is to take advantage of the Help option in your software (this is typically located in the top taskbar). In addition to using the Help function, you can use web searches (e.g., Google) to ask questions about formatting procedures. It is likely that other people have had the same problem, so there may be advice (or a discussion) available on the web. When conducting a web search, we recommend including the software name along with your question or problem. Some simple examples of searches that we have conducted include

- "how to insert page break in word"
- "google docs different header on first page"
- "microsoft word special indent"

iStock.com/bymuratdeniz

TABLE 7.6

Top Ways to Find Help With Common Software Such as Word, Pages, or Google Docs

1. Use the Help function in the program
2. Search the web (e.g., "how to insert page break in word")
3. Search for YouTube video tutorials
4. Take a training course (there are many available online—you can search the web or visit the homepage of the software)
5. Visit a campus computer lab, or your Information Technology help desk, and ask for help

If you prefer to watch someone walk you through a procedure, you can also search for video tutorials. There are quite a few YouTube videos that we have watched. If you are very new to the software, you may find it useful to take an online course that walks you through the basics. For example, we checked on www.microsoft.com and found a lot of helpful training videos for their Office software.

Finally, if computer troubleshooting on your own is not a strong suit for you, there is always the option of asking another person for help. A good resource for students is to visit a campus computer lab and ask a worker for help. One word of warning, though—be careful when seeking help from a person who is not an expert with the software. They may give you advice that leads you astray.

Additional Computer Skills

When it comes to computer skills, most future employers are going to expect you to have the basics covered. So, if you have not done so already, you may want to work on your typing speed (see Logan, Ulrich, & Lindsey, 2016, for a comparison of different techniques) and familiarity with different types of computers (e.g., Macs, PCs). In addition, it is a good idea to practice solid workplace habits of backing up files, using quality passwords, being careful with links in emails, and properly managing privacy and security settings—after all, it only takes one careless employee to create a security problem.

Those are just the basics, though most employers expect more (e.g., Lederman, 2019). If you are considering work in any type of research or business setting, the ability to use spreadsheet software such as Excel, Numbers, or Google Sheets can be very helpful! A more-advanced skill to consider is the ability to program in a common language such as Java, Python, or C++. Unless you want to work as a programmer, you do not have to master the skill, but knowing the basics can be helpful in a lot of occupations. Along this line, you may also want to have some experience setting up a website or as a social media expert.

Take-Home Message

Your professors, future co-workers, and future bosses will assume that you know how to use software programs like those in the Microsoft Office suite. In fact, you will likely be using a word-processing program for your undergraduate courses right now. We recommend two things: (1) be aware of how you can learn to do something in these programs and (2) if you do not already know the basics, take the time to learn now!

Action Steps

1. Do not play the "ignorant" role when an instructor or boss asks you to do a specific task in common software programs like Microsoft Office or Google Docs (i.e., do not respond by asking them how to do it)—practice using this software now and figure out how to do the basics!
2. Search for word-processing shortcuts today, practice them, and then start using them every time you use that program.

7.6 PRESENTATION AND POSTER TIPS

In this module, we share some tips for giving a presentation. Presentations typically come in two styles—oral presentations or posters. Although some students seem to dread public speaking, we want to reassure you that you can get over that fear and you can do a great job. We provide a lot of tips in this module, and we hope that applying them will increase your confidence with giving a presentation (SPOILER ALERT: the most important tip is to practice, practice, practice!). Keep in mind that college courses are a great place for honing your speaking skills. So, use the tips here, and if you want to read more tips about presenting, check out Feldman and Silvia's (2010) book that presents tips in a very humorous way.

iStock.com/monkeybusinessimages

What to Include

Some of you might be wondering what you should include in a research presentation. Whether you are doing an oral presentation or a poster, the simplest advice is to use the sections of an APA-style paper as a guide—that is, start with a title, state your goal, and then review previous studies. If you are presenting a research proposal, include the proposed method, predicted results, and implications of the study. If you are presenting a completed research project, add in the actual method, results, and interpretations.

We also want to share an old piece of advice that you might have heard about presentations. First, tell the audience what you are going to cover. Next, cover your material. Then, at the end remind them of what you covered. Research can be complicated, so it helps the audience to provide them with a guide at the start and a reminder at the end of what was important.[3] Also, remember that, although you are highly familiar with your project, your audience might be learning about your topic for the very first time. In addition, whether you are in class or at a conference, your audience is going to be observing a lot of different posters or presentations—with all of that information, *your message* will only be memorable if it is reinforced to them!

Creating Oral Presentation Slides

Presentation software such as PowerPoint can be helpful, but when used incorrectly, it can have the potential to bore an audience (e.g., Tufte, 2003). There is a reason that people use the phrase "*Death by PowerPoint*" (see Eves & Davis, 2008). So, please heed our warnings here and avoid some common mistakes.

iStock.com/Whiteway

Our first rule for presentation slides and posters is that "less is more" when it comes to the amount of text (e.g., Beyer, 2011). Instead of filling up slides with text, consider focusing on images and graphs instead (e.g., Beyer, 2011). One reason for this is that, if you put text on your slides, your audience will spend their time reading instead of listening to you. Another reason to avoid a lot of text is that some presenters have a tendency to read their slides to the audience—this leads to a boring presentation because the audience could simply read the slides themselves. So, stick with a minimal amount of text—and, instead of reading the slides, *explain* the slides to the audience. We provide even more tips in Table 7.7.

TABLE 7.7

Some Key Things to Keep in Mind When Creating Your Presentation Materials

- Minimize the amount of text—less is more (consider focusing on images or graphs).
- Pick a good (large) font size.
- Have a high contrast between the font and background colors—think black font on white, not red font on blue (see Lane, 2019).
- Minimize the number of slides in a presentation (Eves & Davis, 2008).
- Although special effects might be fun, they can be distracting for an audience (Eves & Davis, 2008).
- If you are going to include (a small amount of) humor, remember to be tasteful with your jokes (to make sure that you will not offend anyone, run it past your grandmother first).
- Include a clear ending—we recommend including a slide that says "Thank you" (this will signify to your audience that you are finished).

[3] By the way, you may have noticed that we are using our own advice—our modules in this book are structured with an opening at the beginning and a take-home message at the end.

Are Notes Okay?

iStock.com/Steve Debenport

Our advice is to avoid notes if you can—in our view, the best presentations are those which are so well-practiced that the speaker looks comfortable and can engage with the audience. However, please do not try to wing it—these scenarios can turn into trainwrecks. If you feel more comfortable presenting with a set of notes, then go ahead and use them as a security blanket. You can use index cards, but another option is to use the presentation software for your notes (most allow you to do this). For your notes, you can create bullet-point highlights or use key phrases as prompts (e.g., "slow down here" or "explain diagram here").

If you are going to use notes, please be careful not to put too much text in them. When there is too much text, you might be tempted to read from your notes—and our advice is to avoid reading if at all possible. Presentations that are read tend to be less engaging because, in most cases, the reading tends to be less natural and more monotone. Also, presenters that read are looking down at their words instead of engaging and making eye contact with their audience!

Overcoming Glossophobia (Public Speaking Anxiety)

© Can Stock Photo / Aleutie

We have met quite a few people who tell us that they dislike giving presentations or speaking in front of a group of people. If this fits you, then rest assured that you are not alone. There are reports that people such as Gandhi and Thomas Jefferson disliked speaking in front of groups (e.g., Mochari, 2013).

In Table 7.8 we list some steps that you can take to minimize the anxiety that accompanies a presentation (e.g., Tsaousides, 2017).

TABLE 7.8

Strategies You Can Try to Help You Overcome a Fear of Presenting

- Avoid negative thinking
- Reframe the situation to make it seem less intimidating
- Use calming techniques (e.g., deep breathing)
- Remind yourself that presenting is a skill and that you can improve this skill
- Be prepared
- Practice, practice, practice!

One approach is to avoid negative thinking—instead of telling yourself that you "hate presentations because people are watching you," reframe the situation and remind yourself that many in the audience are probably not paying close attention. Another strategy is to use calming techniques that work for you—a common one is to control your breathing, typically with deep breaths. You can also try to remind yourself that public speaking, like most activities, is a skill and that you can improve by working at it. Building on this, one way to work on improving is to be prepared. Use the advice that we just provided to improve your slides and, most importantly, practice (more on this to follow)!

Practice, Practice, Practice!

Once you have your slides or poster ready, you must first practice your presentation. Practice it many times—present it to your family, present it to your roommate, present it in front of a mirror, or, if you are shy, present it to your dog—just be sure to practice. Even if you are planning to use notes, you must practice. We have seen *a lot* of presentations, and a practiced presentation is ten times better than one that has not been practiced (presentations that seem natural, like the speaker is winging it, are often the result of a lot of practice!).

What are the benefits of practice? First, you will have more confidence. Second, practicing will help you remember what you want to say—so practicing can help you ditch the notes. Third, practice can help you develop the skills involved in presenting effectively. For example, instead of reading or looking down, you can practice making eye contact with your audience. Finally, if you time yourself while practicing, you can adjust the presentation so that it fits better into the allotted amount of time—trust us on this, students who do not practice tend to go on much longer than they intend to speak.

Be Prepared for Technology or Poster Issues

Technology is great, but it can also fail us. One technology issue that you may encounter is that files saved in one software platform do not always open smoothly (or at all) on a different platform. So, consider saving your presentation in different formats (e.g., PPT, PDF, etc.). A second rule is to bring your presentation with you in different ways—you can email it to yourself AND bring it on a portable USB drive. A final rule is to be prepared so that you can, in a technology-nightmare scenario, give the talk without your slides. To do this, bring a printout of your slides so that you can use them to guide you through the talk—you might also take advantage of a dry erase board or chalkboard to sketch an important diagram or graph. Our point here is that you can overcome any tech obstacle if you are prepared.

© Can Stock Photo / duiwoy55

For poster presentations, there are also a number of ways that things can go wrong.

Here are some tips for avoiding some major problems that we have seen students experience:

iStock.com/asiseeit

- Pay attention to the size—most events will specify the maximum or recommended poster size dimensions (often 36 × 48), so always stay within those specifications!
- If you are traveling, you may have to carry your poster in a long poster tube (recommended) or print it on cloth (this is surprisingly effective) or you will have to get it printed when you arrive (NOT recommended because of the stress of things going wrong).
- Most conferences provide pins for hanging posters, but some do not—be prepared.

Use Presentations to Grow Your Network

Although class presentations are done to satisfy a course requirement, most other types of presentations (conferences, work settings) are done to share your work, educate people on a topic, network with others, and to potentially collaborate in the future. So, it is good to get into the following habits. First, at the end of your talk, share your professional contact information (i.e., your school email address) on your final slide. For example, you could write something like "Any questions? Contact me at jhouska29@school.edu." For posters, we recommend including your email at the end of your poster or a Quick Response (QR) code that links to a PDF version of your poster. In addition to that, be willing to let people take a photo of your poster.

© Can Stock Photo / Aleutie

Take-Home Message

Giving presentations using software such as PowerPoint is an expected skill of 21st-century students and workers. And, as more students become involved in undergraduate research, more and more students will gain useful skills such as thinking on one's feet and conveying complex information in a clear and concise manner. Even if you are terrified right now as you read about public speaking and formal presentations, know that you will get better at it through practice, practice, and more practice!

Action Steps

1. Ask your professors about opportunities to visit research poster sessions that are held at your institution. Visit a poster session and observe how more-senior students present and field questions.
2. If you are a research assistant or a member of a research team, ask your professor about opportunities to present (e.g., on campus or at a conference). One way to reduce the presentation anxiety is to collaborate with another student as presenters—that way you can divvy up the work and practice presenting together.

Student Clubs, Professional Organizations, and Conferences

8

8.0 MEET DHRUV

iStock.com/VikramRaghuvanshi

CHAPTER OUTLINE

Dhruv was approaching his final year in college and was starting to think about applying for jobs. He visited the school's career center to get advice, and one of the career counselors told him that his résumé was a bit light and that it would be better if he could list more experiences or skills. Dhruv thought about what he might do to remedy the situation. Unfortunately, he had missed out on summer internship opportunities. He could look for other internship positions, but there was no guarantee that he would land one for the fall. And, seeing as he had little interest in research, he did not want to join a research team. He was at a loss for what he should do.

The next week, Dhruv was talking to his friend Paul before class, and he mentioned his dilemma. Paul looked over the barren résumé, and he pointed out that there were no extracurricular activities listed. Paul suggested a simple solution—he told Dhruv that he was the new Psi Chi vice president and that they still needed to fill one of the student officer positions (for treasurer). Apparently, very few students had applied for an officer position this year. The best part, according to Paul, was that this kind of position would give Dhruv a variety of experiences that he might be able to talk about on future job interviews—leading a group, working with others, and managing a financial account. Paul's sales pitch worked—Dhruv decided to give it a shot!

Let's fast-forward to the following summer. This story has a happy ending in that Dhruv's action paid off. He landed an interview for a good organization, and during the interview, he was asked to talk about an example that demonstrated how he could work effectively with a team. Without hesitation, Dhruv talked about his experiences working on the Psi Chi leadership group to organize events, raise money, and bring in guest speakers from the community.

Why Did We Tell You This Story?

In our experience, students tend to focus on doing well in class as a way to prepare for their future careers. However, the classroom can be limiting in terms of the ways that you can develop certain skills that are valued by employers. One way to develop these skills is to get involved in co-curricular activities—in this module, we walk you through the benefits of joining (and, most importantly, actively participating in) psychology organizations and student clubs.

8.1 STUDENT CLUBS AND ORGANIZATIONS—THE IMPORTANCE OF THE CO-CURRICULAR

iStock.com/JasonDoiy

Some of the best learning experiences can be outside of the classroom, and educators have picked up on this. For example, high schools are building co-curricular opportunities (see Richmond, 2015, for an example) and college psychology courses are increasingly adding service learning options (e.g., Campbell & Oswald, 2018; Fleck, Hussey, & Rutledge-Ellison, 2017). In this chapter, we want to stress the importance of participating in a club or organization. For the most part, organizations are professional groups in a particular field for both students and professionals, whereas student clubs meet on college campuses and are typically restricted to student members. When we mention clubs and organizations to students, some are willing to hear us out, whereas others tell us that the idea sounds nice but they do not have time for them. So, our goal in this module is to make a case as to why you (and everyone else for that matter) should join clubs and organizations.

Benefits of Student Clubs

iStock.com/designer491

College clubs can benefit students in a number of ways (see Table 8.1). For starters, they tend not to cost much—some are free, some have a small upfront membership fee, and others have nominal dues. There are lots of different student clubs at most schools, and the topics or themes around which they are built will vary. Some are designed around enjoyment and fun, such as clubs for eSports, Ultimate Frisbee, or card games. Others can be political or socially aware, such as a political party group or an environmental group. Finally, other clubs can be based on academic interests, such as a pre-med or psychology club. Our discussion of benefits here is going to focus on the latter category, but they can apply to other types of groups as well.

Besides enjoying yourself, one of the biggest benefits of a student club is a chance to meet others who have similar interests as you as well as to meet others from different backgrounds. Most clubs will also have faculty advisors, so you can meet professors, too. As you will learn later in this book when we provide career and graduate school preparation advice, this is a form of networking that should not be overlooked—you can learn a lot from other people!

Speaking of learning, a second major benefit of student clubs is the chance to learn and grow. This should be obvious when you think about academic clubs—these groups typically host panels or guest speakers on various topics or they share opportunities that you might not have known about. However, even if you joined a club to play video games, you would hopefully be learning (e.g., tips, shortcuts, or strategies). Student clubs can be a great place to develop skills, especially if you are an active participant, such as becoming an officer in the club. Another example is that college radio is not just for communication majors—you can get involved and polish your public speaking skills! In student clubs, you may not realize it, but you are probably acquiring competencies such

TABLE 8.1

Top Benefits to Participating in a College Student Club

- A variety of options from which you can choose
- Most are low cost (or free)
- Networking—meet other students (and possibly faculty)
- Learning and developing skills (especially in leadership positions)
- Some clubs have opportunities for community service

as communicating with others, working well in groups, and perhaps leadership. Do not overlook these "soft skills" because they will serve you well, regardless of your future and individual interests (e.g., Appleby & Ferrari, 2013).

If we have not yet convinced you of the benefits of joining a student club, then we will try one more appeal. When you are an official member of a student group, you can legitimately list this status on a curriculum vitae (CV) or résumé. However, if you do this, we recommend that you only list clubs that you actively participated in, and be ready to talk (at a job interview) about what you gained through your experiences with that club.

Student Clubs—What Is the Time Commitment?

The level of engagement and time commitment will vary widely among student clubs. For instance, if you join your campus podcast club and host your own show, you are probably going to need to go digging for background information, plan your shows, and rehearse before you record it. This endeavor, understandably, will require a greater time commitment than a dance group. If you find yourself interested in serving your local community, student clubs participate in ongoing food pantry distributions, soup kitchens, and monthly assistance to homeless shelters. As you can see, there is a whole lot going on outside of class—see what your campus has to offer!

Another consideration is the club's formal or local expectations. Some clubs will meet often because of a mandate; there may be requirements in the club's bylaws or constitution. In other cases, the faculty advisor sets the expectations for regular meetings and the student officers enforce them. For example, some require that you attend a certain number of events to be deemed an active member, whereas others might not care how often you attend. There also might be different expectations depending on whether you are a club officer or simply a member. Our recommendation, though, is that, if you are going to join a club, you should try to attend as many events as possible.

Benefits of Organizations

The best reason for joining an organization is for the benefits and resources available to members. This might include books that can help with your professional development, videos with interesting talks (see American Student Government Association, 2019), or regular newsletters or trade magazines. Academic organizations will also regularly hold large meetings or research conferences for their members. Finally, some organizations will offer opportunities to apply for funding—this can include scholarships, funding for a research project, or possibly travel money for students who attend and present at a conference. Keep in mind that different organizations have different benefits, so examine them closely to see which ones can be most beneficial to you.

Another benefit we alluded to earlier is the opportunity to lead—this is not just for student clubs; many national, regional, and local organizations also have student officers. Besides academically oriented organizations, you might consider student government as it is where many students first get their start in formal leadership. But, there are many other leadership opportunities for college students. Depending on your campus culture, Greek life (fraternities and sororities) may be worth pursuing for the leadership possibilities and the community service activities (one of your authors can attest to the impact it had on his leadership; see Konnikova, 2014).

ShutterStock/Steve Heap

Organizations to Avoid

Let's finish this section with a warning—keep an eye out for organizations that, for all intents and purposes, are scamming you out of your money by asking you to pay membership dues but are not providing any real benefits in return (e.g., Williams, 2019; Wilson, 2017). For example, we have seen students receive official-looking notifications from honor societies that we (and our colleagues) have never heard of before. If you are ever unsure about the credibility of an honor society, consider the questions in Table 8.2.

Organizations—What Is the Time Commitment?

The time commitment for an organization is going to depend on whether it holds meetings or events on your campus like a student club. However, some have little to no time commitment because you are simply joining the organization by virtue of your major, GPA, or other status. As a member, you may spend some time browsing or taking advantage of the resources that are provided (our recommendation).

Take-Home Message

We highly recommend that most students join at least one or two student clubs or organizations (we will share some of our favorite psychology clubs and organizations in the forthcoming modules). The main reason to join student clubs is to meet other people who have similar interests as you. You can learn, grow, and, must we say it ... simply have some fun. Clubs and organizations can provide tangible benefits, be very enjoyable, help

TABLE 8.2

Questions to Ask If You Are Unsure About an Organization

- Does it have a chapter or presence on your campus?
- Is it a nonprofit?
- Does the organization have a history?
- Are there requirements in order to qualify (e.g., high grade point average)?
- Do your professors think highly of the organization?
- Are there clear (and useful) benefits for you?
- Is it certified by the Association of College Honor Societies (check their website at www.achsnatl.org)?

iStock.com/Olivier Le Moal

you develop soft skills, and sometimes be life-changing. In addition, being a part of student clubs can increase your sense of belonging—this is important because feeling like you belong at an institution can lead to increased persistence toward graduation (e.g., Supiano, 2018). So, please get involved!

Action Steps

1. Most colleges and universities will have lists of student clubs that are active on your campus. Browse through the different clubs that are available—you may be surprised to find some interesting ones that you might want to join!
2. As we discuss various psychology organizations and student clubs in this chapter, consider how each one can benefit YOU! If you are considering more than one club or organization, make a quick list of the ways in which YOU can benefit from each.

8.2 PSI CHI—THE INTERNATIONAL HONOR SOCIETY IN PSYCHOLOGY

If you are reading this book, then that means that you strive to become a high-achieving psychology student and maybe even a psychology superstar. One way in which you can be recognized for your efforts in psychology is to join the biggest and most popular psychology honor society—Psi Chi.[1] As you read this chapter, you will see that some organizations are open to anyone who is willing to pay a membership fee. However, being a member of Psi Chi is more meaningful because you have to earn membership by completing courses in psychology and having a high grade point average. Also, in addition to being a large professional organization, Psi Chi also acts like a student club as most institutions host their very own chapter. In this module, we will describe Psi Chi, how you can benefit from it, and why we STRONGLY recommend that you join (if you qualify)!

© Can Stock Photo/gpointstudio

[1]In addition to Psi Chi, there is a national psychology honor society for students attending community and junior colleges—Psi Beta (www.psibeta.org). If you are attending a community or junior college, we recommend that you look into this organization.

Psi Chi, the International Organization (www.psichi.org)

Psi Chi, which in recent years has expanded to become the *international* honor society in psychology, has been around in some form for approximately 90 years (Hogan & Takooshian, 2004)! Psi Chi has a one-time membership fee that grants you a lifetime membership. According to the "Welcome to Psi Chi" page of its website (the web address is listed previously, in the section header), Psi Chi has well-known members such as *Albert Bandura* (of "Bobo doll" fame), *B. F. Skinner* (operant conditioning), and *Philip Zimbardo* (Stanford Prison Experiment)—in addition, both authors of this book are members, too (at this point you are probably asking yourself, "Will the list of famous psychologists ever end?"). Most of Psi Chi's leaders are psychology professors who do a great job of making sure that the organization is specifically focused to help undergraduates in psychology (e.g., Hogan & Takooshian, 2004).

Psi Chi, the Local Chapter (Student Club)

One of the best parts of Psi Chi is that most colleges and universities that offer a psychology degree have a chapter of Psi Chi on their campus. A Psi Chi chapter is essentially a student club with student officers (such as president, vice-president, and treasurer). Both of us have served in the role of campus faculty advisor for Psi Chi and would highly recommend that you get involved!

Chapters welcome new groups of incoming members by holding induction ceremonies every year (or every semester). Some chapters hold events on a variety of topics, such as what type of research is happening on campus, which research teams are looking for student volunteers, and how to properly prepare application materials for graduate school. Many chapters bring in speakers (either professors or members of the community) to present on topics that students want to learn about. Chapters may organize social events and mixers so you can get to know your fellow psychology high-achievers. Finally, many chapters take part in community service events or organize trips to a nearby regional research conference. The activities at your institution may differ depending on local traditions, the current student officers, member preferences, and the faculty advisor. We not only recommend that you join, but we also recommend that you get involved as an officer. And gaining nuggets of wisdom from a faculty advisor is not so bad either.

Starting a chapter (or revitalizing a neglected one). If your institution does not have a Psi Chi chapter, check out the Psi Chi website for guidelines for starting a new chapter! Also, if your chapter has fallen on hard times with minimal activity and involvement, you can find tips for revitalizing your chapter (e.g., Shaw, 2004). You can also get new ideas by checking out "Chapter Activities," a segment that regularly appears in the *Eye on Psi Chi* magazine. In addition, Kukucka et al. (2016) provide a lot of good ideas by describing a summary of an academic year (August through April) of events and activities for their chapter. As you can see, reviving a dormant chapter of Psi Chi need not be a daunting task—you have many resources at your disposal, and likely other students and faculty who would support your initiative!

Benefits to Joining Psi Chi

In addition to participating in a local chapter of Psi Chi on your campus, there are a lot of other benefits to joining (see Cannon, 2018, for his top reasons; also, other benefits are listed on the Psi Chi website). As we noted earlier, Psi Chi is geared toward undergraduates, so these benefits are for students like you (see Table 8.3). In fact, if you are an undergraduate and are planning to only join one psychology organization, then this is the one we recommend!

For those of you who want to learn more about careers or graduate school, then Psi Chi has your back. They have a Career Center on their website with a lot of features. For example, they include psychology-related career listings and advice for career preparation. In their *Eye on Psi Chi* magazine, we counted at least five career articles for psychology students in the 2018 year alone (e.g., Hettich, 2018; Thomas, 2018). They also provide a number of tips for graduate school preparation on their website and in *Eye on Psi Chi* articles (e.g., Thompson & Fitzgerald, 2017).

iStock.com/Olivier Le Moal

Do you like money? Well, Psi Chi advertises research grants, travel grants, scholarships, and awards on their website. We elaborate on this later in this book, but we want to point this out now—unlike other psychology organizations who mainly advertise funding for graduate students and professors, most of Psi Chi's funding is for undergraduates! The research and travel money can come in handy when you attend the Psi Chi events that are held at a lot of major psychology research conferences (we discuss conferences in more detail later in this chapter).

TABLE 8.3

Top Benefits of Joining Psi Chi

- This is a legitimate honor society—joining shows that you are a high-achieving psychology student.
- There are funding opportunities (research grants, travel grants, scholarships) for undergraduates.
- The organization provides resources for career and graduate school preparation.
- If you participate in your institution's chapter of Psi Chi, you can participate and reap the benefits of participating in a student club (see our discussion of these benefits in the previous module).
- You can purchase Psi Chi graduation regalia so that you can stand out at commencement.

Take-Home Message

If your academic accomplishments meet Psi Chi's requirements, then we strongly recommend that you join and get involved with Psi Chi! Undergraduate members become plugged in to the broader world of psychology outside their institution, and if your school's chapter is active, members can connect more deeply with other psychology superstars—both students and faculty. If your local chapter has fallen dormant or is not as vibrant as it could be, then take the initiative to bring it back to life. It is likely that you can find psychology professors in your department who have had positive Psi Chi experiences and will want to support your energies.

Action Steps

1. Check to see if your department hosts a Psi Chi chapter (affiliated with the international organization) or possibly a Psychology Club (not affiliated with it). In some cases, a department may have both types of clubs—the former is for students who qualify and the latter is typically for students who want to be involved with a psychology club but do not (yet) qualify for Psi Chi.
2. Check the Psi Chi website (www.psichi.org) and also check with your campus chapter to see if you qualify for membership—if you qualify, then join today (seriously, do this)!

8.3 NATIONAL AND INTERNATIONAL PSYCHOLOGY ORGANIZATIONS

When it comes to joining psychology organizations, Psi Chi is our top recommendation—but, there are other psychology organizations that you should consider as well. In this module, we will cover two large psychology organizations. There are quite a few benefits to joining these organizations—this includes access to magazines, journals, books, and conferences. But, as we noted in other sections of this chapter, make a decision to join only if it will benefit you (we think that every student should join at least one).

APA and APS

The two largest professional organizations in psychology are

- American Psychological Association (APA)—www.apa.org
- Association for Psychological Science (APS)—www.psychologicalscience.org

APA has been around for over 120 years (Evans, Sexton, & Cadwallader, 1992) and it is extremely large—according to its website, APA is a national organization with over

100,000 members! In contrast, APS (its original name was the American Psychological Society) was founded 30 years ago (West, 2008) and on its website it is described as an international organization with more than 35,000 members. Both organizations include members from a wide variety of topic areas in psychology, covering almost every area in psychology. A small distinction between these organizations is that APA has a reputation for having a slightly bigger focus on clinical and applied psychology, whereas APS has a broad focus on experimental areas (e.g., social, cognitive, developmental, etc.). But, do not dismiss APA if you are interested in psychological science—APA has a number of divisions that focus on experimental areas; by the same token, APS has plenty of coverage of clinical topics—for example, check out the APS journal *Clinical Psychological Science*.

Benefits of Joining APA and APS

Journals, magazines, and books. At this stage of your education, you might consider joining both organizations! If you explore their websites (the addresses are listed previously), you will see that APA and APS publish popular peer-reviewed journals such as *Psychological Review* and *Psychological Science* (respectively). APA regularly sends its members *Monitor on Psychology* magazine and APS provides its members with *Observer* magazine. APA also publishes a large selection of books, many of which are relevant to students and that build upon the themes of this book. For example, they publish the *Publication Manual of the American Psychological Association* (American Psychological Association, 2020) that describes the official rules for APA-style formatting.

Career information and funding opportunities. In addition, both websites now have extensive information about careers in psychology that can be useful for both undergraduate and graduate students. Both organizations also advertise research and travel grants as well as awards. Although most of these are aimed toward graduate students or professors, some of these are applicable to students at the undergraduate level. We strongly encourage you to look through the awards and grants information on these websites—but keep in mind that these are typically only available to members of the organization (a big reason that you should join!).

Conferences. Both APA and APS hold annual research conferences, usually taking place in the summer or late spring. These events tend to be extremely large with days of research presentations, research posters, and well-known speakers. It is basically the equivalent of a music festival but for psychology nerds.[2] Undergraduates are welcome to attend these conferences, as the talks are interesting and there are usually events geared toward students. For example, the APS Student Caucus (known as the "APSSC") regularly holds panels on student topics, such as applying to graduate school, surviving graduate school, and finding careers in psychology—both authors of this book have participated in these panels and can vouch for their usefulness!

Although we have described the good things about APA and APS conferences, there can be some negatives (from a student perspective). First, because they rotate to different cities across the country, an annual conference might not be nearby—so, there

[2]We like this comparison because there have actually been concerts at APS conferences (which were not bad, considering that the band consisted of psychology professors)!

may be significant travel costs to get there (TIP: see the Past and Future Convention pages on the APA and APS sites to get an idea of conference locations). In addition to the expenses associated with planes, trains, and automobiles, these conferences may have high registration fees. Finally, these conferences tend to be huge events, so, if you are not comfortable with crowds, they might not be a good fit for you. If all these points have gotten you down, do not worry—in the next module we will describe some other research conference options you might consider!

iStock.com/furtaev

Take-Home Message

APA and APS provide student members opportunities to develop professionally. Both publish journals and magazines, and they both maintain websites chock-full of useful information for students. They also host large psychology festivals (also called annual research conferences or "conventions"). Keep in mind that, in order to present at one of these conferences, it is likely that you will have to be a member. Finally, these organizations have low student membership fees (the student fees are MUCH lower than what they charge faculty)—so, it may not be a bad idea to join one (or both) of these organizations.

Action Steps

1. Browse the APA and APS websites—check them out today! There is a lot of information on both websites, so consider setting aside some time so that you can see whether one of them, or possibly both, would be good for you to join.

2. If you can only afford to join one of these organizations, create a list of the benefits from each organization that you value the most. Then use your list to compare the organizations and to make a decision as to which you might join. A final point is to keep your eye out for special opportunities—we have seen the occasional advertisement that includes big discounts or even free membership for a year.

8.4 REGIONAL, LOCAL, AND SPECIALTY PSYCHOLOGY ORGANIZATIONS

In addition to the major psychology organizations that we just discussed in the previous module, there are smaller ones as well. Some of these are regional or local and are centered around a specific geographical location, whereas others focus on a specific

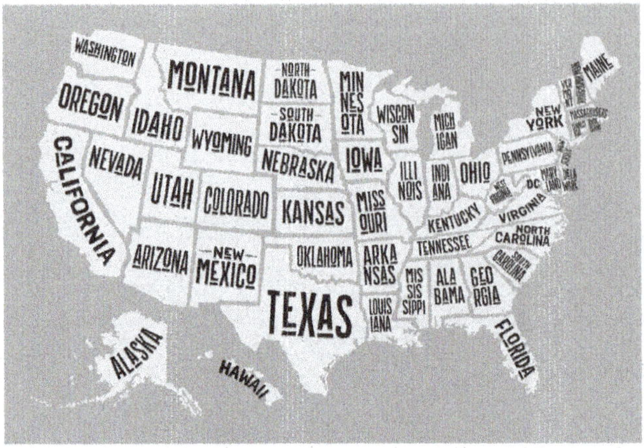

© Can Stock Photo/FoxysGraphic

subfield of psychology. As we noted in the previous module, one potential drawback to national or international organizations is that some people might not feel comfortable within such a large organization. For some people, there can be advantages to being a part of a smaller group. We start this module by describing regional and local psychology organizations, as well as some possible benefits to joining one of these organizations. After that, we describe organizations dedicated to particular subfields in psychology and why some of you might benefit from joining one of them.

Regional Psychology Organizations

Here is a list of some of the different regional psychology organizations along with their current web address:

- Eastern Psychological Association (EPA)—www.easternpsychological.org
- Midwestern Psychological Association (MPA)—www.midwesternpsych.org
- New England Psychological Association (NEPA)—www.newenglandpsychological.org
- Rocky Mountain Psychological Association (RMPA)—www.rockymountainpsych.com
- Southeastern Psychological Association (SEPA)—www.sepaonline.com
- Southwestern Psychological Association (SWPA)—www.swpsych.org
- Western Psychological Association (WPA)—www.westernpsych.org

For most institutions, it should be pretty clear which regional organization fits. Geographically speaking, a school in New York fits in EPA, a school in Florida falls under SEPA, and a school in California would be in WPA. However, some states overlap more than one region—for example, one of our schools, which is located in Nevada, participates in both RMPA and WPA. If you are unsure about which region is connected with your institution, check with your professors.

Student-friendly conferences. These organizations hold annual research conferences that are usually great for undergraduates (e.g., Dunn, 2018)—an added bonus is that the registration fees are typically much lower than for APA or APS. One reason we recommend them is that they tend to be smaller and less intimidating than the gigantic national or international conferences, where an undergraduate might feel lost among the crowd. A second reason is that we regularly see undergraduates presenting research at regional conferences—usually at poster sessions. A third reason is that there are usually events at these regional conferences that are meant specifically for undergraduates—sometimes these are sponsored or held by Psi Chi.

Finally, regional conferences tend to be good fits for undergraduates because of convenience. These regional conferences tend to be close by, possibly within driving distance of your institution. Most of these organizations rotate their conference to different cities within their regions (e.g., EPA has historically rotated among New York City, Boston, and Philadelphia), but some tend to stick with a major city in a centralized location for its region (e.g., MPA typically meets in Chicago).

Student benefits. One drawback to the regional organizations is that they usually do not offer as many benefits as Psi Chi, APA, and APS. For example, there are few, if any, books, magazines, or professional development resources offered to members. It is really all about the annual conference and what attendees can take away from it. Because of that, our recommendation is not to join unless you plan to attend or present at a regional conference (in which case you should definitely join!).

Local Psychology Organizations

If the international, national, and regional psychology organizations are not enough for you, then you should also keep an eye out for local psychology organizations. Often, these are state-based or, in Canada, province-based. These organizations typically offer student memberships and may host their own conference or annual meeting. Because there can be variability as to how much these organizations can benefit students (e.g., some are more focused on professionals), check with the professors at your institution before you join.

Specialty Organizations and Divisions

The international, national, regional, and local psychology organizations that we have discussed thus far (in this module and in the previous module) typically welcome people with interests in any area of psychology. One potential drawback is that including so many areas of psychology can sometimes make it difficult to find resources, publications, conference presentations, or people that share your specific interests. Because of that, APA has a breakdown of nearly 60 divisions (apadivisions.org) and there are also more specialized organizations that focus on a particular subfield of psychology. Some examples include the Society for Neuroscience, Association of Behavioral and Cognitive Therapies, Society for Personality and Social Psychology, and Psychonomic Society—and there are many more out there! These organizations tend to have more professors and graduate students as members, but if you are highly immersed into a psychology subfield, you may want to talk with a faculty mentor as to whether membership or attending one of these specialty conferences can be beneficial for you.

Take-Home Message

If attending a national or international conference is not practical, then regional or local conferences can also be valuable—and at a fraction of the cost with a less-intimidating crowd! Students often return from these events even more energized about psychology, so we highly recommend attending, if feasible. For those of you who are diving deeply into a psychology subfield, a possibility is to look into the more specialized psychology organizations and APA divisions. However, as we noted previously, there is something important to keep in mind—unlike Psi Chi, APA, and APS, the organizations described in this module may not have a lot of general resources for students (e.g., career or graduate school preparation). The main benefit of the regional and local organizations tends to be the student-friendly conferences; for the specialty organizations, the main benefit is immersion into that subfield (including the cutting-edge research being conducted).

Action Steps

1. Determine which of the regional or local psychology organizations is connected to your institution. As we said earlier, you can look on the web or you can ask a professor in your department. At that point, look on the organization's website to see where and when the next conference is occurring. Here is one helpful tip if you are unsure about planning a conference trip alone—it is not uncommon to find Psi Chi members who are planning to attend a regional or local conference, so reach out to them and ask if any members or officers are planning to go.
2. If you are highly focused in a particular subfield of psychology, check with professors or graduate students with whom you work to see if there are any specialty organizations that you should consider.

8.5 ATTENDING A PSYCHOLOGY CONFERENCE AND DOING IT RIGHT

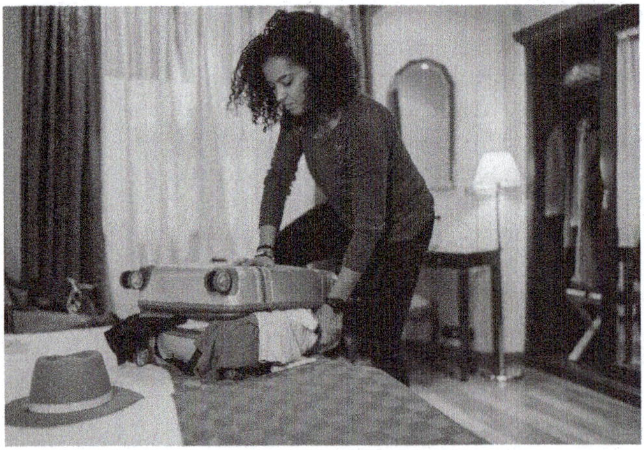
iStock.com/martin-dm

We both love to travel—and money spent on experiences is better than money spent on stuff (e.g., Dunn & Weidman, 2015)! But, before we started "living the dream" as college professors who can afford an occasional trip, much of our traveling consisted of attending psychology conferences. Although business travel is much different from a vacation, there tends to be time to see a tourist trap or two. So, remember that you too can reap the benefits of travel as you develop professionally at academic conferences. This module is designed to introduce you to some of these benefits, provide tips on preparing for conferences, how to get the most out of them when you are there, and some ways to follow up afterward with people that you meet.

Who Can (or Should) Attend?

Conferences can be a great opportunity for any psychology student—and there are a lot of options for you. As we noted in the previous modules, there are the large conferences held by the American Psychological Association and the Association for Psychological Science, the student-friendly regional or local (state-based) conferences, and more specialized conferences (see Table 8.4). In addition, there are also conferences specifically meant for undergraduate research—for example, there is a list of undergraduate psychology conferences on the Council of Undergraduate Research website (https://www.cur.org).

Obviously, if you are presenting research (or co-authoring a presentation), you should attend a conference. However, even if you are not presenting, you should still consider attending one. Conferences are a great way for students to learn about current research studies, attend an event that is geared specifically toward undergraduates (e.g., a Psi Chi event), meet new people from other institutions (students and professors), form stronger bonds with students from your current institution (who are also attending), or learn about graduate programs (e.g., Dunn, 2018).

Before the Conference

iStock.com/marcogarrincha

As we noted in the last module, take your time and pick the conference that is right for you. You might have to take into account the date, location, and type of organization, but choose a conference that works for you. After you register for the conference (look for early-bird registration discounts) comes travel planning. And, remember, due to the positive effects of anticipation, the time before a trip might just be the best part (e.g., Dunn, Gilbert, & Wilson, 2011)!

If you have never attended a conference, you may be wondering how to dress. We recommend dressing nicely—you do not have to wear a suit, but remember that the privilege of presenting in jeans and sneakers is reserved for tenured professors (for more on the inverse relationship between status and attire in academia, see Cham, 2011). Business casual clothing should be fine. If you want

TABLE 8.4

Psychology Conference Options That Students Might Consider

- National or international organizations such as APA or APS
- Regional psychology organizations
- Local (state-based) psychology organizations
- Specialty organizations (typically based on a psychology subfield)
- Psychology undergraduate research conferences

to get another perspective for what to bring with you, read Wong's (2016) tips for what to pack for a conference.

Saving Money

One way to reduce costs is simply to be frugal. There are many travel sites to help you find good airfares—also, check to see if it might be cheaper to drive to a conference rather than fly (but do not forget about gas and parking fees). You can also look for hotels (or other accommodations) that are within walking distance to the conference hotel, as you can sometimes find options that have lower rates (but, check to see if the conference hotel offers a discount to conference attendees).

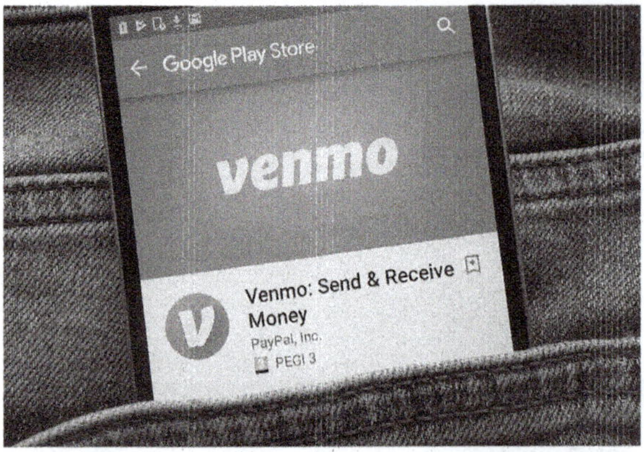

Piotr Swat/ ShutterStock.com

Check with your chapter of Psi Chi (or your Psychology Club) to see if other students are planning to attend a conference. If you are traveling to the conference with friends or other students from your school, you might consider carpooling or splitting a room. We have heard many tales of undergraduates (and grad students alike) who have planned awesome road tips and shared hotel rooms to save on travel costs (these can be the types of college experiences that you will remember). If you are going to do this, be sure that you are comfortable with your travel companions.

In addition to our earlier tips, there are other ways to defray some of the costs (e.g., Morgan, 2007). First, check with your department, an undergraduate research office at your school, or your local chapter of Psi Chi—one of those organizations might have funds to help undergraduates pay for conference travel. If there is money, keep in mind that most of the time it will be prioritized for students who are presenting at the conference, but you never know unless you ask. Another potential source of funding is to check the website of the organization that is hosting the conference or possibly the Psi Chi website—they sometimes offer travel grants (usually for students who are presenting).

Plan Ahead—Download the Conference App

Most conferences will have the conference program available on a downloadable app—if not, the schedule will be posted on the conference website or in a booklet. Before you go to the conference, skim through the program to see which talks seem interesting to you, and take note of which ones you want to attend (Fleck, 2018). If you are going with other students from your school, do not feel obligated to attend the talks that they want to hear—go to the ones that interest YOU and, trust us, you will have plenty of time to hang out with your friends.

At most conferences, talks occur approximately every 15 minutes, and there are likely multiple rooms holding presentation sessions simultaneously. You are allowed to drop in and listen to a talk, and then leave afterward—in other words, you do not have to stay in the same room for hours! But remember, if you are going to enter and exit a room, do so with respect to the speakers and other audience members. Arrive before a talk begins, and then leave after the question-and-answer portion has ended—it is similar to going to the movies; no one likes "that person" who walks in late or disturbs others by leaving in the middle.

Meet "Rock Stars" of Psychology and Lesser-Known Professors (Like Us!)

iStock.com/stocksstudioX

One behavior that you may notice at a conference is name tag viewing. Because most conference attendees are strangers, some people hope that they will recognize a name that they learned about in class. This is okay, but please try to be polite by smiling and making eye contact as well. If you do not want to spend your time name tag viewing, you can feel better knowing that some conferences hold special sessions where students have a chance to interact with well-known researchers. Some of these sessions involve sitting around a table for a casual conversation, and others invite a panel of researchers to answer questions from the audience. Do not be nervous if you get the chance to meet a psychology "rock star" (Palmer, 2016)—just have a normal conversation.

Although it can be exciting to see and possibly meet "rock stars," you can also look for researchers who study topics that interest you. If you are exploring graduate programs, this can be an opportunity for you to interact with a potential mentor. So, do not be afraid to talk with researchers—poster sessions usually work best for this because they are designed for people to have conversations about research.

Presenting

iStock.com/Kritchanut

Presenting a poster or talk at a research conference can be a very satisfying experience for students (Potter, Abrams, Townson, Wake, & Williams, 2010)—it is also a nice topic to discuss during a graduate school interview! Keep in mind that, in order to present at a conference, you have to be involved with research—you need to have an original study that includes analyzed data and an understanding of related studies (in most cases, students will present a study that is co-authored with a professor). Presenting research can lead to improved communication skills and increased confidence (e.g., Potter et al., 2010).

If you are presenting, then it is extremely important for you to practice beforehand (e.g., Palmer, 2016)—and think of it this way, practicing means that you are more likely to do well and have a positive experience! If you want to feel more at ease, check out an undergraduate's perspective of creating, practicing, and presenting a poster (Bivens, 2010) or research talk (Adler, 2010).

Go Out and See Some Sights

As we noted in the opening of this section, one perk of attending a conference is the chance to visit a city. If you visit Chicago, get some deep-dish pizza; in Seattle, visit Pike Place Market; in New Orleans, spend some time in the French Quarter. You do not have to do those activities per se—our point is to get out and spend some time in the city. Most conferences last a few days, so if there is time before or after a conference, or possibly in the evening, go have some fun. But, be smart about it—do not go out until 3:00 a.m. when you know that there are talks that morning (or worse, your plane leaves that morning). Also, remember that the whole point of your trip was to *attend the conference*, so do not play hooky and skip out on large portions of it—after all, it is first and foremost a work (or educational) trip, not a vacation.

Reflect on Your Experience

As you return from a research conference, we recommend that you do a few things:

- First, if you met someone who made a big impression on you, consider following up with a short email thanking the person for the information or advice, or possibly connect on a site like LinkedIn. Do not do this with every single person you met, just the ones with whom you had meaningful interactions.
- Second, jot down any ideas you may have had—possibly a research idea, potential graduate program, research topic you want to read more about, or maybe a career possibility—if you do not write them down, you might forget them.
- Third, if you found an interesting book or two while browsing the selections displayed at most poster sessions, go on the web and order a copy.
- Finally, if you received any help with your preparation or travels—such as funding or guidance from a professor—consider writing a short thank-you note.

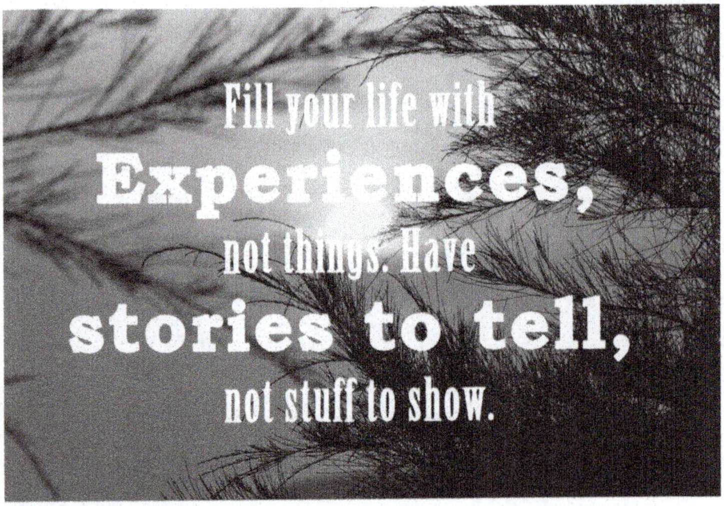

Nokuro/ShutterStock.com

Take-Home Message

Conferences are a great, and often overlooked, learning experience for undergraduates. Use the information in this chapter to select a conference and plan your trip. You can learn about exciting topics, meet researchers, connect with students from other schools, and gather a bunch of free items that are available (both of us have collected way too many stress toys in the shape of a brain). Savor the events leading up to your conferences, but don't forget to do the requisite preparations to ensure you get the most out of them!

Action Steps

1. Start exploring the possibility of attending a conference now! The first step is to find out when and where the next ones are taking place—explore the websites of the major psychology organizations as well as your regional or local psychology organization(s).
2. Ask about funding for conferences. At some institutions, your local Psi Chi or Psychology Club may offer money for student presenters. Similarly, student government or psychology departments may be in a position to defray some costs of attendance. Of course, your mileage may vary! So, do express your interest and ask around campus. What is there to lose? You might just find a source of funding!

8.6 GET INVOLVED—DO MORE THAN SIGN UP!

iStock.com/asiseeit

As we have progressed through this chapter, we hope that you have seen some of the benefits to joining student clubs and organizations. We also hope that you have started to think about or explore some of the possibilities that are available to you—this includes the organizations that we have discussed thus far as well as clubs at your institution. One thing that we want to emphasize is that, in order to get the most out of your memberships, you want to get involved! So, rather than joining a bunch of groups, we recommend joining fewer but taking advantage of what they have to offer you (e.g., Newport, 2008). Keep reading to find out what we mean (see Table 8.5).

TABLE 8.5

Our Top Suggestions for Getting the Most Out of Student Clubs

- Step one is to join (but too many students stop here—keep going!).
- Step two is to show up to events or meetings.
- Step three is to interact with others (ask questions, learn from their experiences).
- Step four is to build meaningful relationships.
- Step five is to work on skill development (consider a leadership position).

Show Up and Learn

When students come to us for research or graduate school advice, one of our first questions is, "Did you join Psi Chi?" Most answer affirmatively but then tell us that they have not attended any events or meetings. This is disappointing for us to hear because one of the big reasons to join a group like Psi Chi is to attend the events and learn. A good chapter of Psi Chi is one that holds events with information on topics that students like you care about. This can include careers, graduate school planning, finding internships, and getting involved with research. So, do not just sign up—show up, too!

Show Up and Talk

Another reason to attend events is to network—networking is not some fancy way of connecting that is only meant for professionals. Networking can be as simple as talking to and meeting other people, who might potentially help each other in some way. For example, if you are a sophomore or junior, it might be a good idea to network with seniors who have been in your position and who are actively in the process of applying for jobs or graduate programs. Where is a great place to find people like this? In student clubs, where you all have common ground (e.g., an interest in psychology).

There is one key to networking like this, though—you cannot go and sit quietly. If you do, you will never meet anyone. Instead, chat with the people around you. Or, even better, find the club officers (or possibly the faculty advisor) and strike up a conversation.

Develop Skills

Instead of simply joining—or even joining and just attending—you might give serious thought to taking a leadership role in a club or organization. Newport (2005, p. 25) goes so far as to say that "Average students join extracurricular organizations. And winning students *run* extracurricular organizations." One of the reasons for this is that a leadership role can help you to develop and demonstrate soft skills, such as managing people, as well as more basic skills like greeting others and having conversations with people you do not know (Newport, 2008).

Building on these ideas, Appleby and Ferrari (2013) reached out to college alumni who had served as Psi Chi officers (e.g., president, treasurer). They asked these alumni if there were skills that they developed as a club officer that helped after graduation in a career or graduate school. Not surprisingly, leadership and working effectively with others were listed by many respondents. Alumni also listed communication, organization, managing time, solving problems, and learning to function effectively in a system. The good news is that these skills just happen to have a lot of overlap with the skills that many employers value (e.g., Hettich & Longnecker, 2015; Slattery & Forden, 2014)!

Some of you may be cringing right now about the thought of campaigning for an officer position and you might not think that you are prepared for a position. Unfortunately, because of this type of thinking, many students do not even put themselves out there for leadership positions. But, keep in mind that most student leaders grow into their roles through mentoring and training by past leaders and advisors—so, you do not need a ton of experience. So, give it a shot—you might be pleasantly surprised.

Take-Home Message

College is a great place to explore your interests because most campuses have a lot of opportunities to participate in clubs, and majors like psychology have professional organizations that you can join. If you are going to participate in a few activities, please do it because you find them interesting and so that you can develop skills (e.g., Newport, 2008). Simply listing clubs and organizations in your application materials can help fill up space on a CV or résumé, but the big take-away should be to enjoy yourself, learn, and develop skills and to better connect with people at your institution (or in your field).

Action Steps

1. Think about clubs and organizations for the resources you can obtain, knowledge you can learn, and skills that you can develop.
2. Brainstorm ideas for what student clubs and organizations you might consider. If your list is longer than three or four, pare the list down so that you can focus on the ones that interest you the most and from which you can benefit the most.

8.7 OTHER CO-CURRICULAR RESOURCES

At this point, some of the key resources on psychology clubs and organizations should be apparent (this book, your professors, and organization websites). But, what about the multitude of co-curricular possibilities? Is there an office for all of that on campus? The good news is that, yes, there just might be one on your campus that goes by a name such as *student life*, *student activities department*, or *student engagement office*. In addition, an office like this might be useful if you find yourself in a position where you want to start a brand-new club—for example, you might discover that there is a large group of students who want to get together to discuss neuroscience research articles, but no club exists for that activity.

Learning From Others

As we close this chapter, let us consider one last idea. Have you ever been in the presence of greatness? That is to say, someone who has a certain amount of productivity, magnetism, or positive energy about them? How about a charismatic leader, thinker, researcher, speaker, or entrepreneur whom you respect? This could be someone on your campus, a relative, someone in your future career field, an alumna (or alumnus) from your school, a family friend, an officer in a psychology organization, or someone you read about online. Take a minute and write down a few people that come to mind—*seriously, write down a few names*; we do not mind waiting a minute while you write them down.

Now, after each of their names, write down a skill or ability you admire about each person. In other words—what is that they can do (or have done) that one day you would like to do or accomplish yourself? Is the person a good leader? A prolific writer or speaker? Great at interacting with others? Sit on this list for a day or two, and add to it or revise it as necessary.

Once you have let your list breathe a bit, decide which person you will contact first! You might be thinking to yourself, "Huh? What? Why?" Now hear us out ... it is very likely that these successful people whom you greatly respect have advice they would be willing to share with you. Sure—it is possible that these busy, successful people will decline. But, if they do, what will you have lost in the process (compared to what nuggets of wisdom you might gain if they do respond)?

So, use your internet sleuthing skills to find the person's email or contact information. Next, use the tips from Table 8.6 to help you compose and refine the message that you are going to send (e.g., Hall, 2019; Vozza, 2016). To help, we provided a simple example here:

> *"Dear [insert person's name here],*
>
> *I have been learning about ways to get the most out of my education as a psychology student at [insert your institution's name here]. Because you [insert the behavior or accomplishment you admire here], I was hoping to pick your brain about things I could do in college to [insert how you would like to improve or the behavior you would like to demonstrate].*
>
> *If you have a few pieces of advice (or action steps I should take) to share with me, you can simply reply to this email. Or, if you prefer, let me know when might be a convenient time for you to chat for a few minutes with me (I am willing to buy you a coffee).*
>
> *Sincerely,*
>
> *[insert your name]*
>
> *[insert your email address],*
>
> *[insert your phone number]."*

That's it—proofread and then send it. As you await the response, here are a few things to keep in mind. Do not be shocked by a non-response if your message is out of the blue to someone you know only superficially or not at all. If that happens, try the next person on your list (do not badger anyone with repeated attempts at contact). However, sometimes you just might be surprised to get a response from someone you do not know. If you already

TABLE 8.6

Tips to Increase the Probability That You Will Get a Response to Your Email

• Make it clear that it is a personalized message (and does not look like a generic email sent to a bunch of people—be transparent about why you are contacting him or her).
• If you have a question, then be direct and clearly ask it (do not be too vague).
• Avoid rambling—be concise and to the point.
• Do not try to write with overly impressive vocabulary—keep it simple.
• Use a clear and informative subject line.
• Proofread it before you send it.

have a rapport with a person, the likelihood that you will have that email conversation or a cup of coffee might be pretty good.

Here are some additional pieces of advice about this process. First, *do your homework*! For instance, if you send your university president an email about how to develop your leadership abilities, think through what you will share and ask when you do meet and chat (or correspond via email). For instance, what is your plan to build your co-curricular transcript (Reed, 2016; Rutter & Mintz, 2016)? What questions will you ask about your president's undergraduate experience? For example, you might ask, "What clubs or organizations were you involved with?" or possibly, "What did you learn from those experiences?" Finally, if you do get a response or have a chat with the person, how will you follow up? We recommend keeping it simple—send a short thank-you note expressing your gratitude for their time and advice (we have more on saying "thank you" in Chapter 15).

iStock.com/george tsartsianidis

Take-Home Message

You have heard, or will likely hear, derivatives of this adage—"People are your greatest resource." And, this is especially appropriate for this chapter on clubs and organizations; after all, these groups are composed of other people who carry out the group's mission and vision. So, as you look to become more involved, work to acquire particular skills, and document your growth—connect with people who have been there and done that before. The general approach we outlined in this module is a safe one that you can modify, based on your personal style or existing rapport with someone. Of course there no guarantees when you are dealing with people ... but you will never know unless you try!

Action Steps

1. Take a few minutes and create your own list of people you admire or who have succeeded in a way that you would like to do one day. Once you have a list, find their contact information (e.g., email). Then follow through by composing your email and—this part is important—actually hitting <send>. With the plan we outlined, this does not take much time, and you never know if you just might get a response!

2. If you find yourself getting no responses at all (or responses of "no"), then read Kruse's (2016) article titled *7 Ways to Say No to 'Pick Your Brain' Meeting Requests* that was published online by *Forbes* (the full reference is listed in the back of the book) to get a better sense of how to interpret replies (or lack thereof).

Career Search

9

9.0 MEET TIA

iStock.com/South_agency

CHAPTER OUTLINE

Tia was a sophomore at her university and was currently enrolled in a Research Methods course. On the first day, Tia arrived to class and sat down in a seat next to a senior named Becca, who was an undergraduate teaching assistant for the class. After some quick introductions, Tia asked Becca for some pointers. Tia was expecting to hear something about multiple-choice exams, what topics to focus on, or about whether the professor took attendance or not. But, instead, what Becca told Tia caught her off guard.

Becca told Tia, "Don't be like me!" and explained that, as long as Tia had already decided on a major, the smartest thing that she could do was to start planning for her future career. At first, Tia thought that she was joking—after all, she was just a sophomore and had at least 2 or 3 more years at the university. Becca, however, was not kidding—she was serious with her advice. Tia decided to hear her out and asked her to elaborate on what she meant.

Becca explained that, for years, she had put off any career planning because graduation and a career seemed like they were far off in the distance. However, now that graduation was one semester away, Becca finally got serious about life after graduation. The downside, though, was that she realized that she had absolutely no idea about what type of career would be a good fit for her—and she was graduating in a couple of months!

Why Did We Tell You This Story?

If you are like Tia (or Becca), you may have thought that deciding on a major was *the* big decision to make in college. However, that is just step number one. In a major like psychology, your exact career (or graduate school) path is not spelled out for you—you have to make some decisions and plan it out. One benefit to psychology is the large number of career options available; but one drawback is that you have to select a path and properly prepare for it. In this chapter, we will walk you through the various career possibilities for psychology students.

9.1 THE CAREER SEARCH—IT IS YOUR CURRENT JOB

iStock.com/fotosipsak

The first thing that we want to address about psychology careers is that earning a bachelor's degree in psychology will not make you a psychologist. In fact, a master's degree will not always give you the title of psychologist either—in a lot of fields, you must earn a doctorate to become a psychologist. This is different from a lot of applied fields—for example, a bachelor's degree in an engineering field allows you to be an engineer, a degree in nursing means that you can apply for jobs to be a nurse, and a computer science degree can lead to programming jobs.

Once we break that news to our students, one of the most common complaints that we hear is that they do not know what they want to do for a career. Some even want us to tell them what they should choose. Well, the bad news is that there is no simple answer that we can give you. Psychology is very open-ended when it comes to jobs. That open-endedness is great in that it gives you a lot of options; however, the cost is that you have to sift through the options and make a choice. If you do not know what you want to do, then you have to do a lot of work if you want to make an informed decision. Psychology majors can find a meaningful career, as long as they put in the work to deciding on one and preparing for it (e.g., Thomas, 2018). So, remember, it is *your* life and *your* future career—you are the one who has to make the decision!

Now, for some good news. In this chapter, we

- Give you lists and descriptions of careers that are related to psychology.
- Tell you about website databases that describe careers in detail, including the skills, education, and training required for those careers.
- Give advice about how to select a career and plan your path.
- Strongly recommend that you visit your career center on your campus as they likely have resources about careers, knowledge about employers, and assessments

to help you choose a career field and can give you advice about finding and preparing for a job.

As you can see, we are providing a lot of help—but, if finding the right career is important to you, then you have to put in the time and effort. We can give you some tips, but we (or your instructors) cannot make the decision for you.

Be Proactive

iStock.com/gustavofrazao

We have known some students who think that choosing a career is something that they can put off until after they graduate—after all, take one step at a time, right? Wrong! In the world of jobs and careers, you never wait until you are unemployed to start looking for a job—you should always start while you are currently employed (or are still in school). In fact, many career centers recommend that you start visiting them when you arrive on campus!

When you put off making decisions and delay taking steps toward goals, you are letting life happen to you rather than designing the life that you want (see Burnett & Evans, 2016, for tips on designing your life!). Our recommendation is that you should become proactive and start the search for a career today—take action! As an analogy, we could choose to run our research teams by waiting until students contact us and then selecting from that limited pool of individuals. Although those students might be excellent research assistants, we also try to be proactive and fill some of our research positions by actively recruiting standout students from honors classes on our campus. Instead of waiting for life to happen to us, we choose to work hard so that we can create a team that we want. You can do the same by taking control of your search for a career. You might not be able to control everything, but you can control many aspects of the process. And start career planning early—even as early as your freshman year (e.g., Martin, 2009)!

iStock.com/gustavofrazao

Do You Have a Passion? Does This Matter?

You have probably heard career advice that tells you to "follow your passion" or to "do what you love and it will not feel like work." We agree with that advice . . . up to a point. For example, if you already know that you want to go to medical school and become a psychiatrist because you are fascinated by the idea of treating serious mental disorders, then we applaud you—go for it! But, keep in mind that there is a danger to locking into one career path as your passion—it may make you less open to other possibilities, and it may also lead you to believe that the passion-path will be easier than it may actually turn out to be (O'Keefe, Dweck, & Walton, 2018).

Another big issue with the idea of "following your passion" is this—*what if you do not have a passion?* We would be rich if we had a nickel for every student who approached us in a panic and complained that they were lost career-wise because they were not passionate about anything. There is good news though—if this describes you, all is not lost!

The idea that everyone should have a passion for a particular career path sounds appealing on the surface, but it really breaks down if you look at it in more detail. For example, we hear about people who "followed their passion" and were successful, but are there people who followed their passion but were not successful? Of course! Also, most people assume that this passion is either innate (inside of them since birth) or that it emerges from some sort of divine intervention. Unfortunately, though, this is just not true. People who love a certain pop star were not born with a passion for that artist—they likely developed it after hearing her music, seeing her on television, or attending one of her concerts.

Passion for a career can be developed—it does not have to already be inside of us before we start a career (Newport, 2012). People can become engaged in their work if they follow three steps (Niven, 2014):

1. Keep challenging yourself to develop new skills.
2. Look for the positive aspects of a job and organization rather than be cynical about the negative parts.
3. Keep track of your achievements, as those can build your self-confidence (see Schaufeli, 2012, for a more detailed coverage of work engagement).

Before we move on, here is one thing to keep in mind about predicting the future about what will make us happy—we are not always good at it! For example, most people think that winning the lottery will bring more happiness than it does in reality (e.g., Gilbert & Wilson, 2007). The take-away here is that you cannot always accurately predict whether a particular career path will be the one to make you happy—you just have to make a choice now and roll the dice. As Trespicio (2015) said, "*You don't create your life first and then live it. You create it by living it, not agonizing about it.*" In other words, do not stress out about waiting for passion to hit you. Instead, explore some options, pick one that seems appealing, and dive into it. As you learn more about it, you may just find that you become more engaged in it!

Take-Home Message

Career center directors and professors alike agree that it is never too early to think through what different career paths would look like. As professors, we can only provide support and point you toward useful information about career paths—much like those cool *Choose Your Own Adventure* books you may have read as a child (see Hendrix, 2011, if you are unfamiliar), only *you* can plot *your* future. So, do all you can to arm yourself with knowledge—enlist many mentors and seek out multiple sources of information now. That way, when you are getting ready to submit your graduation application, your post-grad plan of action is already decided!

Ben_Stevens/ ShutterStock.com

Action Steps

1. Watch Bill Burnett's (2017) TEDxStanford talk that is titled *Designing Your Life* (https://youtu.be/SemHh0n19LA). This talk reiterates some of the key points and suggestions in this module. The next Action Step (below) will also become clearer after watching this video.

2. We recommend that you think through—and design—what different career paths might look like for you (e.g., Lebowitz, 2017). For example, you might follow this approach:

   a. Think about at least three different 5-year plans for yourself (for each year, what are the major action steps you need to take if you are going to be successful in that path?). Be sure to include one that imagines that money or obstacles were not an issue (e.g., Lebowitz, 2017).

   b. Once you write them out, evaluate them (e.g., Are there obstacles in that path? Can you overcome them? Will this plan make you happy? Are there financial costs to the plan? Financial benefits?).

9.2 PICKING A CAREER AND PLOTTING YOUR CAREER PATH

Some of you might already know what you want to do—you may know someone in that career, you may have seen someone doing that career, or you have known that it was the career path for you for as long as you can remember. Even if this description fits you, you may still want to search career paths because you never know if you are going to find something better. And, if you do not, you can always stick with your original choice. For the rest of you, who are unsure about your career choice, we are going to provide some lists that include a lot of possibilities for what you can do with a psychology degree. In the modules that follow, we will give descriptions of some careers that people typically associate with psychology.

Some Considerations While Exploring Career Possibilities

Before we dive into job possibilities, we want to start with some things that you should keep in mind while you think about jobs. The first issue that you need to understand is that different careers have different paths—some careers will require a little bit of graduate school training (e.g., therapist), some will require a lot of graduate training (e.g., psychologist), and others will require none at all (e.g., human resources). Some will require that you become licensed (e.g., clinical psychologist), and others will not (e.g., market research analyst). Some careers and graduate programs are obtainable with the courses you complete in psychology (e.g., experimental psychology), but some might require that you take a few specific courses outside of psychology (e.g., social work, physical therapy). Other career paths might not require courses (or a minor) in another area, but you might clearly benefit from taking courses from a different area (e.g., marketing).

We also hope that you will come to realize that some careers are going to clearly connect to psychology. However, we want you to know right away that not everyone who earns a psychology degree goes into a psychology-related occupation—this is okay! A lot of psychology majors end up in jobs that do not seem to be directly related to psychology (e.g., Slattery, 2018). For example, there are not that many job postings that advertise specifically for someone with a bachelor's degree in psychology. This is where a double-major or a minor can help you develop additional skills and steer you in a direction—for example, you might want to look for a career that blends psychology with that other field (see our discussion of minors and double-majors earlier in this book).

Keep in mind that there are thousands of jobs out there that are very satisfying, and your college training will prepare you to succeed in those jobs. If you do a good job developing skills in college (writing, presenting, working in groups, critical thinking, problem solving, leadership, etc.), then those skills will be applicable to a wide variety of careers. One of the benefits of earning a psychology degree is that, like other degrees in the liberal arts, the skills that you develop are broad and can be applied to many different jobs (e.g., Zakaria, 2015).

Step 1—Identify a Possible Career

Step 1 is to identify a possible career for you—we provide a lot of suggestions throughout this chapter, but feel free to look elsewhere for ideas (toward the end of this chapter, we describe some websites and resources that you can use). At this point, do not worry if you are not certain about your choice—you can do these steps for a number of different career possibilities! The key idea, though, is that you want to start your evaluation of a career path by first identifying a possible career.

© Can Stock Photo / AlphaBaby

Step 2—Plot the Path to That Career

After you identify a possible career, your second step is to determine whether a career path is right for you. You need to determine the skills, experiences, and educational requirements for that career. To do this, you

TABLE 9.1

When You Start by Selecting a Career, Here Are Some Questions to Ask That Can Help You Plot Your Path to That Career

What career do I find interesting?

- What degree do I need?
- What skills must I develop?
- What courses do I need (or would be helpful)?
- What knowledge must I gain?
- What training or experience do I need?

want to examine the career path by starting at the desired outcome (that is, the particular career you have identified) and working backward to your current status (e.g., Ginat, 2005). This type of thinking can help you manage your career or any other types of long-term projects. After all, working backward from a deadline is common in project management (Harvard Business Review, 2013). You can do the same thing by working backward from a career possibility—see Table 9.1. When you have that information, ask yourself whether you can realistically qualify for that position. If not, then move on and look for a different career.

If you think you can qualify for a career, then the next step is to determine whether you can realistically be competitive for a job in that profession. In other words, are you going to meet the minimum requirements or are you going to be a superstar? For most jobs, you will not be the only one applying for the position—because of this, you want to do what you can to be an attractive applicant who is highly desired by potential employers (relative to other applicants for that job). If you do not think that you would excel in a possible career path, then you may want to consider other possibilities.

Step 3—Is That Career Desirable (to You)?

If the career path seems realistic for you, then step 3 is to determine if this is a career that you would really want. We include a lot of items to consider in Table 9.2. These are all important data points that can help you decide whether a career is a good fit for you. You can research this information online (again, we provide some recommended resources at the end of this chapter) or you can reach out to people to learn from them—in the next chapter, we will provide some tips for how to do this (e.g., an informational interview)!

Take-Home Message

As you go through the process of plotting and assessing career paths, one thing that you might discover is that this might cause you to reassess your choice of major. For example, if you find a career where you would greatly benefit from courses in a different major, you may find that you want to double-major in psychology and something else (or possibly have a minor). Some of you may find that you need to change your major so that you can

TABLE 9.2

Questions to Consider When Trying to Determine If a Career Is Desirable to You

• Is the job projected to be in demand for the foreseeable future—you do not want to pick a career path that is going to be obsolete as a result of automation (e.g., Samuelson, 2018).
• What are the salary expectations?
• What is the normal work environment?
• How many hours does someone typically put in each week?
• How flexible are the hours?
• Do you work independently or directly with a supervisor?

be on the right path to develop the knowledge and skills for your career plan. This is okay, but keep in mind that what you learn in psychology can be applicable to a lot of different career paths!

Action Steps

1. List several career paths you are interested in right now (or, if you completed the Action Step activity in the previous module, refer to it). Now, do your research to find out the educational requirements and skills necessary to meet the minimum job requirements. For instance, will you need graduate school to become a viable candidate? What are the skills you will need to demonstrate to land the job?

2. Draft an action plan to achieve those outcomes. Include the types of classes you will need to take and complete and the experiences you will need to develop the necessary skills. Do not forget to identify milestones or checkpoints to determine whether or not you are on the right path! Keep in mind that this planning document will be a *work in progress* and revisited from time to time. The key point is that you are starting your career planning NOW; do not worry about it being perfect—you are bound to revise and improve it over the next few years (and you might do so as you continue reading the upcoming modules).

iStock.com/tumsasedgars

9.3 JOBS WITH A PSYCHOLOGY DEGREE

In this module, we have included lists of psychology-related careers that you can consider. These lists were accumulated for the American Psychological Association (APA) by psychology professors from various universities (American Psychological Association, 2013; see also Landrum, 2018). We (and other psychology professors) hear from some students who express concern about finding a job with a bachelor's degree in psychology—so, it is important for us to reassure you! There are many different career possibilities available for psychology students—you just need to pick one that is realistic for you, and then take steps to prepare yourself.

Career Possibilities for Psychology Students

iStock.com/marchmeena29

The first list is based on a bachelor's degree in psychology (see Table 9.3). Keep in mind two things. First, some of the careers may require special skills or training—this means that, once you earn your bachelor's degree, you cannot simply declare yourself qualified for all of these jobs. So, do your research (e.g., visit your campus career center or conduct an informational interview—we cover this in the next chapter!) to see how you can best prepare for that career. For example, would a specific minor help you become more qualified? Would an internship help? Do you need to focus on learning special skills while in college (statistics, programming, working on research, etc.)?

TABLE 9.3

Psychology-Related Careers—Bachelor's Degree in Psychology

Activities director	Computer programmer
Admissions evaluator	Conservation officer
Advertising sales representative	Correctional treatment specialist
Alumni director	Corrections officer
Animal trainer	Criminal investigator (FBI and other)
Army mental health specialist	Customer service representative supervisor
Benefits manager	Database administrator
Career/employment counselor	Database design analyst
Career information specialist	Department manager
Caseworker	Dietician
Child development specialist	Disability case manager
Child welfare/placement	Disability policy worker
Claims supervisor	Employee health maintenance program specialist
Coach	Employee relations specialist
Community organization worker	
Community worker	

(Continued)

(Continued)

Employment counselor	Psychiatric aide/attendant
Employment interviewer	Psychiatric technician
Financial aid counselor	Psychological stress evaluator
Fundraiser	Psychosocial rehabilitation specialist (PSR)
Health care facility administrator	Public relations representative
Host/hostess	Purchasing agent
Human resource advisor	Real estate agent
Information specialist	Recreational therapist
Job analyst	Recreation leader
Labor relations manager	Recreation supervisor
Loan officer	Research assistant
Management analyst	Retail salesperson
Market research analyst	Sales clerk
Mental retardation aide	Social services aide
News writer	Substance abuse counselor
Occupational analyst	Systems analyst
Patient resources and reimbursement agent	Technical writer
Personnel recruiter	Veterans contact representative
Police officer	Veterans counselor
Polygraph examiner	Victims' advocate
Preschool teacher	Vocational training teacher
Probation/parole officer	Volunteer coordinator
Project evaluator	Writer

Second, remember what we said earlier—a bachelor's degree in psychology will open doors for you in careers that are not necessarily related to psychology. This is because a college degree in psychology, if you take advantage of the opportunities to grow, will help you develop skills in critical thinking and analysis, writing, presenting, working with others, and solving problems.

The second list is based on additional, graduate training (see Table 9.4). Note that there are many jobs in the second list (and none in the first list) that include the words "psychologist," "therapist," or "counselor"—this means that you need a graduate degree for these professions (we provide more info on these "helping" careers in the next module!). As you read through the second list, in some cases the job requires a master's degree; for many, it is a PhD (Doctor of Philosophy) or PsyD (Doctor of Psychology), and others may require a specialized degree such as a JD (Juris Doctor) or MD (Doctor of Medicine). Again, if you are interested in any of these careers, do some research on the skills and training that are required for that path. A final note is that, although these lists are somewhat long, please understand that they are not exhaustive and that there are more possibilities of careers that are not listed.

TABLE 9.4
Psychology-Related Careers—Graduate Degree

Academic counselor	Mathematical/quantitative psychologist
Applied statistician	Medical social worker
Art therapist	Mental health counselor
Assessment professional/program evaluator	Military chaplain
Biogerontologist	Military counselor
Chief psychologist	Minister, priest, rabbi, chaplain, etc.
Child abuse counselor	Multicultural counselor
Child counselor	Music therapist
Child psychologist	Neurologist
Clinical psychologist	Neuropathologist
Clinical social worker	Neuropsychologist
Cognitive neuroscientist	Neurosurgeon
Cognitive psychologist	Occupational therapist
College/university professor	Optometrist
Community psychologist	Pediatrician
Comparative psychologist	Personnel psychologist
Consumer psychologist	Physiatrist
Counseling psychologist	Physical therapist
Developmental psychologist	Physician
Domestic violence counselor	Psychiatric nurse
Educational psychologist	Psychiatric social worker
Exercise therapist	Psychiatrist
Experimental psychologist	Psychological anthropologist
Family counselor/caseworker	Psychologist
Forensic psychologist	Psychometrician
Gerontological counselor	Psychotherapist
Geropsychologist	Rehabilitation psychologist
Guidance counselor	School psychologist
Health psychologist	School social worker
Industrial/organizational psychologist	Social psychologist
Lawyer	Speech pathologist
Licensed professional counselor	Sport psychologist
Marriage and family counselor	Veterinarian
Marriage and family therapist	Vocational rehabilitation counselor

To help you out even further, we explored the U.S. Department of Labor's Bureau of Labor Statistics website. One cool feature is that they monitor the careers that college students enter, broken down by major. Of interest to you, Angeles and Roberts (2017) created a list of the top five occupations for those with an undergraduate degree in psychology:

1. Social workers
2. Elementary and middle school teachers
3. Counselors
4. Managers (miscellaneous)
5. Registered nurses

iStock.com/sharrocks

The U.S. Department of Labor's Bureau of Labor Statistics website also creates projections for careers at the bachelor's degree level. According to Torpey (2018), the most projected openings over the 10-year period between 2016 and 2026 are in the following fields:

- Business (e.g., market research analysts, human resources)
- Community and social service (e.g., social workers)
- Engineering and architecture (e.g., civil and mechanical engineers)
- Financial (e.g., accountants, loan officers)
- Healthcare and science (e.g., registered nurses, sales representatives)
- Information technology (e.g., software developers, computer systems analysts)
- Management-related (e.g., general managers, management analysts)
- Sports, communication, and design (e.g., coaches, public relations)
- Teaching (e.g., elementary, secondary)

Although some of these positions (such as engineering) are not commonly connected to psychology, you can find a number of these "most projected openings" occupations in Tables 9.3 and 9.4. This tells you that there are realistic career paths out there with projected job openings for students with a psychology degree. But, as we noted earlier, keep in mind that, for some of these careers, you may need to combine your psychology degree with skill development (and specialized coursework) targeted for that particular career—hence, the importance of plotting out your career path!

Take-Home Message

There are a variety of career paths that you can pursue with a degree in psychology. However, keep in mind that the traditional careers that people associate with psychology (e.g., psychologist, therapist, counselor) require additional, graduate training (in case you missed it earlier—we cover these "helping" careers more in the next module!). When you are considering careers, it is up to YOU to research that career to determine if it is the right one for YOU. Look for information online and visit your school's career center. Make an informed decision about your career choice so that you can choose wisely and know what you need to do in order to prepare yourself to be competitive for a job in that area!

Action Steps

1. Read through Tables 9.3 and 9.4 and select a few possible careers from them. If the lists seem too long and intimidating, start by crossing out ones that are clearly not a good fit for you. This will reduce the number of possibilities, making it easier for you to think about relevant options.
2. Research the careers that you selected. Write out the pros and cons for each of them based on the factors that are most important to you (money, skills required, education/degree needed, independence, etc.).

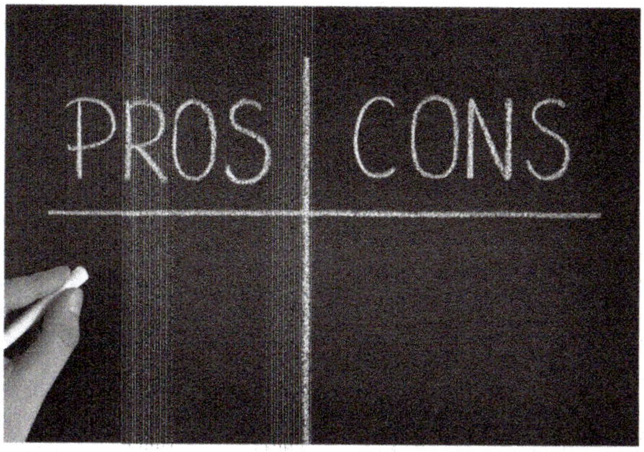

iStock.com/anilakkus

9.4 THE HELPING PROFESSIONS

Every semester, we see students who tell us that they are majoring in psychology because they really want to help people. However, many of these students do not know the differences among some of the most common "helping" careers (e.g., Metz, 2016). If you were not already aware of this, there are a number of different jobs that are thought of as under the umbrella of helping professions. This includes careers such as psychiatrist, clinical psychologist, counselor, and therapist—and there are even more! As we said earlier, this is common as students are just getting into psychology, so do not feel bad about not knowing the differences among them. In this module, we are going to go over some of these careers so that you can have a better idea of whether any are a good fit for you!

iStock.com/EvgeniyShkolenko

How These Professions Are Similar and Different

The obvious thing that these careers have in common is that they are careers in which you can help other people. However, they differ in terms of how you help—for example, do you work with an individual or do you work with both the individual and a partner (or close family members)? Some deal with a problem from a medical perspective, whereas others approach a problem from different psychological perspectives. They may also differ in terms of their settings, the types of problems they address, and the levels of severity that are treated.

These careers are similar in that they are connected to the field of psychology. But, these different careers require different paths, different training, and different degrees—importantly, most require training beyond a bachelor's degree (see Table 9.5). In the following sections, we have provided short summaries of these seemingly similar "helping professions" so that you can have a better idea of which might interest you.

Psychiatrist

A psychiatrist has a medical degree (MD) and is a doctor who specializes in mental health issues. Psychiatrists can work in hospital settings as well as in private practice. Burton (2012) pointed out that psychiatry avoids the repetitiveness of some medical specialties (e.g., one knee surgery is like every other knee surgery) because each patient can be unique with a different problem. One thing that separates psychiatrists from other "helping" professions is that psychiatrists can explore underlying physical causes and can treat problems using both therapy and medication (because of their medical training). Because of their medical knowledge and ability to treat patients with medication, psychiatrists can often focus on very serious cases of mental disorders.

Clinical Psychologist

Most clinical psychologists hold a doctoral degree—typically this is either a PhD or a PsyD (we will elaborate on these later in the book when we discuss graduate programs). Depending on their degree and their training, clinical psychologists can do research, treatment, clinical assessments, or therapy (e.g., Wang, 2008). According to Metz (2016), clinical psychologists can work in a variety of settings, including hospitals, prisons, mental health clinics, private practice, or a university. Clinical psychologists can work with people who have a variety of disorders, such as bipolar, depression, or anxiety (just to name a few). Depending on one's training, clinical psychologists work with individuals, groups, couples, or families—most clinical psychologists will specialize in one area, depending on their training and expertise.

TABLE 9.5

A Quick Breakdown of the Typical Degrees That Are Required for Different "Helping" Careers (See the Text for More Information About These Various Careers)

Career	Typical Degree(s)
Psychiatrist	MD
Clinical psychologist	PhD or PsyD
Counseling psychologist	PhD or PsyD
Mental health counselor	Master's degree
Marriage and family therapist	Master's degree
Social worker	Master's degree (in some cases, a bachelor's degree)

Counseling Psychologist

Counseling psychologists are fairly similar to clinical psychologists. Counseling psychologists also tend to have a doctoral degree, and like clinical psychologists they can do research, treatment, or therapy (e.g., Karazsia & Smith, 2016). The main difference between clinical and counseling psychologists is that the former tends to work with populations who have mental disorders, whereas counseling psychologists are less likely to do this—that is, counseling psychologists are less likely to work with pathological populations and they are more likely to work from a humanistic perspective (e.g., Norcross, 2000). Vazquez (2007) stated that counseling psychologists focus on the well-being of a person and that they often help people deal with issues in their lives (perhaps vocational issues). But, as Price (2009) notes, these traditional lines between clinical and counseling psychologists are becoming blurred—so, don't rule out one path or another at this stage of your career planning.

Mental Health Counselor

In contrast to counseling psychologists, there are many mental health counselors who have master's degrees (e.g., Metz, 2016). Although clinical and counseling psychologists are likely to treat people who deal with mental disorders, the majority of mental health counselors work with relatively healthy people. For example, they may provide school or college counseling, guidance with careers, or help with addictions and they can also work with families or couples who are having problems.

Marriage and Family Therapist (May Also Be Named Couple and Family Therapist)

The marriage and family therapist career is similar to mental health counseling in that most therapists have a master's degree. Although some marriage and family therapists work in mental health clinics, government agencies, universities, or hospitals, most work in private practice (Metz, 2016). Marriage and family therapists are trained not only to work with an individual but also to consider how interactions with a partner or family influence the individual (e.g., Lebow, 2013). Therapists tend to work with a goal of a finite number of sessions (e.g., there might be a certain number of sessions that are designed to reach a particular solution) and can focus on topics such as relationship issues, depression, personal psychological issues, and family interactions (American Association for Marriage and Family Therapy, 2018).

Social Worker

The first thing to understand about social work is that there are different types of social workers, and social workers are involved in a variety of different settings (see Grobman, 2011, for examples). One way to break down the types of social work careers is to use the categories of macro, mezzo, and micro (e.g., Grobman, 2011). Although these terms describe different types of social work, they can work together in some situations (e.g., Knight & Gitterman, 2018).

When we talk to students about social work, they typically think of the micro category; Metz (2016) breaks this category up into subtypes—clinical and direct service. A clinical social worker has some similarities to a mental health counselor or therapist.

Most clinical social workers will have a master's degree and will have training in counseling or therapy, helping people to cope with everyday problems (e.g., Torpey, 2018). This may also include issues such as health or substance abuse, and it can involve specific populations such as children or older adults. Clinical social workers can work in mental health clinics or private practice. A direct service social worker works with individuals to match them up with programs and assistance that can be beneficial (Metz, 2016). To do this, a direct service social worker might conduct screenings and, in some cases, small amounts of counseling—but, it is important to note, direct service social workers do not do formal therapy with clients. Direct service social workers may work in government departments that have names with terms such as "child welfare" or "family services." One unique aspect of this career is that it is possible to start with a bachelor's degree in social work!

In the mezzo and macro categories, social workers focus less on helping an individual and typically have a master's degree. For the mezzo category, social workers will focus more on groups of people. This can involve working with families, but it is not limited to that—this type of social work might look at issues that involve school settings, the community, or possibly a workplace. Macro social workers are different because they typically work on bigger-picture community issues or public policy—this type of social worker is the most removed from helping individuals, as the focus is more on promoting or developing programs. Social workers in this position can serve as part of an agency or possibly as a lobbyist to influence government programs.

Take-Home Message

One key take-away here is that the grand majority of the helping professions that people associate with psychology require some graduate training—either a master's degree or a doctoral degree. However, there are some opportunities to help others that are possible without graduate training (see Table 9.6). So, there are opportunities to help others without furthering your education in graduate school, but some of these positions that we listed here may even require some graduate training depending on the specific position and circumstances.

TABLE 9.6

"Helping" Careers That May Not Require an Advanced Degree

- Social and community service manager (e.g., overseeing a community program)
- Psychiatric aide or technician
- Childcare worker
- Child behavior specialist (e.g., behavioral interventions for children with autism)
- Substance abuse or rehabilitation counselor
- Social and human service assistant (e.g., helping people who need assistance to obtain benefits and social support)
- Clergy
- Teacher
- Social work positions (some)

Action Steps

© Can Stock Photo / Ieremy

1. If you are interested in the helping professions, use the information that we just provided as a starting point. Do even more research on these options so that you can rank the options as to which would be the best fit for your goals. For example, if you know that you do not want to be in graduate school very long, then you may want to eliminate the possibilities of psychiatrist or clinical psychologist. However, if you like the possibility of helping people and also working as a professor, then you might rank a PhD in clinical psychology at the top of your list. Explore the options and find the best fit for you!

2. As you are designing your career plan, do not do this in isolation! Share what you are learning with your classmates. Find classmates who are aspiring to similar career paths and connect with them. It is worth having a support team and collaborators upon which you can bounce ideas, share information and approaches, and ask for feedback on your plans.

9.5 MORE PSYCHOLOGY CAREERS

iStock.com/Pixsooz

As we noted in the previous module, many students declare psychology as their major because they find human behavior fascinating and they are interested in helping people. But, there is a significant portion of psychology students who are not interested in providing therapy or administering treatment. These careers are not "anti-helping"—they simply work with people in different ways than the traditional "helping" professions that we discussed in the last module. So, let's explore some of these—as you read, keep in mind that, like most of those "helping" careers, these careers typically require graduate training.

Industrial/Organizational Psychology

Industrial/organizational psychology, commonly abbreviated as I/O, is the application of psychology to workplace settings. The goal is to improve worker performance and efficiency and to consider worker happiness as well. I/O psychologists can work for a company or organization, consult with different organizations, or perhaps work in an academic setting as a researcher. In fact, as more businesses recognize the importance of organizational health (e.g., Lencioni, 2012), more I/O-minded types may find themselves working in human resources offices.

iStock.com/monkeybusinessimages

To paint a better picture of what I/O psychologists do, let's consider some examples (e.g., Pass, 2007). In the first example, an I/O psychologist is called in as a consultant to solve a retention problem for a company, where too many workers are leaving for other jobs. In the second example, an I/O psychologist works for a company and is asked to help design a system for screening and hiring employees for a new project. As you can see, these types of research questions are applicable to many work settings—not just for the benefit of executives at the helm of for-profit businesses.

School Psychology

School psychologists primarily work to help children in school settings—for example, those who have special needs or those who engage in disruptive or problem behavior. This can include behaviors such as bullying, violence, and substance abuse. The role of school psychologists can be multifaceted (e.g., Barringer & Saenz, 2007)—in this occupation, school psychologists can design schoolwide strategies to prevent problem behaviors among the students, they can intervene with individual students by assessing negative behaviors and developing a plan for improvement, and they can provide intensive treatments for students when there are extreme behavior issues. In the latter scenario, this might include working with the child's family as well.

Forensic Psychology

We have noticed over the past several years that forensic psychology is becoming increasingly popular among students. However, because of movies and television shows, forensic psychology is sometimes one of the most misunderstood careers. For example, movies like *Silence of the Lambs* and television shows like *CSI* or *Criminal Minds* sensationalize aspects of it, and some of these may even add psychic components to it (e.g., Huss, 2001; Ward, 2013)—in case you already forgot what you learned in your General Psychology course, there is no consistent evidence to support abilities such as extrasensory perception (e.g., Stanovich, 2010).

So, what is the reality of forensic psychology? To put it simply, it is the application of psychology to legal issues (e.g., Ward, 2013). In some cases, forensic psychology can involve experimental psychology—for example, one of the authors of this book has worked with attorneys to explain cognitive psychological research on the accuracy (or inaccuracy) of eyewitnesses. However, in most cases, forensic psychology work is focused around clinical psychology skills, such as assessments and evaluations of individuals and their behavior. Forensic psychologists can work in a variety of settings, including universities, prisons, police departments, law firms, or private practice (e.g., Mauro, 2019). Although there are some graduate degree programs in forensic psychology, a lot of people who work in this field have degrees in areas of psychology such as clinical psychology and have gained forensic experience through internships and co-ops (Clay, 2009).

Sport Psychology

Sport psychology involves the application of psychological theories and research to sports and exercise (e.g., Appleby, 2007). Sport psychology can involve a wide range of issues, such as expert performance (e.g., Swann, Moran, & Piggott, 2015), choking under pressure (e.g., Beilock & Carr, 2001), and the effects of sex stereotypes on sports performance (e.g., Chalabaev, Sarrazin, Fontayne, Boiche, & Clement-Guillotin, 2013), just to name a few. According to Appleby and colleagues (2011), there are a few different career paths that people can follow within the field of sport psychology—coaching athletes, teaching students about how psychology can be involved in sports, motivation and goal-setting, and individual work with athletes to improve performance or to overcome an obstacle. People working in this field can have advanced degrees from a number of different areas, including sport and exercise psychology, counseling psychology, or kinesiology (Appleby, Appleby, & Polenske, 2015).

Human Factors and Engineering Psychology

Another interesting career area in psychology is human factors (the term *engineering psychology* is sometimes used as well). Human factors involves assessing and improving the design of general products, technology, or transportation so that a user's experience is more effective and possibly safer (for an interesting read on this topic, see Norman, 2013). In this career, people apply psychological research in areas such as visual perception, decision-making, behavior, or biases to make improvements. For example, human factors and engineering psychologists might study people's tendencies when interacting with a smartphone to help design the hardware as well as where to put buttons or icons. They might also apply visual perception research to workplace scenarios that involve identifying people in poor-visibility conditions. A lot of the work in this field builds from cognitive science, and some level of graduate training (at the master's or doctoral level) is typically needed.

Experimental Psychology

The term experimental psychology is a broad term that includes a variety of psychological research areas. Experimental psychology will typically include areas such as cognitive, developmental, neuroscience, quantitative, and social psychology. These subfields of experimental psychology tend to focus on basic theoretical research, but findings can be applied to real-world situations. Also, training in an experimental psychology field (e.g., a graduate degree) can be applied to a variety of work settings.

Many people who earn advanced degrees in areas of experimental psychology work in research—for example, many of your professors might be considered experimental psychologists. However, as more and more universities have offered and increased the number of doctoral degrees that they confer, there are more qualified experimental psychologists than there are professor positions. Because of that, experimental psychologists have started to move into different career settings, such as government agencies, nonprofits, and businesses. Quantitative analysis skills (e.g., statistics) and knowledge of experimental methods make experimental psychologists useful when it comes to designing studies, analyzing data, making sense of it, and conveying it to a variety of constituents. On a college campus, you may even see experimental psychologists in positions other than professor—for example, it is not surprising to see experimental psychologists in the office of institutional research

(Furlong & Vick, 2017), where they might assess student learning or perhaps evaluate the effectiveness of university retention programs.

Take-Home Message

We hope that this module has increased your understanding of some additional—and perhaps lesser-known—career paths in psychology. A big thing that we want you to take away from this module is that there are a lot of psychology-related career possibilities that do not fit into the "helping" professions category. If you find any of these pathways particularly intriguing, we encourage you to seek out more information by taking a class on the topic or by talking to professors who have expertise in those areas. As a reminder, if you browse your institution's website for psychology, you can look up the background, training, and publications of your professors to see who has expertise in which areas. Finally, remember that, although it is okay to get career ideas from movies or television shows, you need to do some homework so that you can see what they are like in real life!

Action Steps

1. Browse through the upper-level psychology course options (you can probably find them in the undergraduate course catalog)—a lot of psychology courses offer electives in unique topics (including some of the topics we covered in this module). So, if one of those areas interests you, and you find a course on the topic, find out how often and when it is offered so that you do not miss it!

2. If you are interested in one of the topics we covered in this module, look up psychology professors on your college or university website AND look up professors from other departments that might be related to your topic of interest. Often departments will feature biographies of their teaching faculty, and you can use these to learn more about your professors' training and experiences. It is possible that you will find faculty in your department or other departments who might have useful advice for your career plan. For example, if you have interests in sport psychology, look at professors from psychology and kinesiology programs; if you enjoy forensics, consider professors from psychology and criminal justice programs.

9.6 CHOOSE YOUR OWN ADVENTURE—DESIGN YOUR OWN CAREER PATH

While growing up, we read books that were called *Choose Your Own Adventure* (e.g., Hendrix, 2011). These books were different from your standard novels such as *Harry Potter* or *Hunger Games*—instead of passively following a story plot, at various points in the story you are presented with two options such as, "See what is behind the door (go to page 28) or move on without opening the door (go to page 36)." In other words, you can tailor the story by actively making choices about what happens.

The same thing can happen with your career planning. You could follow a prescribed path, such as doing X, Y, and Z, in order to enter a certain profession. Or, you can actively design your own career by taking your own path.[1] We want to be clear—there is nothing wrong with either pathway! However, because most career advice is based on the former, in this module, we are going to provide some examples of unique career building for psychology students.

Ben_Stevens/ ShutterStock.com

Combining Psychology With Something Else

In an earlier chapter in this book, we encouraged you to consider adding a minor to your psychology training. Well, one of the reasons that we made that recommendation was because it can be helpful when it comes to career preparation, especially if you are not going into a career that is directly within the confines of psychology (such as clinical or experimental psychology). For example, Hettich (2017) recommends combining the general skills you acquire as a psychology student with area-specific skills of the career you want; he notes that area-specific skills can be added through college courses, work experience, or an internship. Thomas (2018) notes that some psychology-related graduate programs, such as counseling or social work, may want you to build upon your psychology courses by completing courses in that area (or possibly a minor). So, if you are interested in a particular graduate program, do some homework now so that you know what you need to do in order to get into that program!

Unique Psychology Career Paths

We can expound upon this idea even further by saying that a psychology degree can be applied with other skills and interests to create unique career paths! For example, Dittman (2005, 2013) described a few different nontraditional career outcomes for psychology students. For each of these paths, people combined training in an area of psychology (at the graduate level) with training or skills in another area. These nontraditional careers included

Photo by U.S. Air Force Master Sgt. Adam M. Stump Via Wikimedia Commons

- Director of animal programs for Disney (industrial/organizational psychology + experimental psychology involving animals; Dittman, 2013)
- Epidemic intelligence service officer (clinical psychology + epidemiology training; Dittman, 2013)
- Motivational speaking related to addictions (clinical neuropsychology + stand-up comedy; Dittman, 2013)

[1]One example is a psychology major who created his own path in entertainment to become a stand-up comedian, movie actor, director, two-time host of the Oscars, and host of *The Daily Show* (Phillips, 2015).

- Coordinator of a clinical research program in anesthesia (health psychology + behavioral oncology training; Dittman, 2013)
- Catholic priest and a forensic psychologist (counseling + law enforcement; Dittman, 2013)
- User experience researcher at State Farm (human factors psychology + computer science; Stringer, 2016)
- Performance psychologist for Cirque du Soleil (sport psychology + amateur gymnast; Clay, 2011)
- Director of a Fear of Flying program (cognitive psychology/human factors + flight attendant skills; Chamberlin, 2015)

In the past, most experimental psychology professors trained their graduate students to become clones of themselves—future professors and experimental researchers. But, psychology graduate programs are starting to recognize the variability in career outcomes for students. One reason is that graduate programs are recognizing that there are not enough job openings in colleges and universities for all new PhDs to become professors (Beilock, 2015). Because of this, faculty in these programs are taking steps to prepare doctoral students to be ready for a variety of different career paths by offering more internship opportunities and connecting them with alumni (Beilock, 2017).

In addition to graduate students, we have seen plenty of undergraduates who have forged their own career paths after graduating. As we noted earlier in this chapter, a major like psychology prepares students for a wide variety of career possibilities (e.g., Zakaria, 2015). We have seen former psychology students enter fields such as marketing, business, institutional research, writing, animal training, and entertainment, just to name several areas. In fact, a significant percentage of jobs in Silicon Valley is going to people who had a liberal arts major like psychology—those tech companies need more than programmers and engineers; they need creative people who can communicate effectively and solve problems (e.g., Anders, 2015). The point here is that you too can be creative by combining knowledge and training from different areas to reach a unique career!

Other Professional Career Pathways for Psychology Students

Medical school. You might be surprised to learn that psychology is the third most popular undergraduate major among medical doctors (e.g., Abadi, 2017)! Golding and Lippert (2017) shared a student's account of deciding to major in psychology to prepare for medical school, and an important take-away is that any major that interests you can work, as long as you still take the standard pre-med courses (i.e., a handful of courses from biology, chemistry, and physics). On a side note—the student from the article was using our recommendation from earlier (in this chapter) to plot her path by determining the end goal—medical school—and then working back to figure out what majors and what coursework could work (see, it works!).

There are a number of reasons that psychology can be helpful for a career in medicine (e.g., Kong, 2017). First, medical doctors typically interact with people from diverse backgrounds; psychology can help with that. Second, psychology majors and minors focus on research design and statistics; these are relevant for medicine because of the need to read and keep up with the latest research. Third, a significant portion of medical issues can involve behavioral (e.g., getting patients to follow treatments) or mental components (e.g., psychological states, like depression, can influence physical functioning). Finally, in case you have not heard, as of 2015 the Medical College Admission Test (MCAT) includes a focus on psychology.

Law school. Psychology is also one of the top majors among applicants to law school (Law School Admission Council, 2018). Harvard Law School (2018), which is consistently rated as a top law program, advises students that there is no perfect major to prepare for law school. In other words, you do not have to major in pre-law or political science—students coming from many different majors (including many students from psychology) are admitted into law school. We think that psychology can be great preparation for law school because you develop communication and critical thinking skills and you learn about a number of topics that are relevant to law, such as human thought (including rationality and biases) and behavior (e.g., Golding & Lippert, 2016).

Physical therapy or occupational therapy. Similar to a career path in medicine, we see a growing number of psychology students who are interested in either physical therapy or occupational therapy. According to the American Physical Therapy Association (2016), psychology is one of the top five majors of students who enter a graduate program in physical therapy. Just like the pre-med route, students interested in physical or occupational therapy can major in psychology but need to do a little bit more outside of the psychology coursework. For example, students who want to attend a graduate program in one of these areas need to take some additional science courses and they should also look into volunteer or shadowing experiences during college. A final point to mention is that there are also career possibilities as either a physical therapy assistant or occupational therapy assistant that does not require graduate school work.

Entrepreneur

For those not familiar with this term, it is just a fancy name for people who run their own business. A business can be operated in a physical location such as a factory, office, or restaurant or it can be an online business. The skills you can develop as a psychology major can be very useful as an entrepreneur (do not just take our word for this—see Dahl, 2014). As a psychology major, you develop communication skills, skills to work effectively with others, and skills to critically think and solve problems and you can learn about persuasion in a Social Psychology course (which can be useful for

iStock.com/MaxRiesgo

marketing and selling). If you are considering this route, you may want to combine your psychology degree with some business and finance courses, but you could possibly team up with others who have business training. Finally, keep in mind that anyone can be a part-time entrepreneur by creating a side business that brings in extra money.

Take-Home Message

The key take-away for you here is this—start thinking now about your career path. And, importantly, do not limit yourself by thinking that you cannot do anything with a psychology degree. As we illustrated in this module (and elsewhere in this chapter), there are a lot of options, and you can also be creative as to how you build your career. However, keep in mind that, if you are someone who likes to "color outside the lines" or who prefers to take "the [road] less traveled" (Frost, 1916), then you may have to do a little bit more planning to set your path. The earlier you decide on some possibilities, the more time you have to adequately prepare to make yourself competitive for that path!

Action Steps

1. Reflect upon what types of workplace settings interest you the most. Are you interested in business? Health care? Educational settings? Technology? Entertainment? Sports? Jot down some potential workplace settings to guide your career plan. If you could craft your "dream" job, what would it be? Plot a path (degree[s]), experiences, skills, etc.) to get you there! You might still choose a traditional or defined route, but why not at least consider a unique path?
2. Take your Introductory Psychology textbook, and think about how some of the content conveyed (e.g., personality, persuasion, memory, attention) might apply to the workplace settings you find to be the most interesting. We hope you will find relevant applications of psychological concepts and studies that guide your exploration and career reflection!

9.7 RESOURCES FOR FINDING CAREERS

Up to this point, we have provided you with a lot of information about psychology career possibilities. But, we are humble enough to admit that we cannot capture all of the information you might need inside this book. Because we want all of you to succeed, we want to share some additional resources that you can use to learn about career possibilities and what you can do to achieve your desired outcome (i.e., to design a career). So, in this module, we will walk you through a large number of resources that can help you make the most informed and well-thought-out decision when it comes to selecting a career and executing your career plan.

Career Services, Career Fairs, and Career Tests

Let's set things straight right away—regardless of how confident you are in your career path, we want every single one of you to contact your career center today to set up an appointment.

iStock.com/sshepard

If you are a freshman, great (e.g., Hannon, 2018; Koenig, 2018)! If you are a sophomore, it's too bad that you waited a year to do this, but do it this semester! If you are a junior or senior, what are you waiting for? Do it now! This is our number one recommendation for you as a resource.

While you are waiting for the actual appointment, be sure to check out their career center website. What you find will vary from institution to institution, but you will likely find some very useful information and tools (see Table 9.7). We browsed some career center websites from different schools and we saw information such as (a) jobs and internship listings, (b) information about graduate school preparation, (c) lists of workshops for career preparation, (d) interview tips, (e) advertisements for career fairs, and (f) résumé advice. We will talk about some of these topics in more detail in the coming chapters, but we wanted to introduce them to you now.

In addition, some campus career center websites will have career and personality tests that you can take. These tests attempt to match your interests and personality characteristics to possible careers. Try one of these tests today to see what kinds of career options are recommended for you. You may find some ideas that you never heard of or never considered! Keep in mind that you can take the same test multiple times, tweaking your answers so that you can possibly see more career recommendations.

O*NET

Another strategy that you can use is to browse a website such as O*NET (onetonline .org). This database allows you to enter various keywords and, based on those search terms, it will produce a variety of occupations that you can browse through. The great part of this database is that, when you click on a career, it will provide a lot of detail, including a description of the basic career, specific job titles associated with that career, and what types of skills and education are needed. There are a lot of options on this site for searching, so

TABLE 9.7

Some Ways That a Campus Career Center Can Help

- Meeting with a career counselor
- Job and internship listings
- Tips for graduate school preparation
- Workshops related to career preparation
- Interview tips
- Career fairs
- Résumé advice
- Career interest tests

try them all as you might find different pieces of information with different approaches. For example, you can search with keywords, browse by industry, or explore careers by rating your interests (O*NET Interest Profiler)—this last item measures your rated interests for a variety of jobs and then categorizes your results into different interest areas. The O*NET portal is chock full of resources, so be sure to give it a look!

LearnHowToBecome

Another site that students find useful is LearnHowToBecome (learnhowtobecome.org). Although O*NET is great with the data and information that it provides, LearnHowToBecome presents information about various careers in a little more of a user-friendly manner. This site provides descriptions of occupations, education and experience requirements, recommendations, job outlooks, salary information, and when applicable, what you can do in the profession at different degree levels. We encourage you to try this site by exploring a few different careers and learning about them. However, one word of caution: be a critical thinker as you use sites like this as some information can be based on sponsored content (i.e., paid ads).

Other Online Resources

You can also get ideas about potential careers by exploring websites that post job advertisements, such as CareerBuilder (careerbuilder.com), Monster (monster.com), or Indeed (indeed.com). Some of these websites have useful functions that allow you to do a search such as "psychology bachelors" to see job postings for that degree. We also checked with the career centers on our campus and they shared with us a few more websites that you can try: Job Central (us.jobs), JobServe (jobserve.com), LocalJobster (localjobster.com), SimplyHired (simplyhired.com), Snagajob (snagajob.com), and USAJOBS (usajobs.gov). Finally, you might also look to the National Career Development Association (NCDA) website—they share resources that include internet sites that can provide helpful career information.

Psychology Organizations

In the previous chapter, our top recommendations for psychology organizations were Psi Chi, the American Psychological Association (APA), and the Association for Psychological Science (APS). We are going to reiterate that recommendation here because these organizations offer career help. For example, Psi Chi has a "Career Center" page on its website that lists jobs and some career preparation advice. On its website, APA has job postings and career advice and the site points you toward some of the APA books and magazines that feature career guidance. Finally, APS also posts job ads and some resources about careers. One good thing about all of these sites is that (the last time that we checked) you can access some of the resources without even having to be a member—so be sure to check out these sites!

Your Department

Although the psychological organizations can provide helpful resources for careers, do not overlook your own department. You could attend lectures, symposiums offered by your department, or Psi Chi events that focus on careers. For example, our Psi Chi chapters have hosted panels with professionals from the local community with psychology-related careers—the volunteers on these panels spoke candidly about and answered questions about their career experiences. In addition to that, one of our Psi Chi chapters has even organized their very own psychology-themed career event, with presentations and booths from different companies and organizations—students could walk among them to ask questions and learn about jobs.

Some departments might even offer special career workshops, career lectures, or possibly a course on careers. According to data collected by Norcross et al. (2016), a Careers in Psychology course is offered by only 37% of the departments that they sampled. So, if your department offers this course, consider yourself lucky and be sure to enroll in it! However, if your department does not offer a course like this, then nudge your professors to develop one.

Alumni Groups

Most institutions have an alumni association, and the most common way to think about these organizations is that students join after graduation to stay in touch with classmates. BUT, alumni associations are not just for organizing reunions—they can be a great resource for your career, even before you graduate! Many alumni associations allow current students, or students who attended the institution but never graduated, to join. The benefits that alumni groups offer can vary across organizations, but it is not uncommon to see them offer career assistance and networking opportunities (i.e., a way to connect with other alumni members and to talk about careers). Our point here is this: do not disregard this as a resource because you have not graduated yet—check with your alumni group and see if they allow current students to join!

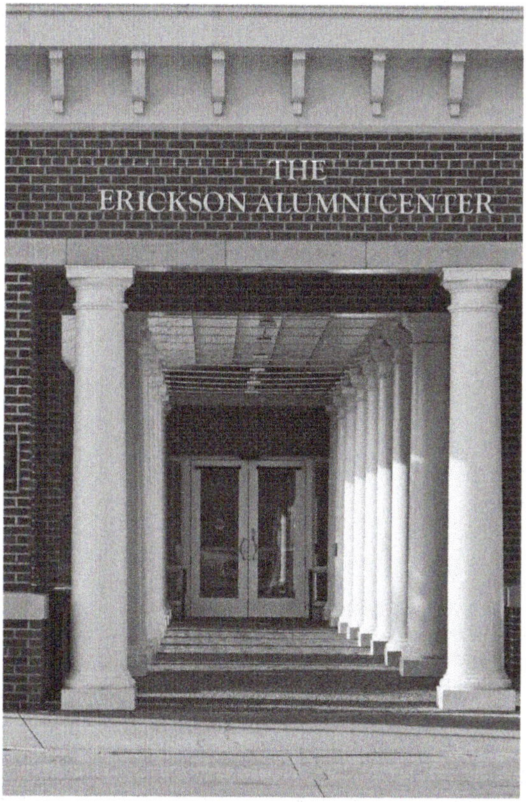

iStock.com/John M. Chase

Take-Home Message

In this module, we provided a lot of tips for resources that can help you explore careers. In addition to those, a final method is to keep your eyes open for opportunities. You can see what types of jobs your friends, family members, or classmates have or are considering. You can also read books or watch movies to see examples of careers; however, keep in mind that these are not always accurate portrayals (e.g., television shows like *CSI* are not always accurate versions of how forensic teams operate in the real world). No matter what approach or which resources you use, remember that your career path is a decision that must be made by you!

Action Steps

1. Even if you think you have a potential career pathway decided already, do complete the O*NET Interest Profiler. This free instrument will provide some insight into your individual preferences and may help you evaluate your potential "fit" with other career paths.

2. Browse your institution's website for career-related programming this academic year (the career center website is the best place to start). Plan to attend at least one event—even if it seems too general or appears unrelated to psychology. You never know what wisdom or insight you can glean from attending these kinds of events, so give them a try!

Career and Professional Development

10

10.0 MEET AKIRA

iStock.com/curtoicurto

CHAPTER OUTLINE

When Akira talked with the career counselor on her campus, she was honest and admitted that she was not interested in graduate school. She knew that it could open up a lot of doors for psychology-related careers, but she just did not have the motivation to complete more years of school.

Akira breathed a sigh of relief when the counselor told her that this was okay—a lot of students in her major did not pursue graduate school. However, Akira's composure was rocked a little when the counselor continued by telling her that it was up to her to take steps to determine a career and find a job.

The counselor read Akira's nervous expression right away (after all, he worked with college students every single day about the career and job-hunting process) and quickly reassured her that it was a very wise decision to meet with him—he was here to provide assistance! He made Akira feel even better when he praised her for setting up this appointment during her junior year and not waiting until right before graduation.

Why Did We Tell You This Story?

Visiting a campus career center is an important step in your career preparation. They can go over a number of steps that you can take to select a career and find a job. For example, they might help by providing career interest tests, assessing your skills and capabilities, developing and polishing your résumé, taking stock of your online presence, determining if an internship or shadowing experience could be helpful, informing you about career fairs, and hosting professional development workshops. The career center is just one step that you can take to prepare for a career—in this chapter, we cover that as well as a number of things that you can do!

10.1 NETWORKING FOR CAREERS

Consider the phrase "it is not always what you know, it is who you know"—this nugget of wisdom suggests that networking is important for career development and advancement.

© Can Stock Photo / iqoncept

However, when we mention "networking" to students, many of them blow it off as if it were some once-trendy and now-outdated professional buzzword such as *synergy*, *millennials*, or *disruption* (see Ryan, 2018, for some buzzwords to drop from your vocabulary). Other students think that networking is only meant for those who are already working in a career field. In this module, we make an argument that college students can benefit greatly from networking (see Table 10.1)—we also provide some ideas for where and with whom to start the networking process.

iStock.com/kali9

Meet Your Classmates

Students often overlook the fact that their fellow students can help them. If you are interested in a psychology graduate program, it is highly likely that you can find other students with the same goal on your campus (e.g., at Psi Chi events). These events are typically filled with high-achieving superstar students—these are the students who can share advice based on what they have already accomplished or learned.

However, student clubs are not the only place to network with other students. Before class—instead of killing time by checking social media—talk to some classmates sitting around you. If you are interested in

TABLE 10.1
Some Reasons That Networking Can Be Helpful for You

- Learn about opportunities that can help you prepare for a career
- Learn about job, internship, or volunteer position openings
- Learn more about a field or career (e.g., pros and cons)
- Build up a group of people who can say positive things about you
- Develop new friendships

TABLE 10.2

Helpful Networking Resources Can Be Easy to Find for College Students

- Classmates
- Relatives, neighbors, and friends
- Professors
- Campus career center
- Campus events (e.g., talks, student clubs)
- Alumni
- Social media

research, ask if any of them are involved in research—if any are, ask about their experience and whether they have tips for getting involved. If you are interested in internships, ask about that. The worst-case scenario is that no one will have done what you are asking about (if this happens, no big deal). But, if someone can provide you with useful information, then that can be a big win.

Your Relatives, Neighbors, or Friends

Your classmates are not your only resource for networking (see Table 10.2 for some networking resource ideas). Most people have friends, neighbors, relatives, and relatives with friends. Think about all of these people in your life and think about whether any of them are in a career field that you want to pursue. You might be surprised to find that one of your connections knows someone in that field (or a closely related field). Ask your relative or friend if they would mind introducing you to that other person. If a face-to-face meeting is not practical, find out if the person is receptive to your reaching out to learn about that career (with a phone call or email).

Talk to Professors

Most of you pay attention to professors in the classroom, but you should also make it a priority to speak with your professors outside of class. In some cases, you might explore your department website and find a professor who is an expert in an area you wish to pursue. If that is the case, do not be shy—stop by during that professor's posted office hours or email him or her to set up a meeting (there is no rule that professors will only help students who are currently enrolled in their courses).

Go to Your Campus Career Center

We can never say this enough—visit your campus career center! Do it now! College career centers are designed to help students like you prepare for and find jobs. Despite this, we are amazed at the number of students who choose not to take advantage of this resource—at most institutions, this is free for students or alumni.

Why should you visit the campus career center? Most will help you through the career selection process, provide feedback on your materials (e.g., résumés and cover letters), share job or internship announcements, and give you advice about interviews. Low-stakes practice sessions to refine your elevator pitch and other components of interview etiquette are worth pursuing even if they take you out of your comfort zone. You might even check to see if you can do a mock interview for practice. In addition to all of that, many career centers host job fairs, workshops, or career panels where you can meet with organizations that are hiring or you can learn about a career from a professional in your community.

Also, many career centers will offer assessment tools that you can use to take stock of your strengths, interests, and possibly even your personality—these tools can be used to offer career possibilities that might be a good fit for you (Schwartz, Gregg, & McKee, 2018). Also, these tools can provide some insight into your behavioral tendencies and how they might shape your workplace interactions with others (see Isachsen & Berens, 1995, for more on this). You can visit your career center to try these tests and, in some cases, you might even find them posted on their website. However, one word of caution—some tests that are used in these settings, such as the *Myers-Briggs* (Myers, McCaulley, Quenk, & Hammer, 1998), may have fallen out of favor among psychological researchers (e.g., Cunningham, 2012). In other words, do not assume that the test results are a definitive answer for who you are and what you should pursue—use them for ideas and getting to know thyself better.

Attend Networking Events

At this point, we hope that you have recognized that college is so much more than simply attending class. Departments and student clubs will regularly hold talks, panels, workshops, or other events each semester. You do not have to go to all of these, but attend some of them. For those interested in graduate school, consider attending a professional conference so that you can learn about research and internships and possibly meet professors from other schools (see our tips on conferences in an earlier chapter).

Most institutions hold job fairs on or near campus, and you may find virtual job fairs, too (e.g., Huang, 2018). Job fairs are a great place to meet representatives from organizations—they can learn about you and, importantly, you can learn about them. To do a job fair right, here are some recommendations (see Yate, 2014): (1) Dress neatly—you are not likely to get hired at a job fair, but you want to impress them because your first impression may potentially lead to an interview. (2) Either bring business cards or be prepared to exchange contact information electronically (see the next module for more on this). (3) Have copies of your résumés to share in case anyone is interested (we cover résumés

iStock.com/GCShutter

in a later chapter). (4) If possible, do your homework beforehand by looking up which organizations will be at a job fair—that way you can ask intelligent questions. And, remember, the main goal of job fairs is to build your network (e.g., Yate, 2014).

Connect With Alumni

Most schools have a large alumni network, so take advantage of this resource! Most alumni groups are organized so that current students (this means you) can meet and contact former students. Alumni were once in your shoes at the very same school, and this common bond means that they are going to be open to helping you (e.g., Cwir, Carr, Walton, & Spencer, 2011). They can tell you about their career, the key skills or experiences needed for that career path, or tips to avoid mistakes that they made. Alums may also be able to tell you whether or not you truly need a graduate degree for a particular job. An easy way to get help from alumni is to see if your school and alumni bodies have some type of alumni mentoring program (e.g., Waitz, 2016).

You might even find that your department stays in contact with or gathers information from their psychology major alumni. For example, some programs might share stories on their website about psychology alumni and their careers. These career profiles of former students can be very helpful because they portray real-life examples of the jobs obtained by psychology students (Lawson, 2018). And, because these alums remain connected and give back to their alma mater, these are people who are likely to welcome inquiries from students like you.

Use Social Media (Wisely)

When it comes to networking, consider using social media to connect with people you meet through other means discussed in this module (for example, if you meet someone at a student club or at a conference, you might connect with them online later). In order to find people, remember that different social media platforms are more popular for different age groups (e.g., Smith & Anderson, 2018). In addition to the traditional platforms (e.g., Facebook or Instagram), look into social media platforms that are oriented around careers (e.g., LinkedIn) or research (e.g., ResearchGate). But, no matter what social media website you use, take steps to maintain a professional image.

iStock.com/mantosh

Cold Call Someone

Even with all of these tips so far, some of you may find that you are having difficulty meeting someone in your ideal career field. In that case, you might try something called a *cold call* (in today's world, this should be updated to a *cold email*). You can do this by searching online and identifying someone in that field and then sending them a short, polite, and professional email with a few questions. Always be brief and crystal clear about who you are and why you are reaching out to them. This is important: do not be vague or ambiguous—be transparent and explicit about who you are and why you are reaching out. For example, you could introduce yourself (e.g., I am a second year student at ____ University majoring in psychology), identify any common ground (this could be a shared interest in a career field), and close with a question (Adeshola, 2017).

Be prepared for the fact that some people may not respond. After all, you are a stranger to them, it is not clear how knowing you can benefit them, and they may be very busy. Also, never feel (or act) like you are entitled to a response (e.g., Ferrazzi, 2005). If a contact suggests a time or location that is not perfect for you, then rearrange *your* schedule to make it work (e.g., Ferrazzi, 2005). Remember, they are helping you out, so always act grateful and always make things easy for them.

Take-Home Message

Joan Garvin via Wikimedia Commons

Do not be someone who eschews networking because you think that hard work is all that should matter. Hard work is important, but networking is also a part of the career development process. When building a network, remember that you are not starting from scratch—you already have friends, family members, social media contacts, classmates, and instructors. The next step is to make new connections. And remember that we are more closely connected to other relevant people than we realize—this should be obvious to anyone who is familiar with the idea of "six degrees of separation" (e.g., Singh, Hansen, & Podolny, 2010). A humorous pop culture take on the idea of six degrees of separation was the game *Six Degrees of Kevin Bacon* (Fass, Turtle & Ginelli, 1996)—in this game, most actors or actresses can be connected to a movie starring Kevin Bacon in a small number of steps (the game can be adapted to use any other popular actor or actress).

Action Steps

1. Start writing out a list of people who can be a part of your network. Use the advice in this module to come up with new people—for example, are any of your current contacts likely to know people who might be worth meeting?

2. Look for events or opportunities at your institution, in the community, or in your field that could be helpful for networking. Start planning now to attend at least one event every semester so that you can nurture and grow your network. In addition, make an appointment this semester to visit your campus career center!

10.2 NETWORKING MYTHS

Now that we have described some useful people and likely places where you can start networking, we are going to address some myths. Years of experiences with students have taught us that there are a lot of misperceptions out there about networking. In this module, we address a number of myths that we consistently hear from students. As we go through each one, we provide tips so that you can take positive steps and become a networking pro. Remember, if you put off building relationships until you need them, it is too late—you want to establish connections now (Ferrazzi, 2005)!

Myth #1: Some People Are Born to Network; Others Are Not

One misperception about networking revolves around the idea that some people are good at it and others are not. This is simply not true—those of you who are quiet or introverted can learn to become great networkers as long as you put yourself out there and practice the right habits. Even if you are an introvert (e.g., Levy, 2018), take a baby step of talking to just one new person—you will be surprised (and proud of yourself) for even a small accomplishment like that. If you need support, find a friend who can attend an event with you. But, do not spend the whole time talking to each other—take time to meet others.

One important component to meeting new people is to be mindful that people make perceptions based on your body language. For body language, make eye contact, stand tall, and keep your arms open—do not avoid eye contact, slump your shoulders, and cross your arms (Misner, 2018). In addition, make an effort to learn names—people appreciate this (e.g., Clifford, 2016). If you have difficulty remembering names, there are a few things you can try: (a) Focus on the name (instead of planning what you will say next), (b) connect the name to something about that person (e.g., "Javier—the chemistry major"), and (c) repeat the person's name during the conversation (e.g., "*It was nice to meet you, Javier*").

Another networking trick is that it is better to be a good listener than a talker. However, do not remain mute—ask some questions to show that you are paying attention. Keep it simple and ask about something relevant to the current situation. Ask follow-up questions to something they just mentioned. You can ask professionals what they like about their field or what skills are most important in their job. With fellow students, you can ask if they are doing some of the steps or activities that you are considering (e.g., research, internship, volunteering, student clubs). At a conference, ask others about their research. And, importantly, after you ask your questions, listen to what they have to say.

Myth #2: Those With the Most Connections Win

A second myth about networking is that having more connections is always better. Be careful with superficial actions that are not very effective, such as sending friend requests to everyone and anyone on social media (e.g., Samuel, 2016). If solid personal

iStock.com/Olivier Le Moal

connections are not made, many of those "new connections" will go nowhere. So, take the time to develop deeper connections. Try to find common ground—is there something that you two have in common? Did you attend the same school? Are you both first-generation college students? Do you have a mutual friend? Engage in similar volunteer activities? Share a research interest or serious hobby? You might be surprised to learn that hobbies are excellent fodder for productive conversations (see Bunea, Khapova, & Lysova, 2018).

Another way to make a contact more meaningful is to follow up a positive encounter with an email thanking the person for taking the time to chat with you. Personalize it by responding to a comment or idea you discussed with that person, or simply say that you appreciated meeting them and hope to chat with them again. This can help reinforce their positive memory of you and what you talked about. You might also consider staying in regular contact with your important connections. Just touch base at least once a year—send a short email to catch up or ask a question. The goal is to keep positive relationships going into the future.

Myth #3: How Can Everyone Help Me?

Some people only think of networking from an egocentric, self-serving mindset (e.g., "how can you help me?"). In reality, networking should be a two-way street that is mutually beneficial (do not forget the rule of reciprocity [Cialdini, 2008] when networking!). Unfortunately, though, as a student, uneven networking relationships are inevitable (e.g., Newport, 2005)—the professional can help you, but how do you as a student help the professional (e.g., Pollak, 2012)? First, do not act needy—do not focus solely on how they can help you. Second, be genuine and sincere about forming a friendship. Use the advice that we provided earlier—spend time listening and not doing all of the talking. In a professor–student relationship (which tends to be one-sided), try to add something of value; for example, professors are much more likely to help you if you have put forth effort in their classes, have been involved with their research, or have listened to their long-winded stories.

iStock.com/CatLane

Finally, whether it is in person or online, if you can help others without needing anything back in return, do it. For example, say you heard about an internship but it is not quite a perfect fit for you. Do not keep it to yourself—tell your friends or classmates who might be interested. You build goodwill with others by doing things like this, plus it will likely make you feel good (Brown, Nesse, Vinokur, & Smith, 2003).

Myth #4: Students Do Not Have Business Cards

When you attend certain events (e.g., job fairs, conferences, or campus events), you might consider bringing business cards. As a student, you can include (a) your name, (b) a school or company logo (you may need to get permission, as some are copyrighted), (c) your email (make sure this is professional—do not include a childish or inappropriate one!), and (d) possibly your phone number. If you have social media contact info, such as LinkedIn or a personal website, go ahead and include that as well—you might consider creating and including a Quick Response (QR) code. Some of you might have a title that you can include, such as "Psychology Research Assistant" or "Psi Chi President," but some of you may not—in the latter case, you can list something like "Psychology Major - Class of 2024."

Another option is to share contact information using your smartphone (see Table 10.3). If you go this route, please make sure that the process is smooth and easy—you do not want to fumble with your phone and make things awkward. This process can be as simple as taking a photo of their contact info (e.g., from a poster or flyer) or jotting down their email address or number. Getting their info is helpful because it allows you to be the one who can reach out right away—thank them for any information they shared with you and communicate that you hope to stay in touch.

Take-Home Message

Anyone, no matter their personality type, can learn how to network successfully—both in-person and online. Practice some simple steps that will make interactions go smoothly. Build quality relationships by showing interest in them. Work on quality, not quantity—try to build friendships instead of superficial contacts. Even if you do not bring much to the relationship, be nice, listen well, and be grateful (if they provide advice or assistance). A strong network can help you find opportunities that you would not normally hear about, so do not overlook this aspect when starting your career. If you want more help with

TABLE 10.3

Pros and Cons of Business Cards and Electronic Networking

	BUSINESS CARDS	ELECTRONIC NETWORKING
Pros	Simple, time-tested method for networking	Most people carry their phones with them (or can easily share their email address)
Cons	It can seem outdated to younger individuals; also, cards can be left at home	It can be an awkward interaction if the exchange of information is not efficient

networking strategies, we recommend a book such as *Never Eat Alone* (Ferrazzi, 2005) or an updated classic such as *How to Win Friends and Influence People in the Digital Age* (Carnegie & Associates, 2011).

Action Steps

1. Figure out a fast and efficient way to exchange contact information with potential contacts—you can create business cards or you can practice a good way to do it on your smartphone.
2. Take an honest assessment of your in-person and online connections. Are the connections superficial? Do you bring anything to help the other person? Take the most important connections to the next level and figure out how you can be a resource for others. Importantly, be specific about the steps that you can take to improve the connections.

10.3 CONDUCT AN INFORMATIONAL INTERVIEW

An informational interview can help you gather useful information about a career path. These are great because they can help you learn some of the pros and cons of a career that you are considering. This is an important step in career preparation because it might help you to decide that a path is right for you, or you might discover a red flag that indicates that the career is not a good fit for you—be prepared for either possibility (e.g., Bolles, 2014). In this module, we are going to walk you through how to conduct an informational interview and what you might ask.

Find Someone to Interview

First, use your network—is there someone you know who is working in the field you want to pursue? If so, reach out to that person. However, you might not be able to find someone in your existing network—if this is the case, you will need to go outside of your network. For example, if you are interested in a career as a counselor or therapist, you could stop by a campus counseling center, you might look up graduate students who are in a counseling or therapy program, or you might ask a psychology professor, especially one who focuses on those topics. If none of those are a possibility, you might refer to a site such as LinkedIn. If that is also a dead end, consider checking with your campus career center to see if they have any contacts, or do an internet search for mental health clinics in your area.

Once you identify some possibilities, you should formally ask if they would let you interview them. Pollak (2012) recommends using email and doing the following:

1. Let them know right away that you are asking for a favor.
2. Briefly explain your career topic interest.
3. Subtly connect with them (e.g., "Because you are already in the field that I am interested in …").

4. Ask if they would be willing to meet with you to chat about their career field.
5. Thank them for any help they can provide.

Importantly, she recommends one more thing: if they are not available, include a request asking whether they know of someone else who might be able to help. This can be helpful because it might change what would be a dead-end situation into a new possible connection!

Finally, and this is important, do not interview someone if you are not actually interested in that career! Remember that you are asking someone to do a favor for you. It is not a good idea to use up someone's valuable time if you are not considering that path. Imagine if a high schooler asked to interview you about college and then, at the end, revealed to you that they are not likely to go to college—most of you would feel like the interview had been a waste of your time.

How to Prepare

Before you meet, do a little bit of homework. First, learn the basics about the career—use the websites (e.g., O*NET) and resources (e.g., your campus career center) that we recommended in the previous chapter. If you find that some aspects of the career are unclear or vague, then this is information that you can ask about during the interview. Second, it is also a good idea to research the person as well. The first place to check is a networking site like LinkedIn. If you cannot find the person on that site, you can try a simple internet search. The goal is to learn a little bit of professional background information about your interviewee.

What Should You Ask?

This is up to you—what do *you* want to learn about that career? The questions that follow are some examples of what you might ask—feel free to use any of these questions or develop your own. We recommend that you avoid asking for personal details—for example, most people will not want to reveal how much money they make (however, see Burkus, 2016, for a perspective on salary transparency). If you are interested in salary information, ask about the topic in a more general way. In our questions that follow, instead of asking how much our interviewee makes, we ask about the expected salary for someone starting out in that job.

- What is your job title?
- In everyday terms, how would you describe your job?
- What is a typical day like?
- What is the expected salary for someone just starting out in this career?
- What are the best and worst parts of the job?
- What kind of education and skills are needed for this job?

- What are your top recommendations for someone interested in pursuing this career path?
- Is there anyone else in this field whom I could contact for an interview like this?

How to Conduct the Interview

Although email or social media can be a good way to initially reach out to someone, we recommend conducting the interview in person. This approach is more personal, the interviewees do not have to type their responses (typing can be more time-consuming than stating answers aloud), and you can adjust or clarify your questions as you go. You can also adjust the number of questions that you ask depending on how things are going. For example, if the interviewee is relaxed and does not seem to mind answering questions, you might throw in a few extra questions.

Try to make the location convenient for your interviewees as they are the ones who are doing you a favor by participating in your interview. We recommend meeting them at their workplace or at a coffee shop (e.g., Bolles, 2014). Coffee shops are great because you can find them anywhere, they are designed for short meetings, and this environment gives you an opportunity to pay interviewees back by offering to buy them something to drink.

iStock.com/Kosamtu

If you are in a different location than your interviewee, then you should probably conduct the interview using video chat such as Skype or FaceTime. This is not as personal as a face-to-face meeting, and it does not make it easy to pay the interviewee back with a caffeinated beverage (although you could send an electronic gift card as a thank you afterward). However, a virtual meeting is still better than an email interview because interviewees do not have to type their answers and because you can still adjust your questions as you go through the interview.

Take-Home Message

Career descriptions that you find in books and websites can be fairly generic—an informational interview is a valuable way to learn about details and the reality of the day-to-day job (you might even consider conducting more than one of these). However, because you are asking people to take time out of their busy schedule, you must keep the following in mind: (1) be polite and professional, (2) take up as little of their time as possible, and (3) be very gracious for their help; in some cases, offer to pay them back. A lot of people will help you just to be kind to someone considering their field, so sometimes thanking them is all that is necessary.

Finally, remember that this is not a sneaky way for you to get a job. Some people think that this is a way to bypass the normal hiring process and they will offer a copy of their résumé. Although it is okay to ask for feedback on your résumé, please do not try to use this process as a backdoor approach to landing a job. The purpose of an informational interview is to learn about the career. Also, most people at companies or organizations are not involved in the hiring process, so you would be wasting your time (and are likely to make the conversation awkward). However, if for some reason, they offer you a position, then go for it (but only if they are the ones to bring it up)!

iStock.com/fizkes

Action Steps

1. Prepare for an informational interview by first identifying a career possibility and then thinking about how you can find someone in that field through your network. If you have to go beyond your current network to find someone, start brainstorming ideas as to how you might find someone (refer back to our earlier modules about expanding and developing a network).

2. Create the list of questions you will ask during your interview. Feel free to use the questions we suggested, modify them, or create your own!

10.4 INTERNSHIPS—WHY YOU NEED ONE

When college students start applying for jobs, they may run into the conundrum that employers want to hire someone who already has relevant work experience. This is an example of a *Catch-22* (Heller, 1961)—how can college students get work experience if the employers are unwilling to hire them so that they can gain experience? Thankfully for you, the solution to this problem is a wonderful thing called an internship (other terms that you might encounter are *co-op* or *practicum*). An internship can be listed on your résumé (we cover résumé in a later chapter) and is something that you can talk about during a job interview (we cover job interviews later in this chapter). In this module, we cover some of the basics about internships, including reasons that you should do (at least) one (e.g., O'Brien, 2010) as well as ways that you can find them.

Internships—Just Do It

In some cases, an internship might be one of the most valued things in a potential job candidate. In one study (Nunley, Pugh, Romero, & Seals, 2016), researchers sent out fictitious résumés for business-related jobs and they manipulated the college major (e.g., business, psychology) and whether or not the person completed an internship while in college. College major did not matter, but those who had completed college internships were 14% more likely to be offered an interview! Another study showed that one of the top predictors of post-graduation employment was the number (more is better) of internships completed (Townsley, Lierman, Watermill, & Rousseau, 2017). Finally, a survey by the National

iStock.com/iQoncept

TABLE 10.4
Some Valuable Reasons to Complete an Internship

- Exposure to and experience in a particular field
- Employers value internship experience
- Development of soft skills (e.g., communication, working in groups)
- Learn whether a career field seems like a good fit for you
- Networking and potential connections for future recommendations
- Possibly connect classroom knowledge to real-world situations

Association of Colleges and Employers (2017) showed that 91% of employers preferred that job candidates have work experience, 65% said they preferred candidates with relevant work experience, and 56% preferred work experience that was an internship. This importance is also recognized by many students, as 61% of students take part in at least one internship while in college (National Association of Colleges and Employers, 2018a).

Internships are valuable because the experiences you gain can separate you from other students who do not complete an internship (see Table 10.4). Most internships are going to be too short for you to develop all of the skills and expertise for a particular career field (e.g., Jones, 2017)—however, internships are important because you can work on soft skills (communication, professional etiquette, etc.). You can also use the experience to decide if a career seems like a good fit for you—some college students even change their career choice after an internship opens their eyes to the negative aspects of a particular career (e.g., O'Brien, 2010). In other words, internships can help you find what you do not like in a job now ... which is much better than finding that out after you graduate!

Another benefit is that, rather than post job ads to the external world, many organizations find it easier to hire people whom they already know (this is consistent with our earlier advice about networking—connections are important!). In fact, some organizations will develop an internship program as a way to funnel talented individuals into full-time positions (e.g., Jones, 2017). Even if an internship does not directly lead to a job, it is a great opportunity to put your networking into overdrive.

While completing an internship, you will likely be around professionals in your field—you can build connections and possibly earn a letter of recommendation from someone who observes you doing excellent work. In addition, this type of letter can nicely complement those from your professors who have known you for several years.

Types of Internships

The laws about internships can be complicated (United States Department of Labor, 2018), but the overly simple breakdown is that an internship is either going to pay you as an employee or else you are getting a clear educational benefit from the experience (but do not get paid). The purpose of the law is to define these positions so that employers cannot have free interns around to do menial tasks (e.g., Greenfield, 2018). There is not much benefit to an internship if you simply fetch coffee and pick up your supervisor's dry cleaning—you want to be networking and getting exposure to a career field.

In an unpaid internship, you should work with either a professor or a campus internship coordinator, as well as your internship supervisor, to clearly define your role, what you will learn, whether you will earn course credit, and whether there are any educational requirements such as papers that you have to write about your experience. For a paid internship, the company or organization pays you an hourly wage or salary for your work. Keep in mind that completing an internship is not the path to riches—most of these positions are going to be at a relatively low pay scale such as minimum wage. So, if your primary goal this summer is to earn good money, then you may want to look for a standard job.

So, which should you do? Recent research has shown that those who completed paid internships were more likely to land a desired job before graduating than those who completed either an unpaid internship or no internship (National Association of Colleges and Employers, 2018b). This is supported by a different study that showed that paid internships tend to have more direction and feedback from supervisors or mentors (McHugh, 2017). However, it should be noted that the Townsley et al. (2017) study we reported earlier showed little to no differences between paid and unpaid internships regarding employment.

Our advice is this—if your goal is to use an internship to lead to a job, you may want to look at paid internships first. But, you might consider unpaid internships if you do not have options for paid positions. If you are considering an unpaid internship, take steps to make sure that it is going to be a good educational and networking experience—be sure that there are clear goals for the position as well as opportunities for useful feedback from a supervisor (e.g., McHugh, 2017)! Some institutions do a better job than others of vetting the quality of an unpaid internship, so if you are receiving help from your institution to find an internship, be sure to ask questions.

Finding Internships

It usually does not take long for us to convince students that internships are something for them to consider. However, the next question that we hear is that they do not know how to find one. To help you with this, here are some steps you can take to find out about internships and positions where you can work with a business, clinic, or organization (here is a heads up—a lot of these ideas are similar to our networking suggestions from earlier!).

1. Set up a meeting with your campus career center and then discuss your goals and interest in finding an internship. Sometimes they know about psychology-related positions, but sometimes they do not. If you have broad interests, then let them know—for example, they might know about opportunities that overlap with psychology, such as marketing, healthcare, or law enforcement. They can also tell you about upcoming career fairs, where you might find employers who are actively looking for interns.

2. Look for opportunities through your network. Does one of your friends or family members work for a company that interests you? Is there someone in your LinkedIn contacts who might be able to help? Does anyone in your student club(s) know about opportunities?

3. Consider joining Psi Chi, the American Psychological Association, or the Association for Psychological Science. These organizations post a lot of career information, including job postings, internships, and summer opportunities. However, please read these carefully to make sure they are meant for undergraduates (some are meant for graduate students or professors).
4. If your institution offers it, take an internship or professional skills course. These courses typically involve career preparation and help finding positions (e.g., Ciarocco, 2018). The professors who teach these courses typically have more knowledge about internships and careers than your average professor (e.g., Vespia, Freis, & Arrowood, 2018).
5. If you have already tried routes such as checking with your campus career center, consider doing your own homework. For example, if you are interested in careers related to mental health, look for mental health clinics in your community or on your campus—reach out to them with a professional email or phone call and ask if they have any positions for college students who want to learn about the field. If they turn you down, ask if they know of any other organizations like theirs that might offer them. They might not have any leads, but you never know unless you ask.

When to Do an Internship

Many college students complete internships during their junior or senior years (or the summer between). This is a good time because you might be able to leverage the internship experience toward your first "real" job after graduation (e.g., Doyle, 2018). It is possible to start internships as early as your freshman or sophomore year, and some students start this early because they want to complete two internships—in some cases, internships may require previous internship experience (e.g., Berger, 2018; Doyle, 2018). However, keep in mind that there can be drawbacks to starting too early—when you are just starting college, an internship on top of your courses might be too much to handle. In addition, you might not yet have a clear idea of your career goals and you likely have not taken upper-division courses that might help you be a better intern (e.g., Schmiede, 2016).

Alternatives to Internships

Job shadowing. Besides (or in addition to) an internship, there are other types of activities that students can do to learn about a career field and gain experience. One is *job shadowing*—this is where you can formally (e.g., arranged through your campus career center) or informally (e.g., arranged on your own) spend time watching someone during an actual work day. If you do this, please take it seriously—another person is helping you by including you in their work world. We encourage you to observe carefully (you are not there to play on your phone) and to jot down questions that arise. If you have time at the end of the day, ask your questions—if not, that gives you an excuse to reach out later (and that can help reinforce that networking connection).

Temp. Another option is to *work as a temp*. If you carefully choose your position, then you can learn about it just like you might as an intern. However, keep in mind that there is a big difference between interning and being a temp. An internship is defined as a learning experience that (hopefully) involves guidance and mentorship—when you temp you are simply hired to work at a job (e.g., Pollak, 2012)!

iStock.com/kobbydagan

Volunteering. You can also develop skills by *volunteering*. For example, you can volunteer with a nonprofit, professional organization, hospital, student club, or research team. As you might guess, what you learn and experience is going to vary from situation to situation. But, one benefit to volunteering (which you typically do not see with internships) is that you might feel good about helping.

Start a business. A final alternative is to work for yourself by *starting your own business* while in college. This option can potentially be the most impressive as it demonstrates incredible motivation, independence, moxie, and skills. You may have heard of some of the following businesses and the college students who started them (e.g., Mulhere, 2016):

- Facebook—Mark Zuckerberg
- Dell Computers—Michael Dell
- Def Jam Records—Rick Rubin
- The Onion—Chris Johnson and Tim Keck
- Reddit—Steve Huffman and Alexis Ohanian
- SnapChat—Evan Spiegel and Bobby Murphy

Starting a business takes work, but remember that not every business needs to have a unique niche or involve complex programming—it just has to be profitable (or break even). It could be as simple as starting a tutoring business, designing websites, selling something you make, or creating an app. Or, a class project may serve as the impetus for your business (see Kausch, 2018). Not everyone has the time to be an entrepreneur, but if you do, college is a great time to take a chance on it—after all, if you fail, you have your college training and degree as your fallback.

Take-Home Message

If you are striving to start a career after you graduate, then completing at least one internship is a very good idea. An internship can give you a closer look into a job, and it can also demonstrate to a company or organization that you might be someone to consider for a full-time job. Research suggests that paid internships might be a better option, but do not discount an unpaid internship if you properly vet it to make sure that you are going to have a quality experience. Employers want work experience (National Association of Colleges and Employers, 2017) and a large proportion of your fellow college students are already out there doing internships (National Association of Colleges and Employers, 2018a)—so, if you want to be competitive for jobs, this might be an important step for you!

iStock.com/marekuliasz

Action Steps

1. Start planning for an internship today. If you are a freshman or sophomore, you do not have to do it this year, but start looking now. Use the suggestions from this module or explore company or organization websites directly.

2. Schedule an appointment with your campus career center and ask to discuss internship possibilities. Keep an open mind as they might not have a position that perfectly matches your interests—but you just might discover a new field of interest. In addition to that, they can also help you prepare materials, such as a cover letter or résumé.

10.5 PREPARING FOR INTERVIEWS

Why do we cover interviews here? After all, if you can land an interview then you have the job, right? Wrong! Though, you do have a *chance* to receive an offer (as do all the other candidates).

Consider this—if they are interviewing three people for a position, your baseline odds of being hired are only 33% (we are not saying this to discourage you, but we simply want to convey the reality). And, if you are not properly prepared for an interview, you are not likely going to be offered the position. In this module, we provide a number of preparation tips, including some mistakes to avoid. A lot of the advice also pertains to job fairs as well—in those scenarios, you are interacting with representatives from an organization, so you want to be prepared to interact in a manner that might help you land a job.

Constantin Stanciu/ ShutterStock.com

Do Your Homework—Know the Organization!

Before an interview, you want to know everything you can reasonably learn about the organization, the job itself, and the people you would be working for (and with) while on the job. Dig deep into the organization website. Re-read the job ad numerous times. Do internet searches of the company or organization name—if it is a company, are there competing companies (e.g., Coke vs. Pepsi, Marvel vs. DC Comics)? Doing some research on the position and the organization can be extremely helpful—you might find information that you like or information that you do not like (possibly leading you to reconsider a position with them).

We also recommend that you create a list of questions that you might ask during an interview (see Green, 2018). Remember, they are not just gathering information about you (and determining fit within their organization)—you are also gathering information about them (and determining how *they* fit into your career plans). One idea is to work from the job advertisement or something you read on their website. For example, you might ask, "I saw in the job ad that the primary responsibility in this position is ___—can you elaborate on any other important responsibilities?" Building on this, you can ask how they define success in this position. You might also ask about the work environment and culture—ask the interviewer why he or she likes working there. If it is the end of the interview and some aspects of the job are not clear to you, ask for clarification. Finally, one question that always works to convey closure is to ask about their next steps in the hiring process and their timeline for making a decision.

iStock.com/milanvirijevic

Mock Interviews and Preparing for Questions

Mock interview. To prepare for interviews, we recommend that you take a lesson from comedians—do not wing it. You might be surprised to learn that comedians often test different types of wording and delivery and then rehearse their jokes many times before a big show—this careful practice can create the appearance of spontaneity (e.g., Morgan, 2015). In a similar manner, the best way to prepare for a job interview is to practice by doing a mock interview—you can do this with peers or, even better, you can see if your campus career center offers this service.

Describe your skills. In an interview, you are likely going to be asked about your skills or your strengths. Prepare (very) short stories that illustrate your abilities, traits, and accomplishments. And do not rely on meaningless descriptive phrases. For example, instead of labeling yourself as a "motivated problem-solver," describe specific examples that demonstrate how you solved problems in the past (see Pinola, 2012, for an overview of the STAR Method). Also, do not answer interview questions by simply restating what you listed on your résumé or curriculum vitae—they already read your application, so you need to expand on it. For a lot of questions, you can describe a problem you encountered,

© Can Stock Photo / iqoncept

the action you took, and then the result (e.g., Pollak, 2012)—we expand on this topic of skills later in the module.

What about this weakness? In some interviews, you may be asked about a flaw or weakness in your record. Be sure that you understand these aspects of yourself and have responses ready to address them. For example, if your grade point average was a tad low, explain why—maybe you did not take courses as seriously during your freshman year, leading to lower grades, but after that you buckled down and improved? Or maybe it took more than 5 years to graduate because you were working a full-time job while taking courses? The point here is to identify what they might think are weaknesses and to have good explanations for them. As you do this, be careful that you do not become defensive or create excuses that place blame elsewhere—use explanations that allow others to understand the situation and that include you taking personal ownership (e.g., Bessette, 2013). We include a quick breakdown of excuses and reasons in Table 10.5.

What is your greatest weakness? In other cases, you might be asked to identify your greatest weakness (e.g., Ryan, 2017). Please do not say that you "work too hard," "care too much," or "have standards that are too high"—these canned responses are somewhat generic and do not convey much about you; at worst, they could be construed as humblebragging.[1] Instead, describe a situation in which you struggled but then took steps to overcome the problem (e.g., Ryan, 2017). For example, if you tend to be shy, you can describe how you overcame that by putting yourself out there and volunteering to do presentations (and now it is no longer a weakness).

Odd questions. In some interviews, be ready to think on your feet with an off-the-wall question (e.g., Fuscaldo, 2014).

TABLE 10.5

Key Differences Between Excuses and Reasons

Excuses • Try to deflect blame • Describe as if it were not your fault at all—other people caused the problem • In some cases, it was some event or thing that caused the problem
Reasons • Take responsibility • Explain what happened—even if you made an error or had poor judgment • Even if something were out of your control (e.g., computer breakdown), was there something you could have done to remedy the situation?

[1] Research by Sezer, Gino, and Norton (2018) suggests that humblebragging can backfire!

- How many ridges are around the edge of a quarter?
- If you could be a superhero, what superpower would you want?
- How would you get an elephant into a refrigerator?
- What kind of bear is best? (Daniels, Forrester, & Einhorn, 2007)

These might sound terrifying (or amusing, depending on your sense of humor), but the best part of these questions is that (typically) there is no right or wrong answer. The interviewer wants to observe how you think creatively, respond to an unusual problem, or apply critical thinking. So, if you get one of these, take a second to think through a reasonable solution—if you get stuck, ask for some clarification to buy a little bit more time to think of a creative answer. Or, better yet, think aloud as you work through the scenario.

Elevator pitch. It is very common at interviews and job fairs to hear the phrase, "So, tell me about yourself." You can deal with this by preparing an elevator pitch, which is a short story to tell about yourself and your goals (in the amount of time you might spend with someone on an elevator). We suggest having two versions ready—a 30-second version and a 5-minute version. You will have to judge for yourself which version is more appropriate for the situation. In either case, keep your pitch positive and hit the highlights of what defines you and where you are going professionally. This is something else that you want to practice—rehearse it so much that it sounds conversational rather than you reciting a memorized speech (remember what we wrote about comedians earlier—they practice so much so that their jokes and stories seem improvised).

Team Oktopus/ ShutterStock.com

Dress and Act Appropriately

Organizations are going to vary in terms of how conservatively or casually employees dress at work, so do some homework to see if you should dress formally or not. If you are completely unsure about how to dress, remember that it is much easier to dress down at the last minute (e.g., remove a jacket or tie, roll up your sleeves) than it is to dress up in a pinch (e.g., you do not want to be in jeans and a t-shirt and then find everyone else in suits). The key is to be professional, clean, and presentable (e.g., O'Brien, 2010).

When it comes to arriving for an interview, we have seen some people who behave rudely, inappropriately, or act overly demanding with administrative assistants. Please do not make a mistake like this! For starters, we think that you should not treat people better or worse based on their position or status—that is not a good life strategy. Second, in this modern world where organizations gather as much information as possible, it is not uncommon for hiring managers to ask administrative assistants or job fair representatives for their input about job candidates (e.g., Koval, 2015).

Our point is this—act professional at all times because organizations are potentially observing you the whole time (e.g., Prossack, 2018). Case in point—we have seen job candidates who have kicked the airport luggage rack out of frustration, berated a restaurant server at a meal, acted condescendingly toward an office worker, and had way too much to drink at a reception following an all-day interview. Did any of those individuals get hired? Of course not—no matter how good their résumé or curriculum vitae looked, those are not positive actions to convey to an organization that is thinking about hiring you.

Assessing Your Skills and Experiences

As you prepare for interviews, some of you may be uncertain about some of your skills, strengths, and weaknesses. If this is the case for you, consider using The Employable Skills Self-Efficacy Survey (Ciarocco & Strohmetz, 2018). This tool can be used to assess your confidence in a variety of skills, such as communication, analytical inquiry, collaboration, and professional development. To access this survey, check out Ciarocco and Strohmetz's (2018) article (we list the full article information in our reference list at the end of this book) or take the test online (employableskills.com/skills.asp).

In addition to that, if you need examples that demonstrate some of your skills, look closely at your college experiences in and out of the classroom (e.g., Shaikh & Camparo, 2018–19). For examples of your critical thinking and communication skills, consider a debate that you participated in or perhaps some of the papers that you wrote. If you completed group projects or presentations, you might be able to come up with experiences that demonstrate your ability to work with others as part of a team. Participating in research, internships, service learning, student clubs, and volunteer work can also be good sources for you to pull from to come up with ways in which you displayed skills that employers value (e.g., Selingo, 2015).

Take-Home Message

Interviews are a chance for you to share a lot of information about yourself and for you to learn about an organization. Before the interview starts, check with your campus career center to see if they offer mock interview opportunities. For the interview itself, we recommend that you always arrive on time—showing up late is a horrible first impression. While there, act confident and motivated, but be careful not to come off as cocky (see David, 2016, for some differences between confidence and cockiness). When the interview is over, send a brief thank-you note (or professional email) to the key people that you met (TIP: even if you do not land the job, this is a great networking move). And, finally, remember that every interview is important, even if you do not think you necessarily want or could possibly land that particular job. At a minimum, every interview is a chance to practice your interview skills and to build your network—plus, you might learn new things and end up wanting the job after all (e.g., Backman, 2018)!

Action Steps

1. Do you have an elevator pitch ready? If not, then start writing out one now—start with your 30-second version. In addition, write out your answers to some common interview questions—what are some brief stories that you can share that illustrate your strengths, your skills, and how you worked on a weakness? Start by brainstorming ideas and then pick the best ones.

2. After completing The Employable Skills Self-Efficacy Survey (Ciarocco & Strohmetz, 2018) that we described in this module, explore the workforce competencies identified in the ETS research report on O*NET (Burrus, Jackson, Xi, & Steinberg, 2013)—we list them for you here. Which ones are strengths for you? Where do you need to grow? Create an action plan to play to strengths and bolster weaknesses.

   Active listening

   Critical thinking

   Judgment and decision making

   Writing

   Social perceptiveness

   Speaking

   Reading comprehension

   Complex problem solving

   Monitoring

   Time management

11 Graduate School

CHAPTER OUTLINE

11.0 MEET AMIRAH

iStock.com/Rawpixel

Amirah thought that she wanted to go to graduate school for a doctorate in clinical psychology. After all, that was the reason she started taking psychology courses. She wanted to learn about mental disorders and to help people, and it was obvious to her that experimental psychology topics were more about laboratory research and did not necessarily explore disorders.

When Amirah met with her academic advisor, she asked him about clinical doctoral programs and explained why she was interested. Her advisor told her that this certainly was one option for her, but that there were a lot of other options that she might want to consider. He explained that there were both PhD and PsyD programs in clinical psychology.

Before moving on, though, he asked her a few more questions because he wanted to check whether a doctoral program was the best fit for Amirah's goals. Amirah did not have an immediate answer to this—she just thought that this was the path that she was supposed to follow because of her interests.

Upon hearing this, the advisor told Amirah that it was now time to explore the variety of possibilities that she could pursue. At first, Amirah seemed a bit unsure about possibly changing her mind, but her advisor was supportive. He told her that it might turn out that a doctorate in clinical psychology would be the best fit, but it was also possible that another option would fit her interests. He told her that they should start by diving more deeply into various career possibilities. From there, they could see which seemed most appealing, and then they could plan the right graduate path for her.

Why Did We Tell You This Story?

As professors, we recognize that students are not always familiar with the variety of paths (even among the "helping" careers) that are available for psychology students. Our point is that, even if you think you know your path, take a little bit of time to explore other possibilities. As with Amirah's situation, you may find that your original line of thinking is the best match for you; however, you might also discover a different path that is a better fit for your goals.

11.1 IS GRADUATE SCHOOL RIGHT FOR YOU?

iStock.com/PeopleImages

We hear from a lot of students that they want to go to graduate school. However, when we press further, some of these students have no answer when we ask about which career they want to pursue. That is, first think about what type of career you ultimately want, and then determine whether graduate school is needed for that career path. In other words, instead of saying "I want to go to grad school … what can I do with that?" ask yourself, "what do I want to do, and does that require graduate school?" This was the advice that we provided in our earlier chapter on careers—think about a career and work backward to plan your path (e.g., Ginat, 2005). In this module, we cover some things that you should consider before you dive headfirst into the adventure that we call grad school (see Table 11.1 for some questions to ask yourself).

TABLE 11.1

To Help Determine If Grad School Is a Good Path for You, Answer the Following Questions

1. Do you have a goal or reason for going? If so, what is it?
2. Are you motivated to work hard in order to succeed?
3. Do you have the potential to work independently (seriously, will you work hard even if a boss or supervisor is not pushing you)?
4. Are you okay with living frugally during graduate school and putting off earning a real income for a few years?
5. Are you open to new locations? Or do you have realistic options nearby if you are not? See Table 6 on pages 26 and 27 of the article by Christidis, Stamm, and Linn (2016) that we mention in the text of this module to get an idea of the number of degrees awarded in a particular state.

What Should NOT Matter?

In the 21st century, this should go without saying, but grad school is open to both men and women—in fact, women outnumber men in psychology programs at both the master's and doctoral levels (Fowler, Cope, Michalski, Christidis, Lin, & Conroy, 2018). The number of doctorates earned in psychology is skewed toward people who identify as white, but the numbers earned by people from diverse backgrounds have been increasing quite a bit in recent years (e.g., Lin, Stamm, & Christidis, 2018). Our point here is this: do not ever place any artificial restrictions on yourself based on gender, race, or ethnicity—if you want to pursue graduate school, then go for it!

Also, be aware that some capable people make it into graduate school but then have feelings that they are not good enough. This is referred to as *imposter syndrome*, and it can happen to both women and men, undergrads, grad students, and even professors (e.g., Pinto-Powell, 2018). Remember this, though—if a program offers to admit you, then you *are* good enough (see Revuluri, 2018, for advice on how to overcome these feelings).

What Degree Do You Need?

You should first determine whether graduate training is needed for your career path. If it is, what type of program and degree is needed? What specialty area are you going to pursue? For example, graduate school in psychology is quite broad as there are a wide variety of subareas from which you have to choose. If you are unsure about the specialty area right now, do not worry—we include some of the most common options in the next module. But, please try to avoid the following mistake—grad school is probably not the best option if you do not have anything else to do and need something to fill the time. You want to think about the plans for your future career and how graduate school can help you get there (e.g., Uscher, 2011).

Are You Ready for More School?

If you are growing weary of school and are barely going to make it to graduation, then you may want to reconsider whether graduate school is the right decision for you (right now). Most master's programs are going to be 2 to 3 years of hard work, and most doctoral programs are going to be 5 to 7 years of hard work. If you are already sick of school now, then you might not make it through those additional years of study.

However, not all hope is lost—did you notice that we included the phrase "right now" in that last paragraph? If you are not ready for grad school right after graduation, you may want to consider a *gap year* to recharge your batteries and better prepare yourself for graduate school (e.g., Hamby, 2015). If you are considering doctoral programs, dive into research. If you are considering master's programs, spend the year gaining relevant work or volunteer experience to help you prepare for your desired field. Or, if you are not completely sure whether you want to join the world of work or go to grad school, you can use that gap year to test drive whether or not you enjoy a particular job.

Can You Commit to the Hard Work?

Graduate school can be a lot of work (you may even have to work on some weekends). Students might be taking classes, teaching their own courses or working as a teaching assistant, conducting research projects, and doing applied work—this certainly requires a great deal of motivation (Thompson & Fitzgerald, 2017). As anyone who has switched college majors can attest, if you are not properly motivated to succeed in a particular field, difficult work can be unbearable. In contrast, if one is highly interested in an area, then it is much easier to find motivation.

iStock.com/MissTuni

One thing about graduate school—as we will discuss later—is that there are more activities that require internal motivation in order to get them done. Unlike undergraduate courses that have set deadlines within a semester (e.g., the paper is due week 12), in graduate school a thesis project can span multiple semesters (or years) and does not have a set deadline. Unfortunately, we have occasionally seen unmotivated students make little progress on projects like these.

If you are reading this book, it is likely that you are highly intelligent. But, in grad school, everyone is intelligent. So, if you have been coasting without much effort because you can get by on your smarts, prepare for a wake-up call in grad school. To succeed in grad school, you will need to use your intelligence and push yourself to work hard (e.g., Henry, 2014). As Ruben (2010) humorously notes—in grad school "you study because you *want* to" (p. 3).

Delayed Gratification

You also have to be okay with hard work now followed by delayed gratification—this is because advanced degrees take time (e.g., Metz, 2016). Also, if you are involved with research, projects take time to complete and take even longer to be accepted for publication. In a clinical context, it may take time to see discernible improvement in someone's symptoms. Our point is this: grad school is not meant for people who always need immediate gratification.

In addition to those aspects of grad school, delayed gratification also comes into play when it comes to money (e.g., Metz, 2016). In most cases, grad students do not live in the lap of luxury—they tend to live a simple, frugal existence as they are putting off earning a real income until a few years (or decade) into the future. This also means that you will delay any real attempts at beefing up a savings account or retirement investments (for more on this, see our chapter on money). Grad school might very well lead to a lucrative job, but remember that not all careers that follow grad school are going to make you wealthy.

Location, Location, Location!

Most institutions of higher learning offer a bachelor's degree in psychology—and if they do not, they offer a degree that is basically the same thing, such as psychological science or behavioral science (e.g., Klatzky, 2012). When it comes to graduate school, some schools are not going to offer a degree or program in the field that you want. Within the United States, there is a large disparity in the number of psychology graduate degrees that

iStock.com/Oleksii Liskonih

are awarded in different states—some states award over 500 psychology doctoral degrees and over 2,000 psychology master's degrees in a year, whereas many other states award fewer than 100 of each degree (Christidis et al., 2016). You might be surprised to learn that the largest percentage growth in the number of psychology doctorates awarded was in the great state of Iowa (a 183% increase between 2004 and 2013!) (Christidis et al., 2016).

On top of that, suppose that one of the institutions near you does offer the graduate program and the degree that you need—that does not mean that you will be admitted. Admission to graduate school can be more competitive than it is for undergraduate programs (more on this later in this chapter). For example, many doctorate programs admit fewer than 10 students each year (see Vonk, 2017, for a firsthand account of an honor student who did not get admitted the first year that he applied; the good news is that he improved his applications and was accepted when he applied the next year).

In addition, there are some academics who think that it is a bad idea to attend the same school for both undergrad and grad school. If you attend different institutions, you will be exposed to a wider range of ideas and perspectives. And do not be shocked if you encounter the phrase "academic inbreeding," which refers to the similar idea of hiring faculty members from one's own doctoral program (e.g., Altbach, Yudkevich, & Rumbley, 2015). There are differing opinions on this issue, so attending the same institution might be okay—but be sure to check with faculty at your institution, and give at least some thought to the possibility of expanding your horizons at a different institution.

So, what is the solution to this dilemma? One possibility is to be open to living in a new place. Remember that a move does not have to be permanent—you can move back after you finish your degree. However, we understand that this is not feasible for everyone—some of you have geographical restrictions because of family, partners, or attachment to a particular region. If that is the case, at least consider nearby cities or neighboring states—after all, a drive or flight home would not take that long. But, for some, relocation is a nonstarter—in this case, you may have to choose graduate programs based on what degrees are offered in your location. In this scenario, you are going to have to be a bit more flexible with your back-up plans.[1]

Take-Home Message

Our number one recommendation is that you make sure that your career path requires that graduate degree before you make the decision to dive into this world. After that, consider whether you have the motivation and the ability to commit fully to it—you do

[1]Another consideration is to look for the possibility of online programs—however, as we note elsewhere in this (and the next) chapter, please be very careful and pay close attention to whether a program is accredited or not. Also, be mindful as to whether this type of education will provide you with the guidance and training that will properly prepare you for your future career.

not want to spend years in graduate school, only to see your motivation fade away (potentially leaving you with an unfinished degree). We hope that we are not painting too bleak of a picture—graduate school was not only important for our careers, but it was also some of the best years of our lives. We simply want to make sure that you are realistic as you plan for this phase of your life.

iStock.com/LemonTreeImages

Action Steps

1. To get a better idea as to whether graduate school should be a possible option for you, return to Table 11.1 in this module and take a minute to answer each of those questions honestly. For how many questions did you answer "yes"?

2. We also recommend that you check out Ruben's (2010) hilarious book that takes a lighthearted perspective of some pros and cons of grad school. This is humorously titled *Surviving Your Stupid, Stupid Decision to Go to Grad School* (see the references at the back of the book for the full citation—also, please note that this book occasionally includes some adult language).

11.2 TYPES OF DEGREES AND PROGRAMS

You might be surprised to learn that, of the people who graduated with a bachelor's degree in psychology, over 40% continued on to earn a graduate degree (American Psychological Association, 2018). When it comes to graduate degrees that are in or related to psychology, we have some good news and some bad news. The good news is that there are many different types of graduate programs and degrees that are available for psychology students. The bad news is that some of them are highly competitive, some can take many years to complete, and, because there are so many programs, it may take some effort to decide on an area that interests you the most. In this module, we introduce some of the degrees and programs that psychology students often consider and explain some key differences among them.

iStock.com/VPanteon

Graduate Programs—A Lot of Options

For graduate training, you need to dig a little deeper than the broad term *psychology*—you need to know a more specific subfield in (or related to) psychology. As you can see in Table 11.2, there are many different subfields for graduate training (keep in mind that some subfields overlap both applied and experimental approaches). Although a lot of students seem to know more about graduate school possibilities in the applied fields (e.g., clinical and counseling), keep in mind that there are a lot of opportunities in the experimental

TABLE 11.2

Graduate Programs in (or Closely Related to) Psychology

Applied psychology		
	Clinical psychology	
		Clinical
		Clinical child psychology
		Gerontology/geropsychology
		Health/medical psychology
		Neuropsychology
		Primary care
		Psychoanalytic
	Community psychology	
	Counseling psychology	
		Community counseling
		Family counseling
		Marriage and family therapy
		Mental health counseling
		Rehabilitation
	Educational psychology	
	Environmental psychology	
	Forensic psychology	
	Industrial/organizational psychology	
	Multicultural psychology	
	Psychiatry	
	School psychology	
		School counseling
		Applied behavior analysis
	Social work	
	Sport psychology	
Experimental psychology		
	Behavioral	
		Animal cognition
	Cognitive psychology	
		Cognitive science
		Engineering psychology
		Human factors/user experience (UX)
		Psycholinguistics
	Developmental psychology	
		Adolescent psychology
		Child psychology
		Gerontology/geropsychology
		Human development and family studies

Neuroscience
- Biological psychology
- Comparative psychology
- Physiological psychology/psychobiology
- Psychopharmacology

Quantitative psychology and psychometrics

Social psychology
- Personality

Note: This table of subfields and areas in psychology is loosely based on the organization used by the National Center for Educational Statistics (2010) and Michalski, Cope, and Fowler (2019).

subfields of psychology. And, in a lot of cases, there are better odds of admission—for example, many experimental psychology doctoral programs receive fewer applicants (i.e., less competition for you) and have higher acceptance rates than clinical and counseling doctoral programs (Michalski, Cope, & Fowler, 2019).

How do you know which subfield of psychology is the right one for you? There is no easy answer for this, as you have to make a decision on your own. However, we strongly encourage you to use the following information to help you decide:

- Which subfield provides the training and degree for your desired career path? Use our recommendations from earlier chapters—explore career websites, visit your campus career center, complete an internship, or conduct an informational interview.
- Do some digging to see what careers people end up in after earning a degree in a particular subfield. Well-organized grad programs will provide information about what their former students end up doing.
- Which topics or courses did you most enjoy learning about as a psychology student?
- Did you get involved with research or learn a whole lot about studies in a particular area? And, if so, did you enjoy it?

iStock.com/USGirl

Overview of Graduate Degrees in (or Related to) Psychology

At a basic level, there are two main options for graduate degrees—master's and doctoral degrees. A lot more master's degrees than doctoral degrees are earned by psychology majors—it is about a 4:1 ratio (American Psychological Association, 2018). Most master's programs are clearly labeled—for example, you might see a Master's in Social Work program or a Master's in Psychological Research. In contrast, doctoral degrees are typically identified by abbreviations such as PhD, PsyD, MD, or JD (the word "doctor" is typically part of the degree's full name). One key difference between master's and doctoral programs is that the former typically takes around 2 to 3 years and the latter takes 5 to 7 years.

Choosing Between a Master's or Doctoral Degree

You might see that some areas of study offer both master's and doctoral programs, and you do not know which to choose (e.g., Fowler, Zlotlow, & Hailstorks, 2014). Your choice of degree depends on the type of program and your future career goals. For example, some states might require you to have a doctorate to earn a license to practice. In other cases, a master's degree might be plenty of training to land a great job. You can also look for which degree is most common for your area. As an example, clinical psychology tends to be the most popular doctoral degree awarded in psychology, but counseling psychology is the top master's degree awarded (Christidis, Stamm, & Lin, 2016)—this suggests that if you are interested in clinical psychology then go for a doctorate, but if you are interested in counseling psychology then you might want to go for a master's. Do some research to learn about the patterns in your chosen subfield. If you only need a master's degree for a desired career, then aim for master's programs. Also, explore graduate program websites—what do their students end up doing after they finish the program? If you are still unsure, ask professors and graduate students at your institution for their perspectives.

Another, related issue is whether you should earn a master's degree first before entering a doctoral program (e.g., Kuther, 2018). Our advice is that, if the doctorate is the ultimate goal, then try to go straight into a doctoral program. Some doctoral programs are designed so that you earn a master's degree along the way, approximately halfway through the program (but not all programs do this). One potential drawback to entering a master's program first is that some coursework or accomplishments from a master's program may not transfer to a doctoral program—also, although earning a master's degree is a great accomplishment, there is no guarantee that having a master's degree will make you a better applicant than people who have just completed a bachelor's degree (e.g., Littleford, Buxton, Bucher, Simon-Dack, & Yang, 2018). Having said all of that, we want to say one more thing on this issue. If you need to (or want to) start with a master's program first before moving into a doctoral program, that is okay—we have personally seen a lot of students (and colleagues) go this route and then find professional success.

PhD vs. PsyD

We meet many students who want to know the difference between PhD (Doctor of Philosophy) and PsyD (Doctor of Psychology) programs. PhD programs have been around longer, and you will see PhD programs in both applied and experimental areas of psychology. In contrast, you are most likely to find PsyD programs in areas of psychology that deal with treatment (e.g., clinical, counseling) but not in experimental areas. Because of this, our discussion differentiates the PhD and PsyD in regard to clinical and counseling

TABLE 11.3

Comparison of Typical PhD and PsyD Programs

PhD	PsyD
• Most subfields in psychology	• Applied subfields in psychology
• Big focus on research	• Smaller focus on research
• Typically found in universities	• Typically found in professional schools or universities
• Smaller class sizes	• Larger class sizes
• Tuition tends to be lower	• Tuition tends to be higher
• Accreditation is important	• Accreditation is important

psychology programs. As we discuss these degrees, remember that one is not necessarily better than the other (see Table 11.3).

Both PhD and PsyD programs focus on mental health treatment, but PhD programs typically involve both treatment and research. Thus, PsyD programs regularly follow the practitioner model and PhD programs will follow the scientist-practitioner model (e.g., Metz, 2016). This is a big difference, so if research (or lack thereof) is an important factor for you, keep this in mind (e.g., Michalski & Fowler, 2016). But, please note that a PhD does not mean that you have to be a researcher—many people with this degree work in applied settings and they use their research training to help them at their jobs.

When you are looking for grad programs, keep in mind that PhD programs are typically found at universities, whereas PsyD programs can be found at professional schools and at some colleges or universities. If you are going to be a mental health practitioner (which is likely if you are thinking about PhD and PsyD programs), it is important that the program is accredited by an organization such as the American Psychological Association (e.g., Golding & Lippert, 2016b). We cover accreditation more later in this chapter, but for now, remember that whether you go the PhD or PsyD route, you want to choose an accredited program.

There are a few other factors to think about when considering PhD and PsyD programs. We discuss this more later, but it is not uncommon for PhD programs to reduce tuition; however, PsyD programs typically do not. Also, PhD programs tend to admit fewer applicants and, because of this, can be more competitive but have better faculty-to-student ratios. Finally, PhD programs, because of the inclusion of research training, can sometimes take slightly longer to complete than a PsyD program (e.g., Golding & Lippert, 2016b).

Other Graduate School Options

You might be surprised to learn that psychology majors are slightly more likely to earn a graduate degree in a field other than psychology (American Psychological Association, 2018). However, this includes any field outside of psychology, even related fields such as social work or marriage and family therapy. Psychology students are able to earn graduate degrees from other areas because of the wide array of skills that are developed as a psychology student. The other great aspect of psychology, because it investigates human thought and behavior, is that it is applicable to most other fields.

Medical school. One of these alternative paths is to pursue a career in medicine (see Kong, 2017, for a discussion of how psychology and medicine overlap). In med school, most students earn an MD (Doctor of Medicine), but some schools will offer other possibilities such as a combined or dual degree. This tends to be more common if a student is interested in research—for example, someone who was interested in medical neuroscience research might earn a dual MD/PhD in Neuroscience.

Although medical students can choose from a long list of specialty areas, most psychology students are familiar with one in particular—psychiatry. You might be surprised to learn that there are subspecialty areas such as psychocardiology or psycho-oncology (e.g., Castelnuovo, 2010). For example, psychocardiology can explore cases of heart disease that are affected by psychological issues such as depression (e.g., Nauert, 2015). One thing to keep in mind about psychiatry is that there is a lot of time spent with medical training (similar to other special areas in medicine)—this is important to know because it can mean less time focusing exclusively on psychological issues compared to, say, someone in a clinical psychology program (e.g., Metz, 2016).

Law school. Another alternative path is to attend law school and earn a JD (Juris Doctor). Similar to medical training, there are also dual degrees available, such as a JD/PhD. It is important to understand that law careers are not exactly what you see on television shows or in movies—only a small percentage of law takes place inside a courtroom (e.g., Lorenz, 2014)—and there are a number of different subfields that students can choose as their area of concentration.

Psychology is a good fit for a career in law because the legal field involves so many aspects of human behavior (e.g., Golding & Lippert, 2016a)—memory, bias, reasoning, and social interactions, just to name a few (TIP: if you are considering law school, be sure to take Cognitive Psychology and Social Psychology courses). A former psychology major who went on to law school argues that the psychology major is great preparation because of the emphasis on writing, conducting searches for relevant articles, and critical thinking (Lorenz, 2014).

Other possibilities. Besides medical school or law school, your education in psychology can also lead to other paths. For example, psychology majors can pursue graduate training in fields such as education, business, physical therapy, or occupational therapy. Keep in mind that (a) this is not a comprehensive list and (b) you may need to complete additional courses or other experiences (e.g., internships, shadowing, etc.) to qualify for graduate programs outside of psychology.

Postdoctoral Research Positions and Clinical Internships

Before we leave this module, we want to introduce two more positions that can be relevant to those of you who are considering graduate school. These occur at the end of or after completing a doctoral program, so you will not be applying to these right after you complete your undergraduate degree. However, because they are so common and because you may have heard of them without having them explained, we are going to introduce them to you here.

Postdoc. The term postdoc is short for postdoctoral researcher or scholar. This is a temporary position (typically 1 to 3 years) for people after they earn a doctorate, and it typically focuses on research. This provides people a chance to improve their research credentials by publishing more, collaborating with new people, or learning to use new research tools or technology. Today, it is very common for graduate students to move into a postdoc in order to be competitive for research or professor positions (e.g., Pelham, 2019). However, the bad news is that the pay is not great and some people end up doing more than one postdoc because they have difficulty landing an academic position (see Ruben, 2013, for a cynical look at postdocs).

Clinical internship. A clinical internship typically occurs during the final year of a doctoral program in clinical psychology. Doctoral grad students apply for a set of ranked internships and then they are (hopefully) matched with one of their choices. The early years of doctoral training are meant to prepare graduate students for this internship experience, and this internship is typically a required step for future licensure and employment (Williams-Nickelson, Prinstein, & Keilin, 2018).

Take-Home Message

iStock.com/JFsPic

As we discussed in our chapters on careers, psychology is unique compared to a lot of other fields in that there is not a single and set path for graduate school—you have options. With there being different degree options in (or related to) psychology, be sure to take a little bit of time to do some research. First, decide on a subfield (or at least narrow it down to a manageable set of subfields). Find out which degree is most common in your topic area. Figure out which degree is needed for what you want to do. And, if you are choosing between PhD and PsyD programs, do even more digging (than what we included here) to see which is best for your situation.

Action Steps

1. If you are considering graduate school, it is very important to identify which subfield(s) are possibilities for you. For some, this will be obvious; but, for others, you might not have a clear idea. If you are early in your college career, remember that this is okay—you have time to take courses and to explore the different areas of psychology. Wherever you are in the college process, start making a list today—even if you think you are certain with a choice, list other possibilities because you never know if you might change your mind as you learn more about a path.

2. After you identify the subfields that seem right for you, the next step is to determine which degree is the best fit. If you have more than one possibility for your subfields, then start making a pro/con list for each one. Also, do not be

afraid to ask professors for their perspective—in some cases, it might be pretty clear to them (based on their experiences and knowledge of the field) which degree makes the most sense for your situation.

11.3 FINDING GRADUATE PROGRAMS

iStock.com/Beeldbewerking

If you are considering graduate options, we want you to be well informed so that you can make wise decisions about whether to go and, if you are going, about where to go. You have to find a program that is a good fit for your skills, interests, and any other factors that are important to you. In this module, we cover some ideas as to how you can find programs as well as some important factors you should consider when deciding which ones are going to make your application list. As you read through this module, keep in mind that some factors may be more important than others, depending on your goals—choosing graduate programs is not a one-size-fits-all endeavor (e.g., Birchmeier, Shore, & McCormick, 2008).

Evaluating Program Fit

We suggest that you first start by identifying programs that fit your basic needs for graduate school. After that, you need to prioritize what is most important to you. In Table 11.4 we list some factors you should consider (we expand on most of these as we move through this module).

TABLE 11.4

Factors to Consider When Searching for and Choosing Graduate Programs

- Your career goals and the type of degree needed
- The grad program topic area
- Admission information (minimum requirements)
- Acceptance rates
- Accreditation (if applicable)
- Faculty areas of expertise and/or a potential mentor's research area
- Program expectations and type of training (e.g., research, clinical hours)
- What program graduates end up doing (i.e., do they get jobs? Internships?)
- Cost and/or financial packages
- Program or school reputation
- Program size
- Program environment or climate (you might not learn this until later, during an interview)

Those are some of the key factors, but you might come up with others that are important to you. Which of these factors should you prioritize? It is difficult to say that one particular factor is more important than another, and keep in mind that this is just *our perspective.* Your priorities might be different, so feel free to consider these based on your situation.

Finding Grad Programs

One resource for finding graduate programs is the book *Graduate Study in Psychology* (American Psychological Association, 2018). This book lists most American and Canadian psychology graduate programs. It also includes information about recent applicants such as the number of applications, number of admitted students, and average scores (GPA, GRE). This is a great book because it is published annually with updated information.

Another great resource is to ask professors for suggestions (yet another reason to get to know your professors!). Cognitive psychology professors are going to know more about cognitive programs, neuroscience professors will know about neuroscience programs, and social work professors have some knowledge about those programs (we think you get the idea). Also, consider asking graduate students—they were recently in your shoes and were looking for programs, so they might be able to provide some tips.

The internet can also be a great resource for finding grad programs. Most program websites will list descriptions of the program, research being conducted, application instructions, and possibly more. There are also sites that let you search through graduate programs (e.g., Gradschools.com). These can be helpful, but we have a warning here—these sites may include ads featuring institutions that are not accredited (we will have more on this) or are "for-profit" schools (see Simon, 2018, for a description of the poorer outcomes at these institutions).

Program Admission Requirements

Graduate programs vary when it comes to admission requirements. At any particular program, these tend to be stable from year to year, but be sure to check with a program for its most up-to-date requirements. Some programs may have minimum cutoff scores, some may provide recommendations, and some may list data for past students who were admitted. And some may include all three—for example, the program might set 3.0 as a minimum GPA, recommend a GPA above 3.3, and regularly admit students who have an average GPA around 3.5.

In our experiences, program requirements or recommendations tend to include

- A minimum grade point average (GPA)
- Minimum standardized test scores (e.g., GRE)
- A bachelor's degree
- A degree specifically in psychology, certain courses completed, or a minimum score on the GRE subject test

Program Acceptance Rates

Besides your qualifications, one big piece of information that can affect your grad school decisions is the likelihood of being accepted—we often use the term *competitiveness.* One piece of good news (which helps your odds) is that the number of institutions awarding master's and doctoral degrees in psychology has been increasing in recent years—also, the number of degrees awarded has been increasing as well (American Psychological Association, 2018). But, which types of psychology graduate programs receive the most applicants and which programs accept the highest percentage of applicants?

To compare master's and doctoral psychology programs, we looked at acceptance data across multiple years (Michalski, Cope, & Fowler, 2015, 2016, 2017, 2019). For master's programs, counseling, clinical, and industrial/organizational programs received the highest numbers of applications, and most psychology master's programs had acceptance rates between 30% and 65%. For doctoral programs, the number of applications for clinical programs was much higher than every other subfield. In terms of acceptance rates to doctoral programs, most subfields were close to 10% to 15%—notably, clinical psychology doctoral programs consistently had one of the lowest acceptance rates (i.e., clinical doctoral programs are very competitive as they receive the most applications and tend to have some of the lowest acceptance rates).

So, in general, the odds of being accepted into a master's program are much better than being accepted into a doctoral program. Keep in mind that these are general trends across degrees and that you will find variability across institutions. To see specific application and acceptance information for a particular program, check to see if a program lists this data on its website. If not, you can also consult a book we have mentioned before—*Graduate Study in Psychology* (e.g., American Psychological Association, 2018). As a reminder, this is published annually with updated information about programs and admissions.

Accreditation

When looking at graduate schools, another consideration is accreditation. This refers to whether an institution has been vetted and approved by an external agency. In our view, accreditation is a must—most reputable institutions of higher education are accredited by a regional organization that approves the quality of the curriculum and training.[2]

Another type of accreditation is for a graduate program—this is mainly for applied programs (e.g., clinical, school, social work, therapy, or counseling). Accreditation of a program is important because you can have more trust in the quality of education and training (Norcross & Karpiak, 2015). Also, grad students from accredited programs are more likely to land an accredited internship (e.g., Callahan, Collins, & Klonoff, 2010) and pass the licensing exam (Norcross & Karpiak, 2015) and they may need a graduate degree from

[2]Some common regional accrediting bodies include the Middle States Commission on Higher Education, New England Association of Schools and Colleges, North Central Association Commission on Accreditation and School Improvement, Northwest Commission on Colleges and Universities, Southern Association of Colleges and Schools, and Western Association of Schools and Colleges.

an accredited program in order to qualify for some jobs—especially for government and academic jobs (e.g., Graham & Kim, 2011). Here are some relevant accrediting agencies for psychology and psychology-related graduate programs:

- American Psychological Association—doctoral programs in psychology
- Council for Accreditation of Counseling & Related Educational Programs (CACREP)—master's in counseling
- Council on Social Work Education (CSWE)—master's in social work
- Commission on Accreditation for Marriage and Family Therapy Education (COAMFTE)—master's in marriage and family therapy

We realize that accreditation can seem confusing—for example, how do you know if an institution or program is accredited? Lucky for you, there are searchable databases available online. Feel free to check out websites for the Council for Higher Education Accreditation (https://www.chea.org/directories), CACREP (https://www.cacrep.org/directory/), CSWE (https://www.cswe.org/Accreditation), COAMFTE (https://www.coamfte.org/), and the American Psychological Association (https://www.apa.org/ed/accreditation/programs/index.aspx)—the latter includes psychology grad program accreditation for clinical, counseling, and school psychology.

Mentors

At this point, we want to make sure that you are aware of a key distinction between different types of graduate programs. In most applied programs that are not focused on research, you may be assigned a mentor or advisor, but you will likely end up working with a variety of professors or supervisors as you take courses and complete a number of milestone experiences. In these programs, the mentor or advisor might provide advice, but you are primarily applying to a program.

In contrast, other grad programs—typically those which focus on research—are mentor-based in that they match up incoming graduate students with a professor with whom they work closely throughout graduate school. Think of a "match" as someone with shared professional (or research) interests and communication style. For these programs, you want to consider both the academic program itself and how well you match up with your potential mentor. The match between a potential mentor and student is a key determinant in both admission decisions and progress—one's relationship with a mentor is one of the most important factors contributing to satisfaction with a PhD program (Woolston, 2017).

iStock.com/digitalskillet

So, choose a mentor carefully (e.g., Scott, 2016; Zimmerman, 2017). Look at the research of a potential mentor—for example, if you want to conduct research related to social cognition, then find a mentor who studies that topic. Dive into faculty web pages and immerse yourself in publications for a specific research topic. You may also want to consider whether you would benefit more from individual attention or if you would rather be part of a larger research team—look at professors' websites to see how many graduate students they currently supervise. Finally, there are other factors you might look for later in the application process (possibly during an interview) such as a potential mentor's communication style or personality (e.g., Ritzer, 2018).

Program Expectations and Type of Training

When looking through grad programs, be sure to do some homework about the program itself. For research programs, are publications and presentations emphasized? Can students collaborate with a variety of professors on research or do they primarily stick with one research team? What major milestone activities are required (e.g., thesis)?

For applied programs, how many hours are you going to spend training or working in applied settings? Also, consider the type of training you are going to receive. Will you learn to treat individuals from a psychodynamic perspective? Or will you learn more about cognitive behavioral methods? One recommendation is that, regardless of the specific type of training that is offered, you may want to make sure that it is evidence-based treatment. This means that, instead of being trained in a treatment approach where everyone *hopes* that it works, you should be trained in an approach that has research or other evidence to support its effectiveness (e.g., APA Presidential Task Force on Evidence-Based Practice, 2006).

What Past Students End Up Doing

One often-overlooked aspect of choosing a grad program is what their past students end up doing. Information like this is important because you want to have a good idea where you are going to end up after finishing a program. For a developmental psychology program, have the past students gone into academic positions (e.g., professors), research positions, or private industry? If you are applying to a clinical psychology doctoral program, you will want to pay attention to information regarding internship placement rates and possibly licensure exam performance (e.g., Norcross & Karpiak, 2015)—do you want to attend a program where a significant proportion of the students is not properly prepared for these next steps? You do not want to spend time and money in graduate school only to not be an attractive candidate for a position that you want. Check program websites for this information. If you cannot find this information, then we encourage you to ask—good programs that are proud of their students' outcomes will gladly share this information with you.

iStock.com/asiseeit

Grad School Finances

The cost of grad school can be another factor to consider, and some grad school tuition can be expensive. However, one thing to know is that many PhD programs drastically cut tuition or, in some cases, waive it completely. That is correct—the graduate programs that might be the most competitive can be the most generous when it comes to tuition costs. You are not likely to see waived or drastically reduced tuition for master's programs, PsyD programs, medical school, or law school.

iStock.com/CREATISTA

Most grad programs will expect that you treat it like your full-time job (and you will likely have to do that, in order to graduate on schedule). One way to deal with costs is to work on campus—many programs offer teaching assistant or research assistant positions that include a small stipend. These stipends are not lucrative, but they help you pay the bills. Also, these roles may allow you to focus on skills that are related to your field, such as conducting research or helping with a class in your topic area. In addition, you can also develop networking relationships by working closely with professors. See our chapter on money for even more tips.

Does the Reputation of an Institution or Program Matter?

Some think that reputation matters—for example, a disproportionate number of billionaires, CEOs, and national politicians attended elite colleges and graduate programs (e.g., Wai, 2014). In addition, 25% of institutions (at the higher end, in terms of prestige) produce approximately 80% of tenure-track professors (Clauset, Arbesman, & Larremore, 2015). However, others argue that where you are educated does not matter—what matters is being exposed to valuable opportunities and then taking advantage of them (e.g., Bruni, 2015). Plenty of people have earned great positions by working hard even though they did not attend a prestigious institution (e.g., Warner & Clauset, 2015).

Our advice is to understand that an institution's reputation can potentially influence future employers. After all, we all tend to be influenced by name brands, and if you ask people to be honest, many wish they could earn a degree from a well-regarded institution. However, this is one very small aspect of what you should use to choose a graduate program—do not spend too much time worrying about rankings such as those in *U.S. News & World Report*. Your career goals, your fit with a mentor or program, and a program's history of placing graduates into good jobs should be much higher on your list of priorities.

Program Size and Environment

You may also want to consider the program size and environment. For example, do you feel more comfortable among a group (or cohort) of 30 new grad students or would you prefer a starting cohort closer to 5? Although you can get an idea of a program's typical cohort sizes from its website, you might not be able to fully evaluate a program's environment until you visit the institution and meet with people. Also, consider reaching out to current grad students and asking for their perspective of the program (and, importantly, do they like it there?).

Take-Home Message

Clearly, there are a lot of factors to consider when choosing possible graduate programs. Because of this, you want to start thinking about which factors are most important to you. You do not have to be picking out potential programs during your freshman and sophomore years, but keep your eyes and ears open. For example, suppose you are interested in

iStock.com/Rawpixel

social psychology and you read a fascinating article in that class that piques your interest—check out who wrote it and if he or she is affiliated with a graduate program and store that away in your head as one program to consider later.

Action Steps

1. Go through our list of factors and rank which ones are most (and least) important for you. For some of you, it might be too difficult to create a true ranking—in this case, differentiate what is "most important" and what is of "lesser importance." Finally, think about if there is anything else that you would add to our list (e.g., location).
2. If you are considering an applied graduate program, we highly recommend that you explore the accreditation websites and databases that we provided earlier in this module so that you can better understand accreditation and why it matters.

11.4 HOW GRADUATE SCHOOL DIFFERS FROM UNDERGRADUATE STUDIES

Graduate school is different from the structure of college during the undergraduate years. There are some big differences in terms of the number of students, the size of classes, the types of classes, and some of the expectations. If you are considering graduate school, we think that it is important that you are informed so that you can make the best decisions and prepare yourself for your future. In this module, we will focus on some of the key ways that graduate school is different.

Classes

As we noted earlier, most graduate programs are selective and admit fewer students than undergraduate programs—because of this, classes tend to be small. One advantage of small classes is that most courses are in a seminar format, meaning that you get to know the professors well. Most seminar courses are built around discussions and have much less lecture (or none at all). With classes being small, it is expected that all students will contribute regularly during discussions (e.g., Freis & Kraha, 2016)—so, you better complete the readings before coming to class (you cannot hide in the back row). In addition, graduate instructors tend to empower students by having them lead class discussions throughout the semester. So, for some weeks, reading before class is not enough—you must prepare thoughtful discussion questions and a presentation for the topic.

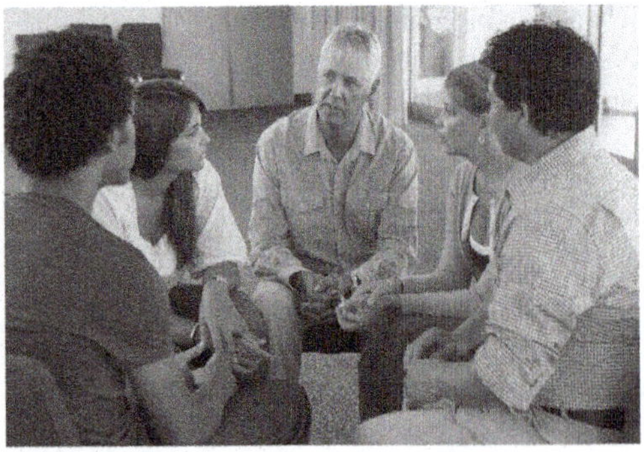

iStock.com/monkeybusinessimages

Other differences revolve around the class requirements. The good news is that many graduate courses do not include exams—but, if exams are required, there is a good possibility that they are take-home exams (NOTE: this is not true for programs related to medicine or physiology, which might have lots of memorization and exams). However, the bad news is that those take-home exams are likely going to be lengthy essays or papers. With less focus on exams, graduate classes typically require discussion participation (as noted earlier), a lengthy paper or two (perhaps in the range of 15 to 20 pages), and class presentations. Depending on the focus of the program, you may see themes for assignments across courses (e.g., research grant proposals in experimental psychology programs or applied consulting projects in an industrial/organizational program).

A final note about classes is that programs will vary in terms of the number of required courses. Some might be class-intensive, with students taking four or five courses each semester. However, other programs may focus more on experiences outside of the classroom, such as research or supervised training (more on these to follow)—in these cases, you may take only one to three courses each semester. In some programs, you can complete the majority of the coursework in the early semesters so that you can focus on other priorities as you get further into the program (e.g., Kraha, Freis, & Longstreth, 2017).

Grades

Many graduate programs require a minimum grade of a B or B– in order to pass a course. This might seem a little daunting, but do not worry—after all, if you are good enough to make it into graduate school, you have likely been earning grades in the A or B range. A second bit of good news is that, for the most part, as long as you are passing your graduate courses, grades do not matter that much (e.g., Freis & Kraha, 2016)—most employers are impressed enough by the advanced degree and do not care about grad school GPA. As the old joke goes, "what do you call the person who graduated last in a medical school class?"—Doctor! One key exception to this is for students entering a master's program first with the intention of applying to doctoral programs afterward—in these scenarios, strive to maintain a high GPA (Littleford, Buxton, Bucher, Simon-Dack, & Yang, 2018).

iStock.com/fatido

Faculty Mentors

One great thing about graduate school is that most programs will assign students a mentor who can help provide advice and guidance. As we noted earlier, in research-intensive graduate programs (e.g., PhD programs), faculty mentors work closely with grad students by providing advice and feedback and by collaborating together on projects. Grad students can benefit a lot from these relationships—they have someone who is guiding their progress, advocating for them, and providing advice and/or resources (e.g., research funding and tools). So, if you have any say in who your mentor is going to be, choose carefully (e.g., Freis & Kraha, 2016). Also, do not be afraid to develop relationships with other professors or supervisors—they can be helpful as well (e.g., Kraha, Freis, & Longstreth, 2017).

Responsibilities Outside of Class

For programs with a research focus, the research demands are fairly high. For applied programs, you will likely spend a lot of time with supervised training. And, for those applied topic areas that include a focus on research (e.g., clinical PhD), you will spend a lot of time doing both. In the following, we go through the research and applied training that is commonly a part of the graduate school experience.

Research. Most graduate programs include research, but the extent of it can vary quite a bit. At one end of the spectrum, grad students might only read about and discuss research in their courses. At the other end of the spectrum, grad students are actively their own research projects. With the exception of clinical psychology PhD programs, programs with more of an emphasis on mental health treatment (or other applied settings) tend to include less research. PhD programs tend to focus a great deal on research, with expectations that graduate students will assist professors with their research and conduct their own projects (with guidance from a faculty mentor).

Most graduate programs will require a thesis for the master's degree and a dissertation for the doctoral degree (if you have a chance, we recommend doing a senior thesis or honors thesis—it is great preparation for these grad school projects). A thesis or dissertation can be as simple as a lengthy review of research or it can consist of an original research project that must be presented to a (sometimes daunting, but often friendly) committee of professors who will ask questions about the project methods, analyses, and conclusions. Specific expectations about theses, dissertations, and other accomplishments may vary across programs—some might be 100+ pages that thoroughly review a topic area, and some might be shorter in length (similar to a research article publication).

Supervised training, practicum, and internships. For applied programs, you are likely going to spend a significant portion of your time outside of class going through supervised training and work experiences. These could take the form of internships or practicums, which may require hours' worth of work. In some mental health treatment programs, grad students may have sessions with clients that are videotaped and then reviewed by a supervisor. For experimental psychology programs, if you are not interested in an academic career, you may want to pursue a summer internship (e.g., Sinche, 2016)—for example, we have seen experimental graduate students work for businesses or even the military. Our point here is that, in most programs, you will be doing activities outside of the classroom that are meant to prepare you for a future career.

Work and Social Life

Graduate school tends to be an immersive experience with high expectations. With all of these demands, you may think that there would not be any time for a social life—and, if you ask graduate students, they may joke about being poor and not having much time to go out. However, graduate students tend to form bonds with their cohort (i.e., the students that enter the program with them) and socialize regularly. Some grad students tell us that one of the things that has helped them survive grad school was the positive support from their peers (e.g., Freis & Kraha, 2016). Although there may not be as much free time as there is during the undergraduate years, there is ample time to relax. And an added bonus is that all of these friendships count as networking relationships.

Take-Home Message

There are some significant changes when you switch from undergraduate to graduate training. Courses have a slightly different structure, and grad students tend to work more closely with faculty. In addition, other things may matter more than course grades (but be sure to put in enough effort so that you pass those courses!), such as research or applied work. Although graduate school can add a lot of stress to your life, it can lead to the development of positive relationships and immense feelings of accomplishment when you reach the end!

Action Steps

1. What is your classroom style? Most grad school classes expect active participation, so, if your current style does not match this, make an effort now to practice speaking up in your courses—ask a question or make a contribution during a discussion. See our classroom tips from an earlier chapter for some more suggestions.

iStock.com/asiseeit

2. As you explore graduate programs, develop a specific idea of what you want to get out of graduate school. As we have noted throughout this chapter, not only does grad school differ from undergrad, but grad programs are different in what you learn and what you experience. So figure out what you want. Is it research? Training in mental health treatment? Both?

11.5 GRAD STUDENTS DESCRIBE THEIR EXPERIENCES

What are the best and worst parts of graduate school? To give you some answers, we spoke with graduate students and put together descriptions of various graduate programs that are connected to psychology. Each section in this module has the same basic structure. First, we list the type of program followed by a description of the best and worst aspects of that program. Keep in mind that these descriptions reflect the perspectives of the people with whom we spoke, but based on our experiences (and our conversations over the years with others who went to graduate school), we think that these descriptions are fairly representative.

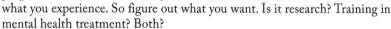

iStock.com/fizkes

- Master's Degree—Industrial/Organizational Psychology
- Master's Degree—Clinical Mental Health Counseling
- Master's Degree—Marriage and Family Therapy
- PhD—Clinical Psychology
- PhD—Developmental Psychology (Child)
- PhD—Experimental Psychology (Cognitive and Social)
- PhD—School Psychology
- MD —Psychiatry

Master's Degree—Industrial/Organizational Psychology

Being a graduate student can be very stressful, overwhelming, and challenging. Unless you specifically make the time, you might not always stay up to date on current events or new movies. You may have to make sacrifices to make time for studying, thesis, working, and preparing for class. To put it simply, graduate school can feel like the craziest thing you will ever put yourself through.

With that said, attending grad school can be a great decision. True, grad school is difficult, but you do not go through it alone. Classmates can feel like family because they are the only ones who understand each other's experiences—attending class together, confiding in one another, socializing, studying, and commiserating together. Beyond those relationships (FYI—that is networking!), you might also be surprised at your development and the speed with which it takes place! Looking back, you can be amazed at your productivity and resiliency.

Master's Degree—Clinical Mental Health Counseling

The best thing about grad school was the exposure to so many brilliant minds. When faced with a tough clinical case, it is particularly helpful to seek out help from experienced professors and members of your cohort (i.e., fellow students). Because clinical work is so diverse and unpredictable, it can be very reassuring to know that there is so much support available. Plus, grad school is an acceptable time to make mistakes and learn from them!

The most difficult thing was achieving balance, particularly when multiple obligations required attention. There were hours of practicum required during the first year and even more hours of internship required during the second year. Additionally, if you have a graduate assistantship (which is extremely helpful for paying bills), that is another 10 to 20 hours per week of work. A final point is to avoid being a perfectionist—learn to do your best by doing a good-enough job and then move on to the next task.

Master's Degree—Marriage and Family Therapy

There are many positive aspects of grad school. First, students can specialize in a number of different areas, depending on their interests. Second, students are exposed to new knowledge and new ways of thinking that can be beneficial both personally and professionally. Third, the cohort of students that enter with you makes it feel like you have support the whole time.

The two worst parts are the fast pace and the cost. Master's programs can be expensive, so make sure that this is what you really want to do. The fast pace is in regards to the courses—at times it feels as if courses go by so quickly that it is difficult to digest all of the information.

PhD—Clinical Psychology

The best thing about a clinical PhD program is knowing that there are a variety of career opportunities. For example, you could be a teaching professor or a research professor, work in a large hospital, or have a private practice. This flexibility is great because it means that you can change your mind while going through the program (but do not do this too late in the process).

The most difficult part about graduate training in clinical psychology is the number of different activities required for students. You are constantly dividing your efforts among clinical work, research, coursework, and service activities. Because of that, it can sometimes seem like you are working all of the time (but there is some occasional down time when you can relax).

PhD—Developmental Psychology (Child)

In a child development program, you have to balance research and coursework. If you enjoy working with children, then a big plus to this program is that you get to work with kids (or babies) when you are conducting studies. You learn a great deal about developmental research as you spend part of the time learning about research and statistical methods and other time focusing on theories of development.

One of the challenges to this type of research is that studies can take a long time—it is more difficult to recruit participants when working with a special population like children. However, there are sometimes opportunities to work with data sets from larger research studies that have already been conducted. It can also be challenging to stay afloat through the program and to keep up with deadlines—it is very important to be self-motivated in order to do well.

PhD—Experimental Psychology (Cognitive and Social)

The best parts of an experimental program are the ability to carry out independent research projects, to explore topics in depth, and the feeling of satisfaction whenever a project is presented or published. In addition, teaching and mentoring can also be rewarding. You also get to learn much more than you could have ever imagined about your specialty area.

The worst part is that the time demands can be overwhelming at times, and the stress is constant—you have to stay on top of things, as projects can take a while to complete. Another issue is that it can be difficult to obtain funding for research or travel. Some students have mentors with grants and, for them, funding is readily available; however, for other students, you have to work hard and sometimes get creative to find funding.

PhD—School Psychology

The major benefit to a school psychology program is the variety of experiences—you have experiences in the classroom and in school settings. Building on that, another benefit is the opportunity to help students—this is a big reason to go into a school psych program. Finally, because grad school is difficult, it is great to have feelings of accomplishment when you finish a major task such as a thesis.

As is the case with any type of graduate work, there are challenges. As a graduate student, you are required to balance a number of classes each semester, hours of practicum time in schools, and engagement in research activities. The training is rigorous but valuable, preparing future school psychologists to work in settings where student success is at the core of every task.

MD—Psychiatry

There are some very good aspects to attending medical school. First, you accumulate a vast amount of knowledge about physiology and diseases. You also have the positive experiences of being able to help others. Finally, there are a large number of options—you can pick a specialty area based on your interests, lifestyle, and personality.

The toughest things about medical school are the long hours and stress. At times, your confidence might be shaken, and some students begin to doubt themselves. People often equate medical school with drinking from a fire hydrant—there is a lot thrown at students all at once with high expectations that they will learn and continue forward.

Take-Home Message

As with most things in life, there are pros and cons to the graduate school experience. Graduate students report that the heightened expectations can be difficult and lead to high levels of stress, but in the end, there are plenty of benefits. For those of you considering mentor-based programs, remember that your relationship with a mentor can either be the best or worst thing about grad school (e.g., Woolston, 2017)—so choose your mentor carefully. Grad school keeps you busy with challenging courses and other activities, it requires motivation, but in the end it can be a rewarding experience!

Action Steps

1. If you are considering graduate school, identify a graduate program that fits your career training plans. Contact a graduate student (explore the program website to find contact information) and offer to buy him or her a cup of coffee if they would be willing to discuss their experiences and impressions of that graduate program.
2. If you end up applying to graduate programs, keep this in mind—talk to grad students who are already in the program that you are considering (or where you are interviewing). They will provide the real descriptions of what the program is like, and this can be very helpful as you make decisions.

Getting Into Graduate School

12

12.0 MEET JERMAINE

iStock.com/michaelpuche

CHAPTER OUTLINE

Jermaine was trying to write a personal statement essay for his graduate school applications, but he was not sure what to write. The instructions were somewhat vague—it said to write about your background and your research interests and to include anything else that might be important for the admissions committee to consider. Jermaine stared at the blank screen for almost an hour but did not come up with anything to write.

The next day, Jermaine decided to seek out help and stopped by the office of one of his professors. The professor welcomed him in and Jermaine told him of the problems he was having with his application essay. His professor told him that this was a common issue and, because of that, the campus Psi Chi chapter held an event each fall that walked students through the important steps. Even better, he also told Jermaine that he would help him get started right away!

Jermaine also told him that he had an idea about what to write about his research interests—after all, that was the whole reason that he was applying to graduate school: to do research projects that explored the fallibility of memory, such as with eyewitness memory. However, he was not sure what to include about his background. What did they want to know about? His grade point average (GPA)? His courses? His favorite horror movie?

He was joking with that last one, but the professor got his point and laughed along with him.

Jermaine's professor told him to pull out his notepad, as he was going to walk him through some ideas that might be a little more relevant for his essay than his interest in zombies!

Why Did We Tell You This Story?

If you have made the decision that graduate school is the right path for you, then the next step is to start preparing. However, you might find yourself in Jermaine's position—motivated to attend graduate school but unsure about how the application process works. The reality is that most institutions do not have a course titled "How to Get Into Graduate School"—you have to figure it out on your own. To help you out, in this chapter we cover the graduate school application process and provide tips to improve your materials.

12.1 WHAT DO GRADUATE PROGRAMS WANT?

If you have made the decision that graduate school is the right path for you, then the next step is to start preparing. Throughout this chapter, we cover the application process as well as the key things that go into an application. In this first module, we cover what graduate schools value and what they use to make admissions decisions. We cover this topic first because it provides an overview of what you will need to think about and work on as you complete your undergraduate degree. In later modules, we go into even more detail on some of these topics—we provide tips so that you can be prepared for this endeavor!

What Grad Programs Want to See

An examination of doctoral programs shows that they typically want and value some key items (Littleford, Buxton, Bucher, Simon-Dack, & Yang, 2018), and we list these items for you in Table 12.1. The main distinctions are between PhD programs, which highly value research and your fit with a mentor, and applied programs (such as PsyD programs), which value research less and give more importance to applied experience (e.g., Pashak, Handal, & Ubinger, 2012). Based on our conversations with faculty from master's programs in counseling, social work, or family therapy, they are more like PsyD programs in what they value.

TABLE 12.1

Most Graduate Programs Want and Value the Following

- Letters of recommendation
- Personal statement (or essay)
- Interview
- Grade point average (GPA)
- Fit (with a mentor or with a program)
- Graduate Record Exam (GRE) scores
- Relevant experience (research and applied experience)

Fit

iStock.com/AleksandarGeorgiev

The term "fit" refers to your fit within a program (as a whole) or your fit with a specific mentor. As we noted in the previous chapter, PhD programs are often mentor-based programs where you will be working on research with a professor. For these programs, it is imperative that you are a good match, interest-wise, with a potential mentor. In many cases, students will apply to a particular program because they want to work with one specific professor on research. Keep in mind that, for mentor-based PhD programs, you must also be a good fit for the program itself.

For other, non-mentor-based graduate programs, your fit with the program is a key component. Do your goals align with the training goals of the program? Does the program match your interests? Does the program prepare you for the type of career that you want to pursue?

Both of these types of fit can be determined through letters of recommendation, personal statements or essays, and an interview. The latter two are clearly under your control—you write your essay and you communicate during an interview. And, even though other people write your letters of recommendation, remember that you are the one who determines what can go into them (e.g., Norcross & Cannon, 2008). In other words, letter writers can only write good things if they see you demonstrate and accomplish good things—so, convey a positive impression and clearly communicate your skills, accomplishments, and goals to them!

Measurable Qualifications

Graduate schools also care about measurable accomplishments and abilities. Grad programs want to see that you did well in undergraduate courses (GPA)—if you did not do well, then they are not confident that you will be able to handle the increased academic demands of graduate school. Some graduate programs may arbitrarily set minimum cutoff values for GPAs, whereas other graduate programs have no minimums at all. Because of this, there is no set guideline for what your GPA must be in order to be competitive—our recommendation is to strive for a 3.5 or higher, but if that is not possible, try to keep it above 3.0.

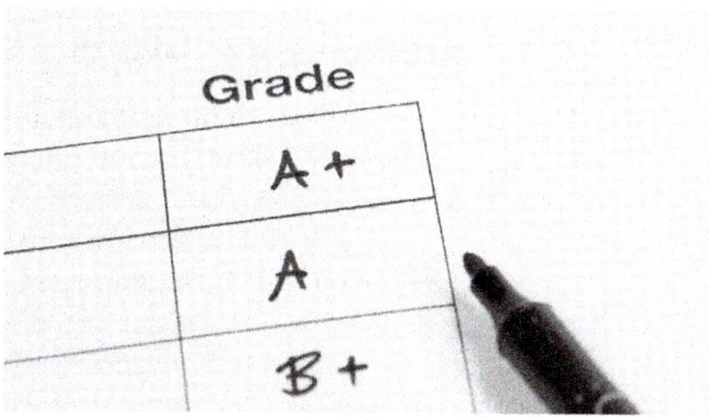

iStock.com/TongSur

Even though a GPA is a number, it is not completely objective—courses differ in their requirements, some instructors grade differently or more leniently than others, and some instructors or institutions inflate grades more than others (e.g., Jaschik, 2016). To address variability in grading, many graduate programs rely on standardized test scores such as the Graduate Record Exam (GRE). The logic is that everyone preparing for graduate school is taking the same basic test, allowing these scores to be directly compared. We cover the GRE in more detail later in this chapter, but for now, just keep in mind two things: (a) you should spend time preparing for this test and (b) different programs give different levels of importance to these scores.

In addition to your GPA and GRE, be aware that some programs are going to have requirements about your undergraduate major or what courses you have completed (e.g., Norcross, Sayette, Stratigis, & Zimmerman, 2014). Some programs may require that you complete a psychology major, and other programs might want you to have completed certain courses (e.g., Abnormal Psychology for a clinical program). Try your best to satisfy these requirements, as having them completed may mean the difference between being admitted or not. There are some programs that may allow you to take a missing undergraduate course (or equivalent) during your first year of graduate school, but do not expect or rely on this.

Experience

If you are considering a PhD program in psychology—regardless of area—you need research experience (e.g., Norcross, Sayette, Stratigis, & Zimmerman, 2014). Some professors even make the case that research experience is the *be-all-end-all A-number-one* factor considered for PhD programs in psychology (e.g., Kashdan, 2015). Because we cover research in an earlier chapter in this book, we will not spend a lot of time on it here.

iStock.com/Viktoriia Oleinichenko

If you are applying to a graduate program that focuses on applied issues (e.g., clinical, counseling, family therapy, or social work), then you should get experience in relevant applied settings (in case you missed it, clinical psychology programs are one of the rare types of program where you need BOTH research and applied experience). Applied experience could be volunteering, shadowing, or interning in a clinic, hospital, or other setting where mental health treatment occurs. For example, you might participate in assessment or treatment assistance, volunteer for your school's crisis hotline, work at a group home, or tutor children with autism. The idea here is to gain some experience and learn about what you *do* and *do not* like about these kinds of roles—and the earlier the better. We have seen past students who have benefited greatly through gaining professional experience (and they earned strong letters of recommendation, too).

Attributes and Skills that Graduate Programs Value

In addition to those factors that we just covered, graduate programs also value certain attributes and skills that you can develop and demonstrate in college (Appleby, Keenan, & Mauer, 1999; see also Appleby & Appleby, 2017). In fact, a number of these overlap with our discussion of skills to develop from earlier chapters in this book (e.g., American Psychological Association, 2013). These are attributes that you want to convey in your application materials and interviews (we include a representative list of attributes in Table 12.2). For example, you can describe your motivation for post-baccalaureate studies in your personal statement or essay. You can also convey strong communication skills by writing a high-quality personal

TABLE 12.2

Knowledge, Skills, and Attributes That Graduate Programs Value (e.g., American Psychological Association, 2013; Appleby & Appleby, 2017)

1. Knowledgeable in psychology
2. Communication skills
3. Motivated and hard-working
4. Research experience and skills
5. Works well in groups or with others
6. Critical thinking
7. Responsible
8. Acts in an ethical manner

statement or essay. In addition, your recommenders may address these in a letter, or they may have to fill out forms rating you on these attributes. So, be sure that you are demonstrating and communicating these when you interact with possible recommenders.

Take-Home Message

iStock.com/Nattakorn Maneerat

Does all of this make you anxious? Dealing with the graduate school application process can cause feelings of anxiety or dread (e.g., Charlton, Ozanich, & Phillips, 2017) and this is okay. We provide a lot of information here to get you started. So, use our advice to get started early (see our timeline in the next module)—do not procrastinate by waiting until your senior year to start planning for your next step. Check out a variety of programs and mentors to find good fits, gain the appropriate experience (research and applied), take time to put together your materials, focus on establishing good measurable scores (GPA and GRE), and build productive working relationships to earn good letters of recommendation (e.g., Charlton et al., 2017)!

Action Steps

1. Reflect upon the types of experiences that might be helpful for the types of graduate programs you are considering. List several that may be worth pursuing. Consult your campus career center, classmates, or professors you know well for potential opportunities.

2. Revisit Table 12.2 from the module and then rate yourself on the following scale: 1 = not at all true of me; 5 = always true of me. For bonus points: have a close friend, classmate, or professor rate you, too, as some strengths or weaknesses of yours might be clearer to them—use this to identify your strengths and areas for growth.

12.2 THE GRAD SCHOOL APPLICATION PROCESS

Even high-achieving students tell us that they have some questions about the grad school application process—and by "some questions," they mean a whole bunch of them. So, let's take a minute and walk you through some important things that you need to know. To help with this, we are going to use the problem-solving strategy that we introduced in the career exploration process—we will start at the end and work backward (Harvard Business Review, 2013; Wiggins & McTighe, 2005) to guide you through the grad school application process.

When Do Graduate Programs Start?

If we are working backward, our starting point (or in this case, our end point) is when you can expect your graduate program to begin. Most graduate programs are going to start at the beginning of the traditional academic year, in either August or September. You might find an occasional program that admits a new class in January, but in our experiences most are going to start in the fall semester or quarter. So, if you are now starting your senior year, then you are potentially 1 year away from day 1 of graduate school.

iStock.com/bfk92

When Do Graduate Programs Finalize Admission Decisions?

A good rule of thumb is to remember the date of April 15—this is the date that a very large number of academic institutions have agreed upon to finalize financial agreements with prospective or current graduate students (Council of Graduate Schools, 2019). In practice, this has turned into the last day for applicants to accept offers and commit to a graduate program. Not all institutions follow this resolution, but there are over 300 schools on the Council of Graduate Schools' list! Also, there are ways to get out of a commitment—typically, both the applicant and the program have to agree on this. But, in most cases, you should remember the April 15 date as the last day to commit to a graduate program.

Interviews, Acceptance Letters, and the Waitlist

Although there tends to be uniformity to the fall start and the April 15 decision date, there is variability when it comes to interviews and acceptance letters. Interviews may occur at any time between the application deadline (more on this in the next section) and April 15. Interviews can be conducted in person, at a conference, on the phone, or by video chat. Also, not all programs are going to conduct interviews—some may make admission decisions based on your application materials alone. Finally, some programs might decide to accept you and then invite you for a campus visit afterward (these visits tend to be more of a recruiting pitch).

Regardless of the interview approach (or lack thereof), programs are going to decide whether they want to offer you a spot in their program. In some cases, this can be an outright acceptance. But in other cases, you might be rejected or placed on a program's waitlist (some programs will tell you that you are on their waitlist, but some will not). The waitlist means that a program likes your application, but due to limited openings, they cannot offer you a spot unless someone who received an acceptance offer declines and creates an opening for you (if the other person accepts, then there may not be a slot for you).

paper_Owl/ ShutterStock.com

This is where things can become interesting—as attractive as multiple offers might seem, navigate this situation carefully! For example, imagine that Program A is your top choice and Program B is your back-up option. Suppose that Program B sends you an acceptance letter, but Program A puts you on their waitlist. This might sound easy—just wait until April 15 to see if Program A eventually offers; if not, accept at Program B at the last minute. However, keep this in mind—there might be others on the waitlist at Program B, wondering whether you are going to accept or not. So, although you are not bound to make a decision until April 15, if you are happy with a program that has accepted you, you might consider ending the process early by accepting their offer.

Application Deadlines

Continuing our path of working backward, let's move on to application deadlines. Some programs have fall deadlines and other programs have winter or spring deadlines. Our observation is that doctoral programs tend to have the earlier deadlines, whereas master's programs tend to have later deadlines (but keep in mind that this is a general observation, not a rule). The important thing, from your perspective, is to submit your materials on time. Some grad programs get so many good applications that it is easy for them to dismiss any that arrive late. And with most grad programs using online portals for applications, the computer may have precise instructions to accept materials until 11:59 p.m. (and 59 seconds) on the deadline date.

Programs will vary when it comes to how quickly they reach out to applicants with interview requests (or acceptance letters). Some may go through their applications and make decisions right away, whereas others might take their time. There is no rhyme or reason for this; it just depends on how an admissions committee decides to operate.

How Many Applications Should You Submit?

Unfortunately there is no perfect one-size-fits-all answer—some suggest applying to five to eight programs (e.g., Martin, 2012) and others give recommendations of four or

iStock.com/YanC

five, eight to 10, or, on the extreme end, one to 25 (e.g., Handelsman, VanderStoep, & Landrum, 2012). It depends on the competitiveness of the programs, your qualifications, how far away you are willing to travel, your available time (applications take time), and your finances (applications cost money).[1] Create a list that includes your most preferred programs ("reaches"), some that are a little less competitive ("good bets"), and at least one or two that you consider back-ups ("safety schools") (but do not apply to programs that you have no intention of attending). Ultimately, the number you apply to is up to you and your situation (but consider asking a professor you trust for advice).

Should You Reach Out to Programs Before Applying?

Before you apply to any program, you should do your homework on that program. If you have any questions that are important to you, you might reach out to a program with a (polite and professional) phone call or email. BUT, before you do, please scour every aspect of the program website first to make sure that your question is not already answered there.

In our view, reaching out is an important step for students who are applying to mentor-based programs. What we mean by reaching out is to send a very brief email to a potential mentor that includes the following:

1. Briefly introduce yourself and describe your interest in that research area.
2. Ask directly if that professor is accepting new students this year.
3. Ask a question about what direction or topic that professor is currently exploring (IMPORTANT: read that professor's website and his or her recent publications first).

Reaching out can help you find out whether potential mentors are taking on new students—if not, you may not want to even bother applying (applications cost money and take time). Also, reaching out might help you get your foot in the door and plant good things about you into the heads of potential mentors—this may help you when they are sorting through the stacks of applications.

[1]However, we recommend students investigate the criteria, policies, and process for submitting application fee waivers at various institutions. See Jaschik (2015) for additional commentary on this issue.

Your Senior Year

Because applications are due in your senior year, that is not the time to *start* building superstar accomplishments that you can brag about in your application materials. A lot of superstar experiences—building a high GPA, volunteering or interning, gaining research experience, presenting a poster at a conference, becoming an officer in a student club, and building up relationships with people who can write you letters of recommendation—take time. If you wait until your senior year to start any of these, you may not be ready to apply.

The general advice is to start planning at least a year before graduating (e.g., Martin, 2012), if not sooner. To help you out, we built a rough timeline for most psychology-related graduate programs (see Table 12.3). Keep in mind that the specifics may vary for your

TABLE 12.3

Graduate School Timeline for Preparation and Applications (Please Note That This Is a Rough Sketch—Your Specific Situation Might Be Slightly Different)

Sophomore year	Explore career path possibilities Build superstar accomplishments
Junior year	Continue building superstar accomplishments Decide whether your career path needs a graduate degree Prepare/study for the GRE Sign up for the GRE (for the summer) Save money for grad school application fees Build relationships with professors who might write you letters
Junior year (summer)	Take the GRE Build a list of schools/programs where you might apply Reach out to potential grad school mentors Build your list of possible letter of recommendation writers
Senior year (fall)	Continue building superstar accomplishments Finalize your list of schools Line up your letters of recommendation Write your personal statement essays Finalize your CV Send out applications (some programs have fall deadlines)
Senior year (spring)	Send out applications (some programs have spring deadlines) Attend grad school interviews Accept an offer from a graduate program
After graduating (fall)	Start graduate school!

situation and the programs to which you apply. We hope that this can help you to avoid procrastination—keep that instant gratification monkey away (Urban, 2016)!

Take-Home Message

Although the process of applying to graduate school does have some unknown variables (e.g., "fit," depth of the applicant pool), try your best to remain focused on what you *can* control. We said it before and we will say it again—do yourself a favor and start planning early. Remember that it is okay to change your mind or to alter your course—this happens and it is okay; as long as you are building up superstar accomplishments, they should be helpful no matter what path you follow. Finally, the *Graduate School Timeline* we shared in Table 12.3 is tried and true—the approach has worked for undergrads like you.

iQoncept/ ShutterStock.com

Action Steps

1. If grad school is a possibility for you, start with our general timeline and personalize it for your situation. For example, when are you going to tackle each step?
2. As you write out your personalized timeline, pay special attention to the accomplishments and actions that will take a lot of time and planning. For example, although we list "Line up letters of recommendation" in the fall of your senior year, you may want to list subgoals for how you are going to build up relationships with potential letter writers in earlier semesters (see the upcoming module on letters of recommendation for additional tips!).

12.3 LETTERS OF RECOMMENDATION

Letters of recommendation are one of the key parts of your graduate school application (American Psychological Association, 2018; Norcross, Kohout, & Wicherski, 2006). We run into too many students who overlook the importance of them (e.g., Nauta, 2000) or fail to plan for them and then end up panicking at the last minute to find any professor who might be willing to write a letter for them—do not let this happen to you. Most graduate programs request three letters of recommendation. You may find some that want two and others that want four or five, but three seems to be the most common (however, it is very important that you do your own research to see how many are requested by a particular program). In this module, we explain the basics of letters of recommendation so that you can improve the odds of earning great letters.

© Can Stock Photo/BeeBright

TABLE 12.4

An Overly Simplistic Comparison of *Great, Good, Okay,* and *Bad* Letters of Recommendation*

	Great	Good	Okay	Bad
Typical length (in pages)	1+	1	½–1	½
Includes positives about you	Yes!	Yes	Yes	No
Includes negatives about you	No	No	Maybe	Yes
Conveys enthusiasm	Yes!	Maybe	No	No

**NOTE:* Some letters may vary from the pattern described here—for example, it is possible for a great letter to be brief but with a very strong recommendation.

Great vs. Good vs. Okay vs. Bad Letters

Not all letters of recommendation are created equal (see Table 12.4). The first type—*great letters*—are glowing recommendations stretching across two pages that enthusiastically cover your major accomplishments and praise you as a top applicant. The second type—*good letters*—will consist of a full page that describes you in a positive manner, discussing how your skills should lead you to success in graduate school. These are the two types of letters that you want.

Other letters might fall into the "okay" or "bad" categories. *Okay letters* might be fairly short (perhaps less than half of a page), they might not include many positive or strong statements about your skills and accomplishments, or they might focus too much on your weaknesses or limitations. Okay letters can occur if a recommender does not know you well or if you did not demonstrate impressive skills or accomplishments. *Bad letters* tend to be short and critical and may explicitly mention that the writer does not recommend you. You never want a bad letter—if you think you might get a bad letter, move on to someone else. In some cases, professors may warn you if the letter is not going to be good or they might decline your request to write a letter (rather than write a bad one).

Obviously, in an ideal world, you would want three great letters, but that is not always realistic. For a highly sought-after clinical psychology doctoral program (with over 100 applications—many from other superstar students), you might need more than one great letter. However, for a lot of programs, you might be fine with one great letter (e.g., Kashdan, 2015) or possibly three good letters. For less-competitive programs, you might get by with two good letters and one okay letter. The quality that you need is going to depend on the competitiveness of a program.

Whom Should You Ask?

Most grad program admissions committees are going to be concerned with your academic accomplishments and, depending on the type of program, possibly your research or applied experiences. For academic or research accomplishments, professors are the obvious choice. If you are applying to an applied program (e.g., counseling, social work, medical school, etc.), you may want to include a letter from someone who supervised or worked with you in a professional setting. For a competitive clinical psychology doctoral program, which includes both research and applied training, our recommendation is to aim for two or three letters from professors and one letter from a professional.

Use the following guidelines to help you decide whom to ask. We also address some frequently asked questions in the following paragraphs—but remember that this is general advice and that your circumstances might be unique (when in doubt, ask a trusted professor for help).

- Who knows you best?
- Who can say excellent things about you?
- Whose opinion would be respected by the admissions committee?

Do my recommenders have to be from my field/major? In some cases, you may have someone from another field who can say great things about you. Our recommendation is this—try to get most of your letters from people in your major/field, but if there is someone else from another field who can say great things about you, then go ahead (the goal is to get great letters).

Does reputation, prestige, or name matter? It might—some people may be impressed to read a letter written by someone who is well known or from an admired institution. If you can get a good or great letter from someone well known, then go for it (we hope that students who worked closely with Skinner, Zimbardo, or Loftus had asked them for a letter). However, do not focus too much on this—choose letter writers who can evaluate you the best.

Can I ask graduate student instructors or part-time instructors? This can be a great option if you have taken multiple courses from them or if you had a phenomenal experience (so they can say great things about you). However, one drawback is that, if you need a letter in a year or two, they may no longer be at your institution—graduate students eventually graduate and part-time instructors are not permanent faculty members.

I worked closely with a graduate student on a research project—is this a good option? This can be okay, but our tip is to see if you can get a letter from the supervising professor. Even better—ask if the graduate student (who knows you well) can help the professor write the letter!

Can I ask a great instructor from a previous institution? If you have a really good relationship with someone from a previous institution and you can still connect with her/him, then go for it. We suggest staying in touch after you transfer to maintain the relationship (see our networking tips from an earlier chapter). However, we recommend that you try to get at least one letter from your current institution where you are earning your degree (some grad programs may have rules or guidelines requiring this).

Can I ask an academic advisor? If you have worked closely with the same academic advisor over a number of years, this might be a possibility. But, although they have seen you progress through college, they may not have directly observed your work or skills. We recommend going with faculty instead, but an academic advisor who could write you a stellar letter might be a good option for a third or fourth letter.

Whom Should You NOT Ask?

There are some people you should avoid using for a recommendation (e.g., Appleby & Appleby, 2017a). Do not ask therapists, counselors, psychologists, or life coaches who are treating/coaching you. Despite the fact that they are in psychology-related professions—which might be connected to what you want to pursue—they are not the best option. Besides, there are possible issues regarding the ethics of disclosure and confidentiality. This last one should go without saying, but do not ask a family member—a family member is not likely going to be completely objective when evaluating you.

Passive vs. Active Approach to Letters

Some students choose a passive approach and leave things to chance or fate when it comes to letters of recommendation. They wait until their senior year and then reflect back to figure out which professors know them best. However, this approach could potentially lead to disaster as you might reach your senior year without having developed any strong relationships.

We prefer a more active approach instead. If you take courses from great professors, take other courses from those same professors so that they can see you accomplish more. Take courses from professors who require projects, papers, and presentations. Think about it, which is going to be more impressive in a letter—a description of your writing, presenting, and leadership qualities or a description of how great you are at multiple-choice exams? Attend office hours (or set up a meeting) so that professors can get to know you better. Take more in-person courses than online courses so that you can more easily make connections with instructors. Get involved in student clubs, service learning projects, or research so that professors can get to know you really well. Taking initiative is not just for recommendation letters—but a way of life!

The Right Way to Ask for Letters

Because letter writers are doing you a favor, you want to ask politely—never demand or expect one (Gomez, 2016). A second consideration is that you might explicitly ask if they can write you a *strong* letter (e.g., Appleby & Appleby, 2017a). Doing this can help you feel more confident that you are going to get a great or good letter rather than an okay or bad letter (e.g., Appleby & Appleby, 2006).

Once you have your letter writers lined up, the next step is to make things easy for them! You can do this by organizing your relevant information into a portfolio for them (e.g., Gomez, 2016) and providing this at least 3 to 4 weeks before your first deadline.

This does not have to be anything formal; just put all of the information together in a neat and organized manner. We recommend sending your writers a single email that has everything they need in one place. If your writers feel rushed by a too-soon deadline or have to search for multiple emails or track you down with questions, then your letter writer might be in a bad mood, which might cause your *great* letter to drop down to just a *good* letter.

What should you provide? Inform them of program deadlines and how to submit their letter. Importantly, you also want to remind them of the great things about

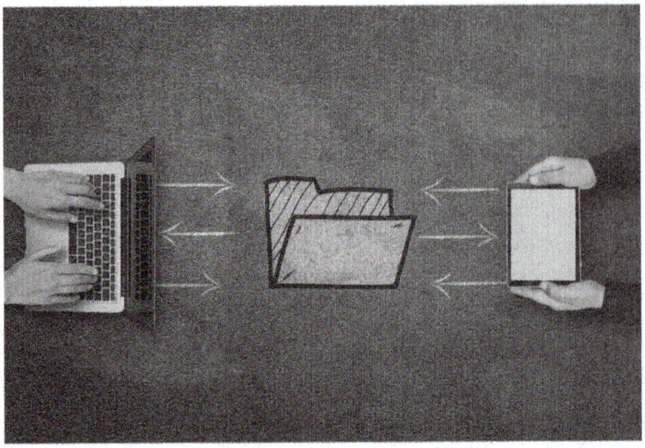

iStock.com/triloks

you that they can include in their letter! Here are some suggestions for what to include (Appleby & Appleby, 2017a; Gomez, 2016):

- A spreadsheet with your list of programs/schools, the type of program (e.g., counseling master's program), each deadline, the method of submitting the letter (e.g., email, snail mail)
- Any required forms—be sure to check whether you need to (a) fill out sections, (b) indicate whether you waive your right to see the letter, or (c) sign it!
- A copy of your curriculum vitae and one of your personal statements or essays
- Reminders of your accomplishments that are relevant to them. If you worked on research with a professor—on which projects and what did you do? If you were in their courses—which courses, which semesters, and what were your big accomplishments? If you volunteered or worked in an applied setting, when were you there and what did you accomplish and learn?

A final idea is to ask if they need a reminder about the letters. We both appreciate this gesture because, as professors, we are always juggling multiple projects and we are also working with a large number of students every semester. A simple reminder can be very helpful to make sure we get your letters written and submitted on time.

Example Letters

If you want to see more of what might be included in letters of recommendation, see the examples in Figure 12.1 and Figure 12.2, or check out excerpts from letters written by Appleby and Appleby (2017b, 2017c)—the information for these sources is listed in our references listed toward the end of the book.

Take-Home Message

Letters of recommendation are very helpful for graduate admissions committees (American Psychological Association, 2018; Norcross et al., 2006), so be sure to take this part of the application process seriously. Letters are important because they are *other people's* evaluations of your accomplishments, strengths, and weaknesses—these tend to be a tad bit more objective than self-assessments where everyone describes themselves as being above average (e.g., Kruger & Dunning, 1999). Finally, please take our advice and use a proactive approach rather than scrambling to find potential recommenders at the last minute.

FIGURE 12.1

Example of a "Great" Letter of Recommendation.

December 2020

To Whom It May Concern,

The purpose of this letter is to strongly recommend Mariah Davis for your doctoral program in Clinical Psychology — I have no reservations about her ability to succeed in graduate school. I met Mariah 3 years ago when she applied to be a research assistant — ever since I met her, she told me that she wants to earn a Ph.D. as that is needed for her to become a clinician with a focus on child behavior disorders. Mariah is an excellent student (overall GPA of 3.9 and psychology GPA of 4.0), earned a number of scholarships that paid for a large portion of her tuition, and was recently recognized by the psychology faculty here at UNLV with an award for Outstanding Senior in Psychology.

Mariah's accomplishments go well beyond these basic qunlifications. She completed a minor in neuroscience to learn more about biological topics that are related to clinical psychology — this included courses such as *Cognitive Neuroscience, Neuropsychology*, and *Neurobiology of Learning and Memory*. In addition, Mariah took upper level seminar courses (including a second statistics course) and was actively involved in independent research. She worked on my research team assisting with data collection, analyzing data, conducting library searches, and creating materials for experiments. Mariah was very responsible and made important contributions to a number of studies — she has repeatedly demonstrated to me that she can think critically about research.

Mariah has co-authored 2 conference presentations with faculty and graduate students. She took an active role by helping to organize the presentations and presenting one of the projects at a national conference. At UNLV, her research activity was recognized by earning 1st place in a Psi Chi (the international honor society in psychology) poster conference. Mariah also has excellent writing skills (with perfect APA Style formatting) and has published an article with the Association for Psychological Science (APS) about an undergraduate's experience with research. In addition, she also earned a $1000 research grant from APS to help her conduct a set of experiments with me over the summer.

Besides her coursework and research, Mariah served as vice-president (last year) and president (this year) for our chapter of Psi Chi. In these roles she took the lead organizing events and meetings and she also developed a mentoring program to help guide freshmen and sophomores who were just starting as psychology majors. As the faculty advisor for Psi Chi at UNLV, I worked closely with Mariah and the other officers — without a doubt, she has been one of the top student officers that I have worked with in my five years as advisor — she is responsible, an effective communicator, works great with others, and generates a lot of ideas.

In conclusion, Mariah has accomplished a lot in college — her achievements are nicely summarized in her curriculum vitae (CV)! On top of that, she works really well with faculty, graduate students, and fellow research assistants. Her enthusiasm about psychology is infectious and has rubbed off on other students — she is usually the first person to volunteer to give a presentation when our research team has meetings. Based on my experiences, I strongly recommend her for your graduate program!

Sincerely,

David Copeland, Ph.D.
Associate Professor of Psychology

FIGURE 12.2
Example of an "Okay" (or Possibly "Bad") Letter of Recommendation.

November 2020

To Whom It May Concern,

This letter is to support Marshall Smith who is applying for your graduate program. Marshall is a student in my *Cognitive Psychology* course this semester. Thus far, he is doing fairly well on the quizzes and assignments, but his grade was brought down by a low score for his paper – he lost a number of points for APA Style formatting mistakes. As long as he does well on the remaining activities, he is on track to earn at least a C and possibly a C+ in this course.

Because I have only known Marshall for a few months, I cannot comment on his skills and potential in much detail. Marshall is almost finished with all of his required psychology courses and electives, and will be graduating this year. My initial impression is that he is interested in graduate school, but I was concerned with the fact that he is not certain about his future career path at this time. While he has not been able to work on research yet, he has stated that he wants to join a research team at some point before he graduates.

If you have any questions about this letter, feel free to contact me.

Sincerely,

David Copeland, Ph.D.
Associate Professor of Psychology

Action Steps

1. If you needed three letters right now, whom would you ask? If you do not think your letters would be good enough, be proactive and either (a) strengthen existing relationships or (b) develop new ones.
2. Apply some of the networking tips from our earlier chapter to maintain and strengthen your professional relationships. For example, stay in contact with past professors who might be good recommenders. Even better, strengthen that relationship by taking another course from that professor or working with that professor—volunteer to help with research, spend time as a teaching assistant, or work in an applied setting.

12.4 THE GRADUATE RECORD EXAM

Most graduate programs will require that you report standardized test scores as part of your application—the Graduate Record Exam (GRE) for many graduate programs, the Medical College Admission Test (MCAT) for medical schools, and the Law School Admission Test (LSAT) for law schools. This is similar to how most high school students take the Scholastic Aptitude Test (SAT) or American College Test (ACT) before applying to college. The idea is that admissions committees can use this (supposedly) objective information to help them determine whether they think you will be successful in their program (however, see Clayton, 2016, for an argument that standardized tests may be biased against students from diverse backgrounds). Because most of our readers will be considering the GRE, we focus this module on it. However, keep in mind that many of the broader principles (e.g., preparation) also apply to the MCAT or LSAT.

What Is on the GRE?

The GRE consists of three major sections (Educational Testing Service, 2018)—Verbal, Quantitative, and Analytical Writing. Older versions of the GRE (before 2011) had a larger focus on how well you memorized vocabulary and mathematical formulas, but the current version is slightly different in its emphasis (e.g., Asbury, 2011). The Verbal section includes items that involve reading a passage and answering comprehension questions, verbal reasoning skills, and understanding word meanings. The Quantitative section involves arithmetic, algebra, geometry, and data analysis—but the good news is that there is no calculus and they provide you with an on-screen calculator. Finally, the Analytical Writing section measures your critical thinking and written communication skills.

There are also subject tests, including one for psychology. This is a multiple-choice test that covers the core content areas—biological, cognitive, social, developmental, clinical, and methods (Educational Testing Service, 2018). However, before you register and start preparing for the subject test, keep in mind that not all graduate programs require that applicants complete this part (American Psychological Association, 2018)—check a program's website for their specific requirements.

GRE Scores

The current version of the test has scores ranging from 130 to 170 on the Verbal and Quantitative sections and 0 to 6 on the Analytical Writing section (e.g., Asbury, 2011). What do you need to score? There is no specific answer to this question because criteria vary for different graduate programs. Some graduate programs post their minimum criteria or the average GRE scores of students admitted in the past—this information can be found on program websites or in a publication such as *Graduate Study in Psychology* (American Psychological Association, 2018). Because the scores themselves are on a fairly meaningless scale, we recommend looking at your percentile scores (i.e., the percentage of other test-takers who scored lower than you did—higher percentile scores are better).

Preparing for the GRE

There are estimates that students who end up being admitted into psychology grad programs study for the GRE for approximately 50 to 100 hours (e.g., Thomas, 2018). We agree that you should practice—start a few months before your test appointment (e.g., Gomez, 2011) and spread out your study sessions (e.g., Kornell, Castel, Eich, & Bjork, 2010). There are many books that contain tips and practice questions—there are also apps that have useful features such as flashcards. Finally, private companies (e.g., Kaplan, 2019) offer preparation courses that include practice tests—however, these courses can be expensive. One way to combat the costs is to work together with your friends by buying different books and then swapping with each other after you finish the practice tests in your book.

TABLE 12.5

Preparation Tips for the Graduate Record Examination (GRE)

General Tips
• Start preparing months in advance
• Use practice books or websites (especially ones with practice questions)
• Adopt a gamifying mindset (see McGonigal, 2010, for more on gamification)
Verbal Section Tips
• Practice with different types of questions
• Review Latin roots
• Read and critique research articles
Quantitative Section Tips
• Master the specific types of math that are included on the test
• Learn to logically narrow down choices
Analytical Writing Section Tips
• Take courses that require papers
• Practice building an outline before writing essays
Psychology Test Tips
• Take courses in core psychology topic areas
• Review a PSY 101 textbook

Another aspect of preparation is to adopt the right mindset (e.g., Gomez, 2011). Instead of stewing in feelings of hatred or anxiety, adopt a gaming mindset (see McGonigal, 2010, for more on gamification). "Gamifying" your learning process can be helpful for a number of reasons. First, game and test performance tends to improve with practice. Second, both game play and standardized test scores can improve if you learn the right strategies and shortcuts. Third, both games and standardized tests can be long—make sure you practice so that you do not end up wanting to tap out after the first few questions during the real test. And, fourth, if you are preparing with friends, a leaderboard (of days studying, hours logged, practice test scores) can motivate one another and foster a playful, supportive sense of camaraderie.

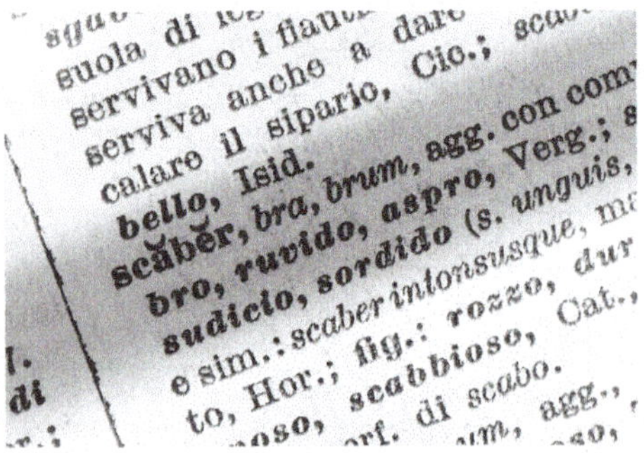

divgradcurl/ ShutterStock.com

When it comes to the test sections, we recommend preparing equally for all of them. But use your judgment based on your own strengths and weaknesses. Different grad programs or potential mentors may prioritize specific sections, but you cannot be certain which ones they value most. We provide some preparation tips for each section of the GRE (also see Table 12.5).

Verbal section. Focus your prep time on becoming familiar with the different types of questions and reviewing Latin roots rather than memorizing the dictionary (so, if you find yourself in a *scabrous* situation, remember that the English language has many Latin words and roots). There are millions of vocabulary words in the English language—what are the odds that the specific words that you study will be on your test? We also recommend practicing your comprehension skills by reading scientific research articles (see our earlier chapter)—this can help prepare you to understand complex passages (e.g., Mahr, 2016).

Quantitative section. There are only so many types of math questions that can be included, so mastering those can prepare you no matter what numbers are inserted into the test questions. Also, learn to think logically so that you can improve your odds by narrowing down multiple-choice options (e.g., squaring a fraction leads to a smaller fraction). Finally, because standardized tests are timed, you may want to practice so that you can get faster—this can save you time to revisit the more-difficult problems on the test.

iStock.com/Bulat Silvia

Analytical writing section. Some argue that this is the most important section for grad programs that are research-focused because it reflects what you will be doing in those programs (e.g., Marton, 2014). To prepare, we highly recommend that you take courses that require papers (to improve your critical thinking and writing skills). You might also want to practice creating outlines before writing because that can help you build an essay that is organized.

Psychology test. To prepare for this test, take a variety of psychology courses that cover the core foundational topics—biological, cognitive, development, abnormal, social, and methods—and focus on long-term learning rather than cramming (see our study tips in an earlier chapter). Second, review Intro Psych (PSY 101) textbooks, as they cover the major concepts in these areas. Finally, take practice tests—remember, testing improves learning (e.g., Roediger & Karpicke, 2006).

Should You Take it Twice?

We hear from students who want to know if they should take the test twice. Some took it once and did not do well; others want to plan ahead *in case* they do not do well. The good news is that you can take the test up to five times, and you can choose which scores get sent to your programs. The Kaplan test prep website (2019) recommends that you should retake the test if (a) your scores do not meet the minimum program requirements, (b) you need a higher score for funding opportunities, (c) you are confident you can do better the next time, or (d) you continue to take all sections seriously—that is, if you did well on the Verbal section, do not blow that off when preparing for your second attempt.

Be prepared for the possibility that your scores may not change very much when retaking the test. Our advice is to prepare your best to do well the first time—but, if you are still anxious about it, take the GRE, MCAT, or LSAT early enough so that you will have time to take it a second time if a disaster scenario occurs. And, finally, remember this—if you take the test again, you are also going to pay to take the test again.

Do Standardized Tests Predict Graduate School Success?

GRE scores correlate with graduate school grades (e.g., Bridgeman, Burton, & Cline, 2008; Burton & Wang, 2005). However, one criticism is that scores are not necessarily predictive if you define success in other ways besides grades, such as the number of grad school research publications (Kuo, 2017). This is a relevant criticism because, as most professors will tell you, as long as you pass your graduate courses, grades do not matter much in grad school or for jobs afterward (e.g., Lambert, 2013). A second criticism is that standardized test scores correlate with socioeconomic status, gender, and ethnicity, and this may make it more difficult for women, minorities, and people from a lower socioeconomic status to gain admission to graduate school (Miller & Stassun, 2014; see also Clayton, 2016).

Cartoon Resource/ShutterStock.com

Take-Home Message

The idea behind standardized tests is that they allow admissions committees to compare candidates on the same standard. Sure, standardized tests have critics, but regardless of what you think about them, most post-baccalaureate programs require you to take the GRE, MCAT, or LSAT. If you find that you are anxious about one of these standardized tests, keep in mind that it is just one of the many pieces of information that admissions committees use for decisions, so take the time to prepare and try your best to do well, but do not put too much pressure on yourself.

Action Steps

1. To reduce standardized test anxiety, focus on gamifying your preparation. Watch McGonigal's (2010) TED Talk titled *Gaming Can Make a Better World* (the complete information about this source is provided in the references at the back of the book) and create a gaming mindset approach to tackling your standardized test.
2. One of the better GRE preparation plans we have seen online (with a study tracking spreadsheet) is by Mahr (2016), who recently completed a computer science grad program. The reference is at the back of the book, but we also included the web address here for you (http://dmahr.com/2016/07/seven-week-gre-study-plan/). You can download his spreadsheet or create your own!

12.5 PERSONAL STATEMENTS AND ESSAYS

Most graduate school applications will require you to write an essay (or two or three essays). Some programs call this a personal statement, some might call it an essay, and others simply ask you to answer a few questions. As with most of the other topics that we have covered thus far, please do not overlook the importance of this step. In fact, personal statements have been rated as the most important component of applicant materials when surveying doctoral programs (Davis, Doll & Sterner, 2018). No matter what type of program you are pursuing, this is not something to write the day before you submit your application—you want to spend some time on this written work. In this module, we will provide some tips to help you with this part of the process.

iStock.com/Maksim Shchur

Demonstrate Your Writing Abilities

The ability to communicate effectively through writing is one of the core competencies in graduate school. In addition to the GRE Analytical Writing score (e.g., Klieger et al., 2018), the personal statement is a common (and efficient) indicator of general writing ability. Therefore, do take this opportunity to demonstrate your skills seriously. The following are a few general tips to strengthen your personal statements and essays.

Start early. Start writing your essay weeks in advance of the application deadline, and work on it at least twice a week. Writing multiple drafts of a paper can improve it greatly. Graduate students and professors do this regularly in order to produce good work (you do not want to know how many drafts we wrote for each chapter of this book).

Use what you learned about writing. Apply all of the good writing techniques and strategies you have picked up over the years. For instance—outline your work, focus on topic sentences and paragraph structure, make one key argument or point per paragraph, "show not tell," use formal tone, check whether all of the questions or prompts were actually addressed in your writing, and read your drafts aloud. And, most importantly, proofread ... proofread ... proofread.

Get Feedback

Although you can ask your peers for basic feedback (e.g., typos and grammar), we highly recommend getting *critical* feedback from a professor or graduate student. You want to send the best statement you can, right? Then ask for constructive feedback that will help you improve your personal statement. Their time is valuable, so do not expect them to read multiple drafts of your paper, but even one round of honest feedback can be very helpful.

For those of you who are not accustomed to receiving critical feedback, here are some tips (e.g., Ahlin, 2017). Do not ask for feedback on the first

iStock.com/Steve Debenport

thing you write—develop it and make it good. Next, specify two or three things to focus on in your paper. Finally, prepare for the possibility that the feedback might recommend major changes. Before you get upset, remember that (a) the person is trying to help and (b) they are critiquing the writing, not you (do not take the criticism personally and do not get defensive). Use the feedback to improve your work.

Follow Their Rules

Graduate programs are going to vary as to how specific they are with their essay instructions. If a program tells you the maximum number of words or pages, then you should use most or all of that space (but do not go over the max). Also, unless they specify that it should be double-spaced, write yours single-spaced so that you can write more.

Some programs are going to ask you to answer specific questions. If they do, be sure that your essay *actually addresses these questions.* In addition, try to balance the amount of space used for each question. If you have five pages to answer two questions, do not use four of the five pages addressing the first question. Unless the questions clearly and drastically differ in terms of their importance, we recommend a more-balanced approach.

Minimal Instructions or "Write a Personal Statement"

In some cases, a graduate program may request an essay but they either provide minimal instructions or else they ask you to write a *personal statement* (without much further instruction). In these cases, we recommend that you write a two- or three-page (single-spaced) essay. What should you write? Great question—let's go through a generic grad school essay now (see Table 12.6 for a summary).

Opening. Start with an opening paragraph that introduces you, states your graduate school and career goal(s), and briefly describes an outline for your essay. You should describe why you are interested in the topic area of this graduate program. This is not the time to try and be too personal or unique or to use clichés. For example, if you are interested in dolphin cognition, try to avoid a line such as *"Ever since I was a child, I wanted*

TABLE 12.6

Recommended Structure for Personal Statement or Essay That Contains Minimal (or No) Instructions

- Write two or three pages (single-spaced)
- Include an opening paragraph
  - Introduce yourself and your goals
  - Briefly describe an outline for the essay
- Include multiple paragraphs in the body
  - Describe your relevant experiences and skills
  - Clearly state why you are a fit for the program
- Include a wrap-up or concluding paragraph
  - Re-emphasize your major points

to swim with dolphins." We have also had clinical psychology colleagues tell us about students who write that they have been interested in mental disorders ever since they were diagnosed with one. There is nothing wrong with having a mental disorder, but it should not be the main motivation as to why you are interested in grad school (see Appleby & Appleby, 2006).

Instead of going those routes, it is okay to be a little boring. Rather than being too personal, write about your college experiences that are relevant to your future career (e.g., Brown, 2004). Maybe you took a class in forensic psychology and it convinced you that this was the field for you? Perhaps you attended a job panel with therapists from your community, and that stimulated an interest in that career path? In some cases, you may have conducted a handful of informational interviews and, from that process, figured out what you wanted to pursue?

Your skills and experiences. After this opening paragraph, use a few paragraphs to describe your skills and the experiences that have prepared you for graduate school. Do not waste time writing about your grades (e.g., Ritzer & Sleigh, 2017)—committees know about those from your GPA and transcript. Instead, talk about research projects, service learning, internships, job shadowing, leadership positions, communication skills, and major accomplishments. Do your best to organize these paragraphs so that the information flows well and presents a positive impression of you.

For some of you, there might be an "elephant in the room" that you might want to address. This could be an F on your transcript, low grades during your first year, a gap in your progress, or something else. If you have an explanation (see Bessette, 2013, for a description of the difference between an explanation and an excuse), you can address it in this portion of your essay. However, keep this very brief—if you spend too much time writing about that, you will have less space to discuss your skills and accomplishments.

Your fit. As you get closer to the end of the essay, you want to discuss why this program is a good fit for you—personalize this part of your essay for each application. This is where you want to answer the question, "*Why are you applying to our program (as opposed to others)?*" If you are applying to a graduate program that is not mentor-based, then describe how that program (as a whole) fits your interests and goals. For example, if you see that their graduates primarily end up in a certain type of job, and that is what you want to do, talk about that in this paragraph. If there is a geographic reason that you want to attend this program, you can mention it here, but do not emphasize this too much—most programs want to hear that you are applying for academic, research, or career reasons. In other words, be sure to discuss your future goals (e.g., Brown, 2004).

If it is a mentor-based program, be sure to identify your first choice for a mentor—which professor would you want to work with if you were admitted? This is important because these programs will admit students based on whether you meet their qualifications and the quality of match between you and a mentor. If there is another professor who does similar research and who would also be a good fit, go ahead and include that second name. You could possibly name a third, but we caution against going this far because you might paint a picture of yourself as being unfocused about what you want to pursue in graduate school.

iStock.com/undrey

Wrap-up. As you probably learned in your English writing course, most good essays will start by briefly stating what is covered in the essay and then they finish by wrapping-up the key ideas. This paragraph should be fairly short, but it is important as it gives your essay closure and it will also re-emphasize your important points. This is also a good time to re-read the opening paragraph to make sure that your essay covered everything that you said you would cover in it.

Take-Home Message

A graduate school essay, or personal statement, is important for a couple of reasons. First, it is a demonstration of your writing abilities. As we noted previously, spend some time working on this. Second, be sure that you follow the instructions carefully—most programs receive a lot of applications and, because of that, they need to narrow down their list. If you do not follow their rules, you might give them a potential reason to disregard your application. Finally, if you encounter a program that provides minimal or vague instructions, then use our guidelines for how to structure your essay!

Action Steps

1. We know that many undergraduates try to avoid classes that include writing, but we encourage you to actively seek out classes that require writing. Think of it as a way to develop and practice your writing skills. The only way to improve your writing is to practice.

2. Think about what accomplishments, experiences, and skills you could include in an essay if you had to write one right now. If you are not satisfied with what you have to work with, then use that to motivate yourself to take action for more superstar achievements.

iStock.com/PeopleImages

12.6 INTERVIEWS AND THE ACCEPTANCE OR REJECTION DECISIONS

At this point, you have written your essay(s), taken the GRE (if needed), requested letters of recommendation, and submitted your materials. We like to (tongue-in-cheek) say that those were the easy steps compared to what comes next—in the words of the brilliant musician Tom Petty, "*the waiting is the hardest part*" (Petty, 1981). So, while you are waiting to hear back from programs, should you sit around and waste time on social media? Of course not—if grad school is truly your goal, then there are still things that you need to do as you prepare for interviews.

Traveling to Interviews, Costs, and Other Options

iStock.com/David-Prado

If a program wants to interview you, this means that you are under strong consideration to be admitted to their program. Some programs are going to invite you to campus—this can be for a few hours or possibly 2 days. Others are going to request a phone or video chat (e.g., Skype or Facetime), and some will want to do an initial phone or video chat interview followed by a campus interview. Programs and schools vary quite a bit here.

There is also variability as to the costs you are responsible for during a campus visit. If you are lucky, a program will pay for your travel and then either pay for your hotel or offer for you to stay the night with a current graduate student from their program. Other programs, though, might not pay for anything or only pay for part of your travel costs. If money is an issue, consider options that can reduce costs—this might include driving instead of flying or staying fewer days (but this minimizes the amount of time you can be there). Another possibility is to ask if you can do a video chat interview instead (e.g., Handelsman, VanderStoep, & Landrum, 2012). However, if you cannot visit a campus, keep in mind that you may have to make a decision about going there without ever having seen it.

Prepare for Interviews

iStock.com/marekuliasz

Before you do any type of interview—in-person, phone, or video chat—you must prepare! Read everything on the program's website. Learn about the background of anyone you might speak with during the interview. Work on your short and long elevator pitches. Plan your clothes (think business casual or possibly a suit). Know that you will be asked questions about your experiences, accomplishments, goals, and (if relevant) research interests. Importantly, act interested and motivated, and be ready to convey why you are a great fit for their program.

We recommend that you develop a list of questions that you can ask. You will likely meet with many faculty members, so feel free to repeat the same questions to different people—no one is going to compare notes about what you asked, plus you want to make sure that you get the same answers from more than one person. Here are some topics that you can ask faculty about:

- The major milestones of the program (e.g., thesis)
- What past graduate students have done after finishing the program

- Their current research projects (for research-intensive programs)
- Funding opportunities
- Their timeline for making admission decisions

If you are interviewing at mentor-based programs, you will want to gather information about your fit with a potential mentor. Prioritize what is most important to you. For example, during an interview, you may want to get a feel for the communication style of a mentor, how much time they spend interacting with their grad students, or personality traits such as enthusiasm (see Ritzer, 2018, for some factors to consider when considering a mentor).

In addition to your interactions with faculty, you may also be interacting with current graduate students as well. You do not want them to feel left out, so consider asking grad students about

- What they like and do not like about the program
- What it is like to work with a certain faculty member (this is very important if you are applying for a mentor-based program!)
- Funding opportunities
- Housing (where do most grad students in this program live?)

Finally, remember that you are being evaluated the whole time you are there. If you meet with graduate students, you are being evaluated. If someone picks you up from the airport, you are being evaluated. In some cases, an interview might also include a social event at the end of the day. This might seem like a chance to let down your guard, but remember that this is still part of the interview.

Dealing With Offers and Accepting

We provide a lot of good advice in this book, but unfortunately we cannot guarantee that you will receive multiple offers of admission. Some of you may only have one offer—in that case, go ahead and accept. Others might get multiple offers around the same time, and still others might get multiple offers that are staggered. For example, you might get a yes from one program, but another program might either be slow to make a decision or they may have you on their waitlist. As a reminder to what we said earlier when discussing the application process, this game typically ends on April 15 (Council of Graduate Schools, 2019). That is the standard deadline, but it is good form to accept or reject an offer earlier if you know your decision (e.g., if you reject an offer early, it can possibly go to another student who might be on a waitlist; Burke & Bottoms, 2017a).

iStock.com/mheim3011

If you are lucky enough to have multiple offers, you will have to make a decision. It might not be as easy as going back to your preference list that you created when deciding on your top choices of programs—there might be new information for you to consider based on what you learned during the interview process! So, take a moment to reassess your options by weighing some of these factors (Burke & Bottoms, 2017a, 2017b):

- Are you a good fit (topic and personality-wise) with a potential mentor or with the faculty in general?
- Does the environment seem like one where you can be successful?
- Will this program help you reach your goals (e.g., what have past grad students ended up doing after finishing that program)?
- Did the current graduate students positively recommend the program?
- What is the funding situation for each program?
- Can you see yourself in that location?

Once you finalize your decision and accept, you can finally take a moment to relax and bask in the triumph of reaching your goal—however, keep in mind that there are still things to do (e.g., Sleigh & Ritzer, 2015).

- If you have not yet graduated, stay focused in your courses—it would be horrible to fail a needed course during your last semester.
- If you are doing research, keep going—if any projects can lead to a conference presentation or a publication, follow through with them (keep building your accomplishments).
- If you want to start preparing for grad school, reach out to your future mentor and see if there are any recommended articles or books that you should be reading.
- Start planning for the transition. If you are going to move, plan for that. If you want to get a head start by working on research the summer before your program starts, check with your future mentor to see if that is a possibility.
- If you have not done so already, send thank-you notes to your letter writers and any other professors or graduate students who helped you. Expressing gratitude is not just a nice thing to do—it can make others feel better, strengthen relationships, and make you feel better (e.g., Morin, 2015)!

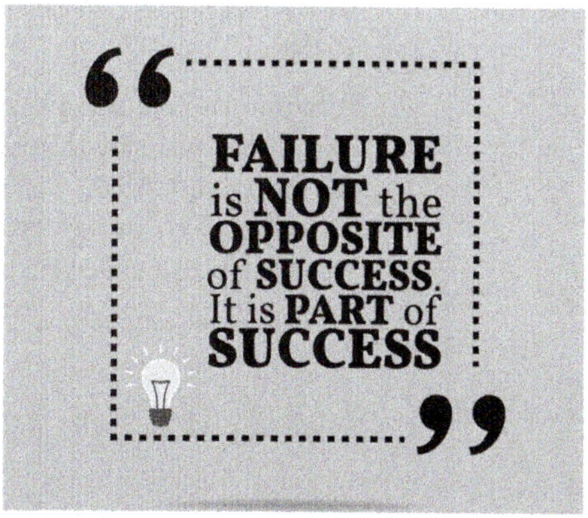
FAILURE
is NOT the
OPPOSITE
of SUCCESS.
It is PART of
SUCCESS

sibgat/ ShutterStock.com

Persistence vs. Finding Something Else

Unfortunately, every year there are some students who do not get admitted into graduate school. So, what should you do if you do not get any admission offers? The first option is to evaluate the situation and to create a plan of attack to go through the process again. For example, were there any weaknesses in your application? Meet with a professor who can give you an honest assessment of what you can do to improve. Maybe you can benefit from additional research experience. If so, dive into that more deeply and see if you can continue to work with a professor for another year. If your GRE scores were low, you might spend time studying before retaking the test. If your letters of recommendation could have been stronger, spend time building stronger relationships. Perhaps your application materials were great, but you fumbled the interviews. If so, work on improving your interviewing skills AND improving your skills and accomplishments. Did you shoot too high when applying to programs? The point here is, if you want to be persistent and try again next year, spend time improving yourself and improving your application strategy—do not make the mistake of being the same person with the exact same approach (but 1 year older).

Another possibility is that you might decide that you do not want to go through the process again. Perhaps you decide that you gave it a good try, but that it just did not work out. This is okay—graduate school is not the best path for everyone. In this scenario, remind yourself that there is nothing to regret because, in most cases, it is better to have tried and failed than to have never tried at all (Gilovich & Medvec, 1995). After you give yourself a short time to get over the disappointment, dive into career preparation—reread our career chapters and be sure to visit your campus career center.

Take-Home Message

Our goal in this final section was to provide you insider tips on the grad school process and food for thought. Essentially, this was a compilation of our "what we wished we had known when applying for grad school." No matter what the future holds for you, keep in mind that we all can work to design and live out *multiple* great lives (see Burnett & Evans, 2017, for more on this notion). So, when the time comes—be sure to take either your graduate school acceptance or other opportunity within this perspective.

Action Steps

1. Just like our advice with giving presentations (from a previous chapter), please spend time preparing—do not try and wing it. It does not get much worse than an interview that consists of periods of silence because you have nothing to say or ask.
2. Whether you get accepted to graduate school or not, take a minute to reassess your future plans by thinking about where you want to be in 5 years. Check out Zadra and Wills's (2009) book (*5: Where Will You Be Five Years From Today?*) that encourages you to be bold when thinking about what you want to accomplish and experience.

Documenting Your Accomplishments

13

13.0 MEET HANNAH

iStock.com/drbimages

CHAPTER OUTLINE

Hannah was finishing her freshman year of college and was considering her options—recently, the idea of graduate school had piqued her interest. She saw an ad for a month-long summer research program, and she thought that this would be a great opportunity. She wanted to apply, but the only problem was that the instructions said to submit a curriculum vitae (CV).

Hannah was nervous because she had no idea what to include. She had heard of the term "CV," but she was never taught how to create one. She looked online and found some of her professors' CVs, and this made her even more anxious—those were all filled with advanced degrees, awards, article publications, presentations, and grants; she had none of those accomplishments.

To get some help, she met with one of her professors during his office hours. When she arrived, she told him about her problems and exclaimed, "I don't have anything to list—I don't have my degree yet, I haven't published any papers, and I have not looked into internships. What do I do?!?" He told her that it was perfectly fine that she did not have much to list in a CV . . . right now. He explained that a CV was a listing of academic accomplishments that would grow each year. In other words, a student's CV (especially a student in her first year of college) was not expected to have as many accomplishments as a professor's CV.

He followed that up by walking her through a list of possible accomplishments that she could include on a CV. He also reassured her that applying for that research program was a great step that would hopefully lead to a lot more achievements that could be listed on her CV in the future!

Why Did We Tell You This Story?

We regularly see students who find themselves in situations similar to Hannah's. Many are not sure what is included on a CV, and some panic that they do not have much that they can list on it. In this chapter, we cover the basics about what can be included on a CV and what should not be included and we also list some examples. We also cover a few other ways that you can document your accomplishments such as by using résumés, portfolios, and websites (including social media).

13.1 RÉSUMÉ TIPS

If you are going to apply for jobs, you will need a résumé. Even if you plan to find your job through your network, you will likely need to supply a copy of your résumé. You can find résumé tips with a simple internet search, but there is so much information out there that it is difficult to sift through all of it. In this module, we tried to summarize tips that we think are helpful. The goal of this module is not to give you a structured template for your résumé (rest assured, though—we do provide some examples) but to give you guidelines to use when editing and building different versions of your résumé (yes, that is correct—we said *different versions*—you want to create a targeted résumé for each job . . . or at least for each type of job you might pursue).

Adopt the Right Mindset for Résumés

To get started, we want you to adopt the right mindset when building a résumé—you can do this by applying the critical thinking skills that you are developing as a psychology student. That is, instead of only thinking about a résumé as a brief story about you, think about résumés from the perspective of the employer who wants to hire someone (e.g., Waters, 2016). Organizations are hiring because they have a problem—they may need someone to fill a defined role, take the organization to another level, or solve an overarching problem. When employers read through résumés, they want to find the best person to help them achieve the organization's desired results. So, as you go through the résumé tips in this module, do not just focus on yourself—consider the employer's needs as well! Think about how your attributes, skills, and knowledge provide value to an organization.

iStock.com/MicroStockHub

Types of Résumés

There are two main types of résumés—chronological and functional. A chronological résumé is the standard type that lists your work experiences in order; start with the most recent occupation and go backward. For a functional résumé, you focus on relevant skills, experiences, and accomplishments, and you de-emphasize your work roles by placing that information toward the bottom with minimal context. So, which should you use?

There are some general rules of thumb about this issue (e.g., Lewis, 2017). The general argument is that, if you have a good work history without any significant gaps in employment, then the chronological format is the way to go. However, if you have major gaps in your employment history, are drastically changing directions in terms of your career, or have no relevant employment history (avoid this by using our advice to complete an internship!), then you might consider a functional résumé. But, keep in mind that functional résumés can have drawbacks. Even if you list your work history at the bottom, employers may still look for that information right away—also, functional résumés have been criticized because, by not listing your employment history right away, it can convey that you are trying to cover up a flaw (e.g., Shields, 2017). For most of you, we recommend sticking with the chronological résumé format, but check with your campus career center for their perspective on your particular situation.

What Goes Into a Résumé?

No matter what format you use, your résumé should be one page. This means that you have to be concise when listing your information. Also, do not focus too much of your efforts on the formatting or try to get cute by doing something unique. Instead, focus on the basics—traditional font, common sections, 1-inch margins—and spend your time and energy on providing the right information. The following is information that is typically included in a résumé (e.g., Doyle, 2018)—use a header for each section (except for the first one—there, your name serves that role).

Identifying information. Start with your name, address, phone, and a professional email address. Be sure that your contact information is up-to-date—if you will lose access to your college email account after graduation, create a professional account (e.g., make a Gmail account with your first and last name in the email address). And, if you are currently employed, you probably do not want to use your current company's email address while on the job market. Some consider using company resources to apply for better jobs to be bad form, and some may think you are apt to "cheat" on them similarly one day.

Objective or summary. For an objective you can describe your career goals. However, keep the employer's perspective in mind—do not include objectives that are important to you but not the employer. An alternative is to include a "Professional Summary" that briefly reviews your important (and relevant) skills, goals, and accomplishments. The LinkedIn profile summary section is often a good model for this; see Reilly (2016) and Wade (2017) for some ideas!

Work experience. In reverse chronological order, list your employment history. As a college student, you can include internships or volunteer positions if they are relevant. Include the organization name, the position you held, and date(s). In addition to activities you conducted in the role, be sure to include any key accomplishments and results you delivered while in that role (this can include demonstrations of soft skills).

Skills. This section is optional, but you can list key skills that you have if they are related to the position (and you did not list this information elsewhere). For example, you might include relevant technological skills, software expertise, domain-specific skills, or proficiencies with a foreign language. But be careful not to oversell your abilities here! If a job requires a particular proficiency, it is likely that you will have to explain your approach or possibly demonstrate it during an in-person interview.

Education. Start with your most recent degree (or expected degree) and list them in reverse chronological order. Include the degree earned, name of institution, and date(s). If you do not yet have a degree, please do not claim that you have it. If you are close, though, you can list that it is "expected" and include the year when you are on track to graduate.

Customize It

Do not submit the exact same résumé for every job. Instead, you should customize your résumé—alter or change the emphasis on skills and accomplishments depending on the particular job description. As you start to build a résumé for a position, you might consider doing two things: (1) consider your strengths, goals, and objectives and (2) think about what the employer wants and what type of person would be a great fit to solve the employer's problems (e.g., Hernandez, 2018). One helpful approach is to keep a "master" résumé for yourself that is somewhat lengthy and has each and every one of your skills and accomplishments described fully. Then, you can refer to that whenever you are creating a customized résumé for a particular job (or general job function).

Be Ready for Applicant Tracking Systems

In some cases, employers use computer systems (e.g., applicant tracking system) to dig through the large number of résumés that they receive (e.g., Hernandez, 2018). So, it is possible that your résumé may not be read by a human unless it is selected as a finalist. Computer programs like this are set to look for certain words and phrases, so it is very important to use keywords from a job ad—use the exact terms, not synonyms (e.g., Marr, 2019). For example, include the job title in your résumé and, if you highlight a specific skill that corresponds to something in the job ad, use the term from the job posting. In addition, be sure to use standard section headers, as a computer program might not recognize creative ones (e.g., Hernandez, 2018).

Focus on Results—Not Activities!

When hiring, employers want to find someone who delivers results—not someone who simply engaged in activities. Most people have job activities and clearly delineated job responsibilities, but not everyone can present a series of meaningful accomplishments! When describing your accomplishments and skills, try not to be vague—be specific by painting a clear picture or using a concrete example to convey the value you would bring to the team. If you can quantify some aspect of your previous experience and accomplishments (i.e., attach numbers as evidence)—then do it (e.g. O'Donnell, 2018). One way to think about this is conveying your job experience in a *results-oriented* manner (rather than being activity-oriented).

Let us give you an example of each to illustrate our point.

Example 1: *An activity-oriented description*

Store Associate, SuperStore *Paradise, NV* (2017–Present)

- Worked 15 hours a week and occasional overtime
- Collected go-backs and stocked shelves
- Mopped store floors and cleaned restrooms
- Greeted customers
- Managed the cash register

Sounds like a regurgitated job description, right?
Example 2: *A results-oriented description*

Store Associate, SuperStore *Paradise, NV* (2017–Present)

- Regularly filled in extra shifts, which allowed the management team to better accommodate changing schedules and address turnover challenges.
- Mopped store floors and scrubbed urinals and toilets, which led to the highest store cleanliness assessment rating in 3 years (May 2018) and contributed to my selection as Employee of the Month (June 2018).
- Greeted customers efficiently at the register, which reduced my average customer transaction time from 2.4 minutes to 1.2 minutes (July 2018 vs. March 2019).
- Effectively managed cash-handling processes, which led to no more than a $2 overage/short rate since I began cashiering in July 2018.

Always think about what happened as a result of your activities!

Be Specific!

Specific descriptions of activities and results achieved are easier to understand and are more likely to be memorable. And, you would like your potential employer(s) to comprehend and recall elements of your résumé, right? To help this point hit home, a Career Builder (2014) survey of hiring managers showed that they hated the following vague résumé buzzwords:

iStock.com/marekuliasz

- Go-getter
- Think outside the box
- Hard worker

- Strategic thinker
- Team player
- Self-motivated

You might be thinking to yourself—"Why? Aren't these good traits and characteristics to have?" Sure! Although possessing these might very well make you a great candidate for the job, listing them as is will not make you stand out from other candidates. Think about what specific behaviors would demonstrate being a "go-getter." What would "team players" do and not do? How would your boss know that you are a "hard worker"? We would suggest not listing traits like these on your résumé, but—if you choose to—be sure you have *specific* examples to demonstrate that you embody those traits.

Another point relevant to specificity is to be aware of A.L.A.A.U.J.—Avoid Listing Abbreviations And Using Jargon (the fact that you did not know that abbreviation was the point that we are making)! Skip abbreviations or acronyms altogether and be specific by spelling them out (e.g., Doyle, 2019). The people reading your résumé may not be familiar with the abbreviations that you use. Also, in some cases, the same abbreviation can have multiple meanings—for example, a quick internet search revealed that APA can stand for any of the following:

- American Psychological Association
- American Psychiatric Association
- American Planning Association
- American Poolplayers Association

Be Accurate!

Companies and organizations typically see a large number of résumés. If your résumé has typos, misspellings, or grammatical mistakes, they will move on to another résumé (e.g., Doyle, 2019). Even if you have an "in" for a job because of networking, these types of mistakes are a huge turn-off. The solution here is simple—use spell-checker, read it yourself (multiple times), and have others provide feedback.

"Are you sure your resume is accurate?"

Cartoon Resource/ShutterStock.com

Also, it is one thing to present yourself in the best way possible, but please make sure that your information is accurate—do not lie or embellish! Even if you hear about other people doing it, please do not do this. And, if that is not enough to convince you not to do it, you should know that employers have ways to catch lies—they look for inconsistencies, conduct background checks, verify information that you list (e.g., college degrees), and, if applicable, they may check to see if you can actually demonstrate skills that you listed on your résumé (e.g., Elliott, 2018).

What Not to Include on Your Résumé

Thus far, we covered a lot of information that you might include on your résumé. However, to be clear, we also want you to know what not to include. Based on common questions that we get from students, here are five things to leave out (e.g., Doyle, 2019):

1. Do not write "Résumé" or the date when you updated it—space is at a premium in a résumé (this is in contrast to a CV, which does include a header and date).
2. Do not include a photograph, personal information (age, race/ethnicity, religion, health or illnesses, etc.), or sensitive identification information (e.g., social security number).
3. Do not include information about high school degrees or accomplishments (unless you have no college experience or it is highly relevant).
4. Do not include unrelated work or skill information—and do not list skills that are assumed (e.g., social media or general word processing software) or obsolete (e.g., expertise with outdated programming languages like Fortran).
5. Do not include names of past supervisors or references—in fact, do not even write something like "References available upon request" (this is assumed).

Finally, know the current practices (these can change across the years). For example, is it standard practice today to include a link to your LinkedIn profile with your contact information (e.g., Bahler, 2018)? Do you list your full home address? Should the résumé be saved as a PDF? Talk to people in the field, career service offices at your school (or alma mater after you have graduated), and professionals that you trust (but understand that people who have not searched for a job in a while might not be up-to-date with current practices).

As this section comes to a close, read on for two example résumés. We think you will see quite a difference between them! Take a few minutes to identify the strong points of the first (Figure 13.1) as well as the pitfalls of the second (Figure 13.2).

Take-Home Message

We encourage you to look at résumé examples, but avoid the temptation to restrict your résumé information to one particular template or example that you found. There is some flexibility in terms of how you can construct your résumé—restricting yourself to modeling from one style may cause you to omit information that might be helpful for your résumé. And, finally, keep in mind that some companies will use an applicant tracking system to initially rate résumés (e.g., Marr, 2019)—and that, when they are viewed by humans, most people sorting through résumés will only spend 6 to 10 seconds scanning your résumé before moving on to others (e.g., O'Donnell, 2018). Make sure that your information is clear and concise and describes someone who would be a great fit for them. As you review and edit your résumé, take the employer's perspective—does your résumé describe someone who fits what they want?

FIGURE 13.1
Example of a Solid Résumé.

Richard Burrhus Wright

1856 Sheridan Way, Apt. 39
Evansville, IL 62008
(312) 469-0578
Richard.Wright@LU.edu

RELATED EXPERIENCE

Social Learning and Evolutionary Research Group, Lombardia University of Southern Illinois — *Research Assistant*

Supervisor: Dr. Ryan J. Kramer
MAY 2019 - AUGUST 2020

Updated the research group webpage and included a sign-up form for new research assistants. This form was shared to social media (Twitter, Instagram, and Facebook) — which led to the largest number of inquiries to date (Fall 2020). Transitioned research participation from paper sign-ups to a *You Can Book Me* page, which led to twice as many sign-ups compared to the prior semester. Trained research assistants to pay participants electronically through their student accounts rather than paper forms (this reduced time spent on payments, and eliminated wasteful use of paper).

PROJECTS

Wright, R. B. (2019). *We're more similar than different: Meta-analysis of distress to different infidelity types.* Poster presented at the 27th annual Lombardia Undergraduate Research Conference, Lombardia, Illinois.

Kramer, R. J., Rando, S., & Wright, R. B. (under review). *Gender differences in distress?* Paper under review for presentation at the 92nd annual meeting of the Upper Midwest Psychological Association, Chicago, Illinois.

EDUCATION

Lombardia University of Southern Illinois, Lombardia, IL — *B.S. Psychology (2021)*
AUGUST 2018–MAY 2021 (Expected)

Mundelein County College, Mundelville, IL — *A.A. Liberal Arts (2018)*
AUGUST 2016–JUNE 2018

SKILLS

Publishing, Presentation and Productivity: Microsoft Office Suite (Word, OneNote, PowerPoint, Forms, SharePoint)

Quantitative Analysis: Excel, SPSS

Website Development: Adobe Dreamweaver, Adobe Photoshop

PROFESSIONAL ORGANIZATIONS AND MEMBERSHIPS

Psychology Club, Lombardia University of Southern Illinois (Spring 2019 - Present)

Illinois Counselors Association (Fall 2020 - Present)

Student Affiliate, Upper Midwest Psychological Association (Fall 2020 - Present)

FIGURE 13.2

Example of a Bad Résumé—Can You Identify How This Can Be Improved?

Rickey B. Wright

1856 Sheridan Way, Apt 39
Evansville, IL 62008
(312) 469-0578
TheGreatest24@gmail.com

I am an energetic and ambitious person who is going to change the world.

EXPERIENCE

Smoke Doggs, Lincoln Shore, IL — *Cashier and Cigartender*
MARCH 2019 - PRESENT
Assist customers upon entry, help customers with cigar choices, maintain cigar lounge cleanliness

Bubba's Big Brews, Wings. and Things, Woodpark, IL — *Security*
JUNE 2017 - MARCH 2019
Worked the door as unarmed security, monitored the bar area and dance floor

Social Learning and Evolutionary Research Group, Lombardia University of S. I. — *Research Assistant*
MAY 2019 - AUGUST 2020
Helped Dr. Kramer with his research, webpage, scheduling participants, and paying participants.

EDUCATION

Lombardia University of S.I., Lombardia, IL — *B.S. (21)*
AUGUST 2018 - MAY 2021 (Expected)

Mundelein C.C., Mundelville, IL — *A.A.*
AUGUST 2016 - JUNE 2013

Oak Forest High School, Oak Forest, IL — *HS. Diploma*
SEPTEMBER 2012 - JUNE 2016

REFERENCES

References available upon request

SKILLS

Microsoft Word - Expert

Microsoft Excel-Expert

Microsoft PowexPoint - Expert

Instagram, Twitter - Expert

AWARDS

Most Valuable Freshman, Mundelein County College Basketball (2017, 2018 seasons)

Who's Who Among American High School Students (2015)

Certificate of Participation, Lombardia Undergraduate Research Conference (Spring 2019)

LANGUAGES

English

iStock.com/sigoisette

Action Steps

1. If you do not already have one, use the tips here to create a draft of your résumé (if you already have one, use the tips here to update or improve it). If you are not sure where to start, use examples or templates to help you.
2. Once you have a draft of your résumé, get feedback from your campus career center. Even if your draft is a mess or just a bare skeleton, bringing a draft (as opposed to bringing nothing) will give the career counselor(s) something to work with when they give you advice.

13.2 CONSTRUCTING YOUR CURRICULUM VITAE (CV)

Most of our students know something about résumés, but they tend to be less familiar with a curriculum vitae (commonly abbreviated as a CV). If you are applying for graduate school, you will likely be submitting a CV (along with a bunch of other materials)—this is because a CV is used by students and professors to document academic accomplishments. A CV is going to (potentially) contain a lot of information because it grows as you have more academic (or academically relevant) experiences. An undergraduate CV might be as short as one or two pages, a graduate student CV might jump up to four to six pages, and some professors are going to have CVs that are over 25 pages. The thing to remember is that, as a student, it is okay for your CV to be short—so do not panic about this. In this module, we walk you through the basic information that you can include in a CV, and we also provide tips for organizing and formatting your CV.

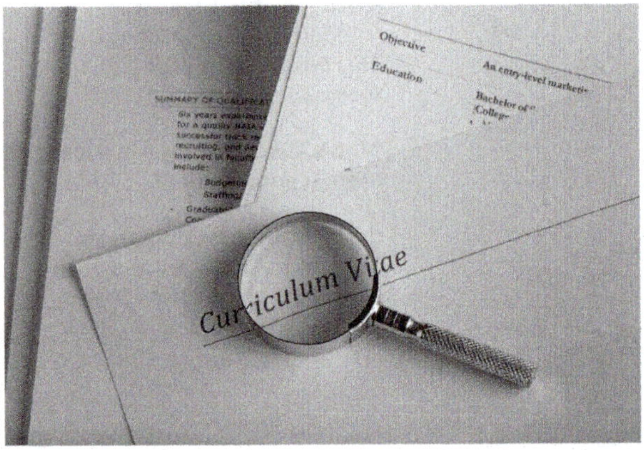

iStock.com/JLGutierrez

Common Sections to Include in a CV

All CVs should include basic information such as your name, contact information, education (i.e., degrees), and references. Other sections are only included if you have relevant accomplishments. For example, if you co-authored a conference poster, then you can list that as a presentation. However, if you have no accomplishments that fit a particular section (i.e., that section would be empty for you), then you should leave it out entirely (not even a section header!). In the following, we cover the most common sections that are included in students' CVs.

1. Name and Contact Information
    - Include your full, professional name.
    - Include an email address, phone number, and perhaps a professional mailing address (this can be your home address if you are a full-time student).
2. Education
    - List each degree you earned (e.g., Bachelor of Arts), the full name of the school where the degree was conferred, when it was earned (year), the years attended, and your major/minor. If you have not yet graduated, you can list it as "Expected ___" (put the expected graduation year in the blank).
    - It is common to list your overall (cumulative) grade point average (GPA)—some people also list the GPA from their major or minor.
3. Awards or Honors
    - Include any awards you earned while in college (and the years you earned them). This can include accomplishments such as the Dean's list.
4. Research Experience
    - List any research assistant positions—include information related to your accomplishments and responsibilities as well as information about your supervisor or collaborator. If your position was in a lab, include the name of the lab.
5. Publications
    - Include any journal or book publications if you were an author or co-author—write it as an APA-style reference (adhere to APA-style formatting).
6. Presentations
    - Include conference presentations if you were an author or co-author. Write it as an APA-style reference (again, use correct APA style).
7. Research or Travel Grants
    - Include any research or travel grants that you earned. List the organization that provided the funding, the year it was earned, the amount of money, and possibly the name of the proposal or project.
8. Scholarships or Fellowships
    - Include any (competitive) scholarships or fellowships that you earned while in college (and the years you had them). List the organization that provided the funding, the year it was earned, and the amount of money. You may also want to include the criteria for the funding (e.g., 3.75 cumulative GPA or higher).
    - Need-based financial aid (e.g., Pell grant) is typically not included.

9. Membership in Professional Organizations or Student Clubs

    - Include any professional organizations or student clubs for which you were an official member. Write out the full name—do not just write an abbreviation. If relevant, indicate the type of membership (e.g., member, associate, student affiliate, etc.).
    - If you had a leadership position, be sure to indicate that as well.

10. GRE Scores

    - Some students include a section with their GRE scores (this could also be MCAT or LSAT scores; if so, rename this section to reflect the appropriate test).
    - Use the all-or-none rule—either include your scores from all test sections or do not include this section at all (i.e., do not just list a score from one section).

11. Work/Internship/Volunteer Experience

    - Describe any relevant work or volunteer experience. For example, if you are interested in a counseling graduate program, you might include that you volunteered or interned in a mental health clinic. Write the name of the company or organization, dates worked, and a brief description of your accomplishments or responsibilities. Be specific about what you did (activities) and what was achieved (results).

12. Skills

    - You can list skills that might be relevant (e.g., native Spanish speaker or proficient in SPSS and R). You can also list any relevant training, experience, or the ability to use specialized tools and technology, such as EEG, fMRI, or eye tracking.
    - Avoid common skills that college students are expected to have, such as experience with Microsoft Office or Google Docs—the only exception is if you are a wizard who can work magic with a particular program!

13. References

    - Include the names, job titles, institutions, and emails of your professional references. It is common to list three references (but in some cases you can list more).

We tried to be fairly exhaustive with the previous list, but there might be additional information that could be included. If you completed an honors thesis or have experience as a teaching assistant, you can add a section for it. It might also be helpful to include a section for relevant coursework (e.g., if applying to a social psychology graduate program, you might list any courses that are related to that topic area or courses that convey that you have research skills).

In addition, keep in mind that these sections and section headers are not set in stone. You can change a section header slightly or you can combine sections if it leads to better organization for your CV (e.g., you might create one section with a header such as, "Honors, Awards, and Memberships"). However, if you get creative like this, ask others for feedback.

What Not to Include in a CV

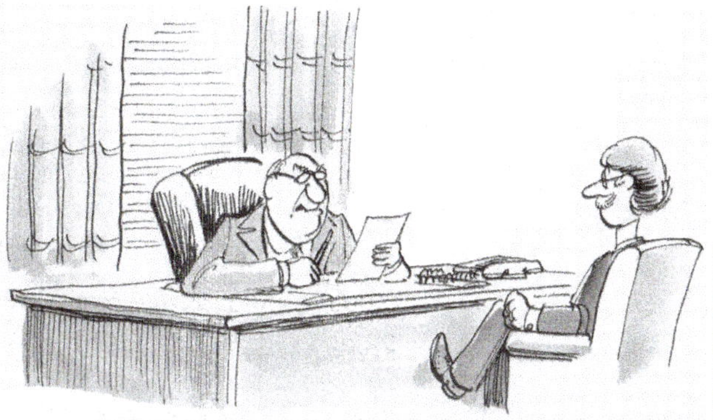
"Summited Mount Everest, did you? Was that just the one time?"

Cartoon Resource/ShutterStock.com

Although it might seem like your entire academic life is included in a CV, there is some information that you should not include. For example, some students think that adding a photo livens up their CV—however, headshot photos are typically not included (save the photos for sites like LinkedIn—more on this later in this chapter). In addition, you do not want to look like you are "padding your CV"—this means adding unnecessary information just to make it look more impressive (e.g., Smith, 2015). Do not list attendance at a conference if you did not do a poster or presentation (any student can attend a conference) or irrelevant volunteer or job positions. People who look at a lot of student CVs (e.g., professors) can spot padding (as well as font boosting and margin trickery) very easily.

Here is a short list of what NOT to include on a CV:

1. Photographs, personal information (e.g., date of birth, gender, ethnicity, religion), or identification numbers (e.g., social security number).
2. Job or volunteer experiences that are not relevant.
3. Section headers if you do not have information for that section—just leave that header and section out completely.
4. As you progress in college, you can drop off most information from high school (except for something big, such as being a valedictorian).
5. Do not double-dip! For example, do not list a presentation twice if it were basically the same presentation given at two different conferences or events.
6. Achievements that are not yours. Do not list awards or degrees that were not earned, and do not list publications or presentations unless you are one of the authors.

Formatting Guidelines for a CV

You might be surprised to learn this, but there are no formal guidelines for how to format a CV. Some people interpret this to mean that you can "do whatever you want" (Greenbaum, 2018), but we think that is a bit extreme. We recommend that you follow the common norms that we describe in the following and that you use examples to help (we provide some in this book, but you can also check to see if your professors list their CVs online).

As you read our formatting tips, you may notice that there are no strict rules regarding fonts and whether or not you should use features such as bullet points or underlining (for example, see Figures 13.3, 13.4, and 13.5). As we noted earlier when discussing résumés, stick with a traditional font and 1-inch margins. And please take the following advice to heart—no matter how you choose to format your CV, be consistent with your formatting, keep things neat, and make sure that it is easy to read and understand (e.g., Doyle, 2019)!

Here are some more formatting guidelines to follow as you build your CV:

1. Unlike a résumé, it is customary to write "Curriculum Vitae" and the date near the top or at the very top. This information can be normal font or large. You can include your name here or with the rest of your contact information.
2. Use headers for all of your sections. In addition, we recommend using page numbers and inserting your name in the top header (this can help if someone prints a copy of your CV).
3. Be consistent! Use the same line spacing for all sections. If you use two places after a decimal in one spot, do that in other spots as well. If one section header is left justified and in bold, then do that for all of your sections. Be consistent!
4. Put your contact information and education sections toward the beginning, and then the references should appear last. The other (middle) sections can be moved around—we recommend putting the sections in an order where the most impressive or relevant accomplishments are listed early.
5. Use tabs or bullet points to make sure that columns and lists line up cleanly.
6. Do not leave a hanging section header at the bottom of a page. If a section header appears at the page bottom without its content, insert a page break and move it to the next page.
7. Except for the most common abbreviations (e.g., GPA), spell things out (this includes the name of your school). Also, write out names, titles, and organizations correctly. For example, "Psychology Honor Society" is a bit generic—be sure to include the full name: "Psi Chi, the International Honor Society in Psychology" (Zlokovich, 2010). Also, keep in mind that different professors have different job titles (see our coverage of professors in an earlier chapter) – usually you can find their job titles on a faculty webpage.
8. When listing multiple items in a section (e.g., degrees, presentations), it is common to write the most recent first and then going back in reverse chronological order.
9. Use APA-style formatting for any publications or presentations. And be accurate with the status of a paper or presentation—for example, if it is only submitted (not yet accepted), clearly indicate this information (do not convey or imply that it is already accepted).
10. Proofread! Typos, misspellings, inconsistencies, and poor formatting will create a negative impression to the reader.

FIGURE 13.3
Example of a Solid One-Page CV.

May 2019

Curriculum Vitae - David J. Matthews

Contact Information

- Address: 41 Grey Street, Henderson, NV 89052
  Phone: (702) 555-3628
  E-mail: matthewsdj36@usen.edu

Education

- Bachelor of Arts in Psychology (2019)
  University of Southeastern Nevada (USEN)
  GPA: 3.78
  Psychology GPA: 3.90

Presentation

- Matthews, D. J, & Koplan, D. C. (2019, March). *The effects of music genre and style on memory for song lyrics*. Poster presented at the meeting of the Nevada Young Researchers Association, Reno, NV.

Research Experience

- Psychology Research Lab Assistant (Fall 2015 — Present)
  University of Southeastern Nevada Memory Lab
  Supervisor: Dr. Dennis C. Koplan
  Software used: E-Prime, Qualtrics, Sona
  Responsibilities: Library searches, programming, data coding

Scholarship

- Radio Corporation of America (RCA) Records Music Research Scholarship: $1000 (2019)

Professional Membership

- Nevada Young Researchers Association: Student Member (2018 — Present)

References

- Dennis C. Koplan, Associate Professor
  Department of Psychology, University of Southeastern Nevada
  dennis.koplan@usen.edu
- Leslie S. Grotowski, Professor
  Department of Psychology, Wilson Community College
  grotowskil@wcc.edu

FIGURE 13.4
Example of an Excellent Two-Page CV.

Montana CV (May 2020) 1

Curriculum Vitae

Jennifer C. Montana
16 Angela Blvd
Mishawaka, IN 46617
(574) 555-1284
montanaj@gmail.com

Education

Magnum Opus University
Bachelor of Science (Expected 2021)
Major — Psychology Minor — Neuroscience
GPA — 3.88

Honors and Awards

Delta Zeta - Midwest Honor Society (2019 — Present)
Outstanding Summer Research Award — Magnum Opus University (2019)

Publication

Johnson, E. S., & Montana, J. C. (2019). Psychological benefits of home field advantage in college sports. *Journal of Sport Psychology in Action, 15*, 181–188.

Presentations

Montana, J. C., & Johnson, E. S. (2019, May). *Psychological effects of home and away games in college sports.* Poster presented at the meeting of the Indiana Psychological Association, Indianapolis, IN.

Johnson, E. S., Schroeder, J. P., & Montana, J. C. (2018, April). *Benefits to imagery and breathing exercises before practice.* Presentation at the meeting of the Major Psychology Association, New York, NY.

Research Funding

Magnum Opus Undergraduate Research Grant (2018) — $1,500
Project title — *Psychological benefits of home field advantage in college sports*

Montana CV (May 2020) 2

Professional Experience

Research Assistant — Sports Psychology Lab (2018 — 2019)
Magnum Opus University
Supervisor — Dr. Emily S. Johnson
Responsibilities — Lab manager, administering surveys, data coding

GRE Scores

Verbal — 168 Quantitative — 166 Writing — 5

Relevant Courses Completed

Sports Psychology
Research Methods
Statistics
Intermediate Statistics
Abnormal Psychology
Cognitive Neuroscience
Psychology of Consciousness

Professional Memberships

Great Lakes Psychological Association — Student Affiliate (2018 — Present)

Volunteer Activities

Young Psychologists — President, Magnum Opus University Chapter (2019 — 2020)

References

Emily S. Johnson, Professor, Department of Psychology, Magnum Opus University
e.s.johnson@mou.edu

Robert C. Rodriguez, Associate Professor, Department of Psychology, Magnum Opus University
r.c.rodriguez@mou.edu

John Paul Schroeder, Assistant Professor, Department of Psychology, Magnum Opus University
r.c.rodriguez@mou.edu

Take-Home Message

Use the advice in this module to create a master copy of your CV, which includes all of your academic achievements. Keep this one and always add to it as you have more accomplishments. However, whenever you are submitting or sharing your CV, be sure to tailor

FIGURE 13.5

Example of a Bad CV—Can You Identify Ways to Improve it?

John T. Vincent
154 Running Meadow Lane
Jackson, NY
(610) 555-3574
potrules420@hotmail.com

Education

UCM
BS Psychology (2020)
GPA: 2.45
Psychology GPA - 2.8
Last 2 YEARS 2.994

Presentations

Robinson, Margaret, Smith, Chris (2019). *Gender Differences In Eating Diorders*. Presented at EPA Conference.

Publication

Vincent, J.T., & Smith, C.D. (2019, June). Why People Like Dogs. *Psychological Science*, 23, pages 121–123

Research Experience

Research Assistant for Chris Smith in ED Lab (2018 — 2019)

I worked in the ED lab for three years and helped a lot with the following tasks:

Run subjects in experiments
Hand out sruveys
Recruit participants
Schedule subjects

I used Word, PowerPoint, and Excel in the lab

VOLUNTEER EXPERIENCE:

March of Dimes Walk for Autism
Runners Club 5k
Psychology Club Member

Member — APA (2019, July)

References

Mr. Morgan, Ph.D. Professor, Department of Psychology, UCM
Mrs. Robinson, Ph.D., Assistant Professor, UCM

it to that situation (e.g., Dittman, 2003). This might mean moving sections around (or perhaps leaving out something that is not relevant). For example, if you have a research publication and are applying to a research-intensive graduate program, then that section should appear early. If you have an impressive award or perfect scores on the GRE, then put that information early. If you did poorly on the GRE (but plan to retake it later), leave that off. One thing to keep in mind, though, is to be sure that there is some organization to the sequence of sections (e.g., do not put research publications early and then research presentations toward the end).

Action Steps

© Can Stock Photo/Gomolach

1. Use the tips here to build your CV. Whether you are a freshman, senior, or somewhere in between, it is good to develop a CV to keep track of your accomplishments. Build a "master version" that includes everything, no matter how small—you can always trim it or customize it when needed. Also, be sure to update your CV as you accumulate more experiences.
2. As a goal-setting exercise, build and save another version of your CV and call it something like "My Dream CV." Here, start with your actual CV, but then insert achievements, experiences, and goals that you want to accomplish in the upcoming years. Make sure that the "goal accomplishments" are written in a way that they stand out from your actual accomplishments—use a different font color or highlight that material.

13.3 BUILDING A PORTFOLIO

Although a résumé and a CV are essentially lists of your achievements, a portfolio can be a much more detailed way to document your accomplishments. In a portfolio, you are collecting and organizing some of the best or most representative examples of your work. Portfolios can be a great educational tool, as students who use portfolios have been shown to have higher grades, more persistence in college, and better graduation rates (Watson, Kuh, Rhodes, Light, & Chen, 2016). Hettich (2019) recommends that psychology students use a portfolio to improve the odds of finding a better job. Remember what we have mentioned earlier—job recruiters and interviewers want to hear examples of how you demonstrated your skills; a portfolio can be a great reminder of your skills (e.g., Hettich, 2016). In this module, we walk you through the reasons that you might want to build a portfolio and we also describe some of the basics about developing one.

© Can Stock Photo/zerbor

© Can Stock Photo/Sosiukin

Why Create a Portfolio?

Suppose that you tell employers that you are proud of your writing and critical thinking skills. They may be intrigued—especially if those skills are needed for the job—but they may want to know if you have any proof for these claims. One solution is to have evidence, such as a psychology research paper that you wrote, that you could share with employers (e.g., Strang, 2015). The majority of employers surveyed said that they would look at a portfolio if an applicant provided a link to it (Leahy & Filiatrault, 2017).

Another reason to build a portfolio as you go through college is that you can use it to take stock of your abilities and accomplishments (e.g., Scartabello, Abate, & Slimak, 2018). For example, you can assess your skills by browsing through your portfolio—your strengths are the things that are clearly present in the portfolio, and your weaknesses may be the areas that are lacking evidence. Doing this can help you describe skills on your résumé or during a job interview (e.g., Hettich, 2019). In fact, students who spend time reflecting on their portfolios tend to perform better in mock interviews, suggesting that their use of a portfolio prepared them to better articulate their skills (Ring, Waugaman, & Brackett, 2017). See Table 13.1 for a recap of why you should create a portfolio.

Creating a Portfolio

What software to use for a portfolio? Although you can create a physical portfolio (e.g., a binder), you might consider developing an *ePortfolio* (sometimes referred to as a digital portfolio). A lot of your accomplishments are going to be electronic (e.g., papers), and if they are not, you can likely scan them to create electronic versions. Also, there are different software platforms that you can use. If you want to be a minimalist and set it up yourself, you could use applications in the Microsoft Office suite (e.g., OneNote, Word). But there is other software out there (e.g., Wordpress) and you might even find that your institution has ePortfolio software available for students (e.g., Digication).

What goes into a portfolio? Start by including any documentation that provides evidence of your skills and accomplishments. You are not restricted to any particular file types in a portfolio—you can include standard files (e.g., PDFs), visual images, videos, or some other format. You could include papers that you wrote as evidence of writing skills.

TABLE 13.1

Top Reasons to Create a Portfolio (or ePortfolio).

1. Share evidence of your skills and accomplishments with employers.
2. Assess your skill development for a better understanding of your strengths and weaknesses.
3. Use it to plan cover letters and rehearse for interviews.

If you created something (e.g., a research poster, website, app) you can put it or a link to it in your portfolio. You might include feedback from a professor as evidence of your ability to give excellent oral presentations. Awards or honors are a great way to document great achievements. If you participated in volunteer activities, service learning, or an internship, you can include feedback or an assessment by a supervisor. If you need ideas for skills that you might want to address in a portfolio, check out our discussion of skills back in our chapter on the psychology curriculum.

In addition to these types of evidence, a portfolio can also include a reflection or summary component. This can help to emphasize key points and provide context for some of the items that you include. Reflecting on your work is also a great way for you to better understand your strengths and weaknesses. As we noted earlier, thinking about your skills and accomplishments like this can lead to better articulation of your abilities and experience (e.g., Ring et al., 2017).

How to organize a portfolio? One thing that is important is that you want some type of structure for your portfolio—you want to avoid the appearance of a disorganized scrapbook (e.g., Birkett, Neff, & Pieper, 2013). Make it user-friendly by presenting your name prominently and including an introduction and table of contents. You can also include links for ease of use—from the table of contents (or main menu) to each document, and then from each document back to the table of contents.

An important component about organizing a portfolio is to think about the goal—is it meant for future employers or for self-assessment? If it is meant for employers, focus on documentation of skills and accomplishments that will be valued for a career or a particular job—you might also include a copy of your résumé. You might also want to be selective and focus on your best work. However, if you are using it for self-assessment, you may want to include more examples of your work so that you can look for patterns (and hopefully improvement).

Portfolios and Ethical Issues

A final note about portfolios is to consider ethical issues related to posting information about others (see Wilson, Slade, Kirby, Downer, Fisher, & Nuessler, 2018, for a review of privacy and ethical issues for portfolios). This is of particular importance in psychology because some of you may participate in scenarios that involve other people—perhaps you worked with adults at a mental health clinic or you ran college students through a psychological experiment. If you want to document these experiences in a portfolio, it is important to respect and maintain the privacy and confidentiality of others—never include identifying information or images of others in your portfolio. If you are ever unsure of what is acceptable to include in a portfolio, seek guidance from professors, supervisors, or your campus career center (e.g., Hettich, 2016).

Take-Home Message

A portfolio (or an ePortfolio) is an organized collection of evidence of your skills and experiences. Even if you never plan to show a portfolio to potential employers, portfolios can be helpful for you to assess your own skills and accomplishments (e.g., Hettich, 2019).

One thing to keep in mind about portfolios is that, if you wait until you are a senior in college, it might be time-consuming to put it all together. In addition, you may not have saved some work, feedback, or other documentation from years past. Because of this, it is recommended that you start a portfolio now and add to it as you build up even more accomplishments.

Action Steps

1. We highly recommend developing a portfolio as a way to be more aware of your learning and skill development. Remember that, when you are doing this for yourself, it does not have to be fancy—start by deciding on a software (check if your institution has ePortfolio software available for students, such as Canvas) or keep it simple and build it in software such as Microsoft OneNote. Then, start collecting evidence of your work and accomplishments.

© Can Stock Photo/SergeyNivens

2. As you put your portfolio together, be sure to include a reflection or summary component as this will help you to assess things such as (a) where you have improved, (b) what you have truly accomplished or demonstrated, and (c) what goals you have for improvement going forward. Remember, anyone can say that they have a skill, but what evidence do you have for demonstrating your skills?

13.4 YOUR ONLINE PRESENCE—SOCIAL MEDIA (LINKEDIN) AND PERSONAL WEBSITES

© Can Stock Photo/iqoncept

In today's world, we not only have to be concerned with the physical world, but we also have to monitor ourselves in cyberspace. Making sure that your online presence is cleaned up and does not *hurt* you is step one—but we think that you should take things further by using your online presence to *help* you! Some sources claim that an online presence today is even more important than a traditional résumé (e.g., Vasel, 2018). In this module, we first reiterate the importance of cleaning up your online image and using social media to your advantage. After that, we cover some possible ways to use the web to help your career development and search—in particular, we focus on using LinkedIn and developing a website.

Your Online Presence and Social Media

© Can Stock Photo/jannoon028

If you wanted to learn more about someone you just met (or were about to meet), what would you do? If you are like most people, then you would do an online or social media search for that person's name. Well, guess what? Employers and graduate school admissions committees are searching for you. We covered this topic earlier when we discussed career preparation advice, so we will only emphasize one key point here: adjust your privacy settings, and make sure your online persona is appropriate for employers or graduate school admissions committees.

When you have taken care of that, the next step is to use social media to your advantage. Nowadays you can find most companies and organizations on popular social media sites like Twitter, Facebook, or Instagram—you will also see professional and student organizations there, too. Use social media to learn about your career field, hear about opportunities, gather information about an organization, and interact with others. Instead of following celebrities (or wannabe celebrities), follow sites or pages that will help you grow. For example, we recommend to our students that they follow our department, the campus career center, and any other organizations related to their future goals.

Use Social Media That Is Meant for Professional Networking

You can go a step further by moving beyond the popular social media sites we just discussed. Consider using a social media platform meant for professional networking such as LinkedIn—after all, 97% of recruiters use it (Han, 2018)! One thing to understand is that LinkedIn is not just an online résumé—yes, some of your profile information will overlap with your résumé, but this is different from a résumé. First of all, a résumé is concise and formal—your online profile will be longer (you can post a lot more information than what you can fit on a résumé) and perhaps a touch less formal (but do not be too casual). Second, your résumé is a static document, but your profile can be updated and have different types of content and allows you to actively connect with others (i.e., network).

© Can Stock Photo/niglaynike

When creating a profile, be sure to do it the right way. One key idea is that, similar to building documents such as your résumé or CV, you should put time and energy into making it better. Take the time to edit it and get feedback from others, and always proofread to make sure that there are no errors. There are a lot of tips out there for designing a good profile (e.g., Ryan, 2018); some of the key pieces of advice include

- Write a targeted headline—do not be too broad or vague, and remember to include keywords (this will help people find you).
- Include a professional looking photo (of your face)—keep it professional (wear a nice shirt or top) and simple.

- Because you have more space than a one-page résumé, provide relevant information that you could not fit on your résumé (e.g., skills, education, and training).
- Upload supporting documents that provide evidence of your abilities (e.g., from your portfolio).
- Make sure that your information (e.g., past jobs) matches the information in your résumé—inconsistencies are a red flag (that you might be lying or embellishing).

There are even tips out there for how college students can use a site like LinkedIn to their advantage (e.g., Babbitt, 2016). One key recommendation is that you can start using career tools like this while you are a student—do not make the mistake of thinking that LinkedIn is social media for adults (e.g., Garriott, 2015). There are a lot of great tips (some overlap with the ones we listed earlier), but here is a quick summary of the key ideas relevant to college students that jumped out to us.

- We stated this earlier, but we will say it again—do not just list skills; be sure to include examples of how you demonstrated skills. And, focus on results achieved rather than simply activities.
- It is expected that you include some type of relevant experience—once again, this shows the importance of activities such as an internship.
- To fill out your profile, you need to have accomplishments—use our superstar tips throughout this book to build these up (e.g., volunteer experiences, awards or honors, memberships in relevant professional organizations, accomplishments in a club or organization, research presentations or publications).
- Be social in a professional manner—use the tools on the site to network with others. Connect with mentors, supervisors, work colleagues, fellow students, professional contacts, and alumni from your school or program.

iStock.com/XtockImages

Consider Developing a Personal Website

Besides using social media platforms such as LinkedIn, another way to supplement your résumé is to develop a personal website (e.g., Frost, 2019). This has similar benefits to what we just described in the last section—you might post items that you collected in your portfolio (see the previous module). One advantage to a personal website is that you can provide evidence of accomplishments in a personalized style—you are not restricted to the structure of a social media platform, and a website can give you freedom to convey your personality in a positive manner.

If you are thinking about a personal website, here are some ideas of what you can include (e.g., Smith, 2015):

- A brief bio of your background and goals
- Your résumé
- Samples of work (e.g., from your portfolio)
- References
- Information that did not fit on your résumé
- Links to additional sites about you (e.g., your LinkedIn profile)
- A blog (good blogs need regular posts and updates—so, think about whether you want to commit to it before you start)

Remember that developing a personal website can be a lot of work. When starting, you need to find a domain name or host, create the website content, proof all of the content, and make sure that everything is professional. Also, you want to make sure that a website looks good, is up-to-date, fits current standards, and has no errors. Our recommendation is that a personal website can be helpful if done right, but only create a personal website if you are willing and able to commit to doing it well—if you are going to be sloppy or not have the time to make sure that it stays updated, it might be better to focus on other things.

Take-Home Message

Similar to what we said earlier about résumés and CVs, one thing to keep in mind about personal websites and using a site like LinkedIn is to depict yourself accurately. Do not embellish and do not pad your accomplishments or skills. Also, be professional. Yes, the internet has few rules and can sometimes seem like the Wild West, but the goal here is to use these methods to launch your career—it is not the place to try and be funny or to act in a juvenile manner. Think about websites and career platforms from an employer's perspective—how are they going to be searching and what do they want to see? And, finally, if you try a personal website or a career-based social media platform, they are only useful if you keep them updated—so, do not make the mistake of creating a profile and then rarely checking in with it.

Action Steps

1. Explore the possibility of using a professional networking site such as LinkedIn. Use the tips we provided to start putting together your information. Browse other people's pages to get ideas, and do not forget to be "professionally social" to build up your network (use our networking tips from an earlier chapter).

2. Delete pictures or social media posts that do not portray you in the best light. Check and adjust your privacy settings, as necessary, across your social platforms. Use different sites to conduct internet searches for your name. Once you have that done, use social media to explore, follow, and possibly interact with companies, professional organizations, student clubs, or your campus (e.g., career services, your department).

Money Issues for Psychology Students

14

14.0 MEET ARIANNA AND BRIANNA

iStock.com/amaster1305

CHAPTER OUTLINE

Arianna and Brianna were identical twins who had a lot of similarities (besides how they looked). Both were about to finish their psychology degrees from a large state university. They both did fairly well in school, earning mostly A's and B's, and both were applying for graduate programs in industrial/organizational psychology.

However, there were also some big differences between them. When Brianna started college, she applied for student loans—forgetting about her mom's financial advice, Brianna borrowed enough to cover her tuition and books, along with a little spending money left over each month. She also avoided working while in school, as she wanted to focus on her studies. In contrast, Arianna had paid attention to her mom's advice about money—she tried to take out the bare minimum. To help, she applied for a large number of scholarships and earned two—one covered part of her tuition and the other helped her pay for books. In addition, Arianna spent two summers completing paid internships—these allowed her to put some of that money toward her tuition.

As graduation approached, the sisters compared notes as they talked about their situations. Brianna admitted that she had not given much thought to how loans would affect her future, and she ended up with $30,000 more in student loan debt than Arianna. On top of that, Brianna was surprised at the impressiveness of Arianna's curriculum vitae (CV)—with the scholarships and internships, Arianna had more accomplishments and experiences listed on her CV!

Why Did We Tell You This Story?

Traditionally, the old advice about conversations was to be polite and avoid topics such as politics, religion, and money. We understand the intention here, but we disagree when it comes to money. Money makes its way into so many aspects of our lives, including many of the topics that we have been covering in this book—careers, decision making, building up academically relevant accomplishments, psychology organizations, paying for your psychology degree, and the costs of graduate school. We focused this chapter on money-related topics for psychology students because we want you to end up more like Arianna than Brianna!

14.1 WHY ARE WE TALKING ABOUT MONEY?

iStock.com/jameslee1

Whether any of us like it or not, money is intertwined with many aspects of our lives including education and careers, and unfortunately colleges tend to drop the ball when it comes to teaching students about money (e.g., Sleigh, Ritzer, & Hamric, 2018). Also, both money issues (e.g., debt) and money accomplishments (e.g., scholarships) can affect your ability to succeed in school and afterward (when you start a career). Do not just take our word for it—a simple search on the American Psychological Association's website (www.apa.org) for the word "debt" led us to numerous articles on how debt affects psychology students:[1]

- *How does psychology doctorates' debt stack up?* (Christidis, Lin, & Stamm, 2018)
- *The debt trap* (Winerman, 2016)
- *New hope for a troubled loan program* (Clay, 2019)
- *Got debt?* (Stringer, 2016)
- *Running start … to a great career: Paying off student loans* (Clay, 2018)

In addition to that topic, there are plenty of other articles that cover money-related topics in relation to psychology, such as the importance of financial literacy for psychology students (e.g., Novotney, 2017; Sleigh et al., 2018). Because money is an important

[1]We want to thank an anonymous reviewer for pointing this out to us!

topic for psychology students, we have included this chapter that covers some important topics that are related to money—particularly for psychology students who are planning for their future. In this module, we cover a few points about debt and paying for college.

High Cost of Tuition

One thing that all college students notice is that tuition and fees can be very expensive (e.g., Boyington, 2018; Hoffower, 2018; Ma, Baum, Pender, & Libassi, 2018). Some of you may receive assistance with tuition (e.g., family support, scholarships), but many of you have to pay all or part of your tuition on your own. There are a variety of ways to get financial support, and some require you to make payments later (which usually include interest), whereas others consist of "free" money that you do not have to pay back (e.g., Christidis, Manjarrez, Stamm, & Lin, 2015). We will cover some of the most popular ways to pay for college in the sections that follow, along with some pros and cons of the different approaches.

Student Loans

One common way to pay for college is by taking out loans. This is great in that it helps students afford college, but one concerning statistic is that the average student loan debt is close to $40,000 (Friedman, 2018a). There are even cases of psychology graduate students finishing with more than $200,000 in debt (e.g., Stringer, 2016; Winerman, 2016)—psychology doctoral programs can lead to some of the highest levels of debt compared to other fields (e.g., Christidis et al., 2018). And, unlike other types of debt, student loans cannot get wiped out by declaring bankruptcy—they will stay with you until they are paid.

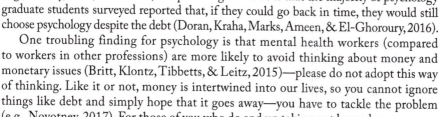

Cartoon Resource/ShutterStock.com

The increase in student loan debt is troubling because students may end up having regrets regarding how much was borrowed—they may have taken too much money (and spent some of it frivolously) or they may have relied on loans to go to an expensive institution when there were less-expensive options (e.g., Safier, 2017). In addition, student loan debt can have negative ramifications for future savings, such as striving to be a millionaire (e.g., Stanley, 2009).[2] However, one piece of good news is that the majority of psychology graduate students surveyed reported that, if they could go back in time, they would still choose psychology despite the debt (Doran, Kraha, Marks, Ameen, & El-Ghoroury, 2016).

One troubling finding for psychology is that mental health workers (compared to workers in other professions) are more likely to avoid thinking about money and monetary issues (Britt, Klontz, Tibbetts, & Leitz, 2015)—please do not adopt this way of thinking. Like it or not, money is intertwined into our lives, so you cannot ignore things like debt and simply hope that it goes away—you have to tackle the problem (e.g., Novotney, 2017). For those of you who do end up taking out loans, here are some tips (e.g., Clay, 2018, 2019; Friedman, 2018b; Novotney, 2017):

[2]We are serious about the term "millionaire"—it is not as difficult to reach this status as you might initially think (and many people should aim for this, especially when it comes to retirement savings).

- Do not be afraid to think about debt—it is a real expense that needs to be addressed.
- Try to borrow as little as possible.
- Take loans out in your name (do not have a family member take out the loan or co-sign with you)—it is your education (not theirs), so do not bring them along for this future debt burden.
- Understand the future payment plan (and any options for changing it).
- Look into student loan forgiveness options.
- When you land a job (and earn an income), avoid increasing your spending—use the new money to help pay down debt right away.

Grants

A better option than taking out loans is securing grants. Unlike loans, grants provide free money that does not have to be repaid and they are typically based on financial need. To qualify for most grants, you will have to fill out the Free Application for Federal Student Aid (FAFSA) and then you can apply for government grants such as a Pell grant—there are also specialized grants including some for veterans and for people pursuing a degree in education (e.g., Nykiel & Helhoski, 2018). Federal and state grants are a great resource and, if you need funding, you really should consider applying for this type of funding—financial aid offices on your campus should be able to help you with this process.

Merit-Based Funding

Although loans and grants are based on need, other types of financial assistance are competitive and merit-based. Most scholarships and research grants fit this latter category (we cover these in more detail in upcoming modules). Organizations providing these funds typically do not care about your current financial situation—instead, they usually award money based on your attributes, accomplishments, or potential. For example, scholarship donors might select a winner based on the quality of an essay, and research grant funding agencies might choose a winner based on the potential outcomes of a proposed project and possibly a "return" on their investment. Competitive funding is important because it is earned and, unlike a loan, you do not have to pay the money back—it is given to you.

One thing of note is that you need to seek these opportunities out and apply for them, and then the people who are selecting the recipient(s) of a scholarship or grant need to see something that they value. Because of this, merit-based funding is a form of recognition or accomplishment (e.g., Mahuron, 2018). Think of it this way: When a funding source is willing to hand you money (which does not have to be paid back), this is a stamp of approval to others that there is something good about you—and this sounds like an accomplishment that superstar psychology students might list on their résumé or CV!

Balancing Work and College

© Can Stock Photo/Pixelbliss

It is estimated that between 70% and 80% of college students are working while attending college (Carnevale, Smith, Melton, & Price, 2015). One important finding is that working small amounts can have benefits over not working at all (e.g., Dundes & Marx, 2006; Wenz & Yu, 2010), as work might help you develop basic skills such as disciplined time management. One caveat to that work benefit is that students who work more than 20 hours per week have lower academic performance than those who work fewer hours (e.g., Dundes & Marx, 2006; Logan, Hughes, & Logan, 2016). Another big finding is that working while in college can be beneficial when the job is related to what you are studying (Carnevale et al., 2015). Paid internships are one option that fits well here—typically the role is temporary (limited hours) and it should be in an area that you want to pursue—this is yet another reason you should look for these!

Unfortunately, limiting the time spent at work is not always feasible. If this applies to you, then there are a few things to keep in mind:

- First, pay careful attention to our study tips from earlier in the book—in particular, find and utilize those brief gaps of time throughout your day to read or study.
- Second, try to stick with a schedule and plan out regular time to spend on your course assignments.
- Third, you may have to make some sacrifices (often by saying "no" to things that are not a priority).
- Finally, work with academic advisors (be honest with them about your work responsibilities) to plan out course schedules—this may mean slightly fewer credits each semester or possibly taking some courses over the summer.

Take-Home Message

The high costs of higher education can lead to a need for supplementary sources of funding. Need-based grants are a great opportunity, but these are not always enough (and some people do not qualify). We recommend first exploring merit-based funding such as scholarships, then considering working while in college (ideally 10 to 15 hours a week), and if needed, borrowing money through student loans (TIP: do not put tuition on a credit card—that is a recipe for destroying your credit score). Keep in mind that ignoring your finances or making uninformed decisions can potentially hinder your ability to reach your true superstar potential.

Action Steps

1. When figuring out how you are paying for college, do not wing it. Make a plan to minimize student loans by applying for need-based grants and scholarships (more on this in the next module). Make an appointment with your financial aid office to explore options that can reduce that tuition bill (even if you have been there before, new opportunities may have become available)!

2. If you are one of the 70% to 80% of college students who also works, please implement some of our suggestions. If possible, minimize the number of hours you work and look for jobs that are relevant to your future career. If you have to work a lot of hours, schedule your time (utilizing small gaps of time for studying) and work with academic advisors to plan your courses.

14.2 SCHOLARSHIPS

© Can Stock Photo/Engdao

Does the idea of free money to help pay for your psychology degree interest you? If you happen to have tuition covered, how about money for books or housing? You might not pay for everything with scholarships (e.g., Singletary, 2018), but remember that every little bit of funding can help. If we have not piqued your interest yet, you should know that earning a scholarship can be a nice superstar accomplishment to add to your résumé or CV! For those of you who do not earn straight A's, do not fret—you can still qualify for plenty of scholarships (e.g., Hatcher, 2012). For psychology students, one of the first places to check out is Psi Chi, as they regularly hand out scholarships (e.g., Psi Chi Awards and Grants, 2019). In this module, we provide you with more tips for finding scholarships and advice that can (hopefully) increase your odds of landing one.

Finding Scholarships

There are a lot of places where you can look for scholarships (e.g., Sethi, 2018), and one of the first places you should look is your institution's financial aid office—in fact, you can probably just go to their website. A great part of these sites is that they often list scholarships that are restricted to students at your institution (which improves your odds of winning—more on this later). A second possibility is to check with your department and college to see if they have any scholarships for students in your major or minor.

Another consideration is to visit your old high school (possibly a career or guidance office). Most high schools help with scholarships because they want their students to succeed in college—and, if you are an alum, then they will likely be willing to help you, too.

Another helpful option is to look into whether a company or organization offers scholarships (or tuition matches) to their employees—in some cases, close family members might also be eligible. So, if you, a parent, sibling, grandparent, spouse, or partner are working, be sure to check to see if the employer offers scholarship opportunities. You can also look into community groups, clubs, or professional psychology organizations (e.g., Psi Chi Awards and Grants, 2019)—many of these groups offer scholarships. Some organizations might not advertise their financial support for higher education openly, so do ask about them.

Books and Websites for Scholarships

Another resource is to check out books that focus on scholarships. Some are published annually and include an updated list of scholarships (or sources where you can look). For example, we found *The Ultimate Scholarship Book 2019* (Tanabe & Tanabe, 2018) and *Scholarships, Grants & Prizes 2019* (Peterson's, 2018).

In addition to books, you can also scour the web for scholarships. Some websites list generic scholarships where almost anyone is eligible, whereas other sites are going to be more restrictive as to who is eligible to apply. So, read carefully as you browse these sites and make sure that you qualify. The following is a small list of scholarship websites to get you started (Speers, 2016):

- Peterson's
- Unigo
- Fastweb
- Cappex
- Chegg
- The College Board
- Niche
- Scholarships.com
- CollegeNET.com
- Scholarship Monkey

Understanding Some Basics About Your Odds

When searching for and applying for scholarships, it helps to adopt a strategic approach and to use your critical thinking skills (see Table 14.1). One general rule of scholarships is that the odds of earning one tend to decrease when more people know

TABLE 14.1
Oversimplified Breakdown of Scholarship Odds

LOW ODDS

- Scholarship is advertised online and it is open to nearly anyone. A lot of these will be on popular websites like *scholarships.com*. In some cases, all that you have to do to apply is to click and submit your contact info.

DECENT ODDS

- Scholarship is only available to people who work for (or who have parents who work for) a company or organization.
- Scholarship is only available to people who attend a particular school.
- Scholarship is only available to people who fit certain criteria (a particular age group, ethnicity, religion, certain accomplishments, etc.).
- Scholarship is open to anyone, but the application process requires some work (e.g., write an essay, be interviewed, report back on an annual basis).

GREAT ODDS

- Scholarship is only available to an *extremely small* group of people, based on some type of specific criteria or very restrictive eligibility.
- Scholarship is only available to a restricted population AND work is involved to *secure* (e.g., essay) and *maintain* it (e.g., attendance at the scholarship gala, annual presentation, thank-you letter).

BEST ODDS

- You find scholarships that fit the "Great Odds" category, and you apply to as many of them as humanly possible!

about them and when more people qualify for them. For example, some scholarships listed on the web have no restrictions and have an easy application process—some are as simple as providing your name and contact information. You are welcome to apply to these because they are easy, but remember that your odds of being selected are fairly low (like playing the lottery). Instead of focusing on easy (to apply for) scholarships like that, we recommend focusing on opportunities that organically narrow the applicant pool.

Consider the following—some students are turned off if a scholarship asks them to do more than type their name and answer a few questions. For example, some scholarships require that you—GASP!—write a short essay! Think about that for a second—many other students might not want to put forth the effort of writing and editing an essay, plus many students are not very good at it (e.g., Strauss, 2017). This might cause the applicant pool to be smaller (which is better for you). And the reality is that essays do not take that long to write (especially once you get some practice with it).

If you are going to write an essay, it is probably a good idea to do it correctly (e.g., Ellis, 2013). First, personalize the essay—make it a story about yourself and your goals. If applicable, indicate how you want to make an impact on others or the world. Consider the perspective of the funding agency or generous philanthropists awarding the scholarship—would they rather give scholarship money to (1) someone who simply needs it to enroll in the fall semester or (2) someone who strives for a career where she can impact the lives of foster children? You know the answer (just in case you did not—it was applicant #2).

When writing these sorts of essays, it is important to stand out (in a good way). So, be careful and try not to include common buzzwords or overly ambitious goals that sound impressive but are out of scope. For instance, avoid a broad and generic answer that most people might give—"*The biggest problem in the world today is global warming.*" Instead—think outside the box a little bit—for example, you might write about how psychological research about human behavior can be applied to address water usage (e.g., Fishman, 2011). Which essay will stand out—the one with the unique answer or the 20 essays that all covered the same theme? And, finally, always revise and proofread your writing! Do you think that someone who submits an essay with loots and lottss of tpyos is deserving of money?

Another way to improve your odds of landing a scholarship is to apply for those with increasingly specific criteria. These restrictions naturally reduce the depth of the applicant pool. For example, you can look for organizations that offer scholarships that are meant for people of certain ethnic or cultural backgrounds. In addition, you might find scholarships based on gender, sexuality, disability, veteran status, having a particular skill or hobby, attending a particular institution, or having a certain major (TIP: look to see if professional organizations in psychology offer funding opportunities). For those of you who are physically talented or skillful, you might consider vying for an athletic scholarship (see Notte, 2018, for probabilities for different sports broken down for men and women).

A final point about scholarship odds is to recognize that you can improve your chances if you simply apply for more of them. Like many things in life, this is a numbers game—apply for as many scholarships as you want (e.g., Sethi, 2018). After writing a few scholarship essays, you will know the common themes that most scholarships want you to write about—this means that additional essays will become much easier! As we noted earlier, pay close attention to the eligibility criteria and the work involved in the application process. Considering these factors will help you better allot your time and increase your overall likelihood of landing a scholarship.

Take-Home Message

With higher education costs seemingly rising every single year, why not look for opportunities to trim those expenses? Also, earning a scholarship can be an achievement in itself! Merit-based scholarships not only help defray your own educational expenses but they can also set you apart from other psychology majors out there. For this reason, make a point of taking shots at competitive scholarships. When looking for scholarships, remember to consider the burden of the application process and how many people will qualify for them—these factors can help you remain strategic in your approach (and ultimately improve your odds). We can almost guarantee that rejection will happen to each and every one of you. But do not worry about rejection—it's simply a numbers game. Keep trying to improve your applications and essays, and remember that, in a lot of cases, if you get rejected you can try again by reapplying the next year.

© Can Stock Photo/deandrobot

Action Steps

1. Start exploring scholarships today—we recommend making a plan to search each month. Search the web, check companies or organizations, scour your state and local entities, and find out whether there are any available through your institution. Narrow your running scholarship list down to those for which you qualify and seem to give you good odds (i.e., relatively narrow applicant pool, some application burden), and then start applying!
2. Every time you write a scholarship essay, get feedback from others so that you can improve it. Also, save your old essays—you may encounter new opportunities that have similar instructions or questions.

14.3 RESEARCH GRANTS, TRAVEL GRANTS, AND AWARDS

Most students are familiar with need-based grants that are typically part of a financial aid package such as Pell grants. Although those are a great source of funding if you qualify, we want to cover other types of grants for psychology students that are merit-based—research and travel grants. Research and travel grants for students are typically offered by professional organizations (e.g., Psi Chi, APA, APS), schools, or governmental agencies for the purpose of funding research activities or travel to present research. This type of funding is competitive (e.g., Rovnyak & Shields, 2017), so if you have a great new idea and can earn funding, it is a major accomplishment to earn a research or travel grant. In this module, we cover some of the basics that might help you find research and travel grants—in addition, we also provide an overview of awards for college students.

Research and Travel Grants—The First Steps

If you are interested in research or travel grants, the first step is to be involved in research, working with a professor or graduate student (see our earlier chapter for tips about getting involved with research). Remember that all undergraduate research is to be supervised (do not go rogue and conduct research on your own). Once you get started with a mentor or collaborator, the next step is to determine if you could benefit from a research or travel grant. Think about if you could benefit from money for (a) summer research, (b) equipment or software used to conduct a research study, (c) paying research participants, or (d) travel to a conference to present your research. If one or more of these possibilities apply to you, have a conversation with your research mentor or supervisor to discuss looking for funding opportunities.

Where to Find Research and Travel Grants

The first place to look for undergraduate grants is psychology professional organizations like Psi Chi (the international honor society in psychology), the Association for Psychological Science (APS), or the American Psychological Association (APA). If you search their websites—especially Psi Chi, which advertises over $40,000 in awards, grants, and scholarships on their website (www.psichi.org)—you will find a number of different opportunities for funding. For travel grants, check to see if the organization that is hosting the conference offers student funding. You can also check to see if your institution offers funds to support undergraduate research. If you are pretty savvy regarding research and travel grants, you can broaden your search to other funding agencies like the National Science Foundation (NSF), National Institutes of Health (NIH), or a military research organization; however, keep in mind that most of those grants are for established researchers like professors or possibly grad students (see Table 14.2).

Is the Research or Travel Grant Meant for Undergraduates?

One key idea to remember is that you must be able to determine whether or not a research or travel grant is applicable to you! Some grant listings might be explicit in that they are meant for someone with an established record of research (e.g., a professor who has published a lot of articles). You can also look for other clues—if the research topic sounds very specific and complex (i.e., over your head), then it is probably meant for experts like professors. Another clue is to look at the amount of money—a research grant for a million dollars (or perhaps hundreds of thousands of dollars) is not meant for an undergraduate who is a novice (funding agencies only give large sums of money to researchers with long track records of productivity).

Other grant advertisements might state that they are intended for "students," but be sure to read the eligibility requirements and expectations closely. Many of those research and travel grants are meant for doctoral or master's (i.e., graduate) students (e.g., Thurmond, 2013). Other keywords in scholarship descriptions that point toward graduate student eligibility are *dissertation*, *thesis*, *early career researcher*, or *internship* (most advertised internship funding is meant for clinical psychology graduate students).

TABLE 14.2

Our Top Recommendations for Where to Look for Student Research or Travel Grants

- Psi Chi
- American Psychological Association (APA)
- Association for Psychological Science (APS)
- Your department, college, or office of undergraduate research
- Other sources, such as the National Science Foundation (NSF) or National Institutes for Health (NIH), might work, but they tend to focus on funding for more-established researchers

If all of this sounds discouraging for finding undergraduate funding, do not fret—keep reading . . .

Research and travel grants meant for undergraduates will typically fit some or all of the following criteria. First, well-written ads may explicitly state that they are meant for *undergraduates*. Second, the listed research topics are going to be broadly described, as they are trying to attract undergraduates who are just starting to get research experience in a variety of areas. Third, look to see who is offering the award. If you find a grant offered by Psi Chi (an organization that mainly helps undergraduates), the odds are good that it is meant for undergraduates. There are a handful of grants offered by APA or APS that are intended for undergraduates, but many are meant for graduate students or professors. Finally, most grants offered by agencies like the NSF are intended for experienced researchers, but you can find some that are meant for graduate students or undergraduates (e.g., Petrella & Jung, 2008).

The key idea here is that you have to think critically to determine if a research or travel grant is meant for you—if you are not sure, ask a professor or graduate student for help (they will know). Here are some questions to ask yourself when searching for undergraduate research or travel grants (these should be an answer of "yes"):

- Does it explicitly state "undergraduates" when describing eligibility?
- Is the topic broad or fitting for undergraduate research?
- Is it offered by an organization known to help undergraduates (e.g., Psi Chi, APS, etc.)?
- Is the amount of money fairly small (e.g., under $20,000)?

Awards

How about a nice, big, official pat on the back for a job well done (which sometimes comes with a cash prize)? In college, formal recognition of your accomplishments may be available in the form of awards or honors (which can be listed on your résumé or CV). Some of you may have already earned some minor awards or recognition by simply being a good student. Most schools recognize students for achieving a certain grade point average and add those students to the Dean's list. In addition, when you graduate, if your grade point average is high enough you may earn Latin Honors with your degree, such as *cum laude* (with honor), *magna cum laude* (with great honor), or *summa cum laude* (with highest honor).

© Can Stock Photo/MoonSafari

Besides these distinctions, there are also many other awards for which you may qualify. If (or should we say "when"?) you join an honor society like Psi Chi, this qualifies as both a membership and an achievement. Your college or university may also have a number of student awards for achievements such as outstanding grades, student service activity (e.g., helping in the department, volunteering in the community), or research accomplishments. Because many students are not aware of these awards, it is sometimes easier to win because there is less competition (good odds)! Also, some awards come with monetary prizes—more free money! Ask your fellow students and your instructors and search your school's website to find out about different awards that might be available.

Writing a Grant Proposal or Award Essay

There are a few rules that you should follow when writing a grant proposal or an essay for an award.[3] We outline these for you as follows:

1. Closely follow the instructions. How long should it be? What should you include or address? What is the deadline? Never deviate from those requirements.
2. Determine what the evaluators consider valuable (and worth funding or awarding). Pore over the details of the ad for the evaluation criteria because they will be using them to pick a winner. So, emphasize key ideas and, in some cases, strategically weave keywords from the ad itself into your application materials.
3. Get feedback from a professor or graduate student—they have more writing experience than you, so use them as a resource to improve your work. Ask for honest feedback to improve—after all, free money or recognition is at stake!
4. Revise your work by writing multiple drafts. Remember the sentiment that has been attributed to Ernest Hemingway here—that first drafts of any work are a piece of crap (Samuelson, 1984). So be sure to allow enough time for editing and drafting!

Take-Home Message

As you get more involved with research, keep an eye out for research and travel grants that can help you pay for new experiences. Because grants involve research projects, these applications typically require more effort than a scholarship, but they can be more impressive to future employers or graduate schools. Finally, when it comes to research grants, travel grants, and awards, we have two pieces of advice. First, make sure that you are a really good match for the qualifications that are listed. Second, if you apply but are not selected, do not get discouraged! Some organizations will provide feedback for grants—if they provide it, use it to make your application even better next year. For instance, examine the characteristics of award recipients—do you have similar accomplishments (if not, can you achieve them before you apply again)?

Action Steps

1. If you are engaged in research, explore possible research or travel grants that are available. Start by going to sites like Psi Chi or check to see if your institution has an office of undergraduate research. You may not qualify for them now, but make a list so that you can go back to them after you gain some experience.

---

[3]We know some undergraduates who got highly involved with professional psychology organizations such as APS and who were asked to evaluate student grant proposals (using rubrics). Doing this can help you see how they are scored, which might help you write a better proposal for yourself!

2. Start making a list of possible awards and what you need to qualify for those awards—check with your department office or scour your institution's website. If you are a good candidate, then apply; if not, keep that list, build up your accomplishments, and check it again next year (but keep adding to the list as you hear about more awards)!

14.4 MONEY, CAREER, AND HAPPINESS

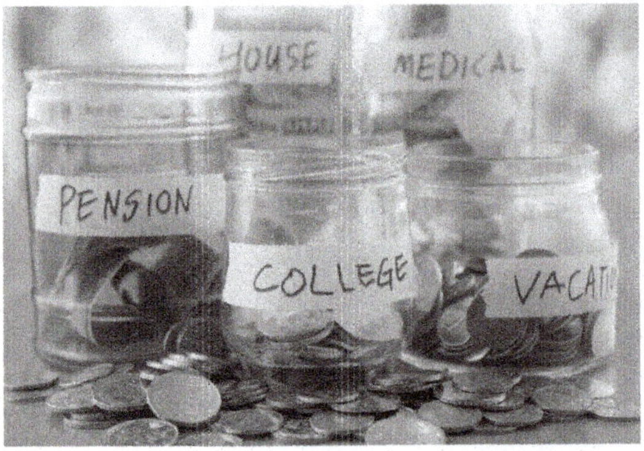

iStock.com/eskaylim

When you are choosing a career path, one consideration that tends to pop up is money. Namely, how much money can one earn by doing a particular job? Keep in mind that salary is only part of the equation when considering the financial benefits of a job—employers differ in terms of what they offer for salary, healthcare, retirement contributions, and perhaps equity in the organization (e.g., stocks). However, because these financial benefits vary from employer to employer and are difficult to predict, we focus most of our discussion on salary here. And please do not be like some mental health professionals who choose to ignore money issues (e.g., Britt, Klontz, Tibbetts, & Leitz, 2015)—money is a factor when it comes to careers. In this module, we discuss the pros and cons of prioritizing money in the process of career choice, some realities about salary in psychology-related careers, and general financial advice.

Importance of Money When Choosing a Career

People vary as to how much importance they place on money (see Table 14.3). On one end of the spectrum are people who value money above everything else—the job could be boring as long as they are getting paid well. On the other end of the continuum are people who do not give much thought to money and who are much more concerned about doing something that they enjoy or that makes them feel good (e.g., Britt et al., 2015). Most of you probably fall somewhere between these extremes—that is to say, you are not ready to work for free, but you are also not obsessed either. To help you figure out where you fall on that continuum, we include arguments *for* and *against* prioritizing money in the process of career choice.

TABLE 14.3

What Is Most Important to You When It Comes to a Career? Rank the Following for Yourself, From Most to Least Important.

- Money (to buy things, pay off debt, etc.)
- Job makes you feel good
- Flexible schedule
- Short/long hours
- Working with good people

Why you SHOULD NOT prioritize money. One big reason NOT to emphasize salary is that the correlation between one's pay and job satisfaction is very small (Judge, Piccolo, Podsakoff, Shaw, & Rich, 2010). Another reason is that there are plenty of other job-related factors—besides how much money one takes home—that might be important. For example, perhaps you care about a flexible work schedule or being able to leave your work world behind when you go home (e.g., White, 2014). Along these lines, there is research that shows that people who value time over money report higher levels of happiness (Whillans, Weidman, & Dunn, 2016).

Other research shows a disconnect between what we value in the present and what we think we would value in the future (e.g., Fishbach, 2017). When people think about future jobs, they think that money will lead to satisfaction—however, when you ask them about what is important about their work in the present, they emphasized wanting to do interesting work and having good co-workers. The point is this—when thinking about a future career, instead of idealizing the role of money, you might instead focus on things that you value in your day-to-day life, such as the potential to be doing interesting things and being part of a winning team.

Why you SHOULD prioritize money. The case *for* money is simple—we need money for a variety of things such as housing, food, transportation, clothing, entertainment, and paying off personal debt (e.g., student loans). And keep in mind that the costs of living can increase if you are supporting others (e.g., family). On top of that, remember that you will also have to earn enough money so that you can save up for retirement—you may not be able to (or want to) work when you are older. Taking a more extreme view—if you focus on earning lots of money, you may be able to retire early, allowing you to explore your passions in your newfound free time (e.g., Baab-Muguira, 2016).

In addition to needing money to live a comfortable life, more income can lead to higher reports of happiness (Jebb, Tay, Diener, & Oishi, 2018). There is a caveat to this, though—once you reach a certain level of income (near $100,000), an increase in salary does not lead to a corresponding increase in happiness. To be sure—having more money can allow you to purchase material items and experiences that are important to you. In addition, you can also pay for services that can save you time (e.g., hire someone for yard work, saving you that time).

Striking a balance. Our advice is to do some self-reflection to determine how important money is to you. Then read about different approaches to life, consumerism, and fulfillment—such as minimalism (see Millburn & Nicodemus, 2011, 2014)—to enrich your perspective. After exploring some of these topics—aim to find a balance among your interests, your skills, and what you consider a good-paying job. Think about the following:

- If you just try to pursue a passion in which you have skills, but ignore how much money you take home, you might not be able to pay the bills.
- If you aim for a job that utilizes your skills and that pays really well, but you find boring, then going to work every day might be a slog.
- And, finally, if you do not have the right skills for a career that is highly interesting and that pays well, you are not going to succeed.

FIGURE 14.1

Venn Diagram Depiction of Finding a Balance Among Your Interests, Skills, and a Good Salary.

As illustrated in Figure 14.1, try to find that sweet spot that balances all three areas (e.g., Hess, 2017). And remember what we mentioned in previous chapters about careers—to succeed in career planning, you have to put in the hard work to get informed about possibilities, develop your skills, and to network like a pro (e.g., O'Donnell, 2018)!

Salaries for Common Careers With a Psychology Degree

Post-graduation salaries differ quite a bit across college majors. Most rankings (e.g., Berry, 2018) have degrees in engineering, science, or business at the top of the list, with liberal arts and social science majors like psychology further down the list—but it should be noted that liberal arts majors can make good money; it just depends on the career that is chosen (Jaschik, 2019). According to data provided by PayScale (2019), people with a bachelor's degree in psychology should expect to earn between $34,000 and $90,000, with an average salary of $57,000—job satisfaction for those with a psychology degree was rated as a 4 out of 5.

Which psychology-related careers tend to lead to the most income? It is probably not surprising that those that require a graduate degree tend to pay more. Some examples of high-paying careers are psychiatrist, industrial/organizational psychologist, neuropsychologist, clinical psychologist, engineering psychologist, forensic psychologist, and counseling psychologist (e.g., Bobnar, 2019; Kelle, 2019). At the low end for pay are occupations that do not require a graduate degree, such as substance abuse counselor, psychiatric technician, social service assistant, and child care worker (Cherry, 2018). Keep in mind that we provided long lists of occupations back in our career chapter, so there are a lot of career possibilities that fall between these notable extremes.

A recent study showed that psychology students' estimates of salaries for specific careers were highly variable compared to industry data, and 11% of those surveyed students did not even try to make an estimate (Strapp, Drapela, Henderson, Nasciemento, & Roscoe, 2018). In other words, psychology students need to become more knowledgeable about salaries so that they are more informed about career preparation! One step that you can take is to talk to your campus career center to learn more about salaries—for example, they might be able to explain that, for some careers, salary may not change much as you gain more experience, but for other careers salary can bump up considerably as you move up the ladder. Also, ask them for tips about negotiating and when (during the interview process) you should ask about salary. If you want to do some digging on your own about average salaries for careers, use websites such as o*net (www.onetonline.org), PayScale (www.payscale.com), or the U.S. Bureau of Labor Statistics Occupational Outlook Handbook (www.bls.gov/ooh/). Additionally, keep an eye out for salary surveys conducted by the American Psychological Association (e.g., Finno, Michalski, Hart, Wicherski, & Kohout, 2010).

Take-Home Message

It is unfortunate, but too many students go through school without any education about the basics of personal finance (e.g., Kovacs, 2016). As an example, a large percentage of students whom we speak with do not know much about topics such as what affects credit scores, different types of debt, and how compound interest works. As we have noted throughout this chapter, money is a part of our lives, including education and careers.

If you are lacking in knowledge about finances, we recommend that you take some time to educate yourself. Do a little bit of reading (we provide some recommendations in the Action Steps that follow) or watch some educational videos. One thing to keep in mind is that, like most things in life, there is not universal agreement on everything related to finances—for example, some people recommend avoiding debt at all costs and others say that a little bit of debt is okay (as long as it is at a low rate and it benefits you in the future). So, learn the basics and recurring themes so that you can make more-informed personal decisions.

Action Steps

1. Take a minute to determine how important salary is to you (e.g., give yourself a rating "salary is extremely important to me" = 5, "salary is not at all important to me" = 1). Also, go back to Table 14.3 and rank those factors—where does money rank for you? Second, do some digging to find out the expected salaries for career paths you are considering.

iStock.com/Brankospejs

2. In our view, ALL college students need to learn the basics of personal finance. We strongly recommend that you spend some time and do some reading. Here are some websites with helpful tips and videos on personal finance:

- TheSimpleDollar.com (e.g., see the piece by Hamm, 2014)
- FoolProofMe.org
- KhanAcademy.org (see the Personal Finance series of videos)

Here are some (reasonably priced) book recommendations that can help you to get started:

- *The Millionaire Next Door: The Surprising Secrets of America's Wealthy* by Stanley and Danko (2010)
- *The Total Money Makeover: A Proven Plan for Financial Fitness* by Ramsey (2013)
- *I Will Teach You to Be Rich* by Sethi (2019)

14.5 MONEY AND GRADUATE SCHOOL

When we talk to students about graduate school, money is not one of the first topics that they ask about—in fact, most rarely bring it up at all. However, there are a number of financial issues that are very important for you to know about before you pursue that path. Some of these are important for graduate school preparation as you complete your undergraduate degree, whereas others are going to be more relevant when you are in graduate school (see Table 14.4). For example, you might want to know about tuition and financial assistance—one great resource for this information is the book *Graduate Study in Psychology* (American Psychological Association, 2018). In this module, we discuss some issues that can affect your preparation and decision making for graduate school.

Money Issues When Preparing for Graduate School

If you are getting ready for graduate school, we want you to know that there are some financial costs that come into play while you are still an undergraduate. First, most graduate programs are going to charge an application fee. Second, if you are

TABLE 14.4
Money Issues Related to Graduate School

Before Starting Graduate School
- Application fees
- Interviews

During Graduate School
- Tuition and fees
- Cost of living (house or apartment, food, transportation)
- Research funding (if applicable)

invited for interviews, you may have to pay all (or part of) your travel costs (i.e., costs of driving or flying there and lodging). Third, you may need to buy professional attire for those interviews. Finally, you might consider attending or presenting at a research conference as an undergraduate (especially if you are aiming for PhD programs that emphasize research).

Let's address each of those incidental costs here. Application fees for graduate programs are typically in the $50 to $80 range (Michalski, Cope, & Fowler, 2019). You can manage these costs by being selective in the number of programs to which you apply. Another approach is to look for funding to help with this—for example, the McNair Scholars program provides research guidance and funding for students from underrepresented groups. In particular, we have seen them pay the grad school application fees for members in their program—go to mcnairscholars.com to see if the McNair program is available at your institution. For grad school interviews, ask if the program can reimburse any of your travel costs or if there are possibilities for free lodging by staying with a current grad student (at worst, if costs prohibit an on-campus interview, you could ask if a video chat interview is acceptable). For clothing, remember that an expensive outfit is not going to make or break the success of your interview—just look neat, presentable, and professional.

Tuition in Grad School

In some cases, institutions rationalize the high price for graduate school with the fact that most people earning a graduate degree increase their earning potential (Marcus, 2017). However, there is some good news—for tuition, one important rule of thumb is that many psychology PhD programs either waive or drastically reduce the price (that is correct, PhD programs tend to have lower tuition costs)! In contrast, master's, PsyD, medical, and law programs typically charge much higher tuition. For master's programs, the bright side is that these experiences typically last only 2 to 3 years. When comparing psychology graduate degrees, debt loads for students earning a master's were just slightly lower than for PhD students (master's programs cost more, but they take fewer years to complete)—however, students earning a PsyD had almost twice as much debt as those who earned either a master's or PhD (Doran, Kraha, Marks, Ameen, & El-Ghoroury, 2016; Stringer, 2016).

An important point to make about graduate school is that, regardless of educational costs, you are not likely going to be working full time while completing your degree. The reason for that is that graduate school is difficult, so you will be spending most of your time and energy working on program activities (courses, research, supervised training, etc.). Because of that, you will not be making (much, or any) money—and the problem is that, just like everyone else in the world, you will likely need money to live. Do not forget to factor in cost of living when considering graduate programs! However, as we noted elsewhere in this book, some programs

iStock.com/Doucefleur

will offer stipends to work as a teaching or research assistant—look for one of these and snatch it up if it is offered to you!

As you learn about graduate programs and go on interviews, be sure to gather as much information as possible about the educational costs (and opportunities) associated with each particular program. If a program does not provide this information to you during an interview, then you should ask. After all, you want to make an informed decision when you choose a graduate program. For example, if you are accepted at two programs that you like equally, you might lean toward the one that is going to put you in the best position financially.

Student Loans for Graduate School

As is the case with your undergraduate studies, student loans are available for graduate school. Taking out loans for graduate school can be okay as long as you keep a few things in mind. First, if you have already financed your undergraduate education through student loans, any additional loans will be added on top of the debt that you are already accruing. Also, although you can get undergraduate loan payments deferred while you are in grad school, additional interest might be accumulating while you are in grad school. Please do not take this lightly by adopting a mindset such as, "I already have $100,000 in loans, what is another $100,000?" This is real money with interest added on top, not pretend money! Give serious thought to the ramifications of this much debt and how much you will have to pay back every single month for years to come (possibly decades!). Loans will reduce your income and affect your ability to afford things such as a home, car, vacations, or child-related expenses.

Our major point here is that we want to make sure that you take your time and make an informed decision by thinking about some of the following issues (e.g., Meyer, 2018). And pay close attention to the likely career outcomes and earning potential for you after you finish a program.

- Can you make some money while in grad school (e.g., can you earn a stipend as a teaching or research assistant)?
- What is the minimum amount possible that you can take out in loans and still get by?
- Can you live somewhere cheaply (or find a roommate to help defray costs)?
- Are there other programs that are less expensive that can help you achieve your goals (i.e., a better value, greater return on investment)?
- And finally, consider the following (e.g., Cautero, 2018)—is that graduate program really worth it for you?
    - Are you going to be happier?
    - Make more money?
    - Is it necessary for the career you want?

Other Ways to Pay for Graduate School

Although there might not be as many available as there are for undergraduate education, there actually are merit-based scholarships available for graduate studies. You should search through professional organizations for your career area—start with Psi Chi, APA, and APS, but expand on those by looking into state or regional organizations as well as organizations for your specific concentration in graduate school (e.g., Novotney, 2015). You might also consider searching sites such as Unigo, Fastweb, Scholarship America, GoGrad, or Sallie Mae's Graduate School Scholarship Search (e.g., Powell, 2018).

In addition to scholarships, you should look into grants, summer funding opportunities, or internships. More common are competitive fellowships to help pay for graduate school—some of these will pay both tuition and a stipend (Kiparsky, 2006). Graduate students who are further along in their program and are more accomplished tend to be the most competitive for these, but some are specifically meant for first- or second-year graduate students. Look into fellowship opportunities offered at your institution and by professional organizations, government organizations, or possibly an organization where you might work after you finish (e.g., Novotney, 2015).

A final (and more unique) approach to locating funding for graduate school focuses on carefully selecting a graduate school mentor. Many professors in research-centric programs are going to be applying for research grants to support their work—and some will budget money to pay for graduate students. So, if you are going into a research-intensive program, you might consider looking for a mentor who has success with grants. However, keep in mind that you cannot always predict when professors will have grants, nor can you know that they will choose you as the recipient of the funding. So, do not rely on this, but keep it in mind as a possibility.

Take-Home Message

Over half of graduate students report that they are stressed about money (Luberecki, 2017). In addition, many grad students report that they do not know much about personal finances (Kovacs, 2016). Although you might not be able to eliminate all financial worries, you can take some steps to ease them (and burying your head in the sand about the issue is not a recommended step!). Figure out the costs, whether or not you are going to take out loans, opportunities for funding, and your expectations for daily living expenses. You might not like the next step, but it is important—create a simple budget and plan to live frugally. Trust us—we have been graduate students and we have worked with lots of graduate students—no one expects graduate students to be living the high life (save that until you graduate, land a job, and pay off any debt!).

To conclude this module, we offer a classic joke about grad school that characterizes the financial situation of most students, "What is the best way to get graduate students to attend an event?" Punchline: "*Advertise free food!*" Do not worry—your authors still attend events solely for the free food. #NoShame

iStock.com/GoodLifeStudio

Action Steps

1. If graduate school is in your future, start a separate savings account (most banks let you do this) and build up a small amount of money for application and interview expenses.

2. As you gather data on possible graduate programs, gather information about tuition, assistantships, fellowships, and any other financial costs or opportunities. Plan to ask about some of these things when you interview—although we recommend posing questions to program directors and potential mentors, do then confirm by asking current graduate students about their experiences.

Closing Advice

15

15.0 MEET JENNY

iStock.com/FangXiaNuo

CHAPTER OUTLINE

Jenny stopped by her professor's office and he welcomed her, asking how he could help. Jenny told him that she did not need any help today but that she had some very good news—she just received an offer of admission to her top choice for graduate school! The professor congratulated her immediately—he knew how hard she had been working these past few years.

After sharing some of the details about the admissions offer, Jenny said that there was one more reason that she stopped by. She wanted to say *thank you* for all of the help and advice that he had provided—ever since she took his Intro to the Psychology Major course, she had listened to his suggestions about preparing for life after college and had followed through by actually doing what he had said. She told her professor that, at first, she was hesitant to visit during his office hours (as she had never spoken to one of her professors outside of class before), but now she was so happy that she did not let her shyness win out.

The professor modestly told her that it was nothing, that he was happy to help as it was part of the job of being a professor. But Jenny told him that it was important to her nonetheless. Some of the advice she had known about, but actually hearing the reasons that she should have those experiences and prepare that way pushed her to actually follow through and do them. And boy did it make a difference—after all, she was now on her way to grad school!

Why Did We Tell You This Story?

Just like Jenny, each and every one of you can apply the advice that we provided in this book to better prepare for your future. We use the phrase *superstar psychology student* in this book as a way to motivate you to dream big, but keep in mind that these are accomplishments and experiences that you can all achieve. So, please, apply the advice that we provide in this book, and—importantly—take action. In this final chapter, we emphasize some key points, provide a few different perspectives that support the ideas we have presented in this book, and sprinkle in a few new tips to help you succeed!

15.1 ARE YOU COMMITTED TO PSYCHOLOGY OR CONSIDERING OPTIONS?

At this point, we have gone through a whole slew of information and shared our best recommendations for succeeding in psychology. In this chapter, we revisit a topic from the opening chapter, and then we emphasize some key pieces of advice for psychology students. Some of this is meant for while you are in college, and some is most helpful for preparing for life after college. We assume that most people who have read this book started off with an interest in psychology, and we hope that this interest has continued (or grown) as you have learned more about what you can do in this field. In this module, we explore some thoughts that college graduates have when they look back on their college experience—we cover this because we want you to learn from their perspectives.

Regrets About College

One piece of good news is that approximately 90% of college graduates report that they received a high-quality education (Marken & Auter, 2017). However, about half of U.S. adults with a bachelor's degree reported that (if they could) they would change a big decision that they made in college. What would they have changed? Approximately 40% of college graduates said that, looking back, they would have studied a different major. There is a range of possible reasons for this regret—it could be that they were not well-informed about job possibilities, they might not be satisfied with the pay in their chosen field, or they might not have known about and properly taken advantage of opportunities in their major (one of our goals with this book was to make you as well informed as possible about psychology!).

What does this mean for you? Most importantly, it means that you should give serious thought to your choice of major—we tried to help you with this throughout this book. If you are happy with your current major and your career trajectory, then it might mean nothing. However, if after learning more about psychology, you are not certain that it is the right path for you, then it is okay to consider a change. Whichever route you choose, keep some things in mind. First, because psychology is the study of thought and behavior, it is applicable to many different fields and careers. Also, as we discussed in the career chapter, just because you major in psychology does not mean that you need to pursue work in the helping professions—you can use your degree to pursue a lot of different options. Third, it is not uncommon for people to change careers over the years—a college major does not have to define the rest of your life (e.g., Gebhard, 2015). Finally, if you are considering a change, then we strongly recommend that you meet with an academic advisor to talk through your options.

Advice From Recent Psychology Graduates

If you are going to continue forward with psychology, then you want to make sure that you do it right. To help, we contacted a large group of recent psychology major graduates and asked them to offer advice for a new psychology major. A lot of what they said supports various ideas we have shared with you in this book, but we include their feedback here so that you can see that this book is not just filled with our unsubstantiated opinions—many others agree with us. These recent graduates provided us with quite a bit of information, and we summarized the most common pieces of advice that they offered.

1. Take advantage of college. You are paying money (and possibly going into debt) for the experience of attending college, so do not waste it. If you want to learn the material, then read! You may be able to pass a course with a minimum amount of reading, but you won't learn as much. Later on, you will appreciate what you learned much more than the grades you earned.

2. Get research or internship experience. Join a psychology research team, and do not put it off until your senior year! If you are considering graduate school, research experience is very important. For those who are going straight into a career, research experience can help you develop skills and improve your résumé—also, you might want to do an internship in order to learn about a career field and gain work experience.

3. Look for Clinical or mental health experiences. If you are interested in applied areas of psychology related to mental health treatment, look for clinical experiences (e.g., volunteer at a mental health clinic). As an undergraduate, do not expect to be treating patients—you will likely be shadowing and observing, although in some cases you may have opportunities such as mentoring adolescents or assisting with children who have behavior issues. Remember that graduate programs are competitive, so a high GPA is not enough to make you stand out.

4. Learn statistics and research methods. You may not like it at first, but build a solid foundation in statistics and research methods as these skills will pay off in upper-level courses, careers, graduate school, and life. Take these classes early as they really will help with later courses. If you are anxious, take active steps to get over your fear of statistics (ask your instructor or teaching assistant for help!).

5. Slowly narrow down your interests. Psychology is a broad field, so take the time to narrow down your academic and professional interests. Start by sampling different courses and then get more specific in the discipline. For example, ask yourself, do you prefer clinical or experimental topics? If experimental, which subarea? If clinical, with which populations would you like to work? By the time you are a junior or senior, you can take more courses in the area that most interests you. Your professional interests—what you want to do when you "grow up"—should be identified now so that you can plan toward that career goal.

iStock.com/Deagreez

6. Start planning early. Start thinking about career plans or grad school early—know what you need to do to be prepared. Set goals—where do you want to be in 1 year? After 2 years? At the end of your 4 undergraduate years? Check your progress as you advance toward your degree. Also, keep an open mind about applying psychology knowledge to careers in other disciplines. Enter a career that interests you—the nice part of psychology is that what you learn in this major can be applied to a lot of different fields!

7. Join clubs and organizations. The most common piece of feedback that we heard was to join a student group like Psi Chi or Psychology Club. Certainly there are many other academic (and social) organizations out there, too. The most important part is getting involved—as the common adage goes, "you get out of it what you put into it." For example, you can gain leadership skills by becoming a club officer. If you are more of an introvert, set modest goals of meeting one new person every time you attend a meeting or event.

8. Meet your professors. Get to know the professors as much as possible—this is important for learning about opportunities and for earning solid letters of recommendation. Make it a goal to build strong working relationships with professors over the college years. You can do this by being active in class, being visible in the department, stopping by during office hours, and working as a research assistant. Get to know these professors above and beyond class because you will learn so much more from them that way. And, when it comes to writing a recommendation letter, your professors will have much more to say about you!

9. Network. Network—not just with professors at your school but with people from other schools and people in your field. You can do this by attending conferences, joining alumni groups, or meeting people in the community. The best jobs are typically found through exercising your networks, not through scavenging through postings on a job board.

10. Act like a professional. Always be professional—act in a way that will encourage people to respect you. Be modest when you succeed and take ownership when you make a mistake. When communicating with professors and others, remember to use titles when addressing them. When someone does something nice for you, be sure to send a thank-you note. Little gestures like that can make a big difference in terms of how people perceive you.

Take-Home Message

In this module, we provided you with a common regret that college graduates have when they look back on their experiences. One of the goals of this book was to give you an honest tour through psychology so that you can decide if it is right for you. We also shared a summary of advice that came directly from students who recently graduated with a bachelor's degree in psychology. Some of the advice that we heard was based on things that they took advantage of and it helped them, whereas other ideas may have been things that they wished they had done while in college. We gathered this information because we want to provide the most useful information that we can for you. These individuals were in your shoes just a few years ago, so please heed their advice.

Action Steps

1. You may already be doing some or all of these ideas, but determine which ones you have overlooked and apply them today. Small daily steps toward your desired outcome (e.g., get to know professor X, build a professional network) will maintain your momentum and empower you.
2. Consider doing something to *Pay It Forward* (Hyde, 1999—there is also a movie based on the book) that can change your psychology program for the better. Work with faculty or with your chapter of Psi Chi to create your own list of advice from graduating seniors to new psychology majors (this could also take the form of social media posts, videos, or seniors visiting freshman classes).

15.2 ADVICE FROM EMPLOYERS AND CAREER COUNSELORS

Sticking with our theme in this chapter of providing advice, this module focuses on advice related to careers. Although you might think that the information in this book makes you an expert on career choice and preparation, it is only the first step on your journey (but it is a big step). So, to build on that, we share some tips and guidance from employers and career counselors in this module. We highly encourage you to continue learning more—after you read this module, visit your career center (again), conduct informational interviews, and gain experiences (e.g., internships).

What Are Employers' Expectations?

First of all, when considering someone for a job, employers tend to value both skills and knowledge (e.g., Hettich, 2016). But, employers think that skills are so important that they actually emphasize them over college major (Hart Research Associates, 2013)! One piece of good news is that students seem to understand the skills that employers value—these include written and oral communication, working with others, ethics, and critical thinking (Hart Research Associates, 2015). In addition, employers have confidence that college is valuable and worthwhile for developing those skills (Hart Research Associates, 2018).

The bad news, however, is that there are clear discrepancies when it comes to assessing these skills. For example, although most students rated themselves as proficient in terms of professionalism, work ethic, leadership, and written and oral communication, employers disagreed—employers indicated that less than half of recent college graduates are proficient in these skills (Bauer-Wolf, 2018; Hart Research Associates, 2018) and that improvement is needed (Hart Research Associates, 2015). In particular, employers think that students need to improve their skills if they have any aspirations of moving up into advanced positions (Hart Research Associates, 2018).

So, what can you take away from this information?

- Be realistic and consider that you might be overestimating your own abilities (over-rating one's abilities is a common psychological finding—see Kruger & Dunning, 1999).
- To address this possible bias, you might ask professors and career centers for help by providing you with honest feedback on your skills.
- You can also try online tools—Hettich (2016) recommends SkillScan (www.skillscan.com) to get a more objective assessment of your abilities (TIP: you may want to work with a career counselor when you do an assessment like this).
- Consider building a portfolio of your college work that illustrates your proficiency in various skills—some employers have noted that portfolios can be helpful for evaluating skills (Hart Research Associates, 2015).
- As you learned throughout this book, there are many activities that you can take part in to continuously improve your skills—for example, you might focus on internships, research, writing papers, and service learning (Hart Research Associates, 2015).

What Career Counselors Wish Students Knew

We talked with representatives from the career centers on our own campuses, and we also did some reading to see if there were any key pieces of information that career counselors wanted students to know (see Table 15.1). Not surprisingly, the biggest thing is that students need to actually visit and use their institution's career center (e.g., Fadulu, 2018)—the career center cannot help you unless you go. It is recommended that you start visiting the career center as early as your freshman year (e.g., Hannon, 2018; Koenig, 2018). Do not be someone who convinces yourself not to go because you are "not ready"—career centers know that students are at different stages of the career preparation process (e.g., McLendon & Reshwan, 2016). Making an appointment at your career center and going (as early as your freshman year) is how you start!

A second piece of advice from career centers is that soft skills and proper interview techniques can benefit from practice (e.g., McLendon & Reshwan, 2016). Take advantage of opportunities at college to improve your critical thinking, leadership, and communication skills. Let your career center help you develop and hone your elevator pitch and

TABLE 15.1

Top Tips From Career Counselors

- Visit and utilize your campus career center—start as early as your freshman year!
- Soft skills and interview techniques can improve with practice—so work on them (your campus career center can help you).
- Ultimately, career preparation is your responsibility—take active steps to prepare.

interview skills. Career centers want you to know that they can help you in a variety of ways (e.g., career ideas, identifying your strengths and weaknesses, refining soft skills, building a résumé, networking, finding internships and other opportunities, etc.) and that proper career preparation should take place across years—not right before graduation (e.g., Koenig, 2018).

Career counselors also want students to know that, although they can help in a lot of ways, some preparation steps are your responsibility. Just as we mentioned back in the career chapters, it is up to you to decide on your path—be proactive! Career centers can administer tests that suggest possible careers that match your interests, but ultimately you are the one who has to select a career to pursue. Career centers can host job fairs (and even help you prepare for them), but you must attend and interact with attendees. Career centers can provide networking tips, but it is up to you to actually go out there and connect with people! The point here is that career centers can help you in many ways, but you must be the one to get things started, to take advantage of their resources, and to apply what you learn.

Take-Home Message

Although we have covered some of these ideas in previous chapters, we included this module because we wanted to provide the perspectives of employers and career centers. In other words, do not just take our word on these topics; you can also trust that this advice is coming from them. When it comes to being prepared for a career, make sure that you emphasize skill development—remember that college is not just about drifting through classes doing the minimum effort to pass; you want to be developing your skills. And, as we noted in this module, an easy way to get some help with that is to use your campus career center!

Action Steps

1. The first step to properly assessing your own skills is to recognize that humans have a bias to overestimate their own abilities (Kruger & Dunning, 1999). Once you accept this, try to be more objective (e.g., get feedback from others) about assessing your skills and where you can improve. Meet with a professor who knows you and your work and ask them to give an honest assessment of some of your skills. Also, use our advice from an earlier chapter to create a portfolio so that you can monitor and assess your skill development as you move through college.
2. Make an appointment with your career center AND GO!!! Even if you have gone before, there are many reasons that you should go more than once. If you happened to have a non-positive experience during a prior visit (e.g., Auter & Marken, 2016), try again and request to meet with a different counselor or representative.

15.3 GET THE MOST OUT OF SUMMERS

If you are going to succeed as a psychology student, then you want to put yourself in the best position to do well. For many students (and some professors), summers are a time for welcome diversions—some people enjoy sleeping in and others spend time on vacation. We also realize that summers may mean more hours at a job or possibly family responsibilities. Although the former activities can be relaxing and the latter can be necessary, the advice in this module focuses on a few different ideas for how you can use your summers more effectively. Some of these ideas require a big time commitment, but others can be implemented easily.

Get a Course (or Two) Out of the Way

We are NOT recommending that you take a full load of courses over the summer—this can potentially lead to burnout when the regular school calendar resumes in the fall (e.g., Anderson, 2017). Instead, we recommend that you focus on one or two courses. On the one hand, some think that this is a good time to take a challenging course because, by taking only one or two courses, you can focus your attention on a difficult topic. However, on the other hand, summer courses tend to be condensed into a shorter time period than the fall or spring, so this means that they move more quickly—and this might not be ideal for tackling a difficult course. So, please use good judgment about what course(s) to take over the summer—we strongly recommend getting input from a professor or academic advisor.

Study Abroad

Study abroad can be greatly beneficial for you as it can lead to both professional and personal growth (e.g., Earnest, 2015). Your authors can personally attest to the impact that traveling abroad has had on their lives. What's more—researchers in the area of student engagement suggest all students engage in two of these high-impact practices prior to graduation—service learning, research with faculty, internship/field experience, *study abroad*, or a senior culminating project (see Kuh, 2008; National Survey of Student Engagement, 2007, for more on this).

Psychology students can be a good fit for study abroad (see Table 15.2) because learning about psychological topics, such as cross-cultural psychology, stereotypes, or diversity, can be good preparation for a study abroad experience (e.g., Goldstein, 2017; Schwebel & Carter, 2010). And you might be surprised to learn that some institutions offer psychology-specific study abroad programs (e.g., Abrams & Ziegler, 2016; Earnest, Rosenbusch, Wallace-Williams, & Keim, 2016). Some institutions offer study abroad options during the summer, and this might be a great time to do it. Keep in mind that every institution is going to have varied study abroad rules (especially regarding financial aid eligibility), so be sure to consult with the office on your campus to learn more.

TABLE 15.2

Top Reasons for Psychology Students to Study Abroad

- Preparation—psychology courses cover cross-cultural and diversity topics
- Professional growth—cultural knowledge, working with people from different backgrounds
- Personal growth—independence, adapting to new environments
- Travel—it is not just about learning, but you can enjoy the experience, too

Get Experience—Volunteer or Do an Internship

As we note in other modules, many organizations (and some graduate programs) prefer applicants who have some relevant work experience. If you are planning on starting a career right after graduation, you can use your college summers to intern—a variety of experiences will allow you to see what different careers are like. If you are planning on going to graduate school in an applied area such as clinical psychology, you may want to volunteer or intern at a clinic. Remember that these experiences are not about the money; they are about developing skills, learning about a career field, and possibly earning a strong recommendation letter. The summer months can be a good time for all of this because you will not have to worry about scheduling your work hours around a full load of classes (e.g., Musulin, 2014). And, this type of opportunity (Kuh, 2008; National Survey of Student Engagement, 2007) can enlighten the rest of your psychology experience!

Get Research Experience

Despite what you might think, not all professors pack up and head to the beach during the summer—many of them spend their summers focusing on research or writing projects. During the spring, ask around and learn which professors will be actively conducting research throughout the summer. Because a lot of other students might be relaxing over the summer, you may have good odds of getting selected to assist with research. See our chapter about participating in research for tips on how to get involved.

If you are already involved with research, then you know that projects take time to complete. So, if you ever want to present a poster at a psychology conference, you need to have started working on research well in advance. For example, most regional psychology conferences take place in the spring months—this means that they are likely to have submission deadlines during the fall months. If you want to submit a proposal, then you need to have results from a research study. This means that the previous year is very important for setting up a study, running it, and analyzing data. Given the time and effort that research requires, summer can be a great time to pursue this excellent educational opportunity (Kuh, 2008; National Survey of Student Engagement, 2007).

Prepare for the GRE (and Take It)

When you are further along in your college career and are considering graduate school, then you need to start planning for the Graduate Record Examination (GRE). You need to ramp up your GRE preparation in the spring and summer before your senior year because the latest you want to take the GRE is during the fall semester of your senior year. Any later, and there may not be enough open testing dates due to all of the other people who have procrastinated as well. We have seen busy students delay taking the GRE until their senior year fall semester and that can lead to high levels of stress. Our recommendation is to use a summer to prepare for and then take the GRE.

Develop a Skill

With more and more students graduating from colleges each year, you need to do something that will help you to stand out from the rest of the pack. One way to do this is to focus on developing a skill over a summer. For example, you may think you know the basics of programs like Google Docs or Microsoft Excel, but you might find that there are short online courses that can teach you shortcuts and commands that can make you much more efficient. Another opportunity is to get an advantage in statistics over your peers by taking an additional statistics course or by watching YouTube tutorials for popular statistical software like SPSS or R—there are hundreds of them out there. A final suggestion is to learn a programming language (e.g., JavaScript, Python, C++). You do not have to become an expert, but some competency with programming can be helpful in a variety of careers (e.g., Bradford, 2016)—think of all of the careers that deal with data, use websites, or develop apps.

Take-Home Message

Although it is important to relax and take some personal time during the summer, it can also be a useful time to improve yourself (see Table 15.3). You can use the summer to get a class out of the way. Use the summer to have a life-changing experience studying abroad. If you want work experience, find an internship or offer to volunteer. If you are pursuing graduate school, you can participate in research, prepare for a conference, or get ready for the GRE. You can also focus on developing a skill that you can retain for the rest of your life. And, finally, everyone has things that they should be doing, but they put them off until a later time—and then continue putting them off indefinitely (e.g., Pychyl, 2013). Use the summer as a way to make up for that procrastination.

TABLE 15.3

A Short List of Activities That Might Be a Good Fit for Your Summers

- Visit the career center
- Meet with an advisor to plan your upcoming semesters
- Meet with a professor
- Search for and apply for scholarships or grants
- Get involved with research
- Explore possible graduate programs
- Get a course out of the way
- Volunteer/intern/job shadow
- Conduct an informational interview
- Prepare for and take the GRE
- Study abroad
- Work on a skill

Action Steps

1. If there is a study abroad office on your campus, take a visit and learn more about their programs. Although some programs might be expensive, there might be scholarships or discounts available that can make it more affordable—you will never know unless you ask questions.

2. Plan out your college years so that you do one important thing each summer. For example, perhaps you spend one summer getting a class or two out of the way. Maybe the next year you get involved in research. And then, the third summer you could do an internship or study abroad. Remember, these summer activities do not have to use up your entire summer—but even doing one thing can help you stand out.

15.4 YOUR PATH TO BEING A SUPERSTAR PSYCHOLOGY STUDENT

Back in Chapter 1, we described what it takes to be a superstar student in psychology (e.g., Martin, 2015). We hope that you have noticed that you do not have to be gifted, a genius, or come from a privileged background to rack up superstar accomplishments—throughout this book, we provided practical tips that anyone could use. In this final chapter, we want to help you out by providing a checklist of recommendations to help you achieve superstar status. We hope that you have been proactive while reading this book and have had some new experiences and accomplishments as you went along. But, even if you have not done that, remember that it is never too late to start. However, do not wait too long—a late start might delay your plans.

And, as you move forward, please pay heed to this mantra: *If you have not taken action yet, then start right now!*

Superstar Accomplishments—Checklist

Goals

- Write out your "why"
- Set superstar goals for yourself
    - Tailor this checklist for your goals
    - Make additions or subtractions to fit it to your situation
    - Remember that (very) specific and concrete goals work best—vague goals or intentions are not very helpful

- Use a planner, calendar, or reminder system
  - Check it regularly (at least once a week, preferably every day)!
  - Update it regularly (at least once a week)

Courses

- Make an appointment with an academic advisor (each year)
  - (Freshman/Sophomore/Junior/Senior)
- Plan your electives (what fits your goals and interests?)
  - Identify high-quality professors and look to take courses that they teach
- Take courses that make you think (and that teach you how to think critically)
- Take at least one course that has a service learning component
- Decide if a minor or second major fits with your goals
- Create an APA template (and actually use it in your future courses)
  - Take courses that help you develop skills (writing, presenting)
- Focus on maintaining a high grade point average
  - Refine your study approach (spread out your reading and studying!)
  - Take exams strategically
  - Set up good classroom habits (where to sit, note-taking)
  - Plan papers and large projects at least 1 week before deadlines
  - Refine your library search skills (PsycINFO, Web of Science)
  - Read published psychology journal articles

Gain Research Experience in College

- Learn about research being done in your department
- Reach out to a professor about becoming a research assistant
- Attend a research conference—even better, present a poster!
  - Apply for research or travel grants
- Complete a senior or honors thesis

Connect With Others and Stay Informed

- Talk to your professors (visit during office hours)
- Identify three (potential) references and help them get to know you better

- Use social media to learn about opportunities at your institution—follow your school, department, and career center
- Get involved with student clubs—we recommend your chapter of Psi Chi
    - Work on soft skills by taking on a leadership position
- Join national and international professional organizations in psychology—Psi Chi, APA, and APS
- Develop a list of network contacts (e.g., use LinkedIn or a spreadsheet so that you have their names and contact information)
    - Maintain solid relationships by reaching out at least once each year
    - Remember that quality trumps quantity when it comes to networks

Career Preparation

- Explore career possibilities and decide on one
- Write out your career path (the current you → what you need to do → where you want to be)
- Visit your campus career center (every year)
    - (Freshman/Sophomore/Junior/Senior)
- Conduct an informational interview (do more than one)
- Take part in volunteer work
- Learn about internships (and job shadowing) and apply
- Go to talks, workshops, and panels about careers
- Identify key skills that are needed in your future career and focus on developing those

Grad School Preparation

- Determine if your career path requires a graduate degree
- Decide on the right degree and field that fits your goals
- Build a list of possible programs
- Prepare for the GRE (or MCAT or LSAT)

Document Your Accomplishments

- Create your curriculum vitae (CV)
    - Update it every semester with new accomplishments
    - Ask a professor for feedback on your CV

- Create your résumé and update it with new accomplishments
    - Ask your career center for feedback on your résumé
- Create an organized portfolio
    - Include items that provide evidence of your accomplishments and skills
- Create a (great) LinkedIn profile (or website)
    - Use it to present yourself professionally and to network

Other Steps

- Apply for at least one scholarship each semester
- Explore opportunities such as study abroad
- Thank people who have helped you

Take-Home Message

Starting in Chapter 1, we introduced the idea of striving to be a superstar student in psychology. And, throughout this book, we have provided a lot of advice for you. This checklist can help you keep track of these various recommendations. However, we understand that your goals are going to be slightly different from the goals of other students. Because of this, be sure to tailor your plan so that you prioritize the experiences and accomplishments that will help you on your journey. If you plan to continue on to graduate school, please note that you can be a superstar in that context as well (see Grover, Leftwich, Backhaus, Fairchild, & Weaver, 2006). And, finally, remember that dreams and wishes are nice, but they will not help you start a career or get admitted into a graduate program unless you take action to turn those dreams into real accomplishments!

Action Steps

1. Use this checklist as a start point, and tailor it to your specific plan and goals—seriously, make a personalized version of this list for yourself! For example, if you are aiming for a career right after you graduate, your priorities might be slightly different from those of someone who wants to attend graduate school. Also, your goals might differ slightly depending on what type of career or what type of graduate program is important to you.

2. Post your personalized version of the checklist in a spot where you will see it regularly.

Even better, work with someone who can keep you accountable—fellow classmates, moms or dads, or relationship partners might fill this role for you. Be sure to check off accomplishments and experiences!

15.5 SAY THANK YOU TO THOSE WHO HELPED YOU

iStock.com/blackred

Our final piece of advice involves adding a positive wrap-up to your experiences. As you make your way through college, you are going to have a lot of experiences and you are going to accomplish a lot. Although a lot of that is a result of your hard work, remember that you are not likely to do it all by yourself. If people help you, then it is a good practice to say "thank you" for the help. Hearing "thank you" can make someone feel better, and it can possibly strengthen your connection with that person. In this module, we make some recommendations about thanking others—this includes whom you should thank, how to do it, and why it is helpful.

Thank Professors and Others at Your Institution Who Helped

Almost all college students have had a professor (or, if you just started college, a high school teacher) who has made a big impact on them. The best professors work hard to present thought-provoking ideas that challenge your beliefs, suggest practical ways to apply what you learned to your life, provide you with helpful advice, or guide you through difficult material—it could be any one of those traits or a combination of them. A Gallup-Purdue University survey (Gallup, 2015) showed that, after graduating, students were nearly twice as likely to rate college as being worth the cost if they had a positive experience with a professor!

Besides professors, there are other people who might impact your life. Some students work with academic advisors who guide them through their courses. Some find a mentor (or guru) who provides copious amounts of wisdom. Some land a job because of the assistance of a career counselor. Some receive career advice or training from an internship or volunteer supervisor. Some learn about a career through an informational interview. And, finally, some learn about a perfect job opportunity from a person in their network. If someone makes a big impact on your path to success, then it is important for you to thank that person for the help!

Thank Family

When we ask students to tell us their "why" for wanting to succeed in college (see Chapter 1), many state family reasons. Some explain that they want to set a good example for children, others want to make a parent proud, and there are those who have a desire to succeed because a family member supported them emotionally or financially throughout college. People are quick to write thank-you letters to strangers or extended family members who give gifts at weddings, birthdays, or baby showers—but they sometimes forget to explicitly say thank you to those closest to them who have helped them succeed on a daily basis.

Thank Any Sources of Financial Support

This piece is advice for those of you who earned financial support while in college, such as a scholarship. Not all students truly recognize this, but your college experience may not have been the same without that financial assistance. Without it, you may have had to take out loans (or additional loans), work long hours at a job, or put books on a credit card—any of these can lead to stress or time away from your superstar accomplishments! For others, a research or travel grant might have helped you attend a research conference that can help you get into graduate school.

Whatever the situation, if you benefited from financial support, then you should let the funder/donor/sponsor know that you are thankful for their assistance. Some financial aid offices require scholarship recipients, as a condition of the award, to send a written thank-you note to donors. Even if your school does not require this, please consider taking this action. Not only are you expressing gratitude, but you are also reinforcing to them that they are doing something good by offering the funding to students like you (e.g., Pierce, 2018).

How to Say Thank You

When thanking a person that you know, we recommend a handwritten letter, note, or card. This does not have to be long—keep it short, include why you thought that the person had an impact on you, and say the words "thank you." One thing that is important is to make sure that you are authentic by writing it in your own words (do not outsource the writing to Hallmark or some other greeting card company).

If you are thanking an organization or donor—for example, in the case of a scholarship—the procedure is slightly different. Instead of a handwritten note, you will want to type up a more-professional letter or email. However, even though it is a professional communication, you should still be authentic with your message of thank you and how the assistance has helped you out. Also, just because this is a letter does not mean that it has to be long—a paragraph or half of a page is plenty. And, finally, be sure that you do not forget to include your name and the exact name of the scholarship or award (just in case they fund a number of different awards).

When NOT to Say Thank You

Although we encourage you to thank the people who have helped you, keep in mind that there are also times when you might not say thank you. First, do not do it if the intention is to curry favor with someone (i.e., flattery because you want something in return). Second, do not do it if you are not truly grateful for the help. And, finally, do not overdo it by writing thank-you notes to anyone and everyone—this would be overly time-consuming and not as authentic and it would make it seem less meaningful or special.

Take-Home Message

Our suggestion is that students should let people know that their help was appreciated. This can have a few benefits. First of all, it is a very nice thing to do. Second, research on happiness suggests that expressing gratitude can have a positive effect on the one who conveys the gratitude (e.g., Emmons & Stern, 2013). Finally, being nice to others can pay off from a networking perspective (e.g., Algoe & Haidt, 2009) in that expressing gratitude can help improve relationships with others. Our guess is that a professor, supervisor, mentor, funding source, or family member who received an authentic, honest, and well-thought-out thank-you letter would remember that act of kindness!

Action Steps

iStock.com/Artur

1. Take a minute to think about the professors, family members, supervisors, or others in your college orbit and determine if any of them truly made a positive impact on you. If there are a few (or one) that stand out, then take 5 minutes to write out a short note or letter saying thank you (handwritten is best)—be sure to include why you thought that the person had an impact on you. Keep the message simple and authentic. If you have received any financial support, such as a scholarship, write a professional letter or email to express your gratitude and how it has helped you.
2. Some students ask if they should give a gift as a way of saying thanks. Our advice is this: gifts are not at all necessary, nor are they expected. A simple note goes a long way!

15.6 FINAL ADVICE FROM THE AUTHORS

As we reach the end of this chapter and this book, we hope that you reflect back on all of the knowledge that we have shared with you. At this point, we want to take a moment to share our top pieces of advice for you. Think of it like this: imagine that this is the last day of the semester and, before you go, we want to emphasize what we think are some of the most important things for you to keep in mind as you continue your journey. We will start with Jeremy's perspective and then move on to David's advice about success.

Jeremy's Final Advice

In this book, David and I share a number of "to-do"s and activities to help you move forward on the path of continuous personal improvement. And, if you have not already gathered this, many of these action steps are not just for psychology majors. As someone who has bounced around a number of majors and programs of study before finding psychology, these skills translate to a number of contexts. So, regardless of your path, focus on sharpening your ability to communicate clearly and effectively in both oral and written form. No matter whether you are pursuing the world of work or graduate study—no skill is more important. So, do take advantage of every writing assignment or class presentation. Use each and every opportunity—whether in psychology or elective courses—to get better as a speaker and writer! Join professional and social organizations that provide opportunities to hone these skills, too. And know that it takes time and effort to improve; writing and public speaking are not easy for many of us.

My last piece of advice speaks to a mindset that was ingrained into me early in my undergrad days. A college advisor used to say time and time again that "the world doesn't care about your excuses—it only cares about *results*." Prioritizing what you are able to do or demonstrate to others—that is, what skills you bring to the table and what value you can add—is of the utmost importance in most professional relationships. This focus on the outcomes you are achieving—rather than on the mere activities you are doing (or the creative excuses being made)—is what can set you apart from others. Tracking everything—not only your successes but also your failures—in a portfolio, journal, app, spreadsheet, or other method can also be enlightening (and addictive!). However you decide to document your personal growth is up to you. But, when you are making strides on that exciting track to personal development, do not keep it to yourself or remain by yourself. Make it a point to find your tribe of like-minded GSD (Get Stuff Done) people who will support and motivate you along this journey!

David's Final Advice

This book is filled with advice, but two things stand out as very important. First, look to the future and figure out where you want to be in 1, 2, or 5 years (see Zadra & Wills, 2009). Seriously, take a minute and visualize where and what you will be like in the future. Doing this can strengthen your purpose and provide you with a "why" for being in college. There is nothing much worse than having to do something but not knowing why you should do it. If you do not have a reason to do something, you might not value its importance and you might not be motivated to do well. This is one of the reasons that some educators think that good course assignments are ones that inform students of the purpose for doing it (e.g., Copeland, Winkelmes, & Gunawan, 2018).

Second, plan the route that is going to connect your current self to that future self. Doing this will set you on a path of being proactive through college because you will know what types of experiences and accomplishments can help you reach your future goals. Too many college students drift through school, not sure of what they are going to do in the future, and not taking action. One reason for this is that they do not have a plan of where they are going. Instead of drifting, plan out what you need to do—this way you can build up accomplishments throughout your college years rather than panicking at the end (e.g., Marcus, 2015)!

I have noticed a big difference in my life when I have focused on those two things compared to when I have not. If I do not have a clear goal for my future self, I tend to put forth less effort and procrastinate more. In contrast, when I have clear goals (e.g., writing this book) with plans on how to get there (writing at least 30 minutes each day), I am often amazed at my progress. I encourage all of you to apply this approach in your own lives—use the information and resources in this book to figure out your future self and to set your plan for getting there!

Take-Home Message

In this book, we provided a lot of detail for how you can succeed as a psychology student. But, we know that not all of you are going to stay in psychology throughout college, and some of you may move into careers that are not psychology-related. That is okay—we want you to follow the path that seems right for you and for you to succeed in your path. The two big-picture pieces of advice that we provide here can be used by any college student to increase the odds of thriving—both in college and afterward!

Action Steps

1. As we mentioned elsewhere in this book, do not avoid opportunities to present and to write—embrace them because this practice can lead to success in your future career. Choose courses that include presentations and papers, and join organizations and get into a leadership position that will allow you to practice your communication skills.

2. If you have not done this already, think about where you want to be in the future—think 2 to 5 years into the future and visualize it! Next, write out the skills, accomplishments, and experiences that the future-you will have at that point. Finally, create a plan for how the current-you can become the future-you (be realistic, but set ambitious goals)!

References

Chapter 1

1.1 The Good (and Bad) About the Psychology Major

Betsch, C., Ulshofer, C., Renkewitz, F., & Betsch, T. (2011). The influence of narrative v. statistical information on perceiving vaccination risks. *Medical Decision Making, 31*(5), 742–753. http://dx.doi.org/10.1177/0272989X11400419

Brinthaupt, T. M., Hurst, J. R., & Johnson, Q. R. (2016). Psychology degree beliefs and stereotypes: Differences in the perceptions of majors and non-majors. *Psychology Learning & Teaching, 15*(1), 77–93. http://dx.doi.org/10.1177/1475725716642116

Goudreau, J. (2012, October 11). The 10 worst college majors. http://www.forbes.com/sites/jennagoudreau/2012/10/11/the-10-worst-college-majors/

Green, M. C., & Brock, T. C. (2000). The role of transportation in the persuasiveness of public narratives. *Journal of Personality and Social Psychology, 79*(5), 701–721. http://dx.doi.org/10.1037/0022-3514.79.5.701

Hart Research Associates (2018). *Fulfilling the American dream: Liberal education and the future of work. Selected findings from online surveys of business executives and hiring managers.* https://www.aacu.org/sites/default/files/files/LEAP/2018EmployerResearchReport.pdf

Jaschik, S. (2015, October 29). Bush questions liberal arts: Psych majors respond. *Inside Higher Ed.* https://www.insidehighered.com/quicktakes/2015/10/29/bush-questions-liberal-arts-psych-majors-respond

Logue, J. (2016, January 20). Psych! *Inside Higher Ed.* https://www.insidehighered.com/news/2016/01/20/florida-governor-wants-know-why-all-psychology-majors-arent-employed

Trattner, E. (2018, October 16). The most worthless college majors you can choose. *MoneyWise.* https://moneywise.com/a/college-majors-with-the-worst-career-prospects

Tversky, A., & Kahneman, D. (1971). Belief in the law of small numbers. *Psychological Bulletin, 76*(2), 105–110. http://dx.doi.org/10.1037/h0031322

Tversky, A., & Kahneman, D. (1973). Availability: A heuristic for judging frequency and probability. *Cognitive Psychology, 5*(2), 207–232. http://dx.doi.org/10.1016/0010-0285(73)90033-9

U.S. Department of Education, National Center for Education Statistics. (2018). *Digest of education statistics, 2016* (NCES 2017-094). https://nces.ed.gov/pubs2017/2017094.pdf

1.2 Does a College Degree Guarantee Success?

Bruni, F. (2018, August 17). How to get the most out of college. *The New York Times.* https://www.nytimes.com/2018/08/17/opinion/college-students.html

Caplan, B. (2018). *The case against education: Why the education system is a waste of time and money.* Princeton University Press. http://doi.org/10.1515/9780691201436

1.3 Superstar Psychology Students

Bain, K. (2012). *What the best college students do.* The Belknap Press of Harvard University Press. https://doi.org/10.4159/harvard.9780674067479

Grover, C. A., Leftwich, M. J. T., Backhaus, A., Fairchild, J. A., & Weaver, K. A. (2006). Qualities of superstar graduate students. *Teaching of Psychology, 33*(4), 271–273.

Martin, R. C. (2015). Undergraduate superstars: What makes them stand out? *Scholarship of Teaching and Learning in Psychology, 1*(2), 107–112. http://dx.doi.org/10.1037/stl0000028

Newport, C. (2005). *How to win at college: Surprising secrets for success from the country's top students.* Three Rivers Press.

1.4 Motivation for College Success—What is Your "Why"?

Miller, M. D. (2014). *Minds online: Teaching effectively with technology*. Harvard University Press. https://doi.org/10.4159/harvard.9780674735996

Nietzsche, F. W. (1889). *Twilight of the idols, or, how to philosophize with a hammer.* Oxford University Press.

1.5 Setting Goals and Creating Systems to Achieve Them

Drach-Zahavy, A., & Erez, M. (2002). Challenge versus threat effects on the goal-performance relationship. *Organizational Behavior and Human Performance, 88*(2), 667–682. http://dx.doi.org/10.1016/S0749-5978(02)00004-3

Kahneman, D. (2013). *Thinking fast and slow*. Farrar, Straus, and Giroux.

Latham, G. P., & Brown, T. C. (2006). The effect of learning vs. outcome goals on self-efficacy, satisfaction, and performance in an MBA program. *Applied Psychology, 55*(4), 606–623. http://dx.doi.org/10.1111/j.1464-0597.2006.00246.x

Locke, E. A., & Latham, G. P. (2006). New directions in goal-setting theory. *Current Directions in Psychology Science, 15*(5), 265–268. http://dx.doi.org/10.1111/j.1467-8721.2006.00449.x

Skinner, B. F. (1948). Superstition in the pigeon. *Journal of Experimental Psychology, 38*(2), 168–172. http://dx.doi.org/10.1037/h0055873

1.6 Overcoming Procrastination and Getting Stuff Done

Ackerman, D. S., & Gross, B. L. (2007). I can start that JME manuscript next week, can't I? The task characteristics behind why faculty procrastinate. *Journal of Marketing Education, 29*(2), 97–110. http://dx.doi.org/10.1177/0273475307302012

Buehler, R., Griffin, D., & Ross, M. (1994). Exploring the "planning fallacy": Why people underestimate their task completion times. *Journal of Personality and Social Psychology, 67*(3), 366–381. http://dx.doi.org/10.1037/0022-3514.67.3.366

Ferrari, J. R. (2001). Procrastination as self-regulation failure of performance: Effects of cognitive load, self-awareness, and time limits on 'working best under pressure'. *European Journal of Personality, 15*(5), 391–406. http://dx.doi.org/10.1002/per.413

Ferrari, J. R. (2010). *Still procrastinating? The no regrets guide to getting it done.* John Wiley & Sons.

Ferrari, J. R., & Tice, D. M. (2000). Procrastination as a self-handicap for men and women: A task-avoidance strategy in a laboratory setting. *Journal of Research in Personality, 34*(1), 73–83. http://dx.doi.org/10.1006/jrpe.1999.2261

Gollwitzer, P. M., & Sheeran, P. (2006). Implementation intentions and goal achievement: A meta-analysis of effects and processes. *Advances in Experimental Social Psychology, 38*, 69–119. http://dx.doi.org/10.1016/S0065-2601(06)38002-1

Lewis, N. A., & Oyserman, D. (2015). When does the future begin? Time metrics matter, connecting present and future selves. *Psychological Science, 26*(6), 816–825. http://dx.doi.org/10.1177/0956797615572231

McCrea, S. M., Liberman, N., Trope, Y., & Sherman, S. J. (2008). Construal level and procrastination. *Psychological Science, 19*(12), 1308–1314. http://dx.doi.org/10.1111/j.1467-9280.2008.02240.x

Mischel, W., Shoda, Y., & Rodriguez, M. L. (1989). Delay of gratification in children. *Science, 244*(4907), 933–938. http://dx.doi.org/10.1126/science.2658056

Pychyl, T. A. (2013). *Solving the procrastination puzzle.* Penguin Group.

Tice, D. M., & Baumeister, R. F. (1997). Longitudinal study of procrastination, performance, stress, and health: The costs and benefits of dawdling. *Psychological Science, 8*(6), 454–458. http://dx.doi.org/10.1111/j.1467-9280.1997.tb00460.x

Urban, T. (2016, February). *Inside the mind of a master procrastinator* [Video]. TED Conferences. https://www.ted.com/talks/tim_urban_inside_the_mind_of_a_master_procrastinator

1.7 Living the "Getting Stuff Done" (GSD) Lifestyle

Grover, T. S. (2014). *Relentless: From good to great to unstoppable.* Simon & Schuster.

Kahneman, D., & Tversky, A. (1979). Intuitive prediction: Biases and corrective procedures. *TIMS Studies in Management Science, 12*, 313–327.

Latham, G. P., & Brown, T. C. (2006). The effect of learning vs. outcome goals on self-efficacy, satisfaction, and performance in an MBA program. *Applied Psychology, 55*(4), 606–623. http://dx.doi.org/10.1111/j.1464-0597.2006.00246.x

Pychyl, T. A. (2013). *Solving the procrastination puzzle*. Penguin Group.

Tracy, B. (2017). *Eat that frog!* Berrett-Koehler.

Urban, T. (2016, February). Inside the mind of a master procrastinator [Video]. TED Conferences. https://www.ted.com/talks/tim_urban_inside_the_mind_of_a_master_procrastinator

Chapter 2

2.1 Due Dates? Grading Policy? It's in the Syllabus!

Bies-Hernandez, N. J. (2012). The effects of framing grades on student learning and preferences. *Teaching of Psychology, 39*(3), 176–180. http://dx.doi.org/10.1177/0098628312450429

Doolittle, P. E., & Siudzinski, R. A. (2010). Recommended syllabus components: What do higher education faculty include in their syllabi? *Journal on Excellence in College Teaching, 21*(3), 29–61.

Harrington, C. M., & Gabert-Quillen, C. A. (2015). Syllabus length and use of images: An empirical investigation of student perceptions. *Scholarship of Teaching and Learning in Psychology, 1*(3), 235–243. http://dx.doi.org/10.1037/stl0000040

Pattison, E., Grodsky, E., & Muller, C. (2013). Is the sky falling? Grade inflation and the signaling power of grades. *Educational Researcher, 42*(5), 259–265. http://dx.doi.org/10.3102/0013189X13481382

Raymark, P. H., & Connor-Greene, P. A. (2002). The syllabus quiz. *Teaching of Psychology, 29*(4), 286–288. http://dx.doi.org/10.1207/S15328023TOP2904_05

2.2 Classroom and Note-Taking Tips

Boch, F., & Piolat, A. (2005). Note taking and learning: A summary of research. *The WAC Journal, 16*, 101–113.

Bohay, M., Blakely, D. P., Tamplin, A. K., & Radvansky, G. A. (2011). Note taking, review, memory, and comprehension. *American Journal of Psychology, 124*(1), 63–73. http://dx.doi.org/10.5406/amerjpsyc.124.1.0063

Brown, P. C., Roediger, H. L., & McDaniel, M. A. (2014). *Make it stick: The science of successful learning*. Belknap Press of Harvard University Press. https://doi.org/10.4159/9780674419377

Bui, D. C., Myerson, J., & Hale, S. (2013). Note-taking with computers: Exploring alternative strategies for improved recall. *Journal of Educational Psychology, 105*(2), 299–309. http://dx.doi.org/10.1037/a0030367

Craik, F. I. M., & Lockhart, R. S. (1972). Levels of processing: A framework for memory research. *Journal of Verbal Learning and Verbal Behavior, 11*(6), 671–684. http://dx.doi.org/10.1016/S0022-5371(72)80001-X

Crede, M., Roch, S. G., & Kieszczynka, U. M. (2010). Class attendance in college: A meta-analytic review of the relationship of class attendance with grades and student characteristics. *Review of Educational Research, 80*(2), 272–295. http://dx.doi.org/10.3102/0034654310362998

Dunn, D. S. (2019, June 3). Unpacking quality class participation [Blog post]. https://www.psychologytoday.com/us/blog/head-the-class/201906/unpacking-quality-class-participation

Finley, J. R., Benjamin, A. S., & McCarley, J. S. (2014). Metacognition of multitasking: How well do we predict the costs of divided attention? *Journal of Experimental Psychology: Applied, 20*(2), 158–165. http://dx.doi.org/10.1037/xap0000010

Kalinowski, S., & Taper, M. L. (2007). The effect of seat location on exam grades and student perceptions in an introductory biology class. *Journal of College Science Teaching, 36*(4), 54–57.

Marshall, P. D., & Losonczy-Marshall, M. E. (2010). Classroom ecology: Connections between seating location, grade performance, and attendance. *Psychological Reports, 107*(2), 567–577.

Morehead, K., Dunlosky, J., & Rawson, K. A. (2019). How much mightier is the pen than the keyboard for note-taking? A replication and extension of Mueller and Oppenheimer (2014). *Educational Psychology Review, 31*(3), 753–780. http://dx.doi.org/10.1007/s10648-019-09468-2

Mueller, P. A., & Oppenheimer, D. M. (2014). The pen is mightier than the keyboard: Advantages of longhand over laptop note taking. *Psychological Science, 25*(6), 1159–1168. http://dx.doi.org/10.1177/0956797614524581

Ravizza, S.M., Uitvlugt, M.G., & Fenn, K.M. (2017). Logged in and zoned out: How laptop internet use relates to classroom learning. *Psychological Science, 28*(2), 171–180. http://dx.doi.org/10.1177/0956797616677314

Slamecka, N. J., & Graf, P. (1978). The generation effect: delineation of a phenomenon. *Journal of Experimental Psychology: Human Learning and Memory, 4*(6), 592–604. http://dx.doi.org/10.1037/0278-7393.4.6.592

Smith, D. P., Hoare, A., & Lacey, M. M. (2018). Who goes where? The importance of peer groups on attainment and the student use of the lecture theatre teaching space. *FEBS Open Bio, 8*(9), 1368–1378. https://doi.org/10.1002/2211-5463.12494

Thornton, B., Faires, A., Robbins, M., & Rollins, E. (2014). The mere presence of a cell phone may be distracting: Implications for attention and task performance. *Social Psychology, 45*(6), 479–488. http://dx.doi.org/10.1027/1864-9335/a000216

Yildirim, C., & Correia, A. (2015). Exploring the dimensions of nomophobia: Development and validation of a self-reported questionnaire. *Computers in Human Behavior, 49*, 130–137. http://dx.doi.org/10.1016/j.chb.2015.02.059

2.3 Study Skills—Study Like a Champion!

Agarwal, P. K., & Bain, P. M. (2019). *Powerful teaching: Unleash the science of learning.* Jossey-Bass. https://doi.org/10.1002/9781119549031

Carney, R. N., Levin, J. R., & Levin, M. E. (1994). Enhancing the psychology of memory by enhancing memory of psychology. *Teaching of Psychology, 21*(3), 171–174. http://dx.doi.org/10.1207/s15328023top2103_12

Cerbin, W. (2018). Improving student learning from lectures. *Scholarship of Teaching and Learning in Psychology, 4*(3), 151–163. http://dx.doi.org/10.1037/stl0000113

Chan, J. C. K., McDermott, K. B., & Roediger, H. L. (2006). Retrieval-induced facilitation: Initially nontested material can benefit from prior testing of related material. *Journal of Experimental Psychology: General, 135*(4), 553–571. http://dx.doi.org/10.1037/0096-3445.135.4.553

Copeland, D. E., Scott, J. R., & Houska, J. A. (2010). Computer-based demonstrations in cognitive psychology: Benefits and costs. *Teaching of Psychology, 37*(2), 141–145. http://dx.doi.org/10.1080/00986281003626680

Howe, J. E., Warm, S. R., & Dember, W. N. (1995). Meta-analysis of the sensitivity decrement in vigilance. *Psychological Bulletin, 117*(2), 230–249. http://dx.doi.org/10.1037/0033-2909.117.2.230

Hunter, A. S., & Lloyd, M. E. (2018). Faculty discuss study strategies, but not the best ones: A survey of suggested exam preparation techniques for difficult courses across disciplines. *Scholarship of Teaching and Learning in Psychology, 4*(2), 105–114. http://dx.doi.org/10.1037/stl0000107

Kornell, N., Castel, A. D., Eich, T. S., & Bjork, R. A. (2010). Spacing as the friend of both memory and induction in young and older adults. *Psychology & Aging, 25*(2), 498–503. http://dx.doi.org/10.1037/a0017807

Roediger, H. L., & Karpicke, J. D. (2006). The power of testing memory: Basic research and implications for educational practice. *Perspectives on Psychological Science, 1*(3), 181–210. http://dx.doi.org/10.1111/j.1745-6916.2006.00012.x

Slamecka, N. J., & Graf, P. (1978). The generation effect: Delineation of a phenomenon. *Journal of Experimental Psychology: Human Learning and Memory, 4*(6), 592–604. http://dx.doi.org/10.1037/0278-7393.4.6.592

Son, L. K., & Kornell, N. (2008). Research on the allocation of study time: Key studies from 1890 to the present (and beyond). In J. Dunlosky & R. A. Bjork (Eds.), *A handbook of memory and metamemory* (pp. 333–351). Psychology Press. https://doi.org/10.4324/9780203805503.ch17

von Restorff, H. (1933). On the effect of sphere formations in the trace field. *Psychologische Forschung, 18*, 299–342.

2.4 Quiz and Exam Tips

Clinton, V., & Meester, S. (2019). A comparison of two in-class anxiety reduction exercises before a final exam. *Teaching of Psychology, 46*(1), 92–95. http://dx.doi.org/10.1177/0098628318816182

Ramirez, G., & Beilock, S. (2011). Writing about test worries boosts exam performance in the classroom. *Science, 331*(6014), 211–213. http://dx.doi.org/10.1126/science.1199427

Roediger, H. L., & Karpicke, J. D. (2006). The power of testing memory: Basic research and implications for educational practice. *Perspectives on Psychological Science, 1*(3), 181–210. http://dx.doi.org/10.1111/j.1745-6916.2006.00012.x

Vul, E., & Pashler, H. (2007). Incubation benefits only after people have been misdirected. *Memory & Cognition, 35*(4), 701–710. http://dx.doi.org/10.3758/BF03193308

2.5 Learning From Graded Activities

Cheng, K.-H., Liang, J.-C., & Tsai, C.-C. (2015). Examining the role of feedback messages in undergraduate students' writing performance during an online peer assessment activity. *The Internet and Higher Education, 25,* 78–84. http://dx.doi.org/10.1016/j.iheduc.2015.02.001

Kruger, J., & Dunning, D. (1999). Unskilled and unaware of it: How difficulties in recognizing one's own incompetence lead to inflated self-assessments. *Journal of Personality and Social Psychology, 77*(6), 1121–1134. http://dx.doi.org/10.1037/0022-3514.77.6.1121

Stanglin, D., & Gross, E. M. (1997, March 31). Oprah: A heavenly body. *U.S. News and World Report, 122*(12), 18.

Wiggins, G. (2012). Seven keys to effective feedback. *Educational Leadership, 70*(1), 10–16.

2.6 Advantages and Disadvantages of Being an Online Student

Blaisman, R. N., Larabee, D., & Fabry, D. (2018). Distracted students: A comparison of multiple types of distractions on learning in online lectures. *Scholarship of Teaching and Learning in Psychology, 4*(4), 222–230. http://dx.doi.org/10.1037/stl0000122

Chesley, B. (2013, August 6). My problem with MOOCs. *Inside Higher Ed.* https://www.insidehighered.com/views/2013/08/06/essay-mooc-debate-and-what-really-matters-about-teaching

Derousseau, R. (2015, April 14). End of California's digital campus is a blow for MOOCs. *U.S. News & World Report.* https://www.usnews.com/news/college-of-tomorrow/articles/2015/04/14/end-of-californias-digital-campus-is-a-blow-for-moocs

Margaryan, A., Bianco, M., & Littlejohn, A. (2015). Instructional quality of Massive Open Online Courses (MOOCs). *Computers and Education, 80,* 77–83. http://dx.doi.org/10.1016/j.compedu.2014.08.005

Trammell, B. A., Morgan, R. K., Davies, W., Petrunich-Rutherford, M. L., & Herold, D. S. (2018). Creating an online course shell: Strategies to mitigate frustration and increase student success across multiple campuses. *Scholarship of Teaching and Learning in Psychology, 4*(3), 164–180. http://dx.doi.org/10.1037/stl0000109

Chapter 3

3.1 Approaches to Learning

American Psychological Association. (2013). *APA guidelines for the undergraduate psychology major: Version 2.0.* http://www.apa.org/ed/precollege/undergrad/index.aspx

Anderson, L. W., & Krathwohl, D. R. (Eds.) (2001). *A taxonomy for learning, teaching, and assessing: A revision of Bloom's taxonomy of educational objectives.* Allyn & Bacon (Pearson Education Group).

Arum, R., & Roksa, J. (2014). *Aspiring adults adrift: Tentative transitions of college graduates.* University of Chicago Press. https://doi.org/10.7208/chicago/9780226197142.001.0001

Bain, K. (2012). *What the best college students do.* Belknap Press of Harvard University Press.

Bloom, B., Englehart, M. D., Furst, E. J., Hill, W. H., & Krathwohl, D. R. (1956). *Taxonomy of educational objectives: The classification of educational goals. Handbook I: Cognitive domain.* Longman.

Craik, F. I. M., & Lockhart, R. S. (2008). Levels of processing and Zinchenko's approach to memory research. *Journal of Russian and East European Psychology, 46*(6), 52–60. http://dx.doi.org/10.2753/RPO1061-0405460605

Fendrich, L. (2009, October 12). Midterm exam in grade-grubbing. [Blog post]. *The Chronicle of Higher Education.* http://chronicle.com/blogs/brainstorm/midterm-exam-in-grade-grubbing/8420

Gerow, J. R. (2010). Learning objectives for introductory psychology: May I object? In S. A. Meyers & J. R. Stowell (Eds.), *Essays from excellence in teaching* (Vol. 9, pp. 62–64). http://teachpsych.org/Resources/Documents/ebooks/eit2009.pdf

Hard, B. M., Lovett, J. M., & Brady, S. T. (2019). What do students remember about introductory psychology, years later? *Scholarship of Teaching and Learning in Psychology, 5*(1), 61–74. http://dx.doi.org/10.1037/stl0000136

Landrum, R. E., & Gurung, R. A. R. (2013). The memorability of introductory psychology revisited. *Teaching of Psychology, 40*(3), 222–227. http://dx.doi.org/10.1177/0098628313487417

McCullough, D. (2014). *You are not special: And other encouragements*. HarperCollins.

Radvansky, G. A. (1999). The fan effect: A tale of two theories. *Journal of Experimental Psychology: General, 128*(2), 198–206. http://dx.doi.org/10.1037/0096-3445.128.2.198

Roderick, N. (2011, February 6). In defense of grade grubbers. *The Chronicle of Higher Education*. http://chronicle.com/article/In-Defense-of-Grade-Grubbers/126187/

Vernon, L. (2019, Summer). The secret life of professors revealed part V: What's in a grade? How to play the academic game, get good grades, and have your professor as your advocate. *Eye on Psi Chi, 23*, 48–49. https://www.psichi.org/page/234EyeSum19Vernon

Wiggins, G. P., & McTighe, J. (2005). *Understanding by design*. Association for Supervision and Curriculum Development (ASCD).

3.2 Adopting a Critical Thinking Mindset

Anderson, L. W., & Krathwohl, D. R. (Eds.) (2001). *A taxonomy for learning, teaching, and assessing: A revision of Bloom's taxonomy of educational objectives*. Allyn & Bacon (Pearson Education Group).

Bouvet, R., & Bonnefon, J. F. (2015). Non-reflective thinkers are predisposed to attribute supernatural causation to uncanny experiences. *Personality and Social Psychology Bulletin, 41*(7), 955–961. http://dx.doi.org/10.1177/0146167215585728

Brown, P. C., Roediger, H. L., & McDaniel, M. A. (2014). *Make it stick: The science of successful learning*. Belknap Press of Harvard University Press. https://doi.org/10.4159/9780674419377

Catapano, R., Tormala, Z. L., & Rucker, D. D. (2019). Perspective taking and self-persuasion: Why "putting yourself in their shoes" reduces openness to attitude change. *Psychological Science, 30*(3), 424–435. http://dx.doi.org/10.1177/0956797618822697

Furnham, A., & Hughes, D. J. (2014). Myths and misconceptions in popular psychology: Comparing psychology students and the general public. *Teaching of Psychology, 41*(3), 256–261. http://dx.doi.org/10.1177/0098628314537984

Huber, C. R., & Kuncel, N. R. (2016). Does college teach critical thinking? A meta-analysis. *Review of Educational Research, 86*(2), 431–468. http://dx.doi.org/10.3102/0034654315605917

Huston, M. (2015, March 9). None of the above—An emerging group of transgender people is looking beyond "man" and "woman." *Psychology Today*. https://www.psychologytoday.com/us/articles/201503/none-the-above

Kida, T. (2006). *Don't believe everything you think*. Prometheus Books.

Lilienfeld, S. O., Lynn, S. J., Ruscio, J., & Beyerstein, B. L. (2010). *50 great myths of popular psychology: Shattering widespread misconceptions about human behavior*. Wiley-Blackwell.

Nisbett, R. E. (2015). *Mindware: Tools for smart thinking*. Farrar, Straus, and Giroux.

Pennycook, G., Fugelsang, J. A., & Koehler, D. J. (2015). Everyday consequences of analytic thinking. *Current Directions in Psychological Science, 24*(6), 425–432. http://dx.doi.org/10.1177/0963721415604610

Stanovich, K. E. (2018). *How to think straight about psychology*. Allyn & Bacon.

Urban, T. (2014, May 7). Your life in weeks. *Wait But Why*. https://waitbutwhy.com/2014/05/life-weeks.html

Young, M. E. (2016). The problem with categorical thinking by psychologists. *Behavioural Processes, 123*, 43–53. http://dx.doi.org/10.1016/j.beproc.2015.09.009

Zwaan, R. A. (1999). Situation models: The mental leap into imagined worlds. *Current Directions in Psychological Science, 8*(1), 15–18. http://dx.doi.org/10.1111/1467-8721.00004

3.3 Regrets, Failure, and Luck—Challenge Yourself!

Ashcraft, M. H., & Moore, A. M. (2009). Mathematics anxiety and the affective drop in performance. *Journal of Psychoeducational Assessment, 27*(3), 197–205. http://dx.doi.org/10.1177/0734282908330580

Dweck, C. S. (2006). *Mindset: The new psychology of success*. Random House.

Gilovich, T., & Medvec, V. H. (1995). The experience of regret: What, when, and why. *Psychological Review, 102*(2), 379–395. http://dx.doi.org/10.1037/0033-295X.102.2.379

Kipman, S. (2018, September 20). 15 highly successful people who failed on their way to success. *Lifehack*. https://www.lifehack.org/articles/productivity/15-highly-successful-people-who-failed-their-way-success.html

Ng, T. W. H., Sorensen, K. L., & Eby, L. T. (2006). Locus of control at work: A meta-analysis. *Journal of Organizational Behavior, 27*(8), 1057–1087. http://dx.doi.org/10.1002/job.416

Rotter, J. B. (1966). Generalized expectancies for internal versus external control of reinforcement. *Psychological Monographs, 80*(1), 1–28. http://dx.doi.org/10.1037/h0092976

Wiseman, R. (2004). *The luck factor: Four simple principles that will change your luck and your life*. Arrow Books.

3.4 Thinking About Ethics in College and in Psychology

Adams, M. (1999). The dead grandmother/exam syndrome. *Annals of Improbable Research, 5*(6), 3–6.

American Psychological Association. (2017). Ethical principles of psychologists and code of conduct. *American Psychological Association*. https://www.apa.org/ethics/code/

Anderman, E. M., & Won, S. (2019). Academic cheating in disliked classes. *Ethics & Behavior, 29*(1), 1–22. https://doi.org/10.1080/10508422.2017.1373648

Bartlett, T. (2012, September 5). Former Harvard psychologist fabricated and falsified, report says. [Blog post]. *The Chronicle of Higher Education*. https://www.chronicle.com/blogs/percolator/report-says-former-harvard-psychologist-fabricated-falsified/30748

Bartlett, T. (2015, June 22). Can a longtime fraud help fix science? *The Chronicle of Higher Education*. https://www.chronicle.com/article/Can-a-Longtime-Fraud-Help-Fix/231061

Callahan, D. (2004). *The cheating culture: Why more Americans are doing wrong to get ahead*. Harcourt.

Carucci, R. (2016, December 16). Why ethical people make unethical choices. *Harvard Business Review*. https://hbr.org/2016/12/why-ethical-people-make-unethical-choices

Davy, J. A., Kincaid, J. F., Smith, K. J., & Trawick, M. A. (2007). An examination of the role of attitudinal characteristics and motivation on the cheating behavior of business students. *Ethics & Behavior, 17*(3), 281–302. https://doi.org/10.1080/10508420701519304

Dinich, H. (2009, March 7). NCAA penalties extend to 10 FSU sports. *ESPN*. http://www.espn.com/college-football/news/story? id=3958292

Handelsman, M. M. (2017). A teachable ethics scandal. *Teaching of Psychology, 44*(3), 278–284. http://dx.doi.org/10.1177/0098628317712789

John, L. K., Loewenstein, G., & Prelec, D. (2012). Measuring the prevalence of questionable research practices with incentives for truth telling. *Psychological Science, 23*(5), 524–532. http://dx.doi.org/10.1177/0956797611430953

McCabe, D. L., Butterfield, K. D., & Trevino, L. K. (2012). *Cheating in college: Why students do it and what educators can do about it*. Johns Hopkins University Press.

McKibban, A. R., & Burdsal, C. A. (2013). Academic dishonesty: An in-depth investigation of assessing measurable constructs and a call for consistency in scholarship. *Journal of Academic Ethics, 11*(3), 185–197. https://doi.org/10.1007/s10805-013-9187-6

Miller, A. D., Murdock, T. B., & Grotewiel, M. M. (2017). Addressing academic dishonesty among the highest achievers. *Theory Into Practice, 56*(2), 121–128. https://doi.org/10.1080/00405841.2017.1283574

Robbins, R. D. (2012, August 30). Harvard investigates "unprecedented" academic dishonesty case. *The Harvard Crimson*. https://www.thecrimson.com/article/2012/8/30/academic-dishonesty-ad-board/

Schmelkin, L. P., Gilbert, K., Spencer, K. J., Pincus, H. S., & Silva, R. (2008). A multidimensional scaling of college students' perceptions of academic dishonesty. *Journal of Higher Education, 79*(5), 587–607. https://doi.org/10.1080/00221546.2008.11772118

Wamsley, L. (2019, April 8). Felicity Huffman and 12 other parents to plead guilty in college cheating scandal. *National Public Radio*. https://www.npr.org/2019/04/08/711136472/felicity-huffman-and-12-other-parents-to-plead-guilty-in-college-cheating-scanda

You, D., Ruiz, A., & Warchal, J. (2018). The presentation of ethics in undergraduate psychology syllabi: A review.

Teaching of Psychology, 45(4), 346–350. http://dx.doi.org/10.1177/0098628318796921

Chapter 4

4.1 Typical Psychology Courses

Ashcraft, M. H., & Moore, A. M. (2009). Mathematics anxiety and the affective drop in performance. *Journal of Psychoeducational Assessment, 27*(3), 197–205. http://dx.doi.org/10.1177/0734282908330580

Dweck, C. S. (2006). *Mindset: The new psychology of success.* Random House.

Gurung, R. A., Hackathorn, J., Enns, C., Frantz, S., Cacioppo, J. T., Loop, T., & Freeman, J. E. (2016). Strengthening introductory psychology: A new model for teaching the introductory course. *American Psychologist, 71*(2), 112–124. http://dx.doi.org/10.1037/a0040012

Landrum, R. E., Shoemaker, C. S., & Davis, S. F. (2003). Important topics in an introduction to the psychology major course. *Teaching of Psychology, 30*(1), 48–51.

Norcross, J. C., Hailstorks, R., Aiken, L. S., Pfund, R. A., Stamm, K. E., & Christidis, P. (2016). Undergraduate study in psychology: Curriculum and assessment. *American Psychologist, 71*(2), 89–101. http://dx.doi.org/10.1037/a0040095

Peterson, J. J., & Sesma, A., Jr. (2017). Introductory psychology: What's lab got to do with it? *Teaching of Psychology, 44*(4), 313–323. http://dx.doi.org/10.1177/0098628317727643

Pfund, R. A., Norcross, J. C., Hailstorks, R., Aiken, L. S., Stamm, K. E., & Christidis, P. (2016). A dubious distinction? The BA versus the BS in psychology. *Teaching of Psychology, 43*(1), 32–37. http://dx.doi.org/10.1177/0098628315620874

Rocchi, M., Beaudry, S. G., Anderson, C., & Pelletier, L. G. (2016). The perspective of undergraduate research participant pool nonparticipants. *Teaching of Psychology, 43*(4), 285–293. http://dx.doi.org/10.1177/0098628316662756

Roscoe, L. J., & McMahan, E. A. (2014). Outcomes of introduction to the psychology major: Careers and opportunities course. *Teaching of Psychology, 41*(2), 110–114. http://dx.doi.org/10.1177/0098628314530340

Vigen, T. (2015). *Spurious correlations.* Hachette Book Group.

4.2 Skills You Develop as a Psychology Major

American Psychological Association. (2013). *APA guidelines for the undergraduate psychology major: Version 2.0.* https://www.apa.org/ed/precollege/about/psymajor-guidelines.pdf

Boucher, E. (2016, August 22). It's time to ditch our deadlines. *The Chronicle of Higher Education.* https://www.chronicle.com/article/It-s-Time-to-Ditch-Our/237530

Feldman, D. B. (2017, October 6). Is psychology really a science? [Blog post]. *Psychology Today.* https://www.psychologytoday.com/us/blog/supersurvivors/201710/is-psychology-really-science

Flaherty, D. K. (2011). The vaccine-autism connection: A public health crisis caused by unethical medical practices and fraudulent science. *Annals of Pharmacotherapy, 45*(10), 1302–1304. https://doi.org/10.1345/aph.1Q318

Friedrich, J., Childress, J., & Cheng, D. (2018). Replicating a national survey on statistical training in undergraduate psychology programs: Are there "new statistics" in the new millennium? *Teaching of Psychology, 45*(4), 312–323. http://dx.doi.org/10.1177/0098628318796414

Hettich, P. (2014, September). APA guidelines for the undergraduate psychology major, version 2.0: Your covert career counselor. *American Psychological Association's Psychology Student Network.* https://www.apa.org/ed/precollege/psn/2014/09/career-counselor.aspx

Kreuter, N. (2012, August 1). Deadlines matter. *Inside Higher Ed.* https://www.insidehighered.com/advice/2012/08/01/essay-academics-and-importance-deadlines

LoCascio, R. (2016, August 23). Why the most successful people fail the most often. *Inc.* https://www.inc.com/rob-locascio/4-spectacular-failures-from-the-most-successful-entrepreneurs.html

Newman, K. (2017, August 11). Here are the most loved (and hated) college courses. *USA Today.* http://college.usatoday.com/2017/08/11/here-are-the-most-loved-and-hated-college-courses/

Nisbett, R. E. (2015). *Mindware: Tools for smart thinking.* Farrar, Straus, and Giroux.

Singer, N. (2018, April 11). What you don't know about how Facebook uses your data. *The New York Times.*

https://www.nytimes.com/2018/04/11/technology/facebook-privacy-hearings.html

Watson, J. B., & Rayner, R. (1920). Conditioned emotional reactions. *Journal of Experimental Psychology, 3*(1), 1–14. http://dx.doi.org/10.1037/h0069608

Zimbardo, P. (2007). *The Lucifer effect: Understanding how good people turn evil.* Random House.

4.3 Double Majoring or Picking Up a Minor

Del Rossi, A. F., & Hersch, J. (2016). The private and social benefits of double majors. *Journal of Benefit-Cost Analysis, 7*(2), 292–325. https://doi.org/10.1017/bca.2016.14

Makridis, C. (2017, March 28). Does it pay to get a double major in college? *The Conversation*. http://theconversation.com/does-it-pay-to-get-a-double-major-in-college-74420

Pitt, R. N., & Tepper, S. A. (2012). *Double majors: Influences, identities, and impacts.* Prepared for the Teagle Foundation, Curb Center, Vanderbilt University.

Sadigh, M. (2017, August 23). Stop calling it a minor. *The Chronicle of Higher Education.* https://www.chronicle.com/article/Stop-Calling-It-a-Minor/240984

Slatalla, M. (2008, April 20). What's your minor? *The New York Times.* https://www.nytimes.com/2008/04/20/education/edlife/guidance.html

Zafar, B. (2011). Double majors: One for me, one for the parents? *Economic Inquiry, 50*(2), 287–308. https://doi.org/10.1111/j.1465-7295.2011.00403.x

4.4 Meet Your Professors

Clauset, A., Arbesman, S., & Larremore, D. B. (2015). Systematic inequality and hierarchy in faculty hiring networks. *Science Advances, 1*(1), e1400005. https://dx.doi.org/10.1126/sciadv.1400005

Condis, M. (2016, November 1). Making office hours matter. *Inside Higher Ed.* https://www.insidehighered.com/advice/2016/11/01/how-convince-students-attend-office-hours-essay

Hailstorks, R., Stamm, K. E., Norcross, J. C., Pfund, R. A., & Christidis, P. (2019). 2016 undergraduate study in psychology: Faculty characteristics and online teaching. *Scholarship of Teaching and Learning in Psychology, 5*(1), 52–60. http://dx.doi.org/10.1037/stl0000134

Keeley, J. W., Ismail, E., & Buskist, W. (2016). Excellent teachers' perspectives on excellent teaching. *Teaching of Psychology, 43*(3), 175–179. http://dx.doi.org/10.1177/0098628316649307

Newport, C. (2005). *How to win at college.* Three Rivers Press.

Olatunji, B. O. (2000, Fall). Getting to know your undergraduate faculty: A valuable asset. *Eye on Psi Chi, 5*(1), 30. https://www.psichi.org/page/051EyeFall00eOlatunj

Ritzer, D. R. (2018, Fall). Finding a mentor. *Eye on Psi Chi, 23*(1), 18–22. https://www.psichi.org/page/231EyeFall18Ritzer

Vernon, L. (2018a, Spring). The secret life of professors revealed part I: The professor's telltale heart. *Eye on Psi Chi, 22*(3), 10–11. https://www.psichi.org/page/223EyeSpr18fVernon

Vernon, L. (2018b, Summer). The secret life of professors revealed part II: The mystery job. *Eye on Psi Chi, 22*(4), 8–9. https://www.psichi.org/page/224EyeSum18iVernon

Vernon, L. (2018c, Fall). The secret life of professors revealed part III: A professor's room with a view (of students). *Eye on Psi Chi, 23*(1), 16–17. https://www.psichi.org/page/231EyeFall18Vernon

Vernon, L. (2018d, Winter). The secret life of professors revealed part IV: A professor's long-term lodging and how to handle conflicts and concerns. *Eye on Psi Chi, 23*(2), 8–9. https://www.psichi.org/page/232EyeWinter18-19Vernon

Vernon, L. (2019, Summer). The secret life of professors revealed part V: What's in a grade? How to play the academic game, get good grades, and have your professor as your advocate. *Eye on Psi Chi, 23*(4), 48–49. https://www.psichi.org/page/234EyeSum19Vernon

Whitaker, M. (2018, January 2). The 21st-century academic. *The Chronicle of Higher Education.* https://www.chronicle.com/article/The-21st-Century-Academic/242136

4.5 Communicating With Professors (and Others)

Blessing, S. B., Blessing, J. S., & Fleck, B. K. B. (2012). Using Twitter to reinforce classroom concepts. *Teaching of Psychology, 39*(4), 268–271. http://dx.doi.org/10.1177/0098628312461484

Bremen, E. (2012). *Say this, not that to your professor: 36 talking tips for college success*. NorLightsPress.com.

Chamberlin, J. (2013, March). "Like" it, or not: Psychology professors are making their courses a feature of their students' Facebook feeds in an effort to enliven class and enhance learning. *Monitor on Psychology, 44*, 60. https://www.apa.org/monitor/2013/03/like-it.aspx

Crowder, S. B. (2016, April 1). The "sacredness" of social media. *Inside Higher Ed*. https://www.insidehighered.com/advice/2016/04/01/professors-should-be-allowed-keep-their-social-media-communications-limits

Gulliver, K. (2014, March 6). Too much informality. *Inside Higher Ed*. https://www.insidehighered.com/views/2014/03/06/essay-problems-created-students-who-are-too-informal-professors

Kolowich, S. (2010, May 4). Professors and social media. *Inside Higher Ed*. https://www.insidehighered.com/news/2010/05/04/socialmedia

Kreuter, N. (2011, June 3). Doctor, Professor, or "hey you"? *Inside Higher Ed*. https://www.insidehighered.com/advice/2011/06/03/doctor-professor-or-hey-you

Stoloff, M., Sanders, N., & McCarthy, M. (2005). Profiles of undergraduate programs in psychology. *American Psychological Association Undergraduate Education*. https://www.apa.org/education/undergrad/profiles.aspx

4.6 Meeting Others at Your Institution

Gibson, A. (2017, July 31). 3 reasons to get to know your academic advisor [Blog post]. https://www.ucdavis.edu/majors/blog/tips-trends/reasons-know-academic-advisor

Hart, L. A. (2002, February). Undergraduates from a graduate student perspective. *Observer*. https://www.psychologicalscience.org/observer/undergraduates-from-a-graduate-student-perspective

Kim, J. (2014, October 28). The changing roles of academic administrative assistants. [Blog post]. *Inside Higher Ed*. https://www.insidehighered.com/blogs/technology-and-learning/changing-roles-academic-administrative-assistants

Lapowsky, I. (2014, January 28). The most important person in your office isn't who you think. *Inc*. https://www.inc.com/issie-lapowsky/the-most-important-person-in-the-office.html

Newport, C. (2005). *How to win at college*. Three Rivers Press.

Wlotko, E. W. (2002, February). Graduate students from an undergraduate perspective. *Observer*. https://www.psychologicalscience.org/observer/graduate-students-from-an-undergraduate-perspective

Chapter 5

5.1 Succeeding With Research

Cynkar, A. (2007, November). Clinch your graduate school acceptance. *gradPSYCH Magazine, 5*(4). https://www.apa.org/gradpsych/2007/11/cover-acceptance.aspx

Karazsia, B. T., & Smith, L. (2016). Preparing for graduate-level training in professional psychology: Comparisons across clinical PhD, counseling PhD, and clinical PsyD programs. *Teaching of Psychology, 43*(4), 305–313. http://dx.doi.org/10.1177/0098628316662760

Landrum, R. E., & Nelsen, L. R. (2002). The undergraduate research assistantship: An analysis of the benefits. *Teaching of Psychology, 29*(1), 15–19. http://dx.doi.org/10.1207/S15328023TOP2901_04

Lotto, B., & O'Toole, A. (2012, June). *Science is for everyone, kids included* [Video]. TED Conferences. https://www.ted.com/talks/beau_lotto_amy_o_toole_science_is_for_everyone_kids_included

Miles, S. R., Cromer, L. D., & Narayan, A. (2015). Applying equity theory to students' perceptions of research participation requirements. *Teaching of Psychology, 42*(4), 349–356. http://dx.doi.org/10.1177/0098628315603252

Miller, A. (1981). A survey of introductory psychology subject pool practices among leading universities. *Teaching of Psychology, 8*(4), 211–213. http://dx.doi.org/10.1207/s15328023top0804_4

Moyer, A., & Franklin, N. (2011). Strengthening the educational value of undergraduate participation in research as part of a psychology department subject pool. *Journal of Empirical Research on Human Research Ethics: An International Journal, 6*(1), 75–82. https://doi.org/10.1525/jer.2011.6.1.75

Norcross, J. C., Hailstorks, R., Aiken, L. S., Pfund, R. A., Stamm, K. E., & Christidis, P. (2016). Undergraduate study in psychology: Curriculum and assessment. *American Psychologist, 71*(2), 89–101. http://dx.doi.org/10.1037/a0040095

Perlman, B., & McCann, L. I. (2005). Undergraduate research experiences in psychology: A national study of courses and curricula. *Teaching of Psychology, 32*(1), 5–14. http://dx.doi.org/10.1207/s15328023top3201_2

5.2 The Life of a Research Assistant

Bedwell, S. A. (2016). Opinion: Why research using animals is important in psychology. *The Psychologist, 29*(8), 624–627. https://thepsychologist.bps.org.uk/volume-29/august/why-research-using-animals-important-psychology

Capitanio, J. (2017, January). Animal research: Serving a vital role in psychological science. *American Psychological Association Psychology Student Network*. https://www.apa.org/ed/precollege/psn/2017/01/animal-studies.aspx

Hamm, J. (2008). Collaboration: Student perspective. In R. L. Miller, R. F. Rycek, E. Baicetis, S. T. Barney, B. C. Beins, S. R. Burns, . . . M. E. Ware (Eds.), *Developing, promoting, & sustaining the undergraduate research experience in psychology* (pp. 220–223). http://teachpsych.org/Resources/Documents/ebooks/ur2008.pdf

Kardash, C. M. (2000). Evaluation of an undergraduate research experience: Perceptions of undergraduate interns and their faculty mentors. *Journal of Educational Psychology, 92*(1), 191–201. http://dx.doi.org/10.1037/0022-0663.92.1.191

Kennison, S. M., Jacobs, S. C., & Montgomery, Y. (2010, Fall). What the student researcher needs to know about research ethics. *Eye on Psi Chi, 15*, 18–21. https://www.psichi.org/page/151EyeFall10bKenniso

Miller, R. L., Rycek, R. F., Balcetis, E., Barney, S. T., Beins, B. C., Burns, S. R., . . . Ware, M. E. (Eds.). (2008). *Developing, promoting, & sustaining the undergraduate research experience in psychology*. http://teachpsych.org/ebooks/ur2008/index.php

Newport, C. (2005). *How to win at college*. Three Rivers Press.

Woody, W. D. (2008). Collaboration: Faculty perspective. In R. L. Miller, R. F. Rycek, E. Baicetis, S. T. Barney, B. C. Beins, S. R. Burns, . . . M. E. Ware (Eds.), *Developing, promoting, & sustaining the undergraduate research experience in psychology* (pp. 215–219). http://teachpsych.org/Resources/Documents/ebooks/ur2008.pdf

5.3 How to Become a Psychology Research Assistant

Kierniesky, N. C. (2005). Undergraduate research in small psychology departments: Two decades later. *Teaching of Psychology, 32*(2), 84–90. http://dx.doi.org/10.1207/s15328023top3202_1

Lai, B. S., Margol, A., & Landoll, R. R. (2010, Summer). Doing your research: How to make the most out of research experiences. *Eye on Psi Chi, 14*, 24–27. http://www.psichi.org/? page=144EYESum10cLai

Shah, H. J., Savage, R., Ortiz, R., & Lai, B. S. (2018, Winter). Undergraduate research: A valuable experience for expanding your mind and your résumé. *Eye on Psi Chi, 22*, 10–11. https://www.psichi.org/page/222EyeWin18hShah

Wayment, H. A., & Dickson, K. L. (2008). Increasing student participation in undergraduate research benefits students, faculty, and department. *Teaching of Psychology, 35*(3), 194–197. http://dx.doi.org/10.1080/00986280802189213

5.4 Consider Becoming a Teaching Assistant

Appleby, D. C. (2019, January 21). Should you become an undergraduate teaching assistant? *American Psychological Association's Psych Learning Curve*. http://psychlearningcurve.org/should-you-become-an-undergraduate-teaching-assistant/

Ebbinghaus, H. (1885). Über das Gedächtnis. *Untersuchungen zur experimentellen psychologie*. Duncker & Humblot.

Family Educational Rights and Privacy Act (FERPA). (1974). (20 U.S.C. § 1232g; 34 CFR Part 99)

Hogan, T. P., Norcross, J. C., Cannon, J. T., & Karpiak, C. P. (2007). Working with and training undergraduates as teaching assistants. *Teaching of Psychology, 34*(3), 187–190. http://dx.doi.org/10.1080/00986280701498608

Koh, A. W. L., Lee, S. C., & Lim, S. W. H. (2018). The learning benefits of teaching: A retrieval practice hypothesis. *Applied Cognitive Psychology, 32*(3), 401–410. http://dx.doi.org/10.1002/acp.3410

Wolverton, B. (2015, June 10). How athletics and academics collided at one university. *The Chronicle of*

Higher Education. https://www.chronicle.com/article/How-AthleticsAcademics/230795

5.5 Another Type of Experiential Learning—Service Learning

American Psychological Association. (2013). *APA guidelines for the undergraduate psychology major: Version 2.0.* https://www.apa.org/ed/precollege/about/psymajor-guidelines.pdf

Bringle, R., & Hatcher, J. (1995). A service learning curriculum for faculty. *Michigan Journal of Community Service Learning, 2*(1), 112–122. http://hdl.handle.net/2027/spo.3239521.0002.111

Bringle, R. G., Reeb, R. N., Brown, M. A., & Ruiz, A. I. (2016). *Service learning in psychology: Enhancing undergraduate education for the public good.* American Psychological Association. https://doi.org/10.1037/14803-000

Campbell, C. G., & Oswald, B. R. (2018). Promoting critical thinking through service learning: A home-visiting case study. *Teaching of Psychology, 45*(2), 193–199. http://dx.doi.org/10.1177/0098628318762933

Celio, C. I., Durlak, J., & Dymnicki, A. (2011). A meta-analysis of the impact of service-learning on students. *Journal of Experiential Education, 34*(2), 164–181. https://doi.org/10.1177/105382591103400205

Chan, K., Ng, E., & Chan, C. C. (2016). Empowering students through service learning in a community psychology course: A case in Hong Kong. *Journal of Higher Education Outreach and Engagement, 20*(4), 25–36.

Ehrenfeld, T. (2016, September 29). Is it true that "no good deed goes unpunished"? People sometimes withdraw or punish you after you try to help them. [Blog post]. *Psychology Today.* https://www.psychologytoday.com/us/blog/open-gently/201609/is-it-true-no-good-deed-goes-unpunished

Fleck, B., Hussey, H. D., & Rutledge-Ellison, L. (2017). Linking class and community: An investigation of service learning. *Teaching of Psychology, 44*(3), 232–239. http://dx.doi.org/10.1177/0098628317711317

Michaelson, C. (2018). Service-learning in an undergraduate abnormal psychology course: What do students learn? *International Research in Higher Education, 3*(2), 125–130. https://*doi.org/10.5430/irhe.v3n2p125*

Ritzer, D. R., & Sleigh, M. J. (2018–19, Winter). Do your community service projects help as much as you think? *Eye on Psi Chi, 23*, 34–38. https://www.psichi.org/page/232EyeWinter18-19Ritzer

Shor, R., Cattaneo, L., & Calton, J. (2017). Pathways of transformational service learning: Exploring the relationships between context, disorienting dilemmas, and student response. *Journal of Transformative Education, 15*(2), 156–173. https://doi.org/10.1177/1541344616689044

Chapter 6

6.1 Library Skills, Part 1—Evaluating Sources

Association for Psychological Science. (2003, March 14). Classical blunders. *APS Observer.* https://www.psychologicalscience.org/observer/classical-blunders

Baker, M. (2015, August 27). Over half of psychology studies fail reproducibility test. *Nature.* https://www.nature.com/news/over-half-of-psychology-studies-fail-reproducibility-test-1.18248

Bridge, D. J., & Paller, K. A. (2012). Neural correlates of reactivation and retrieval-induced distortion. *The Journal of Neuroscience, 32*(35), 12144–12151. http://dx.doi.org/10.1523/JNEUROSCI.1378-12.2012

EBSCO Help (n.d.). What is the Research Starters feature in EBSCO Discovery Service (EDS)? https://help.ebsco.com/interfaces/EBSCO_Discovery_Service/EDS_User_Guide/What_is_the_Research_Starters_feature_in_EDS

Flaherty, D. K. (2011). The vaccine-autism connection: A public health crisis caused by unethical medical practices and fraudulent science. *Annals of Pharmacotherapy, 45*(10), 1302–1304. https://doi.org/10.1345/aph.1Q318

Lee, C. (2013, January 10). Alligators and academia: The importance of primary and secondary sources. [Blog post]. *APA Style Blog.* https://blog.apastyle.org/apastyle/2013/01/alligators-and-academia.html

Lee, T. L., Gelfand, M. J., & Kashima, Y. (2014). The serial reproduction of conflict: Third parties escalate conflict through communication biases. *Journal of Experimental Social Psychology, 54*, 68–72. http://dx.doi.org/10.1016/j.jesp.2014.04.006

Oldenburg, C. M. (2005). Use of primary source readings in psychology courses at liberal arts colleges. *Teaching of Psychology, 32*(1), 25–29. http://dx.doi.org/10.1207/s15328023top3201_6

Simons, D. J., Boot, W. R., Charness, N., Gathercole, S. E., Chabris, C. F., Hambrick, D. Z., & Stine-Morrow, E. A. L. (2016). Do "brain-training" programs work? *Psychological Science in the Public Interest, 17*(3), 103–186. http://dx.doi.org/10.1177/1529100616661983

Stanovich, K. E. (2010). *How to think straight about psychology* (9th ed.). Allyn & Bacon.

Turabian, K., Booth, W., Colomb, G., & Williams, J. (2013). *A manual for writers of research papers, theses, and dissertations: Chicago style for students and researchers* (8th ed.). University of Chicago Press. https://doi.org/10.7208/chicago/9780226816395.001.0001

Watrin, J. P. (2017) The "new history of psychology" and the uses and abuses of dichotomies. *Theory & Psychology, 27*(1), 69–86. http://dx.doi.org/10.1177/0959354316685450

6.2 Library Skills, Part 2—Using Databases to Find Sources

Bjornsen, C. A., & Archer, K. J. (2015). Relations between college students' cell phone use during class and grades. *Scholarship of Teaching and Learning in Psychology, 1*(4), 326–336. http://dx.doi.org/10.1037/stl0000045

Fagan, J. C. (2017). An evidence-based review of academic web search engines, 2014-2016: Implications for librarians' practice and research agenda. *Information Technology and Libraries, 36*(2), 7–47. https://doi.org/10.6017/ital.v36i2.9718

Kolata, G. (2017, October 30). Many academics are eager to publish in worthless journals. *The New York Times*. https://www.nytimes.com/2017/10/30/science/predatory-journals-academics.html

Lee, C. (2015, October 5). The myth of the off-limits source. [Blog post]. *APA Style Blog*. http://blog.apastyle.org/apastyle/2015/10/the-myth-of-the-off-limits-source.html

Lopresti-Goodman, S. M., Rivera, A., & Dressel, C. (2012). Practicing safe text: The impact of texting on walking behavior. *Applied Cognitive Psychology, 26*(4), 644–648. http://dx.doi.org/10.1002/acp.2846

Turabian, K., Booth, W., Colomb, G., & Williams, J. (2013). *A manual for writers of research papers, theses, and dissertations: Chicago style for students and researchers* (8th ed.). University of Chicago Press. https://doi.org/10.7208/chicago/9780226816395.001.0001

Winters, B. (2011, July/August). Wikipedia initiative: Demonstrations. *Observer*. https://www.psychologicalscience.org/observer/wikipedia-initiative-demonstrations

Zahneis, M. (2018, July 19). Some colleges cautiously embrace Wikipedia. *Chronicle of Higher Education*. https://www.chronicle.com/article/Some-Colleges-Cautiously/243968

6.3 A (Relatively Painless) Introduction to APA-Style Formatting

American Psychological Association. (2019). *APA Style*. http://www.apastyle.org/

American Psychological Association. (2020). *Publication manual of the American Psychological Association* (7th ed.). American Psychological Association. https://doi.org/10.1037/0000165-000

Bentley, M., Peerenboom, C. A., Hodge, F. W., Passano, E. B., Warren, H. C., & Washburn, M. F. (1929). Instructions in regard to preparation of manuscript. *Psychological Bulletin, 26*(2), 57–63. http://dx.doi.org/10.1037/h0071487

Bjornsen, C. A., & Archer, K. J. (2015). Relations between college students' cell phone use during class and grades. *Scholarship of Teaching and Learning in Psychology, 1*(4), 326–336. http://dx.doi.org/10.1037/stl0000045

Breitenbach, A. (2014, May 2). But I already learned MLA! Why do I need APA style? [Blog post]. *APA Style Blog*. http://blog.apastyle.org/apastyle/2014/05/but-i-already-learned-mla-why-do-i-need-apa-style.html

Breitenbach, A. (2016, July 14). The origins of APA style. [Blog post]. *APA Style Blog*. http://blog.apastyle.org/apastyle/2016/07/the-origins-of-apa-style.html

Gingerich, A. C., & Lineweaver, T. T. (2014). Omg! Texting in class = u fail:(: Empirical evidence that text messaging during class disrupts comprehension. *Teaching of Psychology, 41*(1), 44–51. http://dx.doi.org/10.1177/0098628313514177

6.4 Practical Advice for Reading Psychology Research Papers

Christopher, A. N., & Walter, M. I. (2006). An assignment to help students learn to navigate primary sources of information. *Teaching of Psychology, 33*(1), 42–45.

Lee, C. (2010, July 15). Five steps to a great title. [Blog post]. *APA Style Blog*. http://blog.apastyle.org/apastyle/2010/07/five-steps-to-a-great-title.html

Miller, G. A. (1956). The magical number seven, plus or minus two: Some limits on our capacity for processing information. *Psychological Review, 63*(2), 81–97. http://dx.doi.org/10.1037/h0043158

Sanbonmatsu, D. M., Strayer, D. L., Medeiros-Ward, N., & Watson, J. M. (2013). Who multi-tasks and why? Multi-tasking ability, perceived multi-tasking ability, impulsivity, and sensation seeking. *PLoS ONE, 8*(1), e54402. Retrieved from https://doi.org/10.1371/journal.pone.0054402

Sego, S. A., & Stuart, A. E. (2016). Learning to read empirical articles in general psychology. *Teaching of Psychology, 43*(1), 38–42. http://dx.doi.org/10.1177/0098628315620875

Yeager, D. S., & Dweck, C. S. (2012). Mindsets that promote resilience: When students believe that personal characteristics can be developed. *Educational Psychologist, 47*(4), 302–314. http://dx.doi.org/10.1080/00461520.2012.722805

6.5 Understanding the Methods and Results

Christopher, A. N., & Walter, M. I. (2006). An assignment to help students learn to navigate primary sources of information. *Teaching of Psychology, 33*(1), 42–45.

Cumming, G. (2008). Replication and p intervals: p values predict the future only vaguely, but confidence intervals do much better. *Perspectives on Psychological Science, 3*(4), 286–300. http://dx.doi.org/10.1111/j.1745-6924.2008.00079.x

Cumming, G. (2013). The new statistics: Why and how. *Psychological Science, 25*(1), 7–29. http://dx.doi.org/10.1177/0956797613504966

Dixson, B. J. W., & Rantala, M. J. (2016). The role of facial and body hair distribution in women's judgments of men's sexual attractiveness. *Archives of Sexual Behavior, 45*(4), 877–889. http://dx.doi.org/10.1007/s10508-015-0588-z

Gosling, S. D., Kwan, V. S. Y., & John, O. P. (2003). A dog's got personality: A cross-species comparative approach to personality judgments in humans. *Journal of Personality and Social Psychology, 85*(6), 1161–1169. http://dx.doi.org/10.1037/0022-3514.85.6.1161

Johnson, V. E. (2013). Revised standards for statistical evidence. *Proceedings of the National Academy of Sciences of the United States of America, 48*, 19313–19317. https://doi.org/10.1073/pnas.1313476110

Reinhart, A. (2015). *Statistics done wrong: The woefully complete guide*. No Starch Press.

Robbins, N. (2011, November 17). What's wrong with this graph? *Forbes*. https://www.forbes.com/sites/naomirobbins/2011/11/17/whats-wrong-with-this-graph/#232af3802a33

Robbins, N. (2012, March 13). Finding examples of misleading and deceptive graphs. *Forbes*. https://www.forbes.com/sites/naomirobbins/2012/03/13/finding-examples-of-misleading-and-deceptive-graphs/#fe7302c73c66

Sego, S. A., & Stuart, A. E. (2016). Learning to read empirical articles in general psychology. *Teaching of Psychology, 43*(1), 38–42. http://dx.doi.org/10.1177/0098628315620875

Wasserstein, R. L., Schirm, A. L., & Lazar, N. A. (2019). Moving to a world beyond "$p < 0.05$." *The American Statistician, 73*(sup1), 1–19. https://doi.org/10.1080/00031305.2019.1583913

6.6 Critically Thinking About Psychological Research

Baumeister, R. F., Vohs, K. D., & Funder, D. C. (2007). Psychology as the science of self-reports and finger movements: Whatever happened to actual behavior? *Perspectives on Psychological Science, 2*(4), 396–403. http://dx.doi.org/10.1111/j.1745-6916.2007.00051.x

Bostyn, D. H., Sevenhant, S., & Roets, A. (2018). Of mice, men, and trolleys: Hypothetical judgment versus real-life behavior in trolley-style moral dilemmas. *Psychological Science, 29*(7), 1084–1093. http://dx.doi.org/10.1177/0956797617752640

Carter, E. R., & Murphy, M. C. (2015). Group-based differences in perceptions of racism: What counts, to whom, and why? *Social and Personality Psychology Compass, 9*(6), 269–280. http://dx.doi.org/10.1111/spc3.12181

Lanagan-Leitzel, L. K., & Diller, J. W. (2018). Teaching psychological critical thinking using popular media. *Scholarship of Teaching and Learning in Psychology, 4*(2), 120–125. http://dx.doi.org/10.1037/stl0000112

Nisbett, R. E. (2015). *Mindware: Tools for smart thinking.* Farrar, Straus, and Giroux.

Stanovich, K. E. (2010). *How to think straight about psychology* (9th ed.). Allyn & Bacon.

Sternberg, R. J. (2006). *Reviewing scientific works in psychology.* American Psychological Association. https://doi.org/10.1037/11288-000

Uttal, W. R. (2003). *Psychomythics: Sources of artifacts and misconceptions in scientific psychology.* Taylor & Francis Group. https://doi.org/10.4324/9781410607614

Vigen, T. (2015). *Spurious correlations.* Hachette Books.

Wilson, T. D., & Brekke, N. (1994). Mental contamination and mental correction: Unwanted influences on judgments and evaluations. *Psychological Bulletin, 116*(1), 117–142. http://dx.doi.org/10.1037/0033-2909.116.1.117

Chapter 7

7.1 Writing a Research Paper

American Psychological Association. (2020). *Publication manual of the American Psychological Association* (7th ed.). American Psychological Association. https://doi.org/10.1037/0000165-000

Ishak, S., & Salter, N. P. (2017). Undergraduate psychological writing: A best practices guide and national survey. *Teaching of Psychology, 44*(1), 5–17. http://dx.doi.org/10.1177/0098628316677491

Madigan, R., Johnson, S., & Linton, P. (1995). The language of psychology: APA style as epistemology. *American Psychologist, 50*(6), 428–436. http://dx.doi.org/10.1037/0003-066X.50.6.428

Truss, L. (2003). *Eats, shoots and leaves: The zero tolerance approach to punctuation.* Gotham Books.

Urban, T. (2016, February). *Inside the mind of a master procrastinator* [Video]. TED Conferences. https://www.ted.com/talks/tim_urban_inside_the_mind_of_a_master_procrastinator

Victor, D. (2018, February 9). Oxford comma dispute is settled as Maine drivers get $5 million. *The New York Times.* https://www.nytimes.com/2018/02/09/us/oxford-comma-maine.html

7.2 Plagiarism—Do Not Do It!

American Psychological Association. (2017). Ethical principles of psychologists and code of conduct. *American Psychological Association.* https://www.apa.org/ethics/code/

American Psychological Association. (2020). *Publication manual of the American Psychological Association* (7th ed.). American Psychological Association. https://doi.org/10.1037/0000165-000

Cooper, H. (2016, May 12). Principles of good writing: Avoiding plagiarism. [Blog post]. *APA Style Blog.* https://blog.apastyle.org/apastyle/2016/05/avoiding-plagiarism.html

Evering, L. C., & Moorman, G. (2012). Rethinking plagiarism in the digital age. *Journal of Adolescent & Adult Literacy, 56*(1), 35–44. https://doi.org/10.1002/JAAL.00100

Gullifer, J., & Tyson, G. A. (2010). Exploring university students' perceptions of plagiarism: A focus group study. *Studies in Higher Education, 35*(4), 463–481. https://doi.org/10.1080/03075070903096508

Ishak, S., & Salter, N. P. (2017). Undergraduate psychological writing: A best practices guide and national survey. *Teaching of Psychology, 44*(1), 5–17. http://dx.doi.org/10.1177/0098628316677491

McCabe, D. L., Butterfield, K. D., & Trevino, L. K. (2012). *Cheating in college: Why students do it and what educators can do about it.* Johns Hopkins University Press.

Morrow, S. (2009, December). Plagiarism: What is it, exactly? *LegalZoom.* https://www.legalzoom.com/articles/plagiarism-what-is-it-exactly

Purdue Online Writing Lab. (2019). Is it plagiarism yet? https://owl.purdue.edu/owl/research_and_citation/using_research/avoiding_plagiarism/is_it_plagiarism.html

Shaw, A., & Olson, K. (2014). Whose idea is it anyway? The importance of reputation in acknowledgement.

Developmental Science, 18(3), 502–509. https://doi.org/10.1111/desc.12234

Sheehan, E. A. (2014). That's what she said: Educating students about plagiarism. In W. Altman, L. Stein, & J. R. Stowell (Eds.), *Essays from excellence in teaching* (Vol. XIII). http://teachpsych.org/Resources/Documents/ebooks/eit2013.pdf#page=46

Turnitin (2016). The plagiarism spectrum: Instructor insights into the 10 types of plagiarism. https://www.turnitin.com/static/plagiarism-spectrum/

7.3 APA Citations and References

Houska, J.A. (2015). Curse of the Billy Goat: An adaptive coping strategy for Cubs fans. *The National Pastime.* https://sabr.org/research/curse-billy-goat-adaptive-coping-strategy-cubs-fans

Hume-Pratuch, J. (2014, February 13). Footnotes for source citations in APA style? [Blog post]. *APA Style Blog.* http://blog.apastyle.org/apastyle/2014/02/footnotes-for-source-citations-in-apa-style.html

McAdoo, T. (2017, September 20). References versus citations. [Blog post]. *APA Style Blog.* http://blog.apastyle.org/apastyle/2017/09/References-versus-citations

Stevens, C. R. (2016). Citation generators, OWL, and the persistence of error-ridden references: An assessment for learning approach to citation errors. *The Journal of Academic Librarianship, 42*(6), 712–718. https://doi.org/10.1016/j.acalib.2016.07.003

Venkatraman, V. (2010, April 16). Conventions of scientific authorship. *Science.* https://www.sciencemag.org/careers/2010/04/conventions-scientific-authorship

Zafonte, M. (2018). Always in style: Using technology tools to help students master APA style. In R. J. Harnish, K. R. Bridges, D. N. Sattler, M. L. Signorella, & M. Munson (Eds.). *The use of technology in teaching and learning.* http://teachpsych.org/ebooks/

7.4 Create Your Own APA Template

American Psychological Association. (2020). *Publication manual of the American Psychological Association* (7th ed.). American Psychological Association. https://doi.org/10.1037/0000165-000

Stevens, C. R. (2016). Citation generators, OWL, and the persistence of error-ridden references: An assessment for learning approach to citation errors. *The Journal of Academic Librarianship, 42*(6), 712–718. https://doi.org/10.1016/j.acalib.2016.07.003

Venkatraman, V. (2010, April 16). Conventions of scientific authorship. *Science.* https://www.sciencemag.org/careers/2010/04/conventions-scientific-authorship

Zafonte, M. (2018). Always in style: Using technology tools to help students master APA style. In R. J. Harnish, K. R. Bridges, D. N. Sattler, M. L. Signorella, & M. Munson (Eds.). *The use of technology in teaching and learning.* http://teachpsych.org/ebooks/

7.5 Computer Skills That You Need to Know

Bahler, K. (2018, April 11). This is the one thing you should never put on your résumé. *Money.* http://money.com/money/5233688/resume-tips-2018-skills-microsoft-office/

Gecawich, M. (2017, August 2). 27 word processing skills all students should know. [Blog post]. *iAcademy.* https://blog.iacademy.com/computer-apps/27-word-processing-skills-students-know/

Hamer, L. (2019). 3 "super basic" résumé skills you should think twice before including. *The Muse.* https://www.themuse.com/advice/3-super-basic-resume-skills-you-should-think-twice-before-including

Lederman, D. (2019, March 14). Report on "new foundational skills" for work force. *Inside Higher Ed.* https://www.insidehighered.com/quicktakes/2019/03/14/report-new-foundational-skills-work-force

Logan, G. D., Ulrich, J. E., & Lindsey, D. R. (2016). Different (key)strokes for different folks: How standard and nonstandard typists balance Fitts' law and Hick's law. *Journal of Experimental Psychology: Human Perception and Performance, 42*(12), 2084–2102. http://dx.doi.org/10.1037/xhp0000272

7.6 Presentation and Poster Tips

Beyer, A. M. (2011). Improving student presentations: Pecha Kucha and just plain PowerPoint. *Teaching of Psychology, 38*(2), 122–126. http://dx.doi.org/10.1177/0098628311401588

Eves, R. L., & Davis, L. E. (2008). Death by PowerPoint? *Journal of College Science Teaching, 37*(5), 8–9.

Feldman, D. B., & Silvia, P. J. (2010). *Public speaking for psychologists: A lighthearted guide to research presentations, job talks, and other opportunities to embarrass yourself.* American Psychological Association.

Lane, R. (2019). Combining colors in PowerPoint—Mistakes to avoid. *Microsoft Office Support*. https://support.office.com/en-us/article/combining-colors-in-powerpoint-%E2%80%93-mistakes-to-avoid-555e1689-85a7-4b2e-aa89-db5270528852

Mochari, I. (2013, December 25). 3 tips to combat anxiety before a presentation. *Inc.* https://www.inc.com/ilan-mochari/3-tips-presentation-anxiety.html

Tsaousides, T. (2017, November 28). How to conquer the fear of public speaking: Are you ready for a standing ovation? [Blog post]. *Psychology Today*. https://www.psychologytoday.com/us/blog/smashing-the-brainblocks/201711/how-conquer-the-fear-public-speaking

Tufte, E. (2003, September 1). PowerPoint is evil: Power corrupts. PowerPoint corrupts absolutely. *Wired*. https://www.wired.com/2003/09/ppt2/

Chapter 8

8.1 Student Clubs and Organizations—The Importance of the Co-Curricular

American Student Government Association. (2019). Multimedia. https://www.asgaonline.com/asga/marketing-manager?taxonomy=44f1d50e-c6c0-404a-bdcd-0484b61431a1

Appleby, D. C., & Ferrari, J. R. (2013, Fall). Psi Chi officers can develop a full portfolio of career-related skills. *Eye on Psi Chi, 18*(1), 12–15. https://www.psichi.org/page/181EyeFall13aAppleby

Campbell, C. G., & Oswald, B. R. (2018). Promoting critical thinking through service learning: A home-visiting case study. *Teaching of Psychology, 45*(2), 193–199. http://dx.doi.org/10.1177/0098628318762933

Fleck, B., Hussey, H. D., & Rutledge-Ellison, L. (2017). Linking class and community: An investigation of service learning. *Teaching of Psychology, 44*(3), 232–239. http://dx.doi.org/10.1177/0098628317711317

Konnikova, M. (2014, February 21). 18 U.S. presidents were in college fraternities: Do frats create future leaders, or simply attract them? *The Atlantic*. https://www.theatlantic.com/education/archive/2014/02/18-us-presidents-were-in-college-fraternities/283997/

Richmond, E. (2015, April 12). Where students learn more outside their classrooms than in them. *The Atlantic*. https://www.theatlantic.com/education/archive/2015/04/where-kids-learn-more-outside-their-classrooms-than-in-them/390297/

Supiano, B. (2018, April 14). How colleges can cultivate students' sense of belonging. *The Chronicle of Higher Education*. https://www.chronicle.com/article/How-Colleges-Can-Cultivate/243123

Williams, T. (2019, April 2). How to recognize a legitimate college honor society? Honor or scam? *ThoughtCo*. https://www.thoughtco.com/legitimate-honor-societies-4135901

Wilson, M. (2017, March 7). How to tell sketchy honor societies from legitimate ones. *USA Today*. https://www.usatoday.com/story/college/2017/03/07/how-to-tell-sketchy-honor-societies-from-legitimate-ones/37428417/

8.2 Psi Chi—The International Honor Society in Psychology

Cannon, B. (2018, January). Seven new reasons to join Psi Chi: Psi Chi offers exciting new programs and opportunities in 2018. *American Psychological Association Psychology Student Network*. https://www.apa.org/ed/precollege/psn/2018/01/psi-chi.aspx

Hettich, P. (2018, Spring). What's YOUR job outlook? *Eye on Psi Chi, 22*(3), 12–13. https://www.psichi.org/page/223EyeSpr18eHettich

Hogan, J. D., & Takooshian, H. (2004, Spring). Psi Chi, The National Honor Society in Psychology: 75 years of scholarship and service. *Eye on Psi Chi, 8*(3), 16–17. https://www.psichi.org/?083EyeSpringaHogan

Kukucka, J., Santoro, A., Clark, S., Blandford, J., Cates, K., Hooper, P., . . . Milstein, J. L. (2016, Fall). A year in the life: Our formula for sustaining an active chapter. *Eye on Psi Chi, 21*(1), 16–19. https://www.psichi.org/page/211EyeFall16bKukucka

Shaw, L. F. (2004, Spring). How to revitalize (or energize) a Psi Chi chapter. *Eye on Psi Chi, 8*(3), 24–25. https://www.psichi.org/page/083EyeSpringeShaw

Thomas, J. H. (2018, Winter). Careers for psychology majors: What every student should know. *Eye on Psi Chi*, *22*(2), 20–23. https://www.psichi.org/page/222EyeWin18aThomas

Thompson, J. A., & Fitzgerald, C. J. (2017, Fall). Some factors to consider before attending graduate school: Intrinsic, extrinsic, and unconscious motivators. *Eye on Psi Chi*, *22*(1), 20–22. https://www.psichi.org/page/221EyeFall17cThompso

8.3 National and International Psychology Organizations

American Psychological Association. (2020). *Publication manual of the American Psychological Association* (7th ed.). American Psychological Association. https://doi.org/10.1037/0000165-000

Evans, R. B., Sexton, V. S., & Cadwallader, T. C. (Eds.). (1992). *The American Psychological Association: A historical perspective.* American Psychological Association. https://doi.org/10.1037/10111

West, C. (2008, August). The history of APS. *Observer.* https://www.psychologicalscience.org/observer/the-history-of-aps

8.4 Regional, Local, and Specialty Psychology Organizations

Dunn, D. S. (2018, March 15). Psychology conferences are for students, too! [Blog post]. *Psychology Today.* https://www.psychologytoday.com/us/blog/head-the-class/201803/psychology-conferences-are-students-too

8.5 Attending a Psychology Conference and Doing it Right

Adler, A. (2010, April). Talking the talk: Tips on giving a successful conference presentation. *American Psychological Association Psychological Science Agenda.* https://www.apa.org/science/about/psa/2010/04/presentation.aspx

Bivens, J. A. (2010, Fall). Standing in front of your poster: A guide for new presenters. *Association for Psychological Science Student Caucus Undergraduate Update.* https://www.psychologicalscience.org/members/apssc/undergraduate_update/fall-2010/standing-in-front-of-your-poster-a-guide-for-new-presenters

Cham, J. (2011, October 17). Dress codes. *PhD Comics.* http://phdcomics.com/comics/archive.php? comicid=1446

Dunn, D. S. (2018, March 15). Psychology conferences are for students, too! [Blog post]. *Psychology Today.* https://www.psychologytoday.com/us/blog/head-the-class/201803/psychology-conferences-are-students-too

Dunn, E. W., Gilbert, D. T., & Wilson, T. D. (2011). If money doesn't make you happy, then you probably aren't spending it right. *Journal of Consumer Psychology, 21*(2), 115–125. http://dx.doi.org/10.1016/j.jcps.2011.02.002

Dunn, E. W., & Weidman, A. C. (2015). Building a science of spending: Lessons from the past and directions for the future. *Journal of Consumer Psychology, 25*(1), 172–178. http://dx.doi.org/10.1016/j.jcps.2014.08.003

Fleck, B. (2018, Winter). Ten tips for student success at conventions. *Eye on Psi Chi, 22*(2), 25–28. https://www.psichi.org/page/222EyeWin18bFleck

Morgan, B. (2007, Fall). Traveling to a conference? Get help footing the bill. *Eye on Psi Chi, 12*(1), 28–29. https://www.psichi.org/page/121EYEFall07eMorgan

Palmer, J. C. (2016, October). Navigating your first academic conference: A guide for first-time conference attendees and presenters. *Psychological Science Agenda.* https://www.apa.org/science/about/psa/2016/10/academic-conference.aspx

Potter, S. J., Abrams, E., Townson, L., Wake, C., & Williams, J. E. (2010). Intellectual growth for undergraduate students: Evaluation results from an undergraduate research conference. *Journal of College Teaching and Learning, 7*(2), 25–34. https://doi.org/10.19030/tlc.v7i2.86

Wong, J. (2016, January 5). The undergraduate researcher's guide to conferences and packing. *UC Santa Barbara Undergraduate Research.* https://undergrad.research.ucsb.edu/2016/01/undergraduate-researchers-guide-conferences-packing/

8.6 Get Involved—Do More Than Sign Up!

Appleby, D. C., & Ferrari, J. R. (2013, Fall). Psi Chi officers can develop a full portfolio of career-related skills. *Eye on Psi Chi, 18*(1), 14–15. https://www.psichi.org/page/181EyeFall13aAppleby

Hettich, P., & Longnecker, H. (2015, Fall). Identifying and communicating your skills from college to career: Part 1. *Eye on Psi Chi, 20*(1), 10–11. https://www.psichi.org/?201EyeFall15bHettich

Newport, C. (2005). *How to win at college.* Three Rivers Press.

Newport, C. (2008, July 23). Dangerous ideas: College extracurriculars are meaningless. [Blog post]. *Study Hacks Blog.* http://calnewport.com/blog/2008/07/23/dangerous-ideas-college-extracurriculars-are-meaningless/

Slattery, J. M., & Forden, C. L. (2014, Fall). What psychology students learn: 10 skills that any employer will appreciate. *Eye on Psi Chi, 19*(1), 14–17. https://www.psichi.org/general/custom.asp? page=191EyeFall14aSlatter

8.7 Other Co-Curricular Resources

Hall, T. (2019, May 25). How to get every email returned. *The New York Times.* https://www.nytimes.com/2019/05/25/opinion/sunday/writing-advice.html

Kruse, K. (2016, May 30). 7 ways to say no to "pick your brain" meeting requests. *Forbes.* https://www.forbes.com/sites/kevinkruse/2016/05/30/7-ways-to-say-no-to-pick-your-brain-meeting-requests/#62dab75a5ccd

Reed, M. (2016, November 29). Co-curricular transcripts? Questions about a potentially good idea [Blog post]. *Inside Higher Ed.* https://www.insidehighered.com/blogs/confessions-community-college-dean/co-curricular-transcripts

Rutter, M. P., & Mintz, S. (2016, October 20). The curricular and the co-curricular: The importance of what takes place outside the classroom [Blog post]. *Inside Higher Ed.* https://www.insidehighered.com/blogs/higher-ed-gamma/curricular-and-co-curricular

Vozza, S. (2016, March 30). 9 surprisingly simple ways to get people to respond to your email. *Fast Company.* https://www.fastcompany.com/3058316/9-surprisingly-simple-ways-to-get-people-to-respond-to-you

Chapter 9

9.1 The Career Search—It Is Your Current Job

Burnett, B. (2017). *Designing your life.* [Video]. https://www.youtube.com/watch? v=SemHh0n19LA&t=5s

Burnett, B., & Evans, D. (2016). *Designing your life: How to build a well-lived, joyful life.* Knopf.

Gilbert, D. T., & Wilson, T. D. (2007). Prospection: Experiencing the future. *Science, 317*(5843), 1351–1354. https://doi.org/10.1126/science.1144161

Hendrix, G. (2011). Choose your own adventure: How *The Cave of Time* taught us to love interactive entertainment. *Slate.* http://www.slate.com/articles/arts/culturebox/2011/02/choose_your_own_adventure.single.html

Lebowitz, S. (2017, January 25). An exercise Stanford professors developed to map out how your life will unfold removes the agony from major decisions. *Business Insider.* https://www.businessinsider.com/no-such-thing-as-one-perfect-life-2017-1

Martin, S. (2009). How to find a job with an undergraduate degree in psychology. *gradPSYCH Magazine.* https://www.apa.org/gradpsych/features/2009/first-job.aspx

Newport, C. (2012). *So good they can't ignore you: Why skills trump passion in the quest for work you love.* Hachette Book Group.

Niven, D. (2014, September 2). I want to enjoy work: Is that possible? [Blog post]. *Psychology Today.* https://www.psychologytoday.com/us/blog/solving-unsolvable-problems/201409/i-want-enjoy-work-is-possible

O'Keefe, P. A., Dweck, C. S., & Walton, G. M. (2018). Implicit theories of interest: Finding your passion or developing it? *Psychological Science, 29*(10), 1653–1664. http://dx.doi.org/10.1177/0956797618780643

Schaufeli, W. B. (2012). Work engagement: What do we know and where do we go? *Romanian Journal of Applied Psychology, 14*(1), 3–10.

Thomas, J. H. (2018, Winter). Careers for psychology majors: What every student should know. *Eye on Psi Chi, 22*(2), 20–23. https://www.psichi.org/page/222EyeWin18aThomas

Trespicio, T. (2015). *Stop searching for your passion* [Video]. TED Conferences. http://www.tedxkc.org/terri-trespicio

9.2 Picking a Career and Plotting Your Career Path

Ginat, D. (2005). The suitable way is backwards, but they work forward. *Journal of Computers in Mathematics and Science Teaching, 24*(1), 73–88.

Harvard Business Review (2013). *HBR guide to project management.* Harvard Business Review Press.

Samuelson, R. J. (2018, February 7). What trucking tells us about the future of work. *The Washington Post.* https://www

.washingtonpost.com/opinions/what-trucking-tells-us-about-the-future-of-work/2018/02/07/70cf8cc8-0c1f-11e8-8b0d-891602206fb7_story.html?utm_term=.a6d4bd2aae39

Slattery, J. M. (2018, Spring). "I don't work in the field." *Eye on Psi Chi, 22*(3), 14-16. https://www.psichi.org/page/223EyeSpr18bSlattery

Zakaria, F. (2015). *In defense of a liberal education*. Norton.

9.3 Jobs With a Psychology Degree

American Psychological Association. (2013). *APA guidelines for the undergraduate psychology major: Version 2.0*. http://www.apa.org/ed/precollege/undergrad/index.aspx

Angeles, D., & Roberts, B. (2017, August). Putting your liberal arts degree to work. *Career Outlook, U.S. Bureau of Labor Statistics*. https://www.bls.gov/careeroutlook/2017/article/liberal-arts.htm

Landrum, R. E. (2018, January). What can you do with a bachelor's degree in psychology? Like this title, the actual answer is complicated. *Psychology Student Network*. https://www.apa.org/ed/precollege/psn/2018/01/bachelors-degree

Torpey, E. (2018, March). Careers in social work: Outlook, pay, and more. *Career Outlook, U.S. Bureau of Labor Statistics*. https://www.bls.gov/careeroutlook/2018/article/social-workers.htm

9.4 The Helping Professions

American Association for Marriage and Family Therapy. (2018). About marriage and family therapists: What is marriage and family therapy? https://www.aamft.org/About_AAMFT/About_Marriage_and_Family_Therapists.aspx

Burton, N. (2012, October 26). Why I chose psychiatry as a career [Blog post]. *Psychology Today*. https://www.psychologytoday.com/us/blog/hide-and-seek/201210/why-i-chose-psychiatry-career

Grobman, L. M. (Ed.) (2011). *Days in the lives of social workers: 58 professionals tell real-life stories from social work practice* (4th ed.). White Hat Communications.

Karazsia, B. T., & Smith, L. (2016). Preparing for graduate-level training in professional psychology: Comparisons across clinical PhD, counseling PhD, and clinical PsyD programs. *Teaching of Psychology, 43*(4), 305–313. http://dx.doi.org/10.1177/0098628316662760

Knight, C., & Gitterman, A. (2018). Merging micro and macro intervention: Social work practice with groups in the community. *Journal of Social Work Education, 54*(1), 3–17. https://doi.org/10.1080/10437797.2017.1404521

Lebow, J. L. (2013). *Couple and family therapy: An integrative map of the territory*. American Psychological Association. https://doi.org/10.1037/14255-000

Metz, K. (2016). *Careers in mental health: Opportunities in psychology, counseling, and social work*. Wiley-Blackwell.

Norcross, J. C. (2000, Fall). Clinical vs. counseling psychology: What's the diff? *Eye on Psi Chi, 5*(1), 20–22. https://www.psichi.org/page/051EyeFall00bNorcros

Price, M. (2009, March). Counseling vs. clinical programs: Similarities abound. *gradPSYCH, 7*(2), 6. http://www.apa.org/gradpsych/2009/03/similarities.aspx

Torpey, E. (2018, March). Careers in social work: Outlook, pay, and more. *Career Outlook, U.S. Bureau of Labor Statistics*. https://www.bls.gov/careeroutlook/2018/article/social-workers.htm

Vazquez, M. J. T. (2007). The diverse and intriguing career opportunities for counseling psychologists. In R. J. Sternberg (Ed.), *Career paths in psychology: Where your degree can take you* (pp. 135–160). American Psychological Association. https://doi.org/10.1037/15960-000

Wang, S. (2008). So you want to be a clinical psychologist? *APSSC Undergraduate Update*. https://www.psychologicalscience.org/apssc/uu/fall_2008/area_focus.cfm

9.5 More Psychology Careers

Appleby, K. M. (2007, Fall). Sport psychology: History, professional organizations, and professional preparation. *Eye on Psi Chi, 12*(1), 22–24. https://www.psichi.org/page/121EyeFall07bAppleby

Appleby, K. M., Appleby, D. C., Cook, A., Christensen, B., Scorniaenchi, J., Bastin, C., & DeLion, J. (2011, Spring). Preparing for success in sport psychology graduate programs. *Eye on Psi Chi, 15*(3), 24–27. https://www.psichi.org/page/153EyeSpr11aAppleby

Appleby, K. M., Appleby, D. C., & Polenske, A. D. (2015, Summer). Meet the professionals! Preparing for a career in sport psychology. *Eye on Psi Chi, 19*(4), 16–19. https://www.psichi.org/page/194EyeSum15gAppleby

Barringer, M., & Saenz, A. (2007). Promoting positive school environments: A career in school psychology. In R. J. Sternberg (Ed.), *Career paths in psychology: Where your degree can take you* (2nd ed.) (pp. 249–257). American Psychological Association. https://doi.org/10.1037/15960-000

Beilock, S. L., & Carr, T. H. (2001). On the fragility of skilled performance: What governs choking under pressure? *Journal of Experimental Psychology, 130*(4), 701–725. http://dx.doi.org/10.1037/0096-3445.130.4.701

Chalabaev, A., Sarrazin, P., Fontayne, P., Boiche, J., & Clement-Guillotin, C. (2013). The influence of sex stereotypes and gender roles on participation and performance in sport and exercise: Review and future directions. *Psychology of Sport and Exercise, 14*(2), 136–144. http://dx.doi.org/10.1016/j.psychsport.2012.10.005

Clay, R. A. (2009, November). Postgrad growth area: Forensic psychology. *gradPSYCH Magazine,* 7(4). http://www.apa.org/gradpsych/2009/11/postgrad.aspx

Furlong, J. S., & Vick, J. M. (2017, August 30). From doctoral study … to institutional research. *Chronicle of Higher Education.* https://www.chronicle.com/article/From-Doctoral-Study-to-/241033

Huss, M. T. (2001, Spring). What is forensic psychology? It's not Silence of the Lambs! *Eye on Psi Chi, 5*(3), 25–27. https://www.psichi.org/page/053EyeSpring01cHuss

Lencioni, P. (2012). *The advantage: Why organizational health trumps everything else in business.* Jossey-Bass.

Mauro, M. (2019, June). What is forensic psychology? [Blog post]. *Psychology Today.* https://www.psychologytoday.com/us/blog/take-all-prisoners/201006/what-is-forensic-psychology

Norman, D. (2013). *The design of everyday things.* Basic Books. https://doi.org/10.15358/9783800648108

Pass, J. J. (2007). Industrial/organizational (I/O) psychology as a career: Improving workforce performance and retention. In R. J. Sternberg (Ed.), *Career paths in psychology: Where your degree can take you* (2nd ed.) (pp. 249–257). American Psychological Association. https://doi.org/10.1037/15960-000

Stanovich, K. E. (2010). *How to think straight about psychology* (9th ed.). Allyn & Bacon.

Swann, C., Moran, A., & Piggott, D. (2015). Defining elite athletes: Issues in the study of expert performance in sport psychology. *Psychology of Sport and Exercise, 16*(1), 3–14. https://doi.org/10.1016/j.psychsport.2014.07.004

Ward, J. T. (2013, September). What is forensic psychology? Learn more about careers involving psychological research and applications in the legal arena. *American Psychological Association Psychology Student Network.* https://www.apa.org/ed/precollege/psn/2013/09/forensic-psychology.aspx

9.6 Choose Your Own Adventure—Design Your Own Career Path

Abadi, M. (2017). A surprising number of doctors were undergrad English majors—and it's not just about GPA. *Business Insider.* https://www.businessinsider.com/english-major-medical-school-doctors-2017-11

American Physical Therapy Association. (2016, June 22). Physical therapist (PT) admissions process. http://www.apta.org/ProspectiveStudents/Admissions/PTProcess/

Anders, G. (2015, July 29). That "useless" liberal arts degree has become tech's hottest ticket. *Forbes.* https://www.forbes.com/sites/georgeanders/2015/07/29/liberal-arts-degree-tech/#507dc906745d

Beilock, S. L. (2015). Preparing PhDs for diverse careers. *Inside Higher Ed.* https://www.insidehighered.com/advice/2015/12/18/helping-phds-prepare-diverse-careers-essay

Beilock, S. L. (2017, March 1). Preparing students for diverse careers in our science [Blog post]. *Association for Psychological Science Career Resources.* https://jobs.psychologicalscience.org/blog/11/preparing-students-for-diverse-careers-in-our-science/

Chamberlin, J. (2015, November). Odd jobs: Psychology and aviation. *gradPSYCH Magazine, 13*(4), 28. https://www.apa.org/gradpsych/2015/11/aviation.aspx

Clay, R. A. (2011, November). Odd jobs: Meet a circus psychologist. *gradPSYCH Magazine, 9*(4), 12. https://www.apa.org/gradpsych/2011/11/odd-jobs.aspx

Dahl, W. (2014, March 10). What's the best degree for becoming an entrepreneur? *Great Business Schools: A Guide to the Best Business Programs.* https://www.greatbusinessschools.org/whats-the-best-degree-for-becoming-an-entrepreneur/

Dittmann, M. (2005, September). Creative careers: Some psychologists are using their psychology training in unique ways. *gradPSYCH Magazine, 3*(3). https://www.apa.org/gradpsych/2005/09/cover-careers.aspx

Dittmann, M. (2013). Non-traditional psychology career profiles. In E. Ulloa and K. Cole (Eds.), *Introduction to academic and career opportunities in psychology* (pp. 169–176). Cognella.

Frost, R. (1916). *The road not taken*. Poetry Foundation. https://www.poetryfoundation.org/poems/44272/the-road-not-taken

Golding, J., & Lippert, A. (2016, January 26). Psychology and the law: How this psychology major found his niche in the legal arena [Blog post]. *Psychology Today*. https://www.psychologytoday.com/us/blog/careers-in-psych/201601/psychology-and-the-law

Golding, J., & Lippert, A. (2017, April 19). Preparing for medical school: What should be your major? [Blog post]. *Psychology Today*. https://www.psychologytoday.com/us/blog/careers-in-psych/201704/preparing-medical-school-what-should-be-your-major

Harvard Law School. (2018, August 2). 5 tips for high schoolers thinking about law school. https://hls.harvard.edu/5-tips-for-high-schoolers-thinking-about-law-school/

Hendrix, G. (2011). Choose your own adventure: How *The Cave of Time* taught us to love interactive entertainment. *Slate*. http://www.slate.com/articles/arts/culturebox/2011/02/choose_your_own_adventure.single.html

Hettich, P. (2017, Winter). Increase your odds of employment: Add a career-specific skillset. *Eye on Psi Chi, 21*(2), 4–5. https://www.psichi.org/page/212EyeWin17kHettich

Kong, R. (2017, Spring). Psychology as a stepping stone: Opportunity for further study in medicine. *Eye on Psi Chi, 21*(3), 6–8. https://www.psichi.org/page/213EyeSpr17hKong

Law School Admission Council. (2018). Applicants by major: 2017-2018. https://www.lsac.org/docs/default-source/data-(lsac-resources)-docs/2017-18_applicants-major.pdf

Phillips, I. (2015, August 7). How Jon Stewart went from Jersey kid to one of the most influential comics of all time. *Business Insider*. https://www.businessinsider.com/jon-stewart-bio-2015-8

Stringer, H. (2016, April). Odd jobs: Keeping app users happy. *gradPSYCH Magazine, 14*(2), 32. https://www.apa.org/gradpsych/2016/04/app-users.aspx

Thomas, J. H. (2018, Winter). Careers for psychology majors: What every student should know. *Eye on Psi Chi, 22*(2), 20–23. https://www.psichi.org/page/222EyeWin18aThomas

Zakaria, F. (2015). *In defense of a liberal education*. Norton.

9.7 Resources for Finding Careers

Hannon, K. (2018, November 22). College career centers up their game as parents focus on "outcomes.". *The Seattle Times*. https://www.seattletimes.com/explore/careers/college-career-centers-up-their-game-as-parents-focus-on-outcomes/

Koenig, R. (2018, March 12). How to make the most of your college career center. *U.S. News & World Report*. https://money.usnews.com/money/careers/applying-for-a-job/articles/2018-03-12/how-to-make-the-most-of-your-college-career-center

Norcross, J. C., Hailstorks, R., Aiken, L. S., Pfund, R. A., Stamm, K. E., & Christidis, P. (2016). Undergraduate study in psychology: Curriculum and assessment. *American Psychologist, 71*(2), 89–101. http://dx.doi.org/10.1037/a0040095

Chapter 10

10.1 Networking for Careers

Adeshola, A. (2017, September 13). Three insanely simple email templates for networking with strangers. *Fast Company*. https://www.fastcompany.com/40465285/three-insanely-simple-email-templates-for-networking-with-strangers

Cunningham, L. (2012, December 14). Myers-Briggs: Does it pay to know your type? *The Washington Post*. https://www.washingtonpost.com/national/on-leadership/myers-briggs-does-it-pay-to-know-your-type/2012/12/14/eaed51ae-3fcc-11e2-bca3-aadc9b7e29c5_story.html?noredirect=on&utm_term=.7dac2651e4cd

Cwir, D., Carr, P. B., Walton, G. M., & Spencer, S. J. (2011). Your heart makes my heart move: Cues of social connectedness cause shared emotions and physiological states among strangers. *Journal of Experimental Social Psychology, 47*(3), 661–664. http://dx.doi.org/10.1016/j.jesp.2011.01.009

Fass, C., Turtle, B., & Ginelli, M. (1996). *Six degrees of Kevin Bacon*. Penguin Group.

Ferrazzi, K. (2005). *Never eat alone*. Currency Doubleday.

Huang, G. (2018, March 22). 5 reasons you should attend a virtual career fair. *Forbes*. https://www.forbes.com/sites/georgenehuang/2018/03/22/5-reasons-you-should-attend-a-virtual-career-fair

Isachsen, O., & Berens, L. V. (1995). *Working together: A personality-centered approach to management* (3rd ed.). Institute for Management Development.

Lawson, T. J. (2018). Tapping into alumni as a source of authentic information and advice on careers in psychology. *Teaching of Psychology, 45*(1), 67–74. http://dx.doi.org/10.1177/0098628317745452

Myers, I. B., McCaulley, M. H., Quenk, N. L., & Hammer, A. L. (1998). *MBTI manual: A guide to the development and use of the Myers-Briggs Type Indicator*. CPP.

Ryan, L. (2018, January 5). Ten business buzzwords that make you sound like an idiot. *Forbes*. https://www.forbes.com/sites/lizryan/2018/01/05/ten-business-buzzwords-that-make-you-sound-like-an-idiot

Schwartz, B. M., Gregg, V. R., & McKee, M. (2018). Conversations about careers: Engaging students in and out of the classroom. *Teaching of Psychology, 45*(1), 50–59. http://dx.doi.org/10.1177/0098628317745247

Singh, J., Hansen, M. T., & Podolny, J. M. (2010). The world is not small for everyone: Inequity in searching for knowledge in organizations. *Management Science, 56*(9), 1415–1438. https://doi.org/10.1287/mnsc.1100.1201

Smith, A., & Anderson, M. (2018, March 1). Social media use in 2018: A majority of Americans use Facebook and YouTube, but young adults are especially heavy users of Snapchat and Instagram. *Pew Research Center*. http://www.pewinternet.org/2018/03/01/social-media-use-in-2018/

Waitz, S. (2016, April 28). Alumni mentoring: 3 keys to success [Blog post]. *CASE Blog*. https://blog.case.org/2016/04/28/alumni-mentoring-3-keys-to-success/

Yate, M. (2014, July 8). How job seekers should use job fairs. *Forbes*. https://www.forbes.com/sites/nextavenue/2014/07/08/how-job-seekers-should-use-job-fairs

10.2 Networking Myths

Brown, S. L., Nesse, R. M., Vinokur, A. D., & Smith, D. M. (2003). Providing social support may be more beneficial than receiving it: Results from a prospective study of mortality. *Psychological Science, 14*(4), 320–327. http://dx.doi.org/10.1111/1467-9280.14461

Bunea, E., Khapova, S. N., & Lysova, E. I. (2018, October 8). Why CEOs devote so much time to their hobbies. *Harvard Business Review*. https://hbr.org/2018/10/why-ceos-devote-so-much-time-to-their-hobbies

Carnegie & Associates (2011). *How to win friends and influence people in the digital age*. Simon & Schuster Paperbacks.

Cialdini, R. B. (2008). *Influence: Science and practice* (5th ed.). Allyn & Bacon.

Clifford, C. (2016, September 21). 11 memory hacks to remember the names of everyone you meet. *CNBC*. https://www.cnbc.com/2016/09/21/11-memory-hacks-to-remember-the-names-of-everyone-you-meet.html

Ferrazzi, K. (2005). *Never eat alone*. Currency Doubleday.

Levy, J. (2018, April 20). 8 networking tips for introverts from a superconnector. *Forbes*. https://www.forbes.com/sites/jonlevy/2018/04/20/8-networking-tips-for-introverts-from-a-superconnector

Misner, I. (2018, July 11). How to display the ideal body language when networking. *Entrepreneur*. https://www.entrepreneur.com/article/315358

Newport, C. (2005). *How to win at college: Surprising secrets for success from the country's top students*. Three Rivers Press.

Pollak, L. (2012). *Getting from college to career: Your essential guide to succeeding in the real world* (rev. ed.). Harper.

Samuel, A. (2016, May 5). The more people we connect with on LinkedIn, the less valuable it becomes. *Harvard Business Review*. https://hbr.org/2016/05/the-more-people-we-connect-with-on-linkedin-the-less-valuable-it-becomes

10.3 Conduct an Informational Interview

Bolles, R. N. (2014). *What color is your parachute? 2015: A practical manual for job-hunters and career-changers*. Ten Speed Press.

Burkus, D. (2016, January). *Why you should know how much your coworkers get paid.* [Video]. TED Conferences. https://www.ted.com/talks/david_burkus_why_you_should_know_how_much_your_coworkers_get_paid

Pollak, L. (2012). *Getting from college to career: Your essential guide to succeeding in the real world* (rev. ed.). Harper.

10.4 Internships—Why You Need One

Berger, L. (2018, October 21). The difference between interning at a small company vs. large company. *The Balance Careers.* https://www.thebalancecareers.com/small-vs-large-company-internship-3959662

Ciarocco, N. J. (2018). Traditional and new approaches to career preparation through coursework. *Teaching of Psychology, 45*(1), 32–40. http://dx.doi.org/10.1177/0098628317744963

Doyle, A. (2018, August 20). The best time to apply for an internship. *The Balance Careers.* https://www.thebalancecareers.com/when-to-apply-for-an-internship-2059852

Greenfield, R. (2018, January 13). Unpaid internships are back, with the Labor Department's blessing. *Los Angeles Times.* http://www.latimes.com/business/la-fi-unpaid-internships-20180112-story.html

Heller, J. (1961). *Catch-22.* Simon & Schuster.

Jones, J. (2017, November 2). What would be more valuable than a summer co-op/internship for a current college student? [Blog post]. *Quora.* https://www.quora.com/What-would-be-more-valuable-than-a-summer-co-op-internship-for-a-current-college-student

Kausch, K. (2018, February 26). Dalcourt's Desserts opening first storefront in Hackettstown. *Hackettstown Patch.* https://patch.com/new-jersey/hackettstown/dalcourts-desserts-opening-first-storefront-hackettstown

McHugh, P. P. (2017). The impact of compensation, supervision and work design on internship efficacy: Implications for educators, employers and prospective interns. *Journal of Education and Work, 30*(4), 367–382. https://doi.org/10.1080/13639080.2016.1181729

Mulhere, K. (2016, March 17). 8 super successful businesses that were created by college students. *Money.* http://time.com/money/4243766/successful-businesses-started-by-college-students/

National Association of Colleges and Employers (2017, April 5). Employers prefer candidates with work experience. *NACE Center for Career Development and Talent Acquisition.* http://www.naceweb.org/talent-acquisition/candidate-selection/employers-prefer-candidates-with-work-experience/

National Association of Colleges and Employers (2018a, February 15). Trend is toward paid internships. *NACE Center for Career Development and Talent Acquisition.* https://www.naceweb.org/about-us/press/2018/trend-is-toward-paid-internships/

National Association of Colleges and Employers (2018b, March 1). Type of internship experience affects job offer rates, salary. *NACE Center for Career Development and Talent Acquisition.* http://www.naceweb.org/about-us/press/2018/type-of-internship-experience-affects-job-offer-rates-salary/

Nunley, J. M., Pugh, A., Romero, N., & Seals, R. A., Jr. (2016). College major, internship experience, and employment opportunities: Estimates from a résumé audit. *Labour Economics, 38*, 37–46. https://doi.org/10.1016/j.labeco.2015.11.002

O'Brien, P. S. (2010). *Making college count: A real world look at how to succeed in and after college.* Patrick O'Brien Enterprises.

Pollak, L. (2012). *Getting from college to career: Your essential guide to succeeding in the real world* (rev. ed.). Harper.

Schmiede, A. (2016, November 18). Timing is everything: When to do an internship. *WayUp.* https://www.wayup.com/guide/community/timing-is-everything-when-to-do-an-internship/

Townsley, E., Lierman, L., Watermill, J., & Rousseau, D. (2017). The impact of undergraduate internships on post-graduate outcomes for the liberal arts. *National Association of Colleges and Employers.* https://www.naceweb.org/job-market/internships/the-impact-of-undergraduate-internships-on-post-graduate-outcomes-for-the-liberal-arts/

United States Department of Labor (2018, January). Fact sheet #71: Internship programs under the Fair Labor Standards Act. *Wage and Hour Division (WHD).* https://www.dol.gov/whd/regs/compliance/whdfs71.htm

Vespia, K. M., Freis, S. D., & Arrowood, R. M. (2018). Faculty and career advising: Challenges, opportunities, and outcome assessment. *Teaching of Psychology, 45*(1), 24–31. http://dx.doi.org/10.1177/0098628317744962

10.5 Preparing for Interviews

Backman, M. (2018, November 2). Why you should never discount a job interview. *Fast Company*. https://www.fastcompany.com/90261263/why-you-should-never-discount-a-job-interview

Bessette, L. S. (2013, October 22). Reasons versus excuses: What's the difference? [Blog post]. *Inside Higher Ed*. https://www.insidehighered.com/blogs/college-ready-writing/reasons-versus-excuses

Burrus, J., Jackson, T., Xi, N., & Steinberg, J. (2013, November). Identifying the most important 21st century workforce competencies: An analysis of the Occupational Information Network (O*NET). Research Report: Educational Testing Service: RR-13-21. https://www.ets.org/Media/Research/pdf/RR-13-21.pdf

Ciarocco, N. J., & Strohmetz, D. B. (2018). The employable skills self-efficacy survey: An assessment of skill confidence for psychology undergraduates. *Scholarship of Teaching and Learning in Psychology, 4*(1), 1–15. http://dx.doi.org/10.1037/stl0000102

Daniels, G. (Writer), Forrester, B. (Writer), & Einhorn, R. (Director). (2007). Product recall [Television series episode]. In B. Silverman (Executive producer), *The Office*. NBCUniversal.

David, T. (2016, December 19). Confident or cocky? [Blog post]. *Psychology Today*. https://www.psychologytoday.com/us/blog/the-magic-human-connection/201612/confident-or-cocky

Fuscaldo, D. (2014, January 17). Weird, funny and strange interview questions HR should be asking [Blog post]. *Glassdoor*. https://www.glassdoor.com/employers/blog/why-hr-should-consider-asking-oddball-interview-questions/

Green, A. (2018, November 6). 10 impressive questions to ask in a job interview. *The Cut*. https://www.thecut.com/article/questions-to-ask-in-a-job-interview.html

Koval, R. (2015, August 24). Want to ace a job interview? Be nice to the receptionist. *Fortune*. http://fortune.com/2015/08/24/robin-koval-building-a-strong-team/

Morgan, N. (2015, March 5). The public speaking secrets of comedians. *Forbes*. https://www.forbes.com/sites/nickmorgan/2015/03/05/the-public-speaking-secrets-of-comedians

O'Brien, P. S. (2010). *Making college count: A real world look at how to succeed in and after college*. Patrick O'Brien Enterprises.

Pinola, M. (2012, November 13). Use the STAR technique to ace your interviews. *LifeHacker*. https://lifehacker.com/use-the-star-technique-to-ace-your-interviews-5960201

Pollak, L. (2012). *Getting from college to career: Your essential guide to succeeding in the real world* (rev. ed.). Harper.

Prossack, A. (2018, July 26). How to turn your job interview into a job offer. *Forbes*. https://www.forbes.com/sites/ashiraprossack1/2018/07/26/how-to-turn-your-job-interview-into-a-job-offer

Ryan, L. (2017, March 29). How to answer the "greatest weakness" question. *Forbes*. https://www.forbes.com/sites/lizryan/2017/03/29/how-to-answer-the-greatest-weakness-question

Selingo, J. J. (2015, January 26). Why are so many college students failing to gain job skills before graduation? *The Washington Post*. https://www.washingtonpost.com/news/grade-point/wp/2015/01/26/why-are-so-many-college-students-failing-to-gain-job-skills-before-graduation/

Sezer, O., Gino, F., & Norton, M. I. (2018). Humblebragging: A distinct—and ineffective—self-presentation strategy. *Journal of Personality and Social Psychology, 114*(1), 52–74. http://dx.doi.org/10.1037/pspi0000108

Shaikh, A., & Camparo, L. B. (2018-19, Winter). Real-world skills: How to develop marketable career competencies and sell yourself to employers. *Eye on Psi Chi, 23*(2), 18–22. https://www.psichi.org/page/232EyeWinter18-19Shaikh

Chapter 11

11.1 Is Graduate School Right for You?

Altbach, P. G., Yudkevich, M., & Rumbley, L. E. (2015). Academic inbreeding: Local challenge, global problem. *Asia Pacific Education Review, 16*(3), 317–330. http://dx.doi.org/10.1007/s12564-015-9391-8

Christidis, P., Stamm, K., & Lin, L. (2016, December). Psychology master's and doctoral degrees awarded by broad field, subfield, institution type and state (2004–2013): Findings from the integrated postsecondary education data system. *American Psychological Association Center for Workplace Studies*. https://www.apa.org/workforce/publications/2016-postsecondary-data/report.pdf

Fowler, G., Cope, C., Michalski, D., Christidis, P., Lin, L., & Conroy, J. (2018, December). Women outnumber men in psychology graduate programs. *Monitor on Psychology, 49*(11), 21. https://www.apa.org/monitor/2018/12/datapoint.aspx

Ginat, D. (2005). The suitable way is backwards, but they work forward. *Journal of Computers in Mathematics and Science Teaching, 24*(1), 73–88.

Hamby, S. (2015, July 28). Should you take a gap year before grad school? [Blog post]. *Psychology Today*. https://www.psychologytoday.com/us/blog/the-web-violence/201507/should-you-take-gap-year-grad-school

Henry, A. (2014, July 23). Seven things I wish I knew before going to graduate school. *Lifehacker*. https://lifehacker.com/seven-things-i-wish-i-knew-before-going-to-graduate-sch-1609488711

Klatzky, R. L. (2012, November). When it comes to department name, "Psychology" is #1. *APS Observer*. https://www.psychologicalscience.org/observer/when-it-comes-to-department-names-psychology-is-1

Lin, L., Stamm, K., & Christidis, P. (2018, February). How diverse is the psychology workforce? *Monitor on Psychology, 49*(2), 18. https://www.apa.org/monitor/2018/02/datapoint.aspx

Metz, K. (2016). *Careers in mental health: Opportunities in psychology, counseling, and social work*. Wiley-Blackwell.

Pinto-Powell, R. (2018, December 20). Imposter syndrome: Not exclusive to women. *Inside HigherEd*. https://www.insidehighered.com/views/2018/12/20/what-colleges-can-do-help-students-avoid-impostor-syndrome-opinion

Revuluri, S. (2018, October 4). How to overcome imposter syndrome. *Chronicle of Higher Education*. https://www.chronicle.com/article/How-to-Overcome-Impostor/244700

Ruben, A. (2010). *Surviving your stupid, stupid decision to go to grad school*. Broadway Books.

Thompson, J. A., & Fitzgerald, C. J. (2017, Fall). Some factors to consider before attending graduate school: Intrinsic, extrinsic, and unconscious motivators. *Eye on Psi Chi, 22*(1), 20–22. https://www.psichi.org/page/221EyeFall17cThompso

Uscher, J. (2011, September). Applier beware. *gradPSYCH Magazine, 9*(3), 22. https://www.apa.org/gradpsych/2011/09/applier.aspx

Vonk, L. (2017, April 5). I was rejected by every PhD program I applied to. This year I got into my top choice. Here's how. *Quartz*. https://qz.com/950763/how-to-get-into-graduate-school-according-to-current-phd-students/

11.2 Types of Degrees and Programs

American Psychological Association. (2018). Degree pathways in psychology [interactive data tool]. https://www.apa.org/workforce/data-tools/degrees-pathways.aspx

Castelnuovo, G. (2010). No medicine without psychology: The key role of psychological contribution in clinical settings. *Frontiers in Psychology, 1*(4), 4. https://dx.doi.org/10.3389/fpsyg.2010.00004

Christidis, P., Stamm, K., & Lin, L. (2016, December). Psychology master's and doctoral degrees awarded by broad field, subfield, institution type and state (2004–2013): Findings from the integrated postsecondary education data system. *American Psychological Association Center for Workplace Studies*. https://www.apa.org/workforce/publications/2016-postsecondary-data/report.pdf

Fowler, G., Zlotlow, S., & Hailstorks, R. (2014, January). Four questions to ask before applying to graduate school. *American Psychological Association Psychology Student Network*. https://www.apa.org/ed/precollege/psn/2014/01/applying-graduate.aspx

Golding, J., & Lippert, A. (2016a, January 26). Psychology and the law: How this psychology major found his niche in the legal arena. [Blog post]. *Psychology Today*. https://www.psychologytoday.com/us/blog/careers-in-psych/201601/psychology-and-the-law

Golding, J., & Lippert, A. (2016b, March 2). Choosing between a PhD and a PsyD: Some factors to consider. [Blog post]. *Psychology Today*. https://www.psychology

today.com/us/blog/careers-in-psych/201603/choosing-between-phd-and-psyd-some-factors-consider

Kong, R. (2017, Spring). Psychology as a stepping stone: Opportunity for further study in medicine. *Eye on Psi Chi, 21*(3), 6–8. https://www.psichi.org/page/213EyeSpr17hKong

Kuther, T. (2018, December 27). Pros and cons of earning a master's degree before a PhD. *ThoughtCo.* https://www.thoughtco.com/earning-a-masters-degree-before-your-phd-1685786

Littleford, L. N., Buxton, K., Bucher, M. A., Simon-Dack, S. L., & Yang, K. L. (2018). Psychology doctoral program admissions: What master's and undergraduate-level students need to know. *Teaching of Psychology, 45*(1), 75–83. http://dx.doi.org/10.1177/0098628317745453

Lorenz, N. T. (2014, Spring/Summer). Lessons learned from a law school graduate with a psychology degree. *Eye on Psi Chi, 18*(3), 26–27. https://www.psichi.org/page/183EyeSprSum14bLoren

Metz, K. (2016). *Careers in mental health: Opportunities in psychology, counseling, and social work.* Wiley-Blackwell.

Michalski, D. S., Cope, C., & Fowler, G. A. (2017, December). Graduate study in psychology 2018 summary report: Admissions, applications, and acceptances. *American Psychological Association Graduate and Postgraduate Education.* https://www.apa.org/education/grad/survey-data/2018-admissions-applications.aspx

Michalski, D. S., Cope, C., & Fowler, G. A. (2019, March). Graduate study in psychology 2019 summary report: Admissions, applications, and acceptances. *American Psychological Association Graduate and Postgraduate Education.* https://www.apa.org/education/grad/survey-data/2019-admissions-applications.pdf

Michalski, D. S., & Fowler, G. (2016, January). Doctoral degrees in psychology: How are they different, or not so different? *American Psychological Association Psychology Student Network.* https://www.apa.org/ed/precollege/psn/2016/01/doctoral-degrees.aspx

National Center for Educational Statistics (2010). Classification of instructional programs: Code 42 psychology. https://nces.ed.gov/ipeds/cipcode/cipdetail.aspx?y=55&cipid=88525

Nauert, R. (2015). Psychocardiology: New medical specialty proposed for depression, heart disease. *Psych Central.* https://psychcentral.com/news/2013/02/19/psychocardiology-new-medical-specialty-proposed-for-depression-heart-disease/51767.html

Norcross, J. C., Ellis, J. L., & Sayette, M. A. (2010). Getting in and getting money: A comparative analysis of admission standards, acceptance rates, and financial assistance across the research-practice continuum in clinical psychology programs. *Training and Education in Professional Psychology, 4*(2), 99–104. http://dx.doi.org/10.1037/a0014880

Pelham, B. (2019). Doing postdoctoral work—should I? *American Psychological Association Academic Careers.* https://www.apa.org/careers/resources/academic/postdoc-work.aspx

Rubin, A. (2013, November 21). The postdoc: A special kind of hell. *Science Magazine.* https://www.sciencemag.org/careers/2013/11/postdoc-special-kind-hell

Williams-Nickelson, C., Prinstein, M., & Keilin, W. G. (2018). *Internships in psychology: The APAGS workbook for writing successful applications and finding the right fit* (4th ed.). American Psychological Association. https://doi.org/10.1037/0000102-000

11.3 Finding Graduate Programs

American Psychological Association. (2018). Degrees in psychology [interactive data tool]. https://www.apa.org/workforce/data-tools/degrees-psychology.aspx

APA Presidential Task Force on Evidence-Based Practice (2006). Evidence-based practice in psychology. *American Psychologist, 61*(4), 271–285. https://doi.org/10.1037/0003-066X.61.4.271

Birchmeier, Z., Shore, C., & McCormick, S. (2008, Summer). Getting in: Finding your fit in a graduate program. *Eye on Psi Chi, 12*(4), 24–27. https://www.psichi.org/page/124EyeSum08bBirchmei

Bruni, F. (2015). *Where you go is not who you'll be: An antidote to the college admissions mania.* Grand Central.

Callahan, J. L., Collins, F. L., Jr., & Klonoff, E. A. (2010). An examination of applicant characteristics of successfully matched interns: Is the glass half empty or half full or leaking miserably? *Journal of Clinical Psychology, 66*(1), 1–16. https://doi.org/10.1002/jclp.20664

Clauset, A., Arbesman, S., & Larremore, D. B. (2015). Systematic inequality and hierarchy in faculty hiring networks. *Science Advances, 1*(1), e1400005. https://dx.doi.org/10.1126/sciadv.1400005

Division 12 of the American Psychological Association (2016). Psychological treatments. *Society of Clinical Psychology Division 12 of the American Psychological Association*. https://www.div12.org/treatments/

Graham, J. M., & Kim, Y. (2011). Predictors of doctoral success in professional psychology: Characteristics of students, programs, and universities. *Journal of Clinical Psychology, 67*(4), 350–354. https://doi.org/10.1002/jclp.20767

Michalski, D. S., Cope, C., & Fowler, G. A. (2015, September). Graduate study in psychology 2016 summary report: Admissions, applications, and acceptances. *American Psychological Association Graduate and Postgraduate Education*. https://www.apa.org/education/grad/survey-data/2016-report.aspx

Michalski, D. S., Cope, C., & Fowler, G. A. (2016, August). Graduate study in psychology 2017 summary report: Admissions, applications, and acceptances. *American Psychological Association Graduate and Postgraduate Education*. https://www.apa.org/education/grad/survey-data/2017-admissions-applications.aspx

Michalski, D. S., Cope, C., & Fowler, G. A. (2017, December). Graduate study in psychology 2018 summary report: Admissions, applications, and acceptances. *American Psychological Association Graduate and Postgraduate Education*. https://www.apa.org/education/grad/survey-data/2018-admissions-applications.aspx

Michalski, D. S., Cope, C., & Fowler, G. A. (2019, March). Graduate study in psychology 2019 summary report: Admissions, applications, and acceptances. *American Psychological Association Graduate and Postgraduate Education*. https://www.apa.org/education/grad/survey-data/2019-admissions-applications.pdf

Norcross, J. C., Ellis, J. L., & Sayette, M. A. (2010). Getting in and getting money: A comparative analysis of admission standards, acceptance rates, and financial assistance across the research-practice continuum in clinical psychology programs. *Training and Education in Professional Psychology, 4*(2), 99–104. http://dx.doi.org/10.1037/a0014880

Norcross, J. C., & Karpiak, C. P. (2015, Spring). Applying to doctoral programs in clinical psychology: Buyer beware. *Eye on Psi Chi, 19*(3), 15–17. https://www.psichi.org/page/193EyeSpr15hNorcross

Ritzer, D. R. (2018, Fall). Finding a mentor. *Eye on Psi Chi, 23*(1), 18–22. https://www.psichi.org/page/231EyeFall18Ritzer

Scott, D. (2016, November 8). Choosing the right advisor [Blogpost]. *Inside Higher Ed*. https://www.insidehighered.com/blogs/gradhacker/choosing-right-advisor

Simon, C. (2018, March 19). For-profit colleges' teachable moment: "Terrible outcomes are very profitable." *Forbes*. https://www.forbes.com/sites/schoolboard/2018/03/19/for-profit-colleges-teachable-moment-terrible-outcomes-are-very-profitable/

Wai, J. (2014). Investigating the world's rich and powerful: Education, cognitive ability, and sex differences. *Intelligence, 46*, 54–72. http://dx.doi.org/10.1016/j.intell.2014.05.002

Warner, J., & Clauset, A. (2015, February 23). The academy's dirty secret: An astonishingly small number of elite universities produce an overwhelming number of America's professors. *Slate*. https://slate.com/human-interest/2015/02/university-hiring-if-you-didn-t-get-your-ph-d-at-an-elite-university-good-luck-finding-an-academic-job.html

Woolston, C. (2017). Graduate survey: A love-hurt relationship. *Nature, 550*, 549–552. https://doi.org/10.1038/nj7677-549a

Zimmerman, L. (2017, January). Seven steps to finding the right advisor. *Monitor on Psychology, 48*(1), 58. https://www.apa.org/monitor/2017/01/right-advisor

11.4 How Graduate School Differs from Undergraduate Studies

Freis, S. D., & Kraha, A. (2016, Fall). You're not in Kansas anymore: How grad school is different than undergrad. *Eye on Psi Chi, 21*(1), 4–5. https://www.psichi.org/page/211EyeFall16dFreis

Kraha, A., Freis, S. D., & Longstreth, M. E. (2017, Fall). You're not in Kansas anymore: More ways that grad school is different than undergrad. *Eye on Psi Chi, 22*(1), 8–10. https://www.psichi.org/page/221EyeFall17hKraha

Littleford, L. N., Buxton, K., Bucher, M. A., Simon-Dack, S. L., & Yang, K. L. (2018). Psychology doctoral program admissions: What master's and undergraduate-level students need to know. *Teaching of Psychology, 45*(1), 75–83. http://dx.doi.org/10.1177/0098628317745453

Sinche, M. V. (2016). *Next gen PhD*. Harvard University Press. https://doi.org/10.4159/9780674974791

11.5 Grad Students Describe Their Experiences

Woolston, C. (2017). Graduate survey: A love-hurt relationship. *Nature, 550*, 549–552. https://doi.org/10.1038/nj7677-549a

Chapter 12

12.1 What Do Graduate Programs Want?

American Psychological Association. (2013). *APA guidelines for the undergraduate psychology major: Version 2.0*. https://www.apa.org/ed/precollege/about/psymajor-guidelines.pdf

Appleby, D. C., & Appleby, K. M. (2017, Winter). Letters of recommendation for graduate school Part I of III: Purpose, preparation, and procedure. *Eye on Psi Chi, 21*(2), 21–25. https://www.psichi.org/page/212EyeWin17cAppleby

Appleby, D. C., Keenan, J., & Mauer, E. (1999, Spring). Applicant characteristics valued by graduate programs in psychology. *Eye on Psi Chi, 3*(3), 39. http://www.psichi.org/? page=033EyeSpr99fAppleby

Charlton, S. R., Ozanich, C., & Phillips, N. (2017, Spring). Conquering graduate application dread: Advice from graduate faculty. *Eye on Psi Chi, 21*(3), 22–25. https://www.psichi.org/page/213EyeSpr17eCharlton

Jaschik, S. (2016, March 29). Grade inflation, higher and higher. *Inside Higher Ed*. https://www.insidehighered.com/news/2016/03/29/survey-finds-grade-inflation-continues-rise-four-year-colleges-not-community-college

Kashdan, T. B. (2015, January 7). 7 tips for applying to a psychology PhD program [Blog post]. *Psychology Today*. https://www.psychologytoday.com/us/blog/curious/201501/7-tips-applying-psychology-phd-program

Littleford, L. N., Buxton, K., Bucher, M. A., Simon-Dack, S. L., & Yang, K. L. (2018). Psychology doctoral program admissions: What master's and undergraduate-level students need to know. *Teaching of Psychology, 45*(1), 75–83. http://dx.doi.org/10.1177/0098628317745453

Norcross, J. C., & Cannon, J. T. (2008, Fall). You're writing your own letter of recommendation. *Eye on Psi Chi, 13*(1), 24–28. https://www.psichi.org/page/131EyeFall08bNorcros

Norcross, J. C., Sayette, M. A., Stratigis, K. Y., & Zimmerman, B. E. (2014). Of course: Prerequisite courses for admission into APA-accredited clinical and counseling psychology programs. *Teaching of Psychology, 41*(4), 360–364. http://dx.doi.org/10.1177/0098628314549713

Pashak, T. J., Handal, P. J., & Ubinger, M. (2012). Practicing what we preach: How are admissions decisions made for clinical psychology graduate programs, and what do students need to know? *Psychology, 3*(1), 1–6. http://dx.doi.org/10.4236/psych.2012.31001

12.2 The Grad School Application Process

Council of Graduate Schools. (2019). April 15 resolution: Resolution regarding graduate scholars, fellows, trainees, and assistants. *Council of Graduate Schools*. https://cgsnet.org/april-15-resolution

Handelsman, M. M., VanderStoep, S. W., & Landrum, R. E., (2012, Winter). Questions (and answers) about graduate school. *Eye on Psi Chi, 16*(2), 12–15. https://www.psichi.org/page/162EyeWin12dHandelsm

Harvard Business Review (2013). *HBR guide to project management*. Harvard Business Review Press.

Jaschik, S. (2015, December 21). Lost fees or lost students? *Inside Higher Ed*. https://www.insidehighered.com/news/2015/12/21/potential-grad-applicant-nyu-goes-public-email-turning-down-fee-waiver-request

Martin, D. (2012, November 12). Grad school application checklist: 12 months out [Blog post]. *U.S. News and World Report*. https://www.usnews.com/education/blogs/graduate-school-road-map/2012/11/12/grad-school-application-checklist-12-months-out

Urban, T. (2016, February). *Inside the mind of a master procrastinator* [Video]. TED Conferences. https://www.ted.com/talks/tim_urban_inside_the_mind_of_a_master_procrastinator

Wiggins, G., & McTighe, J. (2005). *Understanding by design* (2nd ed.). ASCD.

12.3 Letters of Recommendation

American Psychological Association. (2018). *Graduate study in psychology*. American Psychological Association.

Appleby, D. C., & Appleby, K. M. (2006). Kisses of death in the graduate school application process. *Teaching of Psychology, 33*(1), 19–24. http://dx.doi.org/10.1207/s15328023top3301_5

Appleby, D. C., & Appleby, K. M. (2017a, Winter). Letters of recommendation for graduate school Part I of III: Purpose, preparation, and procedure. *Eye on Psi Chi, 21*(2), 21–25. https://www.psichi.org/page/212EyeWin17cAppleby

Appleby, D. C., & Appleby, K. M. (2017b, Spring). Letters of recommendation for graduate school Part II of III: Six paragons. *Eye on Psi Chi, 21*(3), 32–36. https://www.psichi.org/page/213EyeSpr17gAppleby

Appleby, D. C., & Appleby, K. M. (2017c, Summer). Letters of recommendation for graduate school Part III of III: The final six paragons. *Eye on Psi Chi, 21*(4), 28–32. https://www.psichi.org/page/214EyeSum17bAppleby

Gomez, J. (2016, Spring). How to properly request letters of recommendation from your professors: Ask, don't tell. *Eye on Psi Chi, 20*(3), 12–15. https://www.psichi.org/page/203EyeSpr16cGomez

Kashdan, T. B. (2015, January 7). 7 tips for applying to a psychology PhD program [Blog post]. *Psychology Today.* https://www.psychologytoday.com/us/blog/curious/201501/7-tips-applying-psychology-phd-program

Kruger, J., & Dunning, D. (1999). Unskilled and unaware of it: How difficulties in recognizing one's own incompetence lead to inflated self-assessments. *Journal of Personality and Social Psychology, 77*(6), 1121–1134. http://dx.doi.org/10.1037/0022-3514.77.6.1121

Nauta, M. M. (2000). Assessing the accuracy of psychology undergraduates' perceptions of graduate admission criteria. *Teaching of Psychology, 27*(4), 277–280.

Norcross, J. C., Kohout, J. L., & Wicherski, M. (2006, Winter). Graduate admissions in psychology: I. The application process. *Eye on Psi Chi, 10*(2), 28–29. https://www.psichi.org/page/102EyeWin06bNorcross

12.4 The Graduate Record Exam

American Psychological Association. (2018). *Graduate study in psychology.* American Psychological Association.

Asbury, T. (2011, Fall). Revisions in Graduate Record Exam bring good news. *Eye on Psi Chi, 16*(1), 18–19. https://www.psichi.org/page/161EyeFall11bAsbury

Bridgeman, B., Burton, N., & Cline, F. (2008). Understanding what the numbers mean: A straightforward approach to GRE predictive validity. *ETS GRE Board Research Report No. 04-03 ETS RR-08-46.* https://onlinelibrary.wiley.com/doi/epdf/10.1002/j.2333-8504.2008.tb02132.x

Burton, N. W., & Wang, M. (2005). Predicting long-term success in graduate school: A collaborative validity study. *GRE Board Report No. 99-14R ETS RR-05-03.* https://onlinelibrary.wiley.com/doi/epdf/10.1002/j.2333-8504.2005.tb01980.x

Clayton, V. (2016, March 1). The problem with the GRE: The exam "is a proxy for asking 'Are you rich?' 'Are you white?' 'Are you male?'" *The Atlantic.* https://www.theatlantic.com/education/archive/2016/03/the-problem-with-the-gre/471633/

Educational Testing Service. (2018). About the GRE General test. *ETS GRE.* https://www.ets.org/gre/revised_general/about

Gomez, J. (2011, Fall). Bring it on: Preparing for the Graduate Record Examination (GRE). *Eye on Psi Chi, 16*(1), 21–23. https://www.psichi.org/page/161EyeFall11aGomez

Kaplan. (2019). 5 tips for taking the GRE again to raise your score. *Kaplan.* https://www.kaptest.com/study/gre/5-tips-for-taking-the-gre-again-to-raise-your-score/

Kornell, N., Castel, A. D., Eich, T. S., & Bjork, R. A. (2010). Spacing as the friend of both memory and induction in young and older adults. *Psychology & Aging, 25*(2), 498–503. http://dx.doi.org/10.1037/a0017807

Kuo, M. (2017, January 11). Student performance measures that don't perform. *Science.* http://www.sciencemag.org/careers/2017/01/student-performance-measures-don-t-perform

Lambert, N. (2013, October 28). Five truths about graduate school that nobody tells you [Blog post]. *Psychology Today.* https://www.psychologytoday.com/us/blog/publish-and-prosper/201310/five-truths-about-graduate-school-nobody-tells-you

Mahr, D. (2016, July 17). Seven-week GRE study plan [Blog post]. http://dmahr.com/2016/07/seven-week-gre-study-plan/

Marton, R. (2014, March 18). GRE and graduate school success: The key is in the writing [Blog post]. *PLoS Early Career Researcher Community.* https://blogs.plos

.org/thestudentblog/2014/03/18/gre-graduate-school-success-key-writing/

McGonigal, J. (2010, February). *Gaming can make a better world* [Video file]. TED Conferences. https://www.ted.com/talks/jane_mcgonigal_gaming_can_make_a_better_world

Miller, C., & Stassun, K. (2014). A test that fails. *Nature, 510*, 303–304. https://doi.org/10.1038/nj7504-303a

Roediger, H. L., & Karpicke, J. D. (2006). The power of testing memory: Basic research and implications for educational practice. *Perspectives on Psychological Science, 1*(3), 181–210. http://dx.doi.org/10.1111/j.1745-6916.2006.00012.x

Thomas, J. H. (2018, Winter). Careers for psychology majors: What every student should know. *Eye on Psi Chi, 22*(2), 20-23. https://www.psichi.org/page/222EyeWin18aThomas

12.5 Personal Statements and Essays

Ahlin, C. (2017, March 13). 12 tips for getting feedback on your writing. *Bustle*. https://www.bustle.com/p/12-tips-for-getting-feedback-on-your-writing-43119

Appleby, D. C., & Appleby, K. M. (2006). Kisses of death in the graduate school application process. *Teaching of Psychology, 33*(1), 19–24. http://dx.doi.org/10.1207/s15328023top3301_5

Bessette, L. S. (2013, October 22). Reasons versus excuses: What's the difference? [Blog post]. *Inside Higher Ed*. https://www.insidehighered.com/blogs/college-ready-writing/reasons-versus-excuses

Brown, R. M. (2004). Self-composed: Rhetoric in psychology personal statements. *Written Communication, 21*(3), 242–260. http://dx.doi.org/10.1177/0741088304264338

Davis, K. M., Doll, J. F., & Sterner, W. R. (2018). The importance of personal statements in counselor education and psychology doctoral program applications. *Teaching of Psychology, 45*(3), 256–263. http://dx.doi.org/10.1177/0098628318779273

Klieger, D. M., Bridgeman, B., Tannenbaum, R. J., Cline, F. A., & Olivera-Aguilar, M. (2018). The validity of GRE General test scores for predicting academic performance at U.S. law schools. *ETS Research Report No. RR-18-26*. https://onlinelibrary.wiley.com/doi/epdf/10.1002/ets2.12213

Ritzer, D. R., & Sleigh, M. J. (2017, Spring). The link between letters of recommendation and the personal statement. *Eye on Psi Chi, 21*(3), 18–20. https://www.psichi.org/page/213EyeSPR17cRitzer

12.6 Interviews and the Acceptance or Rejection Decisions

Burke, K. C., & Bottoms, B. L. (2017a, Winter). You're admitted! But which program should you attend? Part I of II. *Eye on Psi Chi, 21*(2), 18–20. https://www.psichi.org/page/212EyeWin17dBurke

Burke, K. C., & Bottoms, B. L. (2017b, Spring). You're admitted! But which program should you attend? Part II of II. *Eye on Psi Chi, 21*(3), 29–31. https://www.psichi.org/page/213EyeSpr17fBurke

Burnett, B., & Evans, D. (2016). *Designing your life: How to build a well-lived joyful life*. Alfred A. Knopf.

Council of Graduate Schools. (2019). April 15 resolution: Resolution regarding graduate scholars, fellows, trainees, and assistants. *Council of Graduate Schools*. https://cgsnet.org/april-15-resolution

Gilovich, T., & Medvec, V. H. (1995). The experience of regret: What, when, and why. *Psychological Review, 102*(2), 379–395. http://dx.doi.org/10.1037/0033-295X.102.2.379

Handelsman, M. M., VanderStoep, S. W., & Landrum, R. E., (2012, Winter). Questions (and answers) about graduate school. *Eye on Psi Chi, 16*(2), 12–15. https://www.psichi.org/page/162EyeWin12dHandelsm

Morin, A. (2015, April 3). 7 scientifically proven benefits of gratitude [Blog post]. *Psychology Today*. https://www.psychologytoday.com/us/blog/what-mentally-strong-people-dont-do/201504/7-scientifically-proven-benefits-gratitude

Petty, T. (1981). The waiting. On *Hard promises* [CD]. Backstreet Records.

Ritzer, D. R. (2018, Fall). Finding a mentor. *Eye on Psi Chi, 23*(1), 18–22. https://www.psichi.org/page/231EyeFall18Ritzer

Sleigh, M., & Ritzer, D. (2015, Spring). I got into graduate school! Now what? *Eye on Psi Chi, 19*(3), 10–14. https://www.psichi.org/page/193EyeSpr15gSleigh

Zadra, D., & Wills, K. (2009). *5: Where will you be five years from today?* Compendium.

Chapter 13

13.1 Résumé Tips

Bahler, K. (2018, January 2). What your résumé should look like in 2018. *Money*. http://money.com/money/5053350/resume-tips-free-template/

Career Builder (2014, March 13). Hiring managers rank best and worst words to use in a résumé in new CareerBuilder survey. *Career Builder*. http://www.careerbuilder.com/share/aboutus/pressreleasesdetail.aspx?id=pr809&sd=3/13/2014&ed=03/13/2014

Doyle, A. (2018, December 10). Guidelines for what to include in a resume. *The Balance Careers*. https://www.thebalancecareers.com/guidelines-for-what-to-include-in-a-resume-2061035

Doyle, A. (2019, February 16). What not to include when you're writing a résumé. *The Balance Careers*. https://www.thebalancecareers.com/what-not-to-include-in-your-resume-2063284

Elliott, M. (2018, November 19). Lying on your résumé? Here's how you'll get caught [Blog post]. *Glass Door*. https://www.glassdoor.com/blog/lying-on-your-resume/

Hernandez, J. H. (2018, November 14). 12 résumé writing tips for 2019. *Medium*. https://medium.com/@GreatResumes/12-resume-writing-tips-for-2019-e022e820c477

Lewis, F. (2017, August 16). Chronological vs. functional résumé: Which is right for you? [Blog post]. *JobCluster*. https://www.jobcluster.com/blog/chronological-resume-vs-functional-resume/

Marr, B. (2019, March 25). How to write a résumé to appeal to robot recruiters. *Forbes*. https://www.forbes.com/sites/bernardmarr/2019/03/25/how-to-write-a-resume-to-appeal-to-robot-recruiters

O'Donnell, J. T. (2018, April 3). This 1 résumé mistake makes you look like a liar to hiring managers. *Inc*. https://www.inc.com/jt-odonnell/do-you-look-like-a-liar-on-your-resume-this-1-mistake-could-be-why.html

Reilly, K. (2016, April 21). 7 LinkedIn profile summaries that we love (and how to boost your own) [Blog post]. *LinkedIn Talent Blog*. https://business.linkedin.com/talent-solutions/blog/linkedin-best-practices/2016/7-linkedin-profile-summaries-that-we-love-and-how-to-boost-your-own

Shields, J. (2017, November 6). Why recruiters HATE the functional résumé format [Blog post]. *Jobscan Blog*. https://www.jobscan.co/blog/recruiters-functional-resume-format/

Wade, R. (2017, October 2). The dreaded LinkedIn summary . . . some tips for students [Blog post]. *NACE Blog*. http://community.naceweb.org/blogs/ross-wade/2017/10/02/the-dreaded-linkedin-summarysome-tips-for-students

Waters, B. (2016, May 11). 10 tips for an awesome résumé [Blog post]. *Psychology Today*. https://www.psychologytoday.com/us/blog/design-your-path/201605/10-tips-awesome-resume

13.2 Constructing Your Curriculum Vitae (CV)

Dittman, M. (2003, September). CV dos and don'ts. *gradPSYCH Magazine, 1*(2). https://www.apa.org/gradpsych/2003/09/cv

Doyle, A. (2019, February 14). Academic curriculum vitae (CV) example and writing tips. *The Balance Careers*. https://www.thebalancecareers.com/academic-curriculum-vitae-example-2060817

Greenbaum, H. (2018, April 2). How to format your CV or résumé [Blog post]. *APA Style Blog*. https://blog.apastyle.org/apastyle/2018/04/how-to-format-your-cv-or-resume.html

Smith, B. L. (2015, January). Build a better CV. *gradPSYCH Magazine, 13*(1), 28. https://www.apa.org/gradpsych/2015/01/curriculum-vitae

Zlokovich, M. S. (2010, Fall). Update your chapter: We're international and so are you! *Eye on Psi Chi, 15*(1), 5. https://www.psichi.org/page/151EYEFall10iZlokov

13.3 Building a Portfolio

Birkett, M., Neff, L., & Pieper, S. (2013, February). Portfolios in psychology classes. *Observer, 26*(2). https://www.psychologicalscience.org/observer/portfolios-in-psychology-classes

Hettich, P. (2016, Fall). Program your GPS: Guidelines to proficiency in skills for work and career. *Eye on Psi Chi, 21*(1), 20–24. https://www.psichi.org/page/211EyeFall16cHettich

Hettich, P. (2019, Spring). Planning your first postcollege job: Underemployment and what to do about it. *Eye on Psi Chi, 23*(3), 10–13. https://www.psichi.org/page/233EyeSpring19Hettich

Leahy, R. L., & Filiatrault, A. (2017). Employers' perceptions of the benefits of employment electronic portfolios. *International Journal of ePortfolios, 7*(2), 217–223.

Ring, G. L., Waugaman, C., & Brackett, B. (2017). The value of career eportfolios on job applicant performance: Using data to determine effectiveness. *International Journal of ePortfolio, 7*(2), 225–236.

Scartabello, T., Abate, M., & Slimak, L. (2018). Impact of a portfolio program on self-assessment skills involving general longitudinal outcomes. *International Journal of ePortfolio, 8*(2), 103–114.

Strang, T. (2015, April 29). Three reasons eportfolios matter to today's college students [Blog post]. *Cengage.* https://blog.cengage.com/three-reasons-eportfolios-matter-to-todays-college-students/

Watson, C. E., Kuh, G. D., Rhodes, T., Light, T. P., & Chen, H. L. (2016). Editorial: ePortfolios—the eleventh high impact practice. *International Journal of ePortfolio, 6*(2), 65–69.

Wilson, C. B., Slade, C., Kirby, M. M., Downer, T., Fisher, M. B., & Nuessler, S. (2018). Digital ethics and the use of eportfolio: A scoping review of the literature. *International Journal of ePortfolio, 8*(2), 115–125.

13.4 Your Online Presence—Social Media (LinkedIn) and Personal Websites

Babbitt, M. S. (2016, October 19). 30 things college students should be doing on LinkedIn right now. *LinkedIn.* https://www.linkedin.com/pulse/30-things-college-students-should-doing-linkedin-right-babbitt

Frost, A. (2019). Can a personal website help your job search? What 6 hiring managers really think. *The Muse.* https://www.themuse.com/advice/can-a-personal-website-help-your-job-search-what-6-hiring-managers-really-think

Garriott, O. (2015, February 6). 10 LinkedIn tips for students & new grads. *LinkedIn.* https://www.linkedin.com/pulse/10-tips-students-new-grads-linkedin-omar-garriott

Han, E. (2018, April 5). LinkedIn 101: Why you should use LinkedIn. *The Balance Careers.* https://www.thebalancecareers.com/linkedin-101-the-why-of-linkedin-2062334

Ryan, L. (2018, February 14). Ten things never, ever to put in your LinkedIn profile. *Forbes.* https://www.forbes.com/sites/lizryan/2018/02/14/ten-things-never-ever-to-put-in-your-linkedin-profile/#7d726d9a35e6

Smith, J. (2015, January 14). Here's why every job seeker should have a personal website—and what it should include. *Business Insider.* https://www.businessinsider.com/job-seekers-need-personal-website-2015-1

Vasel, K. (2018, August 14). Is the résumé dead? *CNN Business.* https://www.cnn.com/2018/09/30/success/resume-dead-job-search/index.html

Chapter 14

14.1 Why Are We Talking About Money?

Boyington, B. (2018, September 13). See 20 years of tuition growth at national universities. *U.S. News & World Report.* https://www.usnews.com/education/best-colleges/paying-for-college/articles/2017-09-20/see-20-years-of-tuition-growth-at-national-universities

Britt, S. L., Klontz, B. T., Tibbetts, R., & Leitz, L. (2015). The financial health of mental health professionals. *Journal of Financial Therapy, 6*(1), 17–32. https://doi.org/10.4148/1944-9771.1076

Carnevale, A. P., Smith, N., Melton, M., & Price, E. W. (2015). *Learning while earning: The new normal.* Georgetown University Center on Education and the Workforce. https://1gyhoq479ufd3yna29x7ubjn-wpengine.netdna-ssl.com/wp-content/uploads/Working-Learners-Report.pdf

Christidis, P., Lin, L., & Stamm, K. (2018, September). How does psychology doctorates' debt stack up? *Monitor on Psychology, 49*(8), 19. https://www.apa.org/monitor/2018/09/datapoint

Christidis, P., Manjarrez, D., Stamm, K., & Lin, L. (2015, December). How much (and what kind of) financial aid do undergraduate psychology majors receive? *Monitor on Psychology, 46*(11), 16. https://www.apa.org/monitor/2015/12/datapoint

Clay, R. A. (2018, September). Running start . . . to a great career: Paying off student loans. *American Psychological*

Association Services, Inc. https://www.apaservices.org/practice/business/ecp-column/paying-student-loan?_ga=2.119819080.1946775139.1562610506-1475720771.1561150045

Clay, R. A. (2019, January). New hope for a troubled loan program. *Monitor on Psychology, 50*(1), 22. https://www.apa.org/monitor/2019/01/loan-program

Doran, J. M., Kraha, A., Marks, L. R., Ameen, E. J., & El-Ghoroury, N. H. (2016). Graduate debt in psychology: A quantitative analysis. *Training and Education in Professional Psychology, 10*(1), 3–13. https://doi.org/10.1037/tep0000112

Dundes, L., & Marx, J. (2006). Balancing work and academics in college: Why do students working 10 to 19 hours per week excel? *Journal of College Student Retention: Research, Theory, & Practice, 8*(1), 107–120. https://doi.org/10.2190/7UCU-8F9M-94QG-5WWQ

Friedman, Z. (2018a, June 13). Student loan debt statistics in 2018: A $1.5 trillion crisis. *Forbes.* https://www.forbes.com/sites/zackfriedman/2018/06/13/student-loan-debt-statistics-2018/

Friedman, Z. (2018b, October 16). Here are the 5 biggest student loan mistakes of 2018. *Forbes.* https://www.forbes.com/sites/zackfriedman/2018/10/16/student-loans-mistakes/

Hoffower, H. (2018, July 8). College is more expensive than it's ever been, and the 5 reasons why suggest it's only going to get worse. *Business Insider.* https://www.businessinsider.com/why-is-college-so-expensive-2018-4

Logan, J., Hughes, T., & Logan, B. (2016). Overworked? An observation of the relationship between student employment and academic performance. *Journal of College Student Retention: Research, Theory, & Practice, 18*(3), 250–262. https://doi.org/10.1177/1521025115622777

Ma, J., Baum, S., Pender, M., & Libassi, C. J. (2018). *Trends in college pricing 2018.* The College Board. https://research.collegeboard.org/pdf/trends-college-pricing-2018-full-report.pdf

Mahuron, S. (2018, June 29). How will a scholarship help achieve your education & career goals? *Chron.* https://work.chron.com/scholarship-achieve-education-career-goals-9040.html

Novotney, A. (2017, April). Eight ways to take charge of your finances. *Monitor on Psychology, 48*(4), 66. https://www.apa.org/monitor/2017/04/finances

Nykiel, T., & Helhoski, A. (2018, May 23). Guide to college grants and how they differ from scholarships [Blog post]. *Nerdwallet.* https://www.nerdwallet.com/blog/loans/student-loans/grants-for-college/

Safier, R. (2017, February 24). 6 major student loan mistakes you need to avoid [Blog post]. *Student Loan Hero.* https://studentloanhero.com/blog/6-student-loan-mistakes-you-need-to-avoid/

Sleigh, M. J., Ritzer, D. R., & Hamric, D. (2018, Spring). Everything I needed to know about money I didn't learn in college. *Eye on Psi Chi, 22*(3), 18–23. https://www.psichi.org/page/223EyeSpr18cSleigh

Stanley, T. J. (2009). *Stop acting rich ... and start living like a real millionaire.* John Wiley & Sons.

Stringer, H. (2016, April). Got debt? *Monitor on Psychology, 47*(4), 52. https://www.apa.org/monitor/2016/04/cover-got-debt

Wenz, M., & Yu, W. (2010). Term-time employment and the academic performance of undergraduates. *Journal of Education Finance, 35*(4), 358–374. http://dx.doi.org/10.1353/jef.0.0023

Winerman, L. (2016, April). The debt trap. *Monitor on Psychology, 47*(4), 44. https://www.apa.org/monitor/2016/04/cover-debt-trap

14.2 Scholarships

Ellis, K. (2013). *Confessions of a scholarship winner: The secrets that helped me win $500,000 in free money for college—How you can too!* Worthy.

Fishman, C. (2011). *The big thirst: The secret life and turbulent future of water.* Simon & Schuster.

Hatcher, F. (2012). *The "c" students guide to scholarships.* Peterson's.

Notte, J. (2018, November 7). Here are the best sports for a college scholarship. *Market Watch.* https://www.marketwatch.com/story/these-are-the-sports-your-child-should-play-to-get-a-college-scholarship-2017-05-08

Peterson's. (2018). *Scholarships, grants & prizes 2019.* Author.

Psi Chi Awards and Grants. (2019, Spring). Introducing Psi Chi's fourth annual scholarship recipients! *Eye on Psi Chi, 23*(3), 14–17. https://www.psichi.org/page/233EyeSpring19Scholar

Sethi, R. (2018). How I got $100,000+ in college scholarships [Blog post]. *I Will Teach You to Be Rich.* https://www.iwillteachyoutoberich.com/blog/how-to-get-scholarships/

Singletary, M. (2018, October 16). Your child probably won't get a full ride to college. *The Washington Post.* https://www.washingtonpost.com/business/2018/10/16/odds-your-child-getting-full-ride-college-are-low/

Speers, S. (2016, January 6). The 10 best sites to search for scholarships. *USA Today.* https://www.usatoday.com/story/college/2016/01/06/the-10-best-sites-to-search-for-scholarships/37410585/

Strauss, V. (2017, April 27). Why so many college students are lousy at writing—and how Mr. Miyagi can help. *The Washington Post.* https://www.washingtonpost.com/news/answer-sheet/wp/2017/04/27/why-so-many-college-students-are-lousy-at-writing-and-how-mr-miyagi-can-help/? utm_term=.e1248d33d16b

Tanabe, G., & Tanabe, K. (2018). *The ultimate scholarship book 2019.* SuperCollege.

14.3 Research Grants, Travel Grants, and Awards

Petrella, J. K., & Jung, A. P. (2008). Undergraduate research: Importance, benefits, and challenges. *International Journal of Exercise Science, 1*(3), 91–95.

Rovnyak, D. S., & Shields, G. C. (2017, July 7). How undergraduate research drives science forward. *Inside Higher Ed.* https://www.insidehighered.com/views/2017/07/07/undervaluation-role-undergraduate-research-advancement-scientific-knowledge-essay

Samuelson, A. (1984). *With Hemingway: A year in Key West and Cuba.* Random House.

Thurmond, J. (2013, Summer). Lessons learned: Advice on securing undergraduate travel funding. *APSSC Undergraduate Update.*https://www.psychologicalscience.org/members/apssc/undergraduate_update/undergraduate-update-summer-2013/lessons-learned-advice-on-securing-undergraduate-travel-funding

14.4 Money, Career, and Happiness

Baab-Muguira, C. (2016, October 26). Don't do what you love for a career—do what makes you money. *Quartz.* https://qz.com/819233/do-what-you-love-is-bad-advice-work-for-money-not-for-passion/

Berry, A. (2018, July 8). 50 highest paying college majors [Blog post]. *Glassdoor.* https://www.glassdoor.com/blog/50-highest-paying-college-majors/

Bobnar, A. (2019). The 7 most lucrative careers for psychology majors. *Psychology Degree Guide.* http://psychologydegreeguide.org/highest-paying-careers-in-psychology/

Britt, S. L., Klontz, B. T., Tibbetts, R., & Leitz, L. (2015). The financial health of mental health professionals. *Journal of Financial Therapy, 6*(1), 17–32. https://doi.org/10.4148/1944-9771.1076

Cherry, K. (2018, January 17). 5 of the lowest paying psychology careers. *VeryWellMind.* https://www.verywellmind.com/five-lowest-paying-psychology-careers-2794947

Finno, A. A., Michalski, D., Hart, B., Wicherski, M., & Kohout, J. L. (2010). *Salaries in psychology 2009: Report of the 2009 APA Salary Survey.* APA Center for Workforce Studies. https://www.apa.org/workforce/publications/09-salaries/report.pdf

Fishbach, A. (2017, January 13). In choosing a job, focus on the fun. *The New York Times.* https://www.nytimes.com/2017/01/13/jobs/in-choosing-a-job-focus-on-the-fun.html

Hamm, T. (2014, October 16). Personal finance for college students. *The Simple Dollar.* https://www.thesimpledollar.com/personal-finance-for-college-students-ten-tips-for-realistic-money-management-in-college-without-the-nonsense/

Hess, A. (2017, June 22). 3 ways to be sure you pick the right career. *CNBC.* https://www.cnbc.com/2017/06/21/3-ways-to-be-sure-you-pick-the-right-career.html

Jaschik, S. (2019, February 15). The economic gains (yes, gains) of a liberal arts education. *Inside Higher Ed.* https://www.insidehighered.com/news/2019/02/15/study-documents-economic-gains-liberal-arts-education

Jebb, A. T., Tay, L., Diener, E., & Oishi, S. (2018). Happiness, income satiation, and turning points around the world. *Nature Human Behavior, 2*(1), 33–38. https://doi.org/10.1038/s41562-017-0277-0

Judge, T. A., Piccolo, R. F., Podsakoff, N. P., Shaw, J. C., & Rich, B. L. (2010). The relationship between pay and job satisfaction: A meta-analysis of the literature. *Journal of Vocational Behavior, 77*(2), 157–167. https://doi.org/10.1016/j.jvb.2010.04.002

Kelle, J. (2019). The 25 most lucrative careers in psychology. *BestPsychologyDegrees.com*. https://www.bestpsychologydegrees.com/25-most-lucrative-careers-in-psychology/

Kovacs, K. (2016, November 17). Grad students' financial worries. *Inside Higher Ed*. https://www.insidehighered.com/news/2016/11/17/report-finds-many-graduate-students-are-stressed-about-finances

Millburn, J. F., & Nicodemus, R. (2011). *Minimalism: Live a meaningful life*. Asymmetrical Press.

Millburn, J. F., & Nicodemus, R. (2014). *Everything that remains: A memoir by The Minimalists*. Asymmetrical Press.

O'Donnell, J. T. (2018, January 8). Why 99 percent of people choose the wrong career path (and 4 steps to get you back on path). *Inc*. https://www.inc.com/jt-odonnell/why-99-percent-of-people-choose-wrong-career-path-and-4-steps-to-get-you-back-on-track.html

PayScale. (2019, February 4). Bachelor of Arts (BA), psychology degree. *PayScale*. https://www.payscale.com/research/US/Degree=Bachelor_of_Arts_(BA)%2c_Psychology/Salary#by_Job

Ramsey, D. (2013). *The total money makeover: A proven plan for financial fitness*. Nelson Books.

Sethi, R. (2019). *I will teach you to be rich*. Workman.

Stanley, T. J., & Danko, W. D. (2010). *The millionaire next door: The surprising secrets of America's wealthy*. Taylor Trade.

Strapp, C. M., Drapela, D. J., Henderson, C. I., Nasciemento, E., & Roscoe, L. J. (2018). Psychology students' expectations regarding educational requirements and salary for desired careers. *Teaching of Psychology, 45*(1), 6–13. http://dx.doi.org/10.1177/0098628317744943

Whillans, A. V., Weidman, A. C., & Dunn, E. W. (2016). Valuing time over money is associated with greater happiness. *Social Psychological and Personality Science, 7*(3), 213–222. http://dx.doi.org/10.1177/1948550615623842

White, M. C. (2014, January 6). 5 reasons to consider sticking with a low-paying job. *Time*. http://business.time.com/2014/01/06/5-reasons-to-consider-actually-sticking-with-a-low-paying-job/

14.5 Money and Graduate School

American Psychological Association. (2018). *Graduate study in psychology*. American Psychological Association.

Cautero, R. (2018, August 29). Should I go? My grad school debt will be $40,000. *Her Money from Jean Chatzy*. https://www.hermoney.com/borrow/student-loans/should-i-go-my-grad-school-debt-will-be-40000/

Doran, J. M., Kraha, A., Marks, L. R., Ameen, E. J., & El-Ghoroury, N. H. (2016). Graduate debt in psychology: A quantitative analysis. *Training and Education in Professional Psychology, 10*(1), 3–13. https://doi.org/10.1037/tep0000112

Kiparsky, M. (2006, May 11). How to win a graduate fellowship. *The Chronicle of Higher Education*. https://www.chronicle.com/article/How-to-Win-a-Graduate/46782

Kovacs, K. (2016, November 17). Grad students' financial worries. *Inside Higher Ed*. https://www.insidehighered.com/news/2016/11/17/report-finds-many-graduate-students-are-stressed-about-finances

Luberecki, B. (2017, April 11). Managing finances might be graduate students' toughest test. *The Washington Post*. https://www.washingtonpost.com/express/wp/2017/04/11/managing-finances-might-be-graduate-students-toughest-test/? noredirect=on&utm_term=.25953e7a183f

Marcus, J. (2017, September 18). Graduate programs have become a cash cow for struggling colleges. What does that mean for students? *PBS News Hour*. https://www.pbs.org/newshour/education/graduate-programs-become-cash-cow-struggling-colleges-mean-students

Meyer, C. (2018, July 1). Is taking student loans for graduate school worth it? *Forbes*. https://www.forbes.com/sites/financialfinesse/2018/07/01/is-taking-student-loans-for-graduate-school-worth-it

Michalski, D. S., Cope, C., & Fowler, G. A. (2019, March). Graduate study in psychology 2019 summary report: Admissions, applications, and acceptances. *American Psychological Association Graduate and Postgraduate Education*. https://www.apa.org/education/grad/survey-data/2019-admissions-applications.pdf

Novotney, A. (2015, January). Money for education. *gradPSYCH, 13*(1), 38. https://www.apa.org/gradpsych/2015/01/money-education

Powell, F. (2018, April 16). How to find free money for grad school. *U.S. News & World Report*. https://www.usnews.com/education/best-graduate-schools/paying/articles/2018-04-16/how-to-find-free-money-for-grad-school

Stringer, H. (2016, April). Got debt? *Monitor on Psychology, 47*(4), 52. https://www.apa.org/monitor/2016/04/cover-got-debt

Chapter 15

15.1 Are You Committed to Psychology or Considering Options?

Gebhard, N. (2015, July 31). Four steps to choosing a college major. *The New York Times*. https://www.nytimes.com/2015/08/02/education/edlife/four-steps-to-choosing-a-career-path.html?_r=0

Hyde, C. R. (1999). *Pay it forward.* Simon & Schuster.

Marken, S., & Auter, Z. (2017, June 1). Half of U.S. adults would change at least one education decision. *Gallup & Strada Education Network.* https://stradaeducation.gallup.com/poll/211529/half-adults-change-least-one-education-decision.aspx

15.2 Advice From Employers and Career Counselors

Auter, Z., & Marken, S. (2016, December 13). One in six U.S. grads say career services was very helpful. *Gallup*. https://news.gallup.com/poll/199307/one-six-grads-say-career-services-helpful.aspx? g_source=Education&g_medium=lead&g_campaign=tiles

Bauer-Wolf, J. (2018, February 23). Overconfident students, dubious employers. *Inside Higher Ed.* https://www.insidehighered.com/news/2018/02/23/study-students-believe-they-are-prepared-workplace-employers-disagree

Fadulu, L. (2018, January 20). Why aren't college students using career services? *The Atlantic.* https://www.theatlantic.com/education/archive/2018/01/why-arent-college-students-using-career-services/551051/

Hannon, K. (2018, November 22). College career centers up their game as parents focus on "outcomes." *The Seattle Times.* https://www.seattletimes.com/explore/careers/college-career-centers-up-their-game-as-parents-focus-on-outcomes/

Hart Research Associates. (2013). *It takes more than a major: Employer priorities for college learning and student success.* https://www.aacu.org/sites/default/files/files/LEAP/2013_EmployerSurvey.pdf

Hart Research Associates. (2015). *Falling short? College learning and career success.* https://www.aacu.org/leap/public-opinion-research/2015-survey-results

Hart Research Associates. (2018). *Fulfilling the American dream: Liberal education and the future of work.* https://www.aacu.org/sites/default/files/files/LEAP/2018EmployerResearchReport.pdf

Hettich, P. (2016, Fall). Program your GPS: Guidelines to proficiency in skills for work and career. *Eye on Psi Chi, 21*(1), 20–24. https://www.psichi.org/page/211EyeFall16cHettich

Koenig, R. (2018, March 12). How to make the most of your college career center. *U.S. News & World Report.* https://money.usnews.com/money/careers/applying-for-a-job/articles/2018-03-12/how-to-make-the-most-of-your-college-career-center

Kruger, J., & Dunning, D. (1999). Unskilled and unaware of it: How difficulties in recognizing one's own incompetence lead to inflated assessments. *Journal of Personality and Social Psychology,* 77(6), 1121–1134. http://dx.doi.org/10.1037/0022-3514.77.6.1121

McLendon, L., & Reshwan, R. (2016, September 15). 5 things college career counselors wish students knew. *U.S. News & World Report.* https://money.usnews.com/careers/articles/2016-09-15/5-things-college-career-counselors-wish-students-knew

15.3 Get the Most Out of Summers

Abrams, K., & Ziegler, N. (2016). Facilitating study abroad for psychology students. *Psychology Teaching Review, 22*(2), 4–17.

Anderson, E. (2017, May 25). Pros and cons of taking summer classes. *College Raptor.* https://www.collegeraptor.com/find-colleges/articles/tips-tools-advice/pros-and-cons-of-taking-summer-classes/

Bradford, L. (2016, June 20). Why every millennial should learn some code. *Forbes.* https://www.forbes.com/sites/laurencebradford/2016/06/20/why-every-millennial-should-learn-some-code

Earnest, D. (2015, Winter). Why study abroad? What psychology students have to gain from study abroad opportunities. *Eye on Psi Chi, 19*(2), 8–9. https://www.psichi.org/page/192EyeWin15fEarnest

Earnest, D. R., Rosenbusch, K., Wallace-Williams, D., & Keim, A. C. (2016). Study abroad in psychology: Increasing cultural competencies through experiential learning. *Teaching of Psychology, 43*(1), 75–79. http://dx.doi.org/10.1177/0098628315620889

Goldstein, S. B. (2017). Teaching a psychology-based study abroad pre-departure course. *Psychology, Learning & Teaching, 16*(3), 404–424. http://dx.doi.org/10.1177/1475725717718059

Kuh, G. D. (2008). *High-impact educational practices: What they are, who has access to them, and why they matter.* Association of American Colleges and Universities.

Musulin, K. (2014, February 5). Why summer is the best time to get an internship. *USA Today.* https://www.usatoday.com/story/college/2014/02/05/why-summer-is-the-best-time-to-get-an-internship/37438731/

National Survey of Student Engagement. (2007). *Experiences that matter: Enhancing student learning and success—Annual Report 2007.* Indiana University Center for Postsecondary Research. http://nsse.indiana.edu/NSSE_2007_Annual_Report/docs/withhold/NSSE_2007_Annual_Report.pdf

Pychyl, T. A. (2013). *Solving the procrastination puzzle.* Penguin Group.

Schwebel, D. C., & Carter, J. (2010). Why more psychology majors should study abroad. *Psychology and Education: An Interdisciplinary Journal, 47,* 17–21.

15.4 Your Path to Being a Superstar Psychology Student

Grover, C. A., Leftwich, M. J. T., Backhaus, A., Fairchild, J. A., & Weaver, K. A. (2006). Qualities of superstar graduate students. *Teaching of Psychology, 33*(4), 271–273.

Martin, R. C. (2015). Undergraduate superstars: What makes them stand out? *Scholarship of Teaching and Learning in Psychology, 1*(2), 107–112. http://dx.doi.org/10.1037/stl0000028

15.5 Say Thank You to Those Who Helped You

Algoe, S. B., & Haidt, J. (2009). Witnessing excellence in action: The "other praising" emotions of elevation, gratitude, and admiration. *Journal of Positive Psychology, 4*(2), 105–127. http://dx.doi.org/10.1080/17439760802650519

Emmons, R. A., & Stern, R. (2013). Gratitude as a psychotherapeutic intervention. *Journal of Clinical Psychology, 69*(8), 846–855. http://dx.doi.org/10.1002/jclp.22020

Gallup. (2015). Great jobs, great lives. The relationship between student debt, experiences and perceptions of college worth. *Gallup-Purdue Index 2015 Report.* http://www.gallup.com/file/services/185924/GPI_Report_2015_09.25.2015.pdf

Pierce, B. (2018, January 30). The importance of writing thank you letters for scholarships. *iGrad.* https://www.igrad.com/articles/writing-thank-you-letters-for-scholarships

15.6 Final Advice From the Authors

Copeland, D. E., Winkelmes, M., & Gunawan, K. (2018). Helping students by using transparent writing assignments. In T. L. Kuther (Ed.), *Integrating writing into the college classroom: Strategies for promoting student skills* (pp. 26–37). http://teachpsych.org/ebooks/

Marcus, J. (2015, July 23). Colleges help drifting students map paths to degrees. *U.S. News & World Report.* https://www.usnews.com/news/college-of-tomorrow/articles/2015/07/23/colleges-give-drifting-students-maps-to-help-them-find-their-way-to-graduation

Zadra, D., & Wills, K. (2009). *5: Where will you be five years from today?* Compendium.

Index

Figures, tables, and notes are indicated by f, t, or n following the page number.